# SAUDI ARABIA

GRACE EDWARDS

www.bradtguides.com

Bradt Guides Ltd, UK
The Globe Pequot Press Inc, USA

Bradt GUIDES
TRAVEL TAKEN SERIOUSLY

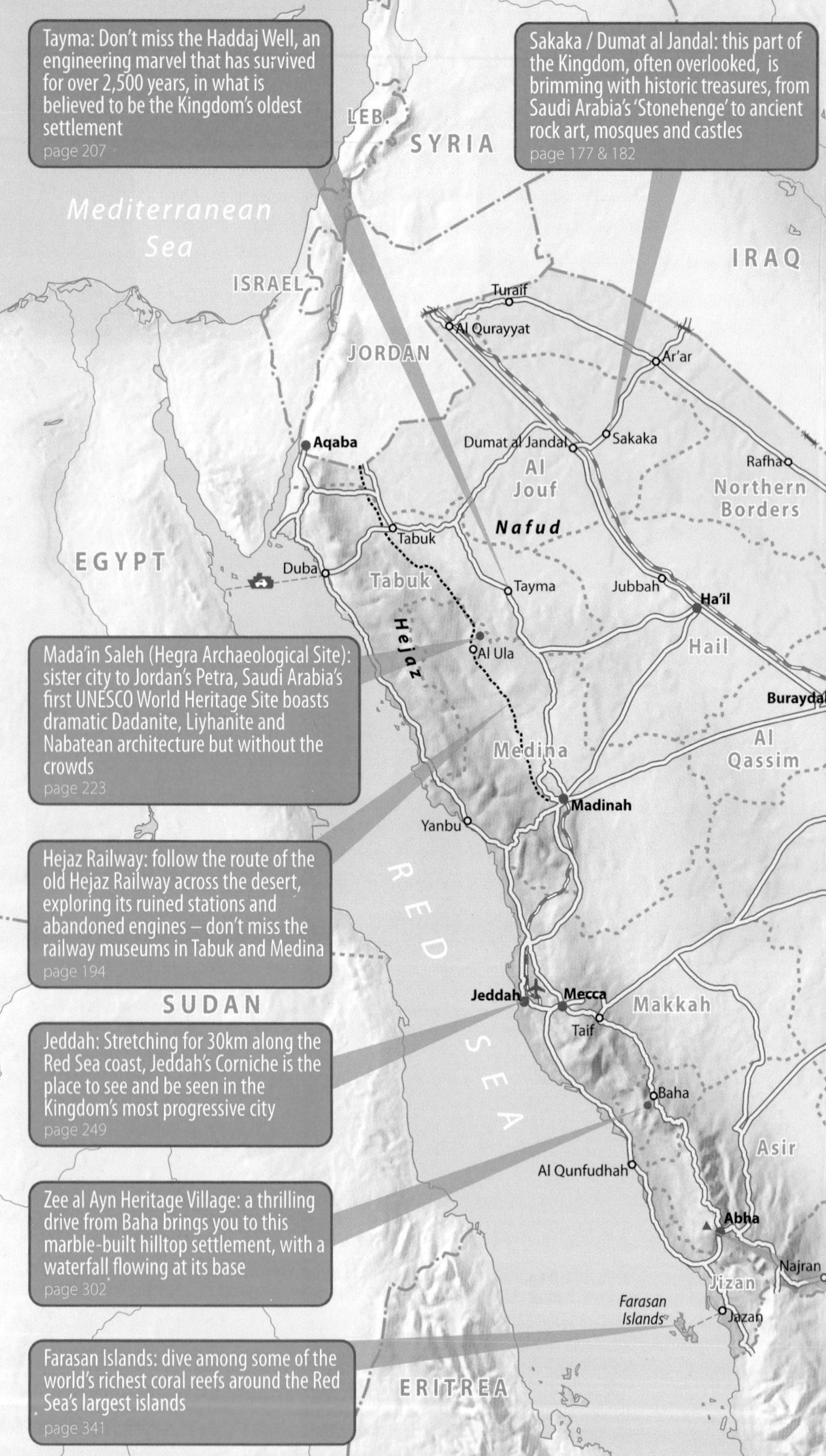

Tayma: Don't miss the Haddaj Well, an engineering marvel that has survived for over 2,500 years, in what is believed to be the Kingdom's oldest settlement
page 207
Sakaka / Dumat al Jandal: this part of the Kingdom, often overlooked, is brimming with historic treasures, from Saudi Arabia's 'Stonehenge' to ancient rock art, mosques and castles
page 177 & 182
Mada'in Saleh (Hegra Archaeological Site): sister city to Jordan's Petra, Saudi Arabia's first UNESCO World Heritage Site boasts dramatic Dadanite, Liyhanite and Nabatean architecture but without the crowds
page 223
Hejaz Railway: follow the route of the old Hejaz Railway across the desert, exploring its ruined stations and abandoned engines – don't miss the railway museums in Tabuk and Medina
page 194
Jeddah: Stretching for 30km along the Red Sea coast, Jeddah's Corniche is the place to see and be seen in the Kingdom's most progressive city
page 249
Zee al Ayn Heritage Village: a thrilling drive from Baha brings you to this marble-built hilltop settlement, with a waterfall flowing at its base
page 302
Farasan Islands: dive among some of the world's richest coral reefs around the Red Sea's largest islands
page 341
LEB.
SYRIA
Mediterranean Sea
ISRAEL
JORDAN
IRAQ
EGYPT
SUDAN
ERITREA
RED SEA
Turaif
Al Qurayyat
Ar'ar
Sakaka
Dumat al Jandal
Rafha
Al Jouf
Northern Borders
Nafud
Aqaba
Tabuk
Duba
Tayma
Jubbah
Ha'il
Hail
Hejaz
Al Ula
Buraydah
Al Qassim
Medina
Madinah
Yanbu
Jeddah
Mecca
Makkah
Taif
Baha
Al Qunfudhah
Asir
Abha
Najran
Jizan
Farasan Islands
Jazan

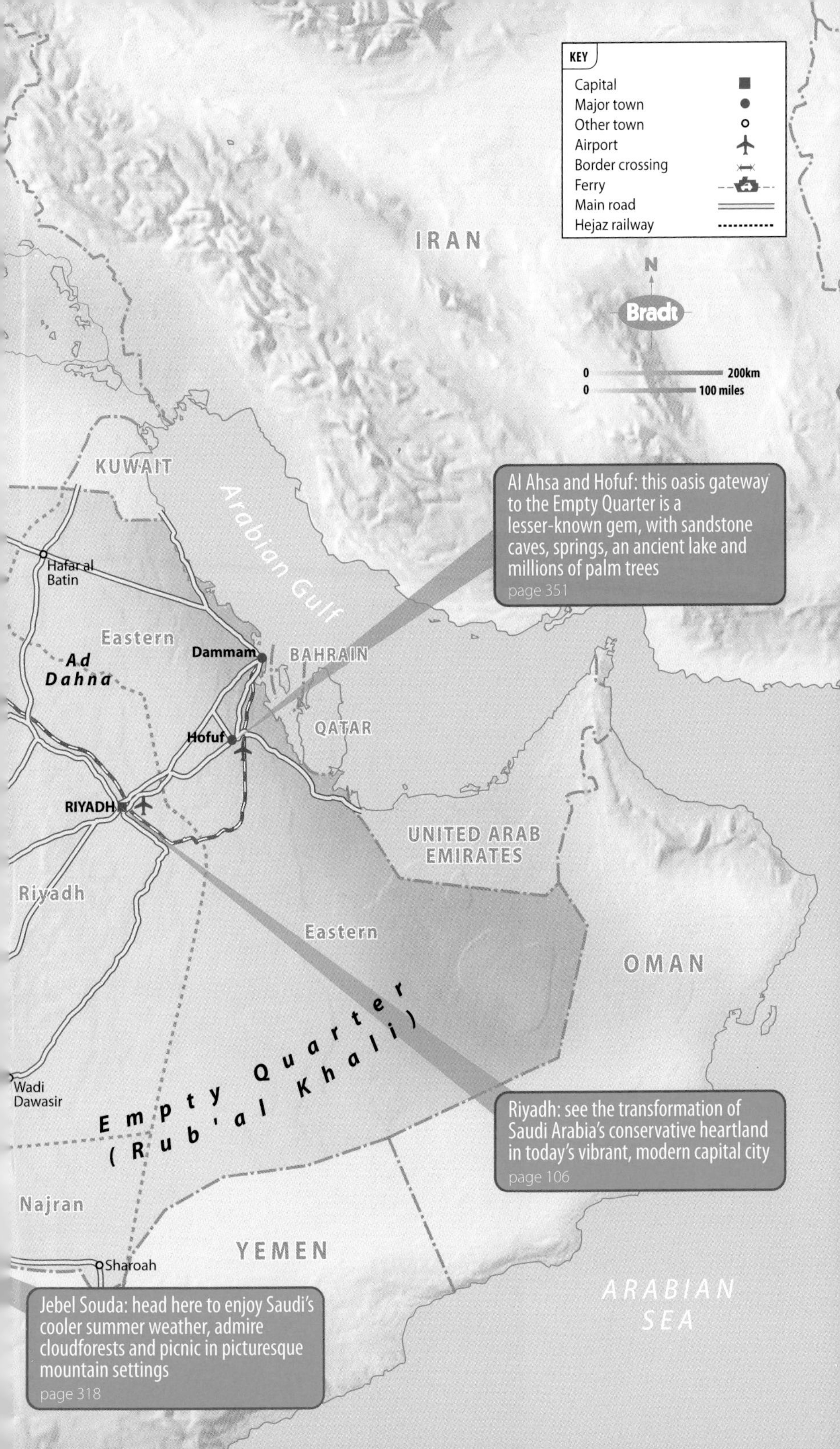
KEY
Capital
Major town
Other town
Airport
Border crossing
Ferry
Main road
Hejaz railway
IRAN
N
Bradt
0 200km
0 100 miles
KUWAIT
Arabian Gulf
Al Ahsa and Hofuf: this oasis gateway to the Empty Quarter is a lesser-known gem, with sandstone caves, springs, an ancient lake and millions of palm trees
page 351
Hafar al Batin
Eastern
Ad Dahna
Dammam
BAHRAIN
QATAR
Hofuf
RIYADH
UNITED ARAB EMIRATES
Riyadh
Eastern
OMAN
Empty Quarter
(Rub'al Khali)
Wadi Dawasir
Riyadh: see the transformation of Saudi Arabia's conservative heartland in today's vibrant, modern capital city
page 106
Najran
YEMEN
Sharoah
ARABIAN SEA
Jebel Souda: head here to enjoy Saudi's cooler summer weather, admire cloudforests and picnic in picturesque mountain settings
page 318

# SAUDI ARABIA
## DON'T MISS...

### RIJAL AL MA'A

Admire the distinctive architecture and local culture of the Flowermen village of Rijal al Ma'a, which aspires to be Saudi Arabia's next UNESCO World Heritage Site PAGE 320

(SS)

### HANGING VILLAGE OF AL HABALA

See where local tribes escaped the Ottomans some 400 years ago in this village once accessed only by rope ladder PAGE 322

(AT/S)

## AL ULA: BEYOND THE ANCIENT SITES

Enjoy al Ula's winter season, with adrenaline-fuelled activities and world-class music, against a magical backdrop PAGE 227
(AHAT/S)

## ROCK ART OF HA'IL

Marvel at Jubbah's ancient petroglyphs depicting everyday life in this region some 10,000 years ago PAGE 174
(SS)

## JEDDAH: AL BALAD

Visit the souqs and house museums of Jeddah's historic old town – a UNESCO World Heritage Site – for a taste of traditional life PAGE 274
(UM/D)

# SAUDI ARABIA
## IN COLOUR

above (OAM/S) Jeddah's Corniche, with views across the Red Sea, is lined with restaurants, coffee kiosks and parks where locals come to exercise, relax and enjoy the city's nightlife PAGE 276

below (MY/S) Riyadh, a modern and vibrant capital city, is Saudi Arabia's seat of government, financial centre and an excellent base from which to explore many sites of interest in Riyadh Province PAGE 106

Creative installations adorn roundabouts across Saudi Arabia. Pictured: *Car Cube*, Jeddah PAGE 277 above left (SS)

Visit Dhahran's King Abdul Aziz Center for World Culture to learn how the oil industry has shaped the Kingdom PAGE 373 above right (AKM/S)

Al Khobar's distinctive water tower is a well-known landmark in Eastern Province PAGE 371 right (JRP/S)

Sunrise over Dammam's Murjan Island PAGE 373 below (AKM/S)

## AUTHOR

**Grace Edwards** has worked throughout the Middle East – including all regions of Saudi Arabia – for decades. As a businesswoman in her own right, she has worked for multinational corporations in a number of key roles and currently provides cross-cultural business consultancy services for people working in Saudi Arabia, as well as for Saudi nationals working with other cultures both domestically and abroad. Over the years, she has explored the whole country, including those regions of the Kingdom less known to outsiders. Her long experience has allowed her to appreciate the nuances of Saudi culture both as a woman and as an 'honorary man' in her professional capacity; and she understands well the ongoing, and significant, changes within the Kingdom and how they impact Saudis and visitors alike. Grace continues to work with a number of prestigious Western, Middle Eastern and multinational organisations across Saudi Arabia, the wider Middle East, and globally. She is the author of *Working and Living in Saudi Arabia* (Grosvenor House, 2020).

### FEEDBACK REQUEST

At Bradt Guides we're aware that guidebooks start to go out of date on the day they're published – and that you, our readers, are out there in the field doing research of your own. You'll find out before us when a fine new family-run hotel opens or a favourite restaurant changes hands and goes downhill. So why not tell us about your experiences? Contact us on 01753 893444 or **e** info@bradtguides.com. We will forward emails to the author who may post updates on the Bradt website at **w** bradtguides.com/updates. Alternatively, you can add a review of the book to Amazon, or share your adventures with us on Facebook, Twitter or Instagram (@BradtGuides).

First published January 2023
Bradt Guides Ltd
31a High Street, Chesham, Buckinghamshire, HP5 1BW, England
www.bradtguides.com
Print edition published in the USA by The Globe Pequot Press Inc,
PO Box 480, Guilford, Connecticut 06437-0480


Cover research: Pepi Bluck, Perfect Picture



ISBN: 9781784779337

**British Library Cataloguing in Publication Data**
A catalogue record for this book is available from the British Library

**Photographs** Alamy Stock Photo: Eric Lafforgue (EL/A); Dreamstime.com: Ulrich Mueller (UM/D); Grace Edwards (GE); Shutterstock.com: adel awad abdallah (AAA/S), Hussam Alduraywish (HA/S), Andrzej Lisowski Travel (ALT/S), Volodymyr Dvornyk (VD/S), enciktat (E/S), Gimas (G/S), H1N1 (HN/S), Hyserb (H/S), iiMOHAMMEDii (IMI/S), Aljohara Jewel (AJ/S), JRP Studio (JRP/S), Kertu (K/S), AFZAL KHAN MAHEEN (AKM/S), malkaa0g (M/S), Osama Ahmed Mansour (OAM/S), Muhammed Hamed Morsi (MHM/S), Rostasedlacek (R/S), Kamarudheen Sallaapam (KS/S), SAMAREEN (S/S), Ahmed Hasan Ali Taher (AHAT/S), Ajmal Thaha (AT/S), Fredy Thuerig (FT/S), Logen Wang (LW/S), Silver Wings (SW/S), Mohammed younos (MY/S); SuperStock (SS).

*Front cover* Mada'in Saleh (Hegra Archaeological Site) (EL/A)
*Back cover, clockwise from top left* Playing an oud, a traditional stringed instrument (HN/S); The Corniche, Jeddah (OAM/S); date palms (IMI/S); detail of a traditional old door, Old Diriyah, Riyadh (HA/S)
*Title page, clockwise from left* King Fahad Road, Riyadh (LW/S); camel ride festival, Buqaiq (AKM/S); interior of dome, Masjid al Nabawi, Madinah (E/S)

**Maps** David McCutcheon FBCart.S. FRGS. Made with Natural Earth. Free vector and raster map data @ naturalearthdata.com

**Typeset by** Ian Spick, Bradt Guides
**Production managed by** Jellyfish Print Solutions; printed in India
**Digital conversion by** www.dataworks.co.in

# Acknowledgements

This book could not have been completed without the support and advice from Bradt Guides which has been received with appreciation and gratitude. I extend a big thank you to the editorial team who helped me achieve the perfect balance of content, context and timekeeping. And to everyone from the Bradt family who gave this project the support it needed.

This book has also benefitted from additional expertise from Jim O'Brien (Native Eye), Professor Madawi al Rasheed, Dr Torsten Wronski and Marianne Taylor, whose comments on earlier drafts of the manuscript and contributions are gratefully acknowledged. Thank you.

Finally, it is impossible to overstate the generosity and hospitality of the people of Saudi Arabia, which can only be truly appreciated by those who visit. To them: I hope this book helps others to appreciate your culture and country in these exciting times. *Shukran jazeelan.*

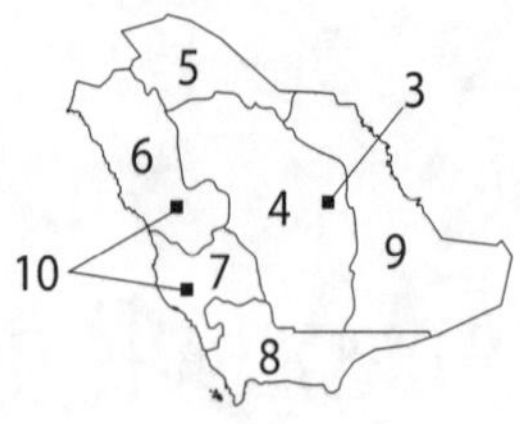


# Contents

## LIST OF MAPS

# Introduction

By the time I visited Saudi Arabia for the first time in the 1990s, I had already been to most countries on the Arabian Peninsula. I almost always travelled alone – as a businesswoman and as an inquisitive tourist. I knew Saudi Arabia would be different. I was right.

Solo women were a rarity in Saudi Arabia in the 1990s and for most of the noughties. When I first travelled in the Kingdom, I once received a handwritten receipt for accommodation that listed me as cargo; later I progressed to being treated with the same status as a child in the male guardianship system. During prayer times, single women needed to be hidden from public view, and I remember being driven around in circles by kind sponsors to avoid being out…and seen by the religious police.

Around a decade into the 21st century, things started to change. As a woman, I knew to behave very cautiously in public, but Saudis were becoming much more comfortable with the idea of a woman travelling unaccompanied, not just in the business world, but also at hotels and restaurants. I, and other women, often found ourselves invited to the front of queues, a demonstration of Saudi-style hospitality.

By the mid-2010s, things were changing rapidly. There were many more solo women travelling for business from overseas, and the male guardianship system rules were no longer being enforced. There were far fewer restrictions for women in public – we could do most things – and doing business was no longer a complete novelty for a growing number of Saudis. We were treated almost as adult women, although we had to work hard – like Ginger Rogers, doing everything men were doing, but backwards and in high heels.

The most significant change for me was the legalisation in 2018 of women driving. No longer dependent on a driver who sometimes knew a city less well than I did, I joined the scrum that is the reality of Saudi traffic. Rather than worrying about being intimidated, or worse, on the roads, I found most men going out of their way to voice their approval. I found it liberating.

Bradt has given me the opportunity to describe what it is really like in Saudi Arabia in the 2020s and to dispel a lot of information that is outdated, biased, or simply wrong. I have researched this book in my usual style mostly as a solo female traveller, driving everywhere from the big cities to the far, remote corners of the Kingdom. I have returned to favourite spots – unchaperoned – and explored places that were until recently effectively off-limits, but which are now welcoming tourists as the Kingdom opens up.

Whether your interest is cultural heritage, archaeology and ancient civilisations, wildlife, watersports, adventure activities in the mountains, desert camping or exploring Saudi's modern cities – from Riyadh's restaurant scene to the hotspots of Jeddah's Corniche – Saudi Arabia has something for everyone.

Yes, there is still a way to go for women – and men – in the Kingdom. But it's a beautiful country that deserves to be a top global tourist destination. Try to go soon and enjoy a magical experience.

## HOW TO USE THIS GUIDE

**AUTHOR'S FAVOURITES** Finding genuinely characterful accommodation or that unmissable off-the-beaten-track café can be difficult, so the author has chosen a few of her favourite places throughout the country to point you in the right direction. These 'author's favourites' are marked with an ✷.

**MUSLIM-ONLY SITES** These sites and places of interest are indicated in the guide by a ☪. Non-Muslims are not permitted to visit these sites.

**PRICE CODES** Throughout this guide we have used price codes to indicate the cost of those places to stay and eat listed in the guide. For a key to these price codes, see page 81 for accommodation and page 84 for restaurants.

**MAPS**

**Keys and symbols** Maps include alphabetical keys covering the locations of those places to stay, eat or drink that are featured in the book. Note that regional maps may not show all hotels and restaurants in the area: other establishments may be located in towns shown on the map.

**Grids and grid references** Several maps use gridlines to allow easy location of sites. Map grid references are listed in square brackets after the name of the place or site of interest in the text, with page number followed by grid number, eg: [114 C3].

**A NOTE ABOUT SPELLING** In Saudi Arabia, road signs, street signs and other types of signage including those at tourist sites often appear in Arabic with a transliteration in English. While we have aimed to keep spellings consistent within the pages of this guide for clarity, on the ground you will find that even for the same place or for similar names used on street signs in different places, the English transliteration may vary.

**WEBSITES AND OTHER CONTACT DETAILS** Telephone numbers and sometimes websites can change frequently and without notice in Saudi Arabia. Saudi businesses often do not have a website or even a landline telephone number. Many also do not have, or do not consistently check, email. Since most Saudi businesses use WhatsApp, we recommend visitors do so too when contacting local venues.

Although all telephone numbers and third-party websites were correct at the time of going to print, some may cease to function during this edition's lifetime. If contact details don't work, you may wish to search online for the most up-to-date information. You can let us know of any issues by emailing **e** info@bradtguides.com.

## KEY TO SYMBOLS

International boundary
Ferry
Airport/airbase
Cable car
Petrol station
Bus station
Museum/art gallery
Castle
Tower
City gate
Bank/ATM
Post office
Hospital
Pharmacy
Hotel
Restaurant
Mosque
Tomb
Cemetery
Hajj/Zirayat site
Historic (archaeological) site
Beach
Cave
Waterfall
Gardens
Viewpoint
Aquarium
Golf course
Horseriding/stables
Border crossing
Summit (height in metres)
Well/spring
Wadi
Sand dunes/desert
Urban market/souq
Urban park
National park/reserve

# Part One

## GENERAL INFORMATION

## SAUDI ARABIA AT A GLANCE

**Location** Arabian Peninsula, Middle East, Western Asia
**Neighbouring countries** Bahrain, Iraq, Jordan, Kuwait, Oman, Qatar, United Arab Emirates, Yemen
**Area** 2,150,000km$^2$
**Climate** Mostly desert, with very long, hot, dry summers and temperatures that can exceed 50°C; and a short winter that ranges from mild in Riyadh (usually 16–24°C), warm on the coasts (mid 20s), and cool in the north, where temperatures can drop to below 10°C. Mountain climates can be at least 10°C cooler than nearby lower elevations in the summer, with snowfall possible in the northwest in the winter. High coastal humidity in the summer; lower humidity inland and in winter.
**Status** Unitary Islamic Absolute Monarchy, with a king obligated to adhere to Basic Law of Saudi Arabia
**Population** Approximately 36 million (World Bank 2021), with up to one-third expatriate workers and their dependents
**Life expectancy** 75.6 years
**Capital (population)** Riyadh (approx 8 million)
**Other main towns** Jeddah (c4.7 million), Mecca (c1.75 million), Tri-cities of Dammam, Dhahran and al Khobar (total c1.7 million), Madinah (c1.4 million), Abha (c1.1 million), Tabuk (c700,000)
**Economy** Largest in the Middle East with a high dependency on oil exports (approx 65%) and expatriate workers (approx 80% in the private sector). GDP US$1 trillion (estimate; IMF 2022), ranked the 18th largest economy.
**Languages** Official language is Arabic. English is widely spoken in major cities; other spoken expatriate languages include several from South Asia and the Philippines.
**Religion** Islam is the official religion of Saudi Arabia. The Salafism branch of Sunni Islam dominates.
**Currency** Saudi riyal (SAR)
**Exchange rate** Pegged to the US dollar at US$1 = SAR3.75, £1 = SAR4.52, €1 = SAR3.92 (October 2023)
**National airline/airport** Saudia (w saudia.com)
**International telephone code** +966
**Time** GMT/UTC +3 year-round
**Electrical voltage** 230V, plug type G (British style with three rectangular pins) being standardised; also 127v, with plug types A, B (both North American blade), C (European two round pins) and the old type D plug (one large and two smaller round pins most commonly associated with South Asia) are still in use.
**Weights and measures** Metric
**Flag** Green, with a white inscription of the *shahada* (profession of the Islamic faith: 'There is no god but Allah and Mohammed is the Messenger of Allah') and a white image of a sword lain horizontally with the handle to the right
**National flower** *Rhanterium epapposum*, known locally as *arfaj* (عرفج)
**National animal** Arabian dromedary camel (*Camelus dromedarius*)
**Public holidays** 23 September (Saudi National Day). For more details, see page 87.

# 1

# Background Information

Often referred to informally as Saudi Arabia, Saudi, KSA or simply the Kingdom, the country's official name – the Kingdom of Saudi Arabia (ٱلْمَمْلَكَة ٱلْعَرَبِيَّة ٱلسُّعُوْدِيَّة; transliteration: al Mamlakah al ʿArabīyah as Suʿūdīyah) – was recognised by royal decree from King Abdul Aziz ibn Saud on 23 September 1932, a date now celebrated as the formal day of independence. The name is a *nisba,* incorporating the name of the ruling family, al Saud.

## GEOGRAPHY

Saudi Arabia dominates the Arabian Peninsula. Covering some 2,150,000km$^2$ (approx 80% of the peninsula's land mass), it is the largest country in the region by far – equating to about one-third the size of Australia, four times the size of France, and nearly nine times the size of the United Kingdom. It also the most populous with approximately 36 million people. The country is bordered to the north by Jordan, Iraq and Kuwait, to the east by Bahrain (via a 25km-long causeway), Qatar and the United Arab Emirates (UAE), and to the south by Oman and Yemen. The geography is mostly desert, but features also mountains, oases and wadis (dry riverbeds). The Kingdom's highest mountain is Jebel Souda (approx 3,000m), also known as Jabal Sawda, and is located in the southwestern Asir Province near the village of the same name.

The west coast is bound by the Red Sea for almost 1,800km from the Yemeni border up to the Straits of Tiran near Ras Gasabah, and from there to the Jordanian border by the Gulf of Aqaba for another 175km. The Red Sea is shallow along the Saudi coastline but has a deep trench further away from land. The narrow coastal plain that runs along the entire length of the Saudi Red Sea coast is known as Tihamah, and is only 80km at its widest point before the Hejaz Mountains rise to the east. This range also includes the Midian Mountains in the northwest and the Sarawat Mountains in the southwest. Many geologists consider the northern end of the entire mountain range to be a part of the Great Rift Valley, which extends from East Africa to Lebanon.

Saudi Arabia's eastern shore runs south for 550km along the Persian Gulf (or Arabian Gulf as it is referred to throughout the Arabian Peninsula and wider Arab world) from just north of Khafji near the Kuwaiti border to just north of al Batha on the border with the UAE, interrupted only by the 87km Saudi–Qatar land border. Until the 2010s, the Gulf produced about 25% of the world's oil – this has declined slightly in recent years with the advent of fracking – with a significant percentage of these oil fields in Saudi waters.

**DESERTS** *Sahra* is the Arabic word for desert and is the origin of the name Sahara in North Africa. However, not all deserts are the same. Saudi Arabia has three major deserts found on the Najd plateau east of the Hejaz Mountains covering the centre of the country. Elevations vary from 1,360m in the west to 750m further east.

**An Nafud** Located in the north of the Kingdom, the an Nafud joins the Syrian desert beyond the Saudi border. It is 290km long and 225km wide, covering a total area of 103,600km$^2$, with sand ridges and sand hills that can reach up to 30m in height. The wind has eroded parts of this desert, leaving a rocky surface. It is broadly bound by Tayma to the west, al Jouf to the north and Ha'il to the south.

**Ad Dahna** The ad Dahna desert is situated to the east of the Najd plateau, running from the east of Buraydah in al Qassim Province to the east of Riyadh and al Kharj in Riyadh Province. It is connected to both the an Nafud and the Rub' al Khali deserts and serves as the buffer between the Najd and al Ahsa regions. The smallest of the three deserts at 100km long and a maximum of 80km wide, it is sandy with high, reddish-coloured dunes called *uruq*.

**Rub' al Khali** Known as the Empty Quarter, this is Saudi's southernmost desert, running south from al Kharj and al Ahsa (Hofuf) and to the east of Najran city in the province of the same name. It is 1,200km long, 500km wide, and covers 650,000km$^2$, making it by far the largest desert on the Arabian Peninsula, extending beyond Saudi Arabia into Oman, the UAE and Yemen. It is a sand sea known as an *urg*, with no oases or other natural water supplies and is one of the world's driest land areas. Some of the sand ridges and hills reach 150m in height. It is effectively uninhabitable in the summer and can be visited at other times only for short periods with all provisions brought in.

**OASES** Oases, known as *waha*, provide a welcome green break in a very tan-coloured country. Saudi Arabia is home to al Ahsa, the world's largest (85.4km$^2$) oasis and a UNESCO World Heritage Site. Some of the Kingdom's other important oases are Unayzah near Buraydah, Tayma on the eastern edge of Tabuk Province, Khaybar about 150km north of Madinah, and al Kharjah about 100km southeast of Taif in Makkah Province.

**WADIS** Though there were rivers in Saudi Arabia in the distant past, none exists in permanent form nowadays and all have become wadis. The most prominent include Wadi Hanifa near Riyadh, Wadi ar Rummah near Buraydah, Wadi as Surr in Makkah Province, Wadi Dawasir in the far southwest of the Najd region and Wadi Najran near the Yemen border.

**LAKES** Lakes, or *bahira*, do exist in the Kingdom, though most are now artificial as natural lakes have largely disappeared due to overuse and to climate change in recent decades. Key lakes include Abha Dam Lake in Asir; al Asfar Lake or Yellow Lake, which is part of the UNESCO World Heritage region of al Asha in Eastern Province; Lake Demah al Jandal in al Jouf; Lake Karrarah (aka the 'Lake of Liquid Light'), Sadus Dam near the Edge of the World and the lake and waterfall at Wadi Namar, all near Riyadh; and the many lakes to the east of Buraydah in al Qassim.

**CRATERS** It is believed that there are about 2,000 dormant volcanoes in Saudi Arabia. Craters, known as *fawhat*, are features of the landscape and are created from some of these volcanoes. They are concentrated in the west of the country, with most in locations that are remote and difficult to visit. Al Wahbha volcano is located nearly equidistant from Madinah and Taif in Makkah Province. Mount al Qadr crater threatened Madinah in the 13th century, but the lava flow stopped short of the city. Much of the central Najd region has *harrat*, volcanic basaltic lava fields that are found in a 180,000km² area of the region (page 169). Hatima (aka Hutaymah) crater is located southeast of Ha'il and is relatively easy to visit. Most craters have left depressions, with the one at al Wahbha as deep as 250m.

In addition to volcanic craters, impact craters caused by meteorites are also found in Saudi Arabia. For centuries, these were rumoured by Bedouin to exist in the Empty Quarter. The first mention by a non-Arab was in 1932 by British explorer and intelligence officer Jack Philby, who referenced a total of five craters. They were named al Wahbha, after the ancient lost city of Ubar. Three circular craters are currently visible in an area of about 500m by 1,000m, depending on the position of constantly shifting sands. As well as sand they are also filled with glass, which was created during the impact out of local sand and iron and nickel from the meteor. Because of the distance needed to travel into the Empty Quarter and the difficulty in finding their precise location, trips to the craters are not advised for independent travellers.

**CAVES** Made of gypsum, limestone, sandstone and other minerals, more than 230 *kahf* or caves are dotted around Saudi Arabia. Some are found in sandy and rocky deserts; others are formed by tunnels between layers of lava rock near volcanoes. A number of these caves can be explored relatively easily. The caves of Jebel Qarah are a key feature of the al Ahsa UNESCO World Heritage Site in Eastern Province, while Shuwaimis Cave, not far from Medina Province, is more than 500m long and home to some of the Ha'il region's UNESCO-listed rock art. Heet Cave, located between Riyadh and al Kharj in Riyadh Province, is also easily accessed and contains fresh water. Further caves are found in many of the harrat northeast of Madinah. Adventurous spelunkers will be delighted to learn that many less well-known caves have been barely explored – but it is important to note that all precautions must be taken as there is no health-and-safety infrastructure.

**OIL FIELDS** Until new sites were discovered in Venezuela in the early 21st century, it was believed that Saudi Arabia had the world's largest oil fields. All of the Kingdom's oil fields are under the control of Saudi Aramco, and many are in Gulf waters, spread along the coast mostly between Dammam and the Kuwaiti border. Land-based oil fields are found mostly in the Eastern and southern Riyadh provinces – the world's largest known land-based oil field is Ghawar, near Buqaiq (or Abqaiq) in Eastern Province between Dhahran and Hofuf.

## CLIMATE

Saudi Arabia has mainly a desert climate with an average of 322 days of sunshine annually. However, temperatures and humidity levels vary across the country. Mountain temperatures from Tabuk to Asir are generally lower than in the rest of the Kingdom. Rainfall averages 129mm per year with most rain falling in the winter months. And it snows in Saudi Arabia too! It can snow most years (usually January or February) in the mountains of Tabuk Province and on occasion at higher elevations on the plateaus of the Northern Borders. Most visitors will find it best to travel to Saudi Arabia from mid-October to March or early April.

In the winter (December to February), temperatures are generally mild during the day. Coastal temperatures are usually in the low to mid 20s (°C) with little drop in temperature in the evenings and with low humidity. In the interior, the desert climate means similar pleasant daytime weather, but overnight the temperature can drop to single digits as in the mountains.

In the short Saudi spring (March to April), temperatures gradually rise to the low 30s. Humidity remains low in most of the country, but it does begin to build in the east. Spring and early summer are the most likely times to encounter sandstorms, which occur most often in the east of the Kingdom. They are caused by the *shamal* winds (*shamal* means north and describes the wind direction from Iraq, where the winds originate).

Summer lasts from May to early October. These months are extremely hot in most of the Kingdom, with temperatures averaging about 40°C along much of the Red Sea coast and reaching 45–50°C in most of Najd and Eastern Province. Although the interior remains relatively dry, it is very humid along the Arabian Gulf coast. Summers are much cooler in Baha and the southern provinces.

The long summer is followed by a short autumn in late October and November. Autumn brings an eventual drop in humidity followed by a drop in temperatures and is a lovely time of year to visit. The *khareef* is a regional monsoon which reaches Oman, Yemen and the southwest Jizan Province of Saudi Arabia, usually occurring between June and early September.

Air conditioning is found throughout the Kingdom and is generally efficient, with some saying that temperatures may even be set too low. Heating is not found in most houses or in some hotels, which may be a bit of a challenge during winter nights in parts of the north.

## NATURAL HISTORY AND CONSERVATION *with Marianne Taylor*

**ECOSYSTEMS** There are 14 distinct terrestrial eco-regions in Saudi Arabia, as well as three marine eco-regions. Of the terrestrial eco-regions, nine have some areas protected for wildlife conservation. The extensive **North Arabian desert** fares best with almost a fifth of its total area under protection

The **Southwestern Arabian coastal xeric shrublands**, also known as the Arabian Peninsula coastal fog desert, runs in a narrow strip along the west coast from the Yemeni border to greater Jeddah and is characterised by the *khareef* (see above). The fog in the south of this region provides adequate moisture to support a diverse community of fauna and flora, including more than 190 plant species.

The **Southwestern Arabian Escarpment shrublands and woodlands**, also known as the Southwestern Arabian foothills savanna, is found in the Asir and southern Hejaz Mountains, up to an elevation of about 2,000m. Its climate is subtropical and semi-arid. Evidence indicates that this area has been farmed for over 5,000 years, using various terracing and irrigation techniques, and has also supported livestock.

An extension of the foothills savanna, the **Southwestern Arabian montane woodlands and grasslands** are present at elevations above 2,000m in the Sarawat and Asir mountains, where grains have been cultivated for millennia. This eco-region includes Jebel Souda, the Kingdom's highest mountain. Cloudforests at least as dramatic as those famously known in Costa Rica are found above 2,500m.

The **Arabian Desert** is the most prominent ecosystem, covering most of the interior of Saudi Arabia and most of the Arabian Peninsula beyond the coasts and mountains – a total of more than 670,000km$^2$. It has a subtropical, hot desert climate and sees very little rainfall. Temperatures in this ecosystem can exceed 50°C during the summer yet can fall to near freezing in the winter. Relief from weather extremes has traditionally been found in desert oases, which have sustained life throughout history. The Arabian Desert is home to more than 900 species of plants, over 300 bird species and about 100 different types of mammals. A significant percentage of

Saudi's wealth derives from the natural resources found in this region, including oil, gas, phosphates and sulphur. The **Arabian Sand Desert** in the east of the country adjoins the Arabian Desert and covers a further 574,000km$^2$.

The **Red Sea–Arabian Desert shrublands** have a hot desert climate and are extremely dry, with rainfall rare or even non-existent in some years. Found along the coastline of the Red Sea, this eco-region extends from the north of Jeddah to the Jordanian border and also covers some interior areas within the Arabian Desert, most notably the Shammar Mountains in the north of the Kingdom. Flora and fauna are limited in this harsh climate. Most of the desert is made of sand and rock, though some shrubs and grasses grow near wadis. Many of the desert plants bloom quickly (if briefly) whenever they benefit from even a small burst of rain.

The **Red Sea mangroves** (which include some protected areas) and the **Indus River Delta–Arabian Sea mangroves** together cover less than 80km$^2$ but provide a vital resource for both land and marine wildlife along the intertidal zone. They provide sheltered nurseries for marine fish and invertebrates, and accordingly offer productive foraging grounds for an array of bird species.

**FLORA** The flora of Saudi Arabia reflects the geographical position of the country at the crossroads of Europe, Asia and Africa. Some 2,250 species of flowering plants have been recorded in Saudi Arabia, with the greatest diversity in the southwestern part of the country. The coastal fog desert climate of southwest Saudi Arabia sustains plants that are also associated with Oman, Yemen and parts of East Africa. Among these are *Commiphora* and *Boswellia* trees, from which myrrh and frankincense (olibanum) are harvested. In total, there are about 190 different species of shrubs and trees in this climate, found both in scrublands and dry tropical woodlands. Jazan is the largest Saudi city in this climate and is known as the fruit basket of Saudi Arabia. It produces more than 30 types of fruit, including fig, guava, papaya and watermelon.

The woodlands of the Southwestern Arabian foothills savanna are found up to an elevation of 1,000m. This environment supports deciduous and evergreen

## THE DATE: A STAPLE OF THE SAUDI DIET

A member of the family Arecaceae (palms), the date tree and its fruits (tamr; التمور) feature prominently in Saudi culture. Archaeologists have found evidence of date farming since the 6th millennium BCE. According to the Visit Saudi website (w visitsaudi.com), date palms are mentioned 22 times in the Qur'an, and the Prophet Mohammed once said that a home with dates is never poor.

When invited to a Saudi home, guests will generally be offered traditional Saudi coffee (kahwa; قهوة) and dates. Dates are also commonly found in hotels and other venues as a welcome ritual. Following the practice of the Prophet Mohammed, during Ramadan it is traditional for Muslims to break their fast by eating an odd number of dates, usually three, along with drinking water.

There are more than 300 varieties of date including the famous medjool date. Other popular varieties are the *ajwa, anbara, barhi, khalas, khudri, mabroom, safawi, saghai, sukary* and *zahidi*. Dates are eaten as they are or covered in chocolate, nuts, or in sweets. Date paste, syrup and juice are all popular as well. They make great gifts and can be purchased in souqs, supermarkets and in the duty-free shops in the international terminals of most airports.

trees, shrubs and grasses that can tolerate a dry climate. Several subspecies of acacia, commiphora, euphorbia, *Grewia tenax*, hibiscus and a variety of aloe plants grow at lower elevations, with acacias and commiphora at elevations as high as 1,800m. When there is sufficient moisture from fog or rain, many wadis bloom with *Breonadia salicina*, a fruit-bearing evergreen tree, and fig (*Ficus vasta*). Another evergreen, *Mimusops laurifolia* also thrives and is the Kingdom's largest tree. At higher elevations between 1,800 and 2,200m, juniper bushes replace the flora of the lower regions, with *Barbeya oleoides* commonly found.

The Southwestern Arabian montane woodlands support evergreens including the *Olea cuspidata* (2,000–2,500m). Above 2,500m, the shrubs *Juniperus procera, Euryops arabicus* and a lichen, *Usnea articulata*, dominate the landscape along with prickly evergreen shrubs such as *Rosa abyssinica*.

Relative to other ecosystems in the Kingdom, the desert has few trees, although some shrubs can be found in wadis in the centre of the country. Common species include *Calligonum crinitum* and saltbush, and sedges also grow in these areas. There are very few plants at all in the Empty Quarter (Rub' al Khali).

## FAUNA

**Mammals** Saudi Arabia is home to about 80 species of wild mammals, many of which are well adapted for life in arid regions. A number of the Arabian Peninsula's most endangered mammals can be found in the coastal fog desert eco-region. These include the caracal (*Caracal caracal*), a reddish, medium-sized cat with striking long-tufted ears. It is a long-legged hunter of birds and mammals, and is a nocturnal loner. The largest cat on the Arabian Peninsula is the Critically Endangered Arabian leopard (*Panthera pardus nimr*). It is smaller than other leopard subspecies, and has not been sighted since the early 21st century, when it was seen in the Asir Mountains. Other predators include the striped hyena (*Hyaena hyaena*), which has long, thick brown fur and appears only in full darkness, and the Arabian wolf (*Canis lupus arabs*), which has a short grey coat and generally hunts in pairs rather than in a pack. Neither is commonly sighted.

Endangered ungulates that dwell in this environment include the Nubian ibex (*Capra nubiana*), a distinctive goat species with tan and white fur and large rippled horns that curl back towards the animal's shoulders, and which can grow to 1m in length in males. Arabian oryx (*Oryx leucoryx*) became extinct in the wild in the

### SAUDI ARABIA'S NATIONAL ANIMAL

The Arabian or dromedary camel (*jamal*; جمل; *Camelus dromedarius*) is the Kingdom's national animal. This one-humped creature can weigh up to almost 700kg and grow to a shoulder height of over 2m, and varies in colour from sandy to dark brown. The hair on its hump, shoulders and throat is longer than that on the rest of the body. Although the truly wild Arabian camel is officially extinct, it is estimated that there are nearly 1 million of them in the Kingdom. They can be found ranging in the wild (feral animals descended from domestic ancestors), on farms, at races (page 133) and even as participants in beauty contests (page 89). Known as 'ships of the desert', camels were domesticated to carry goods and people back in the time of ancient caravans – though transport is not their only use. Camel milk and meat is consumed in Saudi Arabia, and the animal's wool and skin are also used for creating fabrics among other things.

1970s but was reintroduced a decade later due to sufficient numbers in zoos. This beautiful animal has white fur, brown legs, a pattern of black stripes and markings on its head, and long, slender horns. There were formerly three species of gazelle native to the Kingdom: the Arabian gazelle (*Gazella arabica*); the Arabian sand gazelle or reem gazelle (*Gazella marica*), which survives in captivity and fenced reserves but is disappearing in the wild; and the Saudi gazelle (*Gazella saudiya*). Sadly, the last of these officially became extinct in the wild in 1996 (and no captive animals have ever been traced).

Elsewhere, the foothills savanna is home to Arabian leopard, caracal, Arabian wolf, hamadryas baboon (*Papio hamadryas*) and red fox (*Vulpes vulpes*). This is also the preferred habitat of the Arabian gazelle. These species can also be found in the Southwestern Arabian montane woodlands, along with the rock hyrax (*Procavia capensis*) and the striped hyena.

Hoofed mammals found in the Arabian Desert include the Arabian oryx and the Arabian sand gazelle. The desert is also home to the delightful sand cat (*Felis margarita*), a true desert specialist. Smaller than a domestic cat, it has a distinctive square-shaped face and spends the heat of the day in underground burrows. The small (but big-eared) desert hedgehog (*Paraechinus aethiopicus*) is one of the smaller desert mammals, while rodents include an assortment of gerbils, jerboas and jirds. among them the Endangered Arabian jird (*Meriones arimalius*).

Many of these magnificent animals are Endangered or worse, leading the Saudi government to announce conservation strategies as a part of Saudi Vision 2030 (page 28).

**Birds** Almost 500 bird species have been recorded in Saudi Arabia, including non-native (introduced) species, and extreme rarities. Among these are at least 219 regularly breeding species, of which15 breed nowhere else but the Arabian Peninsula. The Kingdom is also an important wintering ground for migratory species that breed further north, and it serves as a staging post for other, longer-distance migrants travelling through the region during spring and autumn. Many of Saudi's special bird species can be found in the Asir Mountains. Included among these is Philby's partridge (*Alectoris philbyi*), named after the British explorer and usually found at elevations between 1,400m and 2,700m. It looks similar to the chukar partridge with its grey plumage, but has black cheeks and throat with a white line below the head, and pink legs and beak. Not to be mistaken for the Philby's partridge is the larger Arabian partridge (*Alectoris melanocephala*). This species displays a distinctly different pattern on the head and nape, with a white band above its black eyes and throat, making a 'V' shape. Male Arabian partridges also have a blunt protrusion (spur) on the lower leg, used when fighting each other to impress females.

The Yemen warbler (*Curruca buryi*) lives on the southeastern slopes of the Sarawat Mountains and is found in dry forest areas. The Arabian or Blandford's warbler (*Curruca leucomelaena*) is often found in acacia on the savanna. It has rounded wings and a long tail which it often flicks. Both sexes of these small songbirds have a white ring around the eyes and fade from black on the upperside to light grey towards the lower parts of their bodies.

The Arabian serin (*Crithagra rothschildi*) is a finch with a conical, seed-cracking beak, which can be found in the dry forests of the Sarawat Mountains, as can the Arabian golden-winged grosbeak (*Rhynchostruthus percivali*) – a considerably heftier finch with a brown body and yellow-flecked wings, and a very sturdy black beak.

Another resident of the Sarawat Mountains is the Arabian or Sarat woodpecker (*Dendrocoptes dorae*), the only breeding woodpecker from the Arabian Peninsula.

It has a brown head and a greyish-brown body with white streaks; the male also has a red crown. It is usually found in ficus and date palm trees and ranges from sea level to 2,800m. The tiny Arabian waxbill (*Estrilda rufibarba*), a finch-like seedeater with a bright crimson eye-stripe, is typically found in the wadis of the Tihamah foothills.

The Southwestern Arabian montane woodlands are home to the Asir magpie (*Pica asirensis*) and raptors including the Barbary falcon (*Falco peregrinus pelegrinoides*), bearded vulture (*Gypaetus barbatus*), griffon vulture (*Gyps fulvus*) and Verreaux's eagle (*Aquila verreauxil*).

The specialist desert birds are a real draw for ornithologically minded visitors to the Kingdom. One of the most striking is the hoopoe lark, a large lark with a long, curved beak and a showy rising-and-diving display flight, showing off its black-and-white wings. Six species of sandgrouse occur; these dove-like birds can be seen in fast-flying flocks. They can nest well away from water, as they wade into oases and soak their belly feathers, and then carry the water back to their chicks. Other desert species include nightjars and thick-knees, and the unusual cream-coloured courser (*Cursorius cursor*), while predators of the desert include the Pharoah eagle owl (*Bubo ascalaphus*) and desert owl (*Strix hadorami*).

A range of interesting seabirds and shorebirds also occur in Saudi Arabia. The crab plover, a large piebald bird with a powerful bill, breeds in colonies on the shores of the Red Sea and Arabian Sea. Many species of plovers and sandpipers visit these shorelines on migration. A long list of breeding and regularly visiting gulls and terns includes the large and impressive Pallas's gull, while offshore trips could provide sightings of various shearwaters, boobies and other seabirds. The sooty falcon (*Falco concolor*) nests on islands in the Red Sea. Inland, wetland areas attract the likes of western reef heron (*Egretta gularis*), squacco heron (*Ardeola ralloides*) and little bittern (*Ixobrychus minutus*).

**Reptiles** Several species of snakes are found in Saudi Arabia, many of which are venomous and potentially dangerous to humans, and most of which are nocturnal. These include the Arabian cat snake (*Telescopus dhara*), which has a reddish-coloured body with varying bands of darker and lighter shades. It inhabits mountains and hills and eats rodents and lizards. The carpet viper (*Echis pyramidum*) lives in rocky terrain in the west of the Kingdom and, although it does not exceed 1m in length, it is extremely venomous. The hook-billed blind snake (*Leptotyphlops macrorhynchus*) is pink in colour with black eyes and is found in Jizan. It eats insects and is not venomous. The puff adder (*Bitis arietans*) prefers a grassy environment and can be yellow, orange or reddish brown with chevron patterns on its body. Its preferred food is small mammals and it is also highly venomous. Other snake species found in Saudi Arabia include the Farasan racer (*Coluber insulanus*), Saudi leafnose snake (*Lytorhynchus gasperetti*), Manser's black racer (*Coluber manseri*) and burrowing adder (*Atractaspis microlepidota*).

In addition to snakes, the Kingdom is also home to other reptiles such as the Saudi cylindrical skink (*Chalcides levitoni*) and Saudi pygmy sand gecko (*Tropiocolotes wolfgangboehmei*).

**Amphibians** Saudi Arabia has several types of frogs and toads that live in oases. These include the indigenous Dhofar toad (*Bufo dhufarensis*), Yemeni toad (*Bufo tihamicus*), Arabian toad (*Bufo arabicus*) and Arabian five-fingered frog (*Euphlyctis ehrenbergii*). The European green toad (*Bufo viridis*), the Middle East tree frog (*Hyla savignyi*) and the marsh frog (*Pelophylax ridibundus*) also live in Saudi Arabia.

**Insects** The 130 or so butterflies found in Saudi Arabia include some easily encountered and striking species, such as the gorgeous blue-spotted arab (*Colotis protractus*); the guineafowl butterfly (*Hamanumida daedalus*), a large species with dark wings speckled with white like its avian namesake; and the yellow pansy (*Junonia hierta*), a striking yellow, black and blue species, along with its plainer but more intricately patterned cousin the golden pansy (*Junonia chorimene*). In wetland areas, look out for interesting dragonflies such as the bladetail (*Lindenia tetraphylla*), a very large species with an unusual body shape, and several colourful skimmer species of the genus *Crocothemis*. The globe skimmer (*Pantala flavescens*), famous for its extreme long-distance migrations, may also be encountered in the Kingdom. You will also find an array of beetles and bees, mantids, moths and more – the insect fauna of Saudi Arabia is not well documented so there is much to discover for enthusiastic entomologists.

## Marine life

***Coral*** Saudi Arabia's western coastline, from the Gulf of Aqaba to the southernmost reaches of the Red Sea, is home to some of the most pristine coral reefs in the world. They are believed to be at least 5,000 years old and contain around 300 different species of corals. Most of the Red Sea coastline contains fringing reef systems and shallow shelves, making them especially attractive to scuba divers. The most dramatic corals are species of *Acropora* and *Porites*, which have a beautiful, branched shape.

For now, the Red Sea coral reefs seem to have developed a particular resilience to high temperatures not found in similar reef systems elsewhere. This is believed to be in part due to a lack of river runoff and low rainfall, and in part due to the low numbers of scuba divers (due to the historic difficulty of travelling to the Kingdom) and live-aboard dive boats.

***Fish, sea turtles and marine mammals*** A wide variety of fish inhabit the sea around Saudi Arabia. Species found in shallow waters include goldsilk seabream (*Acanthopagrus berda),* Persian mullet, which lives along the east coast and eats algae and small invertebrates, and the Arabian sand diver, another east coast inhabitant which has a pointed head and a jutting lower jaw, and dives into the sand when threatened. Further down the reefs, at a depth of at least 20m, are the geometrically shaped Indian threadfish (*Alectis indica*) and the small, brown-and-white Red Sea spiny basslet (*Ancanthoplesiops cappuccino).* There are also almost 50 species of shark – including the whale shark (*Rhincodon typus*), which can reach 12m – as well as sailfish (*Istiophorus platypterus*). Marine mammals present in the Red Sea and Arabian Sea include the plant-eating dugong, a member of the sea cow order Sirenia, Bryde's whale (*Balaenoptera edeni*), the spinner dolphin (*Stenella longirostris*) and Risso's dolphin (*Grampus griseus*). Among the larger fish present are the blue spotted ribbontail ray (*Taeniura lymma*), dorado (*Coryphaena hippurus*), dogtooth tuna (*Gymnosarda unicolor*) and five species of sea turtle, including the green turtle (*Chelonia mydas*). Smaller fish commonly found in the Red Sea include clownfish, the Napoleon fish (*Cheilinus undulatus*) and barracuda. The poisonous tassled scorpionfish (*Scorpaenopsis oxycephala*) is good at camouflage and should be kept at a distance.

**Endangerment and marine conservation** Until recently, there was very little education about conservation and sustainability in Saudi Arabia. This is slowly changing, although it is questionable how much environmental awareness has increased among the general population as it remains commonplace to see everything from water-based littering to spear fishing despite both being illegal.

Saudi Vision 2030 (page 28) has a number of offshore development projects along the Red Sea coast. In particular, Coral Bloom – a new destination geared towards the luxury end of the market, centred on Shurayrah Island off the coast near the village of Hanak – is a flagship project of The Red Sea Development Company (TRSDC). This ambitious project claims to have sustainability and biodiversity considerations at the heart of its plans to develop new beaches, a new lagoon and 11 hotels.

Further up the coast, at the northern end of the Red Sea, it was announced in 2021 that the smart city of NEOM (page 29) and King Abdullah University of Science and Technology (KAUST) plan to jointly build a coral garden around Shusha Island just southeast of the Gulf of Aqaba. Its purpose is to enable the study and preservation of coral reefs by scientists, researchers and eco-tourists – at present, the island's waters sustain over 1,000 species of fish and 300 species of corals. It is difficult to predict what the future holds regarding these massive developments.

**NATURE CONSERVATION AND RESERVES** The National Center for Wildlife (NCW; **w** ncw.gov.sa) has so far recognised 15 designated protected areas at the time of

## NATIONAL CENTER FOR WILDLIFE PROTECTED AREAS

The following list is organised broadly from north to south.

| Protected Area | Location | Attractions |
|---|---|---|
| Al Tubayq Natural Reserve | Northwest Tabuk Province | Rüppell's fox, Arabian and Arabian sand gazelles, hare, ibex, Arabian wolf, falcons, eagles, partridges |
| Harrat al Sham aka Black Desert | Al Jouf and Northern Borders provinces | Arabian and Arabian sand gazelles, striped hyena, Rüppell's fox |
| Al Khunfah Natural Reserve | Al Jouf and Tabuk provinces | Houbara bustard, rock doves, sandgrouse, lappet-faced vultures |
| At Taysiyaa aka Imam Turki bin Abdullah Royal Natural Reserve | Northeast Ha'il Province into al Qassim Province | Arabian oryx, Arabian sand gazelle, houbara bustard (winter) |
| Majami'al-Hadb Reserve | Najd Province | Caracal, Cape hare, white-tailed mongooses, honey badger, rock hyrax, Rüppell's fox, Arabian wolf |
| Nafud al Urayq aka Nafood Aloraiq | Al Qassim Province | Houbara bustard, striped hyena, Arabian wolf |
| Ibex Reserve | Riyadh Province | Ibex, rock hyrax, wild cats, mongooses, eagles, Arabian gazelle |
| 'Uruq Bani Ma'arid | Riyadh and Najran provinces | Arabian oryx, Arabian and Arabian sand gazelles, ostrich being reintroduced to the wild |

writing, though there are dozens of other proposed areas on the list. Most of the NCW protected areas are in remote locations, with little to no infrastructure, so it is advisable to check with someone with local knowledge if you wish to visit. Some require permits.

Some of the protected areas are remote and difficult to access, but there are several national parks and other green venues throughout the Kingdom. If you are short of time or prefer to remain near a city, then these are relatively easy to visit.

**Kharrarah National Park** This national park (page 146) is located about 1 hour's drive southwest of Riyadh, where there are red sand dunes and a lakebed known as the Lake of Liquid Light which is magical after any rain.

**Saja Umm Ar-Rimth Natural Reserve and Mahazat as-Said** These sanctuaries (see below) are adjacent to each other and may be combined with a visit to al Wabah crater, which is just over an hour away. It's a long journey from Taif or Madinah, the nearest cities. But if you are prepared to make a long drive, both are located off Route 80. Others may choose to visit if travelling between Jeddah and Riyadh.

| Protected Area | Location | Attractions |
|---|---|---|
| Jubail Marine Wildlife Sanctuary | Eastern Province | Sea turtles, foxes, corals developed after the pollution from the Gulf War 1991 |
| Saja Umm ar Rimth Natural Reserve | Northeast Makkah Province | Houbara bustard |
| Mahazat as Sayd | Northeast Makkah Province adjacent to Saja Umm ar Rimth | Reintroduction of ostrich, Arabian oryx, Arabian and Arabian sand gazelle; grasslands have regenerated |
| Umm al Qamari Islands | Southwest Makkah Province | Gulls, herons, osprey, pelicans, plovers |
| Jabal Shada Nature Reserve | Al Bahah Province | Might have Arabian leopards, over 500 plant species |
| Raydah Natural Reserve | Asir Province | Caracal, Cape hare, ibex, mongooses, honey badger, rock hyrax, Arabian wolf, partridges; also endemic Arabian birds including Yemen thrush, Yemen woodpecker, Yemen linnet |
| Farasan Islands Protected Area | Jizan Province | Gazelle, European migratory birds, dolphins, dugong, manta ray, green and hawksbill sea turtles, whale shark, whales |

**Saysed National Park** Conveniently located on the eastern outskirts of Taif, this is a pleasant park (page 291) to visit for anyone looking for greenery and running water as there is a stream that runs after the rains. It is also a popular spot for camping outside of winter.

**Asir National Park** Established in 1981, this is the Kingdom's oldest national park (page 318) and is located near Abha. Stretching from the Red Sea to the mountains, it is home to diverse flora and fauna, including the protected ibex. It is very popular in the summer when many Saudis travel to the region for the relatively comfortable weather.

**Farasan Islands Protected Area** The Farasan Islands Marine Sanctuary (page 341) protects much of this archipelago of more than 170 islands and islets, along with the surrounding seas. It is reached via ferry from Jazan Port, which accepts vehicles and foot traffic. These islands are interesting for environmentalists and holidaymakers and are becoming increasingly popular to visit.

## HISTORY

Given the large geography of the Arabian Peninsula, the history of one region of Saudi Arabia can be very different to that of another. More detailed information can be found in each relevant chapter.

**PREHISTORIC TIMES** Much of what is known about the earliest history of what is now Saudi Arabia has been pieced together from a combination of sources, including the analysis of artefacts uncovered in archaeological digs. It is believed that desertification occurred here between 7,300 and 5,500 years ago, and rock art, found in most corners of the Kingdom, provides a window to a very different climactic past. Scenes indicate a much more fertile land, including evidence of farming and the use of domesticated animals which were no longer able to survive in the desert climate when the monsoon rains eventually failed.

One of the oldest examples is the UNESCO World Heritage Site of Rock Art in the Ha'il Region (page 174), which actually comprises two clusters of rock art: one around Jebel Umm Senman Mountain in the Jubbah area, about 120km northeast of Ha'il, and the other at Shuwaimis and Jebel al Manjor, about 370km southwest of Ha'il toward Madinah. The art at both sites dates back more than 10,000 years and is a rich depiction of the life and times of the region, showing how the population used animals, likely spiritual practices, and scenes of war and defence. Both sites are believed to have been located around fresh water which supported these agricultural and pastoral pursuits.

In the north, Akkadian inscriptions from the Assyrians date Dumat al Jandal to 10,000BCE. These inscriptions also refer to at least five queens and female deities of the era, and are considered evidence of the existence of female monarchies during this time. Tayma is believed to be one of the Kingdom's oldest settlements, as Assyrian inscriptions substantiate it to the 8th century BCE. Similarly, petroglyphs in the relatively recently discovered Camel Site near Sakaka date back to 5600BCE. The Rajajil columns, located on the outskirts of Sakaka in al Jouf Province, date back to 4000BCE and are believed to be the remnants of temples where people of the region gathered for religious practices. Pottery shards from the era place this semi-nomadic civilisation beyond the north of the Kingdom, extending to what is now modern-day Iraq, Jordan, Syria and parts of the Sinai Peninsula.

The southern reaches of what is now the Kingdom are also rich in rock art. In 2021, UNESCO recognised the Hima Cultural Area as the Kingdom's newest World Heritage Site. Located deep in Najran Province, this is another treasure trove of petroglyphs which provides information about Neolithic life in this region of the Kingdom. Located on ancient caravan route from Yemen to points north, this rock art chronicles at least 7,000 years of a thriving culture involved in long-distance trade. It also includes hunting scenes and depictions of animal and plant life from these ancient times.

Rock art is prolific elsewhere in the Kingdom, including the al Ula region which was once a major stop on the trade route between the southern Arabian Peninsula and the Levant. Jebel Ikmah, a mountain referred to as the 'outdoor library', contains inscriptions in Dadantic, Thamudic, Minaic and Nabataean languages, charting the rich history of the people who arrived at this caravan spot over the course of many centuries from late pre-Christian times.

**ANCIENT ARAB KINGDOMS** The starting point in understanding the history of Saudi Arabia is recognition of the many kingdoms that ruled various areas of the Arabian Peninsula. Historians have had to rely on written accounts from contemporary empires for their understanding of most of the early Arab kingdoms, as there are no known written records from the kingdoms themselves. These include accounts from the Romans, Greeks, Egyptians and Persians.

**Obaid (5300–3600BCE)** The Obaid or Ubaid period is in evidence in what is now Eastern Province. Shards of pottery from these early Mesopotamian people have been unearthed near Jubail, indicating the presence of some of the first civilisations to have lived a more settled lifestyle.

**Dilmun (2400–1700BCE)** The traders who formed the Dilmun Kingdom lived on the edge of the Arabian Gulf, north from what is now Bahrain and along the eastern Saudi coast, and were known by the Mesopotamians. They controlled trade routes that reached far beyond the Gulf, possibly as far as the Indus Valley and onward to China. The Dilmuns also benefited from agricultural pursuits, as an abundance of freshwater wells meant that the coastal land was fertile during this period. The kingdom is believed to have come to an end after being conquered by the Assyrians.

**Midian (1700–1050BCE)** Midian is a figure mentioned in the Jewish Torah, Christian Bible and the Qur'an, described as a son of Abraham/Ibrahim. Academics differ on whether the term refers to a geographical place or to a collection of tribes from this era who claim descent from Ibrahim's son. The location of Midian is to the east of the Gulf of Aqaba in the far northwest of what is now Saudi Arabia, and into the Midian Mountains, an extension of the Hejaz Mountain range. Artefacts suggest that the Midian people were polytheistic, while the well-preserved Midian tombs (Maghaeer Shwuaib; page 203) are located near al Bad, their presumed capital.

**Qedarite (900–200BCE)** The Qedarite Kingdom – named after Qedar, the second son of the Islamic prophet Ishmael – was an association of mostly nomadic Arab tribes. They covered a large area which included what are now parts of the Northern Borders, al Jouf, Tabuk and Medina provinces, as well as Mesopotamia, the Levant and Sinai. It is believed that the Qedarites were allies of the Nabataeans, and eventually went on to merge with them.

**Dadan (700–100BCE)** Dadan, also known as Liyhan, covered a region from the Gulf of Aqaba (known in the past as the Gulf of Liyhan) in the west to Yathrib (modern Madinah) in the south, Tayma in the east and into the Levant in the north. The people had their own Dadantic language, as found on artefacts in and around al Ula, the modern name for Dadan. They were polytheists and controlled a number of significant caravan routes carrying trade north through the Arabian Peninsula, eventually becoming rivals to the Nabataeans. The Romans later conquered the Nabataeans and supported the continuation of the Liyhanite Kingdom, though the less powerful Liyhanites eventually fell to the Nabataeans as the latter absorbed their land.

**Nabataean (300BCE–100CE)** Nabataean culture is most famously associated with Petra in Jordan, but in fact the Nabataeans were an association of nomadic Arab tribes found along trade routes from Petra to Hegra (Mada'in Saleh) in northwest Madinah Province. They were polytheists, who focused their worship on the god Dushara, and although they spoke a dialect of Arabic, their writing developed from an early Aramaic script. The Nabataean Kingdom was annexed by the Romans for almost 600 years, expanding to most of the Hejaz and acting as a buffer against other Arab tribes hostile to the Romans. They were regarded as part of the wider Thamudic collection of tribes which stretched to the south of what is now Jeddah.

**Mai'in (400–150BCE)** The Kingdom of Mai'in, an early Yemeni kingdom, was centred in the desert south of what is now Najran Province. During the 3rd century BCE, its influence expanded into Najran, Asir and the Hejaz mountains, reaching as far as the Red Sea. The Greek geographer Eratosthenes recorded the Minaeans' existence around 200BCE and also documented the Sabaeans, who similarly expanded their influence into the southwest from the southern reaches of the Arabian Peninsula. He named the region, extending to most of what is now Yemen, Arabia Eudaimon ('Happy, or Flourishing, Arabia') for its fertile ground. The Romans, who controlled much of southern Arabia, adopted the name into Latin as Arabia Felix. Greek and Roman inscriptions still exist in the UNESCO World Heritage Site of Bir Hima in Najran Province.

**Himyarite (110BCE–520CE)** The Himyarite Kingdom absorbed some of the earlier tribes of the southwest region. Initially polytheistic, it converted to Judaism around the turn of the 5th century CE and established several Jewish monarchies that reigned both in Yemen and in Najran, known at the time as al Ukhdood. Christianity, which is believed to have arrived from the Kingdom of Aksum in East Africa, dominated Ukhdood after the defeat of the Jewish king Dhu Nawas, which also signified the end of control by the Himyarites.

**Sassanid (224–651CE)** The Sassanid Empire was a Persian empire that stretched east from Egypt and Turkey to parts of modern Pakistan, as well as down the east coast of the Arabian Peninsula. They were able to control this part of their empire due to their close alliance with the Lakhmids, who were effectively their agents. The collapse of the Lakhmids and the rise of the Prophet Mohammed and his followers led to the end of Sassanid influence in the Arabian Peninsula, culminating in Sassanid defeat by Arab tribes in the Battle of Dhi Qar. The Prophet Mohammed and his followers were involved in a number of battles that ultimately led to the collapse of the empire.

**Lakhmid (300–622CE)** The Lakhmid Kingdom was established in southern Iraq by the Banu Lakhm from the Qahtani tribe in Yemen. Their control reached the Yamama area of eastern Najd to Bahrain and further south along the Gulf to what is now Oman. They were hostile to the Roman Empire and the Byzantines and their allies who were in the west of Saudi Arabia, and were often but not always in alliance with the Sassanids. They were defeated by Arab Najdi tribes.

**Ghassanid (400–700CE)** Originating in southern Arabia, the Ghassanids migrated to the Levant where they formed the Ghassanid Kingdom, which included parts of what is now Tabuk Province. Many of this group were early converts to Christianity. Initially allies of the Romans, they were later aligned with the Byzantines and enemies of the Arab Lakhmids and Persian Sassanids. They were overthrown by the Muslim Rashidun Caliphate at the Battle of Yarmuk in what is now Syria, ending their influence in the region.

**Kinda (450–550CE)** Originating in southern Arabia, the Kinda people were supported by the Sabaeans and then the Himyarites to establish the Kingdom of Kinda, reaching from what is now Eastern Province and Najd region to the west, almost to Yathrib and Mecca. They were an urban people who tried to lead centrally, but ultimately failed due to a series of tribal feuds within the territory and infighting among the great-grandsons of the founder Hujr Akil al Murar.

## LIFE OF THE PROPHET MOHAMMED, PBUH

This is a brief chronology of the Prophet Mohammed's impact on Saudi Arabia from a historical perspective. A more detailed description about key religious events can be found from page 88.

**C570CE** Birth of the Prophet Mohammed. He was born into the al Hashim branch of the Quraysh tribe from Mecca. His father died before his birth; his mother died when he was six and so he was raised by his grandfather and uncle.

**C610CE** The Prophet Mohammed is believed to have received revelations from God via the angel Gabriel/Jibril while praying in al Hira cave near Mecca. He starts to spread the fundamental beliefs of what became the Islamic faith.

**622CE** The Prophet Mohammed and his followers migrate to Yathrib (now Madinah) to escape persecution in Mecca. This became known as the Hijra. The Hijri or Islamic calendar begins with this event, with Day One corresponding to 16 July 622CE in the Western calendar, set posthumously by the Rashidun Caliph Umar.

**624–32CE** A series of visits and military campaigns in much of the Arabian Peninsula leads to the spread of Islam throughout the region. The mostly pagan population converts to Islam; many Jewish residents also convert, while others flee.

**629CE** The Prophet Mohammed returns to Mecca with his army of followers.

**632CE** The Prophet Mohammed dies from illness.

**ISLAMIC CALIPHATES** Caliphates were established from the earliest days of Islam. These religious states encompassed much of what is now the modern Kingdom, other than parts of the southwest, where Yemeni kingdoms were dominant.

**Rashidun (632–61CE)** The Rashidun Caliphate was established after the Prophet's death. Its four successive leaders were Abu Bakr, Umar, Uthman and Ali, who were known as the Rightly Guided Caliphs. The caliphate expanded under Umar and Uthman, reaching west into the Maghreb, north to the Caucuses and east to what is now most of Pakistan and Central Asia. Although Abu Bakr died naturally, Umar and Uthman were assassinated. Growing disagreements about who should lead the caliphate boiled over after the death of Uthman, leading to a de facto civil war between Muslim allegiances and the division of Islam into Sunni and Shi'a sects. Ali, too, was assassinated, and the caliphate collapsed.

**Umayyad (661–750CE)** Founded by Mu'awiya, a relative of Uthman, the Umayyad Caliphate was dominated by a series of leaders from the clan of the same name. They continued growing their territory further into North Africa and into al Andalus, reaching as far as Spain, Portugal and southwest France. Arabic was introduced as the common language. The caliphate was also moved at this time to Damascus. Although there was religious tolerance of Christians and Jews, adherents of those religions were obligated to pay a tax that was not levied on Muslims. This was a period of great influence, but it was also one of continued disagreement about the structure of the caliphate as leaders from various branches of the clans could not unite. It eventually fell to the rival Abbasid family.

**Abbasid (750–1517CE)** The Abbasid Caliphate arose as a result of the Abbasids' success in their revolution over the Umayyads, returning power to the descendants of the Prophet Mohammed's family and moving the caliphate's seat to what is now Baghdad. Centred in several cities in Iraq and Egypt, they continued to control the Arabian Peninsula, but were fractured into various dynasties over the centuries. They notably established the Mamluk Sultanate of Egypt – an army of mostly non-Arabs loyal to the Abbasids, who were based in Cairo and controlled much of the Tihamah plain and Hejaz. They ultimately lost power with the arrival of the Ottomans.

**OTTOMAN RULE: 1517–1918** Ottoman rule of substantial parts of the Arabian Peninsula began in the early 16th century under the reign of Selim I, who conquered

### SHARIFATE OF MECCA: 967–1925CE

The Sharifate of Mecca was established to protect the holiest site in Islam and to protect pilgrims performing hajj. During Ottoman rule, the area of protection expanded to Madinah and was overseen in conjunction with the Ottomans. All sharifs of Mecca descended from the Banu Hashim branch of the Quraysh tribe, from which the Prophet Mohammed also descended; they were, in fact, direct descendants of the Prophet through his daughter Fatima. The last Sharif of Mecca, Ali bin Hussein, was expelled by the conquering al Sauds in 1925. His brothers Abdullah and Faisal, facilitated by the British who ruled Transjordan at the time, became the first kings of Jordan and Iraq respectively.

the Mamluk Sultanate of Egypt. This territory included Mecca and Madinah, where the Ottomans styled themselves as Custodian of the Two Holy Mosques, with the allegiance of the Sharif of Mecca. Ottoman control also extended to what are now parts of southern Saudi Arabia and Yemen to the mouth of the Red Sea. Along the Arabian Gulf, Ottoman rule in al Hasa ran down the coast from the modern Kuwaiti border to south of the port of Uqair. The Ottomans retained power over this area to varying degrees for roughly the next 400 years, before losing control of al Hasa to ibn Saud in 1913 (see below). In 1916, the British supported a pan-Arab revolt against the Ottomans, which, although not initially successful, further weakened the Ottomans, who lost their remaining control at the end of World War I.

**THE THREE SAUDI STATES** There has been a total of three Saudi States. As the name implies, each was under the rule of the al Saud family.

**The First Saudi State (1744–1818)** Led by Emir Mohammed bin Saud al Muqrin and also known as the Emirate of Diriyah, the House of Saud was a powerful family in the agricultural village of Diriyah. In 1744, the family formed an alliance with Mohammed bin Abdul Wahhab, leader of a religious group seeking a stricter interpretation of Islam (page 20). This alliance was also the foundation for expanding the al Saud's power and influence, first through Najd and eventually along the Gulf coast from Kuwait to Oman, into most of the north, and southwest to parts of Asir. The remaining Hejaz continued to be ruled by the Ottomans until the al Sauds challenged them, taking control of Taif, Mecca and Madinah in 1803. In retaliation, the Ottomans organised a military campaign against Diriyah and removed the al Saud Emir from power, causing the state's collapse in 1818.

**The Second Saudi State (1824–91)** Several years later, the Emirate of Nejd or the Second Saudi State was born. The al Sauds were once again in control of the interior of the Arabian Peninsula, but were much less powerful, vying in the region with the al Rashids – rulers of the Emirate of Jebel Shammar to the north of Najd/Nejd – for most of this timeframe. The al Rashids ultimately gained control in 1891, forming an alliance with the Ottomans, absorbing the Emirate of Nejd and forcing the al Sauds into exile in Kuwait.

**The Third Saudi State (1902–present)** The birth of the Third Saudi State began with the recapture of Riyadh by Abdul Aziz bin Abdul Rahman ibn Saud and his supporters, followed by the swift recapture of Nejd. The Ikhwan, a military force comprised of Bedouin tribes loyal to ibn Saud were key to the formation of the Third Saudi State, repelling various enemies during this crucial period. By 1913, ibn Saud's military had won al Hasa from the Ottomans, gaining control from the centre of the Arabian Peninsula to the Gulf Coast. In 1915, the Treaty of Darin was signed between Britain and ibn Saud, agreeing to recognise the borders of the Emirate of Nejd and Hasa. In 1921, ibn Saud's raid on Ha'il led to the surrender of the Emirate of Jebel Shammar and the al Rashids, and the incorporation of the northern reaches into the Emirate of Nejd and Hasa. Momentum continued, with the annexation of the Hejaz in 1924–25. Known as the Kingdom of Hejaz, this emirate was initially run separately from the Emirate of Nejd and Hasa for the next several years. In 1932, they merged into the Kingdom of Saudi Arabia.

**THE KINGDOM OF SAUDI ARABIA** The Third Saudi State developed into the modern Kingdom of Saudi Arabia as it is known today. Key events that have brought the

## IMPACT OF MOHAMMED BIN ABDUL WAHHAB

Born to a family of modest means about 1703 in al Uyaynah near Diriyah, the home of the al Sauds, Mohammed bin Abdul Wahhab was a religious scholar who led a movement to return to the fundamentals of Islam and the purity of the first three generations of Muslims. Practices such as pilgrimages to saints' tombs were seen as idolatry and contrary to monotheism and were banned. As this doctrine took hold among more followers, some powerful leaders in the region tried to expel al Wahhab from Uyaynah, which had now become a religious centre. Mohammed bin Abdul Wahhab asked the Emir of Diriyah, Mohammed bin Saud of the al Saud family, for support. This alliance was formed in 1744. Its key conditions were that the al Sauds would support the doctrine of the al Wahhabs. In return, the al Wahhabs would support the rule and governance of the al Sauds. The al Saud rule of the First Saudi State became stronger with this alliance, and ultimately the al Saud family became the rulers of the Kingdom of Saudi Arabia. Today's descendants of the al Wahhab family are the al Sheikh family. This agreement remains in force to the present time, with varying balances of power and influence. Under the reign of King Salman and the Crown Prince Mohammed bin Salman, the al Sauds currently enjoy a position of significant power, and al Wahhab control over many religious matters has diminished in recent years.

newly united Kingdom to the modern country it has become illustrate the rapid pace of change. Important milestones include:

**1932** The Kingdom of Saudi Arabia is formally established on 23 September with the unification of the Nejd and Hejaz kingdoms. Abdul Aziz bin Abdul Rahman ibn Saud is king.

**1933** Standard Oil of California (SOCAL) is granted a licence to explore for oil.

**1934** The Treaty of Taif settles most of the border disputes between Saudi Arabia and Yemen, with the Saudi provinces of Najran, Asir and Jizan incorporated into the Kingdom.

**1938** CALTEX, a consortium of Saudi, SOCAL and other American companies, discovers oil near Dhahran in Eastern Province.

**1943** Arabian American Oil (Saudi Aramco) is born.

**1953** Ibn Saud dies. His named successor, his son Saud bin Abdul Aziz, becomes king and is quickly seen as extravagant.

**1960** The Organization of the Petroleum Exporting Countries (OPEC) is created, with Saudi Arabia a founding member.

**1962** Slavery is formally abolished.

**1964** King Saud is deposed by his brother King Faisal, who initiates several reforms. These include the introduction of television and considerable changes to fiscal structure within the government to counterbalance the excesses of his predecessor.

**1965** Although the Saudi Arabia–Jordan border was formally defined in 1925 with the Treaty of Hadda, and confirmed in the 1927 Treaty of Jeddah, the area around Qurayyat had remained in dispute; this is resolved by the Amman Agreement of 1965.

**1973** OPEC proclaims an oil embargo targeted at countries supporting Israel in the Yom Kippur War.

**1974** The Treaty of Jeddah defining the Saudi Arabia–UAE border is agreed between King Faisal and the UAE's Sheikh Zayed, but only ratified by the Saudis. As it also impacted the border with Qatar, it has subsequently been in dispute.

**1975** King Faisal is assassinated by his nephew Faisal bin Musaid; King Faisal's brother Khalid becomes the next monarch.

**1979** The Kingdom grows concerned about its Shi'a population in reaction to the Iranian Revolution. In November, a ban on publicly recognising Ashoura, an important time in the Shi'a calendar, results in the Qatif Uprising – a period of civil unrest between Sunni and Shi'a.

Also in November, extremists demanding the overthrow of the royal family gain control of the Masjid al Haram, Islam's holiest site, in what became known as the Siege of Mecca. The siege lasted for nearly two weeks before control was regained, with more than 800 people killed or injured. Many of the militants died during the violence, but some escaped. Nearly 70 others who survived were swiftly tried and beheaded in eight different cities. This event directly led to the tightening of already very conservative social rules, including the closure of cinemas, strict adherence to the dress code and the increased power of the religious police (*mutawa*; page 63) to enforce these edicts.

**1980** Saudi Arabia supports Iraq in the Iran–Iraq War, which lasted until 1988.

**1981** The Gulf Cooperation Council (GCC) is established as a regional alliance promoting intergovernmental and economic unity.

**1982** King Khalid dies of a heart attack; his brother Fahd becomes king.

**1988** Al Qaeda is formed by Osama bin Laden. This movement – an amalgamation of Salafi and modern Islamist thinking – is motivated to bring a back-to-basics view of Islam to the world, regarding other beliefs – including Muslim ones – as illegitimate.

**1990** The Saudi Arabia–Oman border is agreed between King Fahd and Sultan Qaboos.

**1991** The neutral zone along the Saudi Arabia–Iraq border – originally agreed as part of the Uqair Protocol in 1922, and confirmed in the Bahra Agreement of 1925 – is formally split between the two countries, following an agreement reached in 1975. This border has been closed for much of its history, only reopening in November 2020.

**1992** Basic Law of Saudi Arabia is introduced, similar to a constitution. It is based entirely on the Salafist interpretation of Shari'a Law, recognising the Qur'an and Sunnah as its basis and confirming the right of the al Saud family to rule in the Kingdom.

**1990s** Osama bin Laden becomes unhappy with the presence of Western military troops on Saudi soil – seen as sacred to Muslims – as part of the Gulf War in Kuwait.

**1995** King Fahd suffers a major stroke, limiting his ability to rule. His brother Crown Prince Abdullah takes over most duties.

**1999** The G20 is formed, with Saudi Arabia as a member.

**2000** The renewal of the Treaty of Jeddah by the foreign ministers of Saudi Arabia and Yemen finalises the disputed border of Jizan Province.

**2001** The Saudi Arabia–Qatar border agreement is finally signed after decades of discussion.

**2001** The attacks of September 11 in the US are carried out by 19 terrorists, 15 of whom were Saudi nationals. These events immediately set off world-changing responses.

**2005** King Fahd dies; his brother Crown Prince Abdullah becomes king.

**2005** Saudi Arabia joins the World Trade Organization.

**2008** King Abdullah inaugurates the new Princess Nourah bint Abdul Rahman University, the world's largest women's university. Princess Nourah was the influential older sister and confidant of ibn Saud and was known by many as 'the woman who has the brain of 40 men'.

**2009** King Abdullah continues to implement significant educational reforms to expand and modernise education. King Abdullah University of Science and Technology (KAUST), the Kingdom's first co-educational university, is launched in association with leading global scientists with the aim of facilitating the diversification of the economy.

**2009–15** King Abdullah continues further educational reforms, appoints a more moderate head of the religious police and decrees a series of early improvements of women's rights.

**2013** For the first time, a woman is granted a licence to practise law.

**2015** King Abdullah dies at the age of 90; his brother King Salman becomes the seventh Saudi king. King Salman names his nephew Mohammed bin Nayef as Crown Prince and his son Mohammed bin Salman as Deputy Crown Prince, breaking tradition with the line of succession (page 24).

**2016** Saudi Vision 2030 is announced.

**2016** The Saudi Arabia–Egypt border dispute over the islands of Tiran and Sanafir at the mouth of the Gulf of Aqaba is resolved, with both islands now part of Saudi Arabia.

**2017** Mohammed bin Salman, widely known as MBS, becomes Crown Prince after Mohammed bin Nayef is deposed.

**2018–present** Women's rights continue to improve, although they do not include full emancipation in matters of marriage approval or passing citizenship to children. Key reforms that have made a significant difference to women include: gaining the right to drive (2018); participation in more sporting events, both actively and as spectators (2018); leaving the country without permission from their *mahram* (male guardian; 2019); joining the military (2021) and performing hajj and umrah without a mahram if over 45 (2022). In 2019 a woman was granted a commercial airline pilot's licence for the first time and by 2020 women comprised 33% of the Saudi workforce, up from 20% just two years previously in 2018.

**2018** The prominent Saudi journalist Jamal Khashoggi is murdered by Saudi operatives in the Saudi Consulate in Istanbul.

**2019** General tourism opens before being suspended five months later due to Covid-19.

**2021** Tourism reopens.

## GOVERNMENT AND POLITICS

The Kingdom of Saudi Arabia is an absolute monarchy with Riyadh its capital. Since independence, it has been ruled by kings from the al Saud royal family, beginning with Abdul Aziz bin Abdul Rahman al Saud, founder of Saudi Arabia, followed by six of his sons as of 2023. The al Saud family ruled previous Saudi states prior to unification (page 19).

**THE KING** The Saudi king (*melek* or *malik*) uses the title 'Custodian of the Two Holy Mosques' (*khadim al haramayn al sarifayn*) in place of 'His Majesty', emphasising the importance of religious responsibilities in addition to governance of the Kingdom. The king is both head of state and head of government and also holds the title of Prime Minister. At the time of publication, the kings of Saudi Arabia have been:

| | Reigned |
|---|---|
| Abdul Aziz ibn Saud (b1875) | 1953 |
| Saud bin Abdul Aziz (b1902) | 1953–64 |
| Faisal bin Abdul Aziz (b1906) | 1964–75 |
| Khalid bin Abdul Aziz (b1913) | 1975–82 |
| Fahd bin Abdul Aziz (b1921) | 1982–2005 |
| Abdullah bin Abdul Aziz (b1924) | 2005–15 |
| Salman bin Abdul Aziz (b1935) | 2015–present |

**CROWN PRINCE** The crown prince is the second most important figure after the king. For the majority of the history of the modern Kingdom, this position was held by a son of ibn Saud. That changed, however, in 2015, when Mohammed bin Nayef, a grandson of ibn Saud, became the first crown prince from his generation. He held this position until 21 June 2017, when he was deposed by royal decree and replaced by his cousin Mohammed bin Salman, deputy crown prince from 2014 to 2017 and the current crown prince at the time of publication.

**SUCCESSION** The line of succession in Saudi Arabia is not through the familiar system of primogeniture. Instead, the designated successor is the crown prince, who is chosen by the king. The role of crown prince was historically allocated according to agnatic seniority – meaning it went to a younger brother of the king rather than a son – though this all changed when King Salman appointed his nephew in 2015 and then his son in 2017.The succession process is overseen by the Allegiance Council, established by King Abdullah in 2007. Members of the Council are living sons of ibn Saud, grandsons of deceased sons and sons of the king and crown prince.

**STRUCTURE** The king controls all legislative, executive and judicial aspects of governance, issuing royal decrees that are implemented upon receipt. Members of the royal family have substantial presence and influence in these institutions. There are several thousand princes, as well as a number of princesses who have become more publicly active in government in recent years. Saudi governance has no transparency and little accountability as budgets and other important information is not disclosed to the public.

The king is head of the **Council of Ministers**, which comprises the crown prince and 23 ministers with portfolios ranging from foreign affairs to education and other posts. There are also additional ministers of state.

The **Consultative Assembly**, also known as the **Shura Council**, advises the king and proposes laws to the king and cabinet. The assembly has 150 members, appointed by the king, including a minimum of 20% women since 2013. The speaker is traditionally a member of the al Sheikh family. The king has the ultimate power to choose whether to accept the assembly's advice.

The **Supreme Judicial Council** is a seven-member body led by the Minister of Justice; all members are appointed by the king. The council's duties include the supervision of lower courts and judges' performances. It is also involved in reviewing corporal and capital punishment sentences.

The **Council of Senior Scholars**, the ***Ulema***, is the most important religious institution. It has 21 members and is responsible for advising the king on religious matters. The al Sheikh family, descendants of the al Wahhab family (page 20), dominates the Ulema. The Grand Mufti, the Kingdom's most senior religious authority, is head of the council and is directly appointed by the king. His role is focused on issuing *fatwas* (فتوى), which are opinions on legal and social matters.

More informally, other important Saudis, including traditional tribal leaders and prominent merchant families, also have some influence over the Saudi system of governance.

**REGIONS** Saudi Arabia is comprised of 13 regions (*manatiq idāriyya*), often informally referred to as provinces, each of which has an al Saud prince as governor. These regions collectively contain 118 governorates (*muhafazet*) which are further subdivided. All of the 13 regional capitals have the status of municipalities (*amanah*) and are headed by a mayor (*amin*).

**INTERNATIONAL INFLUENCE** The Gulf Cooperation Council, usually referred to as the GCC, is an association of Gulf states which promotes governmental and economic unity. It was established in 1981, with its headquarters located in Riyadh. In addition to Saudi Arabia, its members are Bahrain, Kuwait, Oman, Qatar and the UAE.

Saudi Arabia is also a founding member of the United Nations and a member of the G20, as well as a member of the Arab League and OPEC.

**LAW** The legal system in Saudi Arabia is based on Islamic law known as Shari'a Law. Its constitution is regarded as the Qur'an and Sunnah, or traditions of the Prophet Mohammed. This was codified in the Basic Law of Saudi Arabia in 1992 by royal decree. The Kingdom interprets Basic Law through the Salafist view of Shari'a.

**HUMAN RIGHTS** The topic of human rights in Saudi Arabia can often be of great concern. For some, there is a perception that human rights do not exist at all. Human rights in the Kingdom are based on Shari'a Law, with ultimate power in the hands of the king via a judiciary also controlled by the king. As is permitted under Shari'a Law, Saudi Arabia practises both capital and corporate punishment. In recent years, along with many other matters, the Crown Prince has been at the forefront of many human rights issues.

Saudi Arabia's position on **capital punishment** means it may execute its own citizens or anyone else who commits a capital crime on its soil. Capital crimes in Saudi Arabia include murder, rape, apostasy, blasphemy, armed robbery, illegal drug smuggling, repeated drug use, adultery, sodomy, homosexual sexual activity, witchcraft, sorcery and terrorism. Saudi Arabia's usual method of execution is by beheading. Amnesty International reports 65 people were executed in the Kingdom in 2021, the most recent figure available at the time of writing. This figure represents an increase of 140% from the previous year.

Although all visitors to the Kingdom should have a healthy fear of capital punishment, in reality most people who suffer this fate have been involved in the illegal drug trade or have become entangled in illegal personal relationships with Saudi nationals.

Also sentenced to capital punishment are people who have been involved in terrorist activities or accused of invoking terror within the Kingdom. Most, but not all, have been Saudi, and they include members of al Qaeda. Perhaps the most prominent person to be executed on such charges is Nimr al Nimr, a Shi'a cleric considered by some to have been a fiery advocate for Shi'a minority rights, who was beheaded in 2016. His death sparked similar global outrage to the murder of the US-based Saudi journalist Jamal Khashoggi, an outspoken critic of the Saudi government, in the Saudi Consulate in Istanbul in 2018.

**Corporal punishment** is also used for certain crimes in Saudi Arabia. Punishments for the accused, seen as an eye-for-an-eye retribution for their victim's suffering, include amputations of hands and feet for crimes of robbery; there is also widespread evidence of torture. Lesser crimes such as 'sexual deviance', which were once punished by flogging, now attract jail time and fines. Visitors are not exempt from corporal punishment and cannot rely on their embassies to help them out of trouble.

*Diyya* (blood money) can be negotiated if the aggrieved party is willing and can be paid for both capital and corporal crimes.

Other **common human rights issues** include the ban on any form of protest. This has included protests about women's rights to make autonomous decisions about their choice of education, work, family life and the ability to travel abroad, or even to drive. Thankfully, women are now much more emancipated than they were just a few years ago, but protests about women being allowed to drive made the news for many years in the lead-up to the abolishment of the ban in 2018. And although this reform was announced early in the reign of the crown prince, he was also instrumental in punishing Saudi activists, mostly women, who had been protesting for it – many, such as Loujain al Hathloul, who were arrested in early

## SOCIAL MEDIA RESTRICTIONS

Visitors should be particularly aware of their activity on all social media platforms as there are many instances of people being banned, harassed, driven into exile and imprisoned for comments considered critical of members of the ruling family or Islam, or even those expressing mild criticism of the country. In 2016, a Saudi man was sentenced to flogging, prison and a fine for posts on Twitter that were considered to be anti-Islamic. Rules about social media content considered to violate public order, religious values and public morals mean that substantial fines and prison time can be handed out to anyone who is believed to be in violation of these rules, including visitors, even if the offending posts have been made abroad.

2018 only months before the right to drive was granted in June, were still forced to undergo prison sentences and travel bans as punishment. Some have now left the Kingdom.

Ongoing abuses of some unskilled labourers continue. These include sponsors taking away labourers' passports for 'safe keeping', essentially making them de facto hostages.

**Other rights issues** Attitudes towards animals in the Kingdom, from feral street animals to the most prized horses and camels, include some very unenlightened treatment. And environmentalists have raised concerns about a wide variety of issues such as the impact of the oil industry, the development of luxury properties on pristine beaches and coral reefs, and general litter.

## ECONOMY

Saudi Arabia's economy is ranked as the 18th largest in the world by the International Monetary Fund (IMF) at US$1.04 trillion as of 2022. It is the largest economy in the Middle East and is considered a growing regional power. However, it only ranks 49th in terms of GDP per capita, indicating an imbalance of wealth. Throughout most of history, including the early days of the Kingdom, the majority of Saudis lived a life of subsistence and many were nomadic.

**AGRICULTURE** The transition to food security began in the 1970s with the introduction of modern technology and large government schemes to reach productivity levels not seen before. As a result, Saudi Arabia moved beyond its traditional reliance on dates and olives, creating a thriving dairy industry that exports regionally to the Gulf countries and beyond. The Kingdom also has a successful infrastructure for farming grains, fruit, vegetables and poultry.

**OIL** Most people equate Saudi Arabia's economy with oil and rightly so. Oil exports represent 45% of GDP and 67% of export revenues. The Kingdom is the world's third-largest oil producer after the USA and Russia, and has the world's second-largest known oil reserves after Venezuela. Saudi Aramco is the world's largest oil company and began as a partnership between Standard Oil of California and the Saudi government under ibn Saud. It was originally known as the California Arabian Standard Oil Company, before it joined forces with the Texas Oil company to form CALTEX in 1936. It became the Arabian American Oil Company in 1944 and Saudi Aramco in 1988, when American oil interests were bought out. Today it is comparable in size to American tech company Apple.

**LABOUR FORCE** Saudi Arabia is a young country with rapid population growth. This has presented challenges, especially for the majority of Saudi nationals who have not benefited from a high-quality education from which knowledge and skills can be easily transferred to the practicalities of employment. Steps have been taken in recent years to prioritise employment for Saudi nationals through the *nitaqat* system. This complex system is intended to reserve some jobs for Saudi nationals only and to replace foreign workers in other jobs with Saudi nationals.

**Public and private sectors** In common with other GCC countries, most Saudis prefer to work in the public sector. The reasons can range from more stability, pay and compatible working terms and conditions, to status and prestige. About 70% of all employed Saudis work in the public sector. By contrast, around just 18% of private sector employees are Saudi nationals – though this actually represents a growth from less than 10% in the early 21st century. Even so, the *nitaqat* system remains only marginally successful in recruiting Saudi talent to the private sector. Unemployment remains consistently high at about 12%.

**Expatriate labour** Official statistics about expatriate labour are difficult to validate. It is estimated that about one-third of all residents in Saudi Arabia are expatriate workers and their dependents. All expatriates are subject to the *kafala* system, which sets very specific terms of work and residency rights and restrictions that apply to everyone. Details are determined by job title, renumeration and several other factors. Everyone who is not a Saudi national or a GCC national is an expatriate – not just Westerners.

**Other challenges** Many Saudi nationals have neither a sufficient educational background nor a desire to do some of the jobs that are in greatest demand. These skill gaps mean there is often a substantial mismatch between the potential employee's qualifications and the credentials required for many jobs. It is especially pronounced in sectors requiring science, technology, engineering and medical skills. Many individuals may also be the first in their family to hold such a job and lack a mentor at home, making it sometimes difficult meet the employer's expectations, especially in the private sector.

There is also significant religious sectarian discrimination within the Saudi population which generally favours Sunnis over Shi'a. Finally, there are many jobs that most Saudis would never accept due to perceptions of hierarchy, status and reputation. These are usually service roles such as maids, nannies and drivers, among many others. Youth unemployment remains over 25%.

**Employment and women** Women have historically struggled to access employment, resistance coming both from potential employers and often from their families. Until recently, women needed permission from their male guardian, or mahram, to accept a job. Now, however, they are able to decide for themselves whether they wish to work, and can be seen employed everywhere from retail shops and supermarkets to gender-integrated offices. Female unemployment was as high as 33% as recently as 2017, but is declining as newfound freedoms – including practising law and eligibility for some military roles – have a positive impact. In fact, women now make up an estimated one-third of the Saudi labour force, a total that has doubled since Saudi Vision 2030 (see below) was announced in 2016. Many of the biggest beneficiaries are urban, educated women who are now able to make employment choices unimaginable only a few years ago. But things are also changing for the better for Saudi women living in the provinces, as more families realise the benefits of female employment.

**Employment and people with disabilities** Traditionally, many Saudis regarded disability with something akin to shame. Attitudes are now changing, however, with more people with visible disabilities seen in public than before. About 10% of the Saudi population are believed to have a disability. Saudi Vision 2030 makes provisions for people with disabilities through *tawafuq*, a programme designed to ensure equal employment opportunities for people with disabilities in the private sector. However, it is also important to note that access to buildings and other mobility challenges remain frustrating issues as little practical accommodation has been made.

**SAUDI VISION 2030** (**w** vision2030.gov.sa) It has long been recognised that Saudi Arabia cannot continue to rely on oil revenues forever, nor can it continue with the many social restrictions in the age of global commerce and communication. And while previous kings such as King Abdullah took tentative steps in this direction, for various reasons they were limited in what they could realistically achieve. Saudi Vision 2030 aims to change that, however. Announced in April 2016 by then Deputy Crown Prince Mohammed bin Salman on behalf of King Salman, it aims to balance reform with Saudi Arabia's own cultural values.

Saudi Vision 2030 has three main strategic objectives:

1. **A vibrant society**, with the key focus on strengthening Islamic and Saudi identity and offering citizens a fulfilling and healthy life. This covers a wide range of culture and entertainment, sports, umrah, tourism and other initiatives to improve both life expectancy and quality of life.
2. **A thriving economy**, striving to achieve growth and diversification and to increase employment of Saudi men and women. It has recognised the need for international competitiveness, support of the Public Investment Fund, foreign direct investment, growth and increased participation in the private sector, and an increase in non-oil exports.
3. **An ambitious nation**, enhancing government effectiveness and enabling social responsibility. This encourages support for a robust e-government platform, household savings and income, and additional focus in the non-profit sector and volunteering.

In addition to many gains in women's rights, there has been a significant expansion of entertainment options that have a particular appeal to families and young adults. Cinema, live music and many other activities that were illegal only a few years ago are now available throughout the Kingdom. In general, young, urban, educated Saudi nationals support Saudi Vision 2030 as do many women.

However, there are some segments of Saudi society that are sceptical, suspicious of, or in some cases completely against the reforms and the way they are impacting traditional norms, especially those that they believe contravene conservative Islamic and social values. Others question the realism of the budget and timescales required for such an ambitious initiative. Human rights issues (page 25) are also a major challenge in attracting foreign investment.

**NEOM** (w neom.com; see also page 198) NEOM is a Saudi Vision 2030 project designed to be a world-class tourist and lifestyle destination. The project was announced by Crown Prince Mohammed bin Salman in 2017 and has a giga-budget of US$500 billion. It has been announced that NEOM will fall outside the direct jurisdiction of the Saudi government and will have its own bespoke legal system, leading to speculation that many conservative social codes could be potentially relaxed.

The NEOM site is located in the northwest of Tabuk Province, running along the Red Sea coast for a total of 460km from just south of the town of Haql near the Jordanian border to south of al Muwaileh. Covering a total area of more than 26,500km$^2$, it will include the offshore islands in the Straits of Tiran that approach Sharm el Sheikh in Egypt and a chain of smaller islands further south along the Saudi Red Sea coast. It will also incorporate the Hejaz Mountain range east to Shigry, including Jebel al Lawz. It is claimed that NEOM will be developed with green practices and that it will be designed to maintain a sustainable environment.

Supporters of NEOM note the giga-project contributes to the diversification of the economy and will provide substantial job opportunities. It is also an opportunity to open the Kingdom to visitors from all over the world. However, the list of concerns is long and growing. Accusations of greenwashing and human rights abuses, especially against the local Howeitat people who are being displaced against their will and without compensation, are particularly worrisome. Environmentalists are concerned for the future of pristine reefs and mountains which have traditionally received very few visitors, and questions about the water supply in an already very dry country remain mostly unanswered. It is also difficult to tell if the helicopter pads already in use are for the development of NEOM or will be a permanent form of transport, at least for the well-heeled. Time will tell.

**TOURISM** General tourism is another result of Saudi Vision 2030. Mostly little-known and underdeveloped, even to many expatriate residents, the Kingdom is now hoping to host as many as 100 million tourists by 2030. Although this figure is undoubtedly very ambitious, many well-travelled tourists are already making their way to one of the least explored destinations left in the world. Even pilgrimage tourists, who are generally restricted to the *miqat* zone broadly defined between Mecca, Jeddah and Madinah, will now be able to explore other parts of the Kingdom that were previously off limits, depending on their visa.

**UNESCO World Heritage Sites** Saudi Arabia is home to six UNESCO World Heritage sites and the Kingdom has applied for recognition of a further ten (page 30). At the time of publication, it is still possible to visit many of these sites when no other visitors are present. Infrastructure such as tourist welcome centres do exist in some locations but may not offer the usual services expected elsewhere in the world. This will not last as tourism develops.

**Saudi Seasons** (w saudiseasons.com) Launched in 2019, Saudi Seasons is an initiative to promote Saudi culture and heritage tourism for nationals and visitors alike. Activities range from those that appeal to Saudi nationals and residents such as family days out and regional cuisine programmes, to world-class events such as Formula 1 or Winter at Tantora (page 227). Most but not all 'seasons' are held in the winter months. There are currently 11 seasons held across the Kingdom: al Diriyah, al Soudah, al Ula, Eastern Province, Eid al Fitr, Ha'il, Jeddah, National Day, Ramadan, Riyadh and Taif. Although the official website

## UNESCO WORLD HERITAGE SITES

| | Province | Year recognised |
|---|---|---|
| Al Ahsa Oasis, an Evolving Cultural Landscape | Eastern | 2018 |
| Al Turaif District in ad Diriyah | Riyadh | 2010 |
| Mada'in Saleh (Hegra Archaeological Site) | Medina | 2008 |
| Hima Cultural Area | Najran | 2021 |
| Historic Jeddah, the Gate to Mecca | Makkah | 2014 |
| Rock Art in the Ha'il Region | Ha'il | 2015 |

### UNESCO WORLD HERITAGE SITES TENTATIVE LIST

| | Province | Year applied |
|---|---|---|
| Hejaz Railway | Tabuk, Medina | 2015 |
| Syrian Hajj Road | Tabuk, Medina, Makkah | 2015 |
| Egyptian Hajj Road | Tabuk, Medina, Makkah | 2015 |
| Rijal al Ma'a Village | Asir | 2015 |
| Zee al Ayn Heritage Village | Al Bahah | 2015 |
| Uruq Bani Mu'arid Protected Area | Najran | 2019 |
| Farasan Islands Protected Area | Jizan | 2019 |
| Al Faw Archaeological Area | Riyadh | 2022 |
| Ancient Walled Oases of Northern Arabia | Tabuk, al Jouf, Ha'il | 2022 |
| The Hajj Pilgrimage Routes: Darb Zubaydah | Northern, Ha'il, Riyadh, Medina, Makkah | 2022 |

*For further information, see* **w** *whc.unesco.org/en/statesparties/sa.*

is of varying quality, Visit Saudi Arabia (**w** visitsaudi.com) often has information about the Saudi Seasons calendar. It is also possible to learn about activities from local media during a visit.

## PEOPLE

**Saudi nationals** are broadly defined by bloodline and lineage, mostly through having a Saudi father. There are some exceptions for Saudi mothers and non-Saudi fathers, but these are limited. About 90% of all Saudis are ethnically Arab; the remaining 10% are Afro-Arab, often but not always descendants of enslaved people (slavery was legal in Saudi Arabia until 1962). Most Saudi nationals are not eligible for dual citizenship, which must be granted by the king.

At the time of independence in 1932, the **population** of Saudi Arabia was estimated to be about 2 million. As of 2023, the estimated population is around 36 million people, of which more than 50% are below 25 years old. The current birth rate is 2.27 children per woman – a much lower figure than the seven children per woman average that lasted until the early 1980s.

The population also includes somewhere in the region of 10–12 million **expatriates**, the majority coming from South Asia, the Philippines, Egypt and the Levant. There is also a relatively small number (estimated at around 100,000) of Western expatriates from Europe, North America and the Antipodes.

The largest cities in the Kingdom are Riyadh (population 8 million), Jeddah (population 4.7 million), Mecca (population 1.75 million), Greater Dammam including Dhahran and al Khobar (total population 1.7 million) and Madinah (population 1.4 million).

## LANGUAGE

Arabic is the official language of Saudi Arabia. It has three main dialects. Classical or Quranic Arabic is primarily used for religious purposes and is not generally spoken outside of this context. Modern Standard Arabic (MSA), considered to be 'educated' Arabic, is usually used in more formal situations, such as the media, educational settings and contemporary written works, or sometimes with outsiders who are learning the language. Think of MSA as the King's English or BBC English and you will be close.

Most Saudis speak a regional dialect of Arabic in everyday life. Dialectal or colloquial Arabic has many variations which are not always mutually intelligible. In particular, they vary significantly between the Gulf, Levant, Egypt and Maghreb. There are also different dialects of Arabic spoken within Saudi Arabia among Saudi nationals, as well as by Arabic-speaking expatriates. Key Saudi Arabic dialects include Gulf Arabic in Eastern Province, Najd Arabic in the Najd region including Riyadh, Rashaida Arabic in the Northern Borders and al Jouf, Hejazi Arabic along most of the Red Sea Coast including Jeddah, and Yemeni Arabic in the southwest, especially around Jazan.

English is the language of most global business and, increasingly, of tourism. Many young, well-educated and well-travelled Saudis speak English. However, among the older population and those from less privileged backgrounds or from provincial areas, Arabic is likely to be the only language spoken. There are also many other expatriate languages spoken in Saudi Arabia, most notably Hindi, Urdu, Bengali, Punjabi and Malayalam from South Asia, Tagalog, and Egyptian and Levantine Arabic.

## RELIGION

The official religion of Saudi Arabia is Islam. Unlike in other Middle East countries, no other faith can be openly practised in the Kingdom.

The information in this chapter is not designed to be a crash course towards a deep understanding of the nuances of Islam; rather it is intended to inform readers who may have a general interest in understanding the key concepts and facts about this important and growing faith. Islam, like other faiths, has different values, attitudes, interpretations, behaviours and practices, and the information that follows is in no way meant to divide opinion of Muslims or non-Muslims who may view certain details through their own individual lenses.

**ISLAM BASICS** People who follow the Islamic faith are Muslims, who are known globally as the *ummah* (religious community). The word Islam itself means submission to Allah (God); it has the same root as *salaam*, which means peace. It is a monotheistic, Abrahamic religion, sharing roots with Judaism and Christianity.

Collectively, members of these three faiths are known by Muslims as 'People of the Book'. All three faiths share a belief in prophets including Abraham and Moses, and both Christians and Muslims believe that Jesus was a prophet. Muslims alone believe in the Prophet Mohammed, who they regard as the last prophet.

The Qur'an is the religious text believed to be the literal word of God, delivered orally to the Prophet Mohammed by the angel Gabriel over the course of several years until the Prophet's death in 632CE. Shari'a Law or Islamic Law is based on the Qur'an, as well as the *sunnah* (the teachings of the Prophet Mohammed) and the *hadith* (the accounts of the actions of the Prophet Mohammed).

**Five Pillars of Islam** The Five Pillars of Islam – a set of core beliefs and practices – are considered obligatory for all Muslims. In practice, there are some differences such as how prayer times are calculated.

***Shahada*** The *shahada* is a profession of faith. Recited as part of daily prayers, it is spoken in Arabic (*lā 'ilāha 'illā-llāhu muḥammadun rasūlu-llāh*) and translates as 'There is no god but Allah and Mohammed is the Messenger of Allah'. It is also spoken out loud by anyone converting to become a Muslim, to mark their acceptance of Islam.

***Salat*** *Salat* is the requirement to pray five times a day. The times are relative to the position of the sun: *fajr* (dawn), *dhuhr* or *zuhr* (midday), *asr* (afternoon), *maghrib* (sunset) and *isha* (dusk). Prayer times change from day to day and place to place. Traditionally, the *adhan* or *azhan* (the call to prayer) is made by a man known as a *muezzin*, but in modern times this is mostly pre-recorded. In preparation for each prayer, *wudu* or ritual washing is performed. Prayers themselves are performed in the direction of the Ka'aba (page 381) in Mecca, the holiest site for all Muslims. The direction towards the Ka'aba is known as the *qibla*, which is indicated in mosques by a *mihrab* (niche) in the wall; it is often marked in hotels and other locations, and there are even dedicated qibla apps. Prayers are ritual and vary depending on the time of day. They are said in unison whenever more than one person is present, although men and women do not pray side by side. It is possible to pray anywhere that is clean, not just in a mosque.

The Friday midday prayer is the *jummah*, which replaces the dhuhr prayer. Men are expected to go to mosque. If women go to mosque, which is not as common in Saudi Arabia, they are segregated from men. In addition to prayers, a *khutbah*, broadly similar to a Christian sermon, is given by an *imam* or leader.

***Zakat*** *Zakat* is charitable giving. It is mandatory for every Muslim whose wealth is above a certain threshold, a figure that is calculated in different ways depending on the sect of Islam. In Saudi Arabia, zakat is like a tax collected by the government from individuals and businesses.

***Sawm*** *Sawm* is ritual fasting during Ramadan, the ninth month of the Islamic calendar. Fasting occurs each day from dawn to sunset and lasts for 29 or 30 days, depending on the length of the month. Most Muslims are expected to observe sawm once they have reached puberty, though exemptions are made for those who would suffer from ill health if they fasted, including the elderly and pregnant, breastfeeding or menstruating women. People who are travelling are also exempt. Fasting means not consuming anything: food, drink (including water), smoking, vaping and chewing gum. Many people also refrain from taking medications or injections. At sunset, people traditionally break their fast with dates and water. The meal that follows the breaking of the fast is an *iftar*. Many Muslims also eat a *suhoor*, a meal to sustain them during the day which must be finished before dawn. See pages 88 and 100 for more detailed information about behaviour and practices for those visiting Saudi Arabia during Ramadan.

***Hajj*** Hajj is the pilgrimage to Mecca which all Muslims who are financially and physically able are obliged to perform once in their lifetime. It takes place from the 8th to the 12th days of the twelfth month of the Islamic calendar. A specific pattern of rituals occurs during hajj. Muslims who travel to Mecca at other times of the year are performing *umrah*, which is seen as a good deed but does not replace the obligation of hajj. See page 385 for more detailed information about the hajj pilgrimage.

## OTHER IMPORTANT ISLAMIC CONCEPTS AND PRACTICES

**Hijri calendar** The *hijri* or Islamic calendar is 12 lunar months long, making the Islamic year 10–11 days shorter than the Gregorian calendar used in most of the world. Each month is either 29 or 30 days long, as determined by the sighting of the new moon by a recognised religious authority. This means that dates in the Islamic calendar are only certain for each month once the new moon is sighted, and explains why the timings for Ramadan, Eid al Fitr and other key events cannot be confirmed until this happens. As a result of this system, Islamic festivals occur 10–11 days earlier each year according to the Gregorian calendar, eventually completing a rotation after about 35 years. The beginning of year 1[ah] ([ah] is the abbreviation for the Latin 'anno hegirae', or Hijri year) in the Islamic calendar equates to 16 July 622CE; as of August 2023, the hijri year is 1445[ah]. Sunday is the first day of an Islamic week and Friday is the holy day.

***Halal* and *haram*** The Qur'an, hadith and sunnah all determine what is *halal* (permitted) or *haram* (forbidden). In practical terms, this includes everything from what can be eaten to behaviours that are obligatory, encouraged, discouraged or not allowed – for example, the concept of *hijab*. Although most people in the West think hijab means a woman's headscarf, this is not accurate – in fact, hijab (which means 'barrier') is the idea of modesty and applies to both men and women. The headscarf is just one of many symbols and choices made by modest Muslims. See pages 62, 64 and 100 for practical information about permitted and forbidden behaviour as it applies in Saudi Arabia.

***Insh'allah*** The expression '*insh'allah*' ('if Allah wills') can be heard throughout the day in all contexts of speech and behaviour. It derives from the belief of divine destiny, meaning that all things in the future have already been determined by God. Saudis and Muslims in general will use this term when discussing anything in the future. It should not be interpreted as an excuse or evasion as is commonly misunderstood beyond the ummah.

**BRANCHES OF ISLAM** Most Muslims are either Sunni or Shi'a. The global Muslim population is estimated to be about 85% Sunni and 15% Shi'a, with other branches significantly less than 1%. The division originated after the death of the Prophet Mohammed, when Muslims had differences of opinion about who should succeed him. Fundamentally, the split can be described as an initial political difference at least as important as the eventual diversion of some religious practices.

### PBUH

It is conventional to add *pbuh* (peace be upon him) at the end of any written reference to the Prophet Mohammed as a sign of respect. In Arabic, the initials *saws* (*sallahu alayhi wa salaam*) are the equivalent. The absence of pbuh in this guidebook is for brevity and not as a lack of respect for this Islamic practice.

**Sunni** The Sunni school of thought believes that leaders should be chosen from those who show the ability of continuing the Prophet Mohammed's work. They believe that the first four Rashidun caliphs were chosen by Mohammed's followers and were the rightful successors to the Prophet Mohammed. They were Abu Bakr, Mohammed's closest advisor and father-in-law through his marriage to Aisha; Umar, another father-in-law and senior advisor; Uthman, from a prominent Mecca merchant family; and Ali, the cousin and son-in-law of Mohammed.

There are four Islamic schools of jurisprudence of Sunni Islam: Hanafi, Hanbali, Maliki and Shafi'i. These have their own sub-branches as well, and each branch interprets religious law differently. Sunnis are in the majority in North and sub-Saharan Africa, Turkey, South Asia, Southeast Asia and most Middle East countries, including Syria, Palestine, Jordan, Kuwait, Qatar, the UAE and Saudi Arabia. Lebanon and Yemen are more evenly mixed.

**Shi'a** Followers of Shi'a Islam believe that leaders should come from the descendants of the Prophet Mohammed. They believe that Ali, his cousin and son-in-law, should have been his immediate successor. This schism developed during the earliest days of Islam and remains to this day.

There are two main branches of Shi'a Islam: twelvers, who believe there are 12 divinely ordained imams (the 12th of whom has yet to appear) comprise about 85% of all Shi'a, and Ismailis, who split with other Shi'a over the identity of the seventh imam. There are also further sub-branches, each of which interprets religious law differently. This includes Zaydism, a Shi'a branch found in northwest Yemen and the southwest of Saudi Arabia whose followers believe they are required to obey Imam Zayd bin Ali, an early leader against the Umayyad Caliphate. Many religious practices are interpreted and performed differently to Sunnis, ranging from specific prayer rituals to marriage. Shi'a have a strong concept of martyrdom from the earliest days of the schism, when the killing of revered leaders furthered the division between Islamic beliefs. Many Shi'a days of remembrance derive from this difficult history of suffering many losses. Most of the world's Shi'a live in the Shi'a majority countries of Iran, Iraq, Azerbaijan and Bahrain.

**Ibadi** Ibadism is a third branch of Islam which originated around the same time as the Sunni and Shi'a schools of thought. It developed about 60 years after the death of the Prophet Mohammed, and evolved as an offshoot of the Khawarij movement, which shared some Sunni and Shi'a beliefs yet was distinct from both. Ibadis are known for moderation and tolerance and today make up less than 0.08% of the global Muslim population. An estimated 70% of Omanis are Ibadi, and there are a few small pockets of Ibadi communities in remote areas of Algeria, Libya, Tunisia and parts of the historic Omani empire in East Africa.

**Other branches** There are many other branches of Islam. **Alawites**, sometimes known as Nusayris, are a sect that derives from Shi'a Islam but have distinct practices from other groups. Most Alawites live in Syria, where they comprise about 15% of the population. They also live in smaller communities in northern Lebanon and southern Turkey. The **Druze** is another religious group that derives from Shi'a Islam, though many Druze do not identify as Muslims but rather as People of Monotheism. Most Druze live in Lebanon, Syria, Jordan, Israel and Palestine, although there is a significant diaspora in Venezuela and the USA. Saudi nationals are not Ibadi, Druze or Alawite although some expatriate residents may be.

***Sufism*** Sufism is not a distinct sect but draws on mystic practices that enhance the understanding of Islam. It is found in Sunni and Shi'a communities, most prominently in parts of Africa, Turkey and parts of South Asia. Many of these branches are rejected by some other sects for a variety of theological, political and cultural reasons. In Saudi Arabia, there is a growing increase in tolerance of some Sufi practices, although they are also considered problematic by others.

**ISLAM IN SAUDI ARABIA** Similar to the global population, it is believed that there is a ratio of about 85% Sunni and 15% Shi'a in Saudi Arabia. Official figures are not published, however, so it is impossible to be sure. The al Saud family follows the Salafist movement within the Sunni Hanbali branch of Islam. The Hanbali collection of practices is drawn from tradition and can be perceived as austere relative to other schools of Islam. Salafist beliefs and practices dominate Saudi culture, especially in the central Najd region of the Kingdom. Hanbali Islamic jurisprudence is recognised as the official version of Islam, with other Muslims sometimes restricted or discriminated against, especially Shi'a Saudis. Not all Saudi Sunnis follow Salafism, however. Many Muslims in the Hejaz follow Shafi'i beliefs and practices.

### GOLDEN AGE OF ISLAM

The Golden Age of Islam is usually defined as the period of the Abbasid Caliphate (page 18) from the 8th to the 13th centuries, beginning with the reign of Harun al Rashid and ending with the demise of the caliphate during the conquest of Genghis Khan. Scholars from this era looked to the Qur'an and hadith and placed significant value on knowledge, education and scientific discovery. Early *madrassas* (schools of religious learning) also covered philosophy, law, medicine and mathematics. Significant contributions to the understanding of algebra, calculus, geometry and trigonometry were all advanced during this era. Additionally, the study of scientific disciplines, including agriculture, astronomy, biology, chemistry and physics, created a rich foundation that allowed for the development of advanced engineering practices. And medical knowledge in particular led to substantial gains in providing healthcare basics that are still recognised to this day, including hospitals, chemists and pharmacies, surgery and critical hygiene practices. But the advances weren't just scientific. The beauty of the architecture of the Golden Age can still be seen in the design of mosques and many other buildings, while the art, literature, poetry, and music that developed at this time remain at the root of Islamic culture.

Shi'a Saudis are mostly found in Eastern Province and in Asir, with most Shi'a from Eastern Province followers of the twelver sect of Imamism. Twelvers believe in 12 divine Imams ordained by Allah, the twelfth of whom has not yet appeared and will return at the same time as the Prophet Isa (Jesus). Most of the population who adhere to twelver beliefs and practices have ancestral roots in Persia, modern-day Iran. In the Asir region and along the Yemen border, most Shi'a citizens are Ismaili or Zaidi.

**Saudi expatriates** Most expats are Muslim and of a variety of nationalities and Islamic sects. Most non-Muslim expats are Christian or Hindu, each representing about 15% of the expat population. There are small expat populations from other faiths. A curious paradox for non-Muslim expats in Saudi Arabia is that there is an expectation that everyone has a faith, but any faith other than Islam cannot be openly practised in the Kingdom. Unlike elsewhere in the Middle East, there are no churches or any other places of worship for other faiths. Religious symbols from other faiths are not allowed and could be confiscated if discovered. Moreover, apostacy, the practice of declaring a disbelief of a previous faith, is a capital offence for Muslims, and proselytisation, the attempt to convert someone to another faith (in this case away from Islam), is also a major crime. Atheism is also listed as a capital offence in the Kingdom. Although tourist visas do not require a declaration of faith, unlike other Saudi visas, it is important to keep these rules in mind throughout the Kingdom.

**THE TWO HOLY MOSQUES OF MECCA AND MADINAH** Islam's two holiest mosques are located in Saudi Arabia. The most holy and important, recognised by all branches of Islam, is the **Masjid al Haram** (page 381) in Mecca. At its centre is the Ka'aba, a key focal point of the hajj pilgrimage. The **Masjid al Nabawi** (page 388) in Madinah, also known as the Prophet's Mosque, is Islam's second holiest mosque. It was built during the life of the Prophet, after opposition to Mohammed's beliefs led him and his followers to migrate from Mecca to Madinah.

Throughout the history of Islam, rulers in what is now the Kingdom of Saudi Arabia have periodically used the title **Custodian of the Two Holy Mosques**. King Fahd became the first Saudi ruler to use it in modern times, in 1986, and his two successors, King Abdullah and King Salman, also embraced the title. Thus, the full title of the current ruler of Saudi Arabia is Custodian of the Two Holy Mosques, King Salman bin Abdul Aziz al Saud. Its use is commonplace in newspapers and other media and indicates the importance of royalty in the protection of Islam.

It is forbidden for non-Muslims to travel to Mecca and to the centre of Madinah. For more information, see page 380.

## EDUCATION

Saudi state education is a relatively recent addition to traditional religious education. Historically, the *kuttab* (religious primary school) was mostly accessible to children, nearly all boys, from privileged and well-connected families. As recently as the 1970s, only 15% of Saudi men and 2% of Saudi women were literate, but by 2020 the literacy rate was 98%. Saudi girls are now attending school at the same rate as boys.

**PUBLIC EDUCATION** Public education became available to the general Saudi population in the early 1970s. It is compulsory for boys and girls from the ages of 6 to 14 for a total of nine years. The centralised curriculum is controlled by the state and focuses on religious education, although core subjects including Arabic, mathematics, science, art, social studies and computer science are also taught. English-language classes have also been growing in popularity. Schools are gender-segregated. Only Saudi children have access to public education, though there are a few exceptions for some non-Saudi children who are Muslim and fluent in Arabic.

**Structure** There are three stages to basic public education. Elementary school starts at age six and runs for six years, from Grades 1 to 6. Children who complete elementary school receive a General Elementary School Certificate. Intermediate school runs for a further three years, from grades 7 to 9. Children must pass examinations, earning their Intermediate Education Certificate.

Children who progress to secondary education follow one of three curricula: general, religious or technical-vocational. Exams measure progress during each semester. The General Secondary Education Certificate, known as *thanawiyyah,* is issued to students at the end of their secondary education, documenting all grades and a final cumulative grade point average. These are key for students considering continuing to a Saudi university.

Students of religious schools are expected to be able to memorise and recite the Qur'an in its entirety and earn qualifications to potentially serve as imams. Successful students earn the Religious Institute Secondary Education Certificate. Students following the technical-vocational educational path will focus on practical aspects of specific vocations and will earn a Secondary Vocational School Diploma. As recently as 2018, only 57% of Saudis have earned secondary education credentials.

**UNIVERSITIES** King Saud University was established in 1957 as the Kingdom's first university. Tertiary education has since expanded greatly in the 21st century, with more than 40 universities now in existence. Tuition is free for Saudi nationals. Saudi universities follow a similar course structure to those in the USA, with two-year associate degrees, four-year bachelor's degrees and postgraduate masters and doctorate degrees granted to students who complete each level. It should be noted that only 3% of Saudi university students continue their education beyond their bachelor's degree.

It may surprise some to learn that Saudi women are now among the most educated women in the Muslim world. As of 2018, two-thirds of all university graduates are women. The largest women's university in the world is the prestigious public Princess Nourah bint Abdul Rahman University in Riyadh.

Founded in 2009, near King Abdullah Economic City in Thuwal, about 100km north of Jeddah, King Abdullah University of Science and Technology (KAUST) was the first co-educational university, with relaxed social rules compared to the wider Kingdom. It is affiliated with some of the best research universities in the world.

**University education abroad** Prior to 2005, only royalty and children from elite families had access to foreign education at university level. The King Abdullah Scholarship Program (KASP) was established that year, allowing 200,000 young men and women to enrol in universities abroad through generous scholarships and stipends. This programme was scaled back in 2016 due to crashing oil prices. It is now refocused on sending the most promising students to the top 200 globally ranked universities. Universities in the USA, UK, Canada and Australia are particularly popular for a combination of educational opportunity, English-language practice and, for many students, the opportunity to live in more open cultures.

**OTHER SCHOOLS** Private schools are expensive and generally have a narrower curriculum than public schools, though this may change with a growing population. Expatriate children are mostly limited to study at international schools. They are generally co-educational and have only recently allowed Saudi children to enrol. These fee-paying schools cater to children from many backgrounds. In addition to the International Baccalaureate, Saudi-based international schools teach curricula from the USA, UK, France, Germany, India, Japan, Pakistan and the Philippines. However, each of these curricula must also teach Arabic, Islamic civilisation, Saudi history and geography for a minimum of 1 hour per week.

## CULTURE

Saudi culture has been very conservative since the times of the First Saudi State. Influence from the teachings of the al Wahhab interpretation of what is Islamic (page 20) meant that artistic expressions were limited to a rigid set of practices deemed to be suitable for the Muslim population. As a result, Saudi culture is noticeably more austere than in neighbouring countries. Most contemporary performing arts were banned until very recently, though traditional arts have been practised throughout the ages, albeit mostly by men and boys.

**MUSIC AND DANCE** Traditional Saudi music is often an expression of poetry, folklore or both, and is usually performed in groups – typically by an all-male ensemble in front of an all-male audience. Many Saudis believe that music is *haram* or forbidden, while others believe it should be limited to percussion instruments that are used to produce a rhythm.

**Percussion instruments** include the *ṭabl* (drum) and the *tar*, a tambourine made from goatskin stretched onto a wooden frame. The *duf* or *raq* is a rhythmic instrument that can be square or round and varies widely in size. The *mirwas* is a two-sided cylindrical drum used to set rhythms, often to accompany poetry. The *manjur* is a very interesting tambourine-like instrument with goat hooves along its circumference. It is played by tying it around the around the waist of the musician, who sets a rhythm by making the hooves rattle.

**String instruments** are also popular and include the Bedouin *rehab*, a bowed wooden instrument with horsehair strings used during the recitation of poems; the Hejazi *simsimiyya*, a lyre with steel-wire strings; and the lute-like *oud*, a pear-shaped instrument made of wood (*oud* means 'wood' in Arabic) and strings. The latter is plucked with an elongated pick known as a *risha*, and may also be decorated with ivory (historically) and a range of Islamic symbols.

The *mizmar* is a flute-like wind instrument with five holes. It is usually made of decorated wood. It is key to the traditional Mizmar dance that has been recognised by UNESCO as Intangible Cultural Heritage of Humanity, performed with sticks, drums and clapping to songs.

Other traditional dances include the *ardah*, which involves either two men or lines of men who dance opposite each other, usually holding swords or even rifles, making elaborate movements that were once performed before going to war. This dance is performed with accompanying drums and tambourines. The *samri* is a dance where poetry is sung to the beat of the duf drum with men sitting in two rows, clapping and swaying to the rhythm.

**POETRY** Bedouin poetry is known as *nabati* or the people's poetry. Originating in the Nabataean culture of northwest Saudi Arabia and southern Jordan, it developed into a strong oral tradition whereby history was passed down the generations. Nabati poetry was used to declare war, seek peace and resolve tribal disputes. It is distinct from the more formal Arabic poetry, and is considered unique.

Key styles of classical Arab poetry are *hamasah*, describing military prowess, *tardiyyah* or successful hunting poetry, *madih* or eulogy poems, and *ghazal*, love poems. Poetry has been important since pre-Islamic times, with several 6th-century CE Najdi poets remembered in the Arab world to this day. Imru al Qais al Kindi is regarded as the father of classical Arabic poetry. Particularly prolific was Antarah bin Shaddad al Absi, famous for his poetry commemorating tribal battles. He is one of the poets of the Mu'allaqat, the Hanging Poems on the Ka'aba in Mecca. Another important poet was al Zeir Adi bin Rabia, also known as Abu Layla al Muhalhel. He was a tribal leader of the Banu Taghlib tribe during the War of Basus and the key personality immortalised in the Battle of Adi. His grandson, Amr bin Kulthum, was another Taghlib tribal chief, and one of his poems is also featured on the Ka'aba. The most famous and highly regarded poet was Hatim al Tal in what is now Ha'il Province. In addition to his poetry, he had a reputation for good deeds which gave rise to the saying 'more generous than Hatim', which is still used today.

Poetry has seen a revival from the 20th century up to present times. This probably stems from a combination of improved literacy and the reinforcement of Arab identity in an increasingly globalised world. It is a key element in many Saudi cultural events including major festivals. Poetry contests, often with lucrative awards, are held in in the Kingdom and in other Gulf countries.

**LITERATURE** Due to a combination of illiteracy and a strong oral tradition through poetry, and distinct from other regional Arab cultures, conventional literature in the form of books and other written material has not historically had a strong presence in the Arabian Peninsula. In recent times, censorship has either stifled authors or left them facing criticism, imprisonment, exile or worse. It is still difficult to find anything other than the most benign novels or children's literature in Saudi bookshops today.

## ARTS AND CRAFTS

**Clothing and fabric** The Bedouin tradition of weaving is known as *sadu* and is characterised by weaving striped patterns into fabric. This fabric is usually made of wool and typically features a dark-red design accented by many other colours. Practical items, from blankets, pillows, seat cushions and rugs to animal accessories, bags and even tents are plentiful in modern times. Traditional women's clothing is also typically highly decorated. Usually starting with a black and dark-red base, robes and dresses are embellished with elaborate geometric patterns in contrasting colours, often with metallic thread woven in. Other designs feature elaborate needlework, with wool, cotton, silk and chiffon all popular fabrics. Although many Saudi women today prefer to wear Western styles under their *abayas*, others continue to wear traditional dresses. Such clothing and other items can be easily found in souqs and shops throughout the Kingdom.

**Decorative arts** Saudis have been decorating doors and windows – as well as other features such as ventilation passages, arches, rooftops and walls – for generations. Wood and walls are usually painted in bright colours in geometric patterns, and each region has its own distinct style. Examples of Hejazi features can be found in the centre of Jeddah's old town, al Balad, with its highly decorative protruding windows. In Najd, triangles feature on top of walls and some other flat surfaces, and windows are frequently triangular too. Cooling towers and arches are often highlighted in Eastern Province. Architecture in Asir, meanwhile, is closely associated with that found in parts of Yemen. Here, buildings are constructed with stone into a rectangular shape that resembles a layer cake. These layers are often built into small towers and can reach five or six storeys. They are decorated with contrasting white windows and rooftops.

**Islamic design and calligraphy** Sunni Islam teaches that depictions of people are forbidden. This has led artists to develop a sophisticated set of geometric and abstract designs that can be seen everywhere from architecture to practical

## SAUDI NATIONAL DRESS

Most Saudis wear national dress every day. There are occasions where sport or other activity-appropriate clothing is worn, usually at leisure or when travelling beyond Saudi Arabia and the Gulf countries. It is possible to see some Saudi men wearing loose Western clothing at the weekend, while most women wear national dress whenever they leave their home within the Kingdom.

**MEN** The long robe traditionally worn by men is called a ***thobe***. It is usually white, though many men wear dark-coloured robes in the cooler winter months. Saudi thobes usually have a Nehru-style collar with sleeves finished by cufflinks. Very important people often wear a ***bisht***, the darker open robe, worn over the thobe. Saudi men wear a ***taqiyah*** or rounded white cap on their head, which is then covered by a ***ghutra*** (a white or, more commonly, red-checked folded cloth), which is usually topped by an ***agal*** (double-stranded black cord). Some men also wear the ***sidari***, a heavy gilet made of soft, woolly lambskin or a full-length coat version in the cold winter months. Some very religious men wear their thobe with a high hem which exposes their socks; they may also wear the ghutra without the agal.

**WOMEN** Women wear an ***abaya***, a long black robe that covers the body from shoulders to feet. Until recently these were always plain black, but now you may see them embellished with a range of decorative accents and sometimes the cloth comes in fashionable colours or to suit the styles of the season. Women also wear a headscarf called a ***tarha*** or ***boshya*** (known also as a *shayla* in the UAE). Many religious and very traditional women wear the ***niqab*** or face veil in addition. The most religious may also wear gloves and thick black hosiery.

**PERSONAL GROOMING** Personal grooming is very important to Saudis. Hair and beard care is a priority, although very religious men keep their beards natural. Men and women often wear a complex combination of perfumes and other scent; traditional scents are often made bespoke from their parfumier and are typically blended from traditional oud or frankincense base fragrances. Many of the latest European designer scents can also be popular. Visitors should consider their own standard of personal grooming as this often determines in part how well you may be treated and respected.

items in everyday use. Calligraphy or stylised writing is also a dominant practice throughout Saudi Arabia (and the rest of the Islamic world). Some of the most beautiful artwork found in galleries and exhibitions within the Kingdom features all of these elements.

**Homeware** Basket weaving is a popular practice, which involves shaping palm leaves into geometric designs and then colouring them in similar ways to woven fabrics. Most of these woven items are practical objects for everyday use in the home. They include dowry baskets, which often have a fitted top and were used to contain a bride's treasures, and scales known as *mizan*, which are made with two baskets balanced on a decorated wooden stick. Incense burners are another common household item; these are generally made of wood and lined with lead, with a nest to hold the charcoal and incense. They are painted with bright colours on the outside and are often highly decorated with mirrors or other shiny objects.

**Jewellery** In Saudi culture, most jewellery is worn by women. In addition to earrings, women have traditionally worn ankle bands, arm bands, belts, head adornments and necklaces, all of which symbolise status. Notable items include the *melwi*, a twisted silver bracelet, and a *hizam*, or decorated waist belt, often made with coins, coloured beads and glass. Other styles of jewellery also use some of these materials, depending on the designer and local traditions. In modern times, many women wear gold (sometimes rather a lot of it), and gold jewellery is a popular gift choice. According to Islamic tradition, only women are permitted to wear gold.

**Swords and daggers** Men have decorated swords and some other battle-related items for centuries. Ornamental swords and daggers, such as the *khanjar* traditionally worn by men, can be found in most souqs. The sheaths are decorated with bone, jewels and a range of metals including gold, silver, bronze and copper. They are a work of art and an interesting purchase for tourists up for the challenge of explaining these weapons to their home country's customs officers.

## SPORT

Football is the most popular sport in Saudi Arabia. There are four leagues with 16 clubs in the Professional League and an additional 80 clubs in the first, second and third divisions. The Saudi National Team are known as al Saqour, or the Falcons. They play in the Asian League and have also qualified several times for the FIFA World Cup. Outside of the Kingdom, Saudi royalty have also taken an interest in foreign clubs and currently own Newcastle United and Sheffield United in the English Premier League. Mainly funded by the Saudi Public Investment Fund (PIF), the top division Saudi Pro League (Roshn) has made news recently for attracting high-profile global players.

Popular traditional sports include horseracing, camel racing and falconry. Motor sport is growing quickly in popularity, with Formula E and Formula 1 races held in Riyadh and Jeddah respectively. World Wrestling Entertainment (WWE) events have also been held in Saudi Arabia.

Sports such as cricket, racquet sports and American sports are played by some Saudis, but are often more popular with expatriate communities. Interest in running, cycling, hiking and adventure sports such as paragliding and ziplining is growing. The Kingdom also has world-class snorkelling and scuba diving in the

Red Sea, and both activities are a growing attraction for visitors. Although there are pristine beaches on both coasts, there is no public sunbathing culture due to strict social rules.

Golf has been seen for decades as a sport appealing mostly to Western expatriates, but Saudi Arabia drew significant global attention with the establishment of LIV Golf, also backed by the Saudi PIF. Initially seen as a direct challenge to the established PGA Tour, this was resolved through an agreement reached in June 2023.

Most sport remains gender segregated. Attitudes to **women** participating in sport remain conservative but are evolving, especially where there is a practical solution to the modest dress code. Small steps are being made.

# 2

# Practical Information

## WHEN TO VISIT

It is best to visit Saudi Arabia between mid-October and the end of April, when the weather is most comfortable. The Saudi summer (May to early October) is best avoided as temperatures can soar to at least 50°C during the height of the season, with stifling humidity in the Eastern Province and along the west coast, though coastal temperatures are slightly more manageable, in the low 40s. The winter months (December to February) are usually pleasant, with warm daytime temperatures and relatively low humidity. Early mornings can be chilly in Riyadh during winter. It can snow in the northern mountains in Tabuk Province and can also approach freezing in Najd and the Northern Borders. Spring and autumn can get hot during the day but remain pleasant in the evening. For more on climate, see page 5.

Those who do visit during the summer months may wish to consider focusing their travels in the mountains. The Asir mountain range in al Bahah and Asir provinces is a favourite destination for Saudis wishing to escape the worst of the heat. You may also find the northern Hejaz mountains a good option.

It is very important to take note of the Islamic dates of Ramadan and the hajj. Visiting during Ramadan (page 88) is not recommended for most tourists as restaurants are closed until sunset and everyone, including non-Muslims, is expected to avoid eating, drinking (including water), smoking, vaping and chewing gum in public from dawn to sunset. Violations can lead to serious consequences, including arrest. Work hours are reduced during this period, with many places of interest to visitors operating only for very short times or even remaining closed.

Visiting in the lead-up to or during hajj (page 72) should be considered carefully. With around 3 million pilgrims performing hajj each year, Saudi-bound flights and accommodation here are in great demand at this time. Airfares and hotel rates, especially in and around Jeddah, rise sharply. And there can also be restrictions on visiting Jeddah and within the *miqat* zone for Muslim tourists who are not on pilgrimage.

## HIGHLIGHTS

**MADA'IN SALEH (HEGRA ARCHAEOLOGICAL SITE)** Nabataean sister-city to Jordan's Petra, but without the crowds (for now), this UNESCO-listed site just outside al Ula is a must-see on any Saudi itinerary. Also don't miss nearby Elephant Rock. Try to visit in winter if you want to include contemporary cultural events, such as Winter at Tantora, in your itinerary.

**JEDDAH** Explore the souqs of Jeddah's historic district, al Balad – a World Heritage Site – with its many traditional houses and decorated façades. Don't miss the lavishly ornate hidden gem of Tayebat International City in the Faisaliyah District a bit further north, or a leisurely stroll along the Corniche, stopping for refreshments at a restaurant or coffee shop along the way.

**AL AHSA OASIS** Visit the stunning Qarah Mountain and its labyrinth of caves, and admire the natural beauty of Yellow Lake, here in the world's largest oasis – another of Saudi Arabia's World Heritage Sites – situated on the edge of the uninhabitable Empty Quarter.

**RIYADH** In the Kingdom's conservative heartland, explore the busy capital city, which is undergoing rapid transformation and developing a vibrant social scene. Look to the country's past in the King Abdul Aziz Historical Center's museums, Wadi Hanifa and the UNESCO-listed Turaif district in Old Diriyah and take in an art gallery, lounge or trendy café for a dose of contemporary culture.

**ASIR PROVINCE** Ride the cable car to the hanging village of al Habala or take an exhilarating drive on winding mountain roads to the Flowermen village of Rijal al Ma'a to learn about the region's fierce independence. Asir Province is also home to al Souda National Park – a great hiking destination – and its population of hamadryas baboons.

**JUBBAH ROCK ART** This UNESCO World Heritage Site has some of the world's best-preserved petroglyphs. These depict life in the Arabian peninsula during the earliest days of domestication and before desertification.

**AL BAHAH PROVINCE** Head here for spectacular natural landscapes at their best where hikers, cyclists or those simply seeking a relaxing picnic spot among the greenery will all find their niche.

**DUMAT AL JANDAL** In this ancient ruined city in the Kingdom's northern reaches, be sure to explore Marid Castle and Umar Mosque. If you make it here, then carry on up the road to Sakaka to see Rajajil's ancient standing stones and Za'abal Castle.

**TAYMA** Visit Saudi Arabia's oldest settlement, which was once inhabited by Jewish Arab tribes. Don't miss the engineering marvel of Haddaj well, which is believed to have been built during the time of the Babylonian Empire. Explore nearby Arradam Palace (aka Qasr al Radhm) and al Hambra archaeological sites, which are of similar vintage.

**HEJAZ RAILWAY** Visit any of the Saudi stations on the historic Hejaz Railway line which ran for a very short time in the early 20th century from Damascus to Madinah. The stations at Tabuk and Madinah are recommended for their relatively easy access and informative museums.

**FARASAN ISLANDS** See a mix of Yemeni, Indian and Turkish architecture, as well as flora and fauna unique to the Middle East. Diving and snorkelling among the islands' pristine coral reefs is a special experience.

## SUGGESTED ITINERARIES

With so much to see and do, it can be difficult to decide what places to prioritise. Jeddah and al Ula are must-see destinations even for the shortest visits. Highlights that incorporate the modern and historical, urban and natural can be achieved in ten days, albeit at a very fast pace. Remember that distances are long and are best covered by car if you are not on an organised tour. You might want to consider some internal flights if you are very tight on time.

## TEN DAYS

### Itinerary 1: Riyadh to Jeddah

**Day 1** Arrive Riyadh; al Batha (Masmak Fortress, National Museum, souq) as time permits.
**Day 2** Riyadh; finish al Batha; city tour; al Turaif and Old Diriyah; Edge of the World at sunset.
**Day 3** Ushaiqer Heritage Village; travel to Unayzah.
**Day 4** Unayzah to Ha'il; Jubbah rock art; Ha'il city tour.
**Day 5** Long day travelling from Ha'il to al Ula.
**Day 6** Al Ula; Mada'in Saleh; Dadan Tombs; Jebel Ikmah; al Ula Old Town.
**Day 7** Al Ula; finish highlights if necessary; travel to Madinah by road following the stations of the Hejaz Railway.
**Day 8** Madinah; Hejaz Railway Museum; glimpse of permitted holy sites; train or drive to Jeddah.
**Day 9** Jeddah; al Balad; Tayebat International City; art museum; Corniche; al Rahmah Mosque.
**Day 10** Jeddah; day at leisure, shopping or watersports; depart.

**Itinerary 2: Jeddah to Riyadh** This is the reverse of itinerary 1 and provides sections for itineraries 3 and 4.

**Day 1** Arrive Jeddah; al Balad; Tayebat International City.
**Day 2** Jeddah; finish tour of al Balad if necessary; art museum; Corniche; al Rahmah Mosque.
**Day 3** Jeddah; travel by train or car to Madinah; Hejaz Railway Museum, glimpse of permitted holy sites.
**Day 4** Madinah; travel to al Ula by road along the route of Hejaz Railway stations; al Ula Old Town.
**Day 5** Al Ula; Mada'in Saleh; Dadan Tombs; Jebel Ikmah.
**Day 6** Long day travelling from al Ula to Ha'il.
**Day 7** Ha'il; Jubbah rock art; Ha'il city tour; travel to Unayzah.
**Day 8** Unayzah; travel to Ushaiqer; Ushaiqer Heritage Village; then Riyadh.
**Day 9** Riyadh; city tour; Turaif and Old Diriyah; Edge of the World at sunset.
**Day 10** Riyadh; al Batha (Masmak Fortress, National Museum, souq); depart.

## TWO WEEKS

### Itinerary 3

**Days 1–6** Follow itinerary 2, days 1–6.
**Day 7** Ha'il City Tour; Jubbah rock art; travel to Dumat al Jandal.
**Day 8** Dumat al Jandal; Marid Castle; Umar Mosque.
**Day 9** Dumat al Jandal; travel to Sakaka; Rajajil Columns; Za'abal Castle; Sisra Well.
**Day 10** Sakaka to Unayzah; city tour.
**Day 11** Unayzah to Ushaiqer; overnight in Shaqra.
**Day 12** Shaqra to Riyadh; at leisure, shopping, pampering.
**Days 13–14 or 15** Follow itinerary 2, days 9–10. Option to depart on day 15.

### Itinerary 4

**Days 1–10** Follow itinerary 2, but on day 10 depart instead to Hofuf by train or car.
**Day 11** Hofuf; city tour; forts; al Mulla House; Qasariyah Souq.
**Day 12** Hofuf; al Ahsa; Jebel Qarah and caves; Yellow Lake; Jawatha Mosque.
**Day 13** Al Ahsa to Dhahran; Ithra and Energy Exhibit; al Khobar Corniche; overnight in Dammam.
**Day 14** Dammam; Qatif city tour; Tarout Island and castle; return to Riyadh.
**Day 15** Depart.

## ONE MONTH

### Itinerary 5

**Days 1–14** Follow itinerary 4, remaining in Dammam on day 14.
**Day 15** Fly from Dammam to Taif; visit al Hada resort.
**Day 16** Taif; souq; road journey stopping at old stone villages; Raghadan Forest Park; overnight in Baha.
**Day 17** Baha; day trip to Zee al Ayn Heritage Village; return to Baha.
**Day 18** Baha to Baljurashi; Saturday Historical Market; Bridge Botanical Garden.
**Day 19** Baljurashi to Abha; Wadi al Janabeen Dam; Tanomah Balcony; arrive Abha.
**Day 20** Abha; Shamsan Ottoman Castle; al Basta District; Art Street area; Dabbab Walkway.
**Day 21** Abha; day trip to Jebel Souda; hike, cycle or picnic; stay at a mountain resort in season.
**Day 22** Day trip to Rijal al Ma'a; Sea of Clouds; Rijal al Ma'a Heritage Village.
**Day 23** Abha to Najran; al Habala cable car to village; visit Dhahran al Janoub; continue to Najran.
**Day 24** Najran; al Ukhdud Archaeological Site; circuit of historical sites around Wadi Najran.
**Day 25** Najran; travel to Fayfa or Wadi Lajab; hiking if fit.
**Day 26** Fayfa; mountain drive through Fayfa Mountains to Jazan.
**Day 27** Jazan; ferry to Farasan Islands; House of Riffai; Najdi Historic Mosque.
**Day 28** Farasan; al Qassar Heritage Village; al Ghuzlan Reserve; check out both drivable islands.
**Day 29** Farasan Islands to Jazan; visit the North Corniche area; relax.
**Day 30** Fly from Jazan to Riyadh or Jeddah; depart.

**ESCORTED AND INDEPENDENT TRAVEL** Travelling on an escorted tour will give tourists peace of mind. Like other destinations, tour operators handle most details in your fixed itinerary to make your trip as smooth as possible. It gives time-poor visitors an opportunity to see quite a bit in a limited time. There are some privileges as well, such as a more relaxed dress code and the ability to visit some sites that may be temporarily closed to the general public. It should be pointed out, however, that Saudi Arabia is promoting a polished – some say whitewashed – image through tour operators, including Western ones, who need to maintain their licences to do business. This means that your experience will be managed to show an optimal, but not always wholly realistic, picture of the Kingdom. For details of tour operators, see opposite.

Travelling independently is a completely different experience to travelling with a tour group. Independent travellers will have a much more authentic experience and get to enjoy wonderful encounters with Saudis who may share a wide range of opinions that might come as a surprise at times. Saudis remain superb hosts to guests in their country. But there is a bit less leeway for faux pas. You will experience more by dressing modestly; for women that means wearing the abaya, and for men covering the upper arms and below the knee. Learning basic greetings and courtesies can also be extremely rewarding.

## TOURIST INFORMATION

Many readers may already be aware of how difficult it can be to find reliable information about travel and tourism in Saudi Arabia. Things will change quickly as more tourists visit the Kingdom and when more Saudis gain experience in the conventional tourism industry. In the meantime, here are the official Saudi websites. You may also wish to keep up to date with websites such as Tripadvisor or other reputable websites and blogs.

**Saudi Ministry of Tourism** w mt.gov.sa
**Saudi Tourism Authority** w sta.gov.sa
**Visit Saudi** w visitsaudi.com/en. Another website belonging to the Saudi Tourism Authority which lists telephone contacts in several countries.

## TOUR OPERATORS

It hasn't taken long for many international tour operators to add Saudi Arabia to their list of destinations, and as interest in travel to Saudi Arabia grows, more tour operators are likely to follow suit. Check with your favourite tour operator if it isn't listed below.

Many Saudi-based tour operators are new. Others are specialists in pilgrimages. For the adventurous, this is a great opportunity to support local and regional businesses. Your experience will probably be more immersive in local culture, but it may also be a bit bumpy with some. It is also important to determine whether these companies offer an all-inclusive package or if they are more suitable for providing excursions once you are in Saudi Arabia. Take note that some tour operators may be specialists only for some regions but not necessarily the entire Kingdom. Finally, remember that most tour companies operate Sunday to Thursday and are likely to be closed on Fridays and Saturdays. It is beyond the scope of this guidebook to provide tour operator information for hajj and umrah pilgrims.

### NETHERLANDS

**Culture Road** ☎ +31 6 47 80 4333; w cultureroadtravel.com

### SAUDI ARABIA

**Amazing Tours** w amazingtours.com.sa
**Ghazi Tours** ☎ +966 53 074 5553; w ghazitours.com
**Horizons Tours** ☎ +966 11 231 1057; w saudiarabiatourismguide.com/horizons-tours
**Sana Tourism** ☎ +966 53 660 2030; w sana-tourism.com
**Saudi Arabia Tours** ☎ +966 55 801 8938; w saudiarabiatours.net
**Saudi Arabia Travel Tours** ☎ +966 54 884 3153 (+1 484 320 7442 from US & Canada); w saudiarabiatravelandtours.com
**Saudi Discovery** ☎ +966 800 814 0049; w saudidiscovery.com

### UK

**Abercrombie & Kent** w abercrombiekent.co.uk
**Andante Travels** w andantetravels.co.uk
**Elegant Resorts** w elegantresorts.co.uk
**Explore** w explore.co.uk
**Jules Verne** w vjv.com
**Lupine Travel** w lupinetravel.co.uk
**Native Eye** w nativeeyetravel.com
**Oasis Overland** w oasisoverland.co.uk

**Regent Holidays** w regentholidays.co.uk
**Steppes Travel** w steppestravel.com
**Wild Frontiers** w wildfrontierstravel.com

**USA**

**Adventures Abroad** w adventures-abroad.com
**Original World** w originalworld.com

## RED TAPE

Notoriously one of the most difficult countries in the world to visit as a tourist, Saudi Arabia has now opened its borders. Saudis are a genuinely welcoming people and curious about visitors; and it's an exciting time to consider visiting the Kingdom in these early, fresh, days of tourism. Saudi Arabia is investing significant capital in marketing campaigns aimed at both independent travellers and package tourists, so those seeking authentic encounters with local people may wish to make their trip sooner rather than later.

Once in-country, it is possible to visit nearly all of Saudi Arabia – other than Mecca and parts of Madinah, unless you are Muslim. Although there are anecdotal reports of some non-Muslims visiting these holy sites, the official position remains. You should check your own country's travel advice, as visiting some border areas may invalidate your travel insurance. This is often the case with areas bordering Yemen and until recently also included the border with Iraq. If in doubt, refer to your own government's official website (in the UK: w gov.uk/foreign-travel-advice/saudi-arabia) in advance of travel.

In addition to the visa application, prospective travellers to Saudi Arabia will also be required to sign a declaration demonstrating that they understand several rules that must be followed if entering the Kingdom, including that smuggling illegal drugs into Saudi Arabia attracts the death penalty.

**VISAS** All visitors to Saudi Arabia, other than Gulf Cooperation Council (GCC) nationals (Bahrain, Kuwait, Oman, Qatar and the United Arab Emirates), require a visa prior to travel to the Kingdom. Saudi Arabia issues many types of visa, including those for residency, work and family visits. It is beyond the scope of this guide to provide information on these other visa types. There are also specific hajj and umrah visas issued to religious pilgrims which, unlike other visas, usually impose restrictions on travelling beyond the miqat zone boundary (see page 381 for more information about pilgrimage visas).

### SAUDI TOURISM

Tourism in Saudi Arabia is in its infancy (other than for hajj/umrah pilgrims), and it is estimated that the industry will generate more than 1.2 million jobs for Saudi nationals by 2030, including many for women. More than 3,500 tourist licences have been granted as part of Saudi Vision 2030.

However, it will take time to see the impact of these measures. Saudi Arabia is only just beginning to develop a customer service culture and, although young Saudis are being trained in improving standards to satisfy most international tourists, the application of this training in the real world is relatively new. Infrastructure is still being developed at tourist hotspots, and the provision of hotels in these locations, other than in the big cities, may fall well short of demand. English-language skills are significantly higher within the tourism industry than in the general population.

When visiting, try to manage your expectations. Be both flexible and patient.

**Tourist visas** Saudi Arabia started to issue tourist visas in October 2019, only to be suspended in March 2020 owing to the Covid-19 pandemic. In August 2021, the programme was resumed and tourists from 49 mostly Western, mostly economically developed countries are now eligible to apply for a tourist e-visa through a relatively straightforward online process.

As of August 2023, nationals from the following countries are eligible for a tourist e-visa: in North America – Canada, USA; in Europe – Andorra, Austria, Belgium, Bulgaria, Croatia, Cyprus, Czech Republic, Denmark, Estonia, Finland, France, Germany, Greece, Hungary, Iceland, Ireland, Italy, Latvia, Liechtenstein, Lithuania, Luxembourg, Malta, Monaco, Montenegro, Netherlands, Norway, Poland, Portugal, Romania, Russia, San Marino, Slovakia, Slovenia, Spain, Sweden, Switzerland, Ukraine, UK; in Asia – Brunei, China (including Hong Kong and Macau), Japan, Kazakhstan, Malaysia, Singapore, South Korea, Taiwan (counted separately); and in Oceania – Australia and New Zealand.

At the time of writing, multiple-entry tourist visas are granted for one year with each stay limited to 90 days. Your passport must be valid for at least six months beyond the date of outward travel. Take note of the photograph specifications as detailed in the application process. Applicants under 18 years of age can apply for an e-visa if they are travelling with a legal guardian and are otherwise eligible. There is no upper age limit. The fee at time of writing is SAR535 or approximately US$145.

Israeli passport holders, those born in Israel, and anyone with evidence of having travelled to Israel will almost certainly be rejected if applying to enter Saudi Arabia. Jewish travellers from other eligible nationalities are able to enter Saudi Arabia if they otherwise meet the e-visa criteria. Unlike for other types of Saudi visa, tourist visa applications do not ask your religion.

The e-visa is generally issued within an hour if requested during Saudi business hours or during the next business day if not. Payments are made online with the usual bank card options available. It is strongly advised that prospective visitors apply for their tourist visa through the Saudi Tourism Authority (**w** visa.visitsaudi.com) and not through a third-party website.

Never exceed the time limit per visit or you could become ineligible for future visas to the Kingdom. It is possible to leave Saudi Arabia for only one day and immediately return, even re-entering via a different border, thus restarting the count for the new visit. Tourist visas cannot be extended. However, a new visa can be applied for and obtained once the current visa has expired.

Tourist visas are valid for travel throughout the Kingdom but are not valid for non-Muslims to visit either Mecca or the al Haram area of Madinah. Muslim visitors can perform umrah on a tourist visa if they hold a passport from one of the 49 approved countries. Other nationalities must continue to apply for the traditional umrah visa. However, using a tourist e-visa for umrah is only allowed outside of hajj season.

**CUSTOMS REGULATIONS** Saudi Arabia is serious about keeping contraband from entering the Kingdom. You must present both checked and hand luggage for scanning before you are able to leave the secure area of the arrivals hall and exit the airport. Although the days are over of customs officers routinely asking passengers to show the contents of their laptop or mobile phone, it remains a possibility if they think you are behaving suspiciously. Remember that some items, including content on devices that may be perfectly legal in your home country, may be illegal to bring with you to Saudi Arabia.

While some items fall into a grey area and may be ignored, others will be immediately confiscated if discovered upon entry by customs officers. Other items could prevent you from being granted entry into the country or could result in severe consequences, including imprisonment or, in the case of attempting to import illegal drugs, worse (page 61). It is prudent to assume all items could be taken from your possession. In theory, you should be able to retrieve most confiscated items upon departure, but there's a high chance these will no longer be locatable by the time you want to leave.

**Import and export restrictions** The list below addresses items most relevant to tourists entering Saudi Arabia. If you are relocating to Saudi Arabia, you may also wish to check with your relocation company, who should have this information. Tourism is very new in Saudi Arabia, so there is every possibility that the authorities could change import and export rules at any time, and at short notice. For the latest advice, refer to the official Saudi website detailing prohibited goods for import and export: **w** customs.gov.sa/en/general/prohibited-goods.

The following items may not be brought into Saudi Arabia, or they carry restrictions:

- Alcoholic beverages
- Items containing alcohol (including food items)
- Pork and pork products
- All narcotics
- Medicines without prescriptions (it is best practice to have a copy of your prescription with you)
- Over-the-counter medicines containing codeine
- Chewing tobacco and any other tobacco that is not smoked. Note that vaping is legal for personal use only (be sensible about quantities you bring with you).
- Items associated with gambling, eg: lottery tickets (this could include dice and playing cards, depending on the discretion of the customs officer if discovered)
- Natural pearls
- Fur
- Counterfeit items
- Military items including uniforms and equipment. Camouflage T-shirts and similar could fall into a grey area and are best avoided.
- Radio transmitter/communication equipment (including walkie-talkies, short-wave, VHF, marine, police band equipment, etc)
- Binoculars, night-vision equipment or telescopic equipment, drones
- All weapons and firearms including replicas and children's toys
- Laser pointers
- Pornography (this can be interpreted widely and can include images in fashion magazines)
- Sex toys
- Printed material that is contrary to Muslim or Saudi beliefs or morality
- Symbols from any faith other than Islam – this includes Christian crosses (including jewellery), Christmas ornaments and other decorations, any Judaica, Sikh turbans or any of the five K's, Hindu god statues, artefacts and other symbols, including the *kalava* thread, Buddha bells and prayer wheels, even as souvenirs, or anything else from any other religion that could be interpreted as suspicious

- Anything that could be associated with witchcraft or sorcery
- It is advised that anyone who wishes to carry a Bible does so in e-book format such as on a Kindle device
- Politically sensitive material
- Products made in Israel
- Israeli shekels

## EMBASSIES AND CONSULATES

With the advent of the Saudi tourist e-visa, there is no need to visit a Saudi embassy or consulate in your home country if you are eligible for this visa. Other travellers should contact the Saudi Embassy or a reliable organisation providing visa services such as CIBT (**w** cibtvisas.co.uk) in your country of nationality or residence if you do not hold a passport from one of the eligible countries.

Visitors who need consular assistance while in Saudi Arabia should contact their embassy. Nearly all embassies in Saudi Arabia are located in the Diplomatic Quarter in al Sarafat, Riyadh. A full list of embassies and other diplomatic missions in Saudi Arabia is posted at **w** embassypages.com/saudiarabia.

## GETTING THERE AND AWAY

**BY AIR** Saudi Arabia has a mix of international, regional and domestic airports. Some terminals are modern; others are showing their age. Regional airports connect with capitals of neighbouring countries, commercial centres and some regional tourist destinations. International flights connect to key cities throughout much of Europe and Asia, with a limited number of direct flights to Africa and North America. Most visitors entering Saudi Arabia on tourist visas do so through the Jeddah or Riyadh airports. Current ports of entry into Saudi Arabia that recognise tourist visas are: King Khalid International Airport (RUH) in Riyadh; King Abdul Aziz International Airport (JED) in Jeddah; King Fahd International Airport (DMM) in Dammam; and Prince Mohammed bin Abdul Aziz International Airport (MED) in Madinah (non-Muslims may use this airport as it is situated outside of the al Haram border).

Saudia (page 71) is the national and international carrier of Saudi Arabia. Though better than many Middle East-based carriers, its service record is not of the same standard as some of its full-service Gulf-based competitors. The airline serves key destinations including most capitals in western European countries, Johannesburg, Toronto, and Los Angeles International Airport, JFK (New York) and Dulles (Washington DC) airports in the USA. It also travels to many destinations in south and southeast Asia and Africa. Saudia is a dry airline and does not serve alcohol anywhere in its network or in its al Fursan lounges.

Several other airlines travel to Riyadh and Jeddah from North America and throughout Europe. At the time of writing, it is possible to fly to Riyadh and Jeddah on the national carriers and from the capital cities of France, Germany, Greece, the Netherlands and the UK. KLM and Lufthansa also fly to Dammam.

Some visitors opt to travel on a regional carrier such as Qatar Airways, Emirates or Etihad Airways, especially if they seek a high standard of customer service in the air. Budget-minded visitors may find it economical to travel to Saudi Arabia on a regional budget carrier. Air Arabia, flydubai and flynas are good options. Most of these carriers have scheduled flights to Riyadh and Jeddah, often running throughout the day, evening and overnight.

Flying via Turkey is another option for visitors needing to make a connection when travelling to Saudi Arabia. Turkish Airlines and budget airline Pegasus both offer a wide range of options and both have good reputations for customer service.

Visitors from Asia and the Antipodes often fly to Dubai or Doha and then connect to their destination in Saudi Arabia. Others may prefer to fly directly from or via Hong Kong, Japan, Malaysia, Singapore, the Philippines or South Korea. There are an increasing number of direct flights from a growing number of mainland Chinese cities, including Beijing, Shanghai and many important regional cities.

Airfares can skyrocket during Eid holidays, hajj season, and during some school breaks. Expatriates may also cause airfares to rise when they return home for Christmas or the summer months. Major business and diplomatic events in Riyadh can also have an impact on availability and prices, so plan ahead.

**DRIVING** People entering Saudi Arabia on business and residency visas have more flexibility and should be able to enter through most of the following road crossings. Options are more limited for those entering Saudi Arabia on a tourist visa. Most road border crossings are open 24 hours, seven days a week, but it is best to double-check timings as well as whether your visa type will be recognised at the border where you plan to cross.

**From/to Bahrain (البحرين)** The island country of Bahrain is connected to al Khobar, in Saudi Arabia's Eastern Province, by the King Fahd Causeway, a busy road crossing used by Saudis and expatriates alike. Border formalities take place midway along the causeway on Middle Island. This border recognises tourist e-visas, as well as residency and business visas.

**From/to Iraq (الْعِرَاق)** After some 30 years of closure, the road crossing between Iraq, in al Anbar Province about 50km from al Nukhib, and Ar'ar, in Saudi Arabia's Northern Borders Province, reopened in November 2020. Saudi Arabia reopened the border at al Jumaymah near Rafha in 2021 and there are plans to build additional border crossings between the two countries. However, it is unlikely that any of these will recognise tourist e-visas for their first use.

**From/to Jordan (الأردن)** Visitors can enter Saudi Arabia by road from Jordan through the Durra border crossing along the Red Sea coast, joining Saudi Route 55 towards Haql. It is the main road crossing between Jordan and Saudi Arabia and can be used by holders of residency and business visas (and could eventually be a significant border crossing for the planned NEOM development as well). After Haql the route continues along the coast to Jeddah and beyond, almost to the Yemen border.

Other road crossings are via Mudawara–Hallat Ammar, joining Saudi Highway 15 towards al Haditah and Tabuk, and via Umari–al Haditah, joining Saudi Highway 65 in the direction of al Qurayyat in the remote far north of al Jouf Province. People travelling on a residency or business visa are permitted to use these crossings but may be a curiosity to border officials as most people making this crossing are from the haulier business.

**From/to Kuwait (الكويت)** Kuwait has two road crossings into Saudi Arabia. The coastal crossing between al Nawasib in Kuwait towards Khafji Saudi Arabia is a well-travelled road, and joins Saudi Route 5 towards Jubail, Dammam and other points on the Eastern Province coast. The inland crossing between al Salmi in

Kuwait towards al Ruqi in Saudi Arabia joins Saudi Highway 50 towards Hafar al Batin in the interior of the Eastern Province and continues into the central Najd region's Riyadh Province between Buraydah and Riyadh. Both road crossings can be used by holders of a residency or business visa. Tourist e-visas may be recognised at these road crossings, but visitors should confirm their chosen route before attempting it.

**From/to Oman (عُمان)** The only land border between Oman and Saudi Arabia is Ramlet Khaliya, which opened in December 2021. It is located in the Empty Quarter, which covers parts of both countries. There are no settlements on either side of the border. The nearest town in Saudi Arabia is Shaybah, which supports a major oil field and is located more than 200km from the border; while the nearest town in Oman is Ibri, approximately 160km from the border. Despite these apparent long distances, this road saves 16 hours' journey time compared with before the border opened, when drivers had to go all the way through the UAE to get to Oman. This border recognises tourist e-visas as well as residency and business visas.

**From/to Qatar (قطر)** Qatar has one road crossing into Saudi Arabia, between abu Samra in Qatar and Salwa in the Eastern Province of Saudi Arabia. It joins Saudi Route 615, leading to Hofuf. This border recognises tourist e-visas, as well as residency and business visas.

**From/to the United Arab Emirates (الإمارات العربية المتحدة)** There is one road crossing into Saudi Arabia from the UAE. It is located between al Ghuwaifat in Abu Dhabi Emirate and al Batha in the Eastern Province of Saudi Arabia and recognises tourist e-visas and residency and business visas. It joins Saudi Route 5, which eventually parallels the Qatari border to Salwa, and also Saudi Highway 10, leading to al Kharj, about 100km south of Riyadh.

**From/to Yemen (ٱلْيَمَن)** Owing to the ongoing conflict between Yemen and Saudi Arabia, all road crossings with Yemen are off-limits at the time of writing. Land borders do exist, but it is unlikely that these border crossings will recognise people travelling on tourist e-visas whenever this conflict settles down.

**BY RAIL** It is not possible to arrive in Saudi Arabia by rail. The Hejaz Railway (page 194) is no longer operational, although the line between Amman and Damascus on the Syrian side is in use. Current lines operated by Saudi Arabian Railway (SAR) only serve domestic destinations.

Although the proposed GCC Railway was announced in 2009, there has been very little development in general and no development across the Saudi borders to other GCC countries. At the time of publication, much of this project has been placed on hold, with some GCC countries yet to start the project within their borders.

**BY BUS** The Saudi Public Transport Company, commonly known as SAPTCO (☎ 800 124 999; w saptco.com.sa) is the national bus company and has been operating since 1979. As well as operating a fleet of intercity buses throughout the Kingdom, along with city routes in Jeddah and Riyadh, it offers services to/from some neighbouring countries: to Manama in Bahrain, al Riggae in Kuwait, Doha in Qatar, to Abu Dhabi, Dubai and Sharjah in the UAE, and to al Durra and al Haditha in Jordan and onward to Amman. SAPTCO also connects to Egypt through ferry crossings on the Red Sea. These must be booked by contacting SAPTCO by telephone or by visiting a ticket office in person.

Buses are clean and comfortable. However, they are generally as expensive as flights, so are not a very popular choice for major routes or for travelling longer distances. For example, a flight from Jeddah to Tabuk is about $150 return at the time of writing and takes 1½ hours in each direction. The bus is about $130 return and takes at least 15 hours in each direction. International bus journeys require check-in 2 hours prior to departure.

**BY SEA** There are no commercial ports of entry for visitors travelling on a tourist e-visa, with the exception of arrangements made for cruise-ship operators. Visitors planning to arrive on a cruise ship are advised to check with their tour operator about what requirements must be met to disembark in port, as well as any limitations imposed. Nearly all cruise ships with Saudi Arabia as part of their itinerary will dock in the Jeddah Islamic Port in Jeddah's historic al Balad district. A few may stop in Dammam.

## HEALTH *with Dr Daniel Campion*

Healthcare facilities are generally of a high standard in Saudi Arabia, including excellent hospitals in major cities and other private healthcare facilities. Pharmacies can provide sound medical advice, and well-trained, English-speaking medical professionals can be found throughout the Kingdom.

### PREPARATIONS

**Travel clinics and health information** A full list of current travel clinic websites worldwide is available on **w** istm.org. For other journey preparation information, consult **w** travelhealthpro.org.uk (UK) or **w** cdc.gov/travel (USA). All advice found online should be used in conjunction with expert advice received prior to or during travel.

**Medical insurance** Saudi residents and all foreign visitors are required to have medical insurance, which gives you access to the medical facilities that accept the particular insurance purchased. When applying for a tourist visa, you will be required to select mandatory insurance coverage from a short list of Saudi providers. However, you are strongly recommended to organise your own additional, comprehensive, travel insurance appropriate to your needs, including coverage for evacuation and for any high-risk activities if these are in your plans.

**Vaccinations** There is no risk of **yellow fever** in Saudi Arabia. Under International Health Regulations, a yellow fever vaccination certificate is required for travellers over nine months of age arriving from countries with risk of yellow fever transmission such as parts of sub-Saharan Africa and South America, and for all travellers who have transited for more than 12 hours through an airport in a country with risk of yellow fever transmission. A valid certificate is active ten days after vaccination and lasts for life. Since 11 July 2016, all countries must accept any certificate, no matter how long ago the vaccine was given.

It is important to be up to date with your **tetanus**, **diphtheria**, **polio** and **measles**, **mumps** and **rubella** jabs. Long-term visitors and expatriate residents are usually advised to have a hepatitis A vaccination and a course of hepatitis B injections.

Those travelling to rural locations far from health facilities, or those working with animals, should consider a rabies vaccine before travelling. In the UK, a course of three rabies vaccinations over at least 21 days is recommended (although this may differ in other countries).

Meningococcal ACWY vaccine (page 57) is compulsory for seasonal workers and hajj or umrah pilgrims: the risk is highest at mass gatherings. It is given as a single dose and protects for five years. Outbreaks of other respiratory infections have also occurred during hajj, and vaccination against influenza would be a wise precaution for participants, especially for those at higher risk.

**Personal first-aid kit and medication** If you are planning to travel to remote locations, contents of a personal fist-aid kit might include antiseptic cream or spray, palsters, high-factor sunscreen, insect repellent, paracetamol (acetaminophen), antifungal cream (eg: clotrimazole), antibiotic eye drops, tweezers and a digital thermometer.

It is straightforward enough to create your own first-aid kit after arrival in Saudi Arabia if you do not wish to take up valuable luggage space, as there are well-stocked pharmacies in even the smallest of villages. However, sunscreen can be difficult to come by in the Kingdom, so do remember to bring some from home, with a factor of 30 SPF or above, and a four- or five-star UVA protection rating.

Many drugs, including over-the-counter and prescription medications, are illegal to bring into Saudi Arabia and could lead to arrest if discovered. For more information, check these websites: w saudiembassy.net/bringing-prescription-drugs-kingdom-saudi-arabia; w my.gov.sa/wps/portal/snp/agencies/agencyDetails/AC070. Several narcotic and psychotropic medications are restricted, so check with the embassy before travel. All prescription medication should be clearly labelled with a note from your doctor: you should only take enough for your personal use during the stay. A helpful guide to travelling with medication can be obtained from IAMAT: w iamat.org/travelling-with-medications.

## MEDICAL PROBLEMS

**Dehydration, heat exhaustion and heatstroke** The biggest health risk for most visitors to Saudi Arabia is **dehydration** during the hot summer months. High temperatures, humidity, exertion and a lack of adequate fluids can all result in dehydration, heat exhaustion and possibly heatstroke. Summer is long, running from April to September, and temperatures can reach 50°C in the Eastern Province and Najd region, including Riyadh. The Eastern Province also experiences high humidity from about June to mid-October, making it nearly impossible to spend any significant amount of time outdoors during these months.

The modest local dress code helps protect from sunburn as you will already be covering your skin. Choose loose-fitting clothes made of natural, breathable fabrics such as loosely woven cotton and use sunscreen; wearing sunglasses is also recommended. Try to keep out of the sun between 11.00 and 15.00 when the sun is strongest, and be sure to drink plenty of water. Certain medications (including various blood pressure tablets, antidepressants and antihistamines) may increase your risk of heat illness, so extra caution is advised. If you visit during Ramadan, find a way to drink water away from public view as it is forbidden to drink openly, even in your car. Small children can drink water in public, but try to find a discreet place away from other people.

It's easy to become dehydrated in a hot desert climate although the colder nights provide some relief. Most people don't even realise that their irritability, weariness and dizziness may be due to a lack of water. When out walking in the heat, take as much water as you can carry.

**Heat exhaustion** occurs when the body's cooling system hits overdrive. Profuse sweating, pale clammy skin, fast shallow breathing, nausea, headaches, rapid weak pulse and stomach cramps are all signs of heat exhaustion. It's important to counter this quickly by trying to cool the body down. Sit in the shade, take a dip in a pool, drink plenty of water and relax.

**Heatstroke** can be fatal. This occurs when the body's cooling system has broken down completely. Skin becomes hot and red, breathing slows and confusion and dizziness lead to unconsciousness. Cooling the body down is paramount and immediate medical assistance is essential.

**Malaria** Transmitted by night-biting *Anopheles* mosquitoes, malaria exists in the border areas of Asir, Jizan and Najran near Yemen, but is not found in cities or elsewhere in the country. While malaria tablets for prophylaxis are not recommended for most travellers to Saudi Arabia, it is crucial, nevertheless, to protect yourself from mosquito bites, so keep a DEET-containing insect repellent to hand (50% concentration is ideal). Acceptable alternatives to DEET include icaridin, p-menthane diol or 3-ethlyaminopropionate (IR3535). At night, use a mosquito net impregnated with insecticide if you are not in air-conditioned accommodation. People with certain health conditions which put them at higher risk from malaria may be advised to take prophylactic medication when visiting these provinces – seek advice from a travel health professional.

**Dengue fever** There is a risk of dengue in the provinces of Madinah, Jizan and Makkah including the cities of Mecca and Jeddah. This virus is transmitted by a day-biting mosquito (*Aedes aegypti*), which is why it is important to use insect repellents (see above) during the day. Use your sunscreen first and the insect repellent second. There are four types of dengue fever for which there is currently no cure. Dengue is rarely fatal if you have not had it before. However, even a primary infection can be unpleasant and causes a fever, with a headache, joint and muscle pains and sometimes a rash. Repeated infections with different strains can lead to a more serious haemorrhagic form of the disease, which can result in death. It is important, therefore, to avoid mosquito bites whenever possible by applying a good insect repellent during the day as well as in the evening to avoid other biting insects. A new vaccine against dengue has, at the time of writing, recently been licensed in the European Union and the UK.

**Leishmaniasis** Although uncommon in travellers, a parasitic skin disease called cutaneous leishmaniasis is endemic in parts of Saudi Arabia. (A more dangerous 'visceral' form of the disease is far less common.) It is transmitted by tiny, blood-sucking, low-flying insects called sandflies. Again, insect bite prevention with repellents and an impregnated mosquito net at night are key to preventing infection. Consult your doctor if you notice a persistent skin lesion or an open sore in the weeks and months after travel.

**Respiratory illnesses** As the world emerges from the emergency phase of the Covid-19 pandemic, it is worth remembering that a related but less contagious respiratory virus, Middle East respiratory syndrome coronavirus (MERS-CoV), has been reported in Saudi Arabia since 2012. MERS-CoV can cause severe illness and death, but cases are uncommon. Travellers should avoid close contact with camels and consumption of raw milk or any other camel products.

**Meningococcal disease** The most common forms of meningococcal disease are meningitis (infection of the protective lining around the brain) and septicaemia (blood poisoning). Transmitted by close contact and respiratory droplets, this bacterial infection can kill within hours of the appearance of initial symptoms, typically a combination of a blinding headache, light sensitivity, blotchy rash and high fever. Admission to hospital and prompt antibiotic treatment are required. Outbreaks can occur at mass gatherings and vaccination against the A, C, W and Y strains of the meningococcus is compulsory for seasonal workers and pilgrims taking part in hajj.

**Rabies** Rabies is a risk in Saudi Arabia and has been found in both domestic and wild animals, especially bats. A course of pre-exposure rabies vaccine is advised for long-term visitors who will be in rural areas as it simplifies any post-exposure treatment if needed.

This deadly disease can be carried by any mammal and is usually transmitted to humans via a bite or a scratch that breaks the skin. Do not approach stray dogs or cats. Assume that any mammal that bites or scratches you (or even licks an open wound) might be rabid even if it looks healthy. First, scrub the wound with soap under a running tap for 10–15 minutes, or while pouring water from a jug, then apply an antiseptic or strong alcohol solution, which will guard against infections and might reduce the risk of the virus entering the body.

Whether or not you underwent pre-exposure vaccination, it is vital to obtain post-exposure prophylaxis as soon as possible after the incident. Tell the doctor if you have had pre-exposure vaccine, as this will change the treatment you receive. Death from rabies is probably one of the worst ways to go, and once you show symptoms it is too late to do anything – the mortality rate is almost 100%.

**Schistosomiasis** Also known as bilharzia, schistosomiasis is an unpleasant parasitic disease transmitted by freshwater snails. It cannot be caught in hotel swimming pools or the ocean, but may be present in lakes, oases, swamps and streams in rural areas. Saudi Arabia has implemented schistosomiasis control and elimination programmes resulting in reduced prevalence of the disease, so it is rare in travellers. The infection is often asymptomatic in its early stages, but some people experience an intense immune reaction, including fever, cough, abdominal pain and an itching rash, around four to six weeks after infection. Later symptoms vary but often include a general feeling of tiredness and lethargy. If you are exposed by swimming or wading in fresh water, schistosomiasis can be tested for and treated at specialist travel and tropical medicine clinics, ideally at least six weeks after exposure.

**Altitude sickness** The Asir Mountains in Asir Province are home to several peaks above 2,500m. Altitude sickness can occur above this elevation. To minimise the risk of developing altitude illness, sensible precautions can be adopted. Try not to travel from sea level to high altitudes in a short space of time but give yourself some time to acclimatise instead to the lower levels of oxygen. An ascent that is too rapid can lead to: **acute mountain sickness** (AMS), symptoms of which include headache, loss of appetite, nausea, vomiting, poor sleep, fatigue and weakness; **high altitude cerebral oedema** (HACE), whose symptoms include confusion, altered consciousness and poor co-ordination; and **high-altitude**

**pulmonary oedema** (HAPE), whose symptoms include increasing breathlessness, breathlessness when lying down, a cough which is initially dry and then wet, and the production of frothy, blood-stained sputum. It is essential to be aware of symptoms of altitude illness and to consider symptoms to be caused by altitude illness until proven otherwise. Severe AMS, HACE and HAPE are medical emergencies that require urgent treatment. Acetazolamide is a prescription medication that can assist acclimatisation but it should never replace appropriate precautions including a gradual ascent. For more detailed advice on altitude sickness, see **w** travelhealthpro.org.uk/factsheet/26/altitude-illness.

## OTHER HEALTH CONCERNS

### Snakes and scorpions

**Snakes** are very secretive and bites are a genuine rarity. However, Saudi Arabia is home to a variety of venomous species including the Arabian cobra. Local members of the viper family include the sawscale viper, the carpet viper and horned vipers. Certain spiders and scorpions can also deliver venomous bites and stings. In all cases, the risk is minimised by wearing closed shoes and trousers when walking in the bush, and watching where you put your hands and feet, especially in rocky areas. Shake out boots before putting them on to ensure no creatures have taken up residence. If bitten, you are unlikely to have received venom; keeping this fact in mind may help you to stay calm.

Many 'traditional' first-aid techniques do more harm than good: tourniquets are dangerous; suction and electrical inactivation devices do not work. The only treatment is antivenom. In case of a bite that you fear may have been from a venomous snake:

- Try to keep calm – it is likely that mild venom or no venom (a dry bite) has been dispensed.
- Remove any jewellery or tight-fitting clothes from the bitten limb (most dangerous snakebites cause severe swelling).
- Prevent movement of the bitten limb by applying a splint.
- If trained to do so, apply a crêpe pressure bandage to the affected limb – this should not be too tight.
- Evacuate to a hospital, ideally on a stretcher to limit movement.

And remember:

- Never give aspirin or other non-steroidal anti-inflammatory drugs like ibuprofen, which may exacerbate bleeding. Paracetamol is safe.
- Never cut or suck the wound.
- Do not apply ice packs or electric current.
- Do not apply a tourniquet.
- Do not try to capture or kill the snake, as this may result in further bites.

**Scorpion** stings are intensely painful and may cause generalised toxic effects. Pain relief is essential and hospital treatment may be needed. Specific antivenom against some species of scorpion may be available.

### Food and drink

Most travellers to Saudi Arabia do not need to take specific food or water precautions beyond the basic hygiene principles (such as washing hands before eating) they would employ at home. Food safety is taken seriously in Saudi Arabia and must meet rigorous standards. Ingredients must be labelled, and expiry dates are displayed on all food products sold in supermarkets. Loose items such as nuts and spices are now selected and measured by employees, avoiding possible contamination by other customers. It remains a rule of travel that freshly prepared food is generally safer than food served at a buffet, especially as the day wears on.

If you do get diarrhoea, in most cases it will settle down after 24 hours with rest, drinking plenty of fluids and taking rehydration salts (eg: Electrolade or Dioralyte). If diarrhoea comes with a fever and/or blood and/or slime then you should seek medical help immediately as it is important to get the correct diagnosis and if necessary the appropriate antibiotics.

***Water*** As Saudi Arabia has no rivers and limited underground water resources, most water comes from desalinated sea water. Desalinated water is safe to drink but many people limit its use to the bathroom and for cleaning as it has an unpleasant taste. Many people purchase bottled water for drinking.

### MEDICAL SERVICES IN SAUDI ARABIA

**Emergencies** The national number for an ambulance is 997. You should contact your insurance or medical assistance provider promptly if you are referred to a medical facility for treatment. Most hospitals have accident and emergency facilities, and air ambulances can be accessed by visitors with the necessary insurance to cover this service (or who can afford it independently).

**Hospitals** Visitors are expected to use private hospitals that accept their medical insurance. Hospitals with an excellent reputation include those listed below. As these hospitals can be found in multiple cities throughout the Kingdom, please refer to the relevant chapter for the nearest hospital in your location.

**Dallah Hospital** w dallah-hospital.com
**Dr Sulaiman al Habib Medical Group** w hmg.com
**King Fahd Medical City** w kfmc.med.sa
**King Faisal Specialist Hospital & Research Centre** w kfshrc.edu.sa
**Saudi German Hospital** w saudigermanhealth.com

**Pharmacies** Even the smallest of towns across Saudi Arabia have pharmacies, which sell the usual over-the-counter products, as well as some health and beauty items. Reputable pharmacies, among many more, include al Dawaa (w al-dawaa.com), Nahdi (w nahdionline.com), Boots (w sa.boots.com) and Whites (w whites.net).

Pharmacists are generally very knowledgeable, trained to a high standard and able to give practical advice for many medical conditions that can be treated with over-the-counter products. If needed, you should be able to find the same medications you use at home, although possibly under different branding. Do be aware that opiates and most psychotropic drugs are severely restricted in Saudi Arabia. Birth control is readily available, but tampons may be difficult to find even in some pharmacies.

## SAFETY

You are probably safer in Saudi Arabia than you are in London, New York or Paris. Stay alert if you are travelling near the Yemeni border and, as long as you don't violate the most important social and religious rules (page 62), you should have a safe visit. Your biggest problems are not terrorism or similar fears, but atrocious drivers and dehydration.

## EMERGENCY NUMBERS

Ambulance 997
Police 999, 911
Road security 996
Road accidents 993

**OUT AND ABOUT** Visitors should be aware that health-and-safety practices that are commonplace elsewhere in the world may be lacking in Saudi Arabia. For example, guardrails may be old, broken or poorly secured, or even absent, at the edge of sheer drops at tourist and other sites; and if they are present, they may have wide gaps that a child could fall through or may not be strong enough to hold the weight of a person leaning on them. Steps do not always have handrails. Monuments and ruins that you are permitted to climb on may have unprotected edges and loose rubble underfoot. Litter is rife, unfortunately, including in parks and areas of natural beauty.

Footpaths are often in poor condition and may be strewn with broken glass or other hazards. City streets may have broken pavements that are unsuitable for prams and wheelchair users, and may also force pedestrians out into the road. Be especially careful if it has rained as there are many slippery surfaces.

**PERSONAL SAFETY** Saudi Arabia is generally safer than most other countries when it comes to personal safety matters. Although pickpockets, theft and assaults are rare, use common sense and take care of your valuables.

Sexual harassment is not unknown in Saudi Arabia but, since it is regarded as shameful, it is seldom witnessed in public. It is usually targeted at women, especially women who may be alone somewhere in public where others would not be able to observe the offender. Sexual harassment often occurs when a Saudi perceives behaviour or demeanour as un-Islamic. Observe the dress code (page 100) and refrain from being too open in a way that can be interpreted as an invitation to something more.

**ROAD SAFETY** Although the streets in the oldest city centre districts are sometimes in need of repair, most roads in Saudi Arabia are of good quality. Motorways are reasonably well signposted in both Arabic and English, with a good number of services along the way. City road signs are less consistent and may not always be in English. The roads themselves are not usually the problem – it's the drivers!

It is difficult to fully appreciate driving conditions in Saudi Arabia until you see them for yourself. Flagrant disregard for speed limits, poor lane discipline, sudden turns across multiple lanes of traffic, drivers travelling in the wrong direction for hundreds of metres, children jumping on seats or even riding with their head outside a window or sunroof, 12-year-old drivers, and camels on the road can all be encountered – these all in addition to deteriorating road conditions during sandstorms, rain or fog. Seatbelts may or may not be worn despite the law requiring them to be worn by the driver and front seat passenger. Using a mobile phone while driving almost seems to be the norm even though this behaviour risks points on your licence and a fine. Never rely on a driver to stop for a pedestrian, including in the middle of a designated crossing.

According to World Health Rankings, Saudi Arabia's annual road traffic death rate is among the highest in the world at 34.57 per 100,000. Comparative figures per 100,000 are 10.92 in the USA, 5.96 in New Zealand, 5.17 in Canada, 4.62 in Australia, 3.01 in Ireland and 2.42 in the UK.

**Weather conditions** It doesn't **rain** very often in Saudi Arabia, but it is usually very welcome when it does. However, it brings with it challenges for road users. Oil from vehicles tends to collect on the roads and so they become very slippery when it rains. Water doesn't drain from the roads properly and the remaining puddles can conceal all sorts of dangers from pot-holes to submerged items. Drivers may hydroplane. Since drivers tend not to allow the extra distance between vehicles necessary in wet conditions, and windscreen wipers are often not maintained, it can be a better idea to stay off the roads altogether when it rains if you can.

It is possible to encounter **fog** in the summer months. It is common in al Bahah and Asir provinces, and sometimes along the coast of the Eastern Province, most often in the spring. It is strongly recommended that you do not drive whenever the fog rolls in as visibility can be radically reduced and driving becomes dangerous.

It **snows** on occasion in Saudi Arabia, limited to the higher elevations of Tabuk Province. Snow is celebrated, but drivers should take all necessary precautions, especially as most Saudis are unfamiliar with driving on snow, controlling sliding and clearing the vehicle.

**Sandstorms** occur often between March and June and can cause visibility to drop to practically zero. They tend to be more more severe in the north, declining in severity the further south along the Arabian Gulf coast you go, but they do occur inland as well, including in Riyadh. Try to avoid driving during a sandstorm.

## CRIME

**Corporal and capital punishment** Saudi Arabia practises capital punishment. The following crimes can be punishable by death: murder, rape, apostasy, blasphemy, armed robbery, illegal drug smuggling, repeated drug use, adultery, sodomy, homosexual activity, witchcraft, sorcery and terrorism. The Kingdom also practises corporal punishment, which once involved flogging with a set number of lashes, and still includes amputation of a hand or foot in some instances. It is imperative for foreign nationals to understand that they are not exempt from these punishments if found guilty of violating Saudi law.

**Political crime and threat of terrorism** Saudi Arabia is not immune to terrorism. From a Saudi perspective, the worst act of terrorism in modern times took place on home soil in 1979, when a group of Saudi national extremists seized the Grand Mosque and surrounding area in Mecca. Several people were killed; and the perpetrators were swiftly executed. This led directly to a much stricter interpretation of expected Islamic behaviour in the Kingdom that has only over the past few years begun to relax. From a Western perspective, the terrorist bombings of several Western compounds within Saudi Arabia in the early 2000s caused some expatriates to reassess their comfort levels working and living in the Kingdom. At the time of writing, the last of these occurred in 2004.

The Saudi government takes domestic terrorism very seriously and has stepped up activities to prevent incidents from happening within its borders. Although they provide no guarantee, security measures are in place in high-profile locations, including most high-end hotels, offices and compounds where Western expatriates live.

**Cybercrime** Saudi Arabia takes a dim view of cybercrime, which includes data theft, similar crimes recognised globally and also political and social judgements considered anti-Saudi, anti-Islamic or both. Take care when posting comments on social media or online more generally. The Saudi Anti-Cybercrime Law was announced by Royal Decree in 2007, with the aim to ensure data security and to protect the legitimate use of information technology. Punishments are determined by the Saudi Ministry of Interior and the Communications and Information Technology Commission. It is a prudent assumption that Saudi authorities can access information from your accounts if they really want to, if you attract their attention.

As in most of the world, social media is very popular in Saudi Arabia. However, most Saudis know they also must stay safe. There is no specific suggestion that all visitors are routinely monitored simply by visiting the Kingdom. However, visitors are strongly advised to be sensitive to these matters and to consider deleting anything that could be considered remotely offensive or in violation of Saudi law. This could include posts on social media that would be interpreted as benign in many other countries, even if these statements were written outside of Saudi Arabia. Most people would be well advised to use maximum privacy settings on social media and to keep any comments about the Kingdom to a minimum. Of course, enthusiastic, positive comments about Saudi Arabia are fine.

**POLICE** The telephone numbers for police emergencies are 999 and 911. Although many Saudis speak and understand English, they may struggle to understand a native English speaker in a moment of crisis. Try to find an Arabic speaker to help you if possible if you cannot make yourself clearly understood.

Regular police uniforms are either tan/sand in colour or black. Male officers wear a shirt and matching trousers with a belt. Their uniform also includes a name badge, epaulets, insignia designating rank, and a beret with badge towards the wearer's left side. The badge has a silvery white background with a gold crown at centre top and the black and gold Saudi crossed swords and palm tree symbols that are used throughout the Kingdom. Some police officers wear a formal jacket and stiff hat with a brim, with the same badge in the centre of the hat above the brim. Female police officers wear uniforms that include a long military-style abaya or a long tunic over baggy trousers, again with a name badge, epaulets and insignia designating rank, similar to their male counterparts. They wear a headscarf under their beret and may also opt to wear the niqab.

**PERSONAL CONDUCT AND PUBLIC DECENCY** Although routine challenges from the mutawa (see opposite) are now a thing of the past, it is still possible to get into trouble (possibly very serious trouble) if you breach the rules. The following behaviours are not permitted:

- Possessing alcohol or illegal drugs.
- Public intoxication. This applies from the time you enter Saudi airspace until you leave the Kingdom and applies to alcohol, psychoactive drugs such as cannabis and, especially, narcotic drugs.
- Extreme violations of the dress code. Women should wear the abaya or other suitably baggy clothing; women should not wear tight or revealing clothing, including sleeveless tops, tops that show cleavage or midriff, or skirts and cropped trousers or shorts that expose the legs above the knee. Men could find themselves in difficulty if they wear shorts above the knee or sleeveless tops or vests. How the code is interpreted depends on where you are and who you are. Wearing militaria or garments containing slogans deemed to be un-Islamic or insulting are also forbidden.

## THE MUTAWA

Some visitors may have heard from earlier travellers to the Kingdom about abusive punishment meted out by the religious police for infringements of social norms and behaviour. The *mutawa* or *hai'a* are officially known as the Committee for the Promotion of Virtue and the Prevention of Vice (CPVPV; *hay'a al-'amr bil-ma'rūf wan-nahī 'an al-munkar*), and are a mostly volunteer organisation established to enforce the Islamic concept of hisba. In brief, hisba means upholding community morals based on the Qur'an and to enjoin good and forbid wrong. The mutawa have applied this doctrine to all people in Saudi Arabia, including non-Muslim visitors and expatriates.

Existing in its current form since 1976, the mutawa gained significant powers after the siege of Mecca in 1979. They were particularly active in Riyadh and the more remote regional provinces, often concentrating on their perception of women's morals. They also accelerated enforcement of their rules during Ramadan. Reforms started in the modern era in 2006 under the reign of King Abdullah, and by which the mutawa's powers were significantly restricted. They were now no longer allowed to interrogate anyone arrested for un-Islamic behaviour, and instead were obliged to turn the alleged offender to the police, who would then determine what action, if any, would take place.

A public relations exercise of sorts first occurred in 2012, training the mutawa on how to treat the public with politeness and respect. Power was further reduced during the 2016 reforms under the rule of King Salman. The Saudi Council of Ministers issued a royal decree that stripped the religious police of its privileges, banning its members from pursuing, questioning, arresting and detaining anyone suspected of a crime, or asking for their identification. The mutawa is now responsible only for reporting any violations they may witness to the police.

Members of the mutawa do not wear official uniforms. However, they can be identified by their ID badges worn around their neck on a lanyard containing the official logo. The CPVPV logo design includes a gold outer rim containing the words General Presidency of the Promotion of Virtue and the Prevention of Vice, in Arabic on the top and in English on the bottom. The interior of the badge has a light blue background and contains a stylised depiction of the map of Saudi Arabia intertwined with an open Qur'an in sand and white colours. They are also likely to wear a short thobe worn above the ankles, a ghutra with no agal, and a natural, ungroomed beard. In reality, visitors no longer have any reason to fear the mutawa unless they do something obviously and publicly disrespectful of the rules (see opposite).

- Cross-dressing and costumes. Obvious cross-dressing is taboo, as is wearing fancy dress. In theory, all Muslim men including visiting Muslim men who wear items made of gold or silk could be in violation of the dress code as these are considered feminine items. The authorities do not make the same judgement for non-Muslim men.
- Sexual behaviour in public. This could even include hand holding and hugging but the rule is much more likely to be enforced if a man and a woman are kissing on the mouth, touching or placing hands elsewhere on the body and beyond. Shaking hands is permitted if both the man and the woman agree.

- Ignoring gender mixing restrictions in venue areas where it remains forbidden, and resisting separation. These rules continue to be relaxed at a fast pace, but there are some places where they remain.
- Very loud music.
- Some dancing, mostly non-traditional dancing or dancing that can be interpreted as too intimate. Traditional dances such as the ardah are permitted.
- Anything *perceived* to be blasphemous. Be aware that this can include using otherwise benign words and phrases to replace expletives including in foreign languages, such as 'holy moley'.
- Anything seen to be proselytising a faith other than Islam.
- Ignoring additional rules during Ramadan. This includes eating, drinking, smoking, vaping or chewing gum in public. Bear in mind that the dress code for women and men is more strictly enforced during Ramadan than at other times of the year.
- Attempting to travel to the al Haram areas of Mecca and Madinah, unless you are Muslim.

In 2019, new **public decency laws** were decreed. The Resolution provides that people in public places must pay respect to the values, customs, traditions and culture of the Kingdom of Saudi Arabia. It is important to note that different regions of the Kingdom may interpret these laws in different ways, especially in very conservative areas. The Ministry of the Interior has issued this summary of what it entails, which visitors should keep in mind in addition to the rules of personal conduct listed on page 62:

- Acts of public sexual harassment.
- Playing loud music in residential areas.
- Playing music during prayer times.
- Littering.
- Failing to remove pet waste.
- Occupying seats designated for people with disabilities.
- Bypassing barriers to enter public places.
- Wearing improper dress in public, such as underwear or pyjamas.
- Wearing shirts that display nude pictures.
- Wearing shirts that display phrases offending public decency.
- Writing and drawing on the walls of public places.
- Placing racist stickers on cars.
- Distributing adverts in public without a licence.
- Starting fires in unauthorised places during safaris.
- Threatening people verbally or through gestures.
- Queue jumping in public venues.
- Shining laser pointers into people's eyes.
- Taking people's pictures without their permission.
- Taking photos of a traffic accident without permission from the parties involved in the accident.

## WOMEN TRAVELLERS AND UNMARRIED COUPLES

Some of the most inaccurate information in circulation about Saudi Arabia is to do with **women**. While some is no longer true owing to relatively recent changes in the Kingdom, some of it is long out of date, or simply has just never been true. Women have been working and travelling for business in the Kingdom in increasing numbers over recent years, first with the early reforms of King Abdullah, and accelerating exponentially since the reign of King Salman.

Key points of interest, and relevant to most women considering travel to Saudi Arabia are:

- Women have equal eligibility and can travel to Saudi Arabia on a tourist e-visa the same as men. This is now also true for business visas.
- Women can travel to Saudi Arabia alone, with other women, with their family, in a mixed-gender group, or as part of an organised tour group. There is no need for a woman to travel with a mahram (male guardian such as her father, husband, brother or even her son) unless she wishes to.
- Women can check into hotels and visit museums, restaurants and shopping centres unaccompanied if they wish. Do be aware, however, that there are some places of interest that may still have hours specifically designated for men and others for families. In this context, families mean the presence of women, whether literally in a family or other group, or on her own.
- Women are allowed to drive and can drive with male passengers. However, women (and girls) should never sit in the front seat of a taxi or of any vehicle driven by a professional driver. The driver is likely to move the empty front passenger seat forward – as a gesture of courtesy and respect.
- At the time of writing, buses run by the national company, SAPTCO, are gender segregated, with women and children allocated seats in the rear on intercity buses and seats in the front on intracity buses.
- Sporting activities, exercising and swimming are still mostly gender segregated.
- Women must adhere to the dress code, as must men, which is described in detail on page 100.
- Women are generally treated with a high level of respect by everyone, as long as women return that respect.
- In addition to adhering to the dress code (page 100), women should be mindful of their body language, accepting that there are boundaries of public behaviour that are much more conservative than in the West in particular. Hugging, kissing or other gestures of familiarity or intimacy across the gender line in any public setting are not allowed. This even includes refraining from public displays of affection with your husband; but it is acceptable with very young sons.
- There is no need for single women to wear a wedding ring. Indeed, plenty of married Saudis don't wear one. Practically speaking, wearing a fake wedding ring does nothing to prevent anyone bothering an unmarried woman and instead can create doubt about the honesty of the woman. It is much better to come across as friendly…but not so friendly that it could be misinterpreted as welcoming an approach from a Saudi man. If an unwanted suitor is persistent, it is generally better to ask the man how he would feel if his mother or sister were being treated the same way he is treating you.

The only **legal sexual relationships** in Saudi Arabia are between heterosexual married couples – with each other. Heterosexual (or any other kind of) civil partnerships are not recognised. Unmarried heterosexual couples could potentially fall foul of Saudi law, although a blind eye is often turned for non-Muslim foreigners. It would be prudent not to correct someone who refers to your partner as your husband/wife, and would be reassuring to family-orientated Saudis.

Furthermore, Saudis may have difficulty accepting the idea that some children of overseas visitors are born to unmarried couples or single mothers. Paradoxically, becoming single after the child's birth is not generally a problem from a Saudi perspective. There are many single parents in Saudi Arabia; however, they are almost certainly either divorced or widowed as opposed to never married.

It is illegal for a woman to be unmarried and pregnant in Saudi Arabia. If you think you might be pregnant and are unmarried, it would be wise to postpone your trip or to leave the Kingdom before anyone discovers your pregnancy. Same-sex couples expecting a child will cause even more confusion and possible problems.

## TRAVELLERS FROM DIVERSE ETHNIC BACKGROUNDS

Saudis are very used to receiving visitors from all over the world in their country: religious pilgrims, expatriate residents and business travellers. However, those expats who perform (usually low-paid) service roles, for example, in Saudi Arabia and who traditionally come from south Asia, the Philippines or East Africa are not always treated with the same level of respect as people from other backgrounds. Unfortunately, this can translate to judgements being made about any visitors perceived to be from those regions, which can be problematic in certain situations: gaining access to upmarket restaurants, to shopping malls, at hotel check-in and anywhere there is a queue, such as waiting to hire a car. Visitors who appear to be from these backgrounds but have a Western passport could find it useful to make their nationality clear. Dressing smartly and showing confident body language most closely associated with Western behaviour can also be effective ways to manage this issue.

## LGBTQIA+ TRAVELLERS

Homosexuality is illegal in Saudi Arabia and can lead to severe punishment including the death penalty (page 61). Any sexual orientation other than heterosexuality is not publicly tolerated and same-sex marriages or civil partnerships are not recognised. There is very little awareness or understanding of transgender, transsexual and non-binary identities. Where they feel they need to acknowledge a trans person's identity, the authorities could apply cross-dressing judgements; cross-dressing is strictly taboo in Saudi Arabia and punishable by imprisonment, fines or deportation for foreigners.

Despite these rules, LGBTQIA+ travellers do visit Saudi Arabia trouble-free, but do so with caution. It is strongly advised to be very discreet about your sexual identity if it is not heterosexual, including when dealing with the practicalities of booking hotel rooms and a double versus twin or single beds. With online booking facilities, it is possible to book a double bed, but hotel clerks in your destination may sometimes override your request and assign a room with two beds instead; it would be wise not to challenge this. It is also strongly advised not to use terms such as husband or wife when referring to another person of the same sex in very public settings. 'Friend', 'travelling companion' and similar are safe options.

## TRAVELLING WITH CHILDREN

Most Saudis love children and consider them to be blessings that enrich their lives, and if you choose to travel in Saudi Arabia with children, you will often find yourselves the centre of attention. It is common for Saudis, both men and women, to show open affection to their own children and they might very possibly extend this to your children as well. If this happens with your children, consider it to be a compliment.

You will almost always get assistance when travelling with a small child, for example being helped with your buggy up a flight of stairs. Shops and supermarkets are filled with things for children, from childcare essentials (including nappies) to toys – locally produced soft toys and toys from popular globally recognised brands – which are sold across all price ranges.

There are almost no venues that exclude children. Saudi infrastructure focuses on children's activities in parks, shopping malls and other public spaces, and hotels usually have a wide range of room types, including family suites and adjoining standard rooms with interior doors. Children usually accompany their parents and extended families to restaurants too – whether that's a child-themed fast-food chain or an upscale restaurant that you might think more suitable for quiet conversation with other adults or serious business meetings. Visiting parents should therefore not feel pressured to organise a childminder in the evening unless they genuinely wish to.

There are a few other considerations to bear in mind if you are travelling with children. In particular, the lack of most health-and-safety practices that you may be used to in your home country can be a challenge. It can also be difficult to hire a car seat for younger children. Even though Saudi law bans children under the age of ten from sitting in the front seat of a vehicle and requires child car seats for children in back seats, these rules are widely ignored. You may want to consider bringing your own car seat as there is no guarantee car hire companies will have one, even if you have booked in advance. Car seats should be rear facing until the age of 15 months and can be forward facing if the child weighs more than 9kg. For general safety advice, see page 59.

## TRAVELLING WITH A DISABILITY

Islam teaches that people with disabilities are to be treated with dignity and equality. However, since there has historically been a stigma attached to disability in some parts of Saudi society, the reality on the ground varies. Attitudes are slowly changing, however, and some basic progress has been made in improving accessibility – but there's a long way to go.

Saudi Vision 2030 includes references to making many improvements to Saudi society and tourism, including addressing a wide range of disability issues. The National Transformation Program 2020 is part of the wider Saudi Vision 2030. Its purpose is to provide economic opportunities for people with disabilities and there is a growing number of initiatives supporting groups in the government sector such as institutes for people with visual, hearing and cognitive disabilities.

The infrastructure to support increased mobility is often not present. Pavements rarely have dropped kerbs to allow access for wheelchair users and in general are in poor condition. There is no real consideration for step-free access to hotels or other buildings. Ramps that do exist are often too steep or too narrow to accommodate a wheelchair, or both. Public hearing loops and similar devices are practically unknown. Check with your accommodation or tour operator about what to expect.

Attitudes towards mental health issues have also started to change; but it is early days. If you are planning a trip to Saudi Arabia and usually take prescribed medication for a mental health condition, take particular note that many of these, which may be licensed in your home country, are illegal in the Kingdom. If you are unsure if this applies to you, check with the Saudi embassy in your home country and obtain official advice before you travel.

**AIR TRAVEL** It is possible to book a wide range of services, both on board and in the airport terminals, if you are travelling with a disability. Saudi airports generally have websites that describe their full range of services so you know what to expect.

All Saudi airlines offer a good standard of support for travellers with disabilities, but these services usually start only at the check-in counter. Passengers should be aware that most modern terminals are wheelchair accessible inside, but access to the front of the building may be problematic as they may not always have adequately lowered kerbs, or lowered kerbs are often blocked by inconsiderate drivers. Older terminals may be less well equipped, with ramps and other features not always fit for purpose. Airport employees are generally willing to provide assistance.

**INTERCITY TRAVEL** SAPTCO sells discounted bus tickets for people with disabilities and for a travel companion, and can be booked online as well as at stations. Travellers should be aware that some bus stations do not have step-free access, although there will be assistance available for anyone requiring it. When travelling by rail, staff will provide assistance in the stations and for boarding and disembarking the train, with ramps where needed. Travellers with battery-powered wheelchairs should be prepared to transfer to a wheelchair provided by the station. Reserving mobility assistance in advance is not required, but wheelchair spaces on board the trains are limited and should be booked in advance.

## WHAT TO TAKE

Although most items can be purchased in Saudi Arabia, it is better to bring some things from home. Remember to bring sunscreen and sunglasses; sun visors can be a good idea. Physical books are difficult to find, so bring along whatever you plan to read during your stay. It's a good idea to bring a small stock of toilet paper as it's not always provided in public facilities, especially in more remote areas. If you use tampons, it is recommended that you bring a sufficient supply as tampons are not sold in supermarkets and are not easy to come by in pharmacies. Do check out Nahdi or al Dawaa chemists, though, if you are in a pinch.

Do not forget to take plug adaptors and converters for electronics without a dual voltage configuration, plus suitable chargers for your mobile devices. It can be noisy in Saudi Arabia – bring earplugs or noise-cancelling devices if you think they might make you more comfortable. Finally, if you're an adventure sports enthusiast, you may want to bring your own equipment as you may not always find exactly what you prefer to use sold in sports shops or for hire.

See page 50 for restricted items; and refer to page 100 to ensure you bring appropriate clothing compliant with the local dress code.

**ELECTRICITY** Electricity is supplied by the state-owned Saudi Electricity Company. Historically, the Kingdom has used both a 127V and the 220V/230V/240V systems and is expected to standardise to 230V by 2025. Frequency is 60Hz. The electricity supply is generally reliable with no expectation of routine power outages. Plug configurations in common use are North American plug types A and B, British plug type G, and Continental European plug type F terminators, with British plug type G now standard. The best advice is to travel with an assortment of adapters that can be used for all common mains socket styles.

## MONEY

The official currency of Saudi Arabia is the Saudi riyal (SAR), and it is pegged to the US dollar: US$1 = SAR3.75. There are 100 halalas in a riyal. Coins exist in denominations of 1, 5, 10, 25 and 50 halalas, though these are no longer in wide circulation. Banknotes come in denominations of 1, 5, 10, 20, 50, 100, 200 and 500 riyals, and all denominations are widely used. There are one- and two-riyal coins in addition to one- and five-riyal banknotes. Banknote series six, bearing the image of King Salman, went into circulation in 2016. The exception is the 500-riyal banknote, which has the image of King Abdul Aziz. Some series five banknotes with the image of King Abdullah and series four banknotes bearing the image of King Fahd remain legal tender and remain in circulation, though in diminishing quantities. The oldest banknotes in circulation are those that bear the image of King Faisal, and were first issued in 1976. It is unlikely, though, that you will see these.

**PAYING FOR GOODS AND SERVICES** The Saudi economy is sophisticated. Digital payments, including contactless, chip and pin and the likes of ApplePay, are commonplace and are being used increasingly, especially in major cities and among younger adults. All bankcards used in Saudi Arabia should be chip-and-pin enabled. Visa and Mastercard are widely accepted, and China's UnionPay is accepted in a growing number of locations. American Express and Diners Club cards can be used in higher-end hotels but are otherwise unpopular, including in most restaurants. Some merchants only accept the Saudi bank card Mada, so check and be clear about how you want to pay prior to making your purchase. It is also worth checking if you can purchase prepaid SAR currency cards in your home country as these often have more favourable exchange rates and lower (or no) fees than your regular bankcards.

It is advised that you bring a combination of bankcards and cash. US dollars and euros are best, although most other major currencies can be exchanged in main cities. Since cash may be necessary in remote locations, in locations less used to seeing tourists and in many shops in the souqs, as well as for taxi fares, be sure to bring riyals as well since these merchants are unlikely to accept foreign currencies. And carry some small-denomination riyal banknotes for cash purchases as merchants will rarely have change.

**CHANGING MONEY** Foreign currencies can be easily changed at bureaux de change throughout the Kingdom. Many are located in shopping malls and in other locations popular with expatriate communities. As well as changing your home currency into Saudi riyals, bureaux de change in Saudi Arabia are also good places to get rid of other unwanted currencies you may have left over from previous travels. The bureaux are generally fair and offer similar rates of exchange, while hotel exchange rates are likely to be relatively unfavourable. There is no need to look for unofficial currency black markets as they barely exist and have no added value.

**BANKS** Note that some international banks have different names in Saudi Arabia, such as HSBC, which is branded as SAB. It might be worth checking if your home bank has a partnership with a Saudi bank, as this can save costs for some account holders. Check with your own bank for any charges for exchange rates and international transaction fees as these vary widely. If you should need to visit a Saudi bank, note that most branches have separate men's and ladies' entrances.

ATMs can be found all over Saudi Arabia, including at the usual banks, shopping centres, malls and kiosks on petrol forecourts. Most provide English- and Arabic-language screen options, but be aware that many dispense high-denomination banknotes. You may need to find a way to change these to smaller denomination banknotes, such as at your hotel or a bureau de change.

## BUDGETING

Saudi Arabia is a relatively expensive destination in some regards. International flights into the Kingdom are rarely a bargain. Accommodation is expensive in Riyadh, Jeddah and al Ula, though more reasonable elsewhere. Food prices, both when buying groceries and when eating out, vary widely. Supermarkets are generally more economical as is simple canteen-style dining, where the food is usually delicious. Transport can be very reasonable.

At the time of research, the inflation rate was about 10%. It is recommended that readers take this into account when budgeting for travel as Saudi Arabia is not immune to global economic trends. We have already noticed a substantial price rise for flights and accommodation in particular.

Typical prices for some everyday items are:

| | |
|---|---|
| Two-star hotel | SAR200 excluding VAT (15%). This can drop to SAR150 in provincial cities. |
| 500ml bottled water | SAR1.15 |
| 1.5 litre bottle water | SAR2.50 |
| 330ml soft drink | SAR2.50 if sugar free; SAR3 with sugar |
| 1 litre soft drink | SAR5 |
| glass of fresh juice | SAR5 |
| small coffee from a kiosk | SAR12 |
| bag of Arabic bread | SAR1.15 |
| street snack | SAR6 |
| T-shirt | SAR25–50 |
| 1 litre petrol | SAR2.20 (basic grade 91 RON) |

## GETTING AROUND

**BY AIR** Saudi Arabia is vast, with huge distances between the major cities. Ground travel is time consuming, with relatively few public transport options, and many people choose not to drive. Domestic flights are a routine way to travel these large distances; it is possible to fly between most major cities in Saudi Arabia and between all provinces, and travellers can choose between full-service and budget carriers. Most flights are direct from an airline's hub airport. Connections are relatively frequent even between more remote destinations, with decent procedures at transit airports. Travellers should check if there are separate domestic terminals at the airports on both ends of their journey.

It is best to buy tickets online on your chosen airline's official website as carriers are much more likely to assist you in case of flight changes and refunds than if you've gone with a third-party vendor; and some flights may not show up on popular broker websites such as Expedia, Kayak, etc.

**Airlines** The national airline, Saudia (see opposite), is the only full-service carrier flying within Saudi Arabia. There are several budget carriers operating within Saudi Arabia. As is the case elsewhere in the world, these offer lower fares than full-service carriers, selling additional services, from seat assignments and checked luggage to meals on board, which can push the price up. Ticket prices can also rise significantly in the lead-up to key Islamic dates and holidays, for all airlines. Most operate a hub-and-spoke system, and usually offer direct flights between Riyadh and Jeddah as well. Customer service levels can vary from brilliant to abysmal.

**flyadeal** w flyadeal.com/en; ⌚ 08.00–20.00. This low-cost carrier, an arm of national carrier Saudia, has operated a hub from Jeddah since 2017 & flies to most cities within the Kingdom. An average economy class return ticket between Jeddah & Riyadh is US$130 without additional services.

**flynas** w flynas.com/en; ⌚ 24hrs. Saudi Arabia's first budget airline began operations in 2007. It has its own loyalty programme, naSmile. Its main hub is Dammam airport, & it operates flights throughout the Kingdom & to many international destinations from southeastern Europe, the Caucuses, central Asia, south Asia & elsewhere in the Middle East & North Africa. An average economy class return ticket between Jeddah & Riyadh costs US$120.

**Saudia** w saudia.com; ⌚ 08.00–23.00. The national carrier was founded in 1945 & has an extensive internal network. It is the only full-service carrier flying within Saudi Arabia, offering generous baggage allowances, hot meals on most routes, & more. Saudia belongs to the SkyTeam loyalty programme. Its main hub is Jeddah's domestic terminal, which is now located in the new Terminal 1. It has smaller hubs operating from Riyadh's domestic Terminal 5 & from Dammam airport. Fares are reasonable. An average economy class return ticket between Jeddah & Riyadh is US$180.

## Airports

***Departures and check-in*** Check-in time for domestic flights within Saudi Arabia is 2 hours before departure. It is important that you don't cut it too fine as many Saudi terminals can be chaotic landside – even for the most seasoned traveller. Porters are located kerbside near the front of the terminal entrances and can be very assertive. The going rate is US$1–2 per bag. Trolleys are free in the departure halls and can be used anywhere landside; some airports also allow trolleys to be taken through airside security. Do not be surprised if families are invited to jump the check-in queue. Do not be surprised also if some Saudis queue at the 'premium' desk even when flying economy.

***Airport security*** Make your way through security as soon as you complete check-in and have checked any baggage as security procedures can be very time consuming, especially for men simply on account of passenger gender imbalance.

Going through airport security is a strictly gender-segregated process, other than for very young children. Your travel documents will first be checked by an official, who will then send you through. All passengers place their hand luggage on the x-ray belts. Men and boys go through body scanners similar to elsewhere in the world. Women and girls join a separate queue and enter a screened booth, where female security officers will carry out a wand and/or manual bodycheck for banned items. Your items will be safe from theft even if they are out of sight on the x-ray belt. Be sure to pack laptops and fragile items with extra care to minimise shock and breakage – items will be placed on the x-ray belt by passengers arriving after you and, when the airport is very busy or there is a hold-up at the security checkpoint, can sometimes build up to the point where they collect in a pile at the end of the belt or fall on to the floor.

***Airside terminals*** Airport terminals vary, from modern and clean to old and not very clean at all and all are meant to be non-smoking – a rule followed other than by some Saudi airport employees. Departure gate seating is not always adequate for

> **HAJJ TRAVEL**
>
> Jeddah airport is particularly busy during hajj season. Although there is a dedicated hajj terminal, many pilgrims fly to Jeddah on scheduled airlines. In order to minimise the risk of performing hajj without the correct visa, passengers bound for Jeddah in the lead-up to hajj and who appear to be Muslim may be screened carefully at their departure airport, wherever you are flying from. Muslim visitors should be prepared to prove their visa status if asked. A tour operator's letter or similar should suffice.

the number of passengers. Although airside terminals are not gender segregated other than at security, you will find that many women prefer to sit apart from men at the gates and elsewhere, and you should respect their wishes.

Do not expect a wide range of amenities airside. There are fast-food-style American and Arabic options, limited offerings in duty-free shops, and premium-class lounges at the larger airports that serve hot and cold food and soft drinks, but otherwise it is pretty basic. Most airports provide free Wi-Fi, and an increasing number of airports also offer mobile phone recharging stations. Electrical sockets are usually scarce.

Sometimes Saudi flights are delayed with no reasons given. Announcements are not always made over a tannoy, nor are they always displayed on the flights board. Passengers should regard amended flight times with certain degree of scepticism, at least until the delayed boarding process actually commences. Boarding often descends into a free-for-all, especially after a delay.

***Arriving at your destination*** Domestic arrivals do not require passport checks. Trolleys are plentiful and are free in the arrival halls airside. Porters are available and are usually less aggressive than at departures. Don't be surprised if the arrivals halls are chaotic – similar to other Middle Eastern airports – once you pass through the security doors, with local Saudis waiting to greet their relatives and numerous drivers with names on hand-held signs adding to the bustle. At some airports, taxi touts operate. Never accept a ride with anyone soliciting for your custom. Use an official taxi rank and if you are unsure, ask someone who works at the airport.

**In the air** Some Saudi women may be uncomfortable sitting beside an unrelated man, and on occasion some Saudi men may be uncomfortable sitting next to an unrelated woman. If either situation happens, it is polite to change seats – more than one person may need to move before everyone is happy. There are seats in some rows on some internal routes that can only be reserved by women and are clearly noted on seat maps online.

It is not unusual to find that most of the flight attendants are non-Saudi – this is true for Saudi and many other Gulf carriers. They commence service soon after seatbelt signs are switched off. Announcements are made in both Arabic and English.

**Getting from the airport** Shuttles to Saudi city centres do not exist in the same way they do in other countries. In addition to taxis, private cars, ride-hailing app services, like Uber and Careem, and hiring a vehicle are your options. Be aware that some taxis may try to charge you higher fares, especially if you arrive late at night, if you are carrying a lot of luggage, or there are more than two passengers. Many visitors opt to have their hotel send a car and driver to collect them if the hotel offers this service – this will generally cost about double the usual taxi fares.

***Riyadh*** Riyadh's King Khalid Airport is located about 35km north of the city centre. SAPTCO bus services run from the airport to the city centre every 2 hours at a cost of SAR25. As the bus is not reliable, taxis are the preferred option, with fares from around SAR100. There is an infrequent shuttle bus service between the domestic Terminal 5 and the international terminals 1 and 2.

***Jeddah*** Jeddah's King Abdul Aziz Airport is about 20km north of the city centre. SAPTCO bus services connect the airport's Terminal 1 to the city centre via the Corniche about every 30 minutes at a cost of SAR80. This is an express service, but rarely used by tourists – most people opt to take a taxi to the city centre. Fares run from SAR50 to SAR100 depending on the specific location of your hotel.

***Dammam*** Dammam's King Fahd Airport is situated about 35km north of the city centre and about 95km from Jubail. SAPTCO bus services run from the airport to Dammam city centre every 3 hours (SAR21), but most people choose to take a taxi to their destination. Fares cost between about SAR100 and SAR120, or more if you are going to al Khobar. Fares to Jubail are about SAR155.

***Other airports*** We strongly advise that visitors organise transport to meet them upon arrival. Taxis may be scarce. Some small cities do not yet have Uber or Careem services.

**BY RAIL** The first railway in Saudi Arabia was the Hejaz Railway, built by the Ottomans and opened in 1908. It originated in Damascus and was planned to terminate in Mecca, although it was never completed beyond Madinah. The railway was discontinued in 1920 as the Ottoman Empire fell after World War I, and many of its stations are now tourist attractions. There is talk about reviving this line, but this has been the case off and on for 100 years!

These days there are three train lines in the Kingdom, two passenger lines operated by the state-owned Saudi Arabia Railways (SAR; 9200 22329; w sar.com.sa) and a third known as the Haramain High Speed Railway (HHR). All trains are fast, modern and comfortable, and run several times a day, depending on the specific route, and are a good option for internal travel, although passengers will remain reliant on road transport at their destination.

**Saudi Arabia Railways train services** (SAR; 9200 22329; w sar.com.sa) The **East Train Passenger Line** operates between Riyadh and Dammam. It is an upgrade and expansion of the railway line originally built after World War II by the Bechtel Construction Company for the purpose of serving the Arabian American Oil Company, now Saudi Aramco. There are currently six daily services in each direction, with stops at al Hofuf and Buqaiq (also spelled Abqaiq and Bqaiq).

The **North Train Passenger Line** operates between Riyadh and Qurayyat and is SAR's second train line. It opened between 2017 and 2022. There are two daily services in each direction, with stops at al Majma'ah, al Qassim near Buraydah, Ha'il and al Jouf. There are additional services on Wednesday, Thursday and Saturday. There is an overnight sleeper service northbound on Wednesdays and southbound on Saturdays. Private sleeper cabins can be booked for overnight trains.

All SAR **stations** are modern, clean and secure, and are non-smoking and non-vaping. Amenities at most stations other than Buqaiq include a café, car hire company, ATM, clean toilets and prayer facilities. Station parking is adjacent to the stations, plentiful and free. All Eastern line stations are located near the city centre

### MECCA AND MADINAH STATIONS

Mecca station is off-limits to non-Muslims as it is located within the al Haram boundary (page 381). Madinah's station is located in the al Hamra district, 9km away from the city centre and well away from the al Haram boundary, meaning non-Muslims can use this station.

of each destination, while Northern line stations are all outside the city centres and require a car or taxi to get to and from. If you are travelling **from Riyadh**, note that the East Train Passenger Line runs from the station in the al Sina'iyah neighbourhood. This station is not wheelchair-accessible, though the train service itself does accommodate travellers with disabilities. The North Train Passenger Line runs from the new station near King Khalid Airport and *not* the older Riyadh train station located in the city centre.

Passengers are required to check in no later than 60 minutes before departure. The process closely resembles airport security. Check station opening hours as they may only be open around times when trains are due.

***Tickets and onboard services*** Tickets for economy and business-class seats can be purchased up to 30 days in advance online, through the SAR app, or at the station. It may be more difficult for non-Arabic speakers to buy tickets over the telephone. Whichever method you choose, you will need to provide your passport details. The average cost of a single economy ticket from Riyadh to Dammam is SAR87, and from Riyadh to al Jouf SAR500. A single business ticket on the same route is generally 50% more expensive. Return journeys usually cost the same as two single journeys. There are concession prices for children, students, and some travellers with disabilities but not for pensioners. You will receive a seat assignment when you purchase your ticket. Tickets can be amended or cancelled for free up to seven days before travel, though amended fares may differ from those available at the time the ticket was originally purchased and may attract additional costs.

Trains are modern and comfortable with free Wi-Fi on board; there is also a prayer area in some carriages. Economy seats are reclinable and have a universal plug socket. Economy passengers have access to the restaurant coach and can also use the at-seat trolley service for snacks and beverages. Luggage allowance details can be found on the SAR website. Additional facilities for business-class travellers include access to a business-class lounge, dedicated carriages, newspapers and magazines, fast-track boarding, more luxurious seating with a universal plug socket and USB point, a meal service at your seat, and a more generous luggage allowance with priority luggage delivery at your destination. Private sleeper cabins are available in 'family' and 'single' configurations. Private-sleeper passengers have access to the business-class lounge, and all cabins have a universal plug socket and USB point. Seats can be converted to bunk beds for up to four passengers, including children. Bedding and a sleeping amenity kit will be provided for each passenger. Drinks and snacks are available and will be delivered to your cabin; breakfast will be served prior to arrival in Jouf or Riyadh. Women may travel in family sleeper cabins but are not permitted to make single sleeper bookings and will be re-seated if they do so. Other carriages are not gender segregated.

**Haramain High Speed Railway passenger service** (HHR; ☎9200 04433; **w** hhr.sa) The HHR service, which opened in 2018, is operated by Saudi Spanish Train

Projects Company (SSTPC) and runs between Mecca and Madinah. There are up to eight daily services in each direction, with northbound stops at Jeddah (al Naseem neighbourhood east of the city centre), Jeddah's King Abdul Aziz International Airport, integrated with the main airport terminal, and King Abdullah Economic City (KAEC, approx 18km from the KAEC port near the main road gate).

Tickets for economy class and business-class seats can be purchased up to 30 days in advance online or at the station. Fares are good value, with business-class tickets approximately three times the price of economy. Tickets can be amended or cancelled for a 10% service charge up to 24 hours before travel – be aware that amended fares may differ from those available at the time the ticket was originally purchased and may attract additional costs.

On-board seating is comfortable with good legroom, especially in business class, although seats do not recline. There are luggage racks at the end of each carriage, but luggage sizes are limited to the equivalent of carry-on luggage common to air travel. There is a cafeteria carriage on each train.

The HHR stations are modern and spacious. Except for KAEC station, which has more limited amenities, each has ample parking, ticket offices, food kiosks and business-class lounges. All stations are non-smoking and non-vaping. Access to the station gates is airport-style, requiring travellers to scan their ticket. There are bus transfers (SAR5 pp) to the al Haram areas from both Mecca and Madinah stations.

**BY BUS** SAPTCO (page 53) operates a fleet of clean, comfortable intercity buses throughout the Kingdom, offering both stopping services and express services between major cities, as well as city routes within Jeddah and Riyadh. At the time of writing, SAPTCO buses are gender segregated, with women and children allocated seats in the rear on intercity buses and seats in the front on intracity buses.

**Intercity buses** Destinations from Riyadh include Ar'ar, Buraydah, Dammam, Hafar al Batin, Ha'il, Hofuf, Jeddah, Khamis Mushait, Mecca and Madinah. Most destinations are served by multiple departures every day and make many stops along the route. Special VIP bus services run between Riyadh and al Khobar. Most routes run frequent services, but while fares are reasonable, they may save only a little money on routes that are well served by the airlines. There are on-board toilets, and food and other refreshments are available on some buses, although there are periodic rest stops on most routes. All SAPTCO buses are non-smoking.

Tickets can be purchased up to 30 days in advance online, via the SAPTCO app, at the bus station, or over the phone, though this may prove more difficult for non-Arabic speakers. You will need to provide your passport details. A single ticket from Riyadh to Hofuf/al Ahsa costs SAR72, from Jeddah to al Ula SAR179, and from Abha to Baha SAR99. Return journeys are generally the same price as two single journeys. Concession fares are available for children, students and some people with disabilities, but not for pensioners. There are luggage allowances and limitations that vary by route.

SAPTCO bus stations are almost always located in city centres and passengers should arrive no later than 60 minutes before the scheduled departure time. For more information, visit the SAPTCO website.

**Intracity buses** When travelling by bus in **Riyadh** or **Jeddah**, passengers should purchase a smart card at a ticket kiosk found at the stop or from the driver, which costs SAR10. This includes a SAR5 credit for travel. Single bus journeys cost SAR3,

### TAXI SEATING

Women and girls should *never* sit in the front seat of a taxi or in the front seat of any vehicle driven by a professional driver. Women will notice that the driver is likely to move the empty front passenger seat forward. This is a gesture of courtesy and respect.

with children aged 2–12 years travelling at half price and under twos for free. It is possible to reload your smart card at ticket kiosks, on the SAPTCO app, or with the bus driver. Note that local buses are rarely used by Saudis but are generally used instead by male expatriate manual workers.

For more information and route details in Riyadh and Jeddah, see pages 111 and 253.

**BY METRO** Construction of the Riyadh Metro began in 2014 and was originally announced to open in 2018. At the time of writing, it is projected to open during 2023. For more details, see page 112. Mecca also has a metro with one line in operation since 2010, though a further three lines are planned. Mecca's metro can only be used by Muslim passengers (page 282). Additional metro systems are in the planning phase for Jeddah and Madinah.

**BY TAXI** Taxis are available in all major cities, though finding one is not always easy. There are not many taxi ranks around, so most Saudis either call a taxi company, have a business relationship with a driver, or hope for the best anywhere beyond the busiest city-centre streets. Note that taxis can be notoriously difficult to find at most shopping malls and supermarkets, too, so keep an eye out for shoppers arriving at these destinations by taxi, which you might then hail yourself.

The conventional taxi logo contains stylised Arabic and English words for taxi with part of the Arabic forming the back of the vehicle on the doors of most taxis. Most vehicles are white. There are an increasing number of 'Green Taxis' that can be found at the airport and the city centre. These come equipped with free Wi-Fi and other technology.

The basic rate is SAR5, plus an additional SAR2 per kilometre travelled. Waiting time is charged at SAR30 per hour. These rates can be higher outside of Riyadh and Jeddah. Passengers should ensure that a meter is being used. Payment remains mostly cash, with riyals the only likely currency to be accepted; do have the correct amount if possible as drivers seem to struggle with giving change.

**Ride-hailing apps** Uber is very popular in most major cities in Saudi Arabia, and rates are reasonable. The main challenges for visitors are the possible language barrier, the condition or cleanliness of some vehicles, how experienced some drivers may be, and how well they know the city and your destination. It is generally a good idea to be prepared to show the driver your destination on Google Maps or similar apps. Careem is a popular alternative service to Uber and operates in broadly the same areas of the Kingdom. Originating in Dubai, it operates in 15 countries stretching from Algeria and Egypt in the west to Pakistan in the east. Both Uber and Careem employ Saudi female drivers.

**BY PRIVATE VEHICLE** Many visitors to Saudi Arabia prefer to travel by private vehicle. Vehicles organised from higher-end hotels are generally in better mechanical condition, are usually very clean, are air-conditioned and have working seat belts. Some will offer bottles of water and a newspaper. They are also more likely to be prepared to accommodate infant and child safety seats although it is recommended that you let the hotel and driver know in advance if this is a requirement. They also expect drivers to adhere to the highway code and to other safety standards that may not be observed to the same degree by other drivers. It's OK to inform the driver that you are especially safety conscious and that you expect traffic laws to be adhered to if you do so in a polite and respectful manner. However, do not expect their driving style to be the same that you are used to back home as they must take local driving practices of other, less responsible drivers into account for their and your own safety.

Private cars can often be especially reassuring for solo women travellers or groups of women, especially if they are visiting Saudi Arabia for the first time. It is important to organise your airport transfer, for both arrival and departure, about 24 hours in advance as these runs are in high demand.

Private vehicle drivers, especially those working with hotels, generally speak English to a reasonably good standard and will have a mobile phone so you can contact them if you have arranged for them to wait while you explore your destination. Drivers often struggle to park near many facilities in the cities and so they often retreat to a more remote spot, specifically designated as a drivers' waiting area. Make sure you agree in advance exactly where you will meet your driver once you are ready to be collected and jot down the number plate so you can identify your vehicle when it arrives as many private cars look similar. Be prepared to use WhatsApp to contact your driver; a few will still use the 'send me a missed call' method popular in the days before WhatsApp existed.

Private cars usually need to be organised in advance. Rates are quoted by the hour and tend to be around US$100 per hour. Be careful not to run over the agreed number of hours, even by a few minutes, as you are likely to be charged for an entire extra hour. Daily rates can be negotiated, as well as drop rates within a city. It is also possible to hire a private car and driver for intercity travel, both one way and return, providing a comfortable and flexible way to travel; rates will reflect distance and time and can be expensive, but can be economical if there are two or three people travelling together.

**DRIVING** Saudi Arabia has a comprehensive system of national, regional and local roads. Most roads are in good condition, although there are some exceptions in older city centres and in rural areas. Women can and do drive in Saudi Arabia, and may do so with their family, with other women, with men even if they are unrelated, and alone if they wish.

However, only the brave or foolhardy would attempt to drive in Saudi Arabia on their first visit, with the possible exception of those who have significant driving experience in the larger cities of other GCC countries. You must be a confident driver and recognise that the *real* highway code is far from the official version studied by learner drivers. Driving is Darwinian. If it's bigger than you, it wins. If it's in front of you, it's your problem. If it's behind you, it's their problem. Unfortunately, anyone involved in a road traffic accident will quickly learn another Darwinian rule: if your accident involves a Saudi driver, it will probably be your fault regardless.

**Road safety and regulations** Saudi Arabia implemented the Saher System many years ago. It is a traffic camera system that is meant to detect traffic violations through number plate recognition technology. Violations including speeding, driving through red lights, seatbelt and mobile phone use and many more digressions can be captured, with tickets and fines issued to the owner or driver of the vehicle. In the case of hire cars, the driver will be charged any fees which they must pay when they return the vehicle.

The **speed limit** ranges from 100 to 140kph on major highways and is 50kph in urban areas. Speed limits can suddenly drop on approaches to built-up areas, often accompanied by speed humps which may or may not be easy to see. Speed cameras are positioned near speed humps and many intersections and are also found along most highways and regional roads. They can be found on either side of the road, are painted a dull grey and are generally difficult to spot. There is some use of variable speed limits in major cities when there is traffic congestion.

Use of **seatbelts** is mandatory for the driver and front seat passenger(s). Children under ten years of age must travel in a **car seat**. It is illegal to drive while using a **mobile phone**. It will be noticeable that the latter two rules are mostly ignored by drivers.

Road designs do not always seem logical to foreign drivers. For example, there are two types of legal U-turn, both of which will strike most visitors as downright dangerous. One is a protected left turn just in front of major junctions, but which then requires the driver to merge directly from the far left lane of moving traffic on to the far left lane of moving traffic in the other direction. The other is an unprotected U-turn, often performed by simply reversing direction through a gap in the centre barriers. Speed humps are huge and often appear without warning. Watch other drivers and if they seem to slow down randomly, it is probably due to speed humps, speed cameras or red light cameras. Note that roads outside of built-up areas are not lit, so intercity travel is not advised after dark. Risks you might encounter range from other vehicles travelling without headlamps to camels lying on the warm tarmac. Not all highways have camel fences, so camels go wherever they want – night and day. If you have contact with a camel, the camel wins. Dogs, which are feral and possibly rabid, often run in front of cars or chase vehicles. Cats like to hide under parked vehicles all too often – make a lot of noise to ensure they move before you drive away.

**Road signs** **National routes** are generally referred to as highways, similar to motorways in the UK. Highway signs contain an outline of the country with the highway number inside. It is important to note that many signs are in Arabic only, so learning how to read numbers in Arabic is important for self-drivers. The Saudi sword and palm tree symbol is found in the upper right. South–north highways have a two-digit number that ends in '5', which increases from west to east. West–east highways have a two-digit number that ends in '0', which increases from south to north. **Regional routes** are broadly equivalent to British A roads. The signs for these contain the outline of a *qibla* with a three-digit number in white in the centre. **Local roads** are similar to B roads, signposted with a black number within a white oval. Both include the Saudi sword, and the palm tree symbol is top centre.

Road signs also contain symbols commonly seen on European roads, such as for airports and petrol stations. Hospitals and parking are indicated by the Latin letters H and P respectively. Green direction signs are indicated in Arabic and in English with the Latin letters E, S, W and N. An octagonal red stop sign is used, but note that these are usually only in Arabic. Road sign colour schemes closely follow the UK system, with highways (motorways) with white text on a blue background, regional routes (A and B roads) with white text on a green background and local routes with black text on a white background. Warning and regulatory signs are outlined in red.

Roadworks signs have a yellow background. The Saudi Commission for Tourism and National Heritage does a reasonably good job at providing information (in Arabic and English) at major tourist attractions, but road signs leading to them may not be present, for example at highway exits – where they do exist these signs have a brown background.

You will come across **electronic road traffic signs** in major cities including Riyadh and Jeddah. These are used mostly to manage heavy traffic such as announcing variable speed limits or road accidents. They also direct road users to apps such as WhatsApp and Twitter for up-to-date information.

Within towns and cities, ***street signs*** do not always exist where they are needed. Some are in Arabic only; others are in Arabic and English.

**Car hire** Visitors on a tourist visa or a short-term visit can use their home driving licence to hire a vehicle. There is no need to obtain an international drivers' licence. Others should check with their chosen car hire company in advance of travel as to driving licence requirements. Major global brands including Alamo, Avis, Budget, Enterprise, Europcar, Hertz, National and Sixt are present in the central business district of major cities, at the Riyadh, Jeddah and Dammam airports, and at many but not all regional airports. There are many Saudi brands as well.

Walk around the vehicle with the attendant to ensure you both agree to the vehicle's condition when you start the rental period. Insist on a copy of their notes if they don't offer one. Make sure the seatbelts work.

It is strongly recommended that you accept the most robust insurance. Drivers relying on their car insurance policy from their home country should check to make sure they have sufficient coverage in Saudi Arabia. Drivers should have immediate access to the car hire company if they are involved in a road traffic accident (known as RTA throughout Saudi Arabia). Ensure you have telephone contact details before you drive away. If you are unfortunate enough to be involved in an RTA, contact the police and appropriate emergency number, as well as the car hire company. *Never* sign anything unless you can read it and agree to what is written, keeping in mind that the document will be in Arabic.

**Petrol** Petrol stations are plentiful in most neighbourhoods in built-up areas and are also found at the increasing number of service stations on major highways. However, there may be long distances between petrol stations on remote stretches of road, so take the opportunity to refuel when you can on long journeys. Petrol station forecourts usually have additional services, especially food outlets, mini-markets, coffee kiosks and ATMs. Mosques are almost always present, too, especially outside of major cities.

There are generally two grades of petrol: 91 RON and 95 RON. Pumps are attended by service staff, so drivers rarely need to dispense their own fuel. Major

### CAUGHT SHORT?

Even with the best planning, you may find yourself in need of a loo far away from service stations or a friendly restaurant, especially when travelling long distances in sparsely populated areas. As much as it might be tempting, at least for men, never pee alfresco as this is strictly taboo. Do as the Saudis do and find a mosque. Mosques are everywhere and will have toilets, albeit sometimes quite basic but which will be a relief – literally!

## SWIMMING POOLS AND FITNESS CENTRES

Both swimming pools and fitness centres remain gender segregated throughout the Kingdom except for some properties inside Riyadh's Diplomatic Quarter and in al Ula. References to swimming pools throughout this guide are only for men, and children who have not reached puberty, unless stated otherwise. Women, if accommodated at all, are generally confined to using indoor pools to avoid being seen by the wider public.

Most hotels have added separate fitness facilities for women, but often of inferior quality to and tucked away from the main fitness centre, which is men-only.

Saudi brands include Aldrees, NAFT, Saher and SASCO. Petrol prices are controlled by the government and are very inexpensive compared with prices in most of rest of the world. As of August 2023, the average petrol price in Saudi Arabia is US$0.58 (SAR2.20) per litre.

There are often many lorry drivers at motorway services petrol stations. While it is not unsafe, it can be a good idea for women to wear a headscarf at very remote services which seems to deter attention from those that may otherwise stare.

**ON FOOT** Walking is not the done thing in Saudi Arabia other than in the oldest neighbourhoods of major cities. Broken pavements, weather challenges, and crossing the road when drivers have no respect for pedestrians are enough to put most people off walking anywhere other than the shortest of distances.

**ADDRESSES** There is no conventional address system in Saudi Arabia where street numbers and names are consistently used. Historically, destinations were found by description of key landmarks and, if necessary, the assistance of someone out and about in the neighbourhood. Many people now provide their exact GPS co-ordinates, so it is much easier to find a specific location. There are a number of helpful apps to make this straightforward. What3Words is a popular app that uses a unique set of words to find any $3m^2$ area. Google Maps is also generally very reliable.

# ACCOMMODATION

There is a wide range and variety of accommodation in Saudi Arabia. Accommodation in Riyadh and Jeddah is very expensive. Demand often outpaces supply in these cities and, historically, most hotel guests are business travellers, often with healthy travel budgets provided by their companies. Other cities have much more reasonable rates.

It is generally best to use either the hotel's website direct or a reputable booking website to secure your accommodation. Throughout this guide, if there is limited contact information, that means the property does not use a booking platform and does not have a website. If you want to stay in one of these places, you should be prepared to communicate with the hotel via WhatsApp, especially outside the big cities, in budget accommodation and on the Farasan Islands. Ask for help from an Arabic speaker if you need it.

**Airbnb** operates in Saudi Arabia, as does Couchsurfing. Anyone considering booking this type of accommodation should do so with caution, particularly single women who might inadvertently send the wrong signals to a male Saudi host.

**Hotels** Riyadh, Jeddah and Dammam offer the usual four- and five-star hotels familiar to business travellers around the world. In the most prestigious addresses in Riyadh, you'll find hotels that exude opulence – and in Jeddah a few hotels to match Riyadh's offerings – which would claim more than five stars if they could. Familiar brands from the US, Canada, the UAE and Far East include the Fairmont, Four Seasons, Hilton, Hyatt, Mandarin Oriental, Marriott and Rotana. Some of these properties have had a presence in the Kingdom for decades and could be described as *grandes dames*. Sheraton, Intercontinental and Le Méridien hotels often fall into this category, albeit most have been renovated and updated over the years. Other names are newer arrivals and are pitched to guests who like comfort with modern conveniences. These hotels offer concierge service, upscale dining, 24-hour room service, fitness facilities and swimming pools.

Many bathrooms come complete with bidet, which remain popular in Saudi Arabia. Muslim visitors may appreciate that rooms generally include a prayer rug and a qibla to indicate the direction of Mecca.

International brands such as Ibis, OYO, Park Inn and Tulip Inn cater to the more budget-minded guest. Saudi Arabia also has brand-name hotels familiar to domestic guests that often offer very good value for foreigners, especially those aimed at families. Appealing brands include al Farhan, Boudl and Raoum. Many of these offerings are apartment hotels, designed to accommodate long-stay guests and especially large families. They generally offer a range of room sizes that can be very economical for friends travelling together. Do be aware, though, that some of these properties may request a marriage certificate for foreigners during check-in.

Hotel security for most global brands is robust, starting with access to the property involving a guard who will check under your vehicle with a mirror and ask you to open the boot to ensure nothing dangerous is being brought on to the property, although this has been discontinued at some properties since mid-2022. Airport-style security must be passed through before continuing to the hotel's reception. CCTV cameras are everywhere.

***Resort hotels*** Popular locations such as the Red Sea Coast, along Half Moon Bay in the Eastern Province, and also in oases and farms in the desert, especially in

## NOTES ON ACCOMMODATION

All accommodation listed in this guide is en suite unless specifically noted otherwise. As many hotels offer a variety of rates that may or may not include breakfast, this is only referenced if there is a specifically noteworthy reason. Even the most basic shoestring accommodation will also have free Wi-Fi, although connectivity quality may vary.

**ACCOMMODATION PRICE CODES** Please note that most hotels quote their rates exclusive of VAT at 15%. Some locations also charge additional city and other local taxes.

| | | |
|---|---|---|
| Luxury | **$$$$$** | Over US$250 |
| Upmarket | **$$$$** | US$180–US$250 |
| Mid-range | **$$$** | US$130–US$180 |
| Budget | **$$** | US$70–US$130 |
| Shoestring | **$** | Under US$70 |

Najd, are home to resort hotels. There are mountain resorts in al Bahah and Asir as well. Many of these are unique properties.

**Budget accommodation** Youth hostels do exist in some cities in Saudi Arabia. Many of these are located in sport centres, which are generally men-only facilities. We recommend that women or mixed groups considering a hostel stay communicate with the property prior to booking to ensure they will be allowed to stay. Try Hostelling International (**w** hihostels.com) or The Saudi Network (**w** the-saudi.net/kfia/directory_saudi_arabia/youth-hostels.htm) websites.

Other shoestring-budget properties may not always be an option. Many offer only singles accommodation (ie: for men only) that mostly cater to non-Western expat workers. Many of these establishments may refuse to rent a room to anyone travelling on a tourist visa, especially women. We recommend that travellers looking for shoestring accommodation reset their expectations.

## EATING AND DRINKING

Saudi Arabia is a foodie haven, and everyone will find something they like, from gourmands to the fussiest of eaters. All food and beverages in Saudi Arabia are *halal*, meaning 'permitted'. In the context of food and drink, while some things are halal, others are *haram*, or forbidden. For example, in Islam alcohol and any products containing it are not halal and are therefore banned in the Kingdom. Similarly, pork and any products or ingredients containing or derived from it are also banned. For further information on halal practices, see **w** halalhmc.org.

**TRADITIONAL SAUDI FOOD** It is impossible to provide a complete list of popular Saudi food, but described here are the must-try dishes for visitors to the Kingdom.

**Savoury dishes** ***Kabsa*** is the national dish of Saudi Arabia, though it originates from Yemen and is eaten throughout the Arabian Peninsula. Kabsa starts with a bed of basmati rice, fruit, nuts and spices, with meat – popular are goat and camel, with chicken a more modest alternative – served on top. The meat may be cooked in various ways: the most popular are the *mandi* technique which originated in Yemen and involves cooking the meat in a deep hole in the ground; *mathbi* involves grilling the meat on hot stones. Both result in delicious spice-infused meat that falls off the bone. Eating kabsa is communal, traditionally eaten on a tablecloth spread on the floor and with fresh fruit juice to drink. Arabic bread serves as your utensil and is used to scoop each bite from the main serving platter. Use your right hand only as the left hand is considered to be dirty and thus very rude to use in association with food. Try kabsa at least once during your visit!

Saudis eat numerous variations on the rice-and-meat theme of their national dish. Popular meals include ***ruz bukhari*** (chicken and rice with tomato paste), ***madfoon*** (originally from Yemen, a rice-and-meat dish cooked in an underground pit) and ***gursan*** (rice, meat and vegetables served with a thin bread on top). ***Mutabbaq*** is a stuffed pancake that combines the rice and meat of kabsa or sometimes vegetables. It is then cut into individual portions and can be eaten as a starter or main course. ***Maqluba*** is yet another rice-and-meat (which sometimes is chicken) dish. This one is also cooked underground and usually includes aubergine, cauliflower, potatoes and tomatoes. Most often eaten in the winter, ***ferek*** is a spiced onion paste mixed with sugar and bread, often served with meat on top.

***Harees*** is a porridge-like broth made of cracked wheat with meat and spices, and is particularly popular during Ramadan. ***Margoog*** is another soup made with meat, and flour to thicken it; and **saleeg** is made with rice cooked in milk and broth and topped with chicken or meat. Its origins are proudly Hejazi.

Other food popular in Saudi Arabia is familiar from elsewhere in the Middle East. **Hummus**, known in much of the world, is much smoother than what you may be used to eating back home. ***Moutabal***, an aubergine, garlic and yoghurt dip, is also very popular. Scoop your hummus or moutabal with ***markouk***, the very thin flatbread that can be the size of a napkin. **Shawarma** and **kebabs** come in all sizes and flavours. This is no different in Saudi Arabia. Whether you fancy proper street food or attend a Saudi barbecue, don't miss any place recommended by a local.

**Dates** Dates are very important in Saudi culture. They are served to guests along with *kahwa* (see below) as an important gesture of hospitality, and also have a significant role during Ramadan as Saudis ritually break their fast by eating them. Dates are the pride of each date-growing region across the Kingdom. It is not unusual for Saudis from different regions to have serious conversations extolling the superiority of their dates. We like them all.

**Sweets and desserts** Saudis love sweets and are not short of their own creations, nor have they been shy in adapting neighbouring countries' recipes. Anyone with a sweet tooth will be spoilt for choice. ***Basbousa*** is a semolina cake soaked in rosewater or orange syrup. It is often topped with a single nut and cut into individual servings. ***Areesa***, also known as ***arika*** or ***henainee***, is a dessert made of dates and crumbled bread, flavoured with cream, honey, cardamom and saffron and topped with almonds. It is very popular during Ramadan. ***Kunafa*** is a cheese-based cake soaked with syrup and filled with cream or pistachios. Saudis have also created a version with Nutella. ***Logaimat/lqaymat*** are small ball-shaped dumplings spiced with cardamom and saffron, soaked in date syrup and sprinkled with sesame seeds. They are another Ramadan favourite. ***Ma'amoul*** is a biscuit with a variety of fillings, often dates or figs, and may also contain nuts such as almonds or pistachios. ***Masoub*** is a bread pudding made with bananas, honey and nuts. ***Mohalabeh*** is a pudding made of heated milk and rosewater and topped with pistachios. It can be eaten warm or chilled and has a wobbly texture, not dissimilar to pannacotta. ***Umm ali***, the national dish of Egypt, is also popular in Saudi Arabia. Pastry is broken into pieces and mixed with pistachios, raisins, sugar and cinnamon. Milk or cream is added to the mixture, which is then baked.

**DRINK** Traditionally, hosts serve **kahwa** to guests as a ritual welcome. Guests should always accept this gesture of hospitality. Saudi kahwa is brewed with green coffee beans, flavoured with cardamom, poured from a coffee pot called a ***dallah*** and served in small handleless cups. Café society means that Saudis also drink a wide range of coffees familiar globally such as cappuccino. Prior to the arrival of international coffee chains, Saudis commonly offered 'Nescafé', their generic use of the brand name for instant coffee that some visitors seemed to prefer to the stronger Arabica blends used in traditional Saudi brews. 'Nescafé' is still offered in some places. Other popular drinks include a variety of teas that are not generally served with milk but may be sweetened with sugar.

Popular cold drinks include ***laban***, a fermented milk drink often drunk at breakfast. It may have a plain, yoghurt-like taste or be fruit-flavoured. Many Saudis drink camel's milk, which is produced and sold commercially and easy to find in any supermarket; cow's and goat's milk are also popular and there is a growing market for non-dairy (eg: nut-based) milk alternatives suitable for vegans. Saudis have embraced **freshly squeezed juices** and these are becoming more and more creative. The most popular is probably lemon mint, sometimes served with mint sprigs. Mango, pomegranate, orange, apple, cherry, kiwi and watermelon among others are commonly found. Many juice menus include 'mojitos', which in Saudi Arabia means blended juices. These are especially delicious. **Saudi champagne** is a speciality (non-alcoholic) drink, made of apple juice, 7Up, lemonade, and slices of apple, orange and lemon. Mint and other herbs and spices are added, making each recipe unique to the restaurant or family tradition.

Although desalinated water is safe to drink, most people purchase **bottled water** for drinking, making bottled water a beverage staple.

**MEALS AND MEAL TIMES** Breakfast is typically taken before starting daily activities like work and school, similar to much of the world. Lunch is traditionally taken mid-afternoon around 14.00 or 15.00, and dinner after the last prayer, 21.00 being a popular time. If Saudi families are dining out, they tend to follow the same general timings.

**Breakfast** Breakfast can be a substantial meal for Saudi families. Popular dishes will be a combination of traditional Middle Eastern food from Yemen to Lebanon, as well as Saudi-created options. ***Fuul medames*** is a staple, made by stewing fava beans with olive oil and lemon juice, then topped with chopped onions, tomatoes and parsley. ***Shakshouka*** is the Saudi version of scrambled eggs with onion, garlic, pepper, tomato, *labneh* and traditional spices. Pastries, from the sweetest American recipes to Lebanese croissants topped with za'atar, cheese, sesame or almonds, abound. Most big breakfasts are not complete without **hummus**, ***fatteh*** (toasted shredded bread topped with stewed chickpeas, tahini, labneh, fried garlic and pine kernels) and grilled **halloumi**. **Labneh**, the yoghurt-based cheese found throughout the Middle East, is also eaten at breakfast. Olives, cucumber and tomatoes are often served on their own in addition to ingredients in other breakfast dishes. Although distinctly Lebanese in origin, ***manakish*** is a popular breakfast option, especially for people on the go. It is a flatbread that resembles a pizza, topped with za'atar or Akawi cheese, or both, half-and-half.

**Lunch** Lunch is traditionally the main meal of the day and can involve anything from home-cooked kabsa and its rice-and-meat variations to a trip to a traditional restaurant with the family as a treat. Many Saudis finish work by 14.00. Others

### RESTAURANT PRICE CODES

Please note that restaurants must also charge diners 15% VAT. Some restaurants include this in the price of each item on the menu; others add VAT at the end of the bill.

| | | |
|---|---|---|
| Expensive | $$$$$ | Over US$40 |
| Above average | $$$$ | US$30–40 |
| Mid-range | $$$ | US$15–30 |
| Cheap and cheerful | $$ | US$7–15 |
| Rock bottom | $ | Under US$7 |

### TRADITIONAL SAUDI-STYLE SEATING

Traditional Saudi restaurants serve food on a tablecloth (or sometimes plastic sheet) laid out directly on the carpeted floor. Diners remove their shoes at the edge of the carpet before sitting along the edges of the tablecloth. Etiquette demands that you do not show the bottom of your feet or socks towards another person, so sitting either cross-legged yoga-style or tucking your legs to the side (impossible for all but the most nimble) is expected. A box of tissues will serve as napkins. Dishes are generally shared. While plates will be provided, cutlery may or may not appear; if not, then use your right hand, never the left, to eat. Family sections of traditional restaurants will be private, with curtains or walls fully surrounding the space. Singles sections may be more open, with cushions forming the boundaries between each dining 'table'.

working a split day will also return home for lunch prior to returning to work in the late afternoon.

**Dinner** Dinner is either a light meal or a hearty but simple meal depending on the season. Soups and stews are popular, such as margoog or harees. However, more than any other meal, and influenced by restaurant culture, dinner may end up being very far away from traditional Saudi cuisine.

**EATING OUT** The large expatriate population in Saudi Arabia has had an influence on the food sold in both the supermarkets and restaurants here. Vegetarians in particular will find it relatively easy to dine out as veggie options are commonly found in the many cuisines represented here, ranging from Lebanese to South Indian. Turkish, Italian and Asian fusion restaurants from all over the continent are also options. Vegans will have more of a challenge and may find Indian restaurants that cater to a 'pure vegetarian' diet suitable. There are a number of vegan restaurants popping up in Jeddah and Riyadh, but they remain limited.

In addition to hotels, some good restaurants can also be found in shopping malls.

**Hotel restaurants** Most hotels offer breakfast, which often caters to Saudis but is complemented by items popular with other nationalities. Many hotels offer an 'international' menu that tries to cater to a wide audience for lunch and dinner, often in the form of a large buffet containing a bit of everything. Prices are generally high. Some top-end hotels also have signature restaurants that focus on a specific cuisine and are generally of excellent quality.

**Independent restaurants** Many Saudi restaurants are independent, some with only one location and others with a few venues within the Kingdom. Some gourmet restaurants serve food of an exceptionally high standard. They can be of any cuisine, although Lebanese, Turkish and regional south Asian restaurants and some offering Asian-fusion cuisine are particularly popular. They can be located anywhere from upscale neighbourhoods in the big cities to industrial areas or other modest areas elsewhere.

**Chains** Although it may upset purists, it is important to acknowledge that chain restaurants, both home-grown and imported, are extremely popular in Saudi

## RESTAURANT SEATING RULES

As a part of the wider practice of public gender segregation, Saudi Arabia has a strict set of rules for dining out, though these are beginning to wane, albeit unevenly. Most restaurants are divided into two areas: the singles/bachelors section and the family section. You may occasionally encounter very basic restaurants that are men-only.

Single men or all-male groups only have access to the single/bachelor section. Literal families, all women and pre-pubescent children may access the family section. Mixed-gender groups of any kind, be that a group of friends or work colleagues or a tour group, must also dine in the family section. If you make a mistake, the host will kindly ask you to follow them to the correct section. If an establishment practises gender segregation and does not have a family section, women are unlikely to be seated and may not even have access to take-away service.

Things are gradually changing. Most places in Jeddah other than in the most conservative neighbourhoods stopped this practice a while ago. Many upscale restaurants in Riyadh are also ignoring these rules, as are shopping mall food courts and most hotel restaurants. However, some restaurants will actually veil the table by use of a thick curtain or private booth so that diners are hidden, and where waiters ask permission before serving. This 'veiling the table' practice remains the norm in much of the rest of Saudi Arabia, at least for the time being.

Arabia, and hence you'll find them in any medium-size or larger city, as well as at highway services. There's a whole range to choose from, offering up everything from relatively healthy options to pretty dire, unhealthy fast food with many brand names you'll recognise from home including familiar large-chain coffee shops. They may be your only choice in some remote areas, especially at odd hours, and are often convenient, especially if you are in a hurry. There are loads of Saudi branded drive-thru coffee kiosks in petrol stations and elsewhere that serve familiar coffee styles.

Nearly all Saudi chain restaurants have singles and family sections. Many, but not all, of them are enforced. Many also still close during prayer time. Popular Saudi chains you will notice throughout the Kingdom are listed alphabetically below:

**Al Baik** Many Saudis are especially enthusiastic about this most basic of Saudi fast-food chains. We can't see what the fuss is about, but they do have good garlic sauce. $

✷ **Al Romansiah** This very popular chain serves Saudi cuisine in the traditional way, with gender segregation strictly observed. Seating is also traditional style, on low cushions on the floor. Orders are taken & paid for at the cashier, then delivered to your 'table' – with single-use plastic sheet & a box of tissues to serve as napkins – or family section private area. Don't miss the *laham mandi*, chicken kabsa & pistachio kunafa. $$

**Café Bateel** Popular with Saudis & expats alike, this café attracts those who are comfortable wearing progressive versions of the dress code – many women wear open abayas or modest dress without an abaya; many men wear Western smart casual dress. The café offers a wide-ranging international menu with starters, salads & a variety of main courses that could be described as international cuisine with a Saudi twist. Their unusual fresh juice blend of dates, figs & lemon is delicious. Branches in Riyadh, Jeddah & al Khobar. $$$

**Cone Zone** This is the place to try Saudi-made ice cream. You are in luck if you visit when halwa with rosewater ice cream is on the menu. $

**Herfy** This very popular fast-food joint focuses on deep-fried chicken, with a few beef & shawarma options, Pepsi products & bottled juices. Portions are huge & made to order. Probably one of the better places to try a Saudi chain restaurant & fulfil a fast-food craving at the same time. $

**Jan Burger** Directly competing with Herfy & Kudu, but possibly better, beef & chicken burgers & chips, with a small selection of sauces, & fizzy drinks are the order of the day here. They claim 100% natural ingredients. (Not present in the more remote regions of the Kingdom.) $

**Kudu** This fast-food chain offers the usual beef & chicken burgers & sandwiches, but also has salads, desserts & a b/fast menu. Portion sizes are more manageable than Herfy. $

✷ **Mama Noura** More of a canteen than a restaurant, this no-frills establishment is legendary. Shawarma sandwiches & dishes that include chips or vegetables are served alongside more substantial grills & meat-filled pastries. Place your order at the cashier's station, where you will be given a numbered ticket, & present your ticket to collect your food at the relevant counter. A long list of freshly squeezed juices are on offer too. This is Arab fast food at its best. Everything is delicious – you can't go wrong. Lots of single men eat here, but women & mixed groups are welcome if you plan to eat in. Mama Noura's take-away business is also bustling. There are multiple branches throughout Riyadh, but sadly not elsewhere. $$

**Paul** We know that Paul originated in France in the late 19th century. But Saudis & others throughout the Middle East have adopted this bakery & sandwich shop as their own. There are many healthy choices, as well as several vegetarian & vegan options. Locations in Riyadh, Jeddah & al Khobar. $$

✷ **Shawarmer** This chain offers great value for money, with a basic chicken shawarma costing around SAR6. Most meat dishes are very tasty – but do ask for more sauce if you need it. $

**Shayah** This appears to be the only remaining Iranian restaurant chain in Riyadh, & is Saudi owned. Modestly priced, the menu is filled with good *koobideh* (Persian kebabs) & other grilled meat choices. They also have a wide range of the usual starters including salads, vegetable-based dishes & Iranian bread, but unfortunately don't offer Persian ice cream or other sweets. Order at the counter for dining in (with singles & family sections) or take-away. Branches in Riyadh & Jeddah. $

**Zaatar w Zeit** This popular chain elevates Lebanese street food without making it fussy. Whether you fancy b/fast, a quick lunch or to take away something for dinner, it caters to all requirements. Most branches offer a combination of communal dining, individual tables & curtained booths. 'Eat fresh' is their claim & seems to be the case. If you are there for b/fast, order the manakish. The half-&-half za'atar & cheese is classic. Locations in Riyadh, Jeddah, Dammam & al Khobar. $$

**Take-away and delivery apps** Both are very popular throughout Saudi Arabia whether you are ordering from a fast-food chain or an upscale restaurant. The most popular app is Hungerstation. Talabat and Uber Eats also serve many restaurants.

**Tipping** Saudi Arabia does not have a tipping culture. Most restaurants simply present the diner with the bill at the end of the meal with no expectation of receiving a tip. Bank card machines are presented with no feature to add a tip. If you come from a tipping culture, keep in mind that even if you remain inclined to tip, the waiter is probably the last person likely to receive it. Just pay the bill.

## PUBLIC HOLIDAYS

**FIXED PUBLIC HOLIDAYS** The only fixed public holiday is **Saudi National Day**, on 23 September in the Gregorian calendar. Established in 2005 – by decree of King Abdullah – though officially celebrated for the first time as recently as 2015, this is a patriotic celebration of the official renaming of the country, in 1932, from the Kingdom of Najd and Hejaz to the Kingdom of Saudi Arabia. Traditional festivities, including songs, dancing and other upbeat activities, can be seen throughout the Kingdom. Visitors are welcome to join most events, as long as they are respectful. If 23 September falls on a Friday or Saturday, then celebrations take place on the adjacent Thursday or Sunday respectively.

**ISLAMIC PUBLIC HOLIDAYS AND OBSERVANCES** All Islamic dates and holidays are determined by the Islamic calendar which is governed by the lunar calendar through performing ritual sightings of the new moon. This means that any published future dates are only best approximations and could vary by a day or so in either direction. Islamic calendar dates advance 10–11 days each year compared with the Gregorian calendar. Note that Ramadan is not a public holiday, but most timings, especially opening hours, do change during this month.

Public holidays are decreed by the king and can also vary in length from year to year. It is important to note that Saudi public sector holidays are often several days longer than holidays recognised in the private sector. Keep this in mind if you are dealing with anything bureaucratic in the Kingdom, including all government-sector departments as well as banks. Authorities may grant additional time off some years, usually announced at short notice.

**Ramadan** Ramadan is the ninth month of the Islamic calendar and is either 29 or 30 days long. It is known in some other Muslim countries as Ramazan or Ramzan. Although people work during Ramadan, the days are short. Muslim employees are protected by law from working more than 6 hours per day. This means things slow down. All restaurants and most other shops and businesses are closed during the day. Meals will be available through room service at your hotel, by purchasing food from supermarkets, or through a take-away delivery app. Although many outsiders and non-Muslims often associate Ramadan with hardship, Saudis and indeed other Muslims consider Ramadan a very important time to be at their best and to share and bond with others. Although we don't recommend you visit during Ramadan, if you do, try to join an *iftar* during your stay. An iftar is the meal served at sunset to break the day's fast and is a joyful and inclusive experience. Iftars can be found throughout the Kingdom, at high-end hotels and restaurants and as community meals generously donated by mosques and charities. Wishing Muslims '*Ramadan kareem*' (generous Ramadan) or sometimes '*Ramadan mubarek*' (blessed Ramadan) is appreciated. For more information on the key religious significance of Ramadan, see page 32.

**Eid al Fitr** Eid al Fitr is celebrated at the end of Ramadan. It is also known as the Little Eid or sometimes the Sweet Eid for its focus on sweets and desserts. It equates to the first day of the tenth month of the Islamic calendar and is usually celebrated for two days by the general public, and often for more days for government-sector employees. Traditions include buying new clothes and visiting family and friends, focusing on hospitality and generosity. Children are fussed over and given lots of sweets. Wishing Muslims '*Eid mubarek*' is appreciated.

**Eid al Adha** Eid al Adha is celebrated on the tenth day of the twelfth month of the Islamic calendar. It is also known as the Big Eid and the Feast of the Sacrifice, noting the significance of Ibrahim's willingness to sacrifice his son Ishmail as an act of obedience to Allah. However, it is believed that God provided a lamb instead, which has led to the practice of slaughtering an animal – by a family member or by someone else paid to do it – during Eid al Adha. The animal may be a lamb, goat or even camel which is then shared with those less fortunate and with friends and family. Eid al Adha generally lasts for four days for the general public and often longer for government-sector employees. Similar to Eid al Fitr, Eid al Adha is also celebrated with new clothes, and visits to family and friends, and feasting. Wishing Muslims '*Eid mubarek*' is also appreciated for this Eid.

**Muharram** Muharram is Islamic New Year and marks the first day of the first month of the Islamic calendar, which is a sacred month. Muharram is an observance rather than a public holiday in Saudi Arabia.

**Mawlid an-Nabawī** This is the Prophet Mohammed's birthday. It equates to the twelfth day of the third month of the Islamic calendar in Saudi Arabia. Although this is a public holiday in many neighbouring countries, this is not the case in Saudi Arabia. Although discouraged from observing Mawlid, many Muslim expatriates might do so discreetly. Shi'a Muslims observe on the seventeenth day of the same month instead, but never openly in Saudi Arabia.

## FESTIVALS AND EVENTS

For further information on these events, refer to **w** visitsaudi.com, local newspapers and blogs.

**King Abdul Aziz Camel Festival** ✷ (Rumahiyah, 15km northwest of Riyadh's Thumamah National Park; usually sometime between Dec & Feb; admission free) The King Abdul Aziz Camel Festival has taken place annually (other than during the Covid pandemic) since 2015/16. Part of Saudi Vision 2030, it is held as a celebration of the importance of camels in Saudi and Arab culture and heritage and is sponsored and supported by the royal family. Events are geared to sport and entertainment. Women are now able to participate in the camel racing that takes place during the festival, both as jockeys and as spectators. There is a traditional souq and plenty of entertainment for children and families.

***Camel Beauty Pageant*** Don't miss this special event, held during the King Abdul Aziz Camel Festival (see above). Although many countries have a history of human beauty contests, Saudi Arabia does things differently. Known as 'Miss Camel', this beauty contest is big business, with more than 100,000 daily spectators and over 30,000 camels participating from all over the world. Camels are judged for their physical features, including the length and gracefulness of their necks, the droopiness of their lips, the size of their nose and the shape of their hump. They are also judged by how they perform on the runway. Prize money is big and pride in a owning a winning beauty is even bigger. The idea of a camel beauty contest may be amusing to many outsiders, but they are taken very seriously in Saudi Arabia. In fact, some camels have been disqualified as their owners have taken disallowed measures to enhance their camel's beauty, such as the use of Botox.

**King Abdul Aziz Falconry Festival** (☎011 810 3015; **w** sfc.org.sa/sa/en/event/details?id=3) The King Abdul Aziz Falconry Festival has been taking place since 2017 and is held for two weeks during December at the Malham Falcons Club north of Riyadh. Falconry as a sport can be traced back at least to the 13th century. The festival is designed to promote and educate people about the sport and to recognise its importance in Saudi culture. This festival is also part of Saudi Vision 2030 and is sponsored and supported by the royal family. Remarkably, in addition to speed competitions, a beauty contest is also held for falcons. Two categories of falcons are judged for the physical appearance of their head and shoulders, upper chest, back, leg, claws and colour. The Farkh category is for falcons less than 12 months old. The Qurnass category is for falcons older than 12 months.

## SHOPPING

Until recently, shopping was one of the only leisure activities allowed beyond going to a restaurant or a park. Shopping continues to be a major event for many Saudi families. Most shops found in Saudi Arabia's **shopping malls** are familiar British high-street brands, as well as continental European and American luxury labels. Headless mannequins and no fitting rooms in clothing stores was the norm until very recently and this is still the case outside of the major cities. When not shopping, the malls are a popular place to socialise and can also provide a welcome respite from the blistering heat of the summer months. In addition to shopping malls, there are a few popular standalone shops. Jarir, the bookshop chain, which sells more electronics and office supplies than books, is a good resource for these everyday items.

**Traditional souqs** are disappearing or are catering for expatriates looking for necessities on very tight budgets, especially foreign workers from south Asia or the Philippines. That said, most cities have retained their central souq, even if others have disappeared. There are a few remaining in Riyadh and Jeddah where historical items can be found that are of interest to some tourists, but these items are scarce and more likely to be found in heritage museums dotted all over the Kingdom. If you do decide to go to a souq, sharpen your haggling skills, but keep things polite and respectful.

VAT increased to 15% in July 2020 and applies to everything, including food. It is sometimes included in the marked price, sometimes not. Double-check before finalising any purchases to avoid any unpleasant surprises, including in the souqs.

Throughout Saudi Arabia, it is easy to spot smaller **grocers** by their shop sign, even if the name is only in Arabic. Look for the stylised yellow trolley on a green background.

**SOUVENIRS** Visitors should remember that it's early days for tourism in Saudi Arabia. Most shopkeepers have not bothered to stock items of interest to general visitors as their clientele until recently has been business travellers or pilgrims.

Contemporary items that can make good souvenirs are traditional clothing, jewellery, dallah (coffee pot) sets, food items such as honey, dates and Arabic coffee, 22 carat gold and traditional artefacts such as stone-encrusted silver jewellery. Other ideas include oud – both the fragrance and the musical instrument. Popular perfumes blended with oud, garam oil and other scents that are suitable for men and women can also be a good choice. *Bukhoor* are wood chips that are soaked in perfume oils and burned to provide scent for a room. Arabian Oud is a particularly prominent perfume shop and is found throughout the Kingdom. Keep in mind that your home country may or may not allow some of these items to be imported, especially food, so check before you buy. Visitors brave enough to purchase a sword, and be prepared to answer customs questions back home, may also consider purchasing a *khanjar*, the traditional curved dagger worn by men.

Head to the souqs for traditional artefacts. Traditional clothing for men and women can also be found near most souqs, as well as in shopping malls. Although most items will be reproductions, it is still possible to find a genuine antique in some souqs.

## ACTIVITIES

In addition to shopping and dining, many more activities are now possible due in part to Saudi Vision 2030. Culture vultures will find a growing number of museums, art galleries and heritage centres to explore, as well as pre-Islamic historical sites found in many corners of the Kingdom. Outdoor adventure enthusiasts can choose between scuba diving, horseriding, mountain hiking, desert camping, dune and *wadi* bashing and more. Cyclists can take advantage of stunning scenery during the more pleasant months but should always be especially cautious whenever there is traffic as their presence on the road is not always accommodated properly. Saudi Arabia's national parks are mostly underexplored and will benefit from responsible tourism at some point in future. City parks proliferate and are generally family orientated. Corniches on seaside cities and towns are also popular gathering spots. If you are visiting during the winter months, Saudi Seasons activities should not be overlooked and give an opportunity to be immersed in activities where you can participate with Saudis and expats alike (see below).

**CAMPING** Many people enjoy camping overnight in the desert. This is possible in good weather but be prepared to bring all of your food, plenty of water, tents and layers of clothing. Women do not need to wear an abaya out in the desert unless camping with Saudis who prefer that you do so. You will also need to be prepared to follow desert sanitation best practices for the toilet.

**DESERT SAFARIS** Desert safaris are popular with Saudis and non-Saudis alike. Many Saudi families go to their favourite spot in the desert to have a picnic and for recreation. Picnics can be simple matters where families bring their own food from home or create a simple barbecue. They can also be very elaborate gatherings, traditionally in a Bedouin tent complete with a luxurious diwan and a cooking area staffed by chefs. Desert safaris can take place in the day during the cooler months or in the evening most of the year.

You may want to consider going with a tour operator, especially for your first time in the desert. It can be a great way to meet like-minded visitors as well.

If you plan to go into the desert independently, follow safety precautions. Never go out to the desert alone and only go with a suitable high-clearance 4x4 vehicle. Have some working knowledge of your vehicle – you may have to let some air out of the tyres on some terrain. Know how to get out of being stuck in the sand. Be prepared for both hot and cold weather and go during the appropriate time of day for the season. Make sure you have reliable communication, such as a legal satellite phone, as mobile phone signals only go so far. Tell someone who is not going with you where you are travelling to and when you expect to be back.

### SAUDI SEASONS

Part of Saudi Vision 2030 (page 28), Saudi Seasons is a government initiative to promote a high standard of tourism in the Kingdom. It is held in 11 different regions throughout the Kingdom and was first held in 2019–20. After a pause in 2020–21 due to Covid-19, it reopened for the 2021–22 season and is expected to become an annual event. The focus is on national and regional Saudi culture and heritage. Sports and entertainment also feature.

**DUNE BASHING** Dune bashing involves driving up and down sand dunes as a form of recreation. Many of the same rules for desert safaris also apply to dune bashing, especially if you are going into the desert where you are unlikely to encounter other people.

**WADI BASHING** Wadi bashing is driving along dry riverbeds as a form of recreation. Most of the same rules for desert safaris also apply to wadi bashing. Additionally, it is of critical importance to check the weather forecast to determine if there is any chance of rain as dry riverbeds can quickly become fast-flowing rivers without warning. Learn to determine when wadis are no longer safe and have an escape plan if something is about to go wrong. Local knowledge is essential. Wadis nearest Riyadh are Wadi Hanifa and Wadi Namar. It's a good idea to consider a local guide if you are considering wadi bashing further away in Riyadh Province.

## ENTERTAINMENT

Until reforms were brought in with Saudi Vision 2030, entertainment in the Kingdom was limited to dining out, shopping, visiting public parks, children's playgrounds, sports for men, television and socialising at home. There were bans on most live music and dance, other than all-male traditional performances. Mixed-gender gatherings other than with close family members were not allowed, and cinema, which did exist in the Kingdom until shortly after the events in Mecca in 1979 (page 21) and the strengthening of the religious police, was banned.

The Kingdom has changed beyond all recognition in a few short years. The General Entertainment Authority was formed in 2016 as part of the reforms of Saudi Vision 2030. Men and women are now able to attend concerts that feature Arab, Western and other global artists. Cinemas reopened in 2018 and are now found countrywide, and a number of film festivals have been established. They include the Saudi Film Festival, held at the King Abdul Aziz Center for World Culture (Ithra) in the Eastern Province, with Saudi and GCC-produced films at the competition. The Red Sea International Film Festival was launched in 2021 and features filmmakers from Saudi Arabia and more than 60 other countries. Talented Saudi filmmakers are growing in number but must be mindful during production as censorship is still strong. Many international films are banned due to content that is interpreted as un-Islamic. The same scrutiny is applied to the written word, limiting the number of books, magazines and digital publications that make it into the public domain.

Qiddiya, located about 70km southwest of Riyadh, was announced in 2017 as an entertainment complex on a grand scale. Theme parks, sports arenas including a motor-racing circuit, a performing arts centre, nature trails and a resort infrastructure to support visitors are all part of Qiddiya's master plan. Ground was broken in 2018. A branch of American entertainment chain Six Flags is scheduled to open as a major headliner at the complex.

## PHOTOGRAPHY

Photography was frowned upon in the recent past. However, young Saudis love selfies and anything else remotely associated with their phone cameras, so things are very different now. Visitors should be comfortable when taking photos of tourist sights, architecture, areas of natural beauty and the like. Obvious must-avoids include the airports, anywhere associated with security procedures, police and military bases and anything that could make Saudi Arabia look bad to the outside world. Saudis have been very reluctant in the past to have their photos taken due to both religious and modesty reasons, especially women. Although this is also changing among some young people, always respect anyone's wishes if they do not wish to be photographed.

## OPENING TIMES

Visitors should note that Saudi Arabia operates in a manner that can be very different to your home country. Days are generally 'split days', where facilities open in the morning and close at *dhuhr* prayer around noon. Most businesses remain closed during the afternoon, opening again after *asr* prayer in the late afternoon and often staying open late into the evening. Aside from prayer times, pretty much everything in the Kingdom is far from precise. Do not be surprised if venues do not open when they say or open late. On slow days, some businesses may also close early. Take advantage of places that are open even if it wasn't your original plan – they may not be open later, despite what is advertised. It is also worth noting that a lot of tourist attractions are closed at the weekends even though it might seem to many visitors that these would be popular days to visit.

The main exceptions are restaurants and supermarkets, which can remain open throughout the day, though some still close during prayer times, especially those in very conservative neighbourhoods and in the provinces.

**RESTAURANTS** Although the information provided in the listings in this guide is accurate at the time of research, note that these hours can be unreliable. Some restaurants have seasonal hours that change at different times of the year. Others simply close when their owners go on holiday. During Ramadan restaurants remain closed until sunset, but then stay open much later than at other times of the year.

Prayer times mean that opening hours may be slightly different throughout the year at lunchtime, especially on Fridays. Until very recently, all restaurants, food courts and fast-food outlets were required to close for every prayer time. Diners would either be locked out of an establishment until prayer times were over or locked into a restaurant, where they were permitted to finish their meal but not order anything further nor pay the bill. Things are changing, gradually. Many places in Riyadh, Jeddah and the main cities of the Eastern Province now continue to remain open during prayer times. However, this is not the case in the other provinces and rural areas except for the few establishments catering specifically to foreign guests. It is always a good idea to keep prayer times in mind when planning lunch, and especially dinner.

**SHOPS** Most shops are open for a couple of hours in the morning, from about 09.30 or 10.00 until the midday dhuhr prayer. Other than some of the largest retailers, they remain closed for most of the afternoon, generally reopening after the late-afternoon asr prayer, and finally closing for the day at around 23.00. During Ramadan, most shops open only after sunset, and often only after iftar 1–2 hours later, but with many then remaining open until almost dawn.

It is important to understand that published opening hours are only approximations as shopkeepers who close for prayer times will adhere to the specific prayer times, which vary over each day of the year. Until recently, it was mandatory to close all shops for every prayer time. This is now changing, but practices differ from retailer to retailer and from location to location. Check prayer times just in case if you don't have a lot of time to do your shopping.

Supermarkets are heaving in the evenings and at weekends. Try to go during the day if you want to avoid crowds. They are now remaining open during prayer times throughout the Kingdom, although smaller, independent grocers may still close.

**SOUQS** Most souqs open only for about 2 hours in the morning but come alive again once the sun sets in the evening. Others don't bother to open in the morning at all. Most shops in the souqs close for prayer times.

## SAUDI TIME

Rather than following a rhythm set by the Gregorian year, Saudi Arabia's rhythm is set by the key events of Ramadan, both Eids, hajj and the Islamic New Year. There are many good resources, including websites and apps, for finding specific information you may need when planning your visit. Try **w** islamicfinder.org or **w** muslimpro.com.

**CALENDAR** Although Saudi Arabia uses the Gregorian calendar year in everyday life, the Hijri or Islamic calendar is used for religious and some secular events and dictates the rhythm of the year. The Islamic calendar starts with the month of Muharram.

Month lengths are determined by the sighting of the new moon and are either 29 or 30 days long. The exact length is revealed when it has been confirmed that the new moon has been seen. This can make precise calculations to the day difficult, such as determining the exact dates of Ramadan. Of course, even though Islamic dates cannot be defined precisely in the Gregorian calendar, they are precise in the Hijri calendar. Ramadan always starts on the first day of the ninth month of the Islamic calendar, regardless of whether the eighth month had 29 or 30 days.

**PRAYER TIMES** There are five prayer times a day: at dawn, midday, afternoon, sunset and dusk. Prayer times are always precise since they are determined by exact positions of the sun throughout the day. You will hear the call to prayer a few minutes before each prayer time, and many people will stop what they are doing to go to pray. Prayer times change from day to day and location to location and can be found on websites and apps (see above). It's generally a good idea to be aware of prayer times wherever you are.

**WORKING WEEK** The Saudi work week runs from Sunday to Thursday. The weekend is Friday and Saturday.

**TIME KEEPING** Punctuality doesn't appear to be a particular cause for concern, and people often seem to run late – the reason could be anything from especially bad traffic to running into a friend or relative on the way to an appointment. Make sure you have a contact mobile number for your Saudi host, guide or driver (they are most likely to respond to you via WhatsApp).

Project deadlines should be taken with a healthy amount of scepticism. Announced dates – whether the opening of the Riyadh Metro, the possible resumption of construction of the partially built Jeddah Tower, or the megaproject NEOM – are best regarded as aspirational rather than literal. Planning, labour, time management and shifting priorities often mean overrunning and occasionally abandoning a project altogether. Of course, this is not uncommon elsewhere in the world, but it is particularly important to make allowances in Saudi Arabia. Try to be patient.

## MEDIA AND COMMUNICATION

**POST** Saudi Post (w splonline.com.sa) is the national postal system and known colloquially as *al bareed*. Its signs are in Arabic and English and are green, gold and white. Traditionally, items from a central location were sent to a branch post office near the customer's home, where the customer would then collect it as there were no routine home deliveries. Addresses were not standardised. In fact, most Saudis refer either to their PO Box number or a physical location rather than a conventional address even now.

If you plan to use the post office, we suggest you do so only for low-risk items such as postcards. If you plan to ship anything, then we recommend you use a well-known courier company such as DHL, Fedex or UPS. Aramex is also a good option if it delivers to your parcel's destination.

**NEWSPAPERS AND MAGAZINES** ***Arab News*** (w arabnews.com) and ***Saudi Gazette*** (w saudigazette.com.sa) are the two nationwide newspapers that are published in Arabic and English. They are also available to view online free of charge. Although neither newspaper will publish anything negative about Saudi Arabia or the ruling family, both do have good coverage of global events.

Until recently, most Saudi magazines were business orientated. ***Destination Magazine*** is a lifestyle magazine that offers a window on contemporary culture, with regional editions covering Jeddah, Riyadh and Eastern Province. ***Time Out*** publishes specific magazines for Riyadh and Jeddah. ***What's On Saudi Arabia*** covers more activities throughout the Kingdom. ***Directions KSA*** has similar content. Localised editions of fashion magazines such as ***Vogue*** are also popular. Many magazines are published in Arabic and English. See page 405.

**TELEVISION AND RADIO** Although television was heavily controlled in Saudi Arabia until satellite television arrived in the 1990s, it is now possible to watch television from all over the world. In addition to programmes in Arabic and English, there are many channels broadcasting in other languages. Popular Saudi

### FACE TO FACE

While email and telephone may be the best way of getting in touch with companies and tourist sites back home, do not be surprised in Saudi Arabia if your emails and telephone calls go unanswered. WhatsApp is often the best method of communication, but if that doesn't work, then you may find it easier and quicker simply to go to some venues and ask for the information you need in person if it's important to you.

**RESOLVING PROBLEMS** It is better to discuss problems face to face wherever possible in the Kingdom. The next best choice is usually WhatsApp, although some other social media contacts like Instagram might work. You can try to phone if the person you need to speak to is a good English-speaker or if you speak Arabic sufficiently well. Emails are generally the worst choice – they may not be looked at for a long time and may never be answered.

When communicating a problem, above all be gracious and respectful. Criticism and complaints can be taken personally very easily, which will not help to resolve your issue.

channels include al Arabiya, KSA Sport, MBC, Saudi One, Saudi Two, Rotana, and several stations that are dedicated religious broadcasters. Children's television is also very popular and is usually imported from the US and dubbed into Arabic. Al Ekbariya is the Saudi state news channel. Foreign news channels that broadcast in English in Saudi Arabia include al Jazeera, the BBC, CNN, France 24 (English and French), Germany's DW (Deutsche Welle), Russia Today and Sky News.

Radio was heavily restricted until relatively recently.

**INTERNET** Internet connectivity throughout Saudi Arabia is generally excellent, with robust internet speeds and few outages or other disruptions. Compared with many neighbouring countries, the internet is relatively open, with fewer blocked sites popular with visitors such as VOIP websites. Most sites that are blocked are those that are considered to be un-Islamic or are critical of the Kingdom or its people and especially the ruling family. Although we are not specifically suggesting that Saudi authorities are monitoring every keystroke or swipe, we do recommend that you are very conscious of your internet use. This includes what sites you access as well as what you may be saying. Refer to the cybercrime section on page 61 for further information. Stay safe.

Many Saudi businesses do not have websites or email addresses. Instead, they often rely on social media such as Facebook, Instagram or Twitter as a means of contact.

**TELEPHONE AND MOBILE PHONES** The international dialling code for Saudi Arabia is +966. All Saudi mobile telephone numbers begin with 05. Saudi freephone numbers begin with 800. Universal access numbers begin with 9200.

Saudi Arabia is on the top-ten countries list for mobile phone use in the world. There is excellent 4G and 5G connectivity throughout the Kingdom other than in remote desert locations, and the 5G connectivity is the second most robust in the world after South Korea. It is simply assumed that everyone, from primary school age children to pensioners, has a fully functioning mobile phone. This is also reinforced by the Saudi government, which has gone digital at a rate that most Western countries can only envy. Visitors to Saudi Arabia will struggle to communicate for even the most basic reasons if they arrive without a working phone. You'll also find one useful when eating out, as physical menus are disappearing in restaurants and being replaced by QR codes to scan for the menu instead.

We recommend that you purchase a Saudi handset and SIM card if you do not or cannot enable roaming on your home country mobile. The key service providers are Saudi Telecom (STC; **w** stc.com.sa), Mobily (**w** mobily.com.sa) and Zain (**w** sa.zain.com). SIM cards can be purchased in the arrivals hall of most major airports, and handsets from shopping centres throughout the Kingdom.

The most popular way to communicate in Saudi Arabia is via **WhatsApp**. You'll find that WhatsApp is a must-have as the majority of Saudis use this for most business communication, as well as in everyday life. You will be lost without it, sometimes literally!

## CULTURAL ETIQUETTE

Underpinning much of Saudi culture is the value placed on adhering to shared societal values. In Saudi Arabia, collective expectations of behaviour strongly influence an individual's choices and Saudis will choose the path that best fits with these expectations, even if it means that they don't always get to follow their own personal preference. They know that not only do their choices reflect on themselves, but also that the entire group – be that family, local community, or wider – will also be judged by their behaviour. Visitors should keep in mind that their own behaviour will almost certainly be judged by most Saudis as representative of nationality and will contribute to a growing positive or negative impression of their home country. Your comfort, acceptance and how you will be treated are in great part down to how you choose to fit in.

A 'When in Rome…' attitude can be especially pertinent in Saudi Arabia. You don't always have to agree with or like some of the behaviour rules and requirements that come with visiting the Kingdom, but you are much more likely to enjoy your stay if you are respectful of them.

**HANDS** In Saudi Arabia, as in most Islamic countries, the left hand is considered the 'dirty' hand. Traditionally, many Muslims perform tasks such as toileting functions or touching dirty objects with their left hand. Although it is acceptable to write or play sports using your left hand, it is important to avoid passing something to someone with your left hand or to eat with your left hand when you are directly touching the food, such as a sandwich, or sharing a communal plate of food. Using cutlery is fine as is any action that requires both hands. This left-handed author suggests that other left-handed people consider holding something such as a pen or your mobile in your left hand so that it is already occupied, reducing the chance of instinctively using your left hand at critical moments.

**SHOES AND FEET** Feet are also considered dirty. Shoes should be removed before entering a Saudi home. You may be given house slippers to wear once inside. If not, you should consider the condition of any socks you may be wearing. Footwear must also be removed prior to sitting down on the floor or on low cushions such as those found in traditional restaurants and similar settings. Never cross your legs so that the soles of your feet or shoes are directed towards another person – this equates to the middle-finger gesture and is obviously very disrespectful. This rule applies whether you are sitting on furniture or on the floor. If you are invited into a Saudi home, you will be given slippers for use in the toilet. These slippers are distinct from slippers you may be given to wear elsewhere in the home and are only to be worn for the toilet.

**TOILETS** There are two types of toilet in Saudi Arabia: seated and squat. Seated toilets are found in nearly all hotels and are usually found in restaurants and other mainstream venues. Squat toilets are found in some older buildings, in the provinces, and also at some airports in addition to seated toilets. It's wise to carry with you an emergency supply of loo roll as it isn't always supplied where you need it. Many visitors may be curious about the presence of a hose and a bin near

### OUT AND ABOUT DURING PRAYER TIMES

Similar to restaurants, all shops, supermarkets and offices used to be expected to close during each prayer time, on the assumption that Muslim men will stop what they are doing and go to pray. In the past this was often enforced by the mutawa (page 63). Nowadays, things are changing and you may find that the establishment you are in remains open during prayer time.

For more information, see page 93.

the toilet, in homes as well as public places. Islamic practice is to use the hose for personal hygiene and to dispose of anything used (including your toilet paper and wipes) into the bin rather than down the toilet. This also explains why toilets and toilet cubicles seem to be very wet and why the bins are often very full.

## INTERACTING WITH PEOPLE

**Meeting and greeting** Saudi men greet other men with a handshake. They may also greet close family, friends and associates with two or three kisses on each cheek. Some Saudi men will also greet women with a handshake, especially Western women in a business environment, but others will not as many Saudis follow the convention of not having any physical contact with the opposite sex. In this instance, they will greet the woman verbally and may also place their right hand over their heart, which is a sign of respect. Some Saudi women might greet other women and sometimes men with a handshake; others don't shake hands at all. Like their male counterparts, Saudi women may greet close family, friends and associates with two or three kisses on each cheek and maybe hug as well. Our best advice is for visitors simply to wait and follow the lead of your Saudi counterpart and do the same. If you make a mistake and forget, then simply apologise and move on if someone refuses or is obviously uncomfortable. Saudis know there are different ways of greeting in your home country but will appreciate it if you follow their conventions in theirs.

**Conversation** Saudi men have been taught that they should communicate with other men rather than with women in a public setting. This is why some Saudi men may speak to a man, sometimes even when they are responding to a woman who has asked a question directly to him. Even though it may feel dismissive or even offensive to many visiting women, it is meant as a gesture of respect from the Saudi man's perspective. If it is important to the visitors for a woman to be spoken to directly, then it is a good idea to say so directly and politely, ideally from both the woman and the man. In many cases, the Saudi man may be relieved and will relax his own etiquette rules. Visiting men should be very careful when speaking with Saudi women. Do not be surprised if some Saudi women will not speak directly to a visiting man, especially if he is alone or as part of a male-only group. Saudi women have been taught that their reputation can become tarnished very quickly if they are seen speaking to an unrelated man in public. It is perfectly fine for a visiting man to speak to a Saudi woman in a professional capacity, such as a business colleague or hotel employee.

**Hospitality and generosity** Hospitality and generosity are cornerstones of Saudi culture and in the Middle East in general. Historically, harsh climates and long distances meant that travellers in particular needed to be looked after as their journey was often a difficult one. These traditions have been maintained in modern times, albeit more symbolically. At a minimum, guests will be offered Arabic coffee and dates as a gesture of welcome and generosity. As a guest, your obligation is simply to be a good one and accept all reasonable gestures of hospitality, starting with the coffee and dates. The gesture of acceptance is the important bit here. Accept the offering even if you don't particularly like coffee or dates by taking a sip or a bite. If you do enjoy the offerings, then it is fine to accept a refill, but don't be greedy. Shake the cup or place your (right) hand over the top when you are done. Lift your right hand to indicate no more food. If you are offered something else that will send you straight to A&E, then do mention this. You may refuse cigarettes or the *nargelah*.

It is also a good idea to have a bit of small talk at the ready. General enquiries about the well-being of family are appreciated; but do not ask about individual family members, especially women, unless your host mentions them first. Appreciation of Saudi Arabia is always a good topic. Many people find sport or technology safe topics if you share the same interests. Food and culinary traditions are usually another winner.

**Invitation to a home** People lucky enough to receive an invitation to a Saudi home should feel very honoured and accept the invitation with enthusiasm. Although some Saudi families live modern lives in the big cities which share elements common to other cultures, most families still live more traditionally.

Shoes should be removed at the entrance just inside the home. Other shoes will almost certainly be present in this area, so simply add yours to the collection. Visitors will be invited into a room for receiving guests called a diwan. Expect to be there for a while. Traditional diwans are strictly gender segregated, although it is possible for some foreign women to be invited into the male diwan as an 'honorary man' in this instance. Men should never assume they have access to the rest of the house unless they receive a rare invitation to the contrary. Women may also be invited to the women's diwan and may also be invited to tour other areas of the home.

Visitors will receive the traditional welcome of Arabic coffee and dates and are very likely to be invited for a substantial meal as well. If you need to make your excuses to leave early (after coffee and dates), try to do so as respectfully as possible. In accordance with respecting family/group expectations of behaviour, not wishing to inconvenience others who are waiting for you somewhere else would be an acceptable excuse. If you are able to accept the invitation to dine, then be prepared for a feast. Try a little of everything, but take care not to clear your plate as this indicates you are still hungry, implying that your host has not provided enough. Leave a little on your plate to indicate the generosity of your host.

Be prepared to answer personal questions about yourself, your family and your country. Single visitors beyond early adulthood may wish to adapt the truth to avoid being pitied for the lack of an opposite-sex husband or wife and especially the absence of children. Anyone in a same-sex relationship or who are unwed parents should refrain from mentioning this directly as these life choices are generally not accepted in Saudi Arabia (pages 64 and 66). Keep conversation upbeat and positive, but do not openly admire any specific object in the house as many hosts will feel obligated to give it to you. Once you have visited and eaten, your host will serve another cup of coffee. This is a polite signal that the visit is over. Sip the coffee and get ready to retrieve your shoes and leave. Thank your host for their hospitality and generosity.

**Displays of affection** Public displays of affection between a man and a woman are not the done thing in Saudi Arabia, although you might see some young couples holding hands discreetly in progressive neighbourhoods in Jeddah, Riyadh and parts of the Eastern Province. We advise heterosexual couples to refrain from hugging, kissing and other affectionate behaviour in public. Paradoxically, it is common to see two men openly holding hands in public, leading many visitors to assume they are seeing a same-sex couple which can cause quite a bit of confusion. However, in Saudi Arabia, holding hands between two men is not sexualised but rather simply a sign of friendship and comfort. Similar behaviour can be seen with two women as well.

**DRESS CODE FOR VISITORS** All visitors, Muslims and non-Muslims alike, must adhere to Saudi religious and social norms, no matter the rules in their home country (page 62). Some leeway is usually, but not always, given if an innocent mistake is made. Problems commonly relate to the dress code, for men as well as women. For dress code in Jeddah, see page 254.

**Men** It may surprise some visitors that men, as well as women, have a dress code and are also expected to wear modest clothing. This means covering the upper arms and covering the knees. Sleeveless tops and anything that reveals too much body hair are problematic, although wearing a shirt with the top button undone is not uncommon. Cropped trousers (but never shorts above the knee) are generally fine where casual clothing is otherwise acceptable. Camouflage, militaria and any controversial images or slogans could cause problems and are best avoided. Tattoos are haram in Islam. However, Saudis are aware of the popularity of tattoos in some parts of the world and will tolerate them on foreigners if the design of the tattoo is otherwise non-offensive. Men should be aware that wearing silk and gold are considered inappropriate, though visiting men who are not Muslim will not have any problem wearing a gold watch or wedding band. Visiting men should never wear the thobe as it comes across as mockery. Buying male Saudi national dress is perfectly fine, however, if you wear it in private or bring it home as a souvenir.

**Women** At the time of writing, it is possible for women who are visiting the Kingdom as tourists to wear very modest baggy clothing that covers their legs to their ankles and their upper arms and elbows. Necklines must be high; a standard T-shirt round-neck style is best and adding a scarf around the neckline is even better. If you choose this dress code, you will most definitely stand out as a tourist. Other women find it more comfortable to wear an abaya as this has been the strict norm for decades until tourist visas were first issued. Most Saudis will regard visiting women who wear the abaya with respect. We would strongly advise women to consider wearing the abaya until a significant number of Saudi women stop wearing them, especially if you are visiting Saudi Arabia on business, are not on an organised tour or are travelling alone. Visiting women never need to wear a niqab or cover their hands and feet. Unlike men, women can wear silk and as much gold jewellery as they wish. But some Saudis may find it more difficult to accept tattoos on a woman. For both men and women, be aware if any visible tattoos have a design that could be regarded as offensive.

**Children** Infants and babies can wear pretty much whatever their parents choose as long as they are not nude in public. Nappies should always be worn under a garment. Small children can also wear whatever they please until they reach puberty, and it is common to see young children dressed in shorts and T-shirts. In

### RAMADAN DRESS CODE

If you are visiting during the holy month of Ramadan, you are expected to dress even more modestly than at other times. Men should wear full-length trousers and sleeves that cover the elbow. In more conservative environments, men may be asked to wear long-sleeved shirts to the wrist. Women should (or are strongly advised to) wear an abaya, plain with minimal embellishment, and should be prepared at certain times to put on a headscarf as well.

some Saudi families, older children who have not yet reached puberty dress more modestly, covering their legs and arms.

At around age 12 or when it's obvious that the child has entered puberty, things change. Boys are more likely to wear the thobe in the manner of their male relatives. Boys' casual clothing will now cover their legs at least beyond the knee. Girls wear the abaya and are much more likely to wear a headscarf as well.

Visiting families with younger children should not need to make many adjustments to their clothing. Families with teenage girls and boys will need to ensure their children adhere to the Saudi adult dress code. As with women, girls should carry a headscarf with them but generally do not need to wear it in most places.

**GENDER SEGREGATION** Until recently, Saudi Arabia practised a form of gender segregation regarded as strict even by neighbouring countries. It is an Islamic value for both men and women to behave modestly, especially in public, and not to behave in a way that could be determined as sexualised. From a practical perspective, gender segregation was determined to be the most effective way to accomplish this and was widely enforced. While the gender segregation rules are not as strict as they once were, they still can be enforced if a man and a woman are seen to behave in a manner that is deemed too familiar. In addition to family sections in restaurants (page 86), most institutions from government buildings to banks continue to offer women-only sections so they can conduct their business separately from men. It is still very common practice for groups of women or groups of men to socialise, but mixed-gender groups remain rare other than in the most progressive social circles.

## TRAVELLING POSITIVELY

Saudi Arabia is pulling out all the stops to develop tourism and be tourist friendly. Visitors can do their bit by being respectful of a destination that is unused to hosting tourists other than religious pilgrims. Try to remember that most people you may encounter in the tourism sector have only been working in it for a short time. Leave your assumptions behind and see for yourself what today's Kingdom is all about.

**Charitable activities** are a key cornerstone of Saudi society. In fact, *zakat*, or charitable giving, is one of the five pillars of Islam recognised by Muslims all over the world. Volunteering is promoted in the community. Be aware that charities must be approved by the Saudi government and will be judged by their adherence to Islamic values. It is illegal to raise funds for charity without the correct permissions. Do keep in mind that the concept of human rights is very different in Saudi Arabia than it is in much of the world, with little to no tolerance of outsiders who are perceived to be meddling, and whose actions could lead to them being deported or imprisoned. Visitors planning to become involved in charitable activities during their stay in Saudi Arabia should ensure that they are doing so legally.

**SUSTAINABLE TOURISM** In a country that has no history of general tourism, it could be argued that tourist hotspots have been sustained simply due to the fact that they've had very few visitors. As tourism in Saudi Arabia develops, there are many steps that need to be considered if the Kingdom wishes to promote sustainable tourism.

References to Saudi's claims of sustainability are at the heart of Saudi Vision 2030. These are early days, where responsible travellers can lead by example, reinforcing good behaviour that many local communities will observe and hopefully adopt as

## 'IT DEPENDS'

Most behaviours and judgements of behaviour operate under the mantra of 'It Depends'. You may be treated differently to someone else who has made the identical decision about their behaviour, judged on who you are (or are perceived to be), where you are, what you did, and who saw you do it. Although you may feel that this is unfair and hypocritical, as a visitor you are strongly advised to let the situation pass without comment. No matter how outraged you may feel, challenging what you deem to be unfair behaviour will rarely change the situation or someone's mind, but could cause further problems for you.

Things to keep in mind in Saudi Arabia that can impact 'It Depends' and how you may be treated:

- Nationality or perception of nationality
- Age and gender
- Urban or rural location
- Big cities or provincial capitals
- Tourist, expat or business visitor
- How you are dressed
- Muslim or non-Muslim
- Your general attitude and demeanour
- Level of politeness and respect

their own. Whether performing simple tasks like recycling or politely declining an offer of a plastic straw, little steps help.

Saudi Arabia is a large country with vast distances between major points of interest, and many of the most interesting places are in remote areas. Regardless of how they have arrived, visitors will require ground transport at their destination. Try to minimise your carbon footprint by planning your journey to visit multiple points of interest in the same location before moving on. Try to car share if you can organise this with other visitors. Do take the bus or train if possible and if you have sufficient time, rather than fly – you will have the added bonus of seeing some interesting scenery en route.

Accommodation can be another challenge, with different levels of sustainability practices. Try to stay at reputable, locally owned hotels, where most owners are very enthusiastic about sharing their history and traditions that are sometimes in danger of disappearing. Consider rewarding accommodation providers who make genuinely positive steps towards a better environment by giving them a positive review online. Be aware that restaurants often serve very large portions that can lead to unnecessary food waste. Fortunately, Saudi take-away culture means that asking to package the remainder of a meal to take home is considered normal. It is also possible to order items from most menus for sharing.

It is better to set a clear and noticeable example that shows you are doing your bit to promote sustainable tourism than to be directly critical. Show Saudis your reusable items that promote sustainability. Praise the beauty of clean and beautiful landscapes. These small steps tend to be more effective in the long run than lectures or condescending attitudes. For visitors who plan to visit through a tour operator, try to find an organisation that does its best to promote sustainable tourism, even if it is far from perfect.

There is room for optimism as Saudi Arabia continues to develop its tourism economy. The Kingdom was among the leading countries at the United Nations Climate Change Conference COP26 to build a coalition around the Sustainable Tourism Global Centre (STGC) concept. This initiative aims to transition the tourism industry to net zero emissions, preserve nature and support local communities. Launched by Crown Prince Mohammed bin Salman in October 2021, its aim is to grow the sector and generate jobs for Saudis while achieving climate commitments.

# Part Two

## THE GUIDE

# 3

# Riyadh الرياض

Riyadh, which means 'gardens', is the capital of the Kingdom of Saudi Arabia. Located in the northeast of Riyadh Province in the ad Dahna desert, which connects the Empty Quarter to the south and the an Nafud desert to the northwest, this sprawling city – and the Kingdom's largest – is comprised of 15 municipalities and has a population of about 8 million. More than one third of the population are expatriates from all over the world, with the largest groups from south Asia. Riyadh is also the main financial centre of the Kingdom – the landmark Kingdom Centre and equally distinctive Faisaliyah Center, known for their upscale shopping, restaurants and hotels, are significant business centres.

In the first half of the 20th century, Riyadh was still a very traditional city; but by the mid 20th century, it was well under way to being developed into the modern metropolis it is today under the guidance of King Saud, the second king. King Saud looked to American cities for his inspiration as to what modern Riyadh would

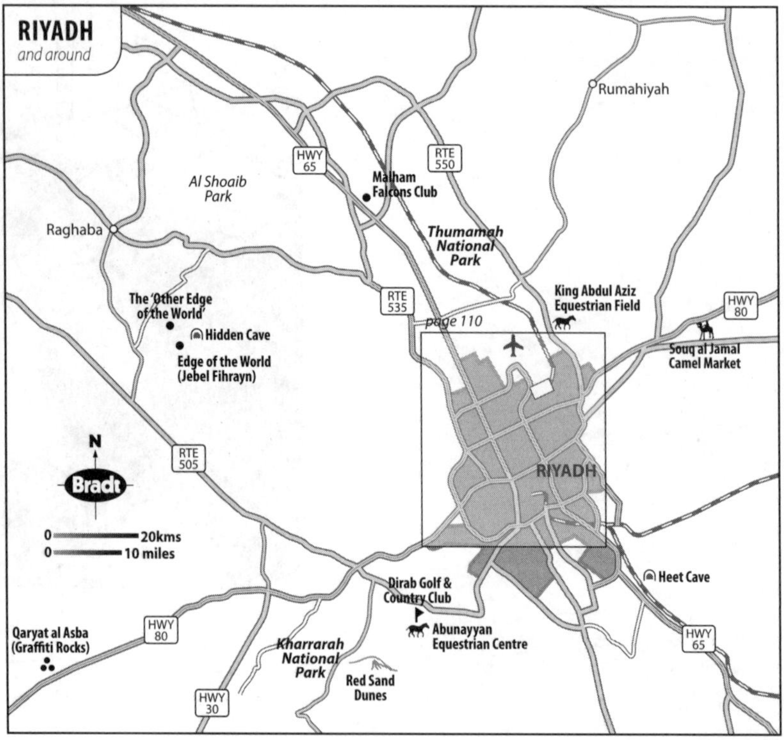

**RIYADH**
*and around*

Rumahiyah
HWY 65
RTE 550
*Al Shoaib Park*
Malham Falcons Club
Raghaba
*Thumamah National Park*
RTE 535
King Abdul Aziz Equestrian Field
HWY 80
The 'Other Edge of the World'
Hidden Cave
page 110
Soug al Jamal Camel Market
Edge of the World (Jebel Fihrayn)
N
Bradt
RTE 505
RIYADH
0 20kms
0 10 miles
Heet Cave
Dirab Golf & Country Club
Abunayyan Equestrian Centre
Qaryat al Asba (Graffiti Rocks)
HWY 80
*Kharrarah National Park*
Red Sand Dunes
HWY 65
HWY 30

become, adopting the grid system that is now in place. Indeed, with its skyscrapers, extensive road networks, limited pavements and lack of a walking culture, some people might say Riyadh resembles Houston more than Jeddah. Even though it does have a bus system – and a much-anticipated metro is under construction – city dwellers are heavily reliant on the car for getting about.

Riyadh's weather is extreme, with summer temperatures reaching 50°C and temperatures in the short winter often dropping to single digits overnight in January and February. There are also occasional sandstorms, usually in the spring months. As expected in a desert climate, rainfall is sparse. When it does rain, roads become chaotic and drainage problems are obvious. Nevertheless, most of the population welcomes these breaks from the intense sun.

Riyadh is an excellent base from which to explore many areas of interest elsewhere in the province, most as day trips from the capital.

## HISTORY

Although first impressions of Riyadh are that of a new, modern city, it has been in existence since pre-Islamic times. It is believed that the city, originally known as Hajr al Yamamah (حجر اليمامة), was first settled as early as the Palaeolithic in about the 1st millennium BCE by the Bani Hanifa tribe and saw the arrival of Islam. They were very early converts to Islam and came under the Rashidun Caliphate.

Hajr then became the capital of al Yamama Province during the times of the Umayyad and Abbasid empires. During the Abbasid period, control of Hajr was lost to the Ukhaydhirites in 866CE, who moved the seat of power to what is now the city of al Kharj, about 100km southeast of Hajr. Hajr then declined for the next several centuries.

In 1590CE, the name Riyadh first appeared. By 1737, it referred to the oases that were walled in for protection by Deham bin Dawwas, who conquered the area from nearby Manfuha. In 1744, the al Saud–al Wahhab alliance was formed, creating the First Saudi State and forcing out other threats including bin Dawwas. Based in Diriyah, it controlled Riyadh and other nearby settlements.

After the destruction of the First Saudi State, control of the region was held by the Viceroy of Egypt under the Ottoman Empire. Riyadh was named the capital of the turbulent Second Saudi State in 1823, and was ruled by the al Saud and rival al Rashid tribes from Ha'il in the northern Najd during most of the 19th century, during which period the Masmak Fortress was built. The Second Saudi State collapsed in 1891.

A key to the existence of the Third Saudi State, now modern-day Saudi Arabia, was the return of Abdul Aziz bin Abdul Rahman bin Faisal al Saud (ibn Saud) from exile in Kuwait in 1902. With the capture of the Masmak Fortress, he regained control of Riyadh and eventually consolidated all of the other regions that make up the Kingdom to this day. Riyadh became the capital of the Kingdom of Saudi Arabia in 1932, the year of independence.

Although the Kingdom is an absolute monarchy, there are government institutions with appointments, mostly made by the king, that look after political, legal and social matters. Riyadh City is led by a governor appointed by the king. The Shura Council (Consultative Assembly), Council of Ministers and Supreme Judicial Council are all in Riyadh.

## GETTING THERE AND AWAY

**BY AIR** King Khalid International Airport (KKIA) serves Riyadh city and the province. It is located approximately 35km from the city centre and is currently reached by road transport, though there are plans to build Riyadh metro stations at the airport.

**Arrivals** As in so much of the Kingdom, Riyadh's airport is undergoing renovation and expansion. Terminals 1 and 2 opened in 1983 and look it, although some modernisation has occurred since then. Terminal 1 has now closed for further development. Terminal 2 serves most international carriers. The arrivals hall has facilities for mobile phones, hire cars, bureaux de change, ATMs, a limited café and convenience shop, and a seated waiting area. Although terminals 3 and 4 were also originally built in 1983, they have not been operational for years, until very recently. Now fully redeveloped into modern facilities, they present a much more modern welcome. Terminal 3 serves the budget carriers flynas and flyadeal's international routes. KLM, Middle East Airlines, Qatar Airways, Turkish Airlines and Wizz Air also operate from Terminal 3. Terminal 4 has also benefited from a similar redevelopment and is dedicated to the national carrier, Saudia, for its international flights. Terminals 3 and 4 have a broader range of facilities in their arrivals halls. It is possible to walk between terminals 2, 3 and 4. Terminal 5, which opened in 2016, is used for domestic arrivals (flynas, flyadeal and Saudia) and has a wide range of amenities and services. A shuttle bus runs, albeit infrequently, to and from Terminal 5 from the other two operational terminals, but expect a long wait time, especially in the evening.

Passengers arriving at KKIA will notice that there are several queues in the approach to the immigration desks. First-time visitors or anyone travelling on a new visa should look for the new visa queue as you will be sent there if you join the wrong queue. Your fingerprints and an iris scan will be taken before you are stamped into the Kingdom. There is also a separate re-entry queue for people who have previously entered the Kingdom on the same visa, including business travellers and residents. There is also another separate queue for Saudi and GCC passport holders. This queue is not an option for other nationalities including *iqama* holders.

Once you finish entry formalities, proceed to the appropriate baggage carousel and retrieve any checked luggage. Free trolleys are available, as well as paid porter service. You will then place all of your luggage – hand and hold – through an x-ray machine. Officials are usually checking for illicit alcohol and contraband drugs, especially from Western countries. Don't do it.

**Departures** KKIA departure halls allow entry only to passengers. All departure halls have luggage wrapping and the usual airline check-in counters. As soon as you have completed check-in, you should proceed to the emigration and security queues as they can take some time when busy. Note that these queues are gender segregated. Men will go through the usual security checks. Women and young children will do so in a curtained booth staffed by female security officials.

Once airside, passengers will find duty free shops with limited products – you can stock up on dates if you haven't already done so.

***Lounges*** Terminal 2's Plaza Premium Lounge is a business-class lounge located on the first floor and can be accessed by eligible passengers or those willing to pay. Eligible domestic passengers will find the al Fursan Golden Lounge (for Saudia passengers) and naSmiles Lounge (for flynas passengers) in terminals 4 and 5. It is possible to purchase access to the al Fursan Golden Lounge for a fee; naSmiles only accepts eligible passengers through a premium class ticket or elite loyalty status.

**Airport transfers** Hotels do not provide shuttle bus services to and from the airport as is usual in many other capital cities. It is commonplace for mid-range and higher-level hotels to organise a private car and driver to collect their guests from the airport for a fee upon request. This fee usually starts from SAR150–200 for a standard vehicle, which is adequate for two or three passengers. Prices rise for a luxury vehicle or a larger vehicle for more than three passengers.

There is a taxi rank outside each terminal. There is a dispatcher outside Terminal 2 who you pay to organise your journey at a fair price with no need to negotiate with or pay the driver at your destination. This is not the case for the other terminals. Ask the driver to switch on the meter as they can sometimes 'forget'.

SAPTCO bus services are scheduled to run from the airport to the city centre every 2 hours at a cost of SAR25. These services are unreliable and rarely used by tourists as they are designed for low-income airport workers travelling to and from their city centre residences.

The Riyadh Metro, when open, will also run to KKIA.

**BY ROAD AND RAIL** For information on travelling to Riyadh overland, see page 52.

## ORIENTATION

Broadly, greater Riyadh is defined by the Northern, Eastern and Southern ring roads, King Khalid Road completing the circle to the west. To the north of the Northern Ring Road to King Salman bin Abdul Aziz Road, which leads to the airport, there is significant new development including the purpose-built King Abdullah Financial District. There are many new neighbourhoods to the east of the Eastern Ring Road, where many global organisations have set up their Saudi offices. Most visitors are likely to be interested in three main areas of Riyadh. Al Batha and Dirah form the historic centre. The developed area to the north of the historic centre, with Olaya Street and King Fahd Road the main thoroughfares running to the Northern Ring Road, is the second area of interest and is where most visitors stay and where most hotels, restaurants and shopping centres are found. Finally, the Diplomatic Quarter, known as the DQ, is home to nearly all of the embassies, as well as to many of Riyadh's best parks and a growing number of restaurants. Note that Old Diriyah, just outside of Riyadh, is geographically close to the DQ and the two areas are treated as a combined district.

**AL BATHA AND DIRAH** Riyadh's oldest neighbourhoods are found in the al Murabba district south of Makkah al Mukarramah Road, bordered by King Fahd Road to the west, al Garabbi Street to the east and al Madinah al Munawwarah Road to the south. This area developed when Riyadh expanded beyond the walls of the Masmak Fortress in the early 20th century.

Key areas of interest to most visitors, and best explored on foot, include al Murabba's **al Futah area** where the King Abdul Aziz Historical Center and the Saudi National Museum are located. About 1km south is **Dirah**, home of the Masmak Fortress, al Safat (aka 'Chop Chop') Square, Souq al Zel and the Thumairi Souq/ Gold Market. The **al Batha** commercial centre is a succession of traditional souqs selling practical household goods and catering mostly to low-income expatriates. They are found along and around the north–south arteries of King Faisal and al Batha roads, and also east of Dirah, from around King Saud Road to the north to al Madinah al Munawwarah Road to the south.

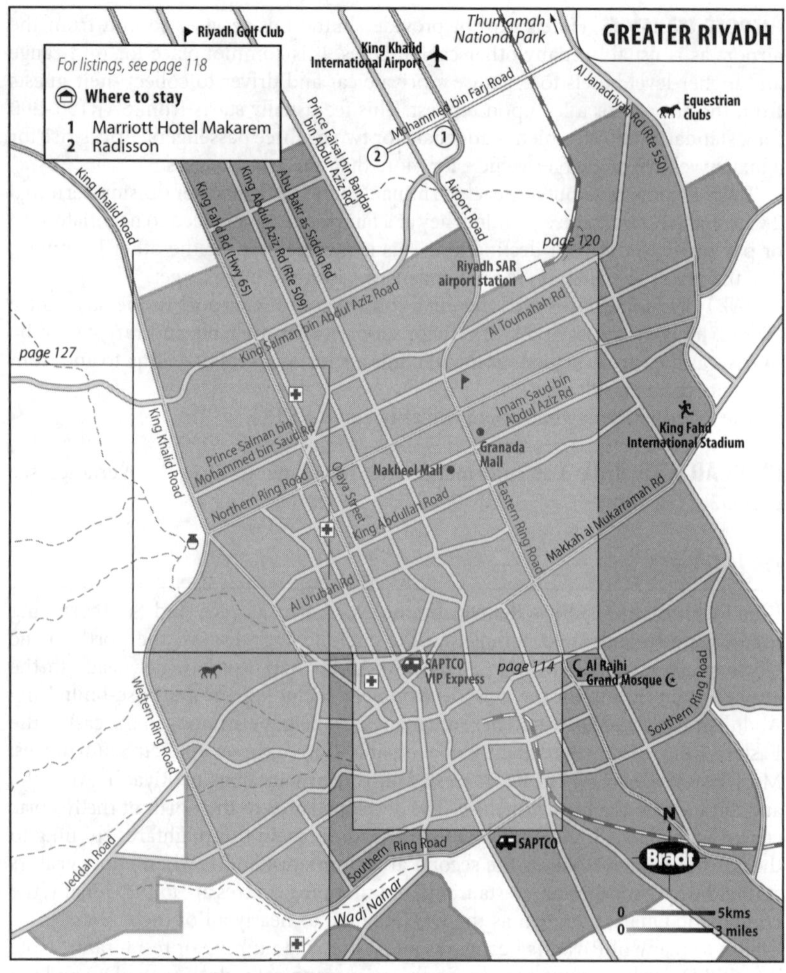


**OLAYA STREET AND THE CITY CENTRE** This area of Riyadh is built on a grid layout and is relatively easy to find your way about, if you can ignore the roadworks, diversions and odd U-turns. Olaya Street is considered by many as the city centre's main artery and is where most hotels are located or are very nearby.

Key north–south arteries are: King Fahd Road/Highway 65 (labelled on some maps as al Hameid), which parallels Olaya Street to the west in the centre of the city; al Takhassousi Street and Prince Turki bin Abdul Aziz al Awwal Road between King Fahd and King Khalid roads; and King Abdul Aziz Branch and Abu Bakr al Siddiq roads, both between Olaya Street and the Eastern Ring Road; key west–east arteries include Makkah al Mukarramah Road, Tahlia Street, Musa bin Nusair Street, al Urubah Road and King Abdullah bin Abdul Aziz Road. Many restaurants can be found along or just off these.

The area near the intersection of King Fahd Road and Olaya Street at Makkah al Mukarramah Road is where most government ministries are situated. It has a traditional, conservative business vibe which should be noted when considering your choice of hotel. If you are looking to be near good restaurants and shopping, consider staying north of this area from about Tahlia Street to the Northern Ring Road. Properties north of King Abdullah bin Abdul Aziz Road tend to have a different, more progressive business feel as they are close to the Financial District.

**DIPLOMATIC QUARTER AND OLD DIRIYAH** The **Diplomatic Quarter** (DQ) is located in the al Sarafat neighbourhood and is bordered by King Khalid and Makkah al Mukarramah roads to the north and east, by Jeddah Road to the south, and by Wadi Hanifa to the west. It has a modern, organised atmosphere and is an oasis of calm. The entire area is gated, with security measures in place to vet all visitors.

The DQ is laid out in a hub-and-spoke format radiating from 11 circles. There are additional roads leading to residential neighbourhoods and several lovely parks. While building of the DQ started in 1979, to accommodate most of the 114 embassies currently in Saudi Arabia, upscale housing, hotels and restaurants continue to be built. A Tamimi supermarket, a branch of the Dr Sulaiman al Habib Medical Centre and dispensing chemist, and a Whites Pharmacy are all up and running. Many new restaurants have recently opened and are mostly found in Oud Square and al Fazari Courtyard. The only two hotels within the gated community are the Radisson Blu (page 118) and the Marriott Hotel and Apartments (page 118), though there are other hotels nearby.

**Old Diriyah** is about 5km north of the DQ, west of King Khalid and King Salman bin Abdul Aziz roads, north of the Western Ring Road. It is the home of the al Turaif UNESCO World Heritage Site, a collection of palaces and other key historic buildings related to the ruling al Saud family. Nearby is al Bujairi Heritage Park and Terrace. Other key features of Old Diriyah and the surrounding area include Wadi Hanifa. The village of modern Diriyah, about 2km to the northwest, with its beautiful panorama of the wadi and historical area, has become a thriving new Arts District in recent years.

## GETTING AROUND

**BY BUS** The local bus service in Riyadh is run by SAPTCO. Local buses are rarely used by Saudis, but are generally used instead by male expatriate labourers. The few women who use these buses will be segregated from male passengers at the front of the bus.

There are six routes: 7, 8, 9, 10, 16 and 17. Most routes travel through al Batha and run approximately every 10 minutes between 05.30 and 23.30, with less frequent service on Fridays. Passengers should purchase a smart card, which costs SAR10 (page 75).

For detailed route information in Riyadh, visit **w** saptco.com.sa/Buses/Transport-Services-within-Cities/Roads-of-Riyadh-City.aspx?lang=en-US.

**BY TAXI** Taxis are available in Riyadh, but they are not always easy to hail on the street; ride-hailing apps are a good alternative. See page 76 for details. Uber is very popular and safe in Riyadh with reasonable rates; and drivers are vetted. Uber offers a Women Preferred View option, where female drivers can choose to accept only female passengers. This is part of Uber's Masaruky initiative to help encourage more Saudi women into the workforce as part of Saudi Vision 2030. Careem is also reliable.

**BY PRIVATE CAR WITH A DRIVER** Many visitors choose to get around Riyadh by hiring a private car and driver through their hotel. The main advantages are flexibility and to minimise hassle with driving violations, accidents, lack of parking facilities, and a whole host of general driving challenges. Do check rates as they are often set by the hour, including any waiting time. For more information about what to expect, see page 76.

**BY METRO** Construction of the Riyadh Metro began in 2014 and was originally announced to open four years later. A soft opening has been announced for late 2023 or early 2024. When built, the system will have six lines known by line number and colour, and 85 stations. The lines will stretch from several city centre locations, to King Khalid Airport in the north, al Batha in the south, Dhahrat Laban in the west and Prince Saad bin Abdul Rahman al Awal Road beyond the Eastern Ring Road in the east. An additional line will run along King Abdullah Road from near the DQ in the west to King Fahd Stadium in the east. Travel will be in first-class, family (suitable for women and families) and singles (male only) carriages. Further information can be found on the Riyadh Metro's website (**w** rcrc.gov.sa/en/projects/king-abdulaziz-project-for-riyadh-public-transport).

Riyadh Metro buses will run dedicated bus lines, community lines and feeder lines that will connect passengers from more remote locations to various Riyadh metro stations. These will be mixed-gender services.

**ON FOOT** In the city centre, most people do not walk for any distance longer than it takes to go from their parked vehicle to their destination, especially in the summer. It is possible to walk around al Batha and Dirah as they are compact, and some people walk short distances in the DQ. If you do walk, be aware of broken pavements and other hazards. Never trust drivers to stop for pedestrians, even if they have the right of way or are already in the road.

## TOURIST INFORMATION AND TOUR OPERATORS

Tourist information can be found on the Kingdom's official website (**w** visitsaudi.com). There are several other websites and blogs of varying quality. For more information, see page 47, where tour operators are also listed.

It is also possible to organise a tour guide through many of Riyadh's more upmarket hotels who can offer a bespoke, comfortable service for where you want to go, what you want to see and for how long. You will need to negotiate the final price so make sure you understand what you have agreed to and what you have not. Be patient and flexible.

## WHERE TO STAY

A wide range of accommodation can be found in Riyadh, from former royal palaces and luxury hotels to the most basic of rooms that may not always accept Westerners or women as guests. As Riyadh is Saudi Arabia's key business and also government hub, hotels are generally orientated to business travellers and are expensive. Since more people these days are travelling on business to Riyadh and most leisure travellers also have Riyadh on their must-visit list, further increasing demand, there has been a shortage of hotel accommodation in recent years. It is important to book accommodation in advance, especially during the working week and if foreign VVIPs are visiting.

The oldest **hotels** are found predominantly in the historic city centre; hotels near the main government buildings at the southern end of Olaya Street are also generally well established. Hotels near the northern end of Olaya Street, especially those near the Northern Ring Road and King Abdullah Financial District are newer and include comfortable Western chain hotels geared towards business guests. The same Western chain hotels are found around the Eastern Ring Road and will generally appeal to business visitors more than to tourists due to their location. Hotels in and around the DQ range from comfortable to luxurious.

Many of the capital's most luxurious hotels can be found near Olaya Street, between the Faisaliah Tower and King Abdullah Road. **Luxury hotels** fall in the categories of either 'blingy' or 'understated'. A few of the well-established hotels have become the *grandes dames* of the capital and remain favourites owing to periodic refurbishment and good customer service. **Mid-range** hotels are generally comfortable and practical and are usually business orientated. Some **budget and shoestring** hotels, generally found in and around al Murabba, may not accept female guests or Westerners. Some hotels include breakfast but others don't, often dependent on the specific option you book. It is common to find hotels in all price ranges with a high number of internal connecting rooms, so advise the hotel reception desk if you do not want a connecting room. Hotel room rates are generally quoted before taxes. VAT at 15% and Municipality Tax at 5% are added to the quoted room rates.

For those visitors that find the hotels too expensive or prefer something different, the capital also offers a range of **apartments** for both short stays and long stays, which can be a more economical option for large families or groups. Hotel apartments also attract the same VAT and municipality taxes as standard hotels. Some include breakfast but others do not. Hotel apartments generally have at least one bedroom separate from a living area, and a kitchen, which can be equipped with the simplest amenities of a small fridge, sink and microwave or with more substantial cooking facilities and a full-size refrigerator. They are a good choice for visitors who plan to self-cater some meals. Although hotel apartment facilities have traditionally appealed to Saudi families, they also welcome tourists. Staff are less likely to speak much English than at most hotels.

Alternatively, there are many Airbnb and couchsurfing options in Riyadh. Anyone thinking about booking either option should do so with caution, particularly single women or solo female travellers who might inadvertently send the wrong signals to a male Saudi host.

## HOTELS

### Al Batha and Dirah

#### *Mid-range*

**Four Points Sheraton Khaldia** [115 G3] Souleiman al Qouzai just west of King Faisal Rd; ☎ 011 268 2222; w marriott.com. This is by far the best choice for mid-range hotels in the area. It's an old property but refurbished to a good standard, with an on-site restaurant, 24hr room service & a fitness centre. Located roughly halfway between National Museum & Masmak Fortress, it's also near many excellent, affordable restaurants & take-aways. Valet parking is a big bonus in this crowded neighbourhood. **$$$**

**Gloria Inn** [114 D5] East side of al Batha Rd just north of al Madinah al Munawwarah Rd, al Marqab; ☎ 011 510 0222; w gloriainn.sa. This is a good alternative to the Four Points Sheraton, with similar amenities & the added advantage of being the nearest hotel to the Masmak Fortress & surrounding souqs. **$$$**

#### *Budget and shoestring*

**Al Salam Hotel** [114 D4] al Garawi Center, al Batha Rd; ☎ 053 526 0260; w canaltasuites.com. Basic hotel with en-suite rooms & a small coffee bar.

**Hotel Apollo Dimora** [115 H2] Khaif bin Saad Rd; ☎ 011 401 4070; w thedimorahotels.com. This is a modest business-orientated budget hotel with its own restaurant & indoor swimming pool. **$$**

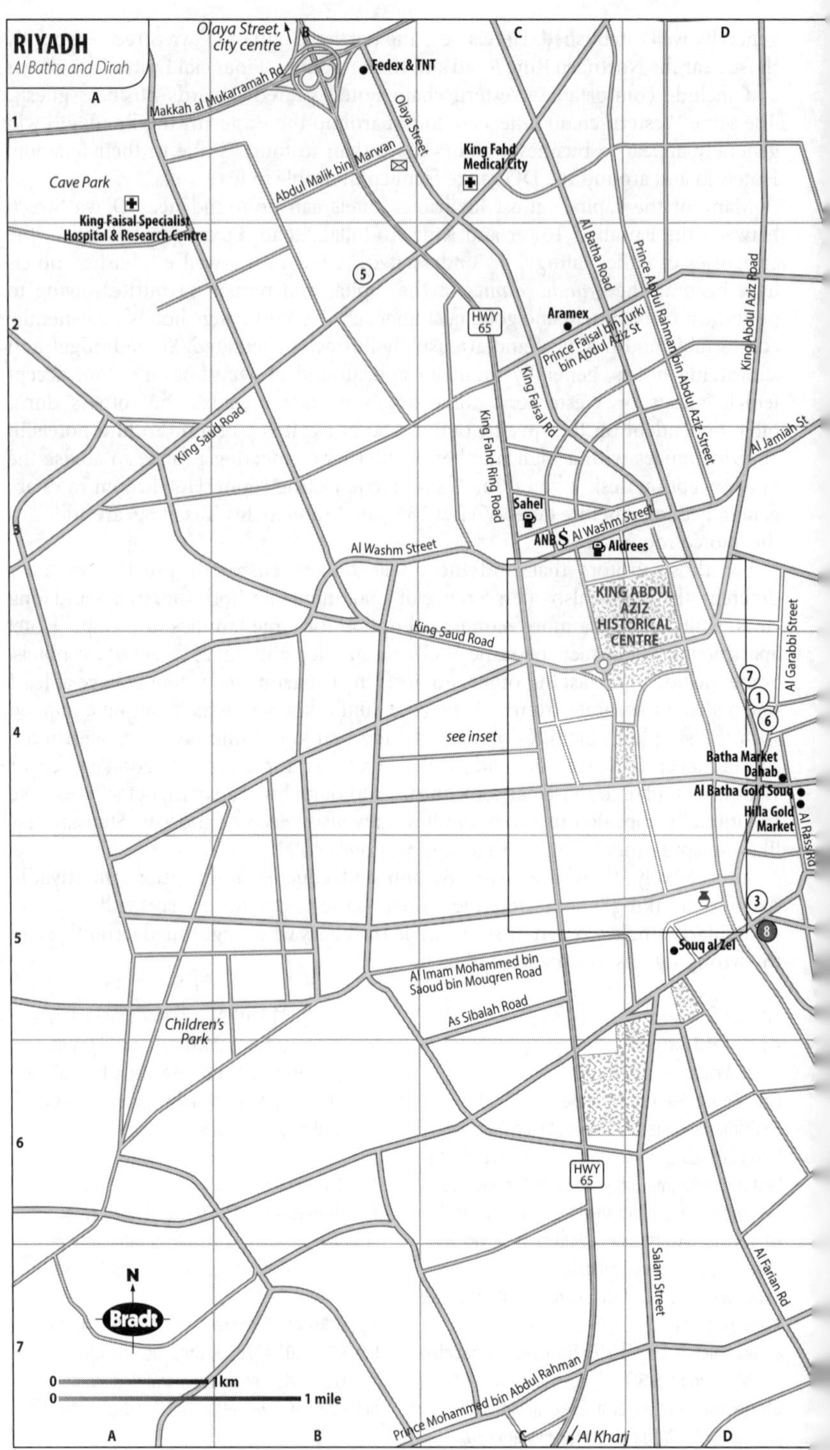

RIYADH
Al Batha and Dirah
Olaya Street, city centre
Makkah al Mukarramah Rd
Fedex & TNT
Olaya Street
Abdul Malik bin Marwan
King Fahd Medical City
Cave Park
King Faisal Specialist Hospital & Research Centre
Al Batha Road
Prince Abdul Rahman bin Abdul Aziz Street
King Abdul Aziz Road
HWY 65
Aramex
Prince Faisal bin Turki bin Abdul Aziz St
King Faisal Rd
King Saud Road
King Fahd Ring Road
Al Jamiah St
Sahel
ANB
Al Washm Street
Aldrees
KING ABDUL AZIZ HISTORICAL CENTRE
Al Garabbi Street
see inset
Batha Market Dahab
Al Batha Gold Souq
Hilla Gold Market
Al Rass Rd
Souq al Zel
Al Imam Mohammed bin Saoud bin Mouqren Road
As Sibalah Road
Children's Park
Salam Street
Al Farian Rd
N
Bradt
0 1km
0 1 mile
Prince Mohammed bin Abdul Rahman
Al Kharj

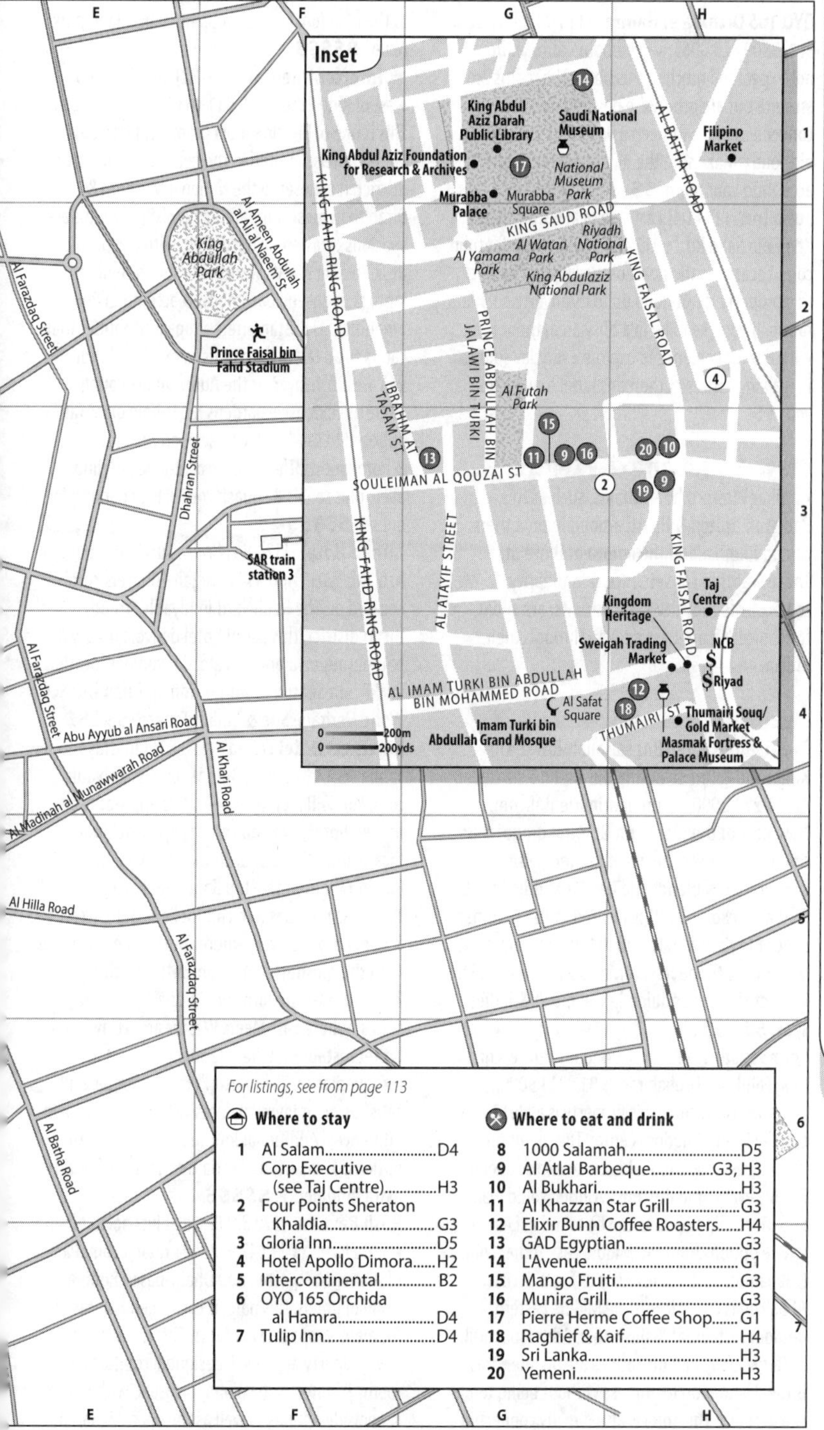

E
F
G
H
1
2
3
4
5
6
7
Inset
King Abdul Aziz Darah Public Library
Saudi National Museum
Filipino Market
King Abdul Aziz Foundation for Research & Archives
National Museum Park
Murabba Palace
Murabba Square
AL BATHA ROAD
KING FAHD RING ROAD
KING SAUD ROAD
Riyadh National Park
Al Watan Park
Al Yamama Park
King Abdulaziz National Park
KING FAISAL ROAD
PRINCE ABDULLAH BIN JALAWI BIN TURKI
IBRAHIM AT TASAM ST
Al Futah Park
SOULEIMAN AL QOUZAI ST
AL ATAYIF STREET
KING FAHD RING ROAD
KING FAISAL ROAD
Taj Centre
Kingdom Heritage
Sweigah Trading Market
NCB
Riyad
AL IMAM TURKI BIN ABDULLAH BIN MOHAMMED ROAD
Al Safat Square
THUMAIRI ST
Thumairi Souq/ Gold Market
Imam Turki bin Abdullah Grand Mosque
Masmak Fortress & Palace Museum
0 200m
0 200yds
King Abdullah Park
Al Ameen Abdullah al Ali al Naeem St
Al Farazdaq Street
Prince Faisal bin Fahd Stadium
Dhahran Street
SAR train station 3
Al Farazdaq Street
Abu Ayyub al Ansari Road
Al Madinah al Munawwarah Road
Al Khar Road
Al Hilla Road
Al Farazdaq Street
Al Batha Road
For listings, see from page 113
Where to stay
1 Al Salam D4
Corp Executive (see Taj Centre) H3
2 Four Points Sheraton Khaldia G3
3 Gloria Inn D5
4 Hotel Apollo Dimora H2
5 Intercontinental B2
6 OYO 165 Orchida al Hamra D4
7 Tulip Inn D4
Where to eat and drink
8 1000 Salamah D5
9 Al Atlal Barbeque G3, H3
10 Al Bukhari H3
11 Al Khazzan Star Grill G3
12 Elixir Bunn Coffee Roasters H4
13 GAD Egyptian G3
14 L'Avenue G1
15 Mango Fruiti G3
16 Munira Grill G3
17 Pierre Herme Coffee Shop G1
18 Raghief & Kaif H4
19 Sri Lanka H3
20 Yemeni H3

**OYO 165 Orchida al Hamra** [114 D4] al Garabbi St ☎ 0800 820 0063; w oyorooms.com/sa. Do not expect too much at this hotel. The rooms are en suite but are otherwise best regarded as a convenient place to sleep if you want to be in the old souqs. Make sure the AC unit works before accepting your room. **$$**

**Tulip Inn** [114 D4] East side of al Batha Rd at Khalf bin Saad Rd; ☎ 011 405 2000; w goldentulip.com. Located in the heart of the Filipino Market, this property is not quite up to its advertised 3-star rating. If you like to be in a busy area, though, with the convenience to explore everyday souqs in walking distance, then this hotel may be for you. **$$**

## Olaya Street and city centre

Familiar Western hotel chains, such as Ibis, Radisson, Hilton & Hyatt, among many others, can be found along the length of Olaya St. Those wanting convenience & familiarity, & to boost their loyalty status credits, are spoilt for choice. All are best booked through their official websites.

### *Luxury*

**Al Faisaliah** [120 B4] Faisaliah Tower, cnr King Fahd & Prince Sultan bin Abdul Aziz rds; ☎ 011 273 2000; w mandarinoriental.com. Now part of the Mandarin Oriental group, this hotel has recently been completely refurbished & upgraded & blends the best of Middle East & Far East hospitality. It is located in the landmark shopping mall & al Faisaliah business complex. Dine in the Globe Restaurant & enjoy a fantastic view of the city. Indulge in the men's & ladies' spas. **$$$$$**

**Four Seasons** [120 B2] Kingdom Centre, cnr King Fahd & al Urubah rds; ☎ 011 211 5000; w fourseasons.com. This property is a part of the equally iconic Kingdom Centre. The rooms are luxuriously appointed without an excess of bling & have every amenity most visitors would want. Superior dining options can be found in Elements, where options from the Middle East, India, China & Japan present a deliciously difficult decision. Al Balcon is a classic upscale Middle Eastern outdoor restaurant & shisha bar. Additional grill, buffet & lobby lounge options are on offer. This is the destination to impress without being too conspicuous. The hotel is also directly connected to the Kingdom Centre shopping mall & landmark tower. **$$$$$**

✷ **Intercontinental** [114 B2] King Saud Rd, west of King Fahd Rd; ☎ 011 465 5000; w ihg.com. This is one of Riyadh's most prominent *grandes dames* hotels. Located in the heart of the ministries district, it is closer to the National Museum & Dirah than most comparable hotels. The rooms are spacious & tastefully decorated, with a welcome desk area for guests wanting to set up their laptops, high-end bathrooms & accompanying amenities. Al Bustan offers a top-notch buffet that caters to all tastes. Don't miss a meal in Mondo if you are a fish lover, or the Addiwan Tea Lounge. There are extensive gardens & a 9-hole grass (as opposed to sand) golf course open to members & hotel guests. There is also a 12-lane bowling alley, plus tennis & squash courts. Free parking for guests. **$$$$$**

**Jareed Hotel** [120 B5] Prince Turki bin Abdul Aziz Rd; ☎ 011 400 4141; w jareedhotels.com. Located on The Boulevard in Riyadh's trendy Hittin district, this Saudi hotel delivers luxury & pampering on a grand scale. Convenient location for Riyadh Season & not far from al Turaif UNESCO World Heritage Site & Bujairi Terrace. **$$$$$**

**Narcissus Hotel & Spa** [120 B3] Cnr Olaya & Tahlia sts; ☎ 011 294 6300; w narcissusriyadh.com. You will feel the vibe of this appropriately named hotel once you spot its eye-catching façade from Olaya St or Tahlia St. If you are looking for over-the-top Saudi opulence, Narcissus provides it in chandeliers, gold accents & general bling everywhere. The theme continues with the plushest of in-room soft furnishings & Versailles-style furniture in guest rooms & suites. Where East Meets West is an extravagant buffet restaurant where requests are not an inconvenience. The rooftop terrace Pampa Grill satisfies meat lovers' palates with its Argentinian influences. Additional lounges offer lighter menu options. Male & female spa treatments offer an extra indulgence. **$$$$$**

**Rosh Rayaan** [120 B3] Olaya St just north of Abi Thalum; ☎ 011 447 9888; w rotana.com. Part of the well-respected Abu Dhabi-based Rotana chain of hotels, this hotel is conveniently located for many shops & restaurants. This is a relatively new property, with well-designed, comfortable rooms & suites. Hotel dining is casual, with buffet & poolside options as well as the open-air Sama restaurant. Valet parking is a welcome service on this busy street. **$$$$$**

### *Upmarket and mid-range*

**Al Mashreq Boutique Hotel** [120 D6] Southeast cnr al Urubah & Prince Turki bin Abdul Aziz al Awwal rds; ☎ 800 122 1222; w almashreq.sa. A member of the Small Luxury Hotels of the World, Al Mashreq delivers the high level of hospitality & customer service you would expect. Located just far enough away from the hubbub of Olaya St, this is an elegant property with all the accoutrements for a comfortable stay at a relatively reasonable price point. The décor is Andalusian, with lovely outdoor gardens & a relaxing Moroccan-style spa (check access times for men & women). The restaurants offer a wide range of cuisines, including Lebanese & salads. An oasis of relative calm. **$$$$**

**Braira Hotel** [120 B4] Olaya St between sts 24 & 26; ☎ 9200 00555; w brairahotels.com/olaya. Part of the well-respected Saudi Boudl group, which is also known for its chain of apartment hotels, Braira offers good value for money for Riyadh in an excellent location. The rooms have additional seating spaces & there is a choice of rooms including several suites that accommodate families. Guests may notice some of the rooms have smaller windows which many Saudis favour. Dining is buffet style. There are 5 other Braira properties in business-friendly locations around Riyadh. **$$$$**

**Fraser Suites** [121 E7] Cnr Olaya St & Makkah al Mukarramah Rd; ☎ 011 263 9333; w frasershospitality.com. This Singaporean-owned hotel group is centrally situated & offers a range of suites, 2 restaurants, & a fitness centre & outdoor pool. Good for those who like the space of a suite & business-like service. **$$$$**

**Le Méridien** [120 B1] Cnr Olaya St & King Abdullah Branch Rd; ☎ 011 826 6666; w marriott.com/en-us/hotels/ruhmd-le-meridien-riyadh/overview. This newer property is on the opposite side of Olaya St from the Sheraton. **$$$$**

**Novotel Riyadh al Anoud Hotel** [120 B2] King Fahd Rd, just south of St 90; ☎ 011 288 2323; w all.accor.com. 2 blocks west of the Dyar property (see right), Al Anoud has a wider selection of suites & is more modern but more expensive. **$$$$**

**Novotel Suites Riyadh Olaya Hotel** [120 B4] Olaya St, north of al Sahriah St; ☎ 011 465 6555; w all.accor.com. A good choice for those prepared to pay a bit more for a modern hotel a bit further south on Olaya St. **$$$$**

**Novotel Suites Riyadh Dyar** [120 B2] St 90 just west of Olaya St; ☎ 011 465 2626; w all.accor.com. This hotel is old & dusty but is less expensive than other Novotel properties nearby. Its location is convenient for the Kingdom Centre & other central attractions & restaurants without being too far from Dirah. Their suites may work for some budget-conscious visitors prepared to share accommodation. Underground & some street parking available. **$$$**

**Sheraton Riyadh Hotel & Towers** [120 B1] Cnr King Abdullah & King Fahd rds west of Olaya St; ☎ 011 454 3300; w marriott.com/en-us/hotels/ruhsi-sheraton-riyadh-hotel-and-towers/overview. When you can't decide which end of Olaya St to stay at, this hotel is a good compromise. Everything about this hotel is reasonable, but a bit tired. **$$$$**

### *Budget and shoestring*

The **Al Diafah Hotel** [120 B3] (St 74 west of Olaya St; ☎ 011 462 7811; **$$$**) & **Taleen Durrat al Nakhil** [120 B4] (Imam Saud bin Abdul Aziz Rd; ☎ 9200 02569; **$$**) are alternative options. Taleen has 8 other locations in Riyadh.

**Ibis** [120 B2] Olaya St opposite the Kingdom Centre; ☎ 011 419 9995; w all.accor.com. This budget hotel from the French Accor group is conveniently located & provides a budget alternative in this pricey area. B/fast café & light dining options on site. **$$$**

**Obaer Hotel** [120 B4] Olaya St at Baljorashi near Faisaliyah Tower; ☎ 011 218 1000. The best thing about this hotel is that it is only metres from Faisaliyah Tower. The rooms are basic but clean. There is room service & a buffet throughout the day. Among the best value for money along the southern end of Olaya St & an excellent choice for women travelling alone. **$$$**

**OYO** w oyorooms.com. This budget Indian chain offers some of the best rates if not always the best service in Riyadh. Rooms are basic with limited food options. Prepare to be self-reliant. Visitors who wish to stay near Olaya St can choose between **OYO 502 Sanam Hotel** [120 B4] (☎ 011 293 2743) on the north side of Makkah al Mukarramah Rd just east of Olaya St & **OYO 562 al Eairy Apartment** [120 B2] (cnr Olaya St &

al Urubah Rd; ☎ 1800 814 6590). An additional 10 OYO properties can be found throughout Riyadh. **$$**

## Diplomatic Quarter and Old Diriyah

At present, there are few options to stay near the al Turaif World Heritage Site in Old Diriyah. Those who wish to do so might try **JAX Holiday Homes** [127 A2] (☎ 053 906 3181), which offers chalet-style accommodation & is located towards the western edge of Diriyah, an area that is becoming part of the trendy JAX Arts District. In January 2022, plans were announced to develop 38 new hotels in & around Diriyah to support the anticipated tourist boom. These properties will be concentrated around Diriyah Gate & to the west of Diriyah in Wadi Safar & are expected to include luxury brands such as Fauchon, Oberoi, Raffles Rosewood & Six Senses.

### *Luxury*

**Aseel Resort** [127 B2] Wadi Hanifa; ☎ 055 702 2222; **w** aseelresorts.com. A traditional, family-orientated farm resort offering villa-style accommodation. **$$$$$**

✷ **Marriott Hotel & Apartments** [127 C7] Abdullah al Sahmi St, near Circle 7 just past the Egyptian Embassy, backing on to Oud Sq, al Safarat; ☎ 011 835 3000; **w** marriott.com. This popular hotel offers the usual high level of amenities expected of a full-service Middle East Marriott: valet parking, several upscale restaurants, concierge lounge & attentive service. Especially welcome is the swimming pool, which permits men & women to swim together. The apartments are connected to the hotel & provide long-stay options mostly for business executives & people in the process of relocating to Riyadh. **$$$$$**

**Radisson Blu Hotel & Residence** [127 C6] Amr bin Omaya al Damri St north of Circle 3 behind al Fazari Sq just south of the Libyan Embassy; ☎ 011 297 9400; **w** radissonhotels.com. The alternative to the Marriott within the DQ gates, this hotel's services tick all the boxes but the vibe is more functional. Indoor pool only. **$$$$$**

**Ritz Carlton** [127 D4] Jeddah Rd (Hwy 40/ Mecca Rd), east of Abdallah bin Houzafah as Sahmi Rd, just past the south entrance gate to the DQ; ☎ 011 802 8020; **w** ritzcarlton.com. This notorious hotel, formerly a palace, with substantial gardens, is located just outside the DQ. It has hosted the famous & infamous & made the news headlines in 2017 when some members of the most influential families in the Kingdom, including some senior members of the Saudi royal family, became involuntary 'guests' as a part of the power shift under King Salman & Crown Prince Mohammed bin Salman. Impeccable service makes each guest feel like royalty, with room rates to match. The hotel's al Orjouan, Hong & Azzurro restaurants are all renowned & worth a visit for anyone looking for a royal dining experience. **$$$$$**

### *Upmarket and mid-range*

**Courtyard by Marriott** [127 D4] Junction of Jeddah Rd 40 at the south entrance gate to the DQ; ☎ 011 281 7300; **w** marriott.com. Recently renovated & business orientated with a much-improved restaurant, this is a good alternative for visitors who want access to the DQ but are on a mid-range budget. The rooftop indoor pool is male only, as is the main fitness centre. Women do have access to a female fitness room. **$$$$**

**Voyage Hotel** [127 D3] al Urubah Rd east of King Khalid Rd just east of Abdullah bin Muammar St; ☎ 011 488 9936; **w** voyagesa.com. Geared to long-stay guests, complete with guest laundry room & 24hr Garden Restaurant. The hotel offers a variety of rooms & suites. **$$$**

**Capital O 162 Brzeen Hotel** [127 D3] al Urubah Rd east of King Khalid Rd just west of the Voyage Hotel; ☎ 011 293 2743. For those on a shoestring budget who want to be near the DQ. Prepare for shoestring customer service experience to go with the shoestring amenities. **$$**

## Airport *Map, page 110*

Hotel choices are currently limited near the airport. At the time of writing, visitors have a choice of the **Marriott Hotel Makarem** (Airport Rd; ☎ 011 220 4500; **w** marriott.com; **$$$$**) or the **Radisson Hotel** (Mohammed bin Farj Rd; ☎ 011 590 2000; **w** radissonhotels.com; **$$$$**). Both are full-service hotels but do not offer shuttle services to the airport terminals.

## HOTEL APARTMENTS

✷ **Boudl** w boudl.com. This hotel apartment group has a good balance of modest prices & good locations, & is comfortable for women travelling alone & groups. Recommended Riyadh properties are the **Boudl Olaya** [121 B3] property on Olaya St, north of St 38 (☎011 217 6666) & the **Boudl al Malaz** [120 F6] (cnr Fatima al Zahraa Rd & al Hamidat, near the zoo; ☎011 206 3050). **$$$**

**Corp Executive Hotel** [115 H3] al Batha St; ☎011 414 1500; w corpinndeira.com. This property is in the Taj Centre complex & is convenient for those who wish to be near Masmak Fortress. It is very basic with en-suite rooms & convenient for the souqs, but don't expect much else. **$$$**

**Sama al Qasr Hotel Apartment** [121 E7] Cnr Hussein al Bawri & Takhassousi St Branch Rd; ☎011 207 7574; w sama-inn.com. The rooms are basic but dark, with reasonably modern furniture. Most rooms include a small kitchenette. There is another branch in the far north of Riyadh at Anas bin Malik Rd, al Yasmin District. **$$$**

**Al Farhan Hotel Suites** [120 C3] King Fahd Rd south of al Imam Saud bin Faysal Rd; ☎011 241 1616; w al-farhan-suites.hotels-riyadh.com/en. Located in the far north of Riyadh opposite the new J W Marriott, this modest property is convenient for the airport & Old Diriyah, especially if you have your own transport. The rooms are spacious but somewhat dark in the Saudi style. Good for those on a budget who are looking for a well-located base for exploration nearby. There are additional properties east of the Eastern Ring Rd along Prince Nayef bin Abdul Aziz Rd, which are in less central locations but with the smaller price tags to match. **$$**

**Bazil Hotel Suites** [121 E6] Olaya St north of Khalid bin Yazid bin Muawiyah St; ☎058 048 1071. The suites are basic with few amenities other than a cash b/fast buffet. Kitchens are equipped with a small fridge, sink, hob & microwave. OK for people who will be eating out or are able to make do with basic facilities. Rooms & suites available. **$$**

# WHERE TO EAT AND DRINK

Many Saudi nationals and expats are foodies and have been embracing a wide variety of cuisines for generations and here you'll find freshness, quality and generous portions. Particularly popular cuisines are Lebanese, Egyptian and other Middle Eastern, regional Indian, Turkish and Asian fusion, served in many top-end venues and often frequented for special occasions. Paradoxically, authentic Saudi restaurants can be relatively difficult to find. Many of Riyadh's best restaurants can be found in luxury and upmarket hotels throughout the city. Other top-end restaurants are in upscale shopping malls; others are independent. Malls also have mid-range restaurants and large food courts that offer more modestly priced options, also with a variety of cuisines.

All of the **Saudi chain restaurants** are in Riyadh. Most have several branches throughout the city. Please refer to page 85 for inspiration.

Friday brunches are popular with families and groups of friends in Riyadh, and in other cities in Saudi Arabia as they are throughout the Gulf, although they are strictly no alcohol in Saudi Arabia. The 15% VAT also applies to restaurants and is included in the bill. There is no expectation to tip. Anyone who is inclined to tip should be aware that the tip is highly unlikely to ever be seen by the waiter.

Coffee culture is strong in Riyadh, and **coffee shops** can be found throughout the city, often in shopping malls and often staying open late, with popular British, US and Canadian brands represented. Saudi favourites include al Masaa Café on al Urubah Road just north of Kingdom Centre, Draft Café in the DQ, Elixir Bunn on King Abdullah Road near al Hamra Mall and near King Saud University, and Joy Café at the junction of al Takhassousi Street and Prince Nayyef Road, not far from Riyadh Gallery Mall. In the east of Riyadh, Moon Shell, Coyard and Prime Coffee

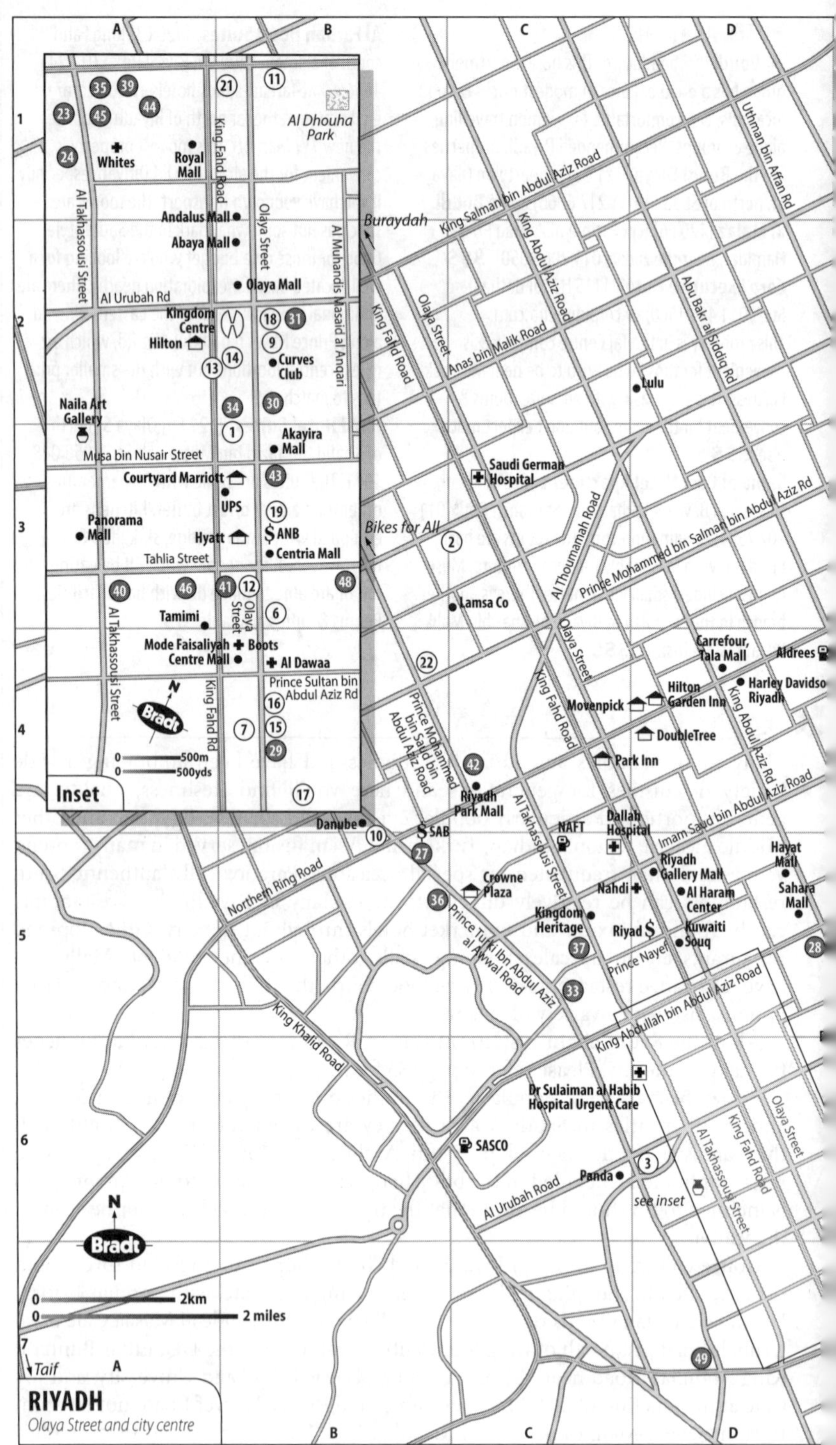
Inset
Al Dhouha Park
Whites
Royal Mall
King Fahd Road
Olaya Street
Al Takhassousi Street
Andalus Mall
Abaya Mall
Olaya Mall
Al Muhandis Masaid al Anqari
Al Urubah Rd
Kingdom Centre
Hilton
Curves Club
Naila Art Gallery
Akayira Mall
Musa bin Nusair Street
Courtyard Marriott
UPS
Panorama Mall
Hyatt
ANB
Centria Mall
Tahlia Street
Tamimi
Mode Faisaliyah Centre Mall
Boots
Al Dawaa
Prince Sultan bin Abdul Aziz Rd
King Fahd Rd
Bradt
500m
500yds
Buraydah
Bikes for All
King Salman bin Abdul Aziz Road
King Abdul Aziz Road
Uthman bin Affan Rd
Abu Bakr al Sidiq Rd
Anas bin Malik Road
Lulu
Saudi German Hospital
Al Thoumamah Road
Prince Mohammed bin Salman bin Abdul Aziz Rd
Lamsa Co
Carrefour, Tala Mall
Aldrees
Harley Davidson Riyadh
Hilton Garden Inn
Movenpick
King Abdul Aziz Rd
DoubleTree
Park Inn
Prince Mohammed bin Saud bin Abdul Aziz Road
Riyadh Park Mall
Imam Saud bin Abdul Aziz Road
Danube
SAB
NAFT
Dallah Hospital
Hayat Mall
Sahara Mall
Northern Ring Road
Crowne Plaza
Riyadh Gallery Mall
Nahdi
Al Haram Center
Al Takhassousi Street
Kingdom Heritage
Riyad
Kuwaiti Souq
Prince Turki Ibn Abdul Aziz al Awwal Road
Prince Nayef
King Abdullah bin Abdul Aziz Road
King Khalid Road
Dr Sulaiman al Habib Hospital Urgent Care
SASCO
Panda
Al Urubah Road
see inset
Al Takhassousi Street
King Fahd Road
Olaya Street
2km
2 miles
Taif
RIYADH
Olaya Street and city centre

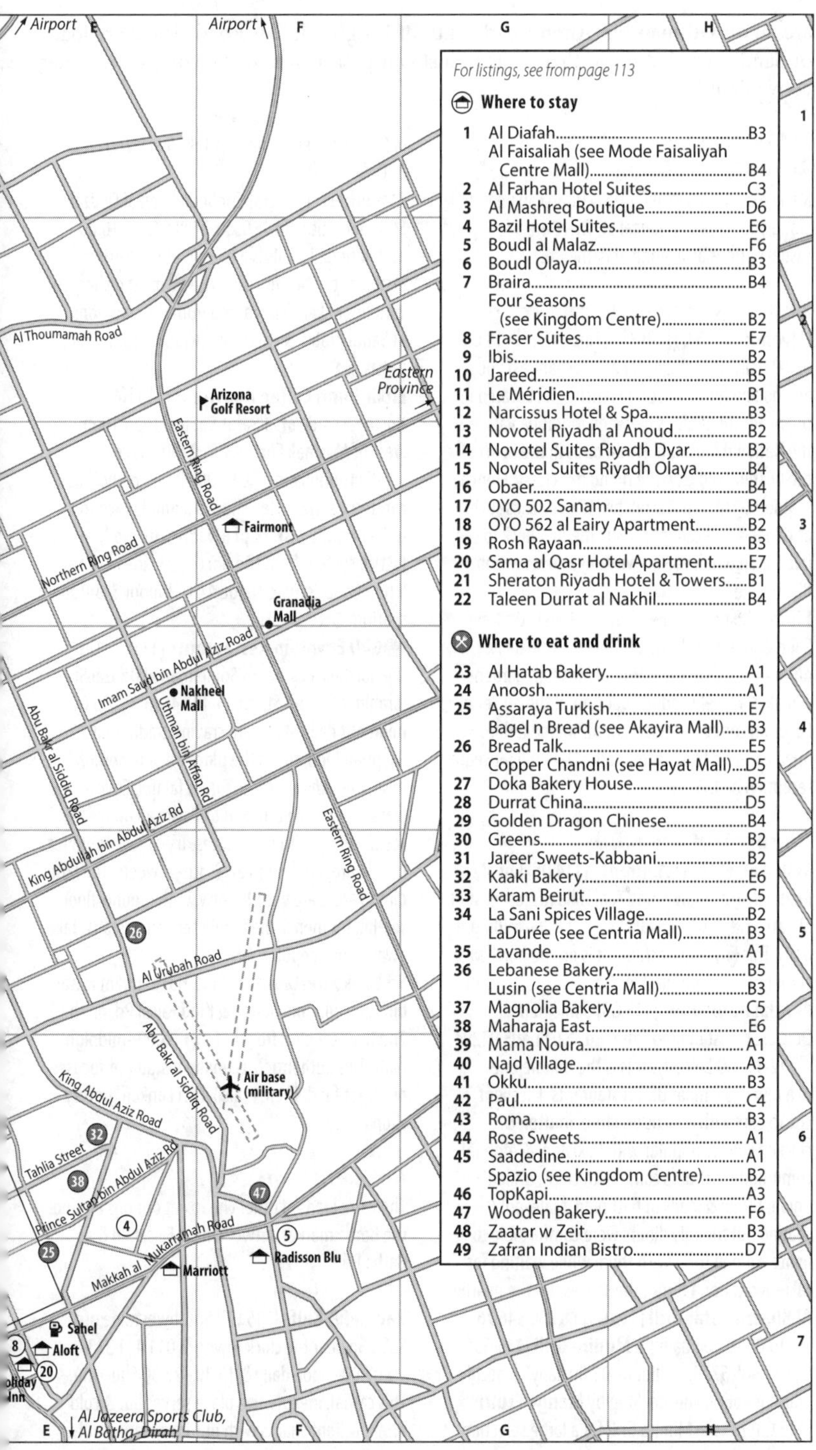

Airport
Airport
E
F
G
H
1
2
3
4
5
6
7
For listings, see from page 113
Where to stay
1 Al Diafah B3
Al Faisaliah (see Mode Faisaliyah Centre Mall) B4
2 Al Farhan Hotel Suites C3
3 Al Mashreq Boutique D6
4 Bazil Hotel Suites E6
5 Boudl al Malaz F6
6 Boudl Olaya B3
7 Braira B4
Four Seasons (see Kingdom Centre) B2
8 Fraser Suites E7
9 Ibis B2
10 Jareed B5
11 Le Méridien B1
12 Narcissus Hotel & Spa B3
13 Novotel Riyadh al Anoud B2
14 Novotel Suites Riyadh Dyar B2
15 Novotel Suites Riyadh Olaya B4
16 Obaer B4
17 OYO 502 Sanam B4
18 OYO 562 al Eairy Apartment B2
19 Rosh Rayaan B3
20 Sama al Qasr Hotel Apartment E7
21 Sheraton Riyadh Hotel & Towers B1
22 Taleen Durrat al Nakhil B4
Where to eat and drink
23 Al Hatab Bakery A1
24 Anoosh A1
25 Assaraya Turkish E7
Bagel n Bread (see Akayira Mall) B3
26 Bread Talk E5
Copper Chandni (see Hayat Mall) D5
27 Doka Bakery House B5
28 Durrat China D5
29 Golden Dragon Chinese B4
30 Greens B2
31 Jareer Sweets-Kabbani B2
32 Kaaki Bakery E6
33 Karam Beirut C5
34 La Sani Spices Village B2
LaDurée (see Centria Mall) B3
35 Lavande A1
36 Lebanese Bakery B5
Lusin (see Centria Mall) B3
37 Magnolia Bakery C5
38 Maharaja East E6
39 Mama Noura A1
40 Najd Village A3
41 Okku B3
42 Paul C4
43 Roma B3
44 Rose Sweets A1
45 Saadedine A1
Spazio (see Kingdom Centre) B2
46 TopKapi A3
47 Wooden Bakery F6
48 Zaatar w Zeit B3
49 Zafran Indian Bistro D7
Al Thoumamah Road
Arizona Golf Resort
Eastern Province
Eastern Ring Road
Fairmont
Northern Ring Road
Granadia Mall
Imam Saud bin Abdul Aziz Road
Nakheel Mall
Uthman bin Affan Rd
Abu Bakr al Siddiq Road
King Abdullah bin Abdul Aziz Rd
Eastern Ring Road
Al Urubah Road
Abu Bakr al Siddiq Road
Air base (military)
King Abdul Aziz Road
Tahlia Street
Prince Sultan bin Abdul Aziz Rd
Makkah al Mukarramah Road
Marriott
Radisson Blu
Sahel
Aloft
Al Jazeera Sports Club, Al Batha, Dirah

are all on Uthman bin Affan Road south of King Abdullah Road. There are loads of Saudi-branded drive-thru coffee kiosks in petrol station forecourts and other convenient locations.

## RESTAURANTS

### Al Batha and Dirah

Many restaurants in al Batha & Dirah can be found along Souleiman al Qouzai St. There are a few very casual options also along al Batha Rd.

#### *Above average and mid-range*

**L'Avenue** [115 G1] Off King Faisal Rd; 🕘 18.00–02.00 daily. This makes for a nice change if you are looking for an upscale French café. Located in the beautiful gardens between Murabba Palace & the National Museum, it's an oasis in the heart of the bustling old city. The menu has classic French seafood & chicken & stretches to delicacies such as caviar & a decadent sweets menu. Check to see if it's open when you are visiting as it is part of Riyadh Season. **$$$$**

**Pierre Herme Coffee Shop** [115 G1] Off King Saud & King Faisal rds; 🕘 18.00–01.00 daily. This outdoor café is in the National Museum gardens & makes a lovely end to your tour of the museum. Focus on coffee & desserts. It's a shame it doesn't open earlier. Access through the National Museum reception hall. **$$$**

#### *Cheap and cheerful*

**1000 Salamah Restaurant** [114 D5] Cnr al Madinah al Munawwarah & al Hilla rds just east of al Batha Rd; 📞 011 204 0041; 🕘 11.00–midnight daily. This Egyptian restaurant is on the northwest corner of al Taamir market. **$$**

**Al Atlal Barbeque** [115 G3] Souleiman al Qouzai St west of King Faisal Rd; 📞 011 403 0229; 🕘 12.30–00.30 daily. This is the middle one of a row of 3 similar BBQ restaurants. Excellent cheap eats with a focus on lamb, mutton & chicken kebabs popular with Pakistani & Afghani communities. Orders come with chips, grilled onion, pickle & loads of flatbread. Male-only seating but friendly diners were comfortable to invite women to sit with them while waiting for take-away. Don't forget the sauces. Try the nearby **Al Khazzan Star Grill** [115 G3] (📞 050 346 7625; 🕘 10.00–01.00 daily) & **Munira Grill** [115 G3] (📞 011 405 5778; 🕘 noon–01.00 daily) & decide which is your favourite. Stop by **Mango Fruiti** [115 G3] next to Munira Grill for a large selection of freshly squeezed juice to take away with your BBQ. **$$**

**Al Bukhari** [115 H3] Cnr Souleiman al Qouzai St & King Faisal Rd; 📞 055 637 8894; 🕘 16.00–midnight daily. This is a highly rated no-frills restaurant with a focus on rice-&-meat dishes with varieties of kabsa flavoured from the traditions of Saudi Arabia & Pakistan, including some spicy twists. **$$**

**Elixir Bunn Coffee Roasters** [115 H4] Northeast side of al Safat Sq, less than 100m west of Masmak Fortress; 📞 9200 13926; **w** elixirbunn.com; 🕘 16.00–23.00 daily. This cafeteria-style coffee shop is a good place to reflect on the history of Riyadh & its modern justice system from the northeast side of al Safat 'Chop Chop' Square (page 141). Indoor & outdoor seating. **$$**

✷ **GAD Egyptian Restaurant** [115 G3] On the northeast corner of Souleiman al Qouzai St & Ibrahim at Tasam St; 📞 011 404 4646; 🕘 06.00–midnight daily. If you are craving traditional Egyptian food, this is the place for you. *Koshari*, *mish*, *mulukhiyah*, *fatta*, *fatier*, falafel, Egyptian pizza, shawarma & mixed grills are all on the menu, along with fresh juices. Try to save room for freshly prepared umm ali & other sweets. The large dining areas are busy & noisy, with ground-floor seating for men & the family section upstairs. Take-away is also popular. **$$**

**Sri Lanka Restaurant** [115 H3] al Imam Faisal bin Turki bin Abdallah St & King Faisal Rd, on the 2nd floor set back from KFC; 🕘 08.00–midnight daily. This authentic Sri Lankan restaurant focuses on street food. There is also a Sri Lankan grocery shop on site. **$$**

#### *Rock bottom*

There are loads of other cheap eat options around the Batha market between King Faisal Rd & al Batha Rd.

**Raghief & Kaif** [115 H4] Southwest side of al Safat Sq near the clock tower; 📞 011 411 3337; 🕘 07.00–noon daily & 15.30–22.30 Sun–Thu. This casual, inexpensive place serves hot & cold drinks & light snacks with outdoor seating only.

Like other restaurants in the area, they are keen to close well in advance of prayer times. $

**Yemeni Restaurant** [115 H3] This is the name of the restaurant directly opposite al Bukhari (see opposite). This is a great place to try a traditional Yemeni b/fast that is also the staple diet of many Saudis. $

## Olaya Street and city centre

Many restaurants are concentrated in this area. In addition to the hotels & shopping malls, the widest variety of cuisines & prices can be found on or near Tahlia, al Takhassousi & Musa bin Nusair sts.

### *Expensive and above average*

**Karam Beirut** [120 C5] Prince Turki bin Abdul Aziz al Awwad Rd, 1.5km north of King Abdullah bin Abdul Aziz Rd; 011 459 5959; w karambeirut.com; 13.00–midnight Sun–Thu, 13.00–01.00 Fri–Sat. This is an upmarket Lebanese restaurant with a Syrian twist, with a refined environment, mixed seating & soft Levantine music in the background. The daily main course house specials are highly recommended. If you are looking for recommendations, try the *kibbe nayeh* Aleppo style. It has just the right punch with finely ground raw lamb & bulgur wheat topped with pine nuts & onion. The spicy lamb cutlets, on the bone, marinated in a hot sauce Tirbali style, served with potato, lemon, tomato & a bone mustard sauce are fantastic. $$$$$

✷ **Lusin** [120 B3] 2nd Fl, Centria Mall, cnr Olaya & Prince Mohammed bin Abdul Aziz sts; 9200 02690; w lusinrestaurant.com; 08.30–midnight Sat–Thu, 12.30–midnight Fri. This well-loved, elegant restaurant with outdoor seating for cooler months, is a favourite destination on Riyadh's increasingly sophisticated restaurant scene. The menu has a perfect blend of authentic Armenian cuisine with just enough Arabic influence to appeal to both palates. The pumpkin soup, grilled kibbe, kebabs with cherry sauce & rose ice cream wrapped in candy floss are brilliant; be sure to order the *gapama* if it is in season. Lusin follows singles/family section social rules, catering predominantly to mixed-gender groups & women. Single men & all-male groups may find more limited availability. Additional branches in Riyadh (Northern Ring Rd & Tallah bin al Mudhaffar St) & Jeddah (Teatro Mall). Booking essential. $$$$$

**Maharaja East** [121 E6] King Mohammed V St just south of Tahlia St; 011 464 1111; w maharajaeast.com; 13.00–midnight daily. If you want a truly upscale dining experience & crave Indian cuisine at its most elegant, Michelin-starred chef Vineet Bahtia will deliver all this & more. The tandoor is the focus, producing Punjabi fare with a modern spin. Starters are plentiful as are the biryanis. The melt-in-your-mouth *raan mussallam* is irresistible. Save room if you can for the *malai kulfi falooda* for a delectable dessert. Vegetarian dishes are plentiful & prepared with the same care & attention. The restaurant is spread over 3 floors & offers open, family & private dining, as well as open terraces when the weather is good. $$$$$

✷ **Okku** [120 B3] Tahlia St just west of Olaya St; 011 442 2929; w okkuriyadh.sa; 13.00–01.00 daily. This modern Japanese fusion restaurant is a place to see & be seen. The indoor décor captures an authentic upscale Japanese restaurant, & outdoor courtyard seating successfully combines Saudi-style cushioned sofas (not on the floor) & discreet tables. You might be surprised by the Japanese heated toilets in the loos, guarded by rows of Japanese warriors plus one huge samurai at the head of the corridor. The full dinner menu options can be mixed & matched & are brought out fresh when they are ready. On offer are salads, *youkoso*, gyoza, noodles & sides, maki sushi & much more. Beef eaters will find many wagyu options attractive. Don't miss the crispy crab gyoza. Desserts are inspired by Japan but are clearly designed for the Saudi palate. There is also a set-price Tezukuri lunch menu. Cocktails are a creative marvel. Indulge in the Kana Chi, a blend of lychee puree, yuzu, cardamom, thyme, rosemary, lime, sugar syrup, ginger & non-alcoholic beer. This Japanese-Saudi fusion shouldn't work, but it does. Impeccable service. Valet parking. Mixed seating. $$$$$

**Spazio** [120 A3] Kingdom Centre; 011 211 1888; w spazio77.com; 09.00–23.30 daily. If your thing is to dine at a restaurant with views from the 77th floor of the Kingdom Centre tower & an all-encompassing VIP guest book that has been signed by royalty, prime ministers & presidents, then look no further. You won't go wrong with any choice on the menu, a compilation of classic French & gourmet northern Italian cuisine. Vegetarian options are limited, but adjustments can be made if requested. The service is excellent as you would expect. $$$$$

**TopKapi** [120 A3] Tahlia St just west of King Fahd Rd; ☎ 011 288 5457; w topkapirest.com; ⏲ 06.30–01.30 daily. Whether you are craving a Turkish b/fast, lunch or dinner, this restaurant won't disappoint with its fresh ingredients & attentive service. B/fasts are hearty. Don't miss the freshly made *pide* (stuffed flatbreads). Lunch & dinner choices range from hummus & salads to more substantial grills & kebabs. The house speciality is *tuzda tavuk*, from the Hatay region of Turkey along the eastern Mediterranean coast. A whole chicken is stuffed with rice & spices, then coated with salt & slow-baked in a wood oven until a hard crust is formed, then ceremoniously cracked with a hammer at the table to open. Enjoy the performance & the delicious result. $$$$

### Mid-range

**Copper Chandni** [120 D5] Hayat Mall; ☎ 011 416 7000; w copperchandni.com; ⏲ 12.30–00.30 daily. Currently found in the southwest corner on the upper floor of the Hayat Mall, this Indian restaurant has been in Riyadh in various locations for a long time. Although the décor is showing its age, the menu continues to deliver even if it's not overly adventurous. There are good selections of salads, tandoori grills & kebabs. It is vegetarian friendly with a few vegan options. Open mixed seating in front of the entrance & private curtained family booths inside. $$$

**Durrat China** [121 D5] King Abdullah Branch Rd opposite Sahara Mall; ☎ 011 470 3799; w durratchina.com.sa/en; ⏲ 13.00–01.00 daily. More upscale than many comparable Chinese restaurants in Riyadh with a more robust menu that fuses Chinese food & Arabic tastes. A focus on fresh ingredients is reflected in their higher prices. In addition to 2 properties in Riyadh, several branches are found throughout Jeddah & most points south. $$$

✷ **Najd Village** [120 A3] al Takhassousi St just south of Musa bin Nusair St; ☎ 9200 33511; w najdvillage.com; ⏲ 11.00–midnight Sat–Thu, 12.15–midnight Fri. This is the place to come for an authentic Saudi dining experience. As soon as you step through the front door, you will be greeted with a visual treasure trove of great artefacts & a traditional Najd atmosphere. Kabsa, the Saudi national dish, is the highlight & best to share with a group, but don't miss other Saudi specialities. Order the Village Sofra if you can't make up your mind. *Henainee* may not be the most visually attractive dessert, but this date-bread-&-butter concoction is a Saudi favourite, so save room. You will be sitting on the floor surrounded by cushions & eating from communal dishes set on the tablecloth placed in the centre. There are three Najd Village locations, all of which now accept mixed groups, families & singles. Try to go to the Olaya branch if you are unable to visit anywhere else in the Najd region. Other branches are in al Waha near Prince Sultan University & King Abdul Aziz Rd north of KAFD. $$$

**Roma** [120 B4] Musa bin Nusair St opposite al Akayira Mall 2; ☎ 011 464 1133; ⏲ 12.30–23.30 daily. This is a good mid-range Italian restaurant in the crowded area around the Akayira Mall. Note that the entrance is around the back from Musa bin Nusair St. Walk through to Shubah bin al Hajjaj St. The menu is robust & incorporates some Saudi tastes such as the basket of assorted Arabic bread with green & Italian black olive spread. Linguini with prawns & asparagus in a pink sauce with chopped tomatoes is tasty. Attentive service at the right price. Saudi champagne in the absence of a good Italian white will have to do. $$$

**Zafran Indian Bistro** [120 D7] Makkah al Mukarramah Rd & umm al Haram al Sharqi, Turki Sq; ☎ 050 339 9181; w zafranrestaurants.com; ⏲ 12.30–midnight Sun–Wed, 12.30–01.00 Thu–Sat. Expect good-quality Indian food at this well-established restaurant on the ground floor of Turki Sq. Try some of their signature dishes. The *papdi chaat* (flour pastries & spiced mashed potatoes, topped with pomegranate, sweet yoghurt, tamarind & mint chutney), *dum ka murgh* (boneless chicken cooked in yoghurt, cashew nut, almond & coconut gravy, flavoured with fresh mint) & the *ajwaini* (carom seed) prawns were delicious. Vegetarians will be spoilt for choice. They also do very good juices. Try the *jal jeera* soda if it's available. It's a delectable concoction of mint, cumin, jal jeera masala, lemon & soda. The service is acceptable but not outstanding. Limited street parking. There are 2 other branches on the Northern Ring Rd. The Rubeen Plaza location is great for people-watching from the outdoor terrace. $$$

### *Cheap and cheerful*

If you aren't sure what you want to eat or how much you want to spend, take a stroll along Tahlia St for several blocks around either side of Olaya St in particular. Something is bound to catch your eye.

**Assaraya Turkish Restaurant** [121 E7] Prince Sultan bin Abdul Aziz Rd west of al Hurrah; ☎011 463 6000; ⏲ 10.30–02.00 Sat–Thu, 12.30–02.00 Fri. The usual starters of hummus, *baba ganouj*, tabbouleh & soups are all recommended, with good meat kebabs & grills to follow, served with Turkish breads. Don't miss the classic dolma, Iskander shawarma & meat cubes & cheese in a clay pot for a different spin. Finish with proper Turkish tea & coffee. **$$**

**Golden Dragon Chinese** [120 B4] Olaya St just north of Makka al Mukarramah Rd; ☎011 464 5136; ⏲ noon–01.00 daily. This generic Chinese restaurant is in the Al Mousa office & retail complex. Keep following the signs to the lifts & you will see the restaurant on the second floor. There's nothing special about this restaurant but it's decent value for money, hits the spot if your party wants a variety of pan-Chinese dishes, & gives a break from Middle East food. The menu includes soups, spring rolls & usual starters, chicken/prawns/beef/fish options, noodles & rice, but few vegetarian options. The service is decent. Family & singles sections are sort of adhered to. Do not mistake this for the Golden Palace just off Olaya St near Roma. **$$**

**Greens Restaurant** [120 B2] Olaya St in 3rd Akayira Mall; ☎050 110 0179; **w** withkoji.com/@greens; ⏲ 07.30–16.00 Sun–Thu. The robust b/fast menu will start your day off well. Lunch options include soups, sandwiches & wraps, salads in a jar, & a 'build-your-own bowl' of clean, healthy ingredients with fresh juices & hot drinks. There are plenty of options on the menu for vegetarians & vegans. **$$**

**La Sani Spices Village** [120 B2] Cnr Wadi al Awsat St & St 76; ☎011 465 5666; ⏲ 24hrs daily. Next to the Dr Sulaiman al Habib Olaya Medical Complex, this is a casual Pakistani restaurant with classic soups, kebabs, samosas & pakoras. Try one of the chicken *handi* specialities. **$$**

✷ **Mama Noura** [120 A1] King Abdullah bin Abdul Aziz Rd east of al Takhassousi St; ☎011 470 8882; **w** linktr.ee/mamanoura; ⏲ 06.00–02.00 Sat–Thu, 06.00–10.00 & noon–02.00 Fri. More of a canteen than a restaurant, this no-frills establishment is popular with Saudis & Arab expats alike. It should be as the food is outstanding. Freshly made shawarma sandwiches & plates are served along with more substantial grills. Meat pastries, along the lines of British meat pies, add to the choice. Go with a group & share if you can. A long list of freshly squeezed juices is also on offer & prepared at a separate station in front of you. The Lebanese sweets station will tempt even the strongest-willed. Go to the order station, take a number & pay, then collect your food at separate stations when you present your number. This is Arabic fast food at its best. Although Mama Noura attracts lots of single men, women & mixed groups are welcome. Large take-away business. There are many other branches throughout Riyadh. **$$**

**Zaatar w Zeit** [120 D3] Tahlia St west of King Mohammed V St; ☎011 810 8377; **w** zaatarwzeit.net/KSA/home; ⏲ 06.00–01.30 daily. This casual Lebanese café is popular in Riyadh & throughout the Middle East. Most branches have communal dining areas, separate tables & curtained booths so everyone is comfortable. Their motto is 'Eat fresh' so dishes are made to order. You won't go wrong with the classic half-&-half manakish with za'atar & cheese. Multiple branches throughout Riyadh. **$$**

## Diplomatic Quarter

Visitors near the DQ will find most restaurants in Oud Sq & al Fazari Sq, as well as in the hotels.

### *Above average*

**Café Bateel** [127 C7] Oud Sq; ☎800 111 0222; **w** bateel.com/en/cafe; ⏲ 07.00–midnight Sun–Wed, 07.00–01.00 Thu–Sat. This branch of the popular café attracts Saudis & expats alike. The international menu has a wide range of starters, salads & main courses. It's also a great place to linger over a trendy coffee. **$$$$**

**Monopoly** [127 C7] Oud Sq; ☎011 810 2324; 📷; ⏲ 17.00–midnight daily. This generic Italian-style restaurant has salads, pasta dishes, pizza & desserts. The food is good but showy. Foodies may be happier with La Rustica in nearby al Fazari Plaza. The outdoor seating has separate smoking & non-smoking areas. You are paying for the atmosphere, to see & be seen. **$$$$**

**Scalini** [127 C6] al Fazari Courtyard; ☎ 011 481 0569; w scalini-riyadh.com; 🕘 noon–23.30 Sat–Thu, 13.30–23.30 Fri. This Italian restaurant was one of the first restaurants to open in the DQ & has maintained its tradition of mostly Neapolitan dishes. The main-course pasta dishes are delicious, but meat eaters & fish lovers are also spoilt for choice. They also do good hot & cold antipasti & salads for those with a smaller appetite. They have also kept up with the times by adding a sushi menu, albeit not Italian; sushi is in such demand in Riyadh. $$$$

### *Mid-range*

**La Rustica** [127 C6] al Fazari Courtyard; ☎ 055 445 8813; w larustica.sa; 🕘 16.00–23.30 daily. This is a great option if you prefer somewhere more budget-friendly than Scalini next door, with a focus on pizza. $$$

**Leila min Lebnan** [127 C7] Oud Sq; ☎ 9200 29039; w pocketres.com/leilaruh; 🕘 07.20–midnight daily. This Lebanese restaurant is good but not outstanding as it once was, although the service remains very good. Inside & outside dining; the latter still allows smoking. Indulge in the mixed grill & Leila Osmalliyeh, an irresistible rosewater halwa & pistachio ice cream covered in toasted vermicelli with dollops of whipped cream. There is another branch in Jeddah that is worth a visit as well. $$$

### *Cheap and cheerful*

Fast food in the DQ is present in the form of Starbucks, Dunkin Donuts, Kudu, Subway & a couple of juice bars.

**Chunk** [127 C7] Oud Sq; ☎ 055 220 2042; 📷; 🕘 18.00–midnight daily. If you like sweet pastries, it will be difficult to walk past Chunk without salivating. This is a very popular place to people-watch while sipping a hot beverage. $$

**Urth Caffé** [127 C7] Oud Sq; ☎ 9200 07498; w urthcaffe.sa; 🕘 17.00–01.00 daily. From crushed avocado on toast to bubble tea to b/fast burritos, this café ticks many boxes for organic produce & sustainability, as well as fabulous trendiness. Eggs also feature heavily on the menu. If you don't fancy an all-day b/fast, then the cake menu may be the answer. Other spots at Riyadh Park, Northern Ring Rd, Riyadh Front Airport Rd & Prince Mohammed bin Abdul Aziz Rd. $$

## Old Diriyah

Until very recently, little was available near al Turaif district other than a few farmers' street stalls. Now, with the development of Bujairi Terrace, dining options for visitors, from simple cafés to branches of Michelin-starred restaurants, offer cuisine from all over the world, as well as Saudi & regional dishes. The vibe here is chic & blends in with its historical surroundings overlooking al Turaif. It has become a trendy destination for Saudis, expatriates & tourists alike.

Those who venture into the modern village of ad Diriyah will find several Saudi fast-food restaurants & a few inexpensive cafés that offer mostly take-aways.

**Long Chim** [127 C2] ☎ 9200 33795; 🕘 17.00–midnight daily. For something different that is scarce on the ground in the Kingdom, try this excellent Thai restaurant. $$$$$

**Maiz Restaurant** [127 C2] w maiz.sa; ☎ 9200 15513; 🕘 noon–01.00 daily. For connoisseurs of very high-end Saudi dining. $$$$$

**Somewhere Bujairi** [127 C2] ☎ 9200 24788; 🕘 13.00–23.45 Sun–Wed, 13.00–00.15 Thu & Sat, 14.00–00.15 Fri. See Somewhere in al Ula (page 218) for a teaser of what will be on offer in this very trendy restaurant. $$$$$

**Takya** ☎ 055 040 2000; w takya.sa; 🕘 17.00–02.00 Sun–Wed, 14.00–02.00 Thu–Sat. Another recommended high-end dining option. $$$$$

**Villa Mamas** [127 C2] ☎ 011 520 1105; w villamamas.sa; 🕘 noon–midnight Mon–Thu, 17.00–01.00 Fri–Sun. An excellent Saudi restaurant run by regionally renowned owner & chef Roaya Saleh, who uses only local, seasonal, organic ingredients. $$$$$

**Brunch & Cake al Bujairi** [127 C2] ☎ 059 265 7843; w sevenrooms.com; 🕘 09.00–23.45 Sat–Wed, 09.00-00.45 Thu–Fri. Casual diners should head directly here to sample delectable all-day b/fasts, as well as lunch & dinner offerings of sandwiches, salads & posh pizzas. Their juice-based mocktails & coffee menu are appealing, as is anything with pistachios. $$$

## SWEET SHOPS AND SNACK SHOPS

For those with a sweet tooth who want a satisfying snack, check out **Anoosh** [120 A1], **Doka Bakery House** [120 B5], **LaDurée** [120 B3], **Lavande** [120 A1], **Rose Sweets** [120 A1] & the famous &

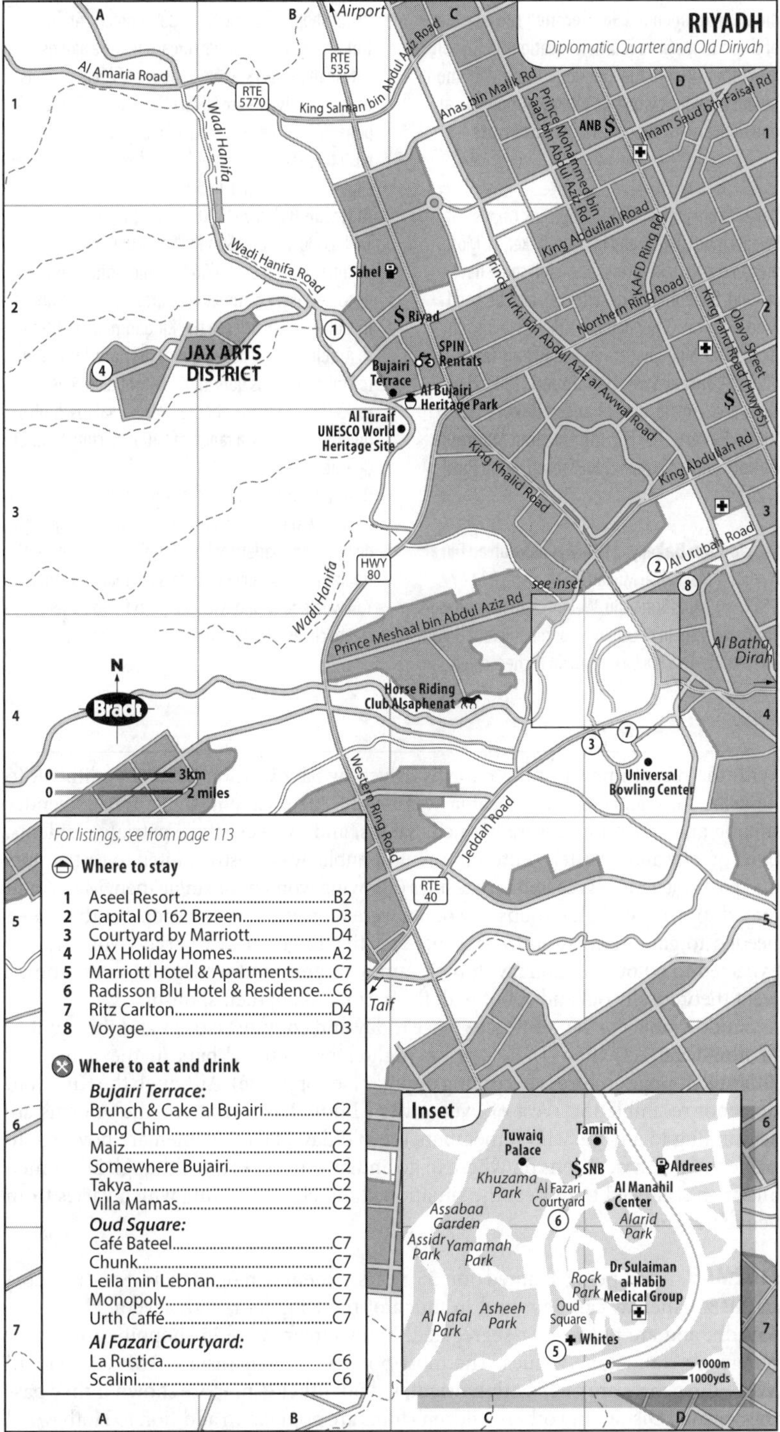
RIYADH
Diplomatic Quarter and Old Diriyah
Airport
RTE 535
RTE 5770
Al Amaria Road
King Salman bin Abdul Aziz Road
Anas bin Malik Rd
Prince Mohammed bin Saad bin Abdul Aziz Rd
Imam Saud bin Faisal Rd
ANB
Wadi Hanifa
Wadi Hanifa Road
King Abdullah Road
KAFD Ring Rd
Northern Ring Road
King Fahd Road (Hwy65)
Olaya Street
Sahel
Riyad
SPIN Rentals
Bujairi Terrace
Al Bujairi Heritage Park
Al Turaif UNESCO World Heritage Site
JAX ARTS DISTRICT
Prince Turki bin Abdul Aziz al Awwal Road
King Khalid Road
King Abdullah Rd
Al Urubah Road
HWY 80
see inset
Prince Meshaal bin Abdul Aziz Rd
Al Batha, Dirah
Horse Riding Club Alsaphenat
Universal Bowling Center
Western Ring Road
Jeddah Road
RTE 40
Taif
0 3km
0 2 miles
For listings, see from page 113
Where to stay
1 Aseel Resort B2
2 Capital O 162 Brzeen D3
3 Courtyard by Marriott D4
4 JAX Holiday Homes A2
5 Marriott Hotel & Apartments C7
6 Radisson Blu Hotel & Residence C6
7 Ritz Carlton D4
8 Voyage D3
Where to eat and drink
Bujairi Terrace:
Brunch & Cake al Bujairi C2
Long Chim C2
Maiz C2
Somewhere Bujairi C2
Takya C2
Villa Mamas C2
Oud Square:
Café Bateel C7
Chunk C7
Leila min Lebnan C7
Monopoly C7
Urth Caffé C7
Al Fazari Courtyard:
La Rustica C6
Scalini C6
Inset
Tuwaiq Palace
Tamimi
SNB
Aldrees
Khuzama Park
Al Fazari Courtyard
Al Manahil Center
Assabaa Garden
Alarid Park
Assidr Park
Yamamah Park
Rock Park
Dr Sulaiman al Habib Medical Group
Al Nafal Park
Asheeh Park
Oud Square
Whites
0 1000m
0 1000yds

highly recommended **Saadedine** [120 A1]. Many of these shops have multiple locations in Riyadh & in other cities in the Kingdom. Those with more savoury cravings won't go wrong stopping in at one of the many branches of **al Rifai nuts**.

### BAKERIES

Bakeries are popular in Riyadh. Think cake & sweets more than bread in many bakeries. Most are geared for take-aways although some have seating. Supermarket bakeries can also be good & economical. Other popular bakeries in Riyadh include the Singaporean-owned **Bread Talk** [121 E5], **Jareer Sweets-Kabbani** [120 B2] for cakes & chocolate, the **Lebanese Bakery** [120 B5], **Kaaki Bakery** [121 E6], the American **Magnolia Bakery** [120 C5] chain & the French group **Paul** [120 C4].

✷ **Wooden Bakery** [121 F6] Cnr Salah ad Din al Ayyubi & Makkah al Mukarramah rds; 011 472 5559; 24hrs Sun–Thu. Weight-watchers beware. This bakery chain of Lebanese origin is like al Hatab on steroids. This is a bakery, meat & cheese deli, sweet shop, patisserie & specialist grocer. Arabic, Turkish, French & German breads feature alongside a fresh manakish station. Varieties of Arabic sweets, crackers & biscuits are all on offer. The well-stocked patisserie would not be out of place in France. We wish there were branches beyond Riyadh. It is rather expensive, but worth it. $$$

**Al Hatab Bakery** [120 A1] Southwest cnr al Takhassousi St & al Suhail; 059 960 6383; w alhatab.com.sa; 06.00–midnight. This is an upscale bakery & more, with branches throughout Riyadh & other cities in the Kingdom. In addition to Arabic & other baked goods, from Turkish *simit* to croissants, this gourmet's delight also sells rusks (bread sticks), cheeses, olives, salads, high-quality oils, jams, a range of Saudi biscuits & other delicacies. $$

**Bagel n Bread** [120 B3] Musa bin Nusair St in Akayira 2 Mall; 059 638 0165; 06.00–midnight daily. A good variety of bagel choices complete with traditional & creative schmears are made to order. You won't go wrong with the everything bagel with cream cheese. Budget-friendly & delicious. $

## ENTERTAINMENT AND NIGHTLIFE

With the recent impact of the reforms driven by Saudi Vision 2030, it is difficult to describe how austere Saudi Arabia was before 2016. Cinemas, live music, gender mixing and much more were banned. Saudis, and by necessity expatriate residents, lived quietly and privately. Entertainment in public was mostly limited to restaurants and parks, strictly segregated for families (allowing women) or single men. Men could attend sporting events. Groups of women were mostly allowed to shop. Saudi women needed to gain permission from a male relative to go out. Expatriate women were expected to go out in public with their family or groups of women; businesswomen went theoretically out and about with the permission of their sponsor.

Saudi Arabia is a very different place today and continues to expand the number of now-legal activities. There are no nightclubs, pubs or bars in the Kingdom, although lounge culture is becoming popular (see opposite). Although the Kingdom does not resemble the West or even other Middle East countries, the reforms are astounding to anyone who remembers the 'old days'. Saudi women are now free to make their own decisions on where to go and how to get there, although all women and men still need to respect the situation about gender mixing which varies from venue to venue.

**CINEMAS** After being banned for 35 years, cinemas reopened in Saudi Arabia in 2018. Cinemas can be found in much of the Kingdom, with several choices in Riyadh, and are not gender segregated. Many cinemas are in shopping malls, but others are standalone venues. The most popular film chains are AMC, Muvi and Vox. Film genres are often action orientated but other genres are shown if they pass the censors. Disney and other children's films are popular. In addition to Hollywood products, films from the Arab world and especially Bollywood and other Indian film industries are very popular.

**LIVE MUSIC** Live music was banned throughout the Kingdom until 2017, when the classic Arab singers Rashed al Majed and Mohammed Abdu performed live to an all-male audience at the King Fahd Cultural Center. Since then, live music has become commonplace and inclusive.

Riyadh Season ran a series of live music events in late 2021 in Banban on the northern outskirts of Riyadh. Global performers at the MDLBEAST Soundstorm music festival included David Guetta, highlighting the monumental social changes that had occurred in just a few years. The female DJ Lujain Bishi, who uses the stage name Biirdperson, grew up in Jeddah and was also on the programme along with many other artists. Men and women were in attendance and were not gender segregated. Back in Riyadh, Lebanon-born Nancy Ajram and other singers from the Arab world performed at Riyadh Boulevard in the trendy Hittin neighbourhood. Folk, classical and popular music can also now be found in multiple venues in Riyadh and beyond.

**LOUNGES** Lounge culture is a relatively new concept in Saudi Arabia and it has come to Riyadh. Whether you are interested in socialising with your friends at a shisha spot or trying your hand at karaoke Saudi-style, you now have some options. There are also open-mike comedy nights to enjoy if your understanding of Arabic is impeccable. Trends and venues change quickly so have a look at Time Out Riyadh (**w** timeoutriyadh.com) and WhatsOn Saudi Arabia (**w** whatsonsaudiarabia.com) to see what's happening on a weekly basis. We're following Time Out Riyadh's guidance and suggest you check out Draft Café, MW Café, Rabbit Hole and Syrup Lounge as notable venues.

**ART** Similar to lounge culture, the art world is now burgeoning in Riyadh. Social rules are relaxing enough that many artists are now more comfortable expressing their creativity, which might have only been possible in Jeddah just a few years ago. But there are still limits as Islamic values must still be adhered to.

The JAX Arts District sits amid an industrial area in Diriyah and has a number of artists' studios. It is being heavily promoted and is a good place to see what's happening with young Saudis if you ask around. The Diriyah Contemporary Art Biennale art exhibition is the first of its kind in Riyadh and was first held in the winter of 2021/22, giving local Saudi and other artists a chance to show their contemporary art. Al Mashtal is another well-supported artist area in the DQ. It hosted Noor Riyadh, its first art light festival, in the spring of 2021 with artists from more than 20 countries. Along with tours of the exhibits, Noor Riyadh also supported several lectures and workshops.

Back in central Riyadh, pop in to one of the growing number of art galleries dotted around the Olaya Street area. Check out **Naila Art Gallery** [120 A3] (al Takhassousi St, Bldg 247, #2, just north of Said bin Khalid St; ☎ 011 880 5352; **w** gallerynaila.com; ⏲ 10.00–22.00 Sun–Thu, 14.00–22.00 Sat) to get a feel for this, a new chance to experience more openness in the Kingdom. They exhibit a range of artists and have a shop where pieces can be purchased.

## SHOPPING

**Shopping malls** can be found throughout Riyadh and are concentrated near Olaya Street and the Northern and Eastern ring roads. Shopping is a popular pastime, and malls a destination in their own right, especially in the summer months to escape the heat. Children's play areas are a main feature of even the most modest shopping centres, and most medium and larger malls have supermarkets, food courts and restaurants in addition to conventional retail shops.

Malls are now usually open throughout the day and well into the late evening, and don't close during prayer times, though they remain shut on Fridays until after Friday prayers. Even though most shopping malls have parking, it is often crowded, especially in the evenings and at weekends. Most car parks get full very quickly once the sun goes down, but it's the best time to visit if you want to witness a slice of everyday Saudi life. Valet parking is available in some locations, but this service adds to the traffic congestion. Although some malls publish telephone numbers and websites, it is better to access most information through social media.

There are other popular shopping destinations that are not always in a shopping mall but have presence in several areas in Riyadh and throughout Saudi Arabia. **Centrepoint** is a clothing chain popular throughout the Middle East, originating in Kuwait. **Extra** is a Saudi electronic goods chain. Saudi Arabia's **Jarir** (**w** jarir.com/sa-en) is a bookstore and so much more. All have multiple branches throughout Riyadh.

There are modern **supermarkets** in every neighbourhood in Riyadh, the most popular being Carrefour, Danube, Lulu, Nesto, Othaim, Panda and HyperPanda and Tamimi. Most of the larger ones sell household goods, small electronics and basic clothing in addition to food. Usually, there are also separate counters for meat, fish, sweets, bakery goods, nuts, spices and specialist deli items. Many supermarkets now also have a hot-food counter with a wide choice of take-away items. There are also a number of convenience shops that are more like a small Co-op or large 7Eleven. MEED and Mini Stop are found throughout Riyadh, and Sahel Marts are found in some petrol stations of the same name. Other convenience shops can be found at other petrol station forecourts.

With shopping malls vastly more popular because of their convenience and variety of products and services, **traditional souqs** are quickly becoming a thing of the past, and are now mostly patronised by people shopping on a minimal budget. As a result, most souqs offer very low-cost products, often made of plastic and imported from China. It is fair to acknowledge, however, that a few souqs specialising in gold or antiques do attract other shoppers, including tourists. Traditional souqs are mostly found in al Batha and Dirah, although there are still-thriving souqs near Riyadh Gallery Mall. Remember that most souqs are only open for about 2 hours in the morning, with most shops closing in the afternoon, but come alive once the sun sets. Do not take any published hours literally. Check prayer times as most shops in the souqs close for about 30 minutes for each one.

There are few shopping options in the DQ and Old Diriyah. Most people who work or live in the DQ go into central Riyadh to shop for anything other than the basic necessities. We expect there will be many shopping options in and around Old Diriyah once refurbishment and developments near completion.

## SHOPPING MALLS

### Al Batha and Dirah

**Taj Centre** [115 H3] Between King Faisal and al Batha rds, with multiple entrances from both streets. Less of a modern shopping mall than a cluster of shops within a nondescript building, the Taj Centre is more of an example of early retail modernisation beyond the souqs. Following tradition, shops orientated to women are mostly on the top floor.

### Olaya Street and city centre

These are listed broadly from south to north on or near Olaya St between Makkah al Mukarramah Rd & the Northern Ring Rd.

**Mode Faisaliyah Centre Mall** [120 B4] Faisaliyah Centre, Olaya St; 011 273 4003; 09.30–23.30 Sat–Thu, 16.00–23.30 Fri. Come here to see what all the hype is about Riyadh's luxury shopping scene. Commonly known as the Faisaliyah Centre, this property was completely refurbished in the early 2020s.

**Panorama Mall** [120 A3] Tahlia & al Takhassousi sts; 9200 09467; w panorama-mall.com; 09.00–01.00 Sat–Thu, 14.00–01.00 Fri. This mall is high end, well established & popular. It has a good selection of shops & restaurants, a Danube supermarket, a cinema & a children's play complex.

**Centria Mall** [120 B3] Olaya & Tahlia sts; 011 216 1111; w centria.com.sa; 10.00–23.00 Sat–Thu, 16.30–23.00 Fri. This is a very high-end mall with a focus on European designer shops & some of the best restaurants in Riyadh.

**Akayira Mall** [120 B3] Olaya & Musa bin Nusair sts; 09.00–22.00 daily. This is an older complex of 3 separate buildings (numbered 1, 2 & 3) which represents early mall shopping in Riyadh from the late 1990s. It's a bit dated, but it's a great way to experience how shopping options have evolved in a short period of time.

**Kingdom Centre** [120 B2] King Fahd Rd; 011 211 2222; w kingdomcentre.com.sa; 09.30–22.30 Sat–Thu, 15.30–22.30 Fri. This mall has a very similar vibe to Faisaliyah Centre with a wide selection of lovely smellies & accessories for silly money. In the past, its women-only top floor appealed to Saudi women looking for a more relaxed shopping experience. It has now become redundant & is now accessible to everyone.

**Olaya Mall** [120 B2] Olaya St; 011 419 2219; 08.00–noon Sat–Thu & 16.30–23.00 daily. Good for women's dressy clothing. Note the traditional split-day opening hours.

**Abaya Mall** [120 B2] Olaya St between sts 98 & 100; 053 491 2222; w abayamall.sa; 09.30–23.00 Sun–Fri, 10.00–midnight Sat. This is the place to come for abaya shops without going to al Batha. It's like a souq in a mall, with an overwhelming amount of choice.

**Andalus Mall** [120 B1] Adjacent to the Abaya Mall; 011 419 2311; 09.30–11.55 Sat–Thu & 16.00–23.55 daily. This mall mostly has women's shoe shops.

**Royal Mall** [120 A1] King Fahd & Ahmad al Ghafi sts; 011 229 7222; w royalmallsa.com; 09.00–midnight Sat–Thu, 12.30–midnight Fri. This mall has even more abayas & more than 50 gold shops.

**Sahara Mall** [120 D5] King Abdul Aziz Rd, north of King Abdullah Branch Rd; 011 452 0400; w saharamall.com.sa; 09.00–midnight Sat–Thu, 13.00–midnight Fri. Shops in this mall are a mix of practical high-street & mid-range brands. Sahara Mall is also an entertainment destination.

**Hayat Mall** [120 D5] Adjacent to Sahara Mall on King Abdul Aziz Rd, north of King Abdullah Branch Rd; 011 205 7401; w hayat-mall.com; 10.00–01.30 daily. Hayat Mall is a favourite with a balanced mix of shops, a good branch of Jarir bookstore & a Danube supermarket.

**Al Haram Center** [120 D5] Olaya & Sanqit sts; 9200 33093; w alharamstores.com; 08.00–midnight Sat–Thu, 14.00–midnight Fri. Stocks inexpensive clothing akin to a Primark or TK Maxx & is especially popular for children's items. Parking is a nightmare.

**Riyadh Gallery Mall** [120 D5] Olaya St & al Imam Saud bin Abdul Aziz Branch Rd; 011 207 8111; 09.00–midnight Sat–Thu, 12.30–midnight Fri. This is big but manageable, with a HyperPanda supermarket & many British high-street & American mid-range brands & a good food court. The smaller Marina Mall is opposite.

**Riyadh Park Mall** [120 C4] Northern Ring Rd, west of al Takhassousi St; 9200 09467; w riyadh-park.com; 10.00–23.00 Sat–Thu, 14.00–23.00 Fri. This is a destination mall to see & be seen in, in the trendy Hittin neighbourhood. The food scene is excellent.

**Tala Mall** [120 D4] Northeast cnr Northern Ring & King Abdul Aziz Branch rds; 9200 00262; 09.30–23.00 Sat–Thu, 13.30–23.00 Fri. This is a smallish mall with a Carrefour & is convenient if you are in the Financial District.

## Near the Eastern Ring Road

**Granadia Mall** [121 F3] Eastern Ring Rd at Imam Abdullah bin Saud bin Abdul Aziz Rd; 9200 35336; w granadia.sa; 10.00–midnight Sat–Wed, 10.00–01.00 Thu, 13.00–02.00 Fri. Popular with Western expatriates, this is just the right size with a variety of practical, good-quality shops, as well as a popular Carrefour supermarket.

**Nakheel Mall** [121 E4] Imam Saud bin Abdul Aziz Branch Rd west of Eastern Ring Rd; 9200 00262; 09.30–23.00 Sat–Thu, 14.00–23.00 Fri.

This upscale mall has the usual clothing shops, a number of coffee shops & a MUVI cinema.

## SOUQS

For gold souqs, see right.

### Al Batha and Dirah

Shops along & near the al Batha Rd from Masmak Fortress north are also good for men's tailoring & places to buy male national dress. You will find a combination of traditional storefront shops, early shopping centres & shops in the souqs. Other souqs heading north from the Masmak Fortress/Taj centre landmarks are the Batha Market Dahab [114 D4], Hilla Gold Market [114 D4] & Filipino Market [115 H1]. Expect mostly to pay cash.

**Sweigah Trading Market** [115 H4] al Imam Turki bin Abdullah bin Mohammed St, just north of Masmak Fortress. This is the place for abayas & other traditional women's garments. There are quite a few children's clothing shops as well.

### Olaya Street and city centre

**Kuwaiti Souq** [120 D5] Between Olaya St & King Fahd Rd opposite the Al Haram Center. Although souqs in general are fading away in popularity in this area of Riyadh, the Kuwaiti Souq (the informal name for Taibah & Uwais Markets) is still thriving. Conveniently located & near the Riyadh Gallery Mall. Bargain hunters often mix a shopping trip between the modern & traditional. Saudis & expats alike come here mostly to buy household goods, traditional clothing & gold. It's a good place to look for souvenirs. The Kuwaiti Souq is very quiet in the morning & closes during the afternoon. Go at night.

## SOUVENIRS

Souvenirs are surprisingly difficult to find, even in Riyadh, although when you consider there was no tourist market until 2019, it makes sense. See page 90 for ideas about what you might want to look for to bring home. Start by having a wander around in the Kuwaiti Souq (see above) as you never know what you may spot.

### Crafts, clothing and homewares

There are 2 well-established souqs on the south side of al Thumairi Abdul Wahid Charafeddine St nearly opposite the Masmak Fortress. Some shops in **Souq al Zel** [114 D5] sell interesting antiques & replicas, so it is probably worth a visit if you like to wander around & try your luck. If you are exploring **Thumairi Souq** [115 H4], pop into **Anas Handicrafts**. This souq also has a collection of gold & jewellery shops.

✷ **Kingdom Heritage** [115 H4] al Thumairi Abdul Wahid Charafeddine St; ☎ 055 116 1722; e info@traditionalksa.com; ⏲ 09.00–noon & 16.00–22.00 Sat–Thu, 16.00–22.00 Fri. Located east of the main entrance to Masmak Fortress, this is the place to go for high-quality, authentic Najd crafts that reflect the heart of the Kingdom's heritage. Traditional jewellery, metalwork, incense burners, ceiling light fixtures & beautiful decorative woodwork items are for sale, from boxes to furniture statement pieces. Look for the 2 large camels at the front of the building.

**Kingdom Heritage** [120 C5] Imam Saud bin Abdul Aziz bin Mohammed Rd, west of King Fahd Rd; ☎ 053 663 3636; ⏲ by appointment only: 09.00–19.00 Sat–Thu. Located in the al Nakheel neighbourhood & tucked away in an office building, this is for serious shoppers only as the items on offer are at the highest price points, reflecting the exclusivity and quality of the artefacts. Enter Gate C of the Al Nemer Center, take the lift to floor 2, then go through the door on the right as you leave the lift.

**Lamsa Co** [120 C3] Tahlia St, west of King Fahd Rd; ☎ 011 423 0656; w lamsa.co; ⏲ 09.00–23.30 Sat–Thu, 16.00–23.00 Fri. Not to be confused with the contemporary furniture shop Lamsa House on King Fahd Rd, Lamsa Co sells traditional clothing, jewellery, homewares & some knickknacks. Note the shop's traditional painted doors & its sign in Arabic & English.

### Gold

Most gold sold in Saudi Arabia is 22 carat.

**Al Batha Gold Souq** [114 D4] West of Souq al Zel, east of al Atayif & north of as Sibalah Rd, Dirah. Riyadh's most famous place to buy gold is here in the al Batha Gold Souq (aka Dirah Souq, Riyadh Souq & sometimes simply the Gold Souq). The small roads nearest the gold souq are unnamed, but if you ask for the Development Market or the gold souq, people will point you in the right direction. Know the official published gold price in grams & the carat weight of the product & start haggling from there.

**Hilla Gold Market** [114 D4] South of abu Ayyub al Ansari Rd, just east of al Rass Rd that runs parallel to al Batha Rd. Another large gold market in Dirah.
**Thumairi Souq/Gold Market** [115 H4] Souq al Zel. This is a convenient place to check out gold jewellery styles & prices if you are visiting nearby tourist attractions, although there are larger gold markets.

### Perfume

There are a number of perfume shops, including the popular Arabian Oud & other shops clustered around al Atayif St between Imam Turki bin Abdullah bin Mohammed St & al Imam Mohammed bin Saoud bin Mouqren Rd west of Masmak Fortress.

## SPORTS AND ACTIVITIES

**BOWLING** Ten-pin bowling has been in Riyadh for decades. Bowling centres are generally orientated to families with Saudi and other women actively participating. Bowling alleys are located at independent properties as well as in several malls. Perhaps unexpectedly, it is also possible to bowl in the very upmarket Ritz Carlton and Intercontinental hotels. Popular bowling facilities that can be found throughout Riyadh include:

**Strike 10** [127 D4] Ritz Carlton hotel off Hwy 40; 011 802 8333; 16.00–midnight daily
**Universal Bowling Center** [127 D4] Southeast cnr King Saud Rd & al Foursan; 050 526 9788; 13.00–01.30 Sat–Thu, 16.00–01.30 Fri
**Yallah! Bowling** [120 C4] Riyadh Park Mall, Northern Ring Rd; 09.00–01.00 daily

**CAMEL RACING** Camel racing season is from November to March. The Janadriyah Cultural and Heritage Festival (page 145) is an excellent place to see camel racing in the context of traditional Saudi culture as this practice dates back to pre-Islamic times. See also the King Abdul Aziz Camel Festival (page 89).

**CYCLING** Only the brave would consider cycling on the streets of Riyadh given the poor quality of driving, the condition of the older roads, dangerous speed humps, ongoing roadworks, summer heat and pollution. Cyclists do ride in the DQ and Wadi Hanifa to Diriyah, though. It is possible to hire bicycles just north of the DQ at **SPIN Rentals** [127 C2] (cnr al Imam Abdullah bin Saud Rd & Hasaan bin Thabit St; 055 973 1117; 15.00–midnight daily). If you do go cycling, wear modest clothing and remember safety considerations, traffic challenges and the weather.

Cyclists might want to contact **Riyadh Wheelers** (w riyadhwheelers.com) for riding with a group and organised events outside of Riyadh. Other cycling groups are **Darrajati** (w dirajiti.com) and **Bikes For All** [120 B3] (KSA Prince Mohammed bin Saad bin Abdul Aziz Rd, south of King Salman bin Abdul Aziz Rd; w bikesforall-ksa.com; 058 365 7688; 09.00–noon & 16.00–23.00 Sat–Thu, 16.00–22.00 Fri).

**EQUESTRIAN SPORTS** Horseriding is a popular pastime throughout Saudi Arabia. There are several equestrian centres around Riyadh for members and guests. Women and men are welcome. Riders can wear their usual riding gear as the dress code is relaxed for this activity.

### Horseriding

There are more equestrian facilities roughly 5–10km east of the King Khalid Airport. **Al Eid** (059 355 5035); **Voyage** (053 414 4444) & **Alareen Equestrian Club** (055 545 5318) are along al Janadriyah Rd, Saudi Rte 550.

**Abunayyan Equestrian Centre** Part of the Dirab Golf & Country Club. See below for contact details.

**Horse Riding Club Alsaphenat** [127 C4] About 1km west of Wadi Hanifa St; ☎ 050 778 2676. In the DQ, & probably the most conveniently located for the majority of Riyadh's hotels.

### Horseracing

**King Khalid Equestrian Field** Outside Thumamah National Park. Horseracing events regularly take place here between 14.00 & 18.00 Fri–Sat from Nov to Mar.

**GOLF** Golf has long been popular among many expat communities and some Saudis. Two well-established golf courses are **Arizona Golf Resort** [121 F2] (Prince Mohammed bin Salman Rd; w agr.com.sa; ☎ 011 248 4444; ⏲ contact the resort for hours), which is off the Eastern Ring Road on the compound of the same name; and the Intercontinental Hotel's **Palms Golf Club** [114 B2] (Jabir bin Abdullah Rd; w intercontinental.com; ☎ 011 465 5000; ⏲ 09.00–23.00 Sun–Thu). Golf courses a bit further out in greater Riyadh are the **Riyadh Golf Club** (☎ 055 739 9900; w riyadhgolfcourses.com; ⏲ 05.30–21.00 daily), to the north of the city about 5km west of King Khalid Airport; and the **Dirab Golf and Country Club** (☎ 055 578 9190; w dirabgolf.com; ⏲ 05.00–19.00 daily), about a 45-minute drive south of the DQ just off Saudi Route 505.

**HEALTH CLUBS AND FITNESS CENTRES** Many mid-range and upscale hotels have fitness centres for men. Most of these hotels have now added fitness areas for women as gender segregation in health clubs and fitness centres remains in force (page 80). Saudi Arabia also has a number of members-only fitness centres. Many of these do sell a day pass to guests, so don't discount them without checking.

If you are looking for a fitness centre beyond your hotel, then here are a few that you might want to check out:

**Al Jazeera Sports Club** [121 E7] Souleiman al Qouzai Rd, west of King Fahd Rd; ☎ 053 289 0067; w sports-club-603.business.site; ⏲ 07.00–midnight Sat–Thu, 16.00–midnight Fri. Men only.

**Al Manahil Center** [127 D6] Bin Zahr St, off Dareen St south of Circle 2; ☎ 011 488 1069; w almanahil.com.sa; ⏲ 10.00–21.00 Sat–Thu, 14.00–21.00 Fri. This is a highly regarded women-only fitness centre & spa.

**Curves Club Sports for Women** [120 B2] Abdullah bin Zamah parallel to Olaya St opposite the Kingdom Centre. Women-only fitness centre.

**Panorama Mall** [120 A3] Cnr Tahlia & al Takhassousi sts; ☎ 9200 09467; w panorama-mall.com; ⏲ 09.00–01.00 Sat–Thu, 14.00–01.00 Fri. A women's fitness centre inside the mall.

**MOTORSPORTS** Formula E took place in Old Diriyah for the first time in the 2018/19 season and has become an annual event. It is known as **Diriyah ePrix**. The circuit is near the World Heritage Site of the Turaif District and takes place in the evening hours. The **Saudi International Motor Festival** (Autoville) takes place in Riyadh's Dirab Motor Park. It has been met with great fanfare among automobile enthusiasts and motorsports fans.

Both male and female motorbike enthusiasts will be pleased to know that Harley Davidson has a shop [120 D4] (Harley Davidson Riyadh; ☎ 011 455 4499; w hdriyadh.com; ⏲ 12.15–21.00 Sun–Thu, 09.15–18.00 Sat) on the Northern Ring Road slip road near the Tala Mall. Check out their website or call the shop if you are interested in joining any events.

**PARKS** In a busy city with little municipal planning, finding relative quiet in a city park is a great way to take a break. Unfortunately, many outside of the DQ can be strewn with litter.

**Al Batha and Dirah** If you are visiting the King Abdul Aziz Historical Center area, you may wish to visit the **National Museum Park** [115 G1] adjacent to the Saudi National Museum. **Al Watan Park** [115 G2] is situated opposite the museum on the south side of King Saud Road. A bit further south is the relatively peaceful **al Futah Park** [115 G2] near the Four Points Sheraton. Many people take their lunch breaks here from nearby office buildings. **King Abdullah Park** [115 F2] is further east and is the dominant park in the al Murabba neighbourhood. This large, multipurpose park is geared to family entertainment, although there are peaceful areas as well. This park is most popular at night. **Cave Park** [114 A1] contains the al Maather Cave and is another popular family park. It is situated along Makkah al Mukkaramah Road adjacent to the King Faisal Specialist Hospital.

**Olaya Street and the city centre** Don't expect to find much greenery in this part of Riyadh. Although you might come across a green square or some outdoor space around your hotel, this is the exception. **Al Dhouha Park** [120 B1] is several streets to the east of Le Méridien Hotel and is a decent option. It is also very popular with families and has facilities for small children. Make your way to one of the parks in the DQ if you want a calmer environment.

**Diplomatic Quarter and Old Diriyah** As the DQ is a planned community, you will be spoilt for choice if you are looking for a place to exercise, relax with small children or have a picnic, or are simply seeking tranquillity. All of these parks are free to enter. **Yamamah Park** [127 C7] is large, shady and very popular with children and families. **Al Nafal Park** [127 C7] is peaceful, with a covered arched promenade at the top and a beautiful view of Wadi Hanifa at the bottom. **Assabaa Garden** [127 C6] is one of several parks that blend classic architecture with green spaces. This park's lower promenade overlooks Wadi Hanifa and provides a lovely view of the Riyadh skyline in the distance. **Asheeh Park** [127 C7] has a walking and cycling track. You may also wish to explore **Rock**, **Khuzama**, **Assidr** and **Alarid parks** and some smaller gardens to find your favourite.

**RUNNING AND JOGGING** Running and jogging is not common practice on the streets of Riyadh and would raise eyebrows, especially for women. However, joggers are a common sight in the DQ, with both men and women wearing Western running gear. It is also possible to run and jog in areas outside of built-up areas such as Wadi Hanifa, but it would be better if done in more modest clothing. Runners might want to connect with the Hash House Harriers (f), who do hold events on occasion around Riyadh. Joining any running group event is a great way to see interesting landscape outside of the city and to socialise with expat residents who can give another insight into living in Saudi Arabia.

**SPORTS STADIA** There are two main stadia in Riyadh. King Fahd International Stadium opened in 1987 and is in the far east of Riyadh. The stadium is used mostly for football matches and some athletics competitions. In recent years, it has also been the main venue for events with a large number of spectators, including WWE (wrestling) and music (South Korea's BTS chose to hold their first concert in the Middle East here). Seating is separated into singles (men only) and family (for women and mixed groups). Prince Faisal bin Fahd Stadium [115 F2] opened in 1971 and is at the southern end of King Abdullah Park off Salah ad Din al Ayyubi Road in Riyadh's al Murabba district. It is used mostly for football matches. Visitors who are interested in attending events in either venue can find further information on the Saudi Ministry of Sport website (w mos.gov.sa/en).

## OTHER PRACTICALITIES

All of the main **banks** found throughout Saudi Arabia can be found in Riyadh. You are never more than a short distance from several branches in all districts. **ATMs** can be found at the banks and are plentiful in shopping centres and especially petrol stations..

### HOSPITALS

Riyadh is a medical hub for Saudi Arabia & the wider GCC. Hopefully a visit to hospital is not necessary & hopefully too you are well insured if it is. Some of the hospitals you might want to research in Riyadh are these top-quality facilities:

**Dallah Hospital** [120 C5] Fas Rd off King Fahd Rd; 9200 12222; w dallah-hospital.com/english/home. Located not far from Riyadh Gallery Mall.
**Dr Sulaiman al Habib Medical Group** [120 C6], [127 D7] w hmg.com.sa. This prominent & well-regarded medical group is found throughout Riyadh & beyond. Convenient locations include DQ: al Safarat, Altawqi & Abu Bakr al Karkhi sts off Circles 5 & 6; 011 216 7711; Olaya Medical Complex, sts 70–79 between King Fahd Rd & Olaya St; 011 525 9999; Khurais Branch Rd ar Rayyan, Makkah al Mukarramah Branch Rd, east of Eastern Ring Rd; 011 490 9999; al Takhassousi, ar Rahmaniyyah neighbourhood on Takhassousi St between Amin Wasif & al Mahazim Riyadh; 011 283 3333
**King Fahd Medical City** [114 C1] Makkah al Mukarramah Branch Rd, near the Marriott Hotel; 011 288 9999; w kfmc.med.sa
**King Faisal Specialist Hospital & Research Centre** [114 A1] al Mathat Ash Shamali; 011 464 7272; w kfshrc.edu.sa/en/home
**Saudi German Hospital** [120 C3] King Fahd Rd, north of Northern Ring Rd, Press District; 011 268 5555; w riyadh.saudigermanhealth.com/en

### PHARMACIES

There is a wide range of pharmacies throughout the city, located in shopping malls, hospitals & separate shops. They are usually open throughout the day & into the late evening. Some of the most popular & well-regarded pharmacies are:

**Al Dawaa** [120 B4] Prince Sultan bin Abdul Aziz Rd; 800 244 4444; w al-dawaa.com; 10.00–03.00 Sat–Thu, 16.00–00.30 Fri
**Boots** [120 B4] Riyadh Gallery Olaya St; 011 510 1410; w me.boots.com; 09.30–23.00 Sat–Thu, 14.00–23.00 Fri
**Nahdi** [120 D5] Junction of Olaya St & Fatima umm al Baha; 9200 24673; w nahdionline.com; 24hrs daily
**Whites** [120 A1] al Takhassousi St, about 700m north of al Urubah Rd; 9200 06648 07.00–03.00 Sat–Thu, 13.00–01.00 Fri

### POST AND COURIER SERVICES

As mentioned on page 95, most people do not rely on the national postal services. For a more reliable (though more expensive) service, use couriers.

#### Post office

**Saudi Post** [114 B1] Cnr Abdul Malik bin Marwan Rd & Olaya St; 9200 05700; w splonline.com.sa; 08.00–21.00 Sun–Thu. 1 of 12 branches scattered throughout the city.

#### Couriers

**Aramex** [114 C2] Prince Faisal bin Turki bin Abdul Aziz St; 800 100 0880; w aramex.com; 09.00–13.30 & 16.00–22.00 Sat–Thu, 16.00–22.00 Fri
**DHL** [121 E6] Cnr al Urubah Rd & Prince Ahmed bin Abdul Rahman St; 011 257 3392; w locator.dhl.com; 10.00–16.00 & 21.00–02.00 Sat–Thu

**FedEx** [114 B1] Olaya St just south of Mecca al Mukarramah Rd; ☎800 850 1520; w fedex.com; ⏲ 09.00–18.00 Sat–Thu

**TNT** [114 B1] Cnr Olaya St & Shaddad bin Aous; ☎800 244 2222; w tnt.com

**UPS** [120 B3] King Fahd Rd, next to the Ministry of Islamic Affairs Bldg; ☎9200 02555; w ups.com; ⏲ 08.00–22.00 Sat–Thu

## WHAT TO SEE AND DO

It is important to remember that mainstream tourism was only permitted in late 2019 and was suspended a few short months later due to the Covid-19 pandemic. During this time, Saudi Arabia continued to focus on building its tourism infrastructure. You may find that some attractions are being developed or renovated and may be temporarily closed. Others are open and are more splendid than ever. Make sure you double-check opening hours prior to visiting to avoid disappointment.

### AL BATHA AND DIRAH

**King Abdul Aziz Historical Center** This is a district at the heart of al Murabba that encompasses the Saudi National Museum, National Museum Park, Murabba Square and the Murabba Palace. The Murabba Palace is in its original location; the museum has been built on the grounds of the palace in a manner sympathetic to its historic setting. On the opposite side of King Saud Road opposite the National Museum, you'll find al Yamama Park, King Abdul Aziz National Park, Children's Park and al Watan Park. Al Watan Park Café is a lovely green area with children's rides and a water tower.

The **King Abdul Aziz Darah Public Library** and **King Abdul Aziz Foundation for Research and Archives** [115 G1] (☎011 401 1999; w darah.org.sa; ⏲ 08.30–14.15 Sun–Thu) are also found within the historical centre. Non-Arabic speakers may struggle with most of the material but can admire the traditional Najd-style architecture.

***Saudi National Museum*** ✷ [115 G1] (King Saud Rd, west of King Faisal Rd; ☎050 236 0060; 𝕏; ⏲ 09.00–19.00 Mon–Thu, 14.00–22.00 Fri; admission free; ample free parking off King Saud Rd, just before the main entrance) This museum is a delight to visit. Trails and arrows marked on the floor guide visitors through each of the eight exhibition halls. The exhibits are reasonably well labelled in Arabic and most also in English; some of the very interesting historical theatre videos are only in Arabic, but non-Arabic speakers will still find them worthwhile to watch. There is good wheelchair access to the reception and ground-floor exhibits, and lifts can take you to the halls on the first floor. While there is no gift shop in the museum, the pleasant reception area contains a meteorite found in the Empty Quarter.

The **Hall of Man and the Universe** is on the ground floor and describes the geology and life on the Arabian Peninsula as far back as the Palaeolithic. Saudi rock art found elsewhere in the Kingdom is on display, as are early forms of Arabic alphabets. This leads to the **Hall of the Arab Kingdoms**, whose focus is on the earliest kingdoms of Dilmun, Madian, Gariah and Tima'a – some important sites remain in what is now Tabuk Province (page 188). Next is the **Hall of the Pre-Islamic Era**, which focuses on key cities of the Arabian Peninsula that were thriving from about 400BCE until the advent of Islam. There is a well-illustrated timeline running the length of these three rooms which helps put things into perspective.

Now to the first floor, where the remaining halls are located. The **Hall of the Prophet's Mission** exhibits matters of importance during the earliest days of

Islam, including family trees of the House of the Prophet, as well as key points in the Prophet's life. This exhibit is very helpful in explaining major events during the earliest days of Islam and is especially beneficial for non-Muslims who may have had limited opportunity to understand this history. Good maps illustrate the Prophet's journeys very clearly. The **Hall of Islam and the Arabian Peninsula** explains the expansion of Islam beyond Mecca and Madinah to the wider Middle East in further detail. It continues with the death of the Prophet and the further spread of Islam across the Maghreb (North Africa) and into what is now Spain, Portugal and southern France. Artefacts from Dumat al Jandal (page 182) are on display. This hall also describes difficult times under early Ottoman rule.

The next hall you will enter is the **Hall of the First Saudi State**, where a short video – in Arabic, followed by English – about the Siege of Diriyah, the ancestral home and origins of the current al Saud ruling family, explains many of the battles that were fought during these early years. It's an interesting watch. The **Hall of the Second Saudi State** displays a rich collection of artefacts that illustrate much of the state's history during this period, covering both military history and domestic life, and the reign and fall of Imam Faisal al Turki. It also introduces Abdul Aziz ibn Saud's early rise to prominence.

The **Unification of the Kingdom Hall** is next on the trail. The exhibits in this hall focus on the history, customs and traditions of each region that was incorporated into the Kingdom of Saudi Arabia, from Abdul Aziz ibn Saud's capture of Riyadh in 1902 to 1932, when the current borders of the Kingdom were made complete. It's worth stepping into the Unification Theatre as it displays a detailed history of the return of ibn Saud from his exile in what is now Kuwait and the battles he led in the successful quest to unify the Kingdom of Saudi Arabia. A comprehensive collection of artefacts representing contemporary life of that era – everything from trade and commerce, agriculture to elaborately carved doors, Bedouin life to the discovery of oil – offer some insight to what life was like in the early 20th century.

The final hall is the **Hall of the Hajj and Two Holy Mosques**. It gives both Muslims and non-Muslims an opportunity to learn more about the history of Mecca and Madinah and of early hajj (pilgrimage) journeys. There are early photographs exhibited of pilgrims on their travels from the Levant and beyond. Various artefacts are on display and are well labelled, including a Ka'aba curtain. There are interesting three-dimensional scale model displays of Mecca Province, Mecca's Holy Mosque (al Masjid al Haram) and the Holy Mosque in Madinah (al Masjid al Nabwi) complete with interactive buttons to highlight different areas of each model.

The way out of the museum is back on the ground floor through a final room that shows large photos of the monarchy since Unification, with all seven kings and the current Crown Prince Mohammed bin Salman depicted.

***National Museum Park*** [115 G1] (🕘 24hrs daily) The park can be accessed through the National Museum during museum opening hours or from al Dalam Street. This green park features colourful plants, lots of shady trees, a cycling path and children's entertainment during popular hours in the evening and weekends. It is a peaceful place in a busy part of Riyadh.

***Murabba Square*** [115 G1] Visitors can walk through this peaceful garden between the National Museum and Murabba Palace. At the edge of the garden towards King Saud Road, many upscale restaurants are open in the winter months as part of Saudi Seasons' Riyadh Season events.

***Murabba Palace*** [115 G1] Off King Saud Rd, adjacent to Murabba Sq; 011 401 1999; w heritage.moc.gov.sa/en/locations/al-murabba-place; 09.00–noon & 17.00–20.00 Sun–Thu, 17.00–20.00 Fri–Sat; admission free) The Murabba Palace was built between 1936 and 1945, and restored in 1999. It became the home of King Abdul Aziz in 1938 when it was partially completed. The king lived there until his death in 1953 along with one of his wives, Hussa bint Ahmed al Sudairi. She was the mother of the future kings Fahd and Salman, as well as Sultan and Nayef, two former crown princes. The palace introduced innovative and modern features to the Kingdom, including the installation of electricity, plumbed bathrooms, early modern air conditioning and the Kingdom's first lift. In addition to being an important tourist attraction, it is also a favoured place for the royal family to host high-profile visitors and dignitaries from abroad.

The palace is constructed in the traditional Najd style, using mud bricks, straw, wood and palm tree fronds. The doors, windows and ceiling are made of wood with the ceiling decorated in geometric painted patterns in black, red and yellow. The exterior is a sand colour with white pillars and window frames. There are two levels with a total of 32 rooms designed around an open courtyard. The ground floor was used as government offices and workers' quarters, while the first floor housed the king's living quarters, as well as summer and winter halls to host guests. There are nine entrances to the palace, with the main entrance to the

## SAUDI SEASONS – RIYADH

Held since 2019, Riyadh Season was temporarily stopped due to the Covid pandemic, returning for the 2021/22 season. To give an idea about what's on offer, between October 2021 and March 2022, more than 7,000 Riyadh Season events took place in 14 different 'season zones' both within the city of Riyadh and in the surrounding area. The opening ceremony took place in Riyadh Boulevard, very much a part of 'new' Riyadh. With parades, fireworks and performances by globally popular K-pop group BTS and the Cuban-American artist Pitbull, it was attended by more than 750,000 people. Top restaurants were established in the Murabba Park historic neighbourhood, and events were also held in the DQ's The Grove entertainment venue, showing culinary and artisanal skills from all over the Kingdom.

Riyadh Season provides similar entertainment annually, so check what's on if you are visiting during the winter months. It also showcases global sporting events such as WWE wrestling, football matches and the debut of Formula 1 in Jeddah but promoted in Riyadh as well. Other attractions include a heritage village, where traditional music can be heard. Another zone could be renamed 'poets corner' for its nightly focus on this long-running Arab tradition. Most zones are free to enter; however, some activities in the zones require a ticket.

Although most events are family orientated with plenty of activities for children, others are clearly aimed at a young adult audience. Live music and concerts from Arab and global artists which would have been unimaginable in the Kingdom only a few years ago are highlights, including during Riyadh Season Founders Day events. These events are expected to be updated for each annual Riyadh Season. Good websites to see what's coming include w riyadhseason.sa and w calendar.visitsaudi.com/en/season/riyadh-season.

south. Visitors will see the permanent exhibition of many of the personal effects and important documents of King Abdul Aziz. The Rolls-Royce gifted by Winston Churchill is also on display.

**Masmak Fortress and Palace Museum** ✱ [115 H4] (al Thumairi St; ☎ 011 411 0091; ⏲ 08.00–21.00 Sun–Thu, 16.00–20.00 Fri, 09.00–20.00 Sat; admission free; wheelchair access is reasonably comfortable as the exhibits are all on the ground level, but floors are uneven in places & some doorways narrow) Masmak Fortress is an architectural and historic gem. As you step away from shiny high-rise buildings and the motorways of the modern capital, the fort and surrounding courtyard retain the feeling of a bygone era and are must-sees for anyone visiting Riyadh. Located to the east side of Deira Square, the fort is prominent but does not feel out of place, even in the company of several modern ministry buildings also found around the square. At 18m, the watchtowers are the tallest feature of the complex, and inside, visitors are likely to note the rooms are surprisingly modest in size. It has been sympathetically restored and in 1995 opened as a museum.

Built in 1865CE under the instruction of the Emir of Jebel Shameer of the House of Rashid, the fortress is historically important as the site of a key power struggle between the House of Rashid and House of Saud. Emir Abdul Aziz bin Abdul Rahman ibn Saud, later the first King of Saudi Arabia, was victorious in the Battle of Riyadh that took place at the fortress in 1902 upon his return from exile in Kuwait. The battle was the turning point that led to the unification of the Kingdom of Saudi Arabia, as further military campaigns were planned and run from the fortress.

Visitors enter the fortress from the west through its large wooden gate, which still contains the embedded spearhead from the future King Abdul Aziz's conquest. The smaller door within the gate, designed to let only one person enter and thus maintaining the security of the fort by keeping the main gate closed, is called *al khokha*.

Once inside the fortress, you will see a passageway leading to the open courtyard that covers the east side, supported by white pillars, with painted doors leading to rooms used for various purposes, including storage of munitions as well as a prison for a period of time after its capture. The passageway to the mosque is immediately to the left. It is no longer possible to visit the mosque but it is possible to look into it from the passageway (take care to avoid stepping on the carpet). The mosque has pillars, decorative triangular ventilation holes and storage space built into the walls, and a *mihrab* indicating the direction of Mecca that all reflect the style of traditional Saudi mosques. Immediately adjacent to the mosque is the meeting room (diwan), where guests typically would be hosted.

In addition to the watchtowers, the courtyard contains a rectangular tower (*burj al murabba*) used to monitor activities within the fort itself, and a well in the northeast corner. Stairs at the edge of the courtyard lead to the first floor's living quarters for key officials, and a guesthouse – but this floor is off-limits to visitors since the stairs are no longer safe to climb.

If you have a keen interest in history, you might prefer to organise a private tour guide, but it is possible to visit al Masmak independently as the exhibits are reasonably well labelled and are displayed with related photographs. It is relatively easy to follow the well-signposted route, where the sequence of exhibits follows the timeline of key events: Riyadh at the Time of Seizure, Raiding al Masmak, The Pioneers, Historic Riyadh, Masmak Fortress, al Masmak Utilisation and the Final Gallery. Throughout the fortress there is a rich collection of artefacts; and also two video clips along the exhibition trail in both Arabic and English. The first clip, about 5 minutes long, is shown in the Raiding al Masmak area and gives a good overview of the history of ibn Saud and the early days of Riyadh. The second clip is shown near The Pioneers area, in a side room indicated by an arrow pointing to the right. It is long at about 15 minutes, but worth watching if you are interested in ibn Saud's efforts at the beginning of unification of the Kingdom of Saudi Arabia.

The final exhibition room displays larger-than-life photos of each Saudi king from the time of unification to the present, along with photos of two crown princes. The fortress also has space for temporary exhibitions, and a room for a gift shop, but this has been moved to the Kingdom Heritage centre nearby (page 132). Once you have finished your tour of the fortress, you might want to explore the narrow roads and many souqs on the south side of the square. For more information about these souqs, refer to page 132. Remember that they are quiet in the morning, closed in the afternoon, and come to life in the evening.

**Al Safat Square** [115 G4] Also known, infamously, as Chop Chop Square, this is where Saudi justice is executed – quite literally – by public beheadings. Some visitors may wish to reflect on what happens here as, ironically, it is otherwise a generally quiet and peaceful space. At other times, events including Riyadh Season activities are also held here. You'll know you are in the right place to enter the area when you spot the Safat clock tower off al Thumairi Street, west of Masmak Fortress.

**Imam Turki bin Abdullah Grand Mosque** [115 G4] Located to the west of al Safat Square, this is one of the largest and oldest mosques in Riyadh. Built in the traditional Najd style, it is striking in appearance and its courtyard setting shows it off to full effect. Funeral prayers of kings and many other members of the royal family upon their death are held here. Only Muslims may enter the interior of the mosque.

### BEYOND DIRAH

☪ **Al Rajhi Grand Mosque** [map, page 110] (Eastern Ring Rd, south of Junction 15; ☎ 011 244 4447; w riyadh.rm.org.sa; ⏰ 04.00–20.00 daily) This beautiful mosque opened in 2004 and is the largest mosque in Riyadh. It was funded by the charitable donations of Saudi Arabia's wealthiest non-royal family, the Al Rajhi, who established what is now the world's largest Islamic banking group. In addition to the grand mosque, where community and social events take place, there are two libraries. Friday prayers are broadcast in seven languages. It should be noted that the mosque is accessible only to Muslims.

**Wadi Namar** [map, page 110] (South of Dirah just off the Southern Ring Rd & al Hameid Hwy) If you want a change of scene, then visiting Wadi Namar is a good choice and is about a 15-minute drive away. Take al Warad Road at the junction of the Southern Ring Road and al Hameid Highway, which after about 2km follows the north side of the dam. You may be able to see the waterfall about halfway along the road if there is water. There are rows of palm trees keeping the promenade pleasantly shaded, making it a good place for gentle exercise. With plenty of parking, it's a clean and calm experience where visitors don't really arrive in numbers until after the sun goes down. Go in the morning and you will have the place nearly to yourself. There are no facilities here, though there are a few supermarkets nearby where you can stock up for a picnic. Visitors should note that the wadi is part of the very conservative as Suwaidi area of Riyadh, so you should consider covering up if you are a man and wear an abaya if you are a woman.

## OLAYA STREET AND THE CITY CENTRE

**Kingdom Centre** [120 B2] (al Urubah Rd between Olaya St & King Fahd Rd; ☎011 211 2222; w kingdomcentre.com.sa; ⏲ 09.30–23.00 Sat–Thu, 16.30–23.00 Fri; adults/under-10s SAR69/23) Fondly nicknamed the 'bottle opener', the Kingdom Centre is a multipurpose complex of restaurants, offices, the Four Seasons hotel, a luxury shopping mall and a cinema. Sitting at a height of 300m at the top of the tower, the Sky Bridge is the main tourist attraction, providing panoramic views of Riyadh. Two high-speed lifts will whizz you up to the Sky Bridge, accessed from the second floor of the shopping mall. Ask the concierge where to find the first lift. There's ample underground parking.

**DIPLOMATIC QUARTER AND OLD DIRIYAH** The Saudi authorities are in the midst of a major development of the Diriyah Gate area including al Turaif and al Bujairi. The entire area is being expanded and will become a mixed-use destination. In addition to continued restoration work, there are plans to develop many luxury hotels (page 118) and to add art galleries, museums, educational institutions, residential neighbourhoods, restaurants, shops, multiple public squares and recreational areas.

**Tuwaiq Palace** [127 C6] Found in the DQ, this sympathetically designed palace and event centre was built in 1985 to fit in with the local culture and geography. The main buildings are linked and feel like tents in an oasis and won the Aga Khan Award for Architecture in 1998. It has expanded from its original use as the Diplomatic Club and is now used for many large social events, cultural festivals and state visits. The buildings incorporate a series of walkways that lead to viewing platforms for stunning vistas overlooking Wadi Hanifa. The lush al Khozama gardens offer relaxing walks surrounding the palace and lead to further trails. There are a host of recreational activities including swimming pools that currently operate on separate days for men and women, as well as fine and casual dining.

**Al Turaif UNESCO World Heritage Site** ✱ [127 C3] Wadi Hanifa Rd, Old Diriyah; ☎9200 02622; w diriyah.sa; ⏲ 10.00–midnight Sat–Thu, 14.00–midnight Fri; from SAR100, seasonal rates; entrance via Bujairi Terrace) This site has just been extensively renovated and has reopened after a long closure. The visitor reception area (opposite the Sheikh Mohammed bin Abdul Wahhab Bridge) is the starting point for your tour and those with a particular interest in learning more about the origins of the al Saud family should plan to spend a few hours wandering around this historic district.

The al Sauds were the leaders of the Emirate of Diriyah during the First Saudi State, dating back to 1744CE. Old Diriyah's historic structures, built from 1766, were once the centre of their power and have been a UNESCO World Heritage Site since 2010. This was also the home of the al Wahhab family at the same time; their religious influence can be felt to this day in the Kingdom and beyond, in the form of Salafism.

The streets of Old Diriyah wind around a series of mud-brick-and-straw-walled buildings that range from huts to palaces. They were built in the traditional Najd style, supported by wood and thatched palm fronds, and several instances of the colourful geometric decorations indicative of this style can be seen throughout the site. There are also four museums: the Diriyah Museum of Salwa Palace, the

Military Museum, Arabian Horse Museum and the Saudi Daily Life Museum. All display artefacts and provide more detail about the history of the Saudi royal family.

***A walking tour of the site*** The first place you will see after the visitor reception area is the **Salwa Palace**. Believed to have been built between 1803 and 1814, the palace is a four-storey construction and served as the first home of the al Saud emirs and imams during the time of the First Saudi State. Old Diriyah's largest palace, it was built in five stages and comprised of four parts: the State's government offices; a circular *majlis* where subjects of the State could consult with the emir on matters important to them; a *mukhtasar* or anteroom for more private matters; and a treasury, to collect zakat. Visitors will be able to view a number of laser shows that highlight additional features and historical notes throughout the palace. The **Diriyah Museum of Salwa Palace** is adjacent to the palace.

Past the Diriyah Museum are the ruins of the **Imam Mohammed bin Saud** Mosque. This mosque is significant as it is where Sheikh Mohammed bin Abdul Wahhab taught his reformed beliefs to students from all over the Arabian Peninsula. Thought to have been originally built around the turn of the 18th century, it fell into ruin in the 19th century, although part of a wall has been preserved.

Next stop along the visitor trail is the **al Turaif Souq** and restaurant, and across from these the **Abdullah Saad bin Saud Palace**. This large palace has an elaborately decorated wooden floor and an impressive courtyard, and also features innovative design to keep airflow moving with its intricately designed triangular window patterns. Continuing clockwise along the curved path you come to the **Arabian Horse Museum**, chronicling the royal family's history with horses and with stables to the rear, and the **Military Museum** which displays a wide range of militaria.

The **Thanayan bin Saud Palace** is found beyond the Military Museum and was the base for an emir of Najd in the 19th century. Leaving the Thanayan bin Saud Palace, walk along the road to the left until you arrive at the building on the right towards the end – this is **al Turaif Nuzul**, a theatre where live performances, from the traditional ardah dance to more contemporary performances showcasing Saudi culture, are held.

Beyond Turaif Nuzul, turn right back in the direction of Salwa Palace and the visitors' reception. You will find the **Museum of Daily Life**, the **Handicraft** and **Wadi markets** and coffee shops. The **Guest House and Bath House** are located in a building with many rooms off a central courtyard. Water would be carried up to the bath house from the nearby wadi well.

**Al Bujairi Heritage Park and Terrace** [127 C2] (✆ 9200 02622; **w** dgda.gov.sa; ⏲ 24hrs daily) The al Bujairi district continues to be developed as a part of the Diriyah Gate Giga Project. It is on the opposite side of Old Diriyah's World Heritage Site and opposite the Sheikh Mohammed bin Abdul Wahhab Bridge from the visitors' centre. The Heritage Park is an open-air museum with many points of interest, with decorative design techniques and calligraphy on show as you walk around, galleries and sword-dancing performances. Visit Bujairi in the evening if you can as it is the perfect spot to see al Turaif lit up, ideally dining on the terrace alfresco.

## EXCURSIONS BEYOND GREATER RIYADH

**The Edge of the World – Jebel Fihrayn** ✱ The Edge of the World, also known as Jebel Fihrayn (جبل الفهرين), is part of the Jebel Tuwaiq escarpment that runs for over

1,000km from Najran in the south to al Qassim in the north, passing through Riyadh Province to the west of the capital city. Ancient caravan routes from Yemen to the Levant and beyond have followed the base of this escarpment for centuries. The Edge of the Word is a spectacular natural attraction where the cliffs are edged with sandstone columns which stand 300m tall. From the top, you are afforded uninterrupted views across the plain below and, since it faces west, unforgettable sunsets.

Understandably, this place has grown very rapidly in popularity since the advent of general tourism, in part due to its proximity to the capital, about 100km away.

***Getting there*** There are two main ways to access the Edge of the World. Most people prefer to take the southern route that passes through al Uyaynah , the village where Mohammed bin Abdul Wahhab was born. Take Route 535 from Riyadh. then turn left off this road east of the village of al Jubaylah on to Route 5762. Turn left at the roundabout past Sodus town centre, then turn left after about 400m. You will see signs in Arabic, where you will turn left on to an unnamed road. You will then see an English sign on the left: 'Al Hussein Wood Houses'. Continue for nearly 3km, where there is an obvious off-road path to the right. If you have reached Sadus Dam at the end of the road, you have missed the turn. The northern route is accessed through the al Shoaib entrance gate (see below). Take Route 535 from Riyadh, continuing past the junction with Route 5762 until reaching the junction with Route 546. Turn left on to Route 546, continuing for about 4km until you reach Route 5762. Turn on to this route until you reach the first roundabout near Sodus; then continue by following the directions detailed in the southern route. Both routes involve a journey of about 15km on unpaved road, which need to be travelled in a 4x4 vehicle with high clearance. The total journey takes about 2½ hours, depending on your skill driving on this terrain.

Note that there is no mobile phone signal once you leave the Sodus village. There is also no public transport. Tour operators run desert safaris from Riyadh. Check on a reputable website to choose a reliable organisation. Horizons Tours and Ghazi Tours (page 47) are recommended, though expensive. Prices range from US$150 to US$360 per adult depending on your tour guide, tour group size, duration and any extras.

**Hidden Cave** About 3km to the northeast of the Edge of the Word is Hidden Cave, which is accessed via a hole in the ground and a ladder. Inside the cave – which allows for only one person at a time – you will be able to see stalactites, crystallised salt formations and its resident bats. Not for the claustrophobic. As this is also reached on unpaved desert tracks, it is best to go with a tour operator or at least with other visitors.

**Al Shoaib Park** (🕘 closes midnight; admission free) Heading out of Riyadh, Route 535 turns into Route 546 a few kilometres after passing the turn-off to al Uyayriah. Turn south off Route 546 just before the village of Huraymila, to find the gates by which to enter the park, where visitors can picnic, cycle, hike and enjoy other outdoor activities. There are other hiking trails in the vicinity. It is also possible to camp near the trails but be aware that the park closes at midnight. There are also wild camping options in other spots along the escarpment within the park. There are no facilities so come prepared.

**The 'Other Edge of the World'** Another stunningly beautiful set of rock formations, known collectively as the 'Other Edge of the World', can be seen not far from Riyadh. Among the formations is a natural spur known as Khasm Zubaydah and a natural pillar known as Qadmat al Saqtah, or Faysal's Finger. It is named after the third king of Saudi Arabia, Faisal bin Abdul Aziz al Saud and rises about 200m from the bottom of the Jebel Tuwaiq escarpment.

Along the track on your way here, you will see some circular stone structures – these are probably tombs (similar structures are also found not too far away from Riyadh in al Kharj), and it is believed they date to the Bronze Age. You will find more elaborate stone burial chambers nearer to Khasm Zubaydah about 10km further along the track. These are taller and are both circular and tower shaped.

***Getting there*** From Riyadh, head west on to the Jeddah highway. Turn right for this site about 2km past the highway checkpoint on to a rough dirt track on a plateau – this is only suitable for 4x4 vehicles. Turn right off this track after about 10km (and after the stone tombs), where you will cross the plain. Go another 10km north, where you will find Faysal's Finger. (Google Maps refers to these sites as 'Near Edge of the World Dhurma side'.)

**Qaryat al Asba (Graffiti Rocks)** Qaryat al Asba, also known as Graffiti Rocks 1 and 2, are believed to date back to the Neolithic period. These sandstone rocks are on the edge of a *khasm* (escarpment) about 140km southwest of Riyadh off the Mecca Highway. Although there is an exit near the rocks, some of which are visible from the highway, the road ends several hundred metres from the site. It is best to approach the site with a 4x4 as this will allow you to get close to the rock art. Otherwise, it's a long walk to the first set of rocks, but this is not advised in the summer months.

***Khasm Musayqirah – Graffiti Rock 1*** Graffiti Rock 1, known more formally as Khasm Musayqirah from the settlement of the same name, has archaeological significance. Carvings of aurochs (water buffalos), unusual elsewhere in the Kingdom, can be found on the rock's east side. The carvings form part of an elaborate battle scene and are of particular interest as aurochs are believed to have

### JANADRIYAH CULTURAL AND HERITAGE FESTIVAL

The Janadriyah Cultural and Heritage Festival has been the highlight of the Riyadh social calendar since 1985. The annual event is a celebration of Saudi culture, not only of Riyadh and the Najd but of all provinces in the Kingdom, and draws over a million visitors each year. It usually runs for two weeks in February.

The festival opens with a camel race and features traditional arts and crafts, folklore troupes, dancers, songs and poetry competitions. This is a great opportunity to try a vast selection of homemade regional Saudi cuisine that doesn't always find its way on to restaurant menus. It is also a chance to see the ardah, a traditional dance usually performed by men, often with swords (page 38) and the *mizmar*, or group dance, performed with sticks, drums and clapping to songs. It is also possible to visit heritage village pavillions.

*The festival site is about 3km south of King Abdul Aziz Equestrian Field, off Route 550, eastbound at the junction of Route 537; admission free.*

disappeared with the last humid period of the Arabian Peninsula more than 8,000 years ago. The east side also contains many handprints. On the southern wall, pre-Islamic Thamudic inscriptions can be clearly seen. The rock's northwest side contains a large panel filled with carvings of ostriches, ibexes, dogs, lions, camels, hunters, warriors, a human skeleton and horsemen. These panels attest to a very different climate to what is found today.

***Khasm al Asmar – Graffiti Rock 2*** Khasm al Asmar, or Graffiti Rock 2, is about 10km east of Graffiti Rock 1 and a bit further from the ar Rayn/Bishah road. One of the most interesting features of this rock is the depiction of two humans facing each other. Each holds a round object in one hand and a long, thin object in the other hand. Whether this is a battle scene, performing arts or something altogether different is open to interpretation. There are also Thamudic inscriptions on this rock, along with *wusum* or specific tribal signs that signify ownership of the camels. Ibex markings can be found at the top of the rock.

As the road is unmarked and often sandy, it is strongly advised that Khasm al Asmar is not visited independently and most definitely not alone.

**Heet Cave** (🕘 24hrs daily; admission free) This cave is also known as Ein Heet Cave due to its eye-shaped entrance – *ein* is the Arabic word for eye. The opening is about 20m wide. At the bottom of the cave is a refreshing pool of water, about 150m long and 30m deep. Bring swimwear, but be prepared to wear a cover-up if there are conservative Saudis present. It is also advised that you bring a torch as you want to watch your footing in the shadows. As usual, bring plenty of water.

***Getting there*** Heet Cave and natural spring are about 50km south of Riyadh just off the al Kharj road, Highway 65. Leave the highway at the Fawran Industrial City junction and turn left, where you enter the small village of Heet. Take a right at the third street, then left, then a final right turn on to Heet Cave Road. Once the road ends, visitors must be prepared to walk about 200m down a very steep incline with loose rocks. Rubber-soled shoes are required. Sadly, there is a lot of rubbish that you will need to overlook and possibly manoeuvre around to get to the cave. This is a daytime trip. If you choose to use a tour guide, expect to pay about US$265–360 pp.

**Kharrarah National Park** Less than 1 hour southwest of Riyadh, Kharrarah National Park makes for a superb day trip or weekend camping trip away from the city. In among the red sand dunes is a lake bed that is created after heavy rainfall. It is known as the Lake of Liquid Light. Without rainfall, the lake evaporates, leaving a green pasture behind that attracts birds and other wildlife. Popular with many Saudi families and nature enthusiasts, it's a great location for a picnic with trees providing shade from the midday sun.

If you are planning to camp, settle in for a beautiful sunset over the lake and then fire up the barbecue. Try to go during the week as weekends are often crowded with sports enthusiasts enjoying dune bashing, quad biking and sand boarding.

***Getting there*** Kharrarah National Park is about 65km southwest of Riyadh off the Mecca Highway (Highway 80). Leave at Junction 7 for Jaww, then reverse direction and take the first slip road. You will see a sign for the park and al Hifna waterfall. The entrance is after 4km, opposite a white mosque. Because of the poor road condition, it is best to travel in a 4x4.

**Souq al Jamal Camel Market** (30km east of Riyadh, off the Dammam Hwy 80, take the Thumamah exit towards al Janadriyyah; ⏲ 24hrs daily, but note that camels are traded during daylight hours; admission free) Camels are still sought after by many Saudis and can cost the equivalent of a mid-range car. This market is the place to go if you love camels and you can't make it to the Camel Festival (page 89). You'll see black, grey, white and sand-coloured varieties of these remarkable single-humped dromedary ships of the desert and it's possible to get up close to the animals if you wish. Otherwise, enjoy a Saudi tea or coffee with the hospitable traders. There are also decorative camel baubles and more for sale – good if you want a unique souvenir from your visit. Go in the afternoon if you want to experience the height of activity in the market. Camels that are purchased are lifted on to the buyer's vehicle via a camel hoist – a truly unusual sight.

**Thumamah National Park** (Approx 80km north of King Khalid airport; admission free) The park offers a range of desert activities from barbecues and picnics to camping, dune bashing, horseriding, quad biking, rock climbing and more. Although camel racing no longer takes place in the park, it's possible for visitors to ride a camel if they wish.

Thumamah National Park is easily reached from Riyadh either from Route 5776, turning east from Banban, or from Route 550 northbound to the east side of the airport.

## Activities

***Camping*** Popular sites for wild camping not far from Riyadh can be found in Thumamah National Park (about 80km north of Riyadh off Rte 550), Kharrarah National Park (about 65km southwest of Riyadh off Hwy 80), and Nufud and Rawdat umm al Shuquq near Raghaba between al Qassim and Riyadh (about 130km northwest of Riyadh). It is also possible to camp near Jebel Fihrayn aka The Edge of the World (100km west of Riyadh).

***Desert safaris*** (Page 91) A reputable operator that runs desert safaris from Riyadh is Saudi Arabia Tours (**w** saudiarabiatours.net).

***Dune bashing*** Dune bashing (page 92) locations near Riyadh include Red Sand Dunes southwest of Riyadh off Highway 30, Nufud and Rawdat umm al Shuquq near Raghaba between al Qassim and Riyadh, and nearly any park with open spaces. It's a good idea to consider a local guide if you are planning on dune bashing further away in Riyadh Province.

***Wadi bashing*** (Page 92) Wadis nearest Riyadh are Wadi Hanifa and Wadi Namar. It's a good idea to consider a local guide if you are considering wadi bashing further away in Riyadh Province.

# 4

# Najd نَجْد

The Najd region is located in the centre of the Arabian Peninsula and contains the provinces of Riyadh, al Qassim and Ha'il. 'Najd' means uplands and describes the landscape that slopes downwards from the west to the east of the region. It is a desert dotted with wadis and oases that have sustained life for millennia and which still today provide a main source of agricultural produce, especially dates and grains. In addition, the Saudi government has facilitated modern trade in the region and is promoting more self-sufficiency.

Rich in history and cultural heritage, Najd has been the heartland of Saudi Arabia since the formation of the modern Kingdom and is home to the country's royal family. The specific Salafist beliefs practised in Saudi Arabia also originated in Najd. Traditional Najd architecture can be found throughout the region, in historical buildings and also modern structures which have continued the design traditions of earlier times.

## HISTORY

The Najd provinces of Riyadh, al Qassim and Ha'il provide evidence of some of the earliest civilisations in the Middle East and Arab world. Archaeologists have unearthed artefacts here from the Neolithic period that date as far back at 9,000 years. It is believed that the al Magar people from this era advanced agricultural practices and were pivotal in domesticating the horse and other working animals.

The earliest people that migrated from the Red Sea coast were the Banu Abs, Banu Amir, Banu Hanifa, Banu Tamim and Tayy tribes. Further groups including the Ghassanids, Kindites and Lakhmids arrived from Southern Arabia and Mesopotamia and were key in establishing tribal alliances with the Kahlani and Qatani kingdoms. During the life of the Prophet Mohammed, many military campaigns took place, resulting in the region being absorbed into the Islamic Empire.

During the 16th century, although not imposing direct rule, the Ottoman Empire had control over the external matters of Najd, with varying levels of interest for the next two centuries. In 1744, the alliance of the al Saud and al Wahhab families led to the creation of the First Saudi State, centred in Diriyah near Riyadh and known as the Emirate of Diriyah. It rapidly expanded from Riyadh Province and incorporated most of Najd, eventually expanding far beyond Najd into most of what is now the Kingdom of Saudi Arabia and north to parts of Mesopotamia, now Iraq. During this era, it also promoted the religious teachings of Mohammed bin Abdul Wahhab, a cornerstone of the conservative practices of Hanbali Sunni Islam dominant in the region to this day. The First Saudi State ended in 1818 with the Egyptian-Ottoman invasion of the state and the execution of its leader, Abdullah bin Saud.

After a few years, the Second Saudi State was established, lasting from 1824 to 1891. During this time, the previous rulers from the al Saud family continued to object to the control of the Ottoman Empire over Najd and its alliance with the al Rashid family. This was a period of battles, assassinations and power struggles as the State expanded to the east, driven by the many rulers loyal to either the Egyptians under Ottoman rule or the al Sauds. In 1891 the Second Saudi State fell under the control of the al Rashid family as a result of their victory in the Battle of Mulayda over the al Saud. Ibn Saud was forced into exile in 1890 in what is now Kuwait.

The Third Saudi State was established following successful seizure, by the House of Saud, of Riyadh from the House of Rashid of the Emirate of Ha'il in 1902. Initially defined as the Emirate of Riyadh, it became the 'Emirate of Nejd' and then the 'Emirate of Nejd and Hasa' in 1913 after further victory in expanding east to the Arabian Gulf. Ibn Saud was able to gain control over the rest of the Najd with the help of the local Ikhwan, tribal soldiers loyal to the Sauds and to their Wahhab-inspired faith. After the creation of the Emirate of Nejd and Hasa, ibn Saud was able to consolidate the Hejaz and Asir regions, completing the boundaries of what is now the sovereign country of the Kingdom of Saudi Arabia.

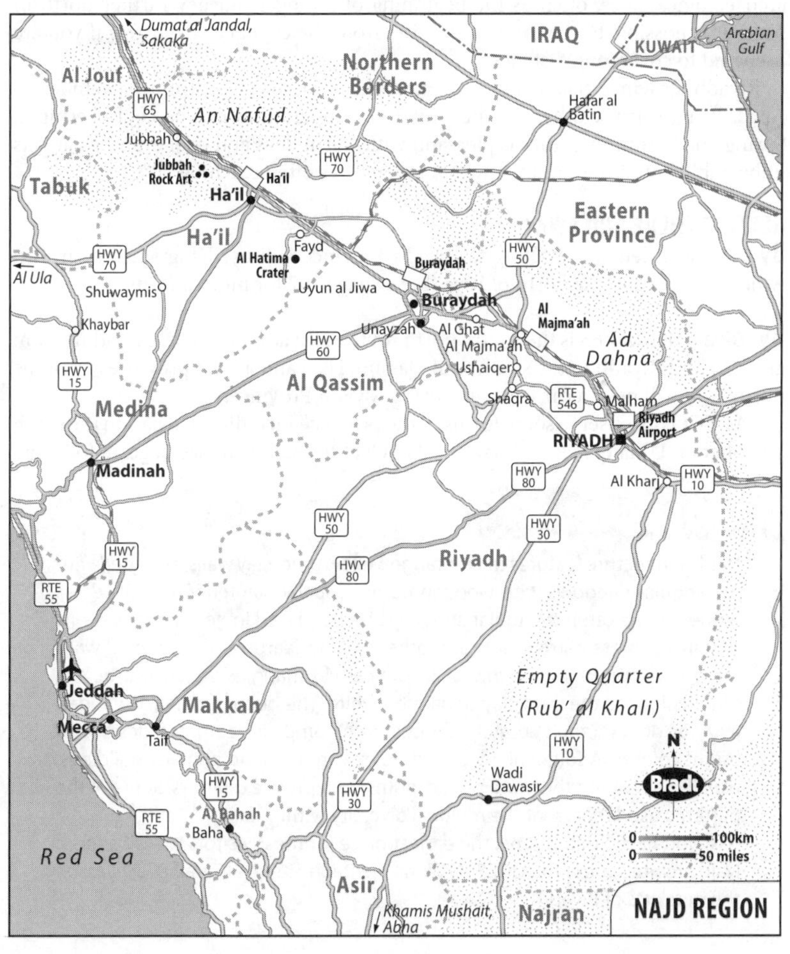

# RIYADH PROVINCE منطقة الرياض

*This section is about Riyadh Province beyond the capital city. See page 106 for more information about Riyadh city.*

Located in the heart of the Najd, where the al Saud ruling family has its origins, Riyadh Province has shaped the culture of the modern Kingdom (page 19). It is the second largest province in the Kingdom, extending from al Qassim Province to the north and well into the Empty Quarter in the south; and it is also the second most populous with almost 9 million people. Agriculture and increasing trade outside the capital are keystones to the economy here, driven by Saudi Vision 2030 (page 28). Although the capital has become much more relaxed socially in recent years, at least by Saudi standards, Riyadh Province remains very traditional and remains proud of its Najd history and traditions.

Riyadh city dominates the interest of many visitors, but the wider province holds some of the most interesting Najd architecture in the region, with many traditional villages open to visitors. Most people venture into Riyadh Province to explore archaeological sites, often as the beginning of a longer journey further north in Najd. It is possible to see some of the sites from the capital as a day trip if you are prepared to cover long distances.

Riyadh Province has a desert climate and is best visited from November to April. Bring warm clothes for the winter as temperatures can be cool overnight. Spring and autumn weather is pleasant, with warm days and cool evenings. It gets unbearably hot in the summer, with temperatures often reaching 50°C.

## GETTING THERE AND AWAY

**By air** Most people travelling to Riyadh Province will use King Khalid Airport, which is located in the north of Riyadh. See page 107 for more information.

**By road** Highway 65 is the south–north route in Riyadh Province, extending from al Kharj and Riyadh to the south to al Qassim, Ha'il and al Jouf provinces from the north. You will need a car when exploring Riyadh Province.

SAPTCO **buses** serve some towns in the province including al Kharj to the south and Shaqra, Ushaiqer, al Majma'ah and al Ghat to the north (see page 53 for more

### NAJD ARCHITECTURE

Najd architecture features thick, orange-yellow mud-clay walls, accented with rectangular windows with wooden frames usually painted white. Windows higher up are often triangular and may also be placed in geometric patterns that incorporate narrow slots and other striking features. The external walls are often topped with a row of pyramid-style triangles which can be the same colour as the mud clay or painted white. The buildings' heavy wooden exterior doors are elaborately painted with complex geometric designs or bright colours. Additional decorated doors can be found in many buildings, usually separating the more public rooms from private quarters. Some of the patterns used represent the regional diversity within Najd.

If you have limited time, the easiest place for most visitors to visit superb Najd architecture is the UNESCO World Heritage Site of al Turaif in Diriyah on the outskirts of Riyadh.

details). **Taxis** can be found easily in al Majma'ah and can be organised in the other towns if they are not present at the bus station.

**By rail** In addition to the Riyadh station located to the north of the city al Majma'ah station is located off Prince Sultan bin Salman Street in the northeast of the city, serving the north of the province. This line runs from Riyadh and al Majma'ah north to al Qassim, Ha'il and al Jouf near Sakaka in the northern provinces of the Najd region. Qurayyat station in the far north of al Jouf Province opened in March 2022. See page 73 for more information.

**SHOPPING** Abdullah al Othaim, Lulu and Panda supermarkets are in al Majma'ah and al Kharj. There are more modest grocers that will sell the basics in most provincial villages, including in Shaqra, Ushaiqer and al Ghat.

**USHAIQER أشيقر** This wonderful example of a typical Najd village brings the past back to life. Ushaiqer (sometimes spelt Ushager or Ushaiger) means 'little blond', describing the mountain to the north of the village. It was settled by Bedouin tribes about 1,500 years ago as the site is enriched with fresh springs, palms and olive trees. Since then, other prominent tribes have lived in the village, including the al Sheikh and al Thani groups of the Banu Tamim tribe. Key figures from the al Sheikh tribe include the religious scholar Mohammed bin Abdul Wahhab (page 20) and the al Thani tribe from which the current Qatari ruling family descends. A small community still lives here, successfully merging traditional and modern lifestyles.

**Getting there and away** Ushaiqer is just over 200km northwest of Riyadh and can be reached by following Route 535 north, which merges into Route 546. After nearly 200km, turn north on to Highway 50 just north of Shaqra. Ushaiqer is about 15km further on Highway 50. Ushaqier is also about 75km south of al Majma'ah on Highway 50.

### Where to stay *Map, page 152*

Included in this listing are accommodation options in nearby Shaqra, about 10km further south on Highway 50.

**Amassi Alref Hotel** Hwy 50, about 700m south of the Heritage Village just past the roundabout; ☎ 011 627 1222. This is a basic but comfortable medium-sized hotel with the usual amenities expected from a 3-star. Recently renovated, it has a mix of rooms & family apartmentts & a good restaurant. Book through a reputable website. **$$**

**Le Park Concord Shaqra Hotel** Unnamed Rd parallel to Hwy 50 (King Faisal Rd), Shaqra; /// advises.contraction.phoned; ☎ 011 628 0014; w leparkshaqra.business.site. Probably the most comfortable choice for those looking for spacious rooms, a few amenities & on-site restaurant in a peaceful location. There is also a small garden & outdoor pool. Great for guests with their own vehicle for easy access to Ushaiqer. **$$**

**Raoum Inn** King Abdul Aziz Rd, just south of King Saud Rd; ☎ 011 622 2322. More centrally located than most other properties, this reliable Saudi brand has good-sized rooms, which can be booked with a small kitchenette. There are limited food options at the hotel, but you will be close to the Basateen Mall & to many fast-food & casual dining places. **$$**

**Shawthabi Heritage Resort** Adjacent to the Heritage Guesthouse, Shaqra; ☎ 056 099 2209. This is an older & more elaborate version of the guesthouse. Traditional shaded & open-air courtyards give this small property an airy feeling. **$$**

✱ **Heritage Guesthouse** Off Hwy 50, about 50m from the Shaqra Heritage Museum; ☎ 050 319 4520. A small, newly built traditional Najd

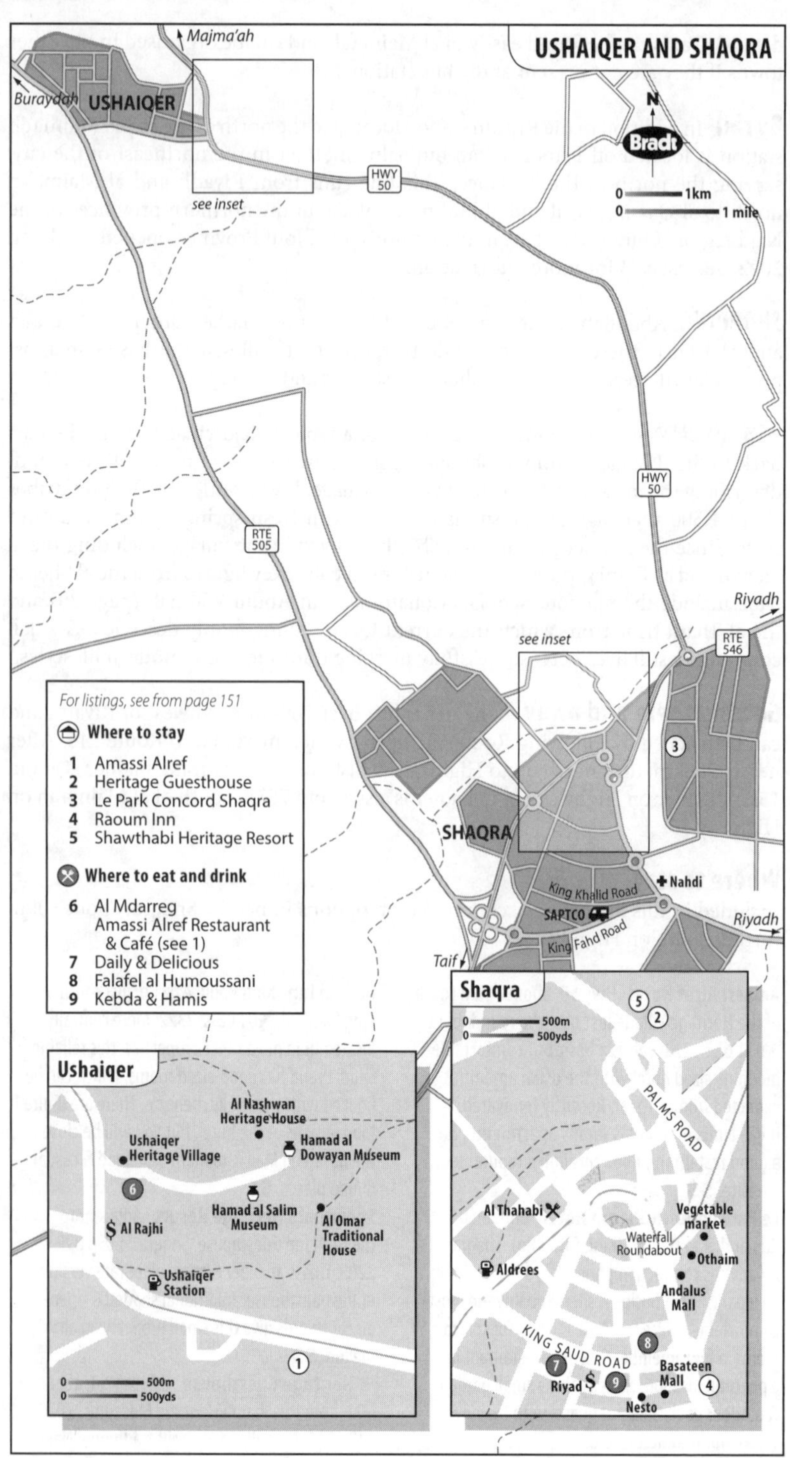
USHAIQER AND SHAQRA
Majma'ah
Buraydah
USHAIQER
HWY 50
see inset
Bradt
1km
1 mile
RTE 505
Riyadh
RTE 546
see inset
SHAQRA
King Khalid Road
Nahdi
SAPTCO
King Fahd Road
Riyadh
Taif
For listings, see from page 151
Where to stay
1 Amassi Alref
2 Heritage Guesthouse
3 Le Park Concord Shaqra
4 Raoum Inn
5 Shawthabi Heritage Resort
Where to eat and drink
6 Al Mdarreg
Amassi Alref Restaurant & Café (see 1)
7 Daily & Delicious
8 Falafel al Humoussani
9 Kebda & Hamis
Ushaiqer
Al Nashwan Heritage House
Ushaiqer Heritage Village
Hamad al Dowayan Museum
Hamad al Salim Museum
Al Omar Traditional House
Al Rajhi
Ushaiqer Station
500m
500yds
Shaqra
500m
500yds
Palms Road
Al Thahabi
Vegetable market
Waterfall Roundabout
Othaim
Aldrees
Andalus Mall
King Saud Road
Basateen Mall
Riyad
Nesto

property in nearby Shaqra, run by a Saudi family that knows how to make guests feel welcome. The décor manages to be cosy & authentic without going over the top. Each room has a private bathroom. The shared kitchen facilities are spotless. B/fast inc. **$**

## Where to eat and drink *Map, opposite*

There are a few places in nearby Shaqra that serve Indian, Pakistani and local food.

**Al Mdarreg Restaurant** Ushaiqer Heritage Village; 055 936 0069; noon–16.00 Fri–Sat. If you are visiting the Ushaiqer Heritage Village during the w/end, then this is a great place to have lunch to continue with the traditional Najd theme. The restaurant is located on the right just past the entrance to the Heritage Village. Follow the steps leading from the road to the garden, where traditional Najd dishes are served buffet-style & priced by weight. Although set up to cater to tour groups, this restaurant also works for independent visitors & families. The family section is located past the buffet, with booths imaginatively created from reeds & seating on the floor on traditionally decorated rugs & cushions. Relaxing. **$$**

**Amassi Alref Restaurant & Café** Hwy 50 about 700m south of Ushaiqer Heritage Village; 011 627 1222; noon–midnight daily. Located in the hotel of the same name (page 151). Good traditional Saudi food, good service & a pleasant ambience. **$$**

**Daily & Delicious** King Saud Rd, about 200m east of King Abdullah Rd, Shaqra; 011 622 4422; w dailyndelicious.com; 12.30–01.00 daily. This casual restaurant & take-away has something for most: grills, salads & pasta, as well as Indian & Arabic snacks. Great for groups. **$$**

**Falafel al Humoussani** King Saud Rd, 100m west of McDonald's, Shaqra; 011 622 3232; w alhummousani.com; 06.00–11.30 & 17.00–00.30 daily. As the name implies, this order-at-the-counter restaurant has a good choice of falafel & hummus dishes. Take-away is popular & there are a few tables for dining in. **$$**

**Kebda & Hamis Restaurant** King Saud Rd, 50m west of Basateen Mall, Shaqra; 053 702 0601; 04.30–23.00 daily. If you are looking for a wide range of Yemeni dishes, then head here. Try a Yemeni b/fast as many Saudis do, or have a hearty dinner after exploring the area. **$$**

## What to see and do

***Ushaiqer Heritage Village*** (24hrs daily; admission to village free; individual museums SAR5–10) The Heritage Village is surrounded by a wall containing watchtowers and small viewing windows. The entrance is through two sets of wooden doors, one that is opened to allow vehicles to enter. Once through the main gates, drive to the end of the road and park near al Salim Museum or al Nashwan House.

The village is in the process of being restored, mostly sympathetically. There are about 400 houses and 25 mosques, all constructed in the traditional Najd style of mud-brick, with a palm-frond roof, highly decorated wooden doors and the distinctive triangular rooftops found throughout the region. Many of the most prominent houses contain a sign bearing the family name. Some of these can be visited if the doors are open during your visit, as they have been turned into intriguing family heritage museums. Visitors can wander along any of the pathways in the village, and may find themselves in gardens, courtyards or the historical Mahasiri market along the way. There is some attempt at making part of the village accessible for wheelchair users but, like the restoration in general, it is a work in progress.

Don't end your exploration without checking out the vendors selling dates, snacks, soft drinks and juices in the main square on the way back to the entrance road.

**Hamad al Salim Museum** (no published opening hours) This house museum is nearest the village entrance to the right. It is well organised, with several rooms containing homewares, clothing, old postage stamps and other artefacts of ordinary life from the recent past. The family is in residence and will happily guide you through their home, although their English is very limited.

The **al Nashwan Heritage House** and **Hamad al Dowayan Museum** are both over the road from the Salim Museum and are worth a quick visit if you find them open. Both give further examples of how everyday life was very different only a generation or two ago.

**Al Omar Traditional House** (🕘 16.00–23.00 daily; small entrance fee) Anyone wandering through the labyrinth of paths is likely to arrive at this house at some point. In addition to some of the other houses and museums, this house also displays many children's items from the second half of the 20th century. Take time to accept the hospitality on offer and share a cup of kahwa on the carpeted seating area.

**AL MAJMA'AH المجمعة** Al Majma'ah is a small, pleasant city with a population of about 50,000 and makes a good base for visiting northern Riyadh Province. It is located on Highway 65 about 100km from the attractions of Ushaiqer. It is about 190km north of Riyadh and about 170km south of Buraydah. Al Majma'ah also has a train station with services from Riyadh and from al Qassim, Ha'il, al Jouf and Qurayyat from the north. Although the train station is handy for fast travel from Riyadh or the north, you will need a vehicle to get around.

**Where to stay and eat** You will find the usual mix of basic Saudi, Lebanese and south Asian restaurants here, mostly catering to the working population. Restaurants are concentrated along Route 535 or King Abdul Aziz Road.

**Boudl al Majma'ah** Cnr King Abdullah Rd & al Imam Mohammed bin Saud St; ☎ 016 421 1780; w boudl.com. This property from the Saudi chain of apartment hotels is a good choice for those looking for comfort & space. Well-appointed rooms & ample parking. Centrally located. **$$$**

**Le Park Concord** Rte 535, just north of Abdul Rahman bin Tariq Rd; ☎ 016 421 0444. This hotel is a bit more business orientated with a conference room & small business centre. There is also an indoor pool for men. Parking on site. **$$**

**Raoum Inn** Hwy 50 north of King Faisal Rd; ☎ 016 431 3637; w raouminn-magmaa.businesssite.com. This medium-size property from the reliable Saudi chain is a good alternative to Boudl for those on a more modest budget but looking for similar features. Conveniently located near the Sport City & al Maqsourah Park. **$$**

**What to see and do** To the west of the **Grand Mosque** (off Hwy 50 & King Faisal Rd), concentrated along al Noor, al Qutaimah and Munikh streets, are a number a small **house museums**, converted homes with mostly 20th-century items on display. Stop by the ruins of **Munikh Castle** and the surrounding 18th-century village which have yet to be restored. A watchtower at the top of the hill dominates the site.

***Al Ghat*** ('The old Deira' on Google Maps; off Hwy 65, 1.5km south on Rte 535; 🕘 village: 24hrs daily, museum: 08.00–15.00 & 16.00–20.00 Sat–Thu, 16.00–20.00 Fri; admission free) Najd is filled with heritage villages in various states of repair and renovation. Al Ghat, just over 50km from al Majma'ah, is one of them and well worth a visit if you are exploring Riyadh Province, or simply travelling along Highway 65 between Riyadh and Buraydah. At more than 1.5km long, this is one of the largest restored Najd villages in the area. With a source of water, the village has been settled since prehistoric times. It remains a fertile area, producing high-quality dates even now. The village is built on a gently sloping hill, giving the visitor a brilliant view of the site. Don't miss key points of interest, including the old souq,

Ousherza Mosque and the Emera Palace, once home to Prince Nasser bin Saad al Sudairy of the influential family that has intermarried with the al Saud royal family. It is now the al Ghat museum, containing tools from the Palaeolithic, as well as agricultural and hunting artefacts.

## AL QASSIM PROVINCE منطقة القصيم

Al Qassim Province is known as the breadbasket of Saudi Arabia, and with a population of about 1.5 million is Saudi Arabia's wealthiest province, thanks in great part to its fertile land around Wadi Rummah and other oases. It may not be the most obvious destination on the developing tourist trail, but it is a good place to learn more about desert agriculture, to attend authentic cultural festivals uninfluenced by tourism, and to relax. Al Qassim has the reputation for being the most conservative province in the most conservative region in the Kingdom – although not progressive like Jeddah, parts of the Eastern Province, or even Riyadh, the province is open and welcoming and much more friendly and relaxed than many might expect.

Al Qassim Province has a desert climate and is best to visit from November to April. Bring warm clothes for the winter as temperatures can be cool overnight. Spring and autumn weather is pleasant, with warm days and cool evenings. It gets unbearably hot in the summer, with temperatures often reaching 50°C.

**HISTORY** Al Qassim Province has been settled since prehistoric times. It became a part of the Islamic Empire during the time of the Prophet Mohammed and was on the old pilgrimage route from Mesopotamia to Mecca. During this time, Princess Zubaydah, wife of the Capilh Harun al Rashid, oversaw the establishment of wells and other water supplies for pilgrims passing through al Qassim. The Emirate of Buraydah was founded by the Banu Tamim tribe in the late 16th century and established the city of the same name. It was led by Rashid al Duraiby. However, the al Sulaim family, based in nearby Unayzah, was opposed and eventually captured the emirate. They stayed in power until the end of the Second Saudi State, when the al Rashids from the Emirate of Ha'il gained control. After further power struggles between the al Sulaims and al Rashids, al Qassim was annexed by ibn Saud in 1907 as part of the Emirate of Nejd and eventually the Kingdom of Saudi Arabia.

### GETTING THERE AND AWAY

**By air** Buraydah's Prince Naif bin Abdul Aziz International Airport serves al Qassim Province and has a range of domestic services on Saudia and flynas. There are also some services on regional carriers from Egypt, Pakistan, Turkey and several other GCC countries.

**By road** Highway 65 is the south–north route into Buraydah from Riyadh Province from the south and from Ha'il and al Jouf provinces from the north. This is the route that visitors would use if coming from Riyadh city. Highway 60 is the west–east route, which visitors would use if travelling from Yanbu or Medina. Be particularly careful to keep your petrol tank topped up and to use the toilets when you have the opportunity as distances east of Medina are long and desolate. You will need a car when exploring al Qassim.

SAPTCO **buses** serve Buraydah, Unayzah and a few smaller towns in the province. **Taxis** and Uber services can be found in Buraydah and to a lesser extent in Unayzah.

**By rail** Al Qassim station is located on Route 7011, nearly 40km to the northeast of Buraydah centre, and serves al Qassim Province. This line runs south to Riyadh and north to Ha'il, al Jouf near Sakaka and Qurayyat. See page 73 for more detail.

**BURAYDAH بريدة** Buraydah is the capital of al Qassim Province with a population of 750,000. For many, Buraydah is the obvious stopover when travelling to Ha'il and points north. It is worth a short visit as there is a fair bit to see and do that many visitors may not be aware of, from well-appointed museums to parks to farm visits.

Despite al Qassim being the agricultural heartland of conservative Najd, Buraydah is modernising at a pace, but still retains its heritage – modern government buildings, for example, have been designed sympathetically to fit in with existing structures and sit side by side quite comfortably with traditional Najd architecture. Many young people in particular are keen to let visitors know that they are more open and welcoming than ever before. There is no doubt that more women are out and about than expected.

**Getting there and away** Highway 65 passes through the city centre and is the main south–north route from Riyadh (350km to the south) and Hai'l (280km) and points north. Highway 60 is the route for those travelling from points west. It is 530km from Madinah.

**Where to stay** Buraydah is a modern city with a surprising number of hotels that meet international standards. There is something to suit everyone's budget in the city and surrounding area. Many older, business-orientated hotels are located near Highway 65, King Abulaziz Road and King Fahd Road, closer to the city centre. The up-and-coming new neighbourhood of ar Rayaan in the northwest of the city is popular with those seeking newer accommodation in a pleasant, convenient location.

For **farm resorts** that offer accommodation, see page 161.

### *City centre*

For shoestring budgets, there are 3 **OYO hotels** (w oyorooms.com; $–$$), all located near the city centre.

**Movenpick** [157 C2] Cnr King Fahd bin Abdul Aziz & King Khalid bin Abdul Aziz rds; 016 316 9999; w movenpick.com. Many consider this large, prestigious property to be Buraydah's premier hotel, with 5-star amenities, including an indoor pool for men, cafés, 24hr room service, a good restaurant & French-style coffee shop. The rooms have been modernised & are luxuriously comfortable. Business travellers will find everything they need. Note that the hotel is at the junction of 2 busy roads. **$$$$**

**Golden Tulip** [157 B2] King Abdul Aziz Rd, 500m west of roundabout at Sinaah Rd; 016 381 7500; w goldentulipbiraidah.com. This decent-sized property has similar amenities to the Movenpick at a more modest price. Buffet b/fast. Good customer service. **$$$**

**Best Western Plus** [157 B2] Prince Faisal bin Misha'l Rd off King Abdul Aziz Rd; 016 382 0606; w bestwesternplusburaidah.com. Located in the same area slightly west of the Golden Tulip, this largish casual hotel is quieter than many others nearby. Modestly priced for the amenities. **$$–$$$**

### *Ar Rayaan and al Nahdah*

In addition to the listings below, there are several Saudi-owned hotels along the same street as the Radisson Blu. These 3-star hotels & apartments include the **Lillian** [157 A1] (016 385 3888; **$$$**), the **Rokn Tala** [157 A1] (055 240 3444; **$$$**) and **Rami's Hotel** [157 A2] (016 330 7777; **$$$**); all are relatively new & clean & offer a less expensive alternative in the same neighbourhood. Book through a reputable website or direct with the hotel via WhatsApp.

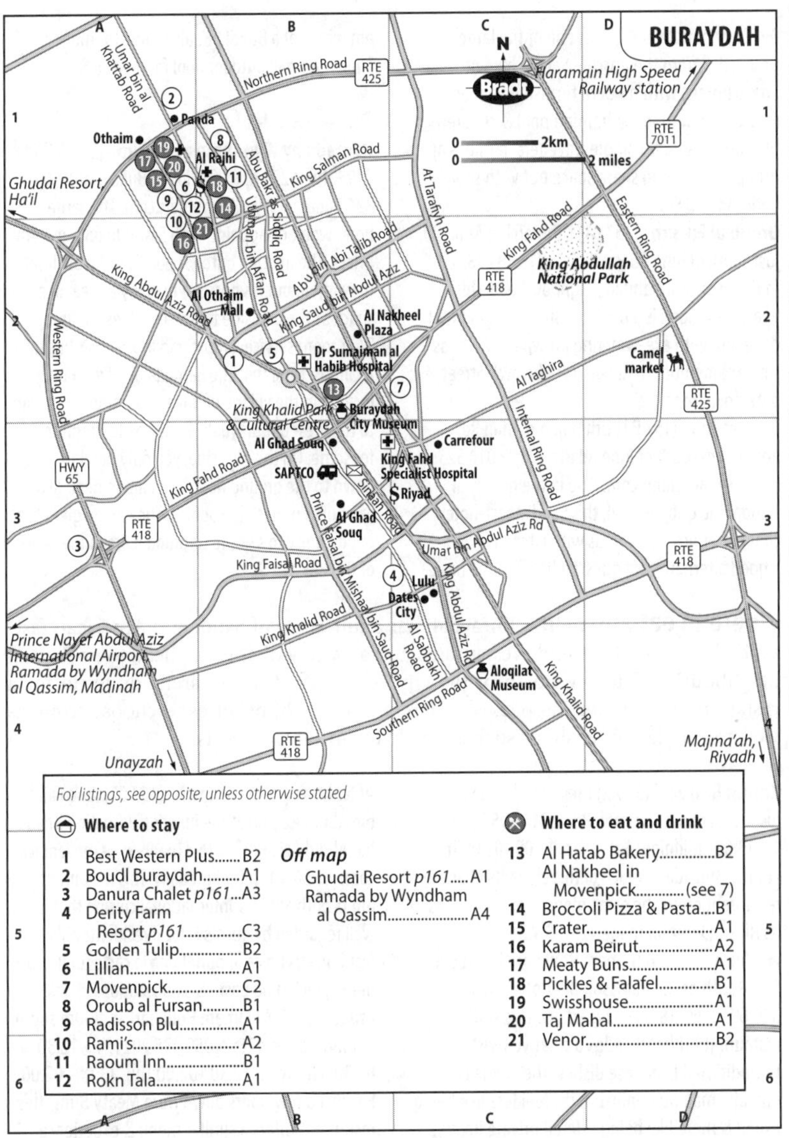




**Radisson Blu** [157 A1] Imam Boukhari St just south of Ring Rd Rte 425; 016 355 5554; **w** radissonhotels.com. Built in 2017, this large property has everything you want in a modern 4-star hotel, with attention to detail from the number of electrical outlets to the finer touches in the bathroom. What really sets this hotel apart is the excellent standard of customer service. The receptionists in particular are very helpful & knowledgeable, going out of their way to advise on everything from recommended restaurants to sightseeing to practical traffic advice. The on-site restaurant provides an excellent buffet b/fast, as well as a good selection of international cuisine for lunch & dinner. The coffee shop to the right of reception serves as a meeting place for well-to-do Saudis. Free parking in an underground car park & on the street. **$$$–$$$$**

**Boudl Buraydah** [157 A1] North of Ring Rd Rte 425 on Umar bin al Khattab Rd; 016 381

0919; w boudl.com. This is one of the larger properties from the upscale Saudi chain of apart-hotels, with modern furnishings, room service, an outdoor swimming pool & children's play area. Good for single travellers, families or groups wanting to share space but with separate bedrooms. **$$$**

**Oroub al Fursan** [157 B1] Uthman bin Affan Rd, just south of Ring Rd Rte 425; ☎ 016 383 3832. In the nearby al Nahdah neighbourhood, this apartment hotel is a medium-sized budget hotel complete with eye-watering brown décor. It has similar amenities to Raoum (see below). Street parking in front. **$$**

**Raoum Inn** [157 B1] Uthman bin Affan Rd, about 2km south of Ring Rd Rte 425; ☎ 016 323 3232; w raouminn.com. Also in the nearby al Nahdah neighbourhood, this Saudi apart-hotel chain offering clean rooms with kitchen facilities is a good alternative for guests who want the basic amenities of a Boudl but also value for money. There's a small outdoor pool for men. **$$**

### *Further afield*

**Ramada by Wyndham al Qassim** [157 A4] Rte 419 & Rte 6252 King Khalid Rd, Bukayriah; ☎ 016 336 6666; w wyndhamhotels.com. This large hotel won't disappoint, with 5-star luxury at 3-star prices. The inviting outdoor pool is sadly off-limits to women, but it's possible to enjoy a meal or a snack at the poolside tables. Good restaurant, 24hr room service, ample parking & basic business facilities. Note that the Ramada by Wyndham is located in the village of Bukayriah, more than 5km to the west of Buraydah, & may be too remote for some. On the plus side, you only need to go down to the ground floor if you are in need of a Starbucks or Baskin-Robbins. The village gives the opportunity to sample traditional life in the heart of Qassim. **$$$**

**Where to eat and drink** Buraydah has a full range of Saudi and American fast-food chains, but for trendy restaurants and a variety of cuisines head to ar Rayaan neighbourhood to the north of the city centre. And if you aren't quite up for a restaurant but are feeling peckish, there are plenty of bakeries to choose from, as well as popular sweet shops such as Saadedin and Rose Sweets.

**Karam Beirut** [157 A2] Imam Boukhari St, just north of King Salman Rd; ☎ 016 355 5552; ⌚ 13.00–midnight Sat–Wed, 13.00–01.00 Thu–Fri. The Buraydah branch of this elegant Lebanese restaurant offers the same menu & experience as its Riyadh location (page 123). **$$$$$**

✷ **Venor** [157 B2] Imam Boukhari St just over 1km south of the Radisson Blu hotel; ☎ 016 326 6060; ⌚ 18.00–03.30 daily. This stylish restaurant brilliantly adds a creative twist to traditional Lebanese dishes. The venue is upscale, making family booths feel less like being exiled & more like being offered private luxury, complete with buzzer to call the waiter. Helpful service if you need a recommendation, though you won't go wrong with the *mutabal ajamy* with spices, pistachio nuts, pomegranate seeds & toasted onion slivers, the cashew *muhamara* with mixed nuts in a spicy pomegranate paste & chilli oil, or falling-off-the-bone lamb in a scrumptious creamy gravy of nutmeg, cinnamon, pomegranate seed, walnut, cashew & pistachio. Indulge in their delicious rose lemonade to complete the meal. **$$$$$**

**Al Nakheel in Movenpick** [157 C2] King Fahd bin Abdul Aziz Rd at the junction with King Khalid bin Abdul Aziz Rd; ☎ 016 316 9999; w movenpick.com; ⌚ 06.30–midnight daily. This restaurant offers both Saudi & international cuisine that is well regarded by guests & local residents alike. B/fast buffet; choice of buffet or à la carte for lunch & dinner, including pasta & salad stations. **$$$$**

**Crater** [157 A1] Imam Boukhari St, 200m south of Ring Rd Rte 425; ☎ 059 436 2021; ⌚ 12.30–01.30 Sat–Wed, 12.30–02.00 Thu, 13.00–02.00 Fri. Just a few doors down from Meaty Buns, this restaurant offers a similar menu & experience. Good alternative if Meaty Buns is busy. **$$$**

**Meaty Buns** [157 A1] Imam Boukhari St, 200m south of Ring Rd Rte 425; ☎ 057 007 1999; w meatybuns.net; ⌚ noon–02.00 Sun–Thu, 13.00–02.00 Fri–Sat. If you need proof that Saudis have a good sense of humour, then look no further than the name of this restaurant. This is the place to go if you want to experience a Saudi take on an American burger bar. They also serve excellent steaks. Although waygu beef is on offer, the tenderloin is excellent at a fraction of the price. Don't miss the cheesy paprika fries. Very casual dining with no separate family section. Outdoor seating during the winter. Fast American-style service. $$$

**Swisshouse** [157 A1] Imam Boukhari St; 9200 05099; w swisshouse-sa.com; noon–02.00 daily. This lovely restaurant serves Arabic cuisine & much more, from light salads & sandwiches to pasta & steaks. If you are a seafood fan, check the several refined dishes on offer that are unlikely to be found at the same level elsewhere in Buraydah. The skewered marinated meats inspired by Portuguese & Brazilian *espetada* are also a very pleasant surprise. Those with a sweet tooth will want to save room for the dessert menu. Branches also in Madinah & Jeddah. $$$

**Taj Mahal** [157 A1] Imam Boukhari St, 100m north of the Radisson Blu hotel; 016 385 5853; 12.30–01.00 daily. Run by Indian & Nepalese staff, this restaurant offers northern Indian, Chinese & Thai cuisine – the south Asian options in particular are very good. The family section upstairs is often full so women may be offered a table with open seating in the singles section if they think you are unlikely to mind. The men dining in the singles section seemed used to this when we went. This restaurant also does a busy take-away business. Service can be a bit slow but a gentle reminder is received with grace. $$$

**Al Hatab Bakery** [157 B2] King Abdul Aziz Rd, at the junction of al Amir Faisal bin Bandar bin Abdul Aziz Rd; 059 582 5454; w alhatab.com.sa; 06.00–midnight daily. This haven of an upscale bakery & more (page 128) has a branch in Buraydah. $$

**Broccoli Pizza & Pasta** [157 B1] Umar bin al Khatab Rd near King Salman Rd aka Old Riyadh Rd; 016 384 4441; 13.00–02.00 daily. If you crave an Italian-style pizza or pasta, Broccoli is the place to go. Casual & moderately priced, this café-style restaurant has the usual singles & family section seating. Many opt for take-away. There are other branches in ar Rayaan & Unayzah. $$

**Pickles & Falafel** [157 B1] Umar bin al Khatab Rd, near King Salman Rd aka Old Riyadh Rd; 9200 02690; 05.00–02.00 daily. Delicious cheap eats with a menu of Middle Eastern street food that goes way beyond falafel. Your order will be a generous size & is freshly made. The seating area is open but we didn't see any women on site, so women & mixed groups might need to be prepared for a few stares. Good take-away business. $

**Shopping** The main shopping malls are **al Othaim Mall** [157 B2] (Uthmain bin Affan Rd) and **al Nakheel Plaza** [157 B2] (King Abdullah Rd). Both are located near the city centre and are open throughout the day until late in the evening (afternoon opening hours on Fri). Buraydah also has Danube, Lulu and Panda supermarkets.

The main souq is **al Ghad** [157 B3], which is located southwest of the junction of King Abdul Aziz and King Fahd roads. Visitors looking for souvenirs might prefer to travel to Unayzah and visit al Musawkaf Market.

## Other practicalities

**Al Rajhi Bank** [157 B1] Umar bin al Khatab Rd; 9200 03344; w alrajhibank.com.sa; 09.30–16.30 Sun–Fri

**Riyad Bank** [157 B3] Cnr King Abdul Aziz & al Taghira rds; 9200 02470; w riyadbank.com; 09.30–16.30 Sun–Thu

**Dr Sumaiman al Habib Hospital** [157 B2] Cnr King Abdul Aziz & Uthman bin Affan rds; 016 316 6666; w hmg.com.sa

**King Fahd Specialist Hospital** [157 B3] King Abdullah Rd, 400m south of King Fahd Rd; 016 325 2000; w kfshb.med.sa

**Al Dawaa Pharmacy** [157 A1] Umar bin al Khatab Rd, ar Rayaan; 800 244 4444; w al-dawaa.com; 09.00–02.00 Sun–Thu, 16.30–01.00 Fri–Sat

**Nahdi Pharmacy** [157 B1] Imam Boukhari St, next to al Rajhi bank; 9200 24673; w nahdionline.com; 07.00–02.00 Sun–Thu, 13.00–01.00 Fri–Sat. There are several other branches throughout the metropolitan area.

**Saudi Post** [157 B3] al Adl Rd, next to Nesto supermarket; w splonline.com.sa; 08.00–21.00 Sun–Thu

## What to see and do

***Aloqilat Museum*** [157 C4] (Nestled in a palm grove on the eastbound lane of busy Rte 418, 200m east of King Abdul Aziz Rd; ☎050 513 3191; ⏲ 08.30–noon & 16.00–18.30 daily; admission free) Although this museum looks underwhelming from the outside, it is well worth the visit for anyone interested in the history of the founding economic leaders of al Qassim. It holds many important documents and photographs from these families alongside the usual artefacts from the past century. The building is a brilliant example of a well-designed and well-preserved Najd home, with a wealth of traditional interior design features, numerous carpets and plenty of seating options on and off the floor. Good manners mean accepting the generous hospitality you are likely to receive from the museum staff. You will be treated with traditional coffee, dates and biscuits.

***Buraydah City Museum*** [157 B2] (King Abdul Aziz Rd at the junction of King Fahd Rd; ☎016 323 1700; ⏲ 08.00–17.00 Sun–Thu; admission free) The building housing this museum is modern and has been constructed in traditional Najd design. It does a good job of displaying a wide range of 20th-century artefacts. Household goods, tools, taxidermy of native animals, early banknotes and coins and militaria are all on display. There is a large collection from previous Saudi kings, as well as interesting family photographs of King Abdul Aziz and his male progeny. King Abdul Aziz's vintage Cadillac will greet you at the entrance to the museum.

***King Khalid Park and Cultural Centre*** [157 B2] (Immediately east of the Buraydah City Museum; ☎016 324 9788; ⏲ 08.00–18.00 Sun–Thu; admission free, though some events may require tickets to be purchased) With its huge dome, King Khalid Cultural Centre, located on the western perimeter of King Khalid Park, is impossible to miss. This is the hub for contemporary cultural events in the region, where there is a theatre and exhibits are displayed. Non-Arabic speakers may struggle to fully appreciate some of the programmes on offer. The dome has an observation deck in its centre, which gives you a good view of the city. The park is peaceful during the afternoon and becomes busy at night. Be aware that single men and all male groups may have limited access to the park on certain days, which can change.

***King Abdullah National Park*** [157 C2] (Southwest cnr at the junction of rtes 425 & 7011 in the northeast of Buraydah; ⏲ 24hrs daily; admission free) This large green space has something for everyone. It's a series of many gardens and parks, with plenty of activities. There is a fountain show complete with dancing water, vendors, food vans, children's play areas and traditional low, cushioned seating for relaxation and perhaps for sharing a picnic with family or friends. Others come to the park for cycling or jogging. There's no obvious gender segregation but look around the area of the park you have chosen to be sure.

***Dates City*** [157 C3] (Southwest junction of King Khalid & King Abdul Aziz rds; ☎016 326 5000; ⏲ 24hrs; admission free) This massive complex is, unsurprisingly, all about the dates. Stop by for a few minutes to take in the whole date world. Bizarrely, in the midst of the market there is a mid-20th-century American pick-up truck complete with canopy over the flatbed adorned with the Saudi crossed-swords emblem – in case you were in need of a diversion from all the dates. If you are visiting in August, check out the **Buraydah Date Festival** activities at Date City and scattered around other areas of the city. Your accommodation will be able to provide further information.

***Camel market*** [157 D2] (East of Buraydah near al Taghira & al Haddyyah rds just west of Rte 425; 🕘 06.00–midnight daily; admission free) Buraydah is believed to be home to the world's largest camel market, more accurately called the cattle market. Visitors can see traders from all over the region buy various livestock – camels, sheep, goats and more – in the early morning hours. Go from sunrise until mid-morning as this is when most of the trading takes place. As is the case elsewhere, you can watch the spectacle of camels dangling in the air as they are being hoisted on to the back of a flatbed truck.

***Farm visits and farm resorts*** With al Qassim's economic reliance on good agricultural conditions enhanced by modern techniques, a farm visit is a good way to understand why this is the Kingdom's wealthiest province, as well as to learn about sustainability in the extreme desert climate. Visitors can participate in a variety of activities such as horseriding and harvesting fruit such as dates, figs and even strawberries. This is a good opportunity to see another side of Saudi life and discover how many urban Saudi families get away from it all – it's a very different experience from museums, archaeological sites or the restaurant scene. Note that some farms offer accommodation, while others welcome day visitors only. The farms listed below all have rooms for guests planning to stay overnight.

A further farm-stay option is the Country Inn Resort (page 163) in Unayzah.

**Danura Chalet** [157 A3] Junction of Hwy 65 & King Fahd Rd; 050 173 6059. This farm resort with lovely grounds, equidistant from Buraydah city centre & the airport, is low-key by Saudi standards. Whether you want to take advantage of the swimming pool at your own chalet or picnic in a Bedouin tent, this is the place to relax. You can choose to self-cater or order from the property's menu. There's also a popular children's playground. Book through a reputable website. **$$$**

✷ **Ghudai Resort** [157 A1] 15km northwest of the airport, off Rte 419 past Qassim University on an unnamed road; ⊕ 26.3695489, 43.7175148; /// carnivore.furthering.sweetens; 050 529 1263; w ghudaifarm.com. One of the Kingdom's first certified organic farms, this is also an eco-friendly operation, with use of clean energy for well-water management, solar energy to generate electricity & other sustainable practices. Thousands of date palm trees have been planted to grow at least 8 different varieties of date & their products. If you have never tasted date paste, this is a great place to try this delicious treat. The resort has 5 rooms, a dining room if you prefer to organise the meal through the resort & an outdoor pool. Intimate & relaxing. This property is not near shops, so bring what you need for your stay. **$$$**

**Derity Farm Resort** [157 C3] al Sabbakh Rd, between King Faisal & King Khalid rds, Buraydah; 0157 050 8884; SAR10 pp for day visitors. Although this is a farm, with horses & livestock, this resort is also a bit like a theme park, with cafés dotted around the property where guests can linger while their children are active on rides, themed playground attractions & a small amusement park. You'll find it crowded during evenings & at w/ends. The accommodation itself is of Najd design with modestly comfortable rooms. Book through a reputable website. **$$**

**UNAYZAH عنيزة** The small city of Unayzah (also spelled Unaizah and sometimes Onaizah) has a population of about 153,000. It is a pleasant city and a relative oasis of calm, with many green parks and lovely examples of Najd architecture. It is located on the eastern edge of Wadi Rummah, the kingdom's longest wadi at more than 600km. Although it's on the historical pilgrimage route from Mesopotamia to Mecca, it is believed that Unayzah has been settled since pre-Islamic times given its plentiful water supply and agricultural success. It's a great alternative for those exploring al Qassim who prefer to avoid staying in the much larger city of Buraydah.

**Getting there and away** Travel on Highway 65 south from Buraydah to Route 414 east. Not long after leaving the southern urban areas of Buraydah, this drive takes you away from the desert and into lush greenery from many date palm farms, complete with their conical watchtowers, some of which date back to Ottoman era. You will cross Wadi Rummah at ar Remah just to the north of Unayzah.

## Where to stay *Map, below*

Although many make a day trip to Unayzah from Buraydah, others may prefer to enjoy the serenity of this historical town for a little longer, perhaps staying at one of Unayzah's many resort hotels.

**Swiss International Resort** Ring Rd Rte 7051 at Abu Bakr al Siddiq Rd; 050 317 4000; w swissinternationalhotels.com. Comprised of a range of 1- to 3-bedroom villas, this resort has the feel of a home away from home, Saudi style. Many villas have an indoor pool, while others have a private outdoor pool. Unlike many other resorts, there is a full-service restaurant with a b/fast buffet & à la carte options throughout the day. Room service is also available. The resort is adjacent to al Hajeb Park, which extends the tranquil ambience. There is also a small grocery shop nearby. **$$$$–$$$$$**

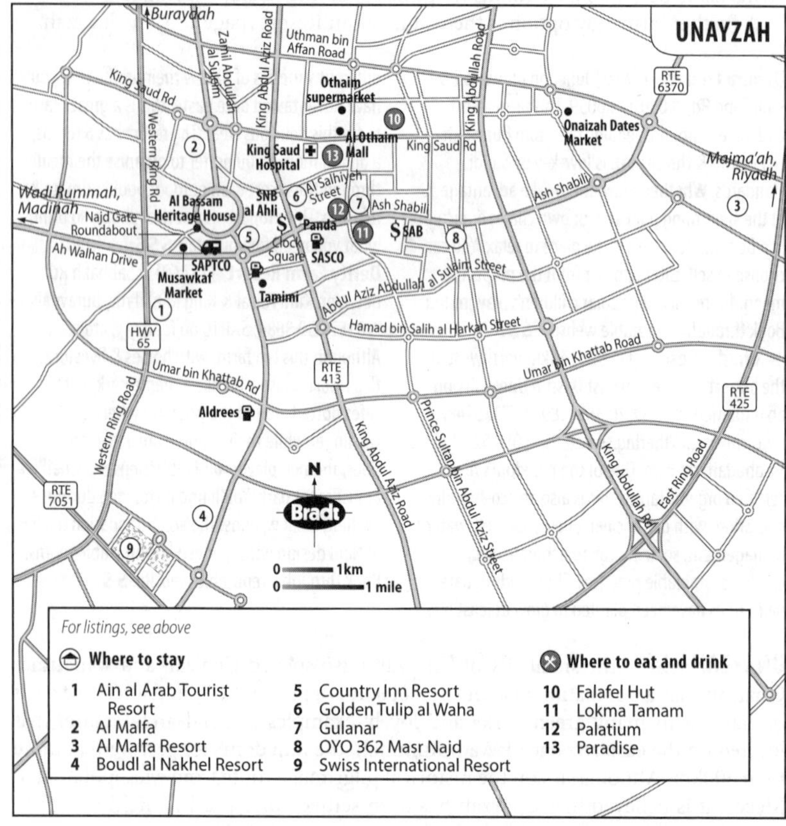

**Ain al Arab Tourist Resort** Western Ring Rd, 800m south of Rte 414; 050 841 0111. More like a sprawling upscale motel, this property is located near the main attractions. Guest accommodation is generous, with suites feeling more like villas. There is an outdoor pool for men & children & a children's playground. Convenient parking. Book through a reputable website. **$$$**

**Al Malfa Resort** Off East Ring Rd & Rte 6373; 016 361 8666; w almalfa.com.sa. This upscale resort hotel is just east of Unayzah. Immerse yourself in the Najd architecture, authentic Saudi meals & greenery in the middle of the desert. Comfortable, spacious rooms with all the usual hotel amenities allow even the busiest guests to relax. **$$$**

**Boudl al Nakhel Resort** Zamil Abdullah al Suleim, about 1.5km north of Ring Rd Rte 7051; 016 363 7121; w boudl.com. Set in well-maintained grounds, this is a great place to get away from it all without being too far from Unayzah. Each chalet has its own private entrance; several also come with a private outdoor pool, allowing women to swim & sunbathe in private. Great for friends or families & excellent value for money; there's also a children's play area. **$$$**

**Country Inn Resort** Zamil Abdullah al Suleim, 200m north of al Madinah Rd; 055 420 2404. This resort provides a very different experience to many others around Unayzah. Built in the Najd style, it offers traditional accommodation with low seating & basic bedrooms. The rooms are small but comfortable enough. Some apartments have private outdoor seating overlooking the gardens, though there are tables in the gardens that can be used by all. On-site farm animals give visitors a glimpse of rural Saudi life. There is also a traditional majlis & an outdoor pool mostly used by children. It is possible to go as a day visitor for a small entrance fee of SAR10. Situated in central Unayzah, this property is conveniently located near Hyperpanda & Onaizah Mall. Book through a reputable website. **$$$**

**Golden Tulip al Waha Hotel** King Abdul Aziz Rd, Rte 413 & al Salhiyeh St; 016 362 0000; w goldentulip.com. From the Dutch chain, this medium-sized hotel is centrally located, with well-appointed rooms, a restaurant, room service, on-site parking & a male-only outdoor pool adjacent to the male-only fitness centre. **$$$**

**Gulanar Hotel** Ash Shabili Rd, east of Prince Sultan bin Abdul Aziz St; 016 365 9777. This central hotel is among the best Unayzah has to offer. Its traditionally designed heritage building has been successfully converted into comfortable rooms, with a luxurious lobby & café, room service & fitness centre. Good customer service. Book through a reputable website. **$$$**

**OYO 362 Masr Najd** Ash Shabili Rd, 600m east of the Gulanar Hotel; 011 293 2743; w oyorooms.com. A centrally located budget option for a very basic stay. The service & cleanliness are above average for this hotel chain. There is another small OYO property 7km to the southwest of this one. **$–$$**

**Al Malfa Hotel** King Abdul Aziz Rd, south of King Saud Rd. Not to be confused with the resort of the same name, this small hotel is a good budget option for those looking for a touch of comfort that won't drain the wallet. There is a basic coffee shop on site with a view of a lovely green space. Restaurants & other amenities are in walking distance or a short drive away. Free parking. Book through a reputable website. **$**

## Where to eat and drink *Map, opposite*

For those looking for cheap eats, al Romansiah, al Baik, Herfy, Kudu and other Saudi chain restaurants are all in Unayzah.

✷ **Lokma Tamam** Ash Shabili Rte 6370 at Prince Sultan bin Abdul Aziz St; 055 700 0380; 12.30–02.00 daily. This is a lovely Turkish Anatolian restaurant in the city centre. Upon entering, you will find the family section to the left, the singles section to the right & a very tempting sweets counter directly in front. Really, though, this is a meat lover's paradise, with kebabs, ribs, burgers, chicken, 1 veg dish & a few salads. Check out the kofte specials, with tahini or cherries. The speciality Cubani salad is an unusual mix of greens, cheese & pomegranate seeds – but it somehow works. Excellent service from the helpful staff who are knowledgeable & happy to answer questions. **$$$$**

**Palatium** Prince Sultan bin Abdul Aziz St, 100m north of Ash Shabili; 055 363 3131; 05.00–01.00 daily. Traditional Arabic cuisine sits comfortably beside a selection of pasta, pizzas & burgers at this popular restaurant. The singles seating is open & airy in contrast to the curtained family section. Good service. They also do a busy take-away business. Parking in front of the restaurant. $$$

**Paradise** King Saud Rd just east of King Saud Hospital; ☎ 9200 06457; ⏱ 13.30–midnight daily. This restaurant has a good range of vegetarian & non-vegetarian Indian dishes. They also offer a choice of Italian pasta, pizza & grills. Stylish seating & private curtained family section. $$$

**Falafel Hut** King Saud Rd at Abdul Rahman al Nogaidan St; ☎ 059 756 3616; ⏱ 06.00–11.30 Sat–Thu, 17.00–23.00 daily. This place does a great take-away business with fresh falafel made to your taste, alongside other Middle Eastern street food. $

## What to see and do

***Al Bassam Heritage House*** (Adjacent to Musawkaf Market; ⏱ hours generally the same as the market) Al Bassam Heritage House is another prominent family home that has been converted to a heritage museum. With a well-organised collection of 20th-century family artefacts, the house has seasonal men's diwans, a family living area, a garden and barn for livestock. As this was historically a grand home, the restoration is as interesting as the antiques on display.

***Musawkaf Market*** (Ah Walhan Dr, just south of the distinctive Najd gate roundabout at Abdullah Khaled al Sulaim St; ☎ 055 982 9449; ⏱ 16.00–22.00 daily) This restored market is of modest size but is filled with shop stalls with a focus on antiques, traditional foods and snacks. If you are looking for souvenirs, this is a good place to find local Najd handicrafts. Wander around the building to find traditional seating when you have had enough of shopping. The market is reasonably wheelchair friendly as the floors, although made of stone, are flat.

***Onaizah Dates Market*** (South of Uthman bin Affan Rd, east of King Abdullah Rd; ☎ 054 566 6590; ⏱ 08.00–23.00 daily) Just in case you didn't get your fill of dates in Buraydah, this large market is also an amazing site.

***Wadi bashing*** Wadi Rummah provides a wonderful landscape for nature enthusiasts. This dry riverbed was once filled with water flowing from Medina Province to the Arabian Gulf not far from the Kuwaiti border. Whether wadi bashing, camping or just getting away from it all, this vast valley is best explored to the west of Unayzah. As described on page 92, take full precautions whenever visiting wadis. Never travel alone, travel only in suitable vehicles, have adequate communication, and always check the weather forecast.

**UYUN AL JIWA عيون الجواء** Uyun al Jiwa (also Jawa), is one of the earliest known settlements in the Kingdom. It has been mentioned in several of the Mu'allaqat, also known as The Suspended Odes or The Hanging Poems, which are said to have been suspended in the Ka'aba in Mecca. Antarah bin Shaddad is one of the best known of these poets, originating from the Bani Abs tribe of the region. Another Mu'allaqat poet, Imru al Qais from the powerful Kindah tribe, also wrote fondly about Uyun al Jiwa. Thamudic inscriptions are found on rocks both at Sakhrat Anatarah and at al Hanadir, about 15km from Uyun al Jiwa.

About 40km northwest of Buraydah just off Highway 65 towards Ha'il, Uyun al Jiwa makes for an easy day trip from Buraydah.

**What to see and do** You will need a car to explore the village and historical areas, many of which are poorly signposted or not signposted at all. Most of the attractions in the area are outdoors, open 24 hours, and with free admission. Some of the key sites have a basic fence to protect them; others remain vulnerable to vandalism – sadly, be prepared to encounter litter and modern graffiti.

***Al Margab watchtower*** Another example of Najd, sand-coloured, mud-brick construction, this tower is situated on the highest point in Uyun al Jiwa. Recently restored, it contains the typical triangular windows, as well as a contrasting white triangular roof. It is possible for visitors to walk up to the tower fence to get a closer look.

***Al Khazzan Heritage Village*** (On an unnamed, paved road at the west end of the modern village; /// runaways.boots.comfortably; ⏲ no fixed hours – enter whenever the doors are open) This traditional Najd village is another restoration in progress. Simply walk through the ornate double wooden doors found in between the two tower gates to enter. From the sweeping entrance rooms lead off the hall to the left and right. The hall leads to a very large courtyard where trade once thrived. The conical watchtower in the right corner attests to the importance of the village's trading past along with the protective thick walls surrounding the village. If you are steady on your feet, it is possible to climb a set of tricky stairs to the first floor, which provides a brilliant view of the courtyard and village houses.

***Hasat al Nusra*** (Just south of the junction of Hwy 65 & Rte 6280) This near-spherical rock, towering several storeys high, appears to defy gravity, balanced as it is on a very narrow base. To get there, take the first unnamed road to the right, where the dramatic rock will already be in view. It sits on a hill that is best reached by 4x4 or by walking about 300m down from the unnamed road. Although it is currently fenced off, it is possible to walk around the entire rock. Afterwards, head to Sakhrat Antarah which is close by.

***Sakhrat Antarah (Antarah bin Shaddad Rock)*** Sakhrat Antarah is much smaller than nearby Hasat al Nusra, but is historically significant: this is where the Arab warrior and revered late 6th-/early 7th-century poet Antarah bin Shaddad allegedly met his lover, Ablah. Its weather-beaten façade contains many recesses interlaced with Thamudic inscriptions that reveal much of the history of the region. Unfortunately, this has been overshadowed by 21st-century graffiti. The rock is about 400m down the hill from Hasat al Nusra and can easily be visited on foot. It can also be accessed from the nearby Route 6280 just off Highway 65.

***Old Uyun*** Located on nondescript streets off Route 6280 about 2km south of Sakhrat Antarah, the old settlement contains a number of mud houses, mostly in poor condition and the old souq, with its shops in a circle. As you are very likely to pass by this area on the way to other sites, have a quick look at these ruins before the tourism authority starts renovation work.

***Ghat al Jawa*** The village of Ghat al Jawa (also known as Gaf al Jawa), some 7km west of Sakhrat Antarah, is home to another precarious rock – this one is a large flat slab balanced on a much smaller base rock, and overlooks a gathering place framed by palm trees. It is near a farm and horse stables to the left. There are tracks to the right of the gathering place leading to other inscribed rocks that dominate the scene. These large rock clusters lead the curious down the track towards flatter desert terrain. From Antarah bin Shaddad, continue south on Route 6280 until the T-junction, where you turn right on to Route 6260. Once you reach the village, turn left on to an unnamed, unpaved road about 100m past the Najd-style mosque on the left. The road is suitable for 2WD vehicles although a 4x4 will give you more opportunity to explore deeper into the desert.

## HA'IL PROVINCE منطقة حائل

Ha'il Province has a population of 700,000. It is bordered by al Qassim Province to the south, Medina and Tabuk provinces to the west, and al Jouf and Northern Borders provinces to the north. Strategically located at the crossroads of ancient pilgrimage routes between the Arabian Gulf and the Red Sea, as well as between Mesopotamia and the ancient kingdoms of what is now Yemen, Ha'il Province was once economically reliant on the pilgrimage trade, but today its main income source is agriculture, producing dates, fruit and grains, especially wheat.

Most people visit Ha'il Province to explore the UNESCO World Heritage Site at Jubbah. But there are other sites that shouldn't be overlooked when visiting this somewhat isolated but historically significant part of the Kingdom. Distances are long and the conditions are harsh in the desert, especially in the summer, but history buffs and nature lovers will be rewarded if the right precautions are taken.

Ha'il Province's desert climate means that the region is best visited from November to April. Bring warm clothes for the winter as temperatures are cool overnight. Spring and autumn weather is pleasant, with warm days and cool evenings. It gets unbearably hot in the summer, with temperatures often reaching 50°C.

**HISTORY** Ha'il Province has been inhabited from as far back as Neolithic times, verified by artefacts discovered in the region dating to 9000–7500BCE. It is very likely this is where the first humans settled in what is now the Kingdom of Saudi Arabia, some think as long as 1 million years ago. The rock art of the era depicts a semi-nomadic, hunter-gatherer civilisation. By the time of the Copper Age (from about 5000BCE), the lifestyle had become more settled, attested to by the differences in the stone tools that have been discovered here. These artefacts also signal major climate change from a more fertile and green environment to the desertification of the region that remains to the present. Arab tribes have lived in the province since pre-Islamic times, with the Ghassanisa and Lakhmis dominant alongside the Nabataeans.

During the earliest days of Islam, this region was absorbed into the Rashidun Caliphate under the force of Abu Bakr. From the 19th century, the province was ruled by emirs of the al Shammar tribe until they were conquered by ibn Saud in 1921, becoming part of the Third and current Saudi State.

### GETTING THERE AND AROUND

**By air** Ha'il domestic airport serves the province and has limited services on Saudia and flynas. There are also limited services on Air Arabia to Sharjah and flydubai to Dubai.

**By road** Highway 65 is the south–north route into Ha'il from Buraydah to the south and from al Jouf Province to the north. This is also the route to use if coming from Riyadh and al Qassim provinces. Highway 70 is the west–east route to use if travelling from al Ula. Drivers should be particularly careful to keep their petrol tank topped up and to use the toilets when available as distances between services are long and desolate. You will need a car when exploring Ha'il. Taxis and Uber can be found in Ha'il city.

SAPTCO **buses** serve Ha'il and a few smaller towns in the province.

**By rail** Ha'il station on Highway 65, about 20km to the north of Ha'il city centre, serves Ha'il Province (see page 73 for more detail). This line runs south to Riyadh and north to Qurayyat near the Jordanian border.

**SHOPPING** Abdullah al Othaim, Danube, Lulu and Panda supermarkets are all in Ha'il. There are also more modest grocers that will sell the basics in Ha'il and Jubbah. Elsewhere, supplies are limited in more remote areas.

**FAYD فيد** Fayd was a major stopping point along the Darb Zubaydah, the old caravan route for pilgrims travelling from Mesopotamia to Mecca. The first Abbasid Caliph, Abdullah abul' Abas, oversaw the building of stopping points along the way where pilgrims could rest and replenish supplies. As recognised by the Caliph, the oasis of Fayd was a perfect location to develop one of the major stations for this very long route. Formerly called Darb Heerah, the entire route was renamed Darb Zubaydah after Zubaydah bint Ja'far, the granddaughter of the Caliph abu Ja'far al Mansour and founder of Baghdad, as she had a key role in the improvement of this route. Fayd was also visited by bin Battuta in 1327 as he continued his explorations after leaving Mecca. Now in ruins in the tiny modern village of the same name, the entire site is unusual for the area as the structures are made of much darker basalt stone from nearby lava fields rather than the traditional light-coloured mud-brick found throughout Najd and elsewhere in the Kingdom.

Fayd is 100km southeast of Ha'il and 180km northwest of Buraydah. Most visitors make Fayd a stop when travelling between these cities. Leave Highway 65 at Route 8818. Travel west for 7km and you will reach the village. The ruins are on the north side of the road opposite the village and are undergoing restoration.

There is one petrol station in the village, useful if you need to top up the tank, but bring your own provisions. Otherwise, visit one of the very basic shops in Ash Shinan, about 15km to the northwest. You can also stop at Link Supermarket along Highway 65 if you are arriving from the north; it's about 25km from Fayd.

## What to see and do

***Fayd Archaeological Museum*** (⌚ Unpredictable hours; admission free) Entrance to the Fayd pilgrimage site is through the museum, which contains various artefacts, from the practical items used during the early Islamic period to more recent coins and jewels. There are a few photos on display giving an overview of the site and of early Islamic inscriptions left by pilgrims. Even without a guide, it is evident how important this site has been since the early days of Islamic pilgrimage.

***The Citadel*** The oasis contains two concentric walls built to protect the settlement. The outer wall has ten towers along its 750m length. Inside this wall used to be residential areas and shops along internal roads which were built parallel to the walls. The high, 350m-long interior wall was built as a military stronghold. Some of the walls have been recently restored, although most of the site remains in various states of ruin.

***Fayd Old City*** Excavations on the south side of the historic site have revealed ovens that are estimated to have produced food for as many as 1,000 people. They have also unearthed large cisterns for gathering water from nearby Harrat umm Hurruj. The northernmost cistern measures 22m in circumference and is 2m deep. South of the excavation site is the mosque built during this time.

## HARRAT

Volcanic craters and lava fields are known in Saudi Arabia as *harrat*. Many of these are found in Ha'il and Medina provinces, and there are a few near Mecca and Taif in Makkah Province. It is believed that the volcanos formed as a result of the Arabian plate shifting the land along parts of the Red Sea Rift, part of the much larger Great Rift Valley that extends from Lebanon through east Africa to Mozambique. Harrats are of significant interest to geologists and for anyone interested in nature.

***Al Hatima Crater*** Also known as Harrat Hutaymah, this crater is about 45km west of Fayd and is worth the visit if you are in the area. The crater was formed by a volcanic explosion and has a distinctive salt circle at its centre. It is possible to walk around the perimeter of the crater top, and also down on to the crater floor if you are fit enough – the descent is about 300m, and you will need to be able to climb down and back up. There are no safety measures in place and the ground is loose. At the bottom, you will also find basalt around the edges. Travel on Route 427 to the village of Tabah. The crater is about 8km from the asphalt near the town of Tabah on a dirt path that is easy to follow. Access is better with a 4x4 but it is possible with a 2WD vehicle.

**HA'IL حَائِل** Ha'il is located on the southern edge of the Nafud Desert. Since the earliest days of Islam, it has enjoyed a reputation for generosity among the Arab world. The ruler of the prominent Tayy tribe, Prince Hatim al Tai, lived in Ha'il. He was also a famous Arab poet and featured in *The One Thousand and One Nights* (*Arabian Nights*). He inspired the saying 'more generous than Hatem' that is used to this day in the Arabic-speaking world.

Ha'il was the capital of the Emirate of Ha'il from 1836 until 1921 and was ruled by the al Rashids, part of the dominant Shammar tribe and rivals of the Sauds. This came to an end when ibn Saud defeated the al Rashids, incorporating the emirate into the Kingdom of Saudi Arabia.

Today most of the city's 600,000-strong population still live conservative, traditional lives. Fewer women are out and about than in Buradyah and even Sakaka. The west side of the city is where many modern facilities are located, including most hotels and restaurants; but much of the city centre can be described as waiting for regeneration, including some tourist attractions. Take the chance to experience a key city in the history of the Kingdom before too much modernisation takes place.

### Getting there and away

See page 166 for details.

### Where to stay

Budget options are limited in Ha'il. It is important to note that many shoestring properties located near the city centre are often booked for labourers and may not be suitable for many visitors. There is no harm in asking, but have a look around the property first and ask to see a room.

#### *Upmarket*

**Millennium** [169 C1] Rte 8560, 5km south of the roundabout at the junction with Hwy 65; ☎ 016 538 6111; **w** millenniumhotels.com. This large 5-star hotel is part of the Singaporean Millennium & Copthorne group & is the city's premier upmarket hotel, catering to both business & leisure visitors. Guests should note that it is located almost 30km north of the city centre adjacent to the University of Ha'il & Ha'il

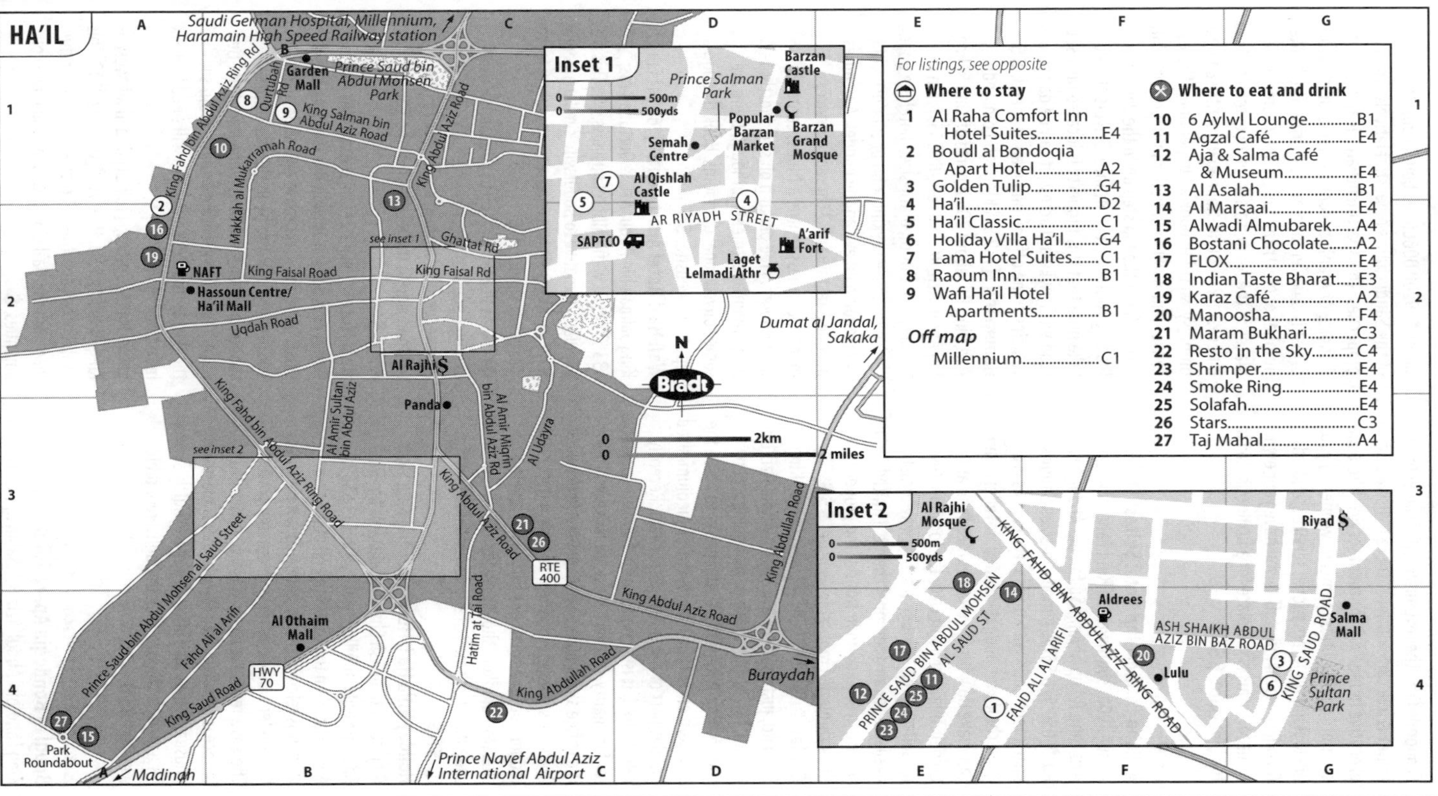
HA'IL
Saudi German Hospital, Millennium, Haramain High Speed Railway station
Inset 1
0 500m
0 500yds
Prince Salman Park
Barzan Castle
Popular Barzan Market
Barzan Grand Mosque
Semah Centre
Al Qishlah Castle
AR RIYADH STREET
SAPTCO
A'arif Fort
Laget Lelmadi Athr
For listings, see opposite
Where to stay
1 Al Raha Comfort Inn Hotel Suites.....E4
2 Boudl al Bondoqia Apart Hotel.....A2
3 Golden Tulip.....G4
4 Ha'il.....D2
5 Ha'il Classic.....C1
6 Holiday Villa Ha'il.....G4
7 Lama Hotel Suites.....C1
8 Raoum Inn.....B1
9 Wafi Ha'il Hotel Apartments.....B1
Off map
Millennium.....C1
Where to eat and drink
10 6 Aylwl Lounge.....B1
11 Agzal Café.....E4
12 Aja & Salma Café & Museum.....E4
13 Al Asalah.....B1
14 Al Marsaai.....E4
15 Alwadi Almubarek.....A4
16 Bostani Chocolate.....A2
17 FLOX.....E4
18 Indian Taste Bharat.....E3
19 Karaz Café.....A2
20 Manoosha.....F4
21 Maram Bukhari.....C3
22 Resto in the Sky.....C4
23 Shrimper.....E4
24 Smoke Ring.....E4
25 Solafah.....E4
26 Stars.....C3
27 Taj Mahal.....A4
Garden Mall
Prince Saud bin Abdul Mohsen Park
Qurtubah Rd
King Salman bin Abdul Aziz Road
King Fahd bin Abdul Aziz Ring Rd
Makkah al Mukarramah Road
King Abdul Aziz Road
see inset 1
Ghattat Rd
NAFT
King Faisal Road
King Faisal Rd
Hassoun Centre/ Ha'il Mall
Uqdah Road
Al Rajhi
Panda
Al Amir Sultan bin Abdul Aziz
Al Amir Miqrin bin Abdul Aziz Rd
Al Udayra
Dumat al Jandal, Sakaka
N
Bradt
0 2km
0 2 miles
see inset 2
King Fahd bin Abdul Aziz Ring Road
King Abdul Aziz Road
RTE 400
King Abdullah Road
Prince Saud bin Abdul Mohsen al Saud Street
Fahd Ali al Arifi
Al Othaim Mall
Hatim at Tai Road
HWY 70
King Saud Road
King Abdullah Road
Buraydah
Park Roundabout
Madinah
Prince Nayef Abdul Aziz International Airport
Inset 2
Al Rajhi Mosque
0 500m
0 500yds
KING FAHD BIN ABDUL AZIZ RING ROAD
Riyad
Aldrees
PRINCE SAUD BIN ABDUL MOHSEN AL SAUD ST
FAHD ALI AL ARIFI
ASH SHAIKH ABDUL AZIZ BIN BAZ ROAD
Lulu
KING SAUD ROAD
Salma Mall
Prince Sultan Park

Economic City. The restaurant offers an extensive buffet & à la carte options. There is also a café, an executive lounge & 24hr room service. There are separate spa facilities for men & women. If you are looking for international service standards & English-speaking staff, & you have your own transport, this is the place for a luxurious stay in Ha'il Province. **$$$$**

### *Mid-range*

**Al Raha Comfort Inn Hotel Suites** [169 E4] About 300m southwest of King Fahd bin Abdul Aziz Ring Rd on al Amir Sultan bin Abdul Aziz Rd; 050 576 5677. A medium-sized Saudi-style apartment hotel with basic services, this is a good choice for budget-minded travellers who can make do with fewer amenities than at the Golden Tulip but appreciate the location. Good for self-caterers, though a take-away b/fast is available for an additional charge. Limited room service; free parking in front of the property. Book through a reputable website. **$$$**

**Golden Tulip** [169 G4] Off west side of King Saud Rd, just south of Ash Shaikh Abdul Aziz bin Baz Rd; 016 541 9999; w hail.goldentulip.com. Suitable for visitors who prefer to be on the southern end of the ring road, this medium-sized hotel is part of the Dutch hotel chain. Recently refurbished, it is a good choice if you are looking for familiarity, comfort & a good location. There is a coffee shop, buffet-style restaurant serving Arabic & some international cuisine, a gym, indoor pool & a small gift shop. Free parking on site. Non-smokers should ensure their room or suite does not smell of smoke before accepting it.. **$$$**

**Holiday Villa Ha'il Hotel** [169 G4] King Saud Rd just south of Ash Shaikh Abdul Aziz bin Baz Rd & the Golden Tulip Hotel; 016 533 5555. Also located on the southern end of the ring road, this relatively large hotel will suit travellers looking for a modern, more international vibe. There is a restaurant, café & room service. The terrace is popular when the weather is pleasant. Unusually, they also offer an airport shuttle service for a modest charge. Book through a reputable website. **$$$**

### *Budget and shoestring*

**Boudl al Bondoqia Apart Hotel** [169 A2] King Fahd bin Abdul Aziz Rd, Salah al Din al Garbi; 9200 00666; w boudl.com. This is one of the Saudi chain's newest, relatively small properties. The apartments are clean & spacious. A choice of Arabic or continental room service b/fast is on offer for a modest price. The limited number of electrical outlets are located in odd places in the room, so ask for an extension lead if necessary. Ground-floor apartments can be a bit noisy, so try to book an upper floor. There's convenient parking in front of the property but be careful of the big step up to the pavement leading to the hotel entrance. Drivers should take note that this property is located on a slip road with awkward access; it can be dangerous if vehicles come off the ring road at speed. **$$**

**Raoum Inn** [169 B1] King Fahd bin Abdul Aziz Ring Rd, about 200m north of King Salman bin Abdul Aziz Rd; 016 536 5555. From the Saudi chain, this medium-sized hotel is a good choice for those seeking a bit of comfort while also keeping an eye on the budget. Amenities include a restaurant, 24hr room service, modest business centre, a fitness centre & games room. Free parking on site. Mostly 1- & 2-bedroom apartments although there are some conventional dbl rooms. Book through a reputable website. **$$**

**Wafi Ha'il Hotel Apartments** [169 B1] Cnr King Salman bin Abdul Aziz & Qurtubah rds; 016 533 5777; w wafihailhotel.business.site. This is a popular alternative to Boudl with similar amenities & prices. Many visitors choose this property for the location & service. **$$**

**Ha'il Classic Hotel** [169 C1] Uqdah Rd, west of King Abdul Aziz Rd, Hwy 70; 055 235 5332. Another very basic small hotel. Look for the misspelt sign to the reception of the 'Calassic Hotel'. **$**

**Ha'il Hotel** [169 D2] Cnr al Amir Miqrin bin Abdul Aziz Rd & ar Riyadh Rd. This very basic small hotel may suit those on a shoestring budget who want to be in the city centre, though women travelling alone might not be comfortable here. Located about 200m south of the Barzan market souqs. You will need to walk in to book. **$**

**Lama Hotel Suites** [169 C1] Uqdah Rd, west of King Abdul Aziz Rd, Hwy 70; 016 532 8112. This simple small apartment hotel is located over the road from the Ha'il Classic with a similar level of amenties. **$**

## Where to eat and drink

### *Southern Ha'il*

Starting in the south of Ha'il, there are a range of restaurants catering to a range of budgets. The usual Saudi chains are present, including a branch of Tazaj, a chicken fast-food chain that used to be more popular throughout the Kingdom. There are shoestring budget restaurants near Barzan Sq, but they may be unused to tourists so be prepared to be a curiosity. Many of these establishments may also have only singles seating.

**Resto in the Sky** [169 C4] King Abdullah Rd, 200m east of Hatim at Tai; 9200 02414; 12.30–01.00 Sat–Thu, 13.00–01.00 Fri. Located on a small hill providing a great view of the city at night, this upscale restaurant also has a nice ambience that is much calmer than many Saudi restaurants. There are tables in the singles section & private booths in the family section. There is also outdoor dining during pleasant weather. The pan-Arab menu has something for everyone, including soups, salads, BBQ & sweets. $$$

**Manoosha** [169 F4] King Fahd bin Abdul Aziz Rd, next to Lulu; 050 056 1687; w mymanoosha.com; 06.00–01.00 daily. This casual restaurant claims to serve healthy choices. We might argue that there are still a lot of calories & ingredients not generally associated with healthy eating on the menu, but the Levantine fast food is certainly delicious. For full indulgence, there is a Baskin-Robbins ice cream shop next door. $$

**Maram Bukhari** [169 C3] Rte 400, King Abdul Aziz Rd northbound about 850m south of Hatim at Tai Rd; 016 532 9851; 11.00–00.30 daily. Just a few doors down from Stars & with a similar clientele, this popular spot is the place to pop into if you like chicken & Bukhari rice served in a variety of ways. Dishes evoke the flavours of central Asia & the Arabian Peninsula; portions are generous so bring your appetite. Take-away is also popular. $

**✱ Stars** [169 C3] Rte 400, King Abdul Aziz Rd northbound about 900m south of Hatim at Tai Rd; 053 944 1430; 11.00–midnight daily. If you want delicious Saudi food without the fuss, then this is place to go. This restaurant enjoys an excellent reputation throughout Ha'il, & the short journey to a more industrial area in the south of the city is worth it. If you eat in during the day, you will almost certainly be mixing with local people on their lunch break. Don't miss the kebabs. Take-away is also popular. $

### *Al Naqrah*

If you are looking for the Ha'il version of trendy, head to the al Naqrah neighbourhood. Extending southwest from the al Rajhi Mosque along Prince Saud bin Abdul Mohsen al Saud St, this is where you will find most upscale restaurants & cafés.

**✱ Al Marsaai** [169 E4] Off King Fahd bin Abdul Aziz Ring Rd northbound at the junction of al Rajhi Mosque; 050 305 6556; 13.00–01.30 daily. This popular upscale restaurant is the place to be & be seen. It also takes the concept of fusion dining to a high level, with imaginative creations showing Indian, Chinese & pan-Arab influences. Dishes include pasta & seafood specialities of salmon, octopus, prawns & crab. Try the California rolls with green & black roe, fresh ginger, wasabi & a white sauce that shouldn't work but does. The singles section occupies the ground floor. There is a separate entrance to the right for access to the family section on the 1st floor. $$$$

**Indian Taste Bharat Restaurant** [169 E3] Opposite al Marsaai on the southbound side of the road; 054 888 5567; 12.30–01.00 daily. Possibly the most popular Indian restaurant in Ha'il. The décor is luxurious, with a blend of Arabic & Indian accents. The mostly Punjabi menu is familiar yet tastes special. $$$$

**Agzal Café** [169 E4] Prince Saud bin Abdul Mohsen al Saud St; 07.00–02.00 daily. Another wide selection of coffee in a great ambience. $$$

**Alwadi Almubarek** [169 A4] Park Roundabout at the jct with al Amir Sultan bin Abdul Aziz Rd, about 200m west of Hwy 70; 054 737 7773; 12.30–01.00 daily. Located near the Saher Complex at the edge of al Naqrah, this restaurant serves traditional Saudi cuisine. Orders are placed at the counter & then delivered where you sit on the floor surrounded by Najd décor. $$$

**FLOX** [169 E4] Prince Saud bin Abdul Mohsen al Saud St; 059 450 1626; 13.00–01.00 daily. Come here for imaginative burgers, volcano fries & other upscale fast food along with a good range of imaginative salads. Note that payment is taken at the time of ordering. $$$

**Shrimper** [169 E4] Prince Saud bin Abdul Mohsen al Saud St; A casual venue for prawns

& much more. Messy enough to ask for a bib. $$$

**Smoke Ring** [169 E4] Prince Saud bin Abdul Mohsen al Saud St; 053 965 5544; 13.00–02.00 daily. Arab BBQ & beef. $$$

**Solafah** [169 E4] Prince Saud bin Abdul Mohsen al Saud St; 06.00–noon & 16.00–01.30 daily. Check out the wide variety of creative coffees, with or without a tempting slice of something sweet. $$$

**Aja & Salma Café & Museum** [169 E4] Off King Fahd bin Abdul Aziz Ring Rd northbound, 1km south of al Rajhi Mosque; 054 737 7773; 15.30–02.00 daily. This venue blends a heritage museum & outdoor café located in lovely green gardens. A great way to get to know a bit more about Ha'il's recent past & to reflect in the garden with a delicious cake & coffee. $$

**Taj Mahal** [169 A4] Park Roundabout at the jct with al Amir Sultan bin Abdul Aziz Rd, about 200m west of Hwy 70; 058 132 1295; 12.30–01.00 daily. A mid-range Indian restaurant with additional Chinese & noodle dishes. $$

### *Northwest ring road*

Many popular hotels are located along the northwest ring road. This area has a wide choice of coffee shops for those looking for a good place nearby for b/fast or lunch.

**6 Aylwl Lounge** [169 B1] On the northbound slip road off King Fahd bin Abdul Aziz Rd, 500m south of King Salman bin Abdul Aziz Rd; 24hrs daily. This coffee shop has a lovely green garden & indoor & outdoor seating with an excellent view of al Salam Park & its prominent hill. Hot & cold drinks, sweets & some light snacks are available. $$

**Al Asalah Restaurant** [169 B1] Jct Hwy 70 & Makkah al Mukarramah Rd; 9200 22281; 10.30–01.00 daily. Although it might not look like it from the outside, this is a traditional Saudi restaurant with singles & family sections, the latter with traditional on-floor seating. The menu includes starters, salads, *mandi*, BBQ kebabs, *maklouba* & many other traditional dishes. Order at the counter & food will be brought to you. There is another branch on King Fahd bin Abdul Aziz Rd at the southeast junction of Ask Shaikh Abdul Aziz bin Baz. $$

**Bostani Chocolate** [169 A2] On the southbound slip road off King Fahd bin Abdul Aziz Rd, 300m north of King Faisal Rd; 055 949 0481; w bostanichocolate.com; 09.00–23.00 Sat–Thu, 16.00–23.00 Fri. More of a shop than a café, this is perfect if you need a sugar rush & are happy to take away your yummies. $$

**Karaz Café** [169 A2] On the southbound slip road off King Fahd bin Abdul Aziz Rd, 300m north of King Faisal Rd; 054 930 7516; 07.00–midnight Sun–Wed, 07.00–02.00 Thu, 14.00–midnight Fri, 16.00–midnight Sat. Lovely coffee shop for your fix of caffeine & cakes. This is also a great place to relax if you need a break. $$

## Shopping

Some mall shops stay open all day but others close from midday prayers until early evening, similar to the souqs. The main shopping malls are listed below. The **Popular Barzan Market** [169 D1] is by the Barzan Grand Mosque and is the main souq. The souq area extends from Ghattat Road in the north to al Imam in the south and along Uqdah Road in the southwest, and includes the usual combination of clothing and home goods shops. The souq is open from mid-morning until midday prayers and again during the evening.

**Al Othaim Mall** [169 B4] Off Hwy 70, King Saud Rd at the first roundabout south of King Abdullah Rd

**Garden Mall** [169 B1] Between Jeddah & King Fahd bin Abdul Aziz rds

**Hassoun Centre/Ha'il Mall** [169 A2] King Faisal Rd, just east of King Fahd bin Abdul Aziz Rd

**Salma Mall by Arabian Centres** [169 G4] On the east side of King Saud Rd, 400m north of Prince Sultan Park

**Semah Centre** [169 D1] On the south side of King Faisal & Uqdah rds, just west of the souqs.

## What to see and do

***A'arif Fort*** [169 D2] (Southeast cnr al Amir Miqrin bin Abdul Aziz & ar Riyadh Rd; exterior access 24hrs daily) The fort was first built during the reign of

Mohammed bin Abdul Mohsen al Ali during the 17th century CE, with additions made by the al Rashid family during their rule. Built on a hill in the centre of Ha'il, the fort's mud-and-clay exterior has been restored. Its walls are filled with round and rectangular windows, with traditional triangular designs on top of the walls, and covers an area of 40m by 11m. Access to the courtyard is through the wooden door. At the time of research, the internal courtyard was closed. Once it reopens, visitors will be able to walk through the residential area, baths and toilets, warehouses, the mosque and prayer area. There is a path along the southern edge of the fort that reaches the top, affording a panoramic view of the city. To the south, a large car park is being built adjacent to the base of the hill.

***Laget Lelmadi Athr (Ha'il Local Heritage Museum)*** [169 D2] (East of Am Amir Miqrin bin Abdul Aziz Rd; /// slimmer.boots.belonged; 055 701 4441; 09.00–noon Sat–Thu & 16.00–midnight daily; SAR20) Located in view of the southern boundary road from A'arif Fort, this heritage museum is a family home and has an extensive collection of local artefacts from the 20th century. Although it is located on an unnamed road, it is easy to find as there is a green 1950s car complete with flat tyres parked at the front door, which looks like it has been there for decades.

***Al Qishlah Castle*** [169 D2] (West off Tareeq al Malik Abdul Aziz Rd, just north of Najd St; exterior access 24hrs daily) This relatively modern landmark was built as a military fortress in 1943 during the reign of King Abdul Aziz, but more recently it was used as a prison. It became a heritage building in 1995. Although the interior of the castle was temporarily closed at the time of research, the exterior is worth a quick visit if you are passing through the area.

Measuring 143m by 141m, and with walls 8.5m high, this large castle is two storeys high and constructed in the traditional Najd style of mud, stone and wood. There are a total of eight watchtowers, and two gates to the south and east. The castle's 142 rooms face on to a courtyard. There is also a mosque with an outdoor prayer area.

***Barzan Castle*** [169 D1] (Off Abdullah al Ali ar Rashid Rd, just north of the Barzan Grand Mosque on the east side, near the large car park surrounded by perfume shops; exterior access 24hrs daily) This palace was started in 1808 and was only finished during the reign of Prince Talal bin Abdullah al Rasheed after 1848CE. It has lain in ruins since 1912, when it was destroyed by ibn Saud as he was overthrowing the al Rashid rulers in the process of consolidating Ha'il into the Kingdom of Saudi Arabia. One tower survived and can be seen by visitors. Although there are signs erected by the Saudi Tourism Authority, there are no other signs of restoration taking place any time soon. The original palace was three storeys high, with reception halls and the kitchens located on the ground floor, surrounded by gardens. The first floor was guest quarters for diplomats and VIP visitors. The top floor was the quarters of the royal family.

Across the road is a wide plaza leading to the Barzan Market.

**AN NAFUD** (Also known as Nafud al Kebir, النفود الكبير, which means 'large sand desert'). Many people visit Ha'il to see the wonders held by this vast and remote part of the Kingdom. An Nafud is a triangulated area located between Ha'il in the south, Tayma in the northwest, and Dumat al Jandal to the north, with a total area of 103,600 km$^2$. It joins the Dahna Desert to the east, connecting to

## ROCK ART IN HA'IL

Jubbah is one of two main locations of the UNESCO World Heritage Site of 'Rock Art in the Ha'il Region', first recognised by UNESCO in 2015. The other main site is Shuwaimis, almost 370km to the southwest.

**JUBBAH** There are two main sites to visit in Jubbah whose petroglyphs UNESCO recognises as among the most important in the world. Depictions on the rocks of people and animals brilliantly illustrate the everyday life of this area as far back as 10,000 years ago. They indicate a time when the area was fertile and able to sustain cattle, deer, gazelles, horses, ibex, lions, oryx and ostriches. The depictions of camels were probably added centuries later as the climate turned drier. The rock art also provides clues to social structures of the time. Of particular interest are depictions of a large figure meting out justice to a smaller figure. Another is the clear depiction of a chariot being pulled by two horses. There are also battle scenes, and more recent Thamudic inscriptions.

The first site is located through a fenced entrance at the end of the car park to the **Visitor Centre**, located on a good but unnamed road in the northwest corner of the village. There is no literature at the Visitor Centre, but there are clear paths that will guide you to the petroglyphs. You will first come across four hills directly in front of you. Walk around these clockwise, weaving around each for your initial exposure to the site's rock art and to get a feel for what comes next. Take the gravel path to the yellow metal steps to your left in the distance and climb them for more fascinating works of rock art including hunting scenes. Descend the stairs and go around anticlockwise. There is another set of yellow metal stairs at the back. Don't think of turning back yet as you would miss some special petroglyphs showing particularly spectacular depictions of animal life and battle scenes.

The second site is **Jebel Sinman**, located 3km south of the Visitor Centre on the same road. Don't miss this site as the petroglyphs continue to illustrate ancient life and are at least as important as those at the first site. This is also where many ancient prehistoric tools and artefacts were discovered.

*Coming from the south, exit Highway 65, turning south towards Jubbah. Turn west at the Dune Bashing Roundabout, go past the Dallah Roundabout, then turn right at al Naif Palace Museum. Turn left at the T-junction to the end of the road, where*

Rub' al Khali to the south. Its beauty is enhanced by the range of colours that change from beige to white, yellow and red, dotted by bushes that turn green after infrequent rains.

This desert is also where researchers from the German Max Planck Institute discovered the oldest fossil belonging to *Homo sapiens* outside of Africa or the Levant, believed to be 85,000 years old. From prehistoric rock art to exploring the mountains, dunes, rock arches and other natural wonders, the Nafud does not disappoint. Whether you are headed to the UNESCO World Heritage Sites of Jubbah and Shuwaimis (see above), or are simply travelling north to Sakaka or northwest to al Ula or Tabuk, you will appreciate this area of outstanding beauty.

**JUBBAH جبة** The village of Jubbah (population 20,000) is located 90km north of Ha'il off Highway 65. It is an oasis in the southern end of the Nafud Desert in a *you will see the Visitor Centre. If you are arriving from the north and wish to take a shortcut, take an unmarked road off Highway 65 southbound that is partly covered with shifting red sand. After about 10km, you will spot the signs to the World Heritage Site. (⌚ 08.00–15.00 Sun–Thu; admission free)*

**SHUWAIMIS** The rock art of Shuwaimis is collectively known as **Rata and Jebel Manjor** and is located in a valley to the northeast of the Harrat Khaybar lava fields, 30km west of the small village of the same name. The earliest rock art here is believed to date as far back as 10,000BCE; it is well preserved, no doubt in great part due to the extreme remoteness of the area.

Like Jubbah, this region was once fertile, with a freshwater lake that was able to sustain substantial wildlife and human settlement. Hunting scenes at Rata and Jebel al Manjor include horses, lions, ibex and – believed to have been inscribed into the rocks at a later date – camels of various sizes. The presence of camels, along with donkeys and ostriches, suggests transition to a desert climate. The rocks also clearly show what might be the world's earliest domesticated cats and dogs, some held by the hunter on leads.

Depictions of other wild animals include cheetah, gazelle, hyena, leopard and Arabian wolfs. Petroglyphs of cows, believed to be from the 6th millennium BCE, are also found here. It is believed that goats and sheep were also tended during this period. Inscriptions in Nabataean and Thamudic alphabets are also found, as are stone tombs in between the two sites that date back to the Bronze Age between the 3rd and 1st millennia BCE.

*The village of Shuwaimis (/// slippage.renewables.hurdling) is in Ha'il Province but is nearer to Madinah (190km) than to Ha'il city (275km). To locate the village on Google Maps, search 'as Shwimes'. Travel on Route 7777 from either direction until you reach Route 8510. Turn west for 40km until you reach al Hait. At the roundabout, turn north on to Route 7900 for about 500m where you will reach another roundabout. Take the second turn off Route 7900 and on to an unnamed road. You will reach the village of Shuwaimis after 30km. Continue for another 30km west to the site, which is at the southern end of the valley and is signposted. The roads are in decent condition. (⌚ 08.00–15.00 Sun–Thu – note that these opening hours cannot be relied on in this very remote location; admission free)*

valley with a water supply. It was on the caravan trail from pre-Islamic times and has been inhabited since the Stone Age, as evidenced by artefacts discovered in the area.

The main reason to visit Jubbah is for its UNESCO-listed ancient rock art. For details, see above.

# 5

# Al Jouf منطقة الجوف and the Northern Borders منطقة الحدود الشمالية

Making up the region of Shammar, al Jouf and the Northern Borders are traditional, remote and sparsely populated areas. They have been a part of all three Saudi states, becoming part of the Kingdom of Saudi Arabia in the 1920s, and are also located, metaphorically, at key crossroads of ancient and modern Arab civilisations. From the Stone Age to the Nabataeans, the various Arab, Assyrian, Roman, Byzantine, Persian, Mesopotamian, Ottoman and British empires have all shaped the region, and the various power struggles it has endured for most of its history mean that it has been in turmoil for much of its existence. In 2019, the Northern Borders finally emerged from restrictions imposed during the early days of the Iraq–Kuwait war of the early 1990s.

Al Jouf, in particular, is a rich resource of archaeological sites that allow academics and the intellectually curious to learn about these early civilisations. These sites also reveal the history of a very different landscape that was much greener and more fertile than nowadays. Two areas of Shammar are on the tentative list of additional UNESCO World Heritage Sites. The Ancient Walled Oases of Northern Arabia date from the Bronze Age – these include Qurayyah, whose ruins can be dated to before the domestication of camels to the rich Nabataean and Roman ages. From the Iron Age, the walled city of Dumat al Jandal and surrounding oasis is also on the list. Dating from the Palaeolithic, its rock art captures its ancient history; and its citadels and castles date back to the 1st century CE.

## AL JOUF PROVINCE منطقة الجوف

Al Jouf means the depression, which describes its location at the edge of Wadi Sirhan. Also referred to as al Jawf, al Jauf or simply Jouf, it is one of the most fertile areas of Saudi Arabia, with its economy focused on growing fruit and olives, as well as livestock production. It has been populated since the Stone Age and currently is home to about 520,000 people.

The Qedar Kingdom dates from the Palaeolithic as far back as the 6th century BCE and is recognised as having some of the earliest organised Arab tribes. It became part of the Christian Assyrian Empire, ruled by the Bani Kalb tribe after conquering the Qedars. Al Jouf was one of the Prophet Mohammed's Islamic conquests from 626 to 630CE, with the population converting to Islam during the

Prophet's life. The Tayy tribe became dominant during the 10th century CE, ruled by the dominant al Fadl family between 12th and 14th centuries.

Al Jouf became part of First Saudi State in 1793, conquered at the time by Imam Abdul Aziz bin Mohammed, and then came under the control of Saud bin Abdul Aziz al Saud during the early 19th century. By the mid 19th century, al Jouf became part of the al Rashid dynasty after being conquered by Talal bin Abdullah al Rashid in 1853, becoming part of the Emirate of Jebel Shammar of the Second Saudi State. At the end of the Ottoman Empire, the Hada Agreement resolved border issues between Transjordan (now parts of Iraq, Jordan and Syria) and Saudi Arabia. Al Jouf became a part of Saudi Arabia's third and current state in 1921. The disputed area around Qurayyat near the Jordanian border was resolved by the Amman Agreement in 1965.

Al Jouf has a desert climate. It is best to visit from November to April. Bring warm clothes for the winter as temperatures drop to near freezing overnight. Spring and autumn weather is pleasant, with warm days and cool evenings. It gets unbearably hot in the summer, with temperatures often reaching 50°C.

## GETTING THERE AND AROUND

**By air** Sakaka al Jouf and Qurayyat domestic airports have limited services on Saudia and flynas. The former serves Sakaka and Dumat al Jandal. There is also a service on flydubai from Dubai.

**By road** Highway 65 is the north–south route into al Jouf and is the road that visitors would use if **driving** from Riyadh, Qassim and Ha'il provinces. Highway 80 is the east–west route from Tabuk Province or from the Northern Borders. Travellers should be particularly careful to keep their petrol tank topped up and to use the toilets whenever there is an opportunity as distances are long and the landscape desolate. You will need a car when exploring the province.

SAPTCO **buses** serve Dumat al Jandal, Sakaka, Qurayyat and many smaller towns. **Taxis** can be found but Uber is less reliable than elsewhere.

**By rail** The al Jouf station on Highway 65 serves the province. Visitors should note, however, that since this station is almost 50km southwest of Sakaka city centre and 25km from Dumat al Jandal, they would need to organise a taxi or hire a car at the railway station to continue their journey. This line now runs to Qurayyat near the Jordanian border.

**SHOPPING** The Abdullah al Othaim supermarket chain is found in Sakaka and Dumat al Jandal. There are also more modest grocers that will sell the basics. Carrefour is present in the Sakaka Cities Mall (southwest cnr Hwy 80 & Arab St; ⏲ 09.00–17.30 & 20.30–02.00 Sat–Thu, 13.00–17.30 & 20.30–02.00 Fri).

**SAKAKA سكاكا** Sakaka has been inhabited for at least 5,000 years and has been the capital of al Jouf Province since 1931. It is located at the northern edge of the Nafud desert. Highway 80, also known as King Fahd bin Abdul Aziz Highway, runs north–south through the city centre. King Khalid Road runs somewhat parallel to the west and is Sakaka's other main thoroughfare. Sakaka's current population of about 280,000 live in a steadily modernising city, surrounded by several significant architectural sites in all directions.

**Where to stay** Hotel choices are limited in Sakaka and may not always have as high a standard of customer service as found in other Saudi cities. Set realistic

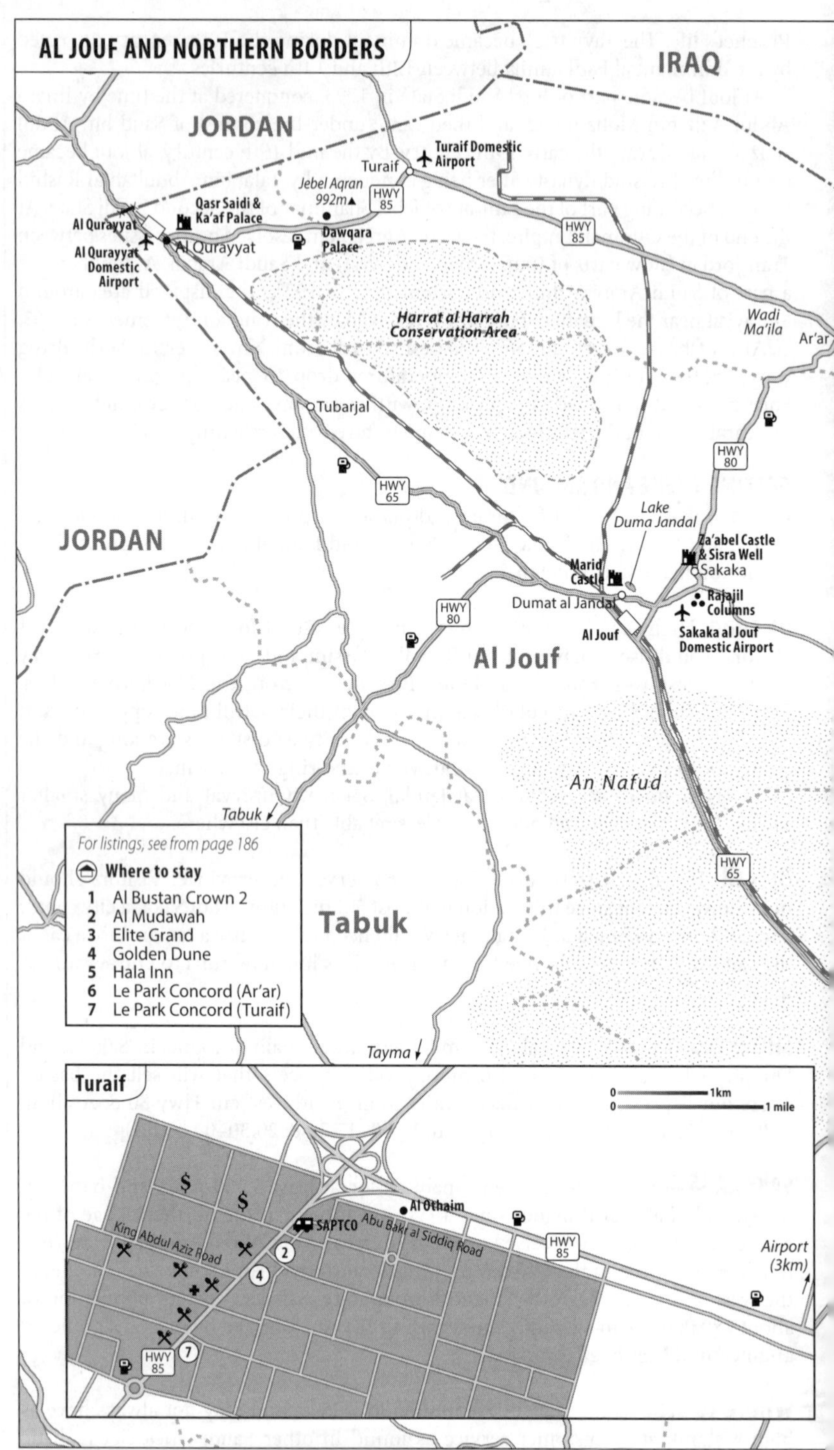
AL JOUF AND NORTHERN BORDERS
IRAQ
JORDAN
Turaif Domestic Airport
Turaif
Jebel Aqran 992m
HWY 85
Qasr Saidi & Ka'af Palace
Al Qurayyat
Al Qurayyat Domestic Airport
Dawqara Palace
Harrat al Harrah Conservation Area
Wadi Ma'ila
Ar'ar
Tubarjal
HWY 65
HWY 80
JORDAN
Lake Duma Jandal
Za'abel Castle & Sisra Well
Sakaka
Marid Castle
Dumat al Jandal
Rajajil Columns
Al Jouf
Sakaka al Jouf Domestic Airport
Al Jouf
An Nafud
Tabuk
Tabuk
Tayma
For listings, see from page 186
Where to stay
1 Al Bustan Crown 2
2 Al Mudawah
3 Elite Grand
4 Golden Dune
5 Hala Inn
6 Le Park Concord (Ar'ar)
7 Le Park Concord (Turaif)
Turaif
0 1km
0 1 mile
Al Othaim
SAPTCO
Abu Bakr al Siddiq Road
King Abdul Aziz Road
Airport (3km)

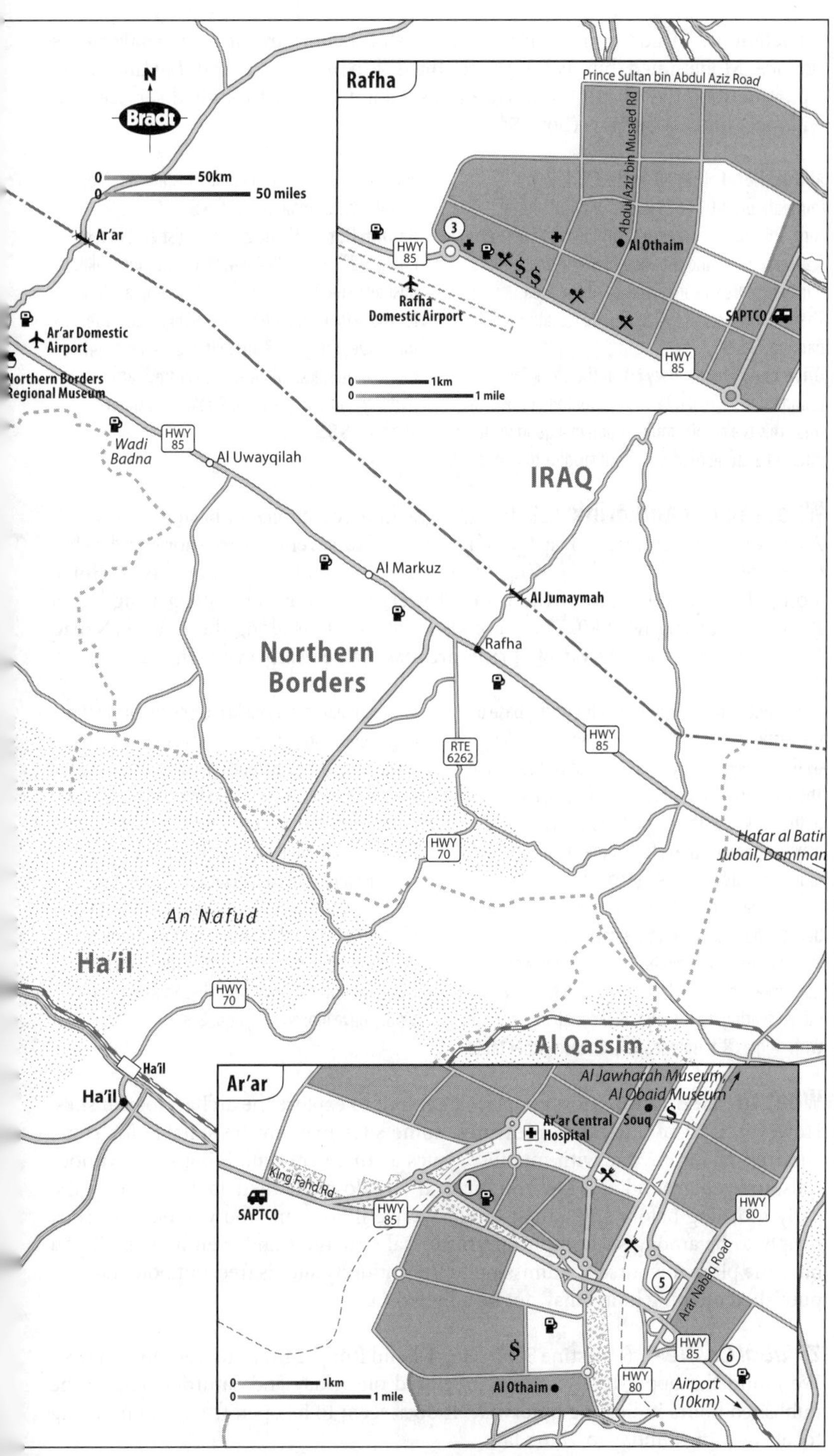
Rafha
Prince Sultan bin Abdul Aziz Road
Abdul Aziz bin Musaed Rd
Al Othaim
HWY 85
Rafha Domestic Airport
SAPTCO
0 1km
0 1 mile
Bradt
0 50km
0 50 miles
Ar'ar
Ar'ar Domestic Airport
Northern Borders Regional Museum
Wadi Badna
Al Uwayqilah
IRAQ
Al Markuz
Al Jumaymah
Rafha
Northern Borders
RTE 6262
HWY 70
Hafar al Batin
Jubail, Damman
An Nafud
Ha'il
Al Qassim
Ar'ar
Al Jawharah Museum, Al Obaid Museum
Ar'ar Central Hospital
Souq
King Fahd Rd
SAPTCO
HWY 80
Arar Nabaq Road
Al Othaim
Airport (10km)
0 1km
0 1 mile

expectations. In addition to those hotels listed here, **Lara al Jouf Apartments** (Prince Mohammed bin Fahd St) to the south of Sakaka and **Lavina Hotel Apartments** (Hwy 80) to the north of Sakaka are basic with limited services but will meet modest budgets (both **$$**).

**Al Nusl Hotel** Hwy 80, at the Clock Tower roundabout; 014 625 0353; w alnusl-hotel.com. This hotel is accented with heritage features & artefacts, setting the mood for visitors heading out to explore the archaeology of the area. There is room service & an on-site restaurant & parking. **$$$**

**Olive Land Hotel** Hwy 80, at the Clock Tower roundabout; 014 624 1211. Situated opposite al Nusl, this is a comfortable option in a good location offering a range of rooms, from studios to larger apartments. There is an on-site restaurant. Most rooms have a small fridge. **$$$**

**Raoum Hotel** Sharie al Malik, just east of King Khalid Rd; 014 625 4444; w raouminnsakaka.business.site. This Saudi chain is a popular choice for those looking for on-site conveniences. The room sizes are good & there is a restaurant, 24hr room service, a small business centre & ample parking – all in a pleasant & relatively quiet location. **$$$**

**Where to eat and drink** Sakaka dining is mostly a choice of basic Saudi, south Asian or some American fast food. There are also several sweet shops and cafés. Check out the options along King Abdul Aziz Road to the north of al Nusl Hotel, along Highway 80 north of the Clock Tower roundabout and along King Faisal Road west of Highway 80. There are also a few options along the Ar'ar-al Nabaq Road to the east of Highway 80. Prices are reasonable nearly everywhere.

✷ **Ta'leel Coffee** King Khalid Rd, at the base of the castle; 053 884 4242; 24hrs daily. Stop by this lovely café if you are visiting Za'abal Castle. There is a street entrance (as well as an entrance to the back near the car park), which is a lovely way to approach the café and the original entrance found directly opposite the base of the castle. This is more than a coffee shop, with pleasant gardens behind the second entrance near the car park. You will see an old double-wheel water well at this entrance, which leads to garden tables with mixed seating. To the right is the main restaurant with singles & family seating. Choose either table or traditional seating on low cushions. The Arabic-only menu is adequate, with an assortment of pizza, sandwiches, burgers, chips & basic Middle Eastern dishes. Staff will help translate or you can go to the counter & ask. The food is reasonable, but this café is all about location, location, location. Not only do you get a spectacular view of the castle, it is also opposite a warren of paths at the base of the castle that visitors might otherwise miss. These timeworn paths give the visitor an excellent impression of how these shops & paths would have looked long ago. **$$**

**What to see and do** Most people visit al Jouf to explore the archaeological sites. However, void of any safety measures, some sites may not be suitable for small children or for anyone with mobility issues as there are crumbling steps without rails, uneven ground and low entrances. If you do make the trip, try to go in the early morning before any tourist groups arrive if you can. You will be awestruck simply to be among such important historical structures and even more so if you have the place to yourself. Admission to the antiquity sites is free, but note that any published opening hours may not be adhered to.

***Za'abal Castle*** ✷ (Palestine St off King Khalid Rd; 24hrs daily; admission free) We found the upper-level castle gates closed on Friday and Saturday despite the published hours indicating otherwise. It does seem to be open from mid morning to late evening Sunday to Thursday.

Za'abal Castle has protected the people of Sakaka for many centuries, and is in various states of ruin. Made of sandstone, it has some original features that date back as far as Nabataean times, about 1st century BCE, although later castles have been constructed on the same site. The current structure dates mostly from the early 18th century. It is built on top of an ancient water well system which is still in use today. The turrets and the top walls are a lighter colour than the rest of the castle due to the use of different combinations of sandstone and clay.

There are two entrances to the castle. One of these is to the right of the Ta'leel café gardens, reached by taking the path from the ground-level car park on the right directly in front of castle. From here you can explore three different maze-like paths, each with rooms leading off. This part of the castle is still in its unrestored, crumbling state.

Access to the upper levels of the castle is via the main gate. From the lower car park, continue along King Khalid Road, taking the first right by Arfag mosque (you might feel like you are on the wrong road as it is a residential neighbourhood, but this is correct), then the second right up a steep hill to the top. Park along the street or on the sand in front of the guardhouse at the castle entrance. If you find the guardhouse open but unstaffed, simply walk in. The pathway and steps leading up to the castle ruins are tricky but not as difficult as in some other castles elsewhere in the Kingdom.

To the left of the guardhouse entrance and behind a pavilion is the ancient **Mount Prince cemetery**. Behind the cemetery is a great example of the effect of the weather on sandstone as evidenced by the stratified layers of the mountain behind the site. Rock art dating as far back as 8,000 years can be found at the base of the mountain. These are found in front of the castle entrance.

To reach the castle entrance after leaving the cemetery area, walk up the long sweeping steps (no handrails), then follow narrow steps to the right. You will be winding along the castle exterior while climbing and will be able to look down to see how much of the castle has been left in its original state. At the top, open the wooden door, then enter the sloping courtyard at the top. There is a room to the left with a locked wooden door that may have been used for administration. Further up, you can walk into the stores tower. The walls have small viewing holes through which you'll have a panoramic view of a remarkably green-looking Sakaka in all directions.

***Sisra Well*** (Off Palestine St between King Khalid Rd & Za'abal Castle; follow the sign from the castle) This restored Nabataean well dates from the 1st century BCE and is just down the road from Za'abal Castle's upper entrance. The well is named after Sisera, the Canaanite military leader who fought the Jewish people in Palestine and is referenced in the Christian Bible and in Jewish traditions in the Talmud. Visitors can approach the fence to see the steps carved into the internal walls of the well, descending to the bottom at about 15m. You will see the tourist sign when returning along the road from the castle.

***Merzouga Heritage Museum*** (King Khalid Rd, eastbound heading back to Hwy 80; 🕘 no published hours) This is a combination museum and souvenir shop displaying everyday artefacts from the mid 20th century. Why not pop in for a few minutes and chat to the friendly owner if it's open. Those looking for traditional clothing to buy, or some crafts, may find something here.

***Rajajil Columns*** ✷ (Unnamed roads; ☎ 055 070 0633; 🕘 09.00–17.00 Sat–Thu) The Rajajil Columns have been described by many as the Stonehenge of Saudi

### SAUDI ARABIA'S 'OLIVE BASKET'

If you are visiting in March/April and you like olives, then stop by the annual **Olive Festival** held in Sakaka's Prince Abdul Elah bin Abdul Aziz Convention Centre. You might also be interested in organising a visit to what is described as the world's largest **olive farm** which has more than 5 million olive trees. The al Jouf Agricultural Development Company is located 200km west off Highway 80 towards Tabuk Province. Ask for directions at the festival as this site does not publish contact information.

Arabia. The 50 monolithic stones on the gently sloping site, some arranged in clusters of four, some with inscriptions, stand about 3m tall and date back to 4000BCE. Although it is clear the site was once a burial ground, a theory supported by the artefacts that have been excavated here, which also validate the very different, pre-desert climate that was in existence at the time, some believe the stones also have astronomical significance. The purpose of the columns, though, ultimately remains a mystery.

There is a small on-site museum located through the metal gates and where you can park your car. It displays a few stone tools, ritual burial artefacts and ancient household items all excavated from the site, with descriptions in Arabic and English. From the museum, follow the paved path that runs alongside the fencing that surrounds the archaeological site, gently ascending to a semi-circular area with concrete benches set immediately in front of a cluster of four of the larger columns. Continue along the path until you near its end. There is an opening in the fence with the Saudi national emblem on each side that allows you on to the site itself. The sand is soft with many jagged rocks strewn around and several ant-hill mounds. You can get as close as you like to the many clusters of pillars, which are mounted in circles and in various conditions – upright, slanted, falling down, fallen down, and broken. There is good access for wheelchair users from the car park, into the museum and on to the paved path along the perimeter of the site where the columns can be viewed.

**Getting there** The routes to the Rajajil Columns are well signposted. From the south, turn southeast at the junction of Highway 80 and the Aramco Petrol Distribution Station. The site will be on the right after about 3km. From the north, turn southeast from Highway 80 and then over the roundabout of the Ar'ar al Nabaq and Prince Abdullah bin Abdul Aziz Road. In just over 2km, turn right at the T-junction. The site will be on the left after about 500m.

**DUMAT AL JANDAL دُومَة ٱلْجَنْدَل** Dumat al Jandal lies at the crossroads of ancient trade routes from the Arabian Gulf settlements of Failaka, Thaj and Bahrain to the southeast and the settlements of Mada'in Saleh and Tayma to the southwest. This fertile area with plentiful well water made it a significant settlement for millennia. Located about 40km southwest of Sakaka, Dumat al Jandal nowadays has a population of about 40,000. It was the capital of al Jouf Province until 1931CE.

Part of the Assyrian Empire, Dumat al Jandal can be traced to the 10th century BCE as attested by the discovery of Nabataean pottery in the town and surrounding area. It was known as Adummatu in Akkadian writings and the capital of the Arab kingdom of Qedar. Dumat al Jandal became part of the Nabataean Empire until the 2nd century CE, when it was incorporated into the Roman Empire for the following four centuries. It then became part of the pre-Islamic Arab Empire of the Kingdom of Kinda in the 5th century CE and was also claimed as part of the Byzantine and the Sasanid empires during this period. In 626CE, the Prophet Mohammed led the first of a series of campaigns to overthrow the Kingdom, believing it was a threat to Madinah. The dominant Benu Kalb people, who worshipped the idol Wadd, also caused offence to the Prophet Mohammed. The town was captured and destroyed by the warrior Khalid bin al Walid. The last of these campaigns, in 630CE, was successful in incorporating Dumat al Jandal into the Islamic Empire and converting the population to Islam.

**Where to stay** Hotel choices are even more limited in Dumat al Jandal than in nearby Sakaka. Most accommodation is conveniently located along Highway 80 near the first roundabout west of Abdullah al Othaim supermarket. Check out **Admato Hotel Apartments** (014 622 6228; **$**), **Dar es Salaam Furnished Apartments** (014 622 3111; **$**), **Wings Dryer Highness Hotel** (055 623 1122; **$**) or the **Inn Hotel Zaba** (**$**). All offer en-suite rooms but are otherwise basic. As they are practically adjacent to one another, visitors might want to compare rooms, especially for cleanliness, before checking in.

**Al Farhan Hotel Serviced Apartments** King Fahd Rd; 014 622 3622. This property is located near Dumat General Hospital between King Abdullah & Prince Sultan bin Abdul Aziz rds. If you are looking for a reasonable level of comfort, this is probably the best choice in town. The building is old & the lighting dim, but the rooms are clean. There is parking to the rear & an attempt at accommodating wheelchair users, although the ramps are a bit narrow & the lifts are small. The very affordable prices include apartment-style accommodation with a kitchen, living room, 1 or more bedrooms & a buffet b/fast. **$**

**Where to eat and drink** Food options are somewhat limited here with mainly Saudi and south Asian restaurants serving local communities. Many restaurants and take-aways are located along the road between Marid Castle and the Clock Tower roundabout, on Highway 80 west of the Clock Tower roundabout, and along Prince Sultan bin Abdul Aziz Road. Be aware that some of these choices may not be comfortable for female travellers as they have been traditionally all-male establishments that remain unused to foreign women. Saudi fast-food options include Kudu, Hungry Bunny and Buns Burger. Try the Manuel Bakery on Prince Sultan bin Abdul Aziz for local baked goods. If you want a different treat, then pop into Cone Zone (King Abdullah Rd) for a taste of Middle Eastern ice cream.

## What to see and do

***Al Jouf Regional Museum of Archaeology and Folklore*** (Cnr King Saud & Prince Sultan bin Abdul Aziz rds; 050 339 3493 ; 07.30–15.30 Sun–Thu) This museum displays artefacts from some of the earliest civilisations from this very important region which are only hinted at in the National Museum in Riyadh. The modern two-storey building is well signposted and wheelchair friendly with lifts to the first floor and very welcome clean toilet facilities. Double check it is open before setting out.

***Marid Castle**** (King Saud Rd, adjacent to the Regional Museum; 054 392 9272; 07.30–17.00 daily; admission free) This castle dominated the ancient city of Dumat al Jandal. It was built for military purposes and dates back to the 1st century CE. Artefacts from this era have been excavated from inside its walls as well as in the surrounding grounds. The castle has survived many battles and was eventually absorbed into the Islamic Empire in 633CE. The two-storey edifice is built of stone on the ground floor, supporting its mud-brick structure on the first floor. Although the site is being restored, you will still see many of the original features. It is possible to climb to the top if you are fit enough to manage about 1,000 stairs. Safety features are practically non-existent, but it is a great adventure to explore if you are prepared. Be especially careful if wearing an abaya.

Access to the castle is to the left of the Regional Museum. Walk to the low wall of the top-level courtyard for a full view of the castle. To the left, at the top of the courtyard, is a three-storey tower. Push open its wooden door and you will see a modern water pump on the ground floor attesting to the provision of a continuous water supply. Walk further left and down more stairs to another courtyard, where there is a bench on the left. It is possible to explore the corner tower in the wall on this level and its traditionally built ceiling of wood beams and palm fronds. Next, turn right to the very uneven and narrow steps to ascend to the top of the tower. Turn right again with care and continue to walk up more narrow stairs hugging the right side of the castle walls. There are a couple of places that are level enough to let others pass. Once you reach the top, you will find a heavy wooden door to the central courtyard. The courtyard gives splendid views of the two jagged mud-brick peaks framed by four 12m-tall round towers, one in each corner. The jagged peaks appear to be defying gravity and add to the ambience while you wonder how they continue to stand. There are other rooms off the courtyard that were used by guards. You will see wooden support beams projecting from the brickwork in many areas of the castle. Upon leaving the main courtyard area at the top, visitors can walk around a restored path along the upper walls for a panoramic view of Umar Mosque, the walled al Dar'i quarter and the Dumat al Jandal wells.

***Umar Mosque*** ✷ (Adjacent to Marid Castle; ☎ 050 339 3493; ⌚ 07.30–15.30 Sun–Thu) As the mosque is located directly behind Marid Castle, once you have finished exploring the castle, find the small door to the left on the ground floor just past the bench at the bottom of the castle steps. Go through the door and turn right, where you will see the ancient minaret about 200m away. There are two sets of steps leading into the mosque – walk down either. Built in the mid-7th century CE shortly after the death of the Prophet Mohammed, this is one of the most significant mosques from the earliest days of the Islamic era. It was built under the orders of Omar bin al Kattab, the third Islamic Caliph, after he returned from Beit al Maqdis in Jerusalem. The floor plan is a key feature of the structure as it is the same pattern originally found in the Prophet Mohammed's house in Madinah. The minaret in the southwest corner is five storeys high, rising to 15m, and is one of the oldest stone minarets in existence.

To the right, you will see rows of prayer rugs, a *mimbar* with stone steps, a qibla carved into the wall and a second pointed indentation resembling another qibla parallel to the first. There are recessed reliefs in the wall where the Qur'an can be placed. There is a separate prayer area for women also with prayer rugs and reliefs for the Qur'an all behind the main prayer area.

***Al Dar'i Quarter*** Upon leaving the mosque, go for a wander through the ruins of the al Dar'i Quarter just below the mosque's entrance. This walled settlement was built during the mid-Islamic Empire, on top of previous settlements dating back to the 1st millennium BCE. An ancient road has also been found beneath the settlement during ongoing excavations. Explore the multiple labyrinthine paths and stone-built homes, storage rooms, archways and the open courtyard area, where trade, including of enslaved workers, was once conducted. Archaeological digs are still taking place to the east of the quarter, and restoration around the site is ongoing. Several wells are signposted and fenced off but can be viewed from all angles from outside the perimeter fence.

***Lake Duma Jandal*** Located about 6km east of Marid Castle, Lake Duma Jandal, with palm trees fringing its western edge, provides a welcome break when you need a wafting breeze and some 'blue'. The adjoining park is a great spot for picnics and popular with local families. You will find coffee and snack kiosks at the entrance after the children's playground. The route along unnamed roads takes you through a few residential neighbourhoods, but the entrance to the park is clearly visible. Follow instructions on Google Maps or similar.

**AL QURAYYAT القريات** Al Qurayyat, or Gurayat, is the nearest town to the al Haditha border crossing 30km northwest towards Jordan. It was part of the Assyrian Empire and, in more recent times, part of Transjordan until becoming part of Saudi Arabia after the collapse of the Ottoman Empire. Its population of about 150,000 has a border-town economy relying on trade along with some agriculture. Travel to Qurayyat on Highway 85 from the Northern Borders or Highway 65 from Najd. Qurayyat is 1,265km from Riyadh and 1,435km from Dammam.

**Where to stay and eat** Hotel options for visitors are limited, and restaurants are concentrated along al Madinah al Munawwarah Road or around the Qurayyat Mall further along King Khalid Road. The cuisine on offer is mostly basic Saudi, Lebanese, Syrian and south Asian, mostly catering to the local working population.

**Al Shaykh Resort** Unnamed roads on the southern edge of town, off Highway 65; ☎050 436 7794. Consider this alternative if you want a more relaxed stay. **$$$**

**Life of the Knights Hotel Suites** King Faisal Rd, northwest of Qurayyat Mall; ☎014 641 3446. Centrally located & probably the best option for a comfortable stay. **$$$**

**Dana North Apartments** Umar bin al Khattab Rd, south of Qurayyat Mall; ☎014 641 1651. This well-situated property is worth checking out for those with a more modest budget. **$$**

## What to see and do

***Qasr Saidi and Ka'af Palace*** (Off Hwy 85 near Am al Arjas; ☎059 578 7050; w heritage.moc.gov.sa/en/points-of-interest/kaf-palace; ⌚ 07.00–15.00 Sun–Thu) If you are travelling towards Qurayyat on Highway 85, take the opportunity to stop at these two sites, which are about 500m apart just off the south side of the road about 10km east of Qurayyat. Saidi Castle dates back to the Nabataean period and served as protection for convoys travelling from Hegra (Mada'in Saleh) to Petra. During much of the Islamic era, it served a similar purpose to protect pilgrims on their journey to Mecca. Located on a strategic hill, it is made of stone and mud-brick. Ka'af Palace was built in 1911 by Prince Nawaf al Shaalan, who ruled the region at that time. Behind the palace walls, there are government facilities, a mosque, prison, warehouses, kitchen, wells, men's and women's residences, and four rooms situated around a private courtyard. The two entrances can be found on the south and east sides of the palace. It was taken over by King Abdul Aziz al Saud when Jouf became part of the Kingdom of Saudi Arabia. The interior of both castles can be explored during the erratic opening hours. If they are closed, it is still interesting to walk around the exterior.

## NORTHERN BORDERS منطقة الحدود الشمالية

As part of the Ottoman Empire until the early 20th century, there was no officially defined border between Saudi Arabia and Iraq until the Uqair Protocol in 1922. There was also a neutral zone defined to the west of Kuwait and formalised in the Bahra Agreement in November 1925. This territory was eventually split between Saudi Arabia and Kuwait in 1975 although the United Nations was only notified in 1991. Travel between Iraq and Saudi Arabia was closed in 1990 due to the Gulf War, and in 2014 a physical, formal border fence between the two countries was built, reopening at Ar'ar only in November 2019, just before the Covid-19 pandemic. The Northern Borders remain focused on security with a noticeable military presence including several checkpoints along the roads.

The Northern Borders of Saudi Arabia is the least populated province in the Kingdom with about 375,000 people. Traditionally the population has been nomadic, the dominant tribes being the Annazah, Rawallah and Shammar, who are also found in significant numbers in Iraq, Jordan and Syria. The provincial capital, Ar'ar, was founded in 1951 as a part of Saudi Aramco's Trans Arabian Pipeline project, known as oil field 'RR', giving Ar'ar its name. It has a population of 160,000. Other settlements include Rafha with a population of 90,000, and Turaif, with a population of 45,000.

The Northern Borders has a desert climate. It is best to visit from November to April. Bring warm clothes for the winter as temperatures drop to near freezing overnight. Spring and autumn weather is pleasant, with warm days and cool evenings. It gets unbearably hot in the summer, with temperatures often reaching 50°C.

Tourism is nearly non-existent in the province. Do be aware that this is a particularly traditional region that may be suspicious of outsiders due to its location and recent history. It should also be noted that gender segregation is strictly enforced, and women are advised to wear an abaya and a headscarf throughout the Northern Borders.

**GETTING THERE AND AROUND** There are no passenger trains anywhere in this province.

**By air** The Ar'ar Domestic Airport has limited services on Saudia and flynas. The Rafha and Turaif domestic airports have limited services on Saudia.

**By road** Highway 85 dominates the Northern Borders Province. This is the route that runs from the Eastern Province and extends to the west for about 900km before entering al Jouf Province and onwards to the Jordanian border. Anyone driving this route should ensure that they stop to top up the petrol tank and to use the toilets wherever possible as distances are long and desolate. It is also possible to drive from Sakaka in al Jouf to the provincial capital of Ar'ar on Highway 80.

SAPTCO **buses** serve Ar'ar, Rafha, Turaif and some smaller towns in the Northern Borders.

### WHERE TO STAY *Map, page 178*

Hotel options for visitors are limited in the Northern Borders, so if you are thinking of staying in the region, you should plan your journey to overnight in Rafha, Ar'ar or Turaif.

In **Rafha**, consider the **Elite Grand Hotel** (Hwy 85; 055 175 1459; **$**), near the roundabout opposite the Rafha Domestic Airport. In **Ar'ar**, options include:

**Al Bustan Crown Hotel 2** (Hwy 85; ☎014 665 0001; **$$**), about 6km west of Highway 80 – don't mistake this for Al Bustan 1 nearer the city centre, which is less female friendly; **Le Park Concord** (Hwy 85, 1km east of Hwy 80; ☎014 665 0900; **$$$**); and **Hala Inn** (Hwy 80, just north of Hwy 85; ☎014 663 4444; **$$$**).

In **Turaif**, try the **Golden Dune Hotel** (☎059 327 1981; **$$**), **Le Park Concord** (☎050 089 4980; **$$**) or **al Mudawah Hotel** (☎014 653 0036; **$**). They are all located on Highway 85 after the major junction southwest of the Saudi Aramco plant.

## WHERE TO EAT AND DRINK *Map, page 178*

Your options here will be mostly basic Saudi and south Asian food, and mostly take-away. In **Rafha**, restaurants are concentrated near the Rafha Circle roundabout by the domestic airport on Highway 85. In **Ar'ar**, you will find most restaurants along Highway 85, near Ar'ar Central Hospital, or near the souq. In **Turaif**, restaurants are near the hotels. You can also check out King Abdul Aziz Road west of Highway 85.

**SHOPPING** The Abdullah al Othaim supermarket chain is found in each of the cities highlighted. Otherwise, look for the yellow trolley signs for the basics.

**WHAT TO SEE AND DO** As a little-touristed area effectively off-limits to visitors until very recently, here is an opportunity to be a true pioneer and explore areas where you may be the first outsider to do so. It is imperative that anyone planning to do this does so with the utmost respect, both from a cultural and a practical perspective, given the difficulties the region most recently endured for more than 30 years.

People interested in history and architecture may wish to check out one of the province's museums. The **Northern Borders Regional Museum** opened in Ar'ar in 2007 and focuses on regional history and culture. **Al Obaid Museum** focuses on historical books and other documents, as well as swords, daggers and old guns. There are also collections of household goods and women's jewellery. The two-room **al Jawharah Heritage Museum** exhibits old newspapers, maps, coins, textiles, carpets and other household items and furnishings. The best way to check opening times is just to head to the museum and see if it's open. If it's not, you may be lucky and a local Saudi will help find the owner to open the museum up for you. If you are travelling through Turaif, then you might wish to explore **Dawqara Palace**. It is believed that these ruins date back to Roman times.

Nature enthusiasts may wish to explore **Wadi Badna** and **Wadi Ma'ila**. Both are near Ar'ar and are best visited in spring. **Jebel Aqran**, 992m high, is located west of Turaif and offers ample opportunity to explore the mountain and for other outdoor activities. Do consider your own safety in case of accident as safety measures are non-existent. Many Saudis travel to the Northern Borders for **falcon and hawk hunts**. **Harrat al Harrah Conservation Area**, which straddles Northern Borders and al Jouf provinces, is the Kingdom's first designated Protected Area. The Saudi Natural Centre for Wildlife describes the protected area's diverse vegetation cover which includes *Tamarix aphylla*, Calligonum, *Lycium shawii* trees, many shrubs, herbs, and perennial and annual plants that are found along flood lines. Animals found in this important area include the reem, or sand gazelle, Arabian wolf, red and sand foxes, striped hyena, cape hare and jerboa rodents. There are also houbara bustards, golden eagles, Eurasian stone curlews, nine species of lark, and other species of migratory birds. There are also many reptiles.

6

# Tabuk منطقة تبوك and Medina منطقة المدينة Provinces

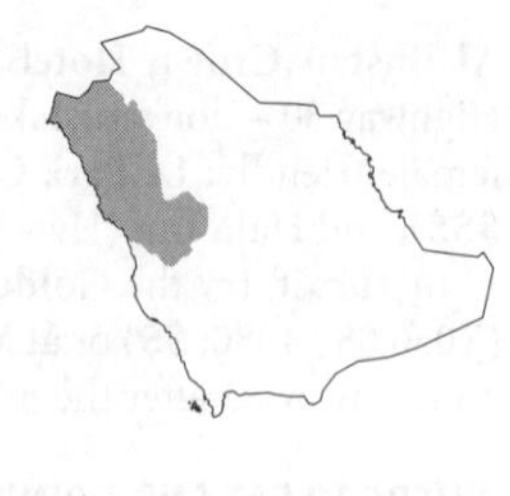

Tabuk and Medina provinces are located in the northwest of Saudi Arabia's Hejaz region. The Tabuk region of the Arabian Peninsula was referred to as Midian in biblical times. It was named after a son of Abraham, and is mentioned in both the Hebrew bible and the Qur'an. However, some scholars believe that Midian refers to a collection of tribes more than a specific geography. The Midian mountains are part of the Hejaz mountain range and are found east of the Gulf of Aqaba.

In the early 20th century, the short-lived Hejaz Railway ran through Tabuk and Medina provinces on the way to the holy city of Madinah. Ruins of these stations can be seen in their various states of decay, terminating in Madinah, where its station is now a very good museum.

## TABUK PROVINCE منطقة تبوك

Archaeologists have discovered evidence that Tabuk (also spelled Tabouk) has been settled for more than 10,000 years, determined by the analysis of rock art found in many areas. In more recent times, Tabuk was a stop on caravan trade routes from pre-Islamic times and was also a major part of the historic pilgrimage route to Mecca and Madinah until the age of aviation. Like much of the north of the Kingdom, Tabuk has been controlled to varying degrees in its early history by Arab tribes, as well as by the Nabataeans, Assyrians, Romans and Persians. During the period of Byzantine control, the Prophet Mohammed led a military operation known as the Expedition of Tabuk, meant to defeat the Byzantines. However, they were never encountered; instead, alliances were made with local leaders from the region. The Ottomans controlled the region during the latter centuries of their power, through the First and Second Saudi States and then, during the late 19th and early 20th centuries, the British Empire held significant influence in the region. Control of Tabuk Province was finally taken by ibn Saud and it was absorbed into the Third Saudi State in 1926. The province's population today is about 910,000.

Tabuk Province is bordered to the west by the Gulf of Aqaba, whose shoreline extends south along the Red Sea; to the east, it shares borders with al Jouf and Ha'il provinces and desert conditions prevail. The region's rich geography encompasses dramatic rock formations, streams as mentioned in the Bible, clutches of idyllic islands and ancient settlements, and numerous wadis which render parts of the province fertile enough to farm.

Whether you like to spend your time by the sea, in the mountains, or exploring the remains of ancient civilisations, Tabuk Province has something to interest most travellers. Some of the world's best scuba diving is to be found here, and boating has begun to increase in popularity in recent decades. Fishing is also popular, both commercially for local residents and for leisure, especially among some expatriate populations.

However, much of Tabuk Province's coastal and mountain region is about to change with the development of NEOM (page 198), probably the most prominent and well-known of Saudi Vision 2030's giga-projects, meant to put Saudi Arabia firmly on the tourist trail. Midian and Nabataean ruins, scattered over a wide area of the province, will sit side by side – or need to make way for – the most aggressive creation of a new city ever planned in the Middle East and likely globally. Visitors should be aware that the development of NEOM is well underway and may cause temporary closures of some places of interest, as well as some roads. The usual caution about unreliable opening hours for places of interest applies to sites throughout Tabuk.

Tabuk Province has a desert climate and is best visited between November and April. It gets unbearably hot in the summer, with temperatures often reaching 50°C in parts, especially in the east around Tayma. The Red Sea coast provides little relief from the summer heat and humidity, although taking a modest dip in the sea does

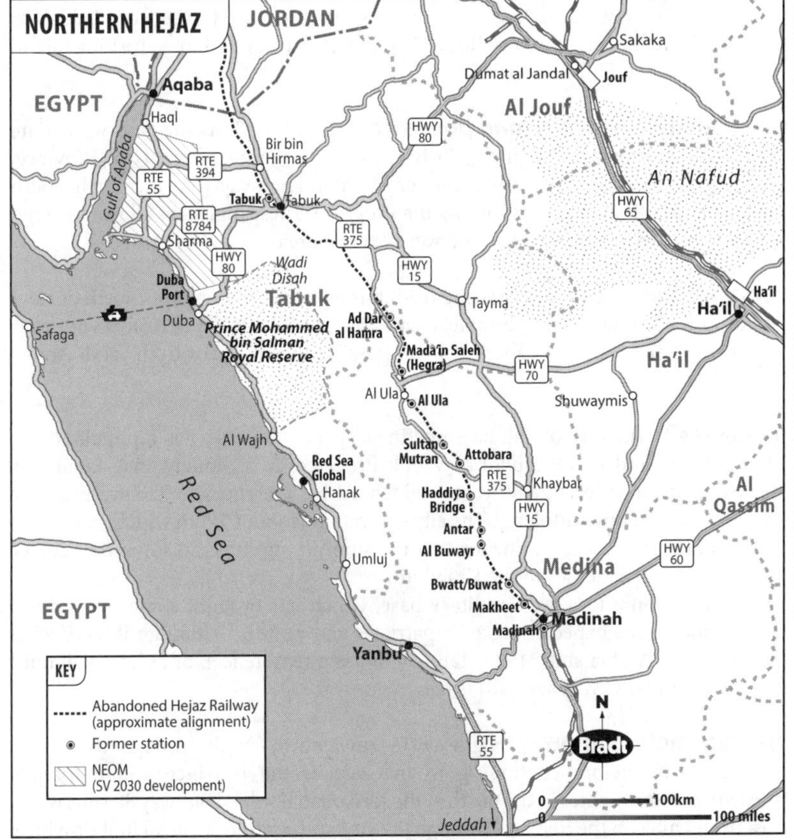

help. If visiting in winter, bring warm clothes as temperatures drop to near freezing overnight. It can snow in Jebel al Lawz and other high peaks of the Hejaz Mountains to the west of Tabuk during the winter. Spring and autumn weather is pleasant, with warm days and cool evenings.

**GETTING THERE AND AROUND** You will need a car when exploring Tabuk Province other than in Tabuk city, where taxis can be found. There are no passenger trains in the province.

**By air** Tabuk's Prince Sultan bin Abdul Aziz domestic airport is located about 2km northeast of the city centre and has services on Saudia, flynas and Egyptian regional carriers. There are limited services to Jeddah and Riyadh on Saudia from al Wajh Airport in the small coastal city of the same name. The NEOM Bay Airport currently serves Jeddah, Riyadh and Dubai and it is expected that flights will increase as the project develops.

**By road** SAPTCO **buses** serve Hanak, al Wajh, Duba, Haql, Tabuk and many smaller towns in the province.

***From Jeddah and the Red Sea coast*** Route 55 is the north–south road running along the entire Red Sea coast and varies between a two-lane road and a dual carriageway. This is the route that visitors are likely to use from Jeddah to NEOM. Travellers may also use Route 55 on their journey to Tabuk, turning inland and eastbound at Duba or Sharma.

***From Medina Province and points east*** Highway 80 is the east–west route from al Jouf Province. Highway 70 is the east–west route from Ha'il Province, entering Tabuk from its extreme southern border. Highway 15 is the north–south road from Madinah and most of Medina Province. These highways all run through remote areas with long distances between service areas.

***From Jordan*** The border crossing from Jordan is a few kilometres north of Haql on Route 55. While you may be able to cross the border into Saudi Arabia with your own vehicle and the right papers, it is not possible to drive to or from Saudi Arabia with a hire car.

**TABUK تَبُوك** The city of Tabuk, sometimes spelled Tabouk, has a population of about 667,00 and is the capital of Tabuk Province. It is thought that Tabuk has been settled for at least 2,000 years, evidenced by references to Tabawa made by the Greek astronomer Ptolemy. The city's elevation is about 770m which, combined with its northern location, means that the summer months are somewhat cooler than in many other cities in the Kingdom.

Tabuk is home to a large military base, which has brought some comforts to accommodate the expectations of expatriates and visitors. Although it has been a part of Saudi Arabia since 1926, Tabuk still has a remote feel, or at least will until the impact of NEOM (page 198) is felt.

**Getting there and away** Highway 15 runs north–south through the centre of Tabuk city before continuing to the east of the province and eventually to Medina. It terminates in the north at the Jordanian border. Highway 80 runs west–east from Duba on the Red Sea, through the city, and continues into al Jouf Province.

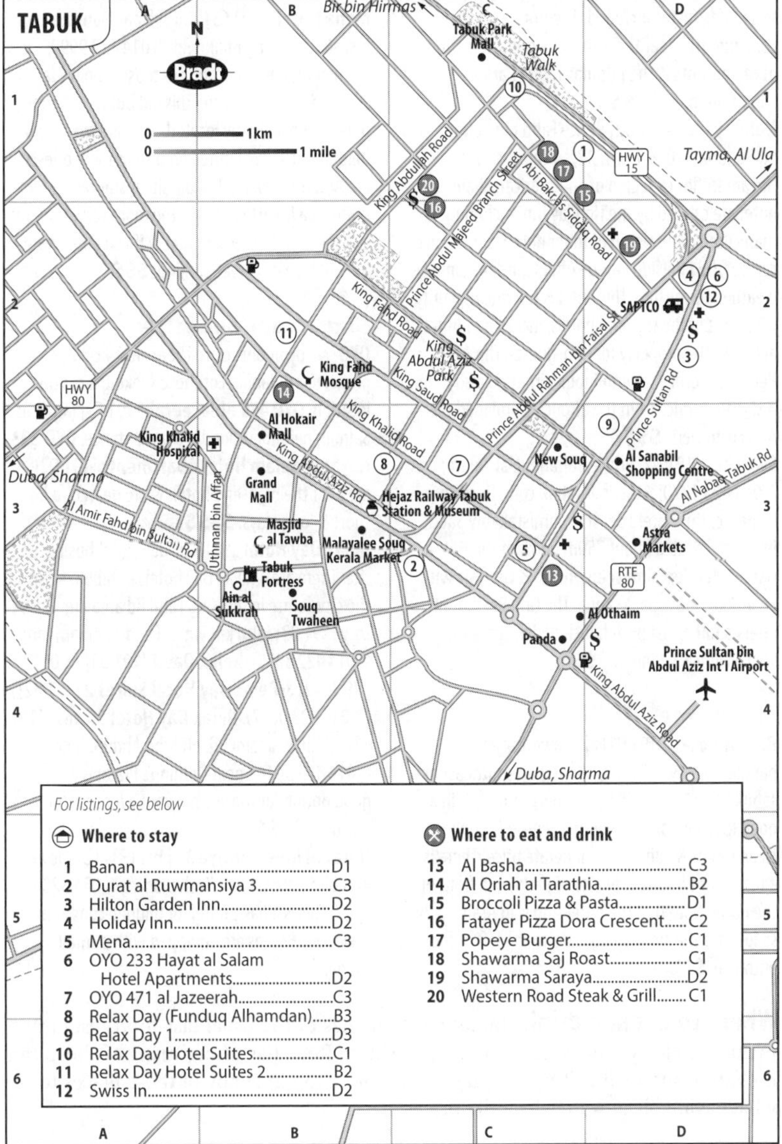




**Where to stay** Top-end Western hotel choices are of a standard similar to those found in other countries. Other hotels provide service ranging from good to abysmal, though they are budget-friendly.

### *Upmarket*

**Hilton Garden Inn** [191 D2] Prince Sultan Rd, al Salam; 📞014 422 6116; **w** ar.hilton.com. This modern property has comfortable rooms & suites, including accessible rooms that will make a stay more comfortable for guests with limited mobility. There is free parking, a rooftop pool, a business centre & a small minimarket on site. A hearty b/fast is served in the buffet restaurant. Check your room rate to see if b/fast is included. The hotel is conveniently near the airbase, a good selection of restaurants & the popular Tabuk Park shopping mall. **$$$$**

**Holiday Inn** [191 D2] Prince Fahd bin Sultan St, Sultana; ☎ 014 422 1212; w ihg.com. All the amenities expected of an American chain hotel are offered by the Holiday Inn, including manicured grounds, an outdoor pool & conference centre. The poolside lounge offers outdoor dining, weather permitting. This hotel is the most security conscious of the top-end hotels, including limited access to the property for non-guests. The Avis Rental Car office serving Tabuk airport is also here. A shuttle service from the airport is provided for Avis customers. **$$$$**

**Swiss In** [191 D2] Prince Sultan Rd, al Salam; ☎ 014 423 1770; w swissintabuk.com. Despite its name, this hotel's décor is unmistakably Saudi inspired. Located about 750m north of the Hilton Garden, it offers similar amenities & comfort with an indoor pool, spa & sauna. The Grill Restaurant offers a full b/fast buffet, included in some rates, as well as lunch & dinner. **$$$$**

### Mid-range

**Banan Hotel** [191 D1] al Khawarazmi Rd, parallel to hwys 15 & 80, about 2km southeast of Tabuk Park; ☎ 014 450 0099. This property is in a good location for those with a vehicle & provides clean rooms & suites at a moderate price. There is a restaurant on site & plenty of parking in front of the hotel. Note that the hotel sign is in Arabic only, so look for the sign saying 'Care' to the left of the entrance. **$$$**

**Mena Hotel** [191 C3] abu Jafar al Mansour St, just south of King Khalid Rd; ☎ 014 422 9999; w menahoteltabuk.com. For those who prefer to stay near the city centre, this old but refurbished hotel is conveniently located. Staff are friendly & helpful but speak limited English as most guests are Arabic speaking. The on-site restaurant offers buffet & à la carte options; the room service menu is somewhat limited but handy if you don't want to go out. Free on-street parking. **$$$**

### Budget and shoestring

**OYO** w oyorooms.com. There are 14 OYO properties in Tabuk. For those seeking a central location, **OYO 471 al Jazeerah** [191 C3] in the as Salman neighbourhood is a good choice. **OYO 233 Hayat al Salam Hotel Apartments** [191 D2] are near the high-end hotels & are geared to both short & long stays. **$–$$**

**Relax Day Hotel** w relax-day-hotel.business.site. There are 4 Relax Day hotels in Tabuk. Near the city centre in the King Fahd Rd area are: **Relax Day** [191 B3] (also known as Funduq Alhamdan; ☎ 014 422 3735), **Relax Day 1** [191 D3] (☎ 055 129 1322) & **Relax Day Hotel Suites 2** [191 B2] (☎ 014 423 0887). **Relax Day Hotel Suites** [191 C1] (al Khawarazmi Rd, off King Abdullah Rd; ☎ 014 425 5444), near Domino's Pizza, is a good option for those who want a less central location. **$–$$**

**Durat al Ruwmansiya 3** [191 C3] al Darae al Aarabii St West, Khalidiyah District; ☎ 054 528 5127. This is a basic hotel for budget-conscious travellers. Rooms are equipped with a small fridge. **$**

## Where to eat and drink

Tabuk has branches of the usual fast-food restaurants including Herfys and Kudu. Abi Bakr as Siddiq Road has a long string of cheap eats including shawarma, burgers, pizza and more. Stop in at any of these places to see what's available at wallet-friendly prices.

**Western Road Steak & Grill** [191 C1] King Abdullah Rd, near TGI Fridays; ☎ 053 313 3753; ⌚ 10.00–01.15 daily. This is the place if you want an American West theme with a bit of Tex-Mex added to the mix – portions are huge even by Saudi standards & will hit the spot if you are craving this sort of food. The décor includes old gas pumps & other mid-century American artefacts. There are b/fast & coffee menus in addition to the main menu. **$$$$**

**Al Basha Restaurant** [191 C3] King Khalid Rd, just east of Prince Sultan Rd; ☎ 014 422 8787; ⌚ 11.00–01.00 daily, closed for prayer times. This large restaurant is popular for both take-away & dining in. The singles section has on-floor cushion seating with a few tables for 2 & plenty of chairs for people waiting for their take-away orders, all with an open kitchen. The food is straightforward & simple, with a good variety of fresh juices, BBQ-grilled chicken & beef, rice & a few salads.

The waiter will help with the Arabic-only menu if necessary. $$$

**Al Qriah al Tarathia** [191 B2] King Khalid Rd, near King Fahd Mosque; 056 120 6666; 11.00–02.00 Sat–Thu, 13.00–02.00 Fri. Also known as al Qaryah al Turathiyah Restaurant, this is similar to other heritage-themed restaurants in other provincial capitals & doesn't disappoint. The Najd-style building hosts an array of artefacts & traditional décor. The food is Saudi with camel kabsa on the menu, & seating is on the floor or at tables. There is a pleasant garden in the centre of the courtyard. $$$

**Broccoli Pizza & Pasta** [191 D1] Abi Bakr as Siddiq Rd; 055 100 4777; 12.30–02.00 daily. Freshly made-to-order pasta dishes with the customer's choice of ingredients make this a popular place. Their pizzas also come with a variety of familiar toppings. Order at the counter & eat in, or take away. Branches also in Ha'il & Jeddah. $$

**Fatayer Pizza Dora Crescent** [191 C2] Prince Mamduh bin Abdul Aziz, next door to McDonald's; 055 166 9990. The menu features Saudi-style pizza & sandwiches on a variety of breads, with several toppings & sauces. The restaurant sign is in Arabic only. $$

**Popeye Burger** [191 C1] Abi Bakr as Siddiq Rd; 054 820 2083; 16.00–02.00 daily. This is a Saudi interpretation of American fast-food burgers & chicken sandwiches, complete with chips & fizzy drinks. Counter service with a few tables if you want to eat in. $$

**Shawarma Saraya** [191 D2] Abi Bakr as Siddiq Rd; 014 429 1136; 17.00–02.00 daily. More shawarma, grills, kebabs & other meaty sandwiches with a few tables. Order at the counter. The restaurant sign is yellow & blue & in Arabic only, as is the menu. Located near the House of Memories wedding hall towards the southeastern end of the road. $$

**Shawarma Saj Roast** [191 C1] Abi Bakr as Siddiq Rd; 014 422 2770; 13.00–midnight daily. This classic take-away shawarma stand also offers cheap & cheerful kebabs. The sign is in Arabic only but you can't miss the stand as the building is bright orange & in front of a large mobile phone mast. Long queues during peak hours attest to its popularity. $

## Shopping

The major supermarket chains Panda, al Othaim and Lulu all have branches in Tabuk, as well as Astra Markets,a regional supermarket chain that sells comparable food and goods.

### *Shopping malls*

**Al Hokair** [191 B3] Cnr King Abdul Aziz Rd & Umar bin al Khattab; 014 422 6699; 09.00–23.30 Sat–Thu, 14.15–23.30 Fri

**Al Sanabil Shopping Centre** [191 D3] King Fahd Rd; 9200 00919; 07.00–23.30 Sat–Thu, 13.00–23.30 Fri. Good if you are looking for sweets.

**Grand** [191 B3] Cnr King Abdul Aziz Rd & Umar bin al Khattab, opposite al Hokair mall; 17.00–23.00 daily

**Tabuk Park Mall** [191 C1] King Faisal Rd, just north of King Abdullah Rd; 9200 09467; 10.00–01.30 Sat–Thu, 13.00–01.30 Fri. Tabuk's most modern shopping mall, with a branch of Jarir. Head here if you are looking for good-quality shops.

### *Souqs*

Popular souqs include **Souq Twaheen**, the **New Souq** [191 C3] (Kaab bin Wail St) & the **Malayalee Souq Kerala Market** [191 B3] (unnamed road off King Abdul Aziz Rd; 09.30–midnight daily), also known as the Indian Souq. Most souqs open for business in the evening with earlier hours unreliable.

**Souq Twaheen** [191 B3] late morning & 16.00–late evening Sat–Thu, late evening Fri. The narrow streets of this souq are about 100m east of the fortress, starting towards the end of al Amir bin Sultan Rd & extending north to King Abdul Aziz Rd. There is nothing remarkable about this souq but it gives a feel of the lives of ordinary shoppers & workers in the area.

## What to see and do

***Tabuk Fortress*** [191 B3] (al Amir Fahd bin Sultan Rd; 014 423 9696; 07.15–13.45 & 16.00–20.00 Sat–Thu, 16.00–18.00 Fri; admission free) This fortress is also known as Tabuk Castle, or as Hab al Aykah (أَصْحَابُ الأَيْكَة), meaning 'Companions of the Wood'. Although other structures have been built on this site dating to the times of the Prophet Mohammed and perhaps much earlier, the fortress you see today was built in 1559 and has been in the custody of the same family for generations. The fortress is easily accessed from the road by walking up the slight hill on the newly paved side road to the right. Look out for the sign in English and Arabic on the wall near the entrance.

You can walk around the fortress independently as there are informational panels throughout, but you could take a guided tour in Arabic or English given by a member of the custodial family. Walk through the wooden doors, then left then right to enter a courtyard, where you will see a tree in front. Along the back wall are a few rooms that contain descriptions of the construction and restoration of the fortress. Many of the ground-floor rooms contain more information about the history of Tabuk going back to the time of Ptolemy in the 1st century CE. Especially informative is a good narrative written about the times of the Prophet Mohammed, explaining his visit to Tabuk and how he met local tribal leaders for the purpose of forming an alliance.

When you have finished exploring the ground floor, look for the steps to the right as you look at the tree from the courtyard entrance. After climbing the stairs, the fortress windows give a view of Ain al Sukkrah, or spring, to the west. Panels describe the significance of the spring from the time of the Prophet's visit, including information about the mosque that was built nearby during the Prophet's life.

## THE HEJAZ RAILWAY

The Hejaz (or Hijaz) Railway has been on UNESCO's Tentative list of World Heritage Sites since 2015, under the cultural category. It was built in the early 20th century by the Ottomans for the purpose of connecting Istanbul with Mecca and Madinah, Islam's two holiest sites. In addition to its religious and military importance, the railway was designed to improve economic and political relationships between the Ottoman Empire and the Arab world.

Loans from a Turkish bank funded the initial construction of the railway. Terrain and working conditions were difficult and progress was hindered by the many Arab tribes who resisted the railway for various reasons, including the fear held by many camel owners of losing pilgrimage business. Some Arab leaders were also concerned about their potential loss of power and influence. In spite of these challenges, the railway opened in 1908, running all the way from Damascus to Madinah by 1913. During the Arab Revolt of World War I, the railway was attacked several times, causing significant damage to many stations and equipment. Vandalism by local residents was also commonplace. In 1920, after the end of World War I and the collapse of the Ottoman Empire, the railway ceased to run. Ibn Saud gained control of the region in 1924, effectively putting an end to the short-lived Hejaz Railway.

**THE STATIONS** Today, it is possible to visit many of the Saudi stations, which you'll find in various states of (dis)repair. From north to south these are: Tabuk, al Ajdar, al Mu'azzam, ad Dar al Hamra, Mada'in Saleh, al Ula, Sultan Mutran, Attobara, Haddiya Bridge, Antar, al Buwayr, Bwatt/Buwat, Makheet and Madinah.

**Tabuk** station is conveniently located in Tabuk city and is a good station to visit, especially if you do not have your own transport to visit other stations. **Al Ajdar**

You will find a series of rooms to the south on the first floor, each containing more information about the city of Tabuk, from the times of the early caravans stopping en route from Syria to pilgrimage routes in more recent times. Learn more about key Islamic figures who wrote about Tabuk, and see collections of artefacts on display. To the east are views towards Souq Twaheen. On the north wall further rooms cover more modern times of Tabuk, including the Ottoman era, and early European visitors. Some rooms contain traditional low seating cushions. The second floor cannot be accessed by visitors.

***Ain al Sukkrah*** [191 B3] (Immediately west of Tabuk Fortress; admission free) Also known as Ayn al Sikr, this is an ancient spring, which dates to the pre-Islamic era known as the Era of Jahiliyyah (جَاهلِيَّة) or ignorance. It is believed that the Prophet Mohammed camped out here for ten days during his visit to Tabuk. Although it is currently fenced in, there is a good view of the spring from all directions. There is no information about the spring on site, but there are good descriptions in Tabuk Fortress on the first floor.

***Masjid al Tawba*** [191 B3] (Less than 200m to the northeast of Tabuk Fortress, ⌚ 24hrs daily for Muslim men, non-Muslim men can visit in between prayer times) Known also as the Repentance Mosque, this is where the Prophet Mohammed prayed during his visit to Tabuk. Originally constructed of bricks, mud and palm fronds, the mosque was reconstructed during the 17th century by the Ottomans

and **al Mu'azzam** are remote stations located several kilometres off-road – they can still be visited, but you'll need a 4x4. **Ad Dar al Hamra** station is about 100km north of Mada'in Saleh, approximately 1km from Route 375 near the village of al Buriekah. The station at **Mada'in Saleh** is now located within the tourist attraction of the same name and is being converted into a luxury hotel. The station in **al Ula** old town still stands but is closed and fenced in. It is possible to get a view from the nearby car park and to see the abandoned carriages on the opposite side of the modern road. **Sultan Mutran** and **Attobara** stations are off Route 375 – the latter has preserved and somewhat restored buildings and is accessible via an unpaved road, but it is about 10km off-road and requires a 4x4.

A visit to **Haddiya Bridge** station is poignant for train enthusiasts. The tipped-over engine in this desolate setting provides hints of the railway's turbulent history at this former major station. It can be accessed from the unnamed road that parallels Route 328 about 3km to the east near the small settlements of Huraymil and Hadiyah. You will also be able to see the Haddiya Bridge ruins to the right as you return from the station back to the road.

Further south on the same unnamed road towards Madinah are **Antar**, which stands alone in front of Jebel Antar, reinforcing the feeling of isolation in this part of the desert, and **al Buwayr** stations. Al Buwayr is currently closed and fenced off as it is being developed as a tourist destination. It is possible to see the station, the locomotive engine and several attached box cars on the rails.

As you continue towards Madinah, you will pass by **Bwatt/Buwat** station and then **Makheet** station in a developing neighbourhood on the outskirts of Madinah. The final station is **Madinah**, where the station museum (page 239) is open for visitors.

and again during the reign of King Faisal – its earlier architecture has not been preserved. In spite of this, there is a sense of history for anyone who has some knowledge of the Battle of Tabuk.

***Hejaz Railway Tabuk Station and Museum*** [191 B3] (King Abdul Aziz Rd, west of Abdullah al Othaim supermarket & shopping centre; ⌚ 08.00–16.00 Sun–Thu; admission free) This compact and well-organised museum displays artefacts from the former Hejaz Railway (page 194). On entering the museum, you will see an original engine and a restored carriage, both positioned on railway tracks. Also on display are photos alongside descriptions of the history of the railway. It is possible to climb on to the engine and carriage to check out the lanterns, communications equipment, time pieces, bells and other tools of the trade from the early 20th century.

The station car park is closed and barricaded, so to access the museum go around the back to the gravel car park in front of a large modern building. The guard is at a desk to the left of the entrance, but you can simply go through the building, exiting through the opposite doors. The museum is to the left.

**THE RED SEA COAST** The Red Sea coast north of Jeddah runs for nearly 1,100km to the Jordanian border and is one of the most pristine stretches of Saudi coastline; and, with KAEC (page 280) and Yanbu (page 243) the main exceptions, it is still mostly untouched. A few traditional towns and villages can be found along the coast, spared from fast-food chain restaurants and glitzy shops and living in the ancient rhythms of long afternoon breaks. Even the usual big-name Saudi supermarkets are absent. However, so are traditional souqs, so the reliance is on locally owned small businesses. With the announcement of NEOM and other Saudi Vision 2030 projects, this is all about to change.

From Jeddah, this journey begins in Makkah Province and continues through the west of Medina Province before reaching Tabuk Province. The roads, with sparse traffic outside towns and cities, are generally very good although they are rife with speed humps and cameras. They should not be driven at night outside built-up areas as they are not lit and camel fences are mostly absent. Petrol stations are also spread out, so it's best to top up where you can once your tank reaches about the halfway mark.

**Umluj أملج** This town is the first substantial settlement in southern Tabuk Province and is a good place to stay if you are passing through on a long journey. From south to north, the **Juman Hotel** (☎ 053 717 5374; **$$**), **HP Red Sea Hotel** (☎ 014 382 5515; **$$**) and **ILAND Hotel** (☎ 050 275 6251; **$$**), all on the Corniche along King Abdullah Road, are the best options for a brief stay and each property has a modest restaurant. Reservations are taken by telephone or WhatsApp. There are a few coffee shops and basic restaurants along the Corniche and Route 55. Take a few minutes to look around the **Old Emirate Palace** next to the Juman Hotel before you leave town. This two-storey palace is one of the few remaining traditional buildings in the area, with wooden doors and windows. Enjoy the small museum (admission free) and courtyard inside if it is open – there are no fixed timings.

**Red Sea Global** (**w** redseaglobal.com) Continuing northbound along Route 55, you will enter the area being developed by Red Sea Global (formerly known as The Red Sea Development Company; TRSDC) near the small town of

Hanak, about 75km from Umluj and 100km from al Wajh. Although less well known than NEOM, this is another Saudi Vision 2030 giga-project expected to be almost 10% larger in total area than NEOM at about 28,800km$^2$. Although little has been built at the time of research, many cranes can be seen from the road along the coast, which has been blocked from Route 55 to the sea with security checkpoints barring entry to the curious. Billboards along the coast promote eco-friendly development, starting with Sheybarah South and Ummahat al Shaykh islands.

According to Red Sea Global, the first phase of the development will open in 2024 and will include 14 luxury hotels offering 3,000 rooms across five islands and two inland locations. It will also include entertainment facilities, an airport and all the necessary infrastructure. In the second phase, scheduled to be completed by 2030, there are also plans to build more than 8,000 hotel rooms on 22 islands and a further six sites on the mainland. It is claimed that visitor numbers will be managed to prevent over-tourism, but no details have been released as to how this will be achieved.

**Al Wajh الوجه** Al Wajh is another good option for those looking for a short stay along this route.

***Where to stay and eat*** Al Wajh has a limited selection of hotels and restaurants which will suit most visitors. Basic restaurants can be found at the southern end of the Corniche along or near Uthman bin Affan Road and along Route 55.

**Raleen Hotel** 053 560 7090. Also known as the Raalin Hotel, this is a newer property on the beach & is a bit more upmarket than the al Wajh Beach Hotel, with private chalets & beach access. **$$**

**Al Wajh Beach Hotel** King Abdullah Rd, Corniche; 014 442 2555. This apart-hotel is opposite the beach & offers good value for money, with adequate bedrooms, living area & kitchen with 2 hobs, a decent-sized fridge, sink & storage. The décor, like the property, is old but serviceable. Ask for the Wi-Fi code at reception. **$**

**Duba ضبا** In future, Duba will be considered the southern gateway to NEOM. It is currently a pleasant seaside town with a small port sheltering small leisure boats. **King Abdul Aziz Castle** is a nice spot on a hill overlooking the old town, the small harbour and the Red Sea. There is no access inside, but it is possible to view all sides of the ruins. North of Duba along the coast many wadis drain into the Red Sea – a spectacular sight when it rains.

Don't confuse this port with the industrial Duba Port about 50km to the north. For those wishing to stay close to NEOM, this is currently the last place for accommodation northbound.

***Where to stay and eat*** The best selection of restaurants can be found along Mohammed bin Ath Thabahi Road and along Route 55. **Blue Fish** (Rte 55) and **al Marjan Fish Restaurant** (in Marsa Diba shopping centre) are good, as is the **Chef Kabsa and Bahri Restaurant** on Mohammed bin Ath Thabahi Road.

**Marsa Diba Hotel** King Abdullah Rd; 050 008 7145. Located in a shopping arcade northeast of Duba town, this hotel offers a comfortable stay & a hearty b/fast buffet. **$$$$**

**Dama Hotel Douba** Tabuk Hwy 80; 056 605 2010. Look for this property at the junction of Hwy 80 & Rte 55. This is a clean 3-star hotel at a mid-range price. **$$$**

**Lille Samar Hotel** Corniche; ☎ 014 433 0045. Those looking for a budget option should consider this hotel, which overlooks the spiral minaret on the Corniche. It is a basic 1-storey motel-style property, but well located south of the harbour near the public beach. **$$**

**Haql حَقْل** Found along the small patch of land between the northern border of NEOM and the Jordanian border is the small city of Haql and the town of al Humidah to its south along the coast. This is the place to stop when planning to cross the Jordanian border if you cannot make it further down the coast past NEOM or to Tabuk. There is a string of beach chalets along the Gulf south of the city centre towards al Humidah which can be hired, though they are unlikely to be used to foreign guests. Each property has its own rules and a very Saudi vibe, with privacy walls and a general feeling of seclusion. Most restaurants can be found in the al Balda al Qadinah neighbourhood along Route 55 and the major streets leading to the al Rajhi mosque in the Alhahrah district. Most supermarkets are little more than corner shops but have the basics.

**NEOM نيوم** (w neom.com/en-us) NEOM is a blended-language acronym, borrowing the Latin 'NEO' for new and merging it with the letter M from the Arabic word *mostaqbal* (مستقبل), which means future. It is advertised as a smart city and global tourist destination, stating that it will be within a 4-hour flight of 40% of the world's population. Its official website claims that 'NEOM will be a destination, a home for people who dream big and want to be part of building a new model for sustainable living, working and prospering'. Announced by Crown Prince Mohammed bin Salman in October 2017, it is a key project under the Saudi Vision 2030 umbrella.

NEOM runs along the Red Sea coast from north of Duba to the south of al Humidah near Haql and the Jordanian border. It reaches inland to the Hejaz mountains, including Jebel al Lawz, and southeast to near the town of Shigry. It has been announced that NEOM will operate under separate legislation from the rest of Saudi Arabia but will remain under the Kingdom's regulations – big social questions ranging from the dress code to alcohol policy remain unanswered at present. Many of the villages referenced in this section have been around for millennia and are being incorporated into NEOM, sometimes with much resistance. Others are targeted for development, often on virginal land. Although it is early days, building works have begun on many projects within NEOM's borders. Others are found only in planning documentation.

NEOM's coastal development plans running broadly from south to north include:

***Oxagon*** Also known as NEOM Industrial City, Oxagon has been advertised as the next generation of industry, with a focus on renewable energy – sustainability, with a reliance on the latest technology. This will incorporate an automated port by upgrading the current Duba Port (NEOM's southern border starts about 25km north of Duba). Octagon-shaped and with nearly 50% designed to be offshore, Oxagon will be 33 times the size of New York City and will also become the world's largest floating structure. Development work is currently underway.

***NEOM Bay*** The initial project has prioritised the building of this NEOM community, which houses people working on the NEOM project and their families. Phases 1 and 2 have been completed enough for residents to move into some properties. It is a combination of a compound and an upscale site camp. The project also includes the NEOM airport, situated about 20km south of Sharma along Route 55, from where Saudia has now started scheduled services to Jeddah, Riyadh and Dubai.

***The Line*** Depending on your perspective, The Line might be considered one of the most imaginative or grandiose projects under the NEOM umbrella, and states it expects to support 1 million residents. Announced in January 2021, it aims to be a linear city with no cars, no streets and no carbon emissions. Its three-level design plans show a lower spine layer intended for ultra-high-speed transport powered by clean energy and controlled with artificial intelligence; the middle layer is the service layer, with the pedestrian layer found at the top. The Line will extend 170km from the mountains to the Red Sea coast at the entrance to the Gulf of Aqaba, with claims of a maximum 20-minute travel time between communities. Inland, significant development is planned, with some already in process.

***Trojena*** (w neom.com/en-us/regions/trojena, neom.directory/what-is-trojena) Trojena is focused around Jebel al Lawz, about 50km inland from the Gulf of Aqaba at an elevation of 1,500–2,600m. Organised in six districts, each designed with different sets of activities and lifestyle choices in mind – including a ski village, a lake for watersports, an observatory for star-gazing, well-being facilities

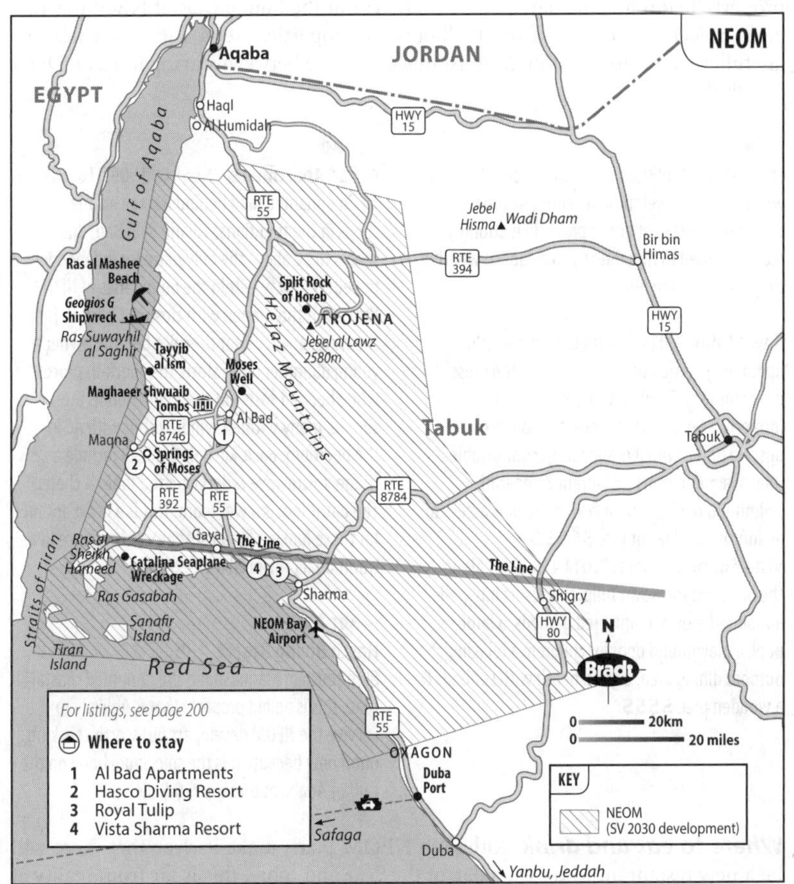


Tabuk and Medina Provinces TABUK PROVINCE 6

and a wildlife reserve – Trojena was announced by Crown Prince Mohammed bin Salman in March 2022 as a year-round destination for tourists. Clean air, protection of the region's biodiversity and scenic vistas are mentioned as priorities. It is also an attractive destination due to having much cooler summer temperatures than elsewhere in the Kingdom. NEOM's official website also indicates a plan to develop 3,600 hotel rooms and 2,200 homes including luxury mansions here, along with a range of restaurants and retail facilities. The Trojena project is scheduled for completion by 2026.

## *Where to stay* *Map, page 199*

Although some housing in NEOM Community near Sharma is now in use, there is currently no accommodation for general visitors unless they are associated with NEOM. Check out the Lulu express supermarket behind the security gates if you are looking for provisions – it is not possible to drive past the security gates without a valid permit, but it is possible to park in the adjacent car park and walk a short distance to the shop.

As NEOM develops, accommodation continues to change. Hotels may close, often permanently. Others are in various states of construction but may be far from ready to host guests. It is of critical importance to check directly with the property before making any plans to stay within the boundaries of NEOM as this giga-project continues to grow. If all of these properties are no longer available or are full, then visitors to NEOM must make a choice between staying in Haql, Duba or Tabuk.

### Sharma

There are 2 established hotels in this small village, which is a key development centre. Anyone considering a stay at either property is strongly recommended to ring directly to establish whether they are accepting guests.

**Royal Tulip** 014 435 1000. Found near the upgraded junction of rtes 55 & 8784, the most direct route to Tabuk city, the Royal Tulip – formerly a Golden Tulip property – is the more upscale hotel, with a grand lobby, comfortable rooms, a good resort restaurant & separate swimming pools for men & women, plus access to an infinity pool & hot tub. **$$$$$**

**Vista Sharma Resort** 014 435 1293. Along the bay from the Royal Tulip, this resort has well-appointed rooms, manicured gardens, a large pool, a playground pool for children, a relaxing outdoor dining area, a good beach with sunbeds & a wooden pier. **$$$$**

### Al Bad

**Al Bad Apartments** 055 690 9095. Located on an unnamed road behind a small arcade of shops in the traditional village of al Bad, this seems to be about the only place for independent travellers to stay within the boundaries of NEOM that is not threatened with closure. Check-in is in the travel agency near the juice bar. The owner's young daughter often starts the check-in process while her dad sorts out the room. Rooms are simple, many without windows but with AC in the bedroom. Basic kitchen facilities include a fridge, microwave & decent-sized table & chairs. The bathroom is a wet room. This is a good option for those looking for an authentic experience in a traditional provincial town. **$$$**

### Maqna

**Hasco Diving Resort** 050 593 8724. About 8km south of Maqna along the unnamed coastal road, this is an old property that is unlikely to survive the NEOM developers but worth checking out if only because it is the sole Saudi hotel on the Gulf of Aqaba at present. **$$$**

***Where to eat and drink*** Although NEOM plans make it clear that there will be a new restaurant to try each day of the year and more, this is far from reality at the time of publication. A few American fast-food pop-up shops including Dunkin Donuts and Hardee's, along with a decent Shawarma Wrappers, can be found at the Aldrees petrol station about 2km northbound from the Vista Sharma Resort. There are also some basic restaurants and small grocers in al Bad and Maqna. Otherwise, when exploring NEOM in its development phase, you might consider packing a picnic from Tabuk, Duba or Haql depending on your direction of travel.

***What to see and do*** Access to tourist sites and other points of interest can be uncertain. At the time of research, the coastal road along the Gulf of Aqaba was blocked by NEOM construction from just after the car park at Tayyib al Ism to about 5km south of *Georgios G* shipwreck. This means that exploring the coast will entail a very large diversion inland via Maqna along Route 55 to al Humidah south of Haql. Intrepid explorers should not be put off by this as there are still many sites that can be visited or at least viewed from outside a fence. Travelling northbound from Sharma, here are some options to consider:

**Gayal** Gayal is a small village with a beautiful coastline along a bay. It is still pristine for the moment but following the controversial removal of local people from the Huwaiti tribe along the coast, the developers have put up their signs along the Corniche.

**Ras al Sheikh Hameed** This is the entrance point to the Gulf of Aqaba about 45km west of Gayal. As there is no coastal road at present, follow Route 55 north, turning west on to Route 392, where you will reach Ras al Sheikh Hameed after about 75km. There is a Saudi Coast Guard station at the end of the otherwise currently desolate road, where the ***Catalina Seaplane* wreckage** can be seen across the bay at the waterline. The wreckage is on the west shore of **Ras Gasabah**, the southernmost end of the peninsula.

**Maqna** Further along the coastal route from Ras al Hameed, Maqna (also known as Magna, Maknah and Maqnah) is a small village about 40km to the north. At the moment the coastal road is seldom travelled, leaving the visitor to their own

### THE GULF OF AQABA

The Gulf of Aqaba is the narrow inlet extending from the Red Sea to the northeast, separating Egypt from Saudi Arabia for most of its length. At its far north shores, small coastal stretches belong to Jordan and Israel. On a clear day, it is possible to see all four countries from the city of Haql.

Ras al Sheikh Hameed and Ras Gasabah are important as they control access to the Gulf of Aqaba from the Red Sea. Situated nearly parallel to Egypt's popular tourist resort of Sharm el Sheikh, Tiran and Sanafir islands were both disputed by Egypt as their land. Ceded to Saudi Arabia in 2016, these islands are now scheduled for development as part of NEOM. Jordan's only port city, Aqaba, and Israel's city of Eilat, also an important shipping port, both rely on economic and military stability to keep these vital routes open.

The unnamed Gulf of Aqaba coastal road runs from the Jordanian border to Ras al Sheikh Hameed for about 175km. It is currently a very pleasant journey as it reveals a series of unspoilt beaches dotted with other areas of outstanding natural beauty. Parts of this road are closed due to the development of NEOM, so this will change shortly.

thoughts when viewing kilometres of empty beaches that abut imaginative rock formations before blending into the desert. Maqna is the only coastal village on the Gulf of Aqaba and within the boundaries of NEOM where simple groceries and other basic provisions can be bought. It also enthusiastically embraces the afternoon siesta – do keep this in mind as nearly everything closes from dhuhr prayer until late afternoon.

Maqna is also believed to be a part of the ancient land of Maydan or Midian. Many believe that the Prophet Moses (Mousa) fled Egypt for Midian after an argument and crossed the Red Sea to live in exile. It is said that Moses, after living in Midian for ten years, subsequently led Egyptians through the Red Sea to Wadi Tayyib al Ism north of Maqna.

**Springs of Moses (Ayn Mousa)** (Just off Rte 8746 towards al Bad, less than 1km from the village of Maqna; admission free) Turn right at the sign into the site, where there is a dirt car park less than 100m from the road. The car park overlooks the springs. It is possible to walk around the site, dip a toe into the water, and walk across a stone-and-wood-built footbridge. There are a total of 12 springs that can be explored among palm trees, with benches scattered around to sit on and reflect.

**Tayyib al Ism** ✷ In a country where places of religious significance seem to be everywhere, Tayyib al Ism (also known as Wadi Tayeb Ism, Tayeb al Ism and more) delivers a brilliant combination of pre-Islamic religious history, as well as references to Exodus in Judaism and Christianity, all in a stunning natural environment. Mormons believe this is the location of the Valley of Lemuel.

Located on the coastal road about 15km north of Maqma, the scenery is dramatic, with the mesmerising shoreline broken only by rocks that seem to be positioned for maximum impact on the eye. Visitors will first encounter a checkpoint about 2km south of the entrance, where security will ask to see passports. You should have no problem passing through if you make it clear you are only going to Tayyib al Ism and not attempting to go further up the coastal road, which is blocked immediately north of the wadi entrance.

Look for the red Arabic-only sign with white script, and a Saudi palm tree and swords symbol. The dramatic rock tower formations and narrow access gap are unmissable. This is where the adventure starts. Park under one of the palm trees at the entrance, which will keep your vehicle relatively cool from the sun. Although it is possible to access the site via 4x4, this is a brilliant hike. The walk starts by passing through the narrow gap between the two rock tower formations. Cross over the wooden pedestrian bridge and follow the path, where you will see many clear water streams that cool your walk. After about 700m, you will reach a valley of palm trees, Setenta Palmera. This is also believed to be the location of Elim as referenced in Exodo or Exodus 15:27. Moses chose well.

**Ras Suwayhil al Saghir** About 35km further north along the coastal road is this beautiful bay. Check to make sure the coastal road is open to the bay as it has been off-limits at times from both the south and north due to NEOM development.

**Ras al Mashee Beach** For those who are prepared to take a very wide diversion before continuing along the Gulf of Aqaba coast, there is a reward about 55km south of Haql. This diversion involves returning to Maqma and taking the inland routes 8746 and 55 before rejoining the coastal route southbound at al Humidah. The reward is a beautiful beach featuring the wreck of the Greek ship ***Georgios G***, a cargo vessel which sank on a coral reef near the shoreline in 1978. Swimming beyond the buoys that surround the shipwreck is not permitted, a rule which is enforced by on-site security. There is a new car park and public toilets but not much else here, so bring everything you need if you plan to stay for a while.

**Al Bad** (also al Bada and al Bada'a) Not everything of interest in Tabuk Province is on the coast or in the mountains. As you move inland, points of interest within the boundaries of NEOM continue to impress – NEOM has claimed desert inland areas of the region, as well as some of the most dramatic mountains towards Bir bin Himas and Tabuk city. Don't miss a visit to al Bad, which is believed to be the centre of Midian and thought by some to have been settled by the descendants of Midian, son of Abraham, perhaps as early as the 8th century BCE. It is located on desert flats of Wadi Afal about 35km inland from Maqna and about 75km north of Sharma off Route 55. There is nothing modern-looking about al Bad, though you will be able to find basic provisions here. Note that there are two settled areas of al Bad running south to north. It is also an excellent stopping-off point to visit pre-Islamic Talmudic, Nabataean and biblical sites. At the time of research, local people were unsure of the future impact of NEOM development plans for their town.

**Moses Well (Al Suaedni Well)** (🕘 24hrs daily; admission free) Not to be confused with the Springs of Moses, this site is to the northeast of northern al Bad on unmarked roads (good driving directions can be found online). Although the entire site is fenced off, visitors may enter the site through a gap in the fence on the west perimeter near the Saudi Tourism Authority sign. To the right almost immediately upon entry is what looks like a modern, pentagon-shaped replica well with stairs descending from the southern side. The signage is confusing as it seems to be describing the historic well, which is not here but is about 200m directly ahead along a stone walkway within the site. The historic well is oblong-shaped and is protected by a rust-coloured fence within the larger site. It has a curving set of eroded stairs that can be seen from outside the rusted fence. There are also ruins of a building in the northeast corner within the fencing.

**Maghaeer Shwuaib Tombs (Madyan)** ✷ (About 1km north of the terminus of Rte 8746 on the thoroughfare to the west of al Bad; 🕘 10.00–18.00 Sun–Thu, 16.00–18.00 Fri–Sat; admission free) Located in hillside caves, these nearly unknown Nabataean tombs are smaller than those of Mada'in Saleh but no less significant. There is a museum in the modern building that leads to the ancient site which does a good job explaining the importance of the tombs and the impact of Midian geography, history and culture regionally. Historical periods are explained from the times of the Midianites, the Adomites and the Prophets, the Land of Aykah, Lehianite and Nabataean periods and finally the Islamic period. Coins from the Greek and Roman periods are also on display. The region has also been controlled by the Umayyads, Fatimids, Mamluks and Ottomans – the caves have survived through all of these periods. This is a great place to get a crash course on tribal history east of the Gulf of Aqaba.

There are about 30 caves in total that date back to the 2nd millennium BCE. Most of the caves that contained the tombs are accessible via a road behind the museum and along stone walkways and stairs. Some of the cave façades are decorated, while others look either undecorated or perhaps have been eroded; and entrance shapes range from rectangular to irregular. It is possible to explore the caves but visitors need to be aware of the low entrance ways and ceilings. For more information about Nabataean culture, see page 16.

**Jebel al Lawz** Jebel al Lawz (also Jabal al Loze, Jebel al Lous) ) is believed by some to be the true location of Mount Sinai. It receives natural snowfall most years during the short winter season. It is a brilliantly beautiful drive to this mountain, or, more accurately, to the checkpoint near the mountain where further access is now forbidden – since the mountain lies within the boundaries of NEOM. Continuing our journey narrative from al Bad, drivers will rejoin Route 55 north of the town by turning east at the junction with Route 394. Turn off from Route 394 after a bit less than 10km, where you can easily spot a collection of heavy roadworks vehicles to the right (this road is undergoing a major 'military upgrade').

Continue for about 40km. Driving on these roads could be compared to a rollercoaster ride, with dramatic switchbacks and steep gradients as you make the ear-popping ascent. The temperature drops at least 10 degrees between Route 394 and the approach to Jebel al Lawz. You are almost guaranteed to see lots of camels at the lower elevations along the mountain route. During research, it was amusing to see a herd deciding to invite themselves on to the premises of the NEOM construction site camp building.

**Trojena** After about 40km after leaving Route 394, you will reach a checkpoint. It is not possible to proceed any further as this is where the massive Trojena project is being developed. If the developers' claims of year-round tourism in a setting of ultra-luxurious family resorts comes to fruition (page 199), Trojena is set to challenge Lebanon's unique claim in the Middle East of offering snow-skiing in the morning and swimming in the sea in the afternoon. The Trojena project also claims to take environmental sustainability into account. No matter what is achieved in this future development, it will look very different to the current natural beauty of the mountain ranges, which are themselves worth this detour.

**Split Rock of Horeb** This rock, about 6m tall, is split almost from top to bottom in a near-vertical line. It has biblical significance for Jews and Christians as the location where Moses received the Ten Commandments during his time in this region of Midian. The rock is situated on top of a rocky hill and accessible only by a combination of 4x4 and climbing on foot. We are not sure if this site has been incorporated into Trojena, but believe it is highly likely.

**WADI DHAM وادي دهام AND JEBEL HISMA جبل حسمة** Leaving NEOM behind, those continuing east from Jebel al Lawz and Trojena will note that the terrain changes dramatically shortly after rejoining Route 394 in the direction of Bir bin Himas. Mountains fade away, replaced by huge rock pillars, some of which reach heights of several hundred metres. The wind has created imaginative rock shapes that appear to change when observed from different angles. Soft sand dances between these rock formations, seemingly changing colour depending on the time of day and direction of viewing. This is Wadi Dham, which stretches from Wadi Rum in Jordan to Wadi Disah to the south of Tabuk. Jebel Hisma, located within the wadi, also contains a treasure trove of rock art and early Islamic Kufic Arabic inscriptions. Wild camping is possible, but heed the usual cautions when travelling in the desert. Even if you don't have much time, do try to pull over to take a few minutes to appreciate one of nature's true spectacles, taking care not to stop on the soft sand.

**BIR BIN HIMAS بئر ابن هرماس** Also known as Bur bin Hirmas/Harmas, Bir bin Himas is the first significant settlement in Tabuk Province along Highway 15 south of the Jordanian border. It is located at the junction of Route 394 and Highway 15, which continues south to Tabuk city and beyond, and is a good place for a break and to refuel before continuing your journey. Although not a tourist attraction, this medium-sized town is a pleasant enough place with numerous olive farms for many kilometres along Highway15 towards Tabuk, and is a good place to stop for petrol and refreshments.

**WADI DISAH (WADI QARAQIR) وادي ديساه** This spectacular wadi lies about 125km east of Duba, 80km as the crow flies but 225km by road to the south of Tabuk and 275km northwest of al Ula. It is hidden away from the main road and accessible only by 4x4. However, there are usually local drivers available for hire who will offer their services for a negotiated fee and present a safe option for those without a suitable vehicle of their own.

Both the east and the west entrances to the wadi are defined by rocky cliffs, reaching 500m in height at the western entrance. Some of the majestic rocks can be conical in shape; others are other-worldly pillars. There is a crystal-clear stream that flows towards the village of Disah a few kilometres to the west. The oasis contains palm trees, tall grass and a year-round spring that nourishes the greenery and provides for a slightly cooler atmosphere than the surrounding area, although prospective visitors should take note that it is still very hot in the summer and cold in the winter. Nature lovers find this a special place for camping, picnicking, hiking and horseriding. There are also examples of 3,000-year-old rock art and petroglyphs to be explored. Some choose to check out the cave just off the dirt road for a closer view of rock art. For the very fit and adventurous, don't miss the opportunity to climb to the Hidden Veranda, where you will be rewarded with a spectacular view of the wadi. As this involves climbing rocks on unmarked trails, it is recommended that a guide is hired if you wish to reach the Hidden Veranda. Local men are usually nearby who can act as guides.

Visitors must bring all camping gear and provisions as this is a very remote location. It is also prudent to keep your eye on petrol levels and top up before turning on to the most remote roads. Wadi Disah is beyond the boundaries of NEOM but is part of the Prince Mohammed bin Salman Royal Reserve and has been announced as targeted for development. Don't delay your visit to see this miracle of nature in its unspoilt form.

**TAYMA تيماء** Tayma is an oasis established on the western edge of the an Nafud desert and east of the Sarawat Mountains. It is the oldest settlement in the Kingdom, with evidence of human habitation here for more than 90,000 years, substantiated by the discovery of a finger bone by Saudi archaeologists working with Oxford University in 2016.

Tayma's abundance of water wells is mentioned in Assyrian inscriptions dating to Mesopotamian times, more than 8,000 years BCE. Cuneiform inscriptions in the region also indicate the presence of Babylonians in Tayma, as does evidence from the Lihyanite or Dadan period. Aramaic writing from the 6th century BCE has also been discovered, most dramatically on the Tayma Stone, which is now housed in the Louvre in Paris. Tayma is also noted in the Hebrew bible; it is believed that Jewish people lived in Tayma at least as far back as the 1st century CE and were possibly prominent for more than a millennium, into the early Islamic period. Tayma has been a well-provisioned stopping place for trade caravans between Yemen and points north from at least Mesopotamian times and later became an important resting place for Muslim pilgrims. European explorers arrived here during the 19th century. Tayma was eventually absorbed into the Third and current Saudi State in 1924.

**Getting there and away** Tayma is 260km from Tabuk in the southeast corner of Tabuk Province, and about 230km from al Ula. Both journeys take about 2½ hours, making for the possibility of a long day trip from either starting point. Whether you approach Tayma from the west from Tabuk or from the south from al Ula, you will know you are approaching the oasis town when you are surrounded by palm tree farms and other agricultural activities in the wadis. The approach from al Ula via Arabah is particularly beautiful, with some stunning rock formations not unlike Monument Valley in the US states of Arizona and Utah. You can make an event of spotting all sorts of rock shapes on the otherwise empty roads.

### Where to stay and eat *Map, below*

For those who find a long day trip unpalatable, it is possible to stay in Tayma, but choices are limited as there is no real infrastructure for tourists. **Alamana Hotel** (Hwy 15, west of Prince Sultan bin Abdul Aziz Rd; 055 610 2370; **$$**) looks very newly built, as does **Jewel Places Hotel** (فندق جوهرة الاماكن; sign in Arabic only; Prince Sultan bin Abdul Aziz Rd, south of the 2nd roundabout southbound off Hwy 15; 050 715 1807; **$$**). Both are budget-friendly, have ample parking, with some rooms containing a kitchenette. They are both on the outskirts of town.

Limited cuisine and local fast food can be found along Prince Sultan bin Abdul Aziz Road, such as at **Kudu Baik** (which is not actually affiliated with either well-known fast-food chain; **$**). The food is unremarkable but will hit the spot if you are very hungry. You can also consider the option of taking away something from the newly opened Abdullah al Othaim supermarket.

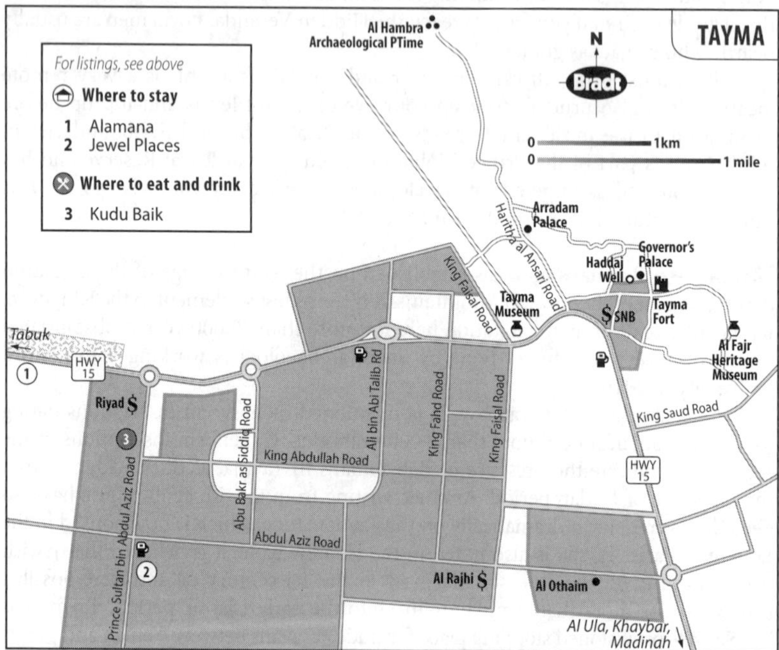

**What to see and do** Unlike at most other historical sites elsewhere in the Kingdom, you will be greeted by security guards at some of Tayma's sites, including Haddaj Well, Arradam Palace and al Hambra Archaeological Site. Visitors are required to present their passport, which is duly logged by the guard along with vehicle registration number.

***Haddaj Well (Bir Haddaj)*** ✱ (Abdullah bin Omar Rd; ⌚ 09.00–17.00 daily; admission free) This well is believed to have been built in the 6th century BCE under the instruction of Nabonidus, the last king of the Babylonian Empire. It was restored after its discovery many centuries later by Suleiman al Gonaim, a prominent Jewish resident of Tayma. King Saud then added four pumps to the well in 1953 for the use of local farmers, putting an excessive burden on the well, causing it eventually to fail. The well was restored to its original design under the instruction of King Faisal after his visit in 1973.

Tayma is worth a visit if only to see this ancient engineering marvel. It is about 18m in circumference with wooden beams supporting wooden wheels all built on stone walls surrounding the pit of the stone-brick well. The water at the bottom of the well is bright green, and trees and other greenery grow along parts of the well wall. The edge of the well is fenced, providing some safety and the area around the well is paved and has benches to sit on. There is a fence around the area that is closed out of hours, but the well remains visible from outside. There is a visitor centre with a few displays and more detailed information.

The location of Haddaj Well is reasonably well signposted from Highway 15. It is situated at the top of Abdullah bin Omar Road just past Old Town Coffee. There is no car park, but street parking is possible to the east near the Governor's Palace.

***Governor's Palace*** (Immediately east of Haddaj Well on the north side of the street; ⌚ 24hrs daily) This mud-brick-and-palm-frond structure is in the Nadj style with triangulated walls on top. Although some wooden doors and stairs have survived, it is largely in a state of advanced ruin but looks like it's in the process of being over-restored to look modern, especially in and around the large courtyard. There are further ruins of what appears to be a village on the south side of the road which you can imagine supported the needs of the palace. Visitors are free to wander around outside the fenced-off area.

***Tayma Fort*** (At the T-junction with al Amir Fahd bin Sultan Rd; ☎ 055 318 8933; admission free) The current fort is built of mud with formidable walls and turrets in the same Najd style with white-framed windows. Saudi Tourism states that the fort has existed for more than 1,000 years, but there are walls within the palace dating from an earlier era. Most of the exterior has been kept to a good standard. A lovely palm grove is situated to the south of the fort. We were unable to explore the interior as it was closed to visitors at the time of research.

***Al Fajr Heritage Museum*** (Off Khalid bin al Walid Rd; ☎ 050 476 8737; ⌚ no regular hours; small entry fee) Of the many heritage museums dotted around the Kingdom, this one has a large number of antiques and is reasonably well organised. The museum is run by a family offering traditional Saudi hospitality, who welcome you through double doors at the front of the building; a sign in Arabic and English to the right of the doors lets you know you are in the right place.

***Arradam Palace (Qasr al Radhm)*** (Haritha al Ansari Rd; ⌚ 09.00–17.00 daily; admission free) These ancient ruins date to the 6th century BCE as determined through the pottery shards found on site. Built to protect Tayma city's western walls from attack, the structure covers an area of about 34m by 25m, with walls over 3.5m high and about 2m thick built of large stones . The site is fenced off, but it can be explored during opening hours. Be careful on the east side as there are open holes caused by collapsed wells. There is a paved viewing area a short distance away with concrete benches, which can be accessed by wheelchair users (but it is not protected from the sun). Look closely and you will find cuneiform writing on some of the stones. There is a visitor centre and a car park at the site.

***Al Hambra Archaeological Site*** ✷ (2km northwest of the Arradam Palace on Haritha al Ansari Rd; ⌚ 09.00–17.00 daily; admission free) Excavated between 1979 and 1986, this palace is thought to date back to the 1st millennium BCE, during the reign of the Babylon Emperor of Tayma. It is built of stone in three sections and overlooks a palm grove that was once a lake. There are early Aramaic inscriptions on site, referencing two deities: the moon god (the bull) and the sun god (the winged disc); the planet Venus, or Ishtar, is represented by a star within a circle. The inscriptions correlate with the Tayma Stone now housed in the Louvre in Paris. Rock art depicting camels and other animals is also present.

The site is about 350m from the visitor centre car park so take this into consideration if you are visiting during the summer months. The unshaded walk is paved with rough stones and is on a gentle incline to reach the site at the top of a hill to the east.

***Tayma Museum*** (Hwy 15 at the roundabout with King Faisal Rd; ☎ 053 818 8209) Unfortunately, this museum is temporarily closed so it could not be visited at the time of research. It contains information, exhibits and much more about Tayma oasis and its importance to the Arabian Peninsula from prehistoric times through the Neolithic, Bronze Age, Babylonian times, Arab tribal conquests, the arrival of Islam and up to current times as part of the Kingdom of Saudi Arabia.

## MEDINA PROVINCE مِنطقة ٱلْمَدِينَة

*Note: There are many spellings for Medina. To avoid confusion, we are using Medina to refer to the province and Madinah for the city.*

Medina Province is home to about 2.1 million people and is significant within the Kingdom of Saudi Arabia for its agriculture and industry, as well as being a global pilgrimage destination. The provincial capital, Madinah, is the second most important site in the Islamic world – the main destination on the Islamic pilgrimage trail after Mecca – and the location of the Masjid al Nabawi mosque complex, which includes the tomb of the Prophet Mohammed. (Do not be surprised if you see a wide range of spellings on the ground for both the city and the province; page viii.) The province is also home to the important industrial city of Yanbu on the Red Sea coast.

Medina stretches from the Red Sea and through the Hejaz Mountains to the Nafud desert. Much of the desert is strewn with basalt, created by centuries-dormant volcanos, creating a blanket of black lava fields which gives a feeling of other-worldliness along the most desolate roads – aside from the frequent herds of camels and goats you're likely to encounter along the way.

There is something here for everyone. Historians and archaeology enthusiasts can visit places that go back to pre-Bronze Age times and observe world-class sites that are only now being revealed to the outside world as Saudi tourism develops. In the north of the province, the Kingdom's first World Heritage Site, Mada'in Saleh, located near the tourist-friendly town of al Ula, boasts rock formations, rock art and much more. Archaeological sites continue to yield new discoveries, with the 4,500-year-old avenues lined with Bronze Age tombs near the oasis of Khaybar a recent example.

Respectfully curious visitors from all backgrounds will learn about the importance of Madinah to religious pilgrims and will be rewarded by viewing sites key to the earliest days of Islam, giving a better understanding of the world's second largest religion. Meanwhile, adventure-seekers and nature lovers can choose from watersports, hiking, desert camping, rock climbing, wadi bashing and more.

Medina Province has a desert climate, with the exception of the coast, which has a hot desert climate, keeping winter temperatures mild. Inland, the summers are scorching hot with temperatures of 50°C and higher. Winters are cool to cold overnight and into the early morning. It is generally best to visit from November to April, when the pleasantly warm days are comfortable for outdoor activities.

**HISTORY** Caravan trade paths have passed through many routes throughout Medina Province since pre-Islamic times, but the province has been settled by indigenous and migrant Arab tribes for millennia. Inscriptions found in al Ula's Jebel Ikmah reveal Aramaic, Dadantic, Thamudic, Minaic and Nabataean languages and provide an insight into these kingdoms.

The area has been controlled by many different rulers throughout its history, including Jewish Arab tribes until their final defeat in Madinah and Khaybar in 7th century CE, although their power peaked in the 5th century CE. The Aws and Khazraj were powerful groups after the decline of the Jews until the arrival of the Prophet Mohammed and the Rashidun in 622CE. They dominated until 660CE, when the Umayyads established their authority until 749CE. The Abbasids (749–1254CE), Mamluks (1254–1517), and Ottomans (1517–1805) followed before the arrival of the First Saudi State (1805–11). After their short tenure, control reverted to Mohammed Ali Pasha (1811–40), then the Ottomans again (1840–1918) and the Sharif of Mecca of the Hashemites (1918–25). Since 1925, Medina Province has been part of the Kingdom of Saudi Arabia.

## GETTING THERE AND AWAY

**By air** The province is served by Madinah's Prince Mohammed bin Abdul Aziz International Airport and Prince Abdul Majeed bin Abdul Aziz Domestic Airport in al Ula. See pages 211 and 234 for details. In addition, Yanbu's Prince Abdul Mohsen bin Abdul Aziz International Airport ( **w** tibahairports.com), receives Saudia flights from Riyadh and Jeddah. Other domestic flights on flynas and flyadeal arrive from Dammam. Air Arabia flies from Sharjah, and Turkish Airlines from Istanbul.

Many visitors to al Ula may find it more convenient to fly into Madinah, or even Tabuk airport (page 190) in the neighbouring province, and then make the road journey, which takes about 3½–4½ hours.

**By road** SAPTCO **buses** serve Madinah, Khaybar, Yanbu, al Ula and some smaller towns along the major highways, mainly from Jeddah and Tabuk.

***From Jeddah and Mecca Province*** Route 55 is the coastal route that runs from Jeddah to Yanbu and further north. Inland, Highway 15 begins north of

### MADINAH AND NON-MUSLIMS

It is possible for everyone to visit the outskirts of Madinah, but the al Haram area in the city centre is officially off-limits to non-Muslims. See pages 235 and 388 for further information about the al Haram boundaries. We have taken the decision to provide information for all visitors to Madinah outside of the First Ring Road al Haram area, highlighting the non-religious sites that fall within this outer area. We will also reference the religious pilgrimage sites in this area, keeping in mind that our viewpoint is one of general tourism and not of religious orientation. For more information about the area within the First Ring Road and religious significance of Madinah, see page 387.

Jeddah and goes to Madinah and Khaybar before continuing north into eastern Tabuk Province. Highway 60 starts along the Red Sea coast about 250km north of Jeddah and passes through Madinah. This is the alternative route for those wishing to stay along the coast for much of their journey to Madinah. The main route to al Ula is from Highway 15 to Highway 70 westbound at the Medina–Tabuk Province border. Many travellers choose to use Route 375 off Highway 15 as an alternative, but this is a particularly desolate route. These are all remote journeys with services few and far between, so it is important to keep an eye on your petrol levels and to take advantage of toilet facilities when the opportunity arises.

***From Tabuk Province*** Route 55 south is the coastal route from Tabuk to Medina provinces. Highway 80 from Tabuk joins Route 55 near Duba. Highway 15 eastbound intersects with Highway 70 and is the main route into Medina Province. For those travelling from Tabuk to al Ula, turn south on to Route 375 from Highway 15. These are also long roads with few services. Be prepared.

***From Ha'il and Riyadh provinces*** Travellers from Ha'il Province will find Highway 70 convenient for journeys to al Ula. If travelling to Madinah, turn south from Highway 70 on to Highway 15. Alternatively, some prefer to travel on Route 7777 between the two cities. All roads from Ha'il to Medina Province are long and lonely but will give the visitor a good perspective on the vast distances and conditions of desert travel. Most people travelling to Medina Province from Riyadh will take Highway 65 north, turning on to Highway 60 west near Buraydah toward Madinah.

**By rail** The Haramain High Speed Railway (page 74) started service in 2018. The Madinah station is located to the east of the city and is modern and well equipped with conveniences for the traveller. There are currently four trains per day that run between Madinah and Mecca via KAEC and Jeddah, which has both city and airport stations.

**AL ULA اَلْعُلا** With Saudi Arabia's first UNESCO World Heritage Site, a wealth of history from many civilisations, and attention to the needs of tourists that surpasses nearly every other region in the Kingdom, the remote oasis town of al Ula is a must-visit destination. Although al Ula was visited very little even by Saudi nationals and residents until relatively recently, the Kingdom continues to focus on the town and the surrounding area, attracting significant interest by hosting world-class performers and events during al Ula Season, which runs in the winter months. There are an increasing number of weather-appropriate activities in the off-season as well, so don't miss out simply because you are visiting the Kingdom outside of winter. See some of the most positive aspects of Saudi Vision 2030 by spending as much time as you can in this beautiful and intriguing location. Here, the right balance has been struck between local heritage and traditions, modern customs and generous Saudi hospitality – and therein lies al Ula's charm.

Al Ula continues to develop, mostly in an environmentally empathetic way, and can be described as a cultural oasis that appeals to Saudi and global tourists alike. Al Ula also enjoys some relaxation of the Kingdom's social rules. The dress code, still very modest, is broader than elsewhere. Some women are comfortable substituting very baggy clothes for their abaya; many men are comfortable with very casual clothing that would be regarded as less appropriate elsewhere in the Kingdom. Gender mixing is the norm, including at resort swimming pools and all but the most traditional restaurants. But remember that this is still in a conservative region of the Kingdom, especially if you are going to more traditional places off the beaten path. Our advice is to err on the side of caution and adapt to what you are comfortable with once you see what others – including Saudi nationals – are wearing.

## Getting there and away

***By air*** Scheduled Saudia flights arrive at al Ula's **Prince Abdul Majeed bin Abdul Aziz Domestic Airport** [212 A7] from Dammam, Jeddah and Riyadh; flynas operates from Jeddah, Riyadh, Dammam and Kuwait; and flydubai also has a service from Dubai. Many of these flights do not operate daily and may have different seasonal timings. Until the flight schedule is increased including arrivals from neighbouring countries – and this is expected over the next few years – many visitors people prefer to fly to Tabuk or Madinah and drive (3½–4½hrs) to al Ula from these cities instead.

Al Ula's airport is more than 45 minutes away from most of the region's attractions. You will need a car upon arrival or to arrange for a pick-up from your accommodation. Although there are car rental company offices at the airport, these are highly unreliable as they open only when flights arrive and only then if they believe someone has a confirmed rental booking. Anyone who thinks they have organised a car should have a contingency plan. There are also car hire companies in al Ula town – ask your hotel for a recommendation.

### *By road*

**Approach from Tabuk** Follow Highway 15 east of Tabuk. Turn south on to Route 375. The total drive time is about 3½ hours.

**Approach from Tayma** Follow Highway 15 south. We recommend taking the road towards Aradah for the spectacular rock formations before joining Highway 70 west to al Ula. This journey takes about 2½ hours.

**Approach from Madinah** Follow Highway 15 north of Madinah. Train enthusiasts may wish to drive along the unnamed road via Shajwa and al Abraq as this most closely parallels the Hejaz Railway and gives the opportunity to visit several station ruins along the route. Without stops, this journey takes about 3½ hours. An alternative route is to follow Highway 15 north past Khaybar before turning west on to Route 375.

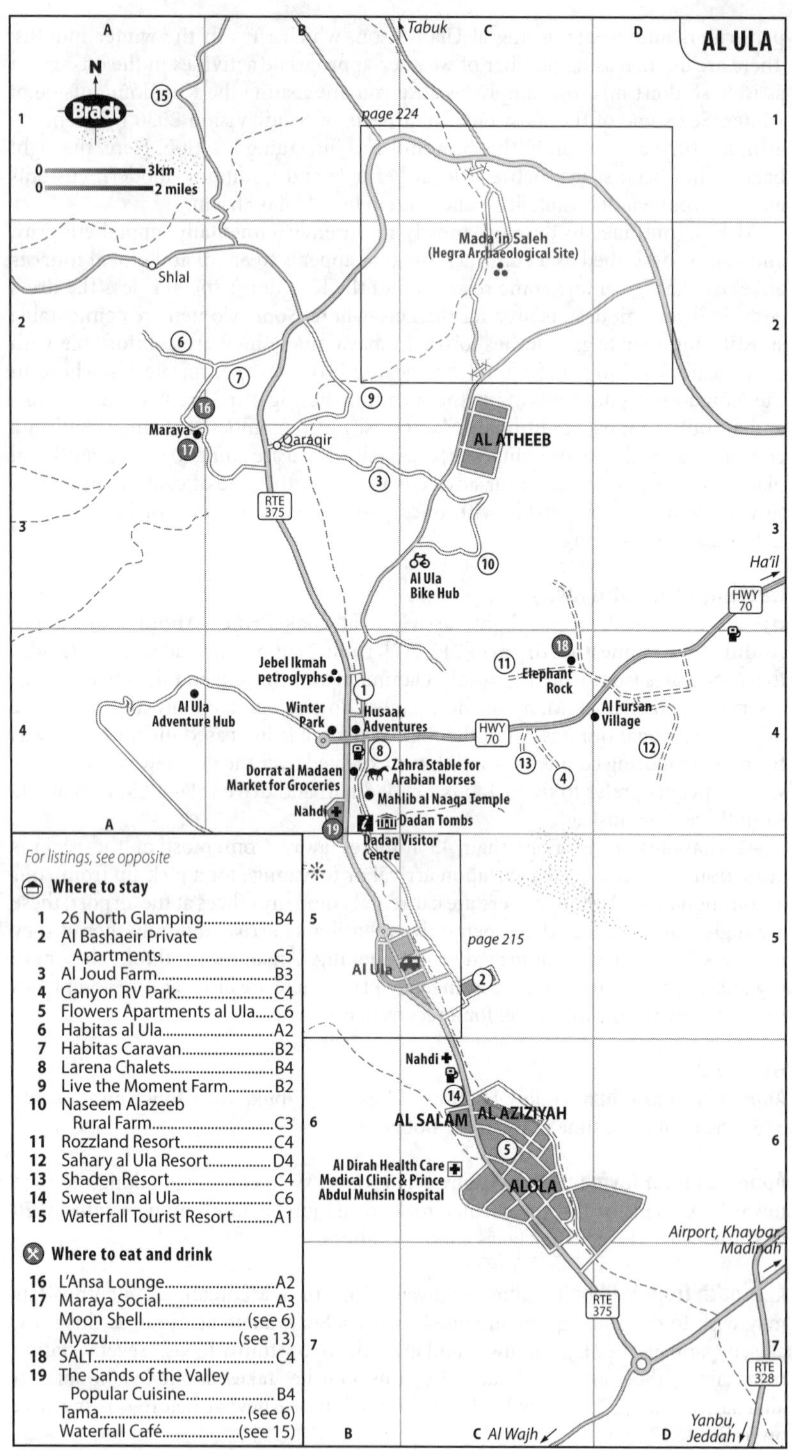
AL ULA
Bradt
N
0 3km
0 2 miles
Tabuk
page 224
Mada'in Saleh
(Hegra Archaeological Site)
Shlal
Maraya
Qaraqir
AL ATHEEB
RTE 375
Al Ula
Bike Hub
Ha'il
HWY 70
Jebel Ikmah
petroglyphs
Elephant
Rock
Al Fursan
Village
Al Ula
Adventure Hub
Winter
Park
Husaak
Adventures
Dorrat al Madaen
Market for Groceries
Zahra Stable for
Arabian Horses
Mahlib al Naaqa Temple
Nahdi
Dadan Tombs
Dadan Visitor
Centre
page 215
Al Ula
Nahdi
AL SALAM
AL AZIZIYAH
Al Dirah Health Care
Medical Clinic & Prince
Abdul Muhsin Hospital
ALOLA
Airport, Khaybar,
Madinah
RTE 375
RTE 328
Al Wajh
Yanbu,
Jeddah
For listings, see opposite
Where to stay
1 26 North Glamping....B4
2 Al Bashaeir Private Apartments....C5
3 Al Joud Farm....B3
4 Canyon RV Park....C4
5 Flowers Apartments al Ula....C6
6 Habitas al Ula....A2
7 Habitas Caravan....B2
8 Larena Chalets....B4
9 Live the Moment Farm....B2
10 Naseem Alazeeb Rural Farm....C3
11 Rozzland Resort....C4
12 Sahary al Ula Resort....D4
13 Shaden Resort....C4
14 Sweet Inn al Ula....C6
15 Waterfall Tourist Resort....A1
Where to eat and drink
16 L'Ansa Lounge....A2
17 Maraya Social....A3
Moon Shell....(see 6)
Myazu....(see 13)
18 SALT....C4
19 The Sands of the Valley Popular Cuisine....B4
Tama....(see 6)
Waterfall Café....(see 15)

**Approach from Yanbu** This route will take about 4 hours without stops. Services are limited, with diminished opening hours especially in the afternoons and at weekends, so keep an eye on your petrol level and fill up when you can if you come this way. Leave Route 55 towards Yanbu al Nakhel. This is Route 328 but you will not see any signs on the road, and it will bring you into al Ula from the south. Once you leave the plains and start to enter the mountains, you will see a few ruins of villages abandoned only decades ago. Head towards al Ays as indicated on the road signs at the beginning of the journey. About halfway, you will reach Wadi Hamd, Wadi Jizal and other substantial wadis. This very green area has many farms and is a very pleasant part of the journey. You will also pass by some salt flats, where road signs now indicate al Ula for the remainder of your drive.

**Orientation** The wider area of al Ula is actually a collection of small settlements. Using Route 375 as a frame of reference, from north to south, you will find Mada'in Saleh, also known as Hegra, Shlal (or Shillal), al Atheeb and several distinct neighbourhoods in al Ula itself. From north to south within al Ula town, you will find the al Jadidah Arts District, Old Town and the modern areas of Saq, al Sukhayrat, and al Ruzayqiyah, al Salam, al Aziziyah and Alola.

**Getting around** While it is much more convenient to have your own vehicle, it is possible to get around in al Ula without one if you are patient. Uber and Careem operate in the area during the high season, as do taxis. Several upmarket hotels provide collection and drop-off services at al Ula airport and can organise private cars with drivers. Most of the organised tours operate from the Winter Park visitor centre [212 B4], taking visitors to the sites by comfortable coach. In fact, many of these sites do not allow access to private vehicles.

Many of al Ula's roads are unnamed, presenting a challenge when visitors unfamiliar with the area attempt to find their hotel, a restaurant or other landmark. As friendly as most local residents are, many people speak only Arabic. They may also give directions by describing another landmark that you may not know. We are using the Winter Park Visitor Centre as a starting point to describe locations when more conventional information is missing. We also advise visitors to use online map services (What3Words may also help in some circumstances), which are generally very accurate and often provide additional information about the destination.

**Where to stay** Luxurious hotels, camping, glamping, chalets, farm stays and resorts are all viable options in and around al Ula, with most accommodation found outside town to the north, often in picturesque settings off the beaten path, including in hidden canyons and valleys and among spectacular rock formations.

Staying in and around al Ula can be surprisingly expensive. Top-end resorts have eye-watering prices even for well-heeled, well-travelled visitors. Happily, you will usually experience top-end luxury, attentive if not always polished customer service and general pampering, especially if you are patient. As al Ula continues to grow in popularity, more accommodation is being developed. Most are at the luxury end of the market with anticipated prices to match. The Hejaz Railway Station in Mada'in Saleh is being converted into a luxury hotel at a rumoured price point of SAR2,000. The Switzerland-based Indonesian Aman Resorts (w aman.com) luxury brand has plans for three locations, each with its own style: look out for their tented camp, desert ranch or more conventional resort to open soon. Singapore's Banyan Tree (w banyantree.com) has assumed ownership of the Ashar Resort and Winter Camp in the Ashar Valley, which will

## BOOKING ACCOMMODATION IN AL ULA

It is especially important to remember that tourism is still very new in Saudi Arabia and that accommodation is limited in relation to demand, especially in al Ula. It is also important to note that most places that offer accommodation do not have their own websites, so plan to book directly via WhatsApp if a mobile phone number is available. Some properties are listed on w booking.com, less so on other third-party platforms. Check out social media such as Instagram or Facebook, as a few places appear on these apps. Otherwise, you may simply need to try your luck once you reach al Ula. You might also ask an Arabic speaker for assistance if you are travelling elsewhere in the Kingdom before heading to al Ula.

Be aware too of seasonal events such as Winter at Tantora (page 227), when accommodation is booked well in advance and can be sold out, and many properties close during the summer months. Plan ahead to avoid disappointment.

be designed along similar lines to Habitas al Ula (see below). Find out more at out each property's website or w experiencealula.com.

The mid-range price point for al Ula is where things get interesting. Channel your inner back-to-nature instincts and you will be rewarded with a wide choice of farm stays, glamping and resorts that dial it back just enough for those who like their stays a bit more casual. Traditional family-run farms allow guests to stay among livestock and fruit trees and experience the best of Saudi hospitality. Many of these come with communal barbecue areas that allow for meeting other guests while still enjoying the privacy of your own en-suite cabin; and a good number have swimming pools where mixed-gender swimming is allowed.

Budget properties in the area are relatively few and at price points that are more suitable for the major cities. However, some chalet and apartment stays can be economical for groups and are often found near the attractions around al Ula's modern neighbourhoods, thus reducing transport costs.

### *Luxury and upmarket*

✷ **Habitas al Ula** [212 A2] Ashar Valley; 014 821 3900; w ourhabitas.com. Habitas can be a bit tricky to find – look for the discreet sign at the first roundabout southbound on Rte 375 about 21km after passing the north entrance of Mada'in Saleh. You will probably notice the sign to Ashar, which indicates the same road. Follow the road for a bit less than 1km until you reach the security gate. You will need to have a booking or otherwise be expected in order to proceed. You will then pass by Habitas Caravan to the left & see a fork in the road. Continue to the right for about another 600m. You have arrived at al Ula's ultimate destination of understated luxury designed for relaxation in a desert environment which can only be described as magical. Leave your vehicle in front of reception for valet parking as transport beyond this point is by golf buggy, e-bikes or walking. Check-in includes a 'Welcome to your home' ritual complete with mystique, a resin similar to frankincense, placed into an incense burner. Try to spot some of the permanent art exhibits (from the Desert X exhibition; page 228) tucked away in the landscape on the hotel grounds – we like the woman meditating on top of the rock resembling a 1960s-style cartoon spaceship near the pool.

There are 100 eco-friendly villas situated between the rock formations that leave the landscape otherwise undisturbed. The eco-friendly focus extends to sustainable building materials & amenities that avoid plastic use. Local handicrafts are used as accent touches. The villas are spacious & include lovely features such as an outdoor rain shower & a shaded outdoor deck where you can stargaze or simply relax. There are no televisions,

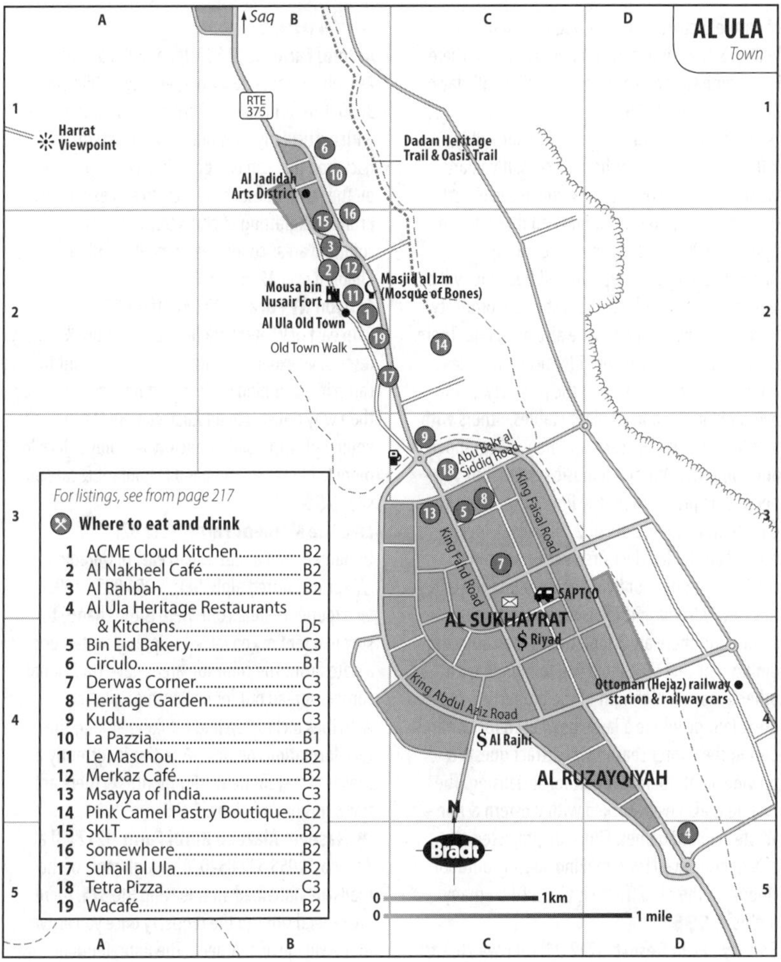

**AL ULA**
*Town*

*For listings, see from page 217*

**Where to eat and drink**



but there is Wi-Fi with very good connection. There is a temperature-controlled infinity pool with sun loungers & umbrellas on the wooden deck & a shaded seating area for lunch alfresco. Meals are served at Tama at Habitas, adjacent to the pool, with a menu that has something for all palates. There is also a branch of Moon Shell featuring its healthy & vegan-friendly menu near reception. You may wish to pamper yourself at the Thuraya Wellness Centre. The top-notch customer service throughout the property makes it even more fabulous. **$$$$$**

**Shaden Resort** [212 C4] Off Hwy 70, east of Rte 375 about 7km from Winter Park; 050 604 3344; **w** shaden-resort.com. The turn to the resort is clearly signposted & is a further 500m off the sealed road. The rooms & suites are in a tent style, some with a private swimming pool. The meals in the main restaurant are good & a branch of Myasu is also on site for fine dining. This is a more understated & genteel experience than nearby Sahary & was once the most luxurious option in al Ula – the customer service, however, remains patchy. **$$$$$**

**26 North Glamping** [212 B4] Athbah Farm, unnamed road running parallel to Rte 375 about 2km north of Winter Park, al Atheeb; 055 220 2721; **w** 26northalula.com. Look for the sign off the main road to al Atheeb. This farm earns the glamping label. The heated & AC tents have been created with an understated design & a terraced deck to take in your surroundings & the sounds of nature. Activities include yoga, horseriding & hiking, & there is a stage for performances. There is an emphasis on healthy food, with an all-day b/fast (inc) on offer. **$$$$**

✷ **Habitas Caravan** [212 B2] Ashar Valley; ☎ 014 821 3900; w ourhabitas.com. If you are looking for more of a social scene in the desert, then this alternative at Habitas might be for you. Opened in 2021, it has a new & exciting vibe. Upon arrival at the reception building, you will be transported throughout the rest of the property by golf buggy. Push bikes are also available. There are 22 caravans, each with identical amenities & décor, along the edges of the property, a few overlooking the horse field & stables, others with a valley outlook. The caravans are well equipped, and come with Wi-Fi & a music system, but you need to be prepared for the limited space inside. Choose from 1 large dbl or 2 sgl beds. A lovely canvassed shaded deck area with traditional seating extends your living space & lets you enjoy the view. Although there is no conventional restaurant, there are 3 food trucks & an adjacent dining tent that will allow you to mingle with other guests. A highlight of the property is the great lounge where a large bowl used for bonfires during the winter season will attract guests & provide a natural focal point for socialising. The lounge is also well stocked with Western & non-Western board games. Films are projected on to a flat-surfaced rock, making a lovely outdoor cinema in the sand. There is also a DJ on many nights. **$$$$**

**Sahary al Ula Resort** [212 D4] Off Hwy 70, east of Rte 375 about 15km from Winter Park; ☎ 014 866 3068, 055 105 3222; w saharyalularesort.com. To get here turn right on to the first road after passing al Fursan village. There are good signs to the resort, which is located in a natural valley surrounded by spectacular rock formations just past the turn for Jebel al Fil. Sahary is a tranquil 3.5km off the sealed road. The al Ghazel Heritage Village rooms & family suites evoke an authentic old town & are appointed with traditional Arab accents; al Reem Civilised Village rooms & suites offer Bedouin-inspired décor. There is a generous buffet-style restaurant & a fine dining restaurant on site. Not quite up to the standards of other properties in this category, but it works for independent travellers on a short visit. **$$$$**

### *Mid-range*

**Al Joud Farm** [212 B3] Unnamed road, al Atheeb; /// table.dusty.perpetually; ☎ 054 000 3600. This farm stay will bring you back to nature with particularly stunning rock formations as a backdrop that can be appreciated from most points on the farm. Guests have a chance to experience pruning & grafting of citrus trees. There are common areas conducive to meeting other guests. Children over 12 only. **$$$**

**Canyon RV Park** [212 C4] Off Hwy 70, about 8km east of Winter Park between Shaden & Sahary resorts; w experiencealula.com. If you want to camp in a stunning location but not under canvas, then why not stay in an Airstream RV? Each one is equipped with a sink & microwave, plus a deck for more living space. There is a restaurant & café on site. **$$$**

**Live the Moment Farm** [212 B2] Unnamed road about 3.5km east of Qaraqir; /// springs.furred.alphabet; ☎ 054 003 7369; w experiencealula.com. Here is the chance to stay in a tent or converted shipping container on a date farm. The common areas have traditional carpets spread out for low cushion seating. Activities include cycling & hiking among the rock formations nearby. Note this is currently a seasonal stay in the winter months & there are few signs or directions. **$$$**

✷ **Naseem Alazeeb Rural Farm** [212 C3] al Atheeb; ☎ 055 532 8540. Although most of the roads are unnamed after leaving Rte 375, there are several signs to the property once you arrive in the village of al Atheeb. The unpretentious accommodation is in converted shipping containers disguised with Saudi decoration on the outside, which somehow works. Options range from sgls to quads & family units. With good AC in summer & with a heater provided in winter, the rooms also have a small fridge, kettle & microwave but no hob. There is a shared kitchen on site for guests. B/fast can be organised in advance for a small charge. Don't miss the glorious swimming pool for both men & women. There are many areas all around the farm with spaces to sit & socialise with others if you wish. Guests are invited to walk around the fruit groves where you can find mangoes, oranges & other citrus trees. Venture over to the animal pens to find ducks, geese, turkeys, chickens & goats. Cat lovers will be thrilled to know the farm has a large family of cats that might come to visit you on your porch. The caves in the mountainside behind the farm are lit up at night for an intriguing effect. This farm stay is an excellent balance of authentic hospitality & value for money. **$$$**

**Rozzland Resort** [212 C4] Unnamed road off Hwy 70; ☎ 053 715 7228. Found in a great location near Elephant & Siamese Conjoined Twins rocks; travel east for about 6km from Winter Park, then turn left (north) off Hwy 70 on to a dirt road. Follow the signs to Elephant Rock, turning left about 100m before reaching the rock, & continue for about 2km. The resort is on the right. The chalets are clean & comfortable & surrounded by lovely grounds. It has a traditional majlis & a small pool. **$$$**

**Waterfall Tourist Resort** [212 A1] Unnamed road about 6km north of the settlement of Shilal or Shlal, 20km from Mada'in Saleh's north entrance off Rte 375; ☎ 055 133 1379. If you are looking for a more remote place to stay, this is a good option. Turn on to the road when you reach the small grocery store on the left. You have gone too far if you reach the village. The rooms are somewhat basic but there is a swimming pool. The real draw is the setting among dramatic rock formations in a region that has plenty of them. There is a waterfall but it usually only flows during part of the winter. The coffee shop set in the cave on the property is popular with residents, non-resident guests & Saudis alike. Adventure-seekers may find the nearby al Ula Adventure Hub (page 220) convenient. **$$$**

### *Budget*

**Al Bashaeir Private Apartments** [212 C5] al Mahash. If you are looking to switch off, then this property may be for you – there is no internet access & children are not allowed. The location is good for the Old Town & the Arts District, with modern al Ula & Winter Park both relatively nearby; but light sleepers should be aware that you will be in between 2 mosques. **$$**

**Flowers Apartments al Ula** [212 C6] al Salam, east of Rte 375 near Azizia Park; ☎ 059 725 0093. This property on an unnamed street works for budget-minded visitors who prefer to stay in the modern town of al Ula. There are 1- & 2-bedroom options with kitchens. The rooms are clean with basic amenities for a short stay & there is a swimming pool & a selection of outdoor seating areas to enjoy the quiet environment. Private parking. **$$**

**Larena Chalets** [212 B4] Off Hwy 70, east of Rte 375 about 2.5km from Winter Park; ☎ 055 279 9407. Turn south on to the dirt road & follow it for about 500m before you arrive at the chalets. This accommodation will appeal to those looking for a basic, clean place to sleep at an affordable price – at least for al Ula. Many rooms have multiple beds, hostel-style, that could suit groups of friends on a budget. There is a small kitchen where guests can prepare simple meals. The chalets have a mountain or garden view. There is a shared lounge & garden & a small swimming pool. It is also possible to visit the farm adjacent to the property. **$$**

**Sweet Inn al Ula** [212 C6] al Salam west of Rte 375; /// distributor.balcony.upcoming; ☎ 055 158 0531. Clean, spacious rooms with the basics in a low-rise building with no lifts. There are kitchen facilities for self-caterers. Conveniently located on an unnamed street at the edge of modern al Ula town. Cash payments or bank transfer only. **$$**

## ✕ Where to eat and drink

A good range of cuisines and price points can be found in restaurants in al Ula, which continues to develop a gourmet scene, complete with branches of popular upscale Riyadh and Jeddah restaurants operating in season. A growing number of fusion restaurants are also developing independently, creating inspired menus that are a must-visit for foodies.

### *Al Jadidah Arts District*

This list is just the beginning – the Arts District will soon be packed with many more trendy restaurants. There is also a growing number of food trucks offering a trendy pop-up experience that make for a great alfresco dining experience during good weather.

**Circulo** [215 B1] Oasis Sq; ☎ 053 335 3201; ⏲ 12.30–midnight daily. If you are looking for a Saudi interpretation of upscale Italian fusion dining, then Circulo is a good find. Inside dining is perhaps a bit too casual for the standard of cuisine. Most people prefer to sit outside on the deck & will be rewarded with a 180° view of the wadi. Don't miss the fabulous linguine with mushrooms & truffles. $$$$$

✷ **Somewhere** [215 B2] Rte 375 towards the southern end of the district; ⌚ 14.00–01.00 daily. 'Let us take you somewhere' is their promise. This very trendy Lebanese fusion restaurant is expensive but worth it for the attentive service & delicious menu. The Lebanese/Chinese beef or chicken bao fusion, hummus with avocado & beetroot fatteh all provide a treat for the taste buds. The indoor seating is welcome when the weather is too hot or too cold to sit outside as it is spacious & has a long floor-to-ceiling window that gives a great view to the back. The comfortable outdoor seating is in a manicured garden with soothing running water & is a perfect setting in the right weather. This spot becomes lively in the evenings. 'Somewhere' is somewhere special. $$$$$

**SKLT** [215 B2] Off Rte 375 towards the southern end of the district; ☎ 053 677 7901; ⌚ 12.30–midnight daily . If you need a beef fix, then your choices range from burgers to steaks. There are also options for seafood lovers & vegetarians. Guests can dine inside or sit out on the deck, which overlooks Old Town. $$$$

**La Pazzia** [215 B1] Oasis Sq; ☎ 050 191 6417; ⌚ from early evening until late. This atmospheric coffee shop on Oasis Sq is a great choice if you aren't up for a full meal but want to enjoy the relaxing vibe. $$

### *Old Town*

All of the following are either in the Old Town on unnamed roads or paths, or along Old Town Walk [215 B2]. Look for signs or ask someone local if you are unable to find your way. There is a convenient map at the entrance to Old Town Walk.

**Le Maschou** [215 B2] Old Town; /// funding.outclassed.interpreted; ☎ 055 158 0829. If you are looking for a romantic spot for a special meal, then consider this French restaurant. The indoor ambience is intimate & is accented by a fireplace that is welcome during the winter. Note that the restaurant operates a fixed menu so if this matters, check in advance. $$$$$

**Suhail al Ula** [215 B2] Old Town Walk; **w** experiencealula.com; ⌚ noon–midnight Mon–Sat. Located at the end of the Walk; you can stroll by the shops or take a short golf buggy ride to the venue. The restaurant is in a restored traditional house with multiple levels of outdoor seating, as well as indoor seating on the 1st floor. Try to book a table on the top floor, where you can soak up the atmosphere & hear the call to prayer bounce off the rocks if you time your meal right. The menu is traditional Saudi cuisine featuring speciality dishes from different provinces. Meat dishes include camel & lamb on the bone. Desserts include a *hneini* cheesecake fusion that is symbolic of the timeless & the modern. $$$$$

**Merkaz Café** [215 B2] Old Town Walk; ☎ 9200 25003; ⌚ 17.00–02.00 daily. This is a good alternative to al Nakheel but with a more mixed menu from around the Arabian Peninsula. $$$$

**ACME Cloud Kitchen** [215 B2] Old Town; /// undertaken.asserting.tortoises; ☎ 9200 27242; **w** acme.com.sa; ⌚ 14.00–02.00 daily. Upscale burger joint with a good range of burgers, sandwiches & sauces & an imaginative choice of fruit juice concoctions. $$$

**Al Nakheel Café** [215 B2] Old Town Walk; ☎ 055 440 1247; ⌚ 09.00–midnight daily. There is no indoor seating so the hours are seasonal & not always posted, but it tends to open in the summer around 18.00, instead of in the morning, when the weather is cooler. The menu is classic Lebanese grill. This is a particularly good location for its great view overlooking the Old Town, perfect for people-watching. $$$

**Al Rahbah** [215 B2] Old Town Walk; ☎ 055 362 3012; ⌚ 09.00–03.00 daily. This casual Egyptian café has plenty of outdoor seating & serves Egyptian tea & coffee popular with the clientele. Shisha smokers will be happy. Lovely heritage décor. $$

**Wacafé** [215 B2] Old Town; /// whirlpool.busters.portrayed; ☎ 053 763 0001; **w** wacafe.sa; ⌚ 15.00–midnight Sat–Wed, 15.00–01.00 Thu–Fri. This is the stop for all things coffee, including coffee-making paraphernalia. Have a browse around the shop when you have finished your coffee & maybe a nibble. This is a good place for gifts for any coffee lovers on your list. $$

### *Saq, al Sukhayrat, al Ruzayqiyah, al Salam, al Aziziyah and Alola areas*

**Msayya of India** [215 C3] Abu Bakr al Siddiq Rd, al Sukhayrat; ⌚ 13.00–01.30 daily. Off Rte 375, just south of the King Abdul Aziz Rd roundabout approaching modern al Ula. When you want a change from gourmet dining, corner-shop snacks or self-catering, then this restaurant is a good break. The mostly Punjabi menu offers a good selection of tandoor, biryani & masala dishes. There are some vegetarian options but this restaurant caters more to non-veggies. There are curtained family sections on both sides of the restaurant, but diners seem to sit wherever they like. $$$

**Al Ula Heritage Restaurants & Kitchens** [215 D5] al Ruzayqiyah al Hamidiyya; 055 837 0888; 11.30–midnight daily. To the south of al Ula. Turn from Tariq bin Ziad Rd at the roundabout; the restaurant is in the northeast quadrant. Not to be mistaken for Heritage Garden Restaurant, this doesn't look like a restaurant from the front. The atmosphere inside is no-nonsense, appealing to those who want a substantial traditional meal without fuss. Expect on-the-floor seating. Good value for not a lot of money. $$

**Derwas Corner Restaurant** [215 C3] Unnamed road, 2 blocks east of King Fahd Rd, al Sukhayrat; /// supervisors.idler.restriction; 014 884 5555; 13.00–01.00 daily. Follow Google Maps or similar, turning near some mobile phone shops for simple, authentic local food with table & floor seating. It's a good choice if you are in the area. $$

**Heritage Garden Restaurant** [215 C3] al Qahira (Cairo) St, al Sukhayrat; 014 884 1444; noon–midnight daily. A mix of Arabic-, Indian- & Chinese-inspired food is on the menu, mostly with a meat-&-rice theme. Orders are placed & paid for at the cashier station first, then your food is delivered to your table or on-floor seating area. $$

**Tetra Pizza** [215 C3] Abu Bakr al Siddiq Rd, northeast junction with Rte 375, al Sukhayrat; 9200 12922; 09.00–04.00 Sat–Thu, noon–04.00 Fri. The pizzas with classic & popular Arabic fusion toppings work well. There are sides that will quickly add to the calorie count, as well as a few pasta dishes that will do the same. It still operates separate singles & family counters for take-away & has a couple of tables for eating in only on the singles side. $$

**Bin Eid Bakery** [215 C3] Unnamed road, 2 blocks south of Abu Bakr al Siddiq Rd, al Sukhayrat; /// animates.antiques.cove; 07.00–midnight daily. Although this bakery is just off Rte 375, the best way to reach it is on small, unnamed neighbourhood streets as the dual carriageway prevents a turn on to the street for quite a distance. Note the entrance is on the street opposite the small supermarket. Although it sounds complicated, a visit to this bakery is worth it. The clientele is a mix of Saudi men collecting tomorrow's b/fast & others selecting sweets as a treat for their children or themselves. The baked goods couldn't be fresher, or more affordable & delicious. The sizes & portions are very generous. $

**Kudu** [215 C3] Rte 375 at the King Abdul Aziz Roundabout, al Sukhayrat; 9200 06999; w kudu.com.sa; 07.30–02.45 Sun–Wed, 24hrs Thu–Sat. At present, this is the only fast-food chain in al Ula, serving a range of mostly chicken sandwiches. $

**The Sands of the Valley Popular Cuisine** [212 B4] Rte 375 southbound, Saq; 058 083 4814. The menu is Yemeni & features classics including fuul, arika, asida, shakshouka adni & milk adni. It's a good choice for b/fast. $

### *In or near the resorts*

Note that many upmarket resorts have appealing restaurants on site. If you haven't already indulged in many of al Ula's terrific restaurants, you might want to book one of the following resort restaurants.

**Maraya Social** [212 A3] Off Rte 375 between Shlal & al Atheeb; 055 005 9161; w marayasocial.com; winter 18.00–midnight Tue–Sat, summer Fri only. If you are attending an event at Maraya, consider a pre- or post-performance meal at this sophisticated spot on the rooftop of the mirrored concert hall. The menu is more limited than many restaurants at this price point but hits the right balance. Beautifully presented dishes extend from light salads to substantial main courses fit for global guests. Turn west on the way to Banyan Tree (formerly the Ashar Resort). $$$$$

**Myazu** [212 C4] Shaden Resort; 050 604 3344; w myazu.com; 18.00–midnight Sun–Tue, 18.00–02.00 Wed–Sat. If you are a connoisseur of classic Japanese cuisine & are also prepared to concede a nod to Saudi tastes, then don't miss Myazu. Refreshing salads & exquisite nigiri, sashimi & maki rolls that are a work of art. There are also branches in Jeddah & Riyadh. $$$$$

**Tama** [212 A2] Habitas al Ula; ☎ 014 821 3900; **w** ourhabitas.com/alula/dining; ⏲ 07.00–17.00 & 18.00–23.30 daily. Inspired Middle East dishes can be enjoyed overlooking the pool with stunning vistas of some of the area's most dramatic, wind-weathered rock towers. Perfectly accompanied by eclectic background music ranging from bossa nova to West African classics. **$$$$$**

**L'Ansa Lounge** [212 A3] Shlal, near Habitas Caravan; ☎ 050 643 2015; ⏲ 18.00–03.00 daily. This open-air venue is hidden away towards Habitas al Ula. Turn left on to the 1st road after passing Caravan instead of continuing towards Habitas al Ula. Enjoy sandwiches, salads & more among some of the most spectacular rock formations in an area loaded with them. **$$$**

**Moon Shell** [212 A2] Habitas Sq; ☎ 050 556 1213; ⏲ 08.00–midnight daily. Moon Shell is more than a coffee shop. It's a destination with indoor, outdoor deck & palm grove seating, all with trendy furnishings. Visitors looking for healthy options will find crunchy b/fast bowls creatively built with fresh fruit. Or you can indulge with Arabic & Western desserts that are not only a work of art, but also delicious. Heaven for veggies & vegans. There is another branch at Muayada Sq (⏲ Oct–Mar). **$$$**

**✷ Pink Camel Pastry Boutique** [215 C2] Along the Dadan Heritage Trail; ☎ 059 040 0902; ⏲ 08.00–midnight daily. Don't miss this wonderful stop in the oasis that feels a world away but is only a few hundred metres on a dirt path east of Old Town. Keep following the signs & you won't miss it. B/fast & sandwiches are popular, but it's their pastries that rise above an already high bar for quality & creativity. It is very easy to hang out on the pleasant covered deck for hours sipping an artisanal coffee & simply soaking in the atmosphere. Indoor & uncovered outdoor tables are also available. This place is a natural chill pill. **$$$**

**SALT** [212 C4] Jebel al Fil (Elephant Rock); ⏲ late afternoon–late evening daily. This branch of the popular mini-burger bar is a great hangout spot for visitors & Saudis alike. The location directly in front of Elephant Rock affords a terrific sunset view if you time it right. Chips smothered with a variety of calorie-laden sauces are particular favourites with the clientele as are a range of imaginative slushies. **$$$**

**Waterfall Café** [212 A1] Waterfall Resort, Shlal; ☎ 053 356 0914; ⏲ 16.00–01.00 daily; SAR10 entrance fee. Walk through narrow passages between rocks & you will find this café in & around a cave. Popular with young Saudis, this is more about the experience & ambience than the coffee. **$$**

**Sports and activities** As with any adventure activities, read all terms and conditions carefully, including dress codes and all safety stipulations.

**Al Ula Adventure Hub** [212 A4] About 4.3km from Winter Park, on the left after the Winter Park roundabout; **w** experiencealula.com; ⏲ hours vary depending on season & activity. Al Ula Adventure Hub works in conjunction with Experience al Ula (page 223) & is *the* destination for adrenaline junkies. Whether you are interested in soaring high, going fast or both, you will be spoilt for choice. Double-check all information, though, as many of the activities offered may be seasonal, running only on certain days or over limited hours during the off-season or due to weather conditions.

**Al Ula Bike Hub** [212 C3] On the main unnamed road just south of al Atheeb village; ☎ 011 880 8855 (Riyadh); **w** experiencealula.com ⏲ 09.00–17.00 Tue–Fri, 09.00–18.00 Sat. A one-stop shop for bike hire, & cycling accessories, with a repair shop & coffee shop. There are 26km of bike trails between al Atheeb and Mada'in Saleh which can be undertaken independently at no cost other than the bike hire, or book through Experience al Ula (SAR75).

**Al Ula Buggies** Part of Husaak Adventures (see below).

**Husaak Adventures** [212 B4] Rte 375, about 2.5km north of Winter Park; ☎ 050 139 6943, 050 139 6942; **w** husaak.com. This organisation works closely with Experience al Ula and is the operator for several adventure activities, including dune bashing and some structured hikes. Their robust team of mostly Saudi and other Gulf nationals has a wealth and depth of knowledge of the area and the skills to lead adventures knowledgably and safely, with enthusiasm that's hard to beat. Check out their website, or WhatsApp the team to book.

### CYCLE LANES CAUTION

Recreational cycling is very popular in al Ula, and there are short distances on a few paved roads that indicate cycling lanes. However, ride with caution, as drivers and other road users cannot be relied upon to respect these.

***Climbing and abseiling*** Al Ula's mountains are perfect for rock climbing and abseiling and different levels of experience are catered for by al Ula Adventure Hub (SAR120–180). Not an experienced rock climber? If you are curious about rock climbing but don't feel confident, then the **Via Ferrata and Canyon Hammock Experience** is a taster that will allow you to find out what all the fuss is about: make your way across a challenging yet rewarding path along rock formations in a safety harness.

***Dune bashing*** For those who like to find their thrills in a motorised vehicle, then dune bashing may give you the adventure you are looking for. Al Ula Buggies (see opposite) offers a guided tour (SAR360 pp), organised via Husaak Adventures, that takes groups of up to three people per buggy through canyons, high sandy dunes and generally bumpy terrain that will make many shriek with joy.

***Helicopter rides*** If you are looking for a moving bird's-eye view of the area, then consider a helicopter ride organised through Experience al Ula (page 223) and run by The Helicopter Company (w experiencealula.com). The fee (SAR500 pp) includes transport from Winter Park to the helipad a few minutes away. It's a 30-minute flight over most of the key sites, including Mada'in Saleh.

***Hiking and walking*** Suitable for older children and adults with a medium level of fitness, the **Ridge Walk** is a 6km hike with a steep beginning but becoming gentler part way up. The **Hidden Valley Hike**, on the other hand, is across soft desert sand, about 4km long and will take an average of 1½ hours. Both activities are available through the Hub and are run by Husaak Adventures (prices from SAR266 pp).

The combined **Dadan Heritage Trail and Oasis Trail** [215 C2] (book through Experience al Ula, SAR35 pp; or do it independently for free) is a gentle, but brilliant, 3km path between al Ula Old Town's Orange Route east off Route 375 to the Dadan Visitor Centre, where parking is available for the start of your walk – this is recommended as there is limited parking in the Old Town. Along this route, you will pass by and through palm groves, farms and ancient mud-walled village ruins. Although this oasis is cooler than the surrounding area, it is best to keep an eye on the temperature as it can be cold in the early hours of the winter and blazing hot from mid-morning in the summer. For those with enough energy to continue south of the end of the Oasis Trail along the Orange Trail, the Pink Camel Pastry Boutique (see opposite) will be waiting for you when you are ready to recharge your batteries with coffee, pastries and a good chance of meeting other active visitors. The guided tour can be arranged through Experience al Ula where you meet local elders who will give more information about the history and significance of the oasis. The trail is also part of a popular cycling route.

***Hot-air ballooning*** Al Ula Skies (w experiencealula.com; SAR100 pp; some height and weight restrictions) usually takes place for about two months in the spring. This is a great opportunity to ride above the monuments and appreciate a bird's-eye view of al Ula's stunning scenery for up to 45 minutes. Double-check with Winter Park when you are planning your visit as this is a seasonal event and is dependent on weather conditions.

***Ziplining*** Ziplining enthusiasts are in for a real treat as al Ula Adventure Hub offers the longest (at 1.5km) and fastest (up to 120km/h) zipline experience in the Kingdom (w experiencealula.com; SAR180 pp).

**Other practicalities** In the absence of familiar Saudi **supermarkets**, Dorrat al Madaen Market for Groceries [212 B4] is decent for the area and conveniently located on Route 375 just south of Winter Park. Remaining open throughout the day, it has good prices and is busier than the competition in the immediate vicinity. There are **pharmacies** including Nahdi in modern al Ula. Most pharmacies close for the afternoon but are then open until late evening. There are also several **petrol stations** along Route 375 including Aldrees, but they also close between approximately noon and 16.00, so plan accordingly.

**Al Rajhi Bank** Cnr King Abdul Aziz Rd & Light St; 9200 03344; w alrajhibank.com.sa; 09.30–16.30 Sun–Thu
**Riyad Bank** Cnr King Fahd Rd & Khalid bin al Waled St; 9200 02470; w riyadbank.com; 09.30–16.30 Sun–Thu
**Al Dirah Health Care Medical Clinic** [212 C6] Rte 375 in the Alola district to the far south of modern al Ula; 014 884 3711. On the premises of Prince Abdul Muhsin Hospital (014 884 3743), these facilities offer basic services & may not live up to standards expected by many Western visitors. Those who plan to undertake rigorous activities should keep this in mind when choosing travel insurance including evacuation coverage.
**Saudi Post** [215 C3] Off King Abdullah Rd behind al Ula General Court bldng; w splonline.com.sa; 08.00–21.00 Sun–Thu, 16.00–21.00 Fri–Sat

**What to see and do** Al Ula's highlight is the Nabataean UNESCO World Heritage Site of Mada'in Saleh. Ancient history is revealed in several other nearby sites that are also awe-inspiring, some of which date even further back in time. The sites themselves live up to expectations even for the most jaded of travellers. Many visitors will feel they have discovered something very special, at least until tourism becomes more mainstream.

Take a scenic drive in and around al Ula and you will see mind-blowing rock formations all to yourself if you set off early enough. We recommend that you start your drive at al Atheeb village, and take Route 375 via al Joud Farm on an unnamed road (///table.dusty.perpetually). Along the way, you will also be able to spot a surprisingly large number of flattened rock faces, perhaps in preparation for future tombs that were never built. Take your time as there are photo opportunities around every corner.

Collectors, from train spotters to geo baggers, may find a new hobby trying to locate some of the most famous rock formations in the region and might stumble across new formations worthy of being added to the list. Have fun searching for Hand Rock, Siamese Conjoined Twins Rock, Vessel Hole Rock and many more. Get started with Face Rock, which is in Mada'in Saleh and part of most organised tours.

Unlike in most of the Kingdom, at least at present, al Ula is a destination where many tourist attractions attract entrance fees, although many others remain free. Tickets for the biggest attractions can be purchased at the Winter Park Visitor Centre or online. They cannot be purchased directly on site at the attractions

## SAUDI TOURISM IN ITS INFANCY

The al Ula area is among the first in the Kingdom to host tourists, and whose numbers are continuing to rise rapidly. Many businesses offering activities are still learning as tourism is new and understanding foreign visitors' preferences and expectations is a work in progress. Saudi hospitality is at its best in al Ula, but visitors should be prepared to exercise great patience. It can be a challenge, especially for those who may be short of time but want to tour at a faster pace than the Kingdom is used to. Infrastructure, including websites and online booking, remains inconsistent. Published contact details may change unexpectedly and without notice. We recommend you try to contact most venues via WhatsApp if you are not already in al Ula, or your Arabic isn't very good. Any telephone number beginning with 05x is a mobile number, whose owner will almost certainly be expecting to communicate via WhatsApp, especially if their English isn't very good. We recommend that you book through the **Experience al Ula** website (w experiencealula.com) if you want the most reliable experiences. They are also good at advising visitors about the area more generally, although this works best once you are in al Ula and can speak with them in person.

themselves. A bus service will take guests from Winter Park to the sites, with proof of ticket mandatory for boarding. The system is well organised with knowledgeable, enthusiastic guides. Guests receive a traditional welcome at each site on the tours, with Arabic coffee, dates and water and a chance to sit and chat. More information can be found on w tickets.experiencealula.com/en/experiences. Hours are dependent on tour schedules which are dependent on the weather and daylight hours.

***Mada'in Saleh (Hegra Archaeological Site)*** ✷ (w experiencealula.com; ⌚ see website for timings; 2hr bus tours SAR95 pp; open top Land Rover tour for up to 7 people SAR700 pp – book through Experience al Ula) Also known as Mada'in Salih, Hegra and al Hijr, this is Saudi Arabia's Nabataean masterpiece and the second city of the Nabataean Kingdom after Petra in Jordan. Declared a UNESCO World Heritage Site in 2008, the area contains a total of 131 monumental tombs within an area of about 15km$^2$.

Owing to the existence of a shallow water table, Mada'in Saleh was populated by the Dadans, Liyhanites, Nabataeans and Romans during its early history. The area became an important stop on the Arabian Peninsula trade route to the north and beyond the Middle East. It is also on the pilgrimage route to Madinah and Mecca, although during the early days of Islam, the population had already moved about 25km away to al Ula Old Town. The Nabataean Kingdom stretched from what is now Jordan to the north, to Dumat al Jandal to the east, and to the modern-day al Ula region at its southernmost edge. The region has been populated from the times of Noah (Nuh) and Abraham (Ibrahim) and Moses (Mousa) but declined after the beginning the 1st century CE. This decline left the area effectively undisturbed for centuries and is why many of the monuments remain in the good condition they can be found in today.

Most of the monuments that remain were built during the 1st century BCE and into the first years of the 1st century CE. A number of them include inscriptions complete with dates, aiding archaeological knowledge. Otherwise, most information about the tombs came not from the Nabataeans themselves but from Greek, Roman and Egyptian visitors. The tombs were constructed by the Thamudic people, an Arab tribe who were considered to be idol worshippers. The stairs at the top of many tombs represent the transportation of the soul to heaven. The façades are hewn from sandstone rock, and the tallest is nearly 22m high. Many are elaborately decorated with Nabataean inscriptions and symbols of life and the afterlife which also contain elements of typical Mesopotamian and Roman depictions, including eagles, griffins, sphinxes and Medusa-like faces surrounded by snakes meant to warn off potential intruders. Some of the inscriptions contain warnings of fines and divine punishments to reinforce this message. Many Saudis have a complicated relationship with the site and may even consider it to be cursed or even taboo to visit.

There are a number of unfinished tombs, including some rocks that contain little more than a smooth façade, similar to having a blank slate on an easel. Many tombs would have contained family groups. There are 2,000 tombs in total in the area. The tombs depict the social status of the occupants, with some of the most elaborate depicting key elements of their lives.

Note that Mada'in Saleh can only be visited on an organised tour with itineraries that give just a taste of the highlights. This may change as the site continues to undergo development; and as archaeologists are still actively working on the site, it is important to understand that some areas will remain off-limits to general tourism. The bus journey from Winter Park to Mada'in Saleh takes 20 minutes. At the time of writing, tours approach the South Gate and include the key sites concentrated in the southwest of the World Heritage Site, including the al Sanea tombs, Tomb of the Lion of Kuza, Jebel al Banat, Jebel Ithlib, al Faqr Tomb and Jebel al Ahmar. There is also a stop at the **Handicraft Pavilion** giving visitors a chance to purchase locally made items that are difficult to find elsewhere and which have links to local heritage.

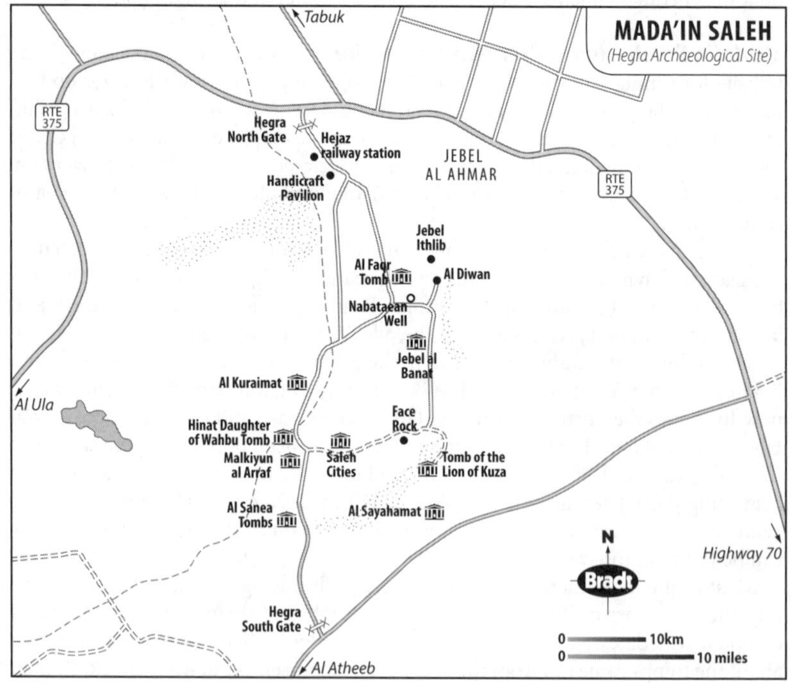

You can partake of more traditional refreshments in the pavilion's indoor seating area. It may also be possible for visitors to participate at the pottery wheel.

Prior to visiting the first attraction, visitors will be greeted by a professional guide known as a *rawi* at a shaded welcome area, where traditional Saudi kahwa, *tamr* and water will be offered. Members of the tours will be able to leave the bus and walk around the designated areas of some of the attractions. At others, you will remain on the bus and drive by.

As Mada'in Saleh continues to be developed for tourism, routes are likely to change with little notice. Other tombs that have featured in the past, including al Kuraimat, al Sayahamat, Hinat Daughter of Wahbu and Malkiyn al Arraf, could feature again in future.

**Al Sanea tombs** The first set of tombs you pass, entering Mada'in Saleh from the southern entrance, contained the remains of military officers and their families. Inscriptions on the tombs indicate the specific families buried there. Next is a drive-by of the **Saleh Cities** tombs, giving a glimpse of the scale of many tombs throughout the site.

**Tomb of the Lion of Kuza** This large monolith towering nearly 22m tall is the first stop where you can disembark and stand in front of this magnificent edifice. It is also known as Qasr al Farid, or lonely castle, as it stands alone at a distance from other clusters of tombs. From the top down, it contains steps, ledges, four columns and a rectangular opening found on many prominent tombs. The rich detail that is found on other tombs of similar status appears to be only partially finished towards the bottom of this tomb. Rock spotters will notice Face Rock near the road on the right-hand side on the approach to the Tomb of the Lion of Kuza. Face Rock is an excellent formation that looks like a person in profile, including the neck, lips, nose and even eyelid.

**Jebel al Banat** Jebel al Banat, or Qasr al Bint, is a cluster of 29 tombs that were owned by or created for women. You will be able to leave the bus to contemplate the elaborate decoration above the doors of the tombs, containing depictions of snakes, birds of prey and other pre-Islamic symbols. Some of the birds' faces have been destroyed. Some inscriptions warn of punishment if the tombs are disturbed. Some of these tomb faces also contain bullet holes, testifiying to more troubled times in the recent past.

**Jebel Ithlib** The Jebel Ithlib area is highlighted by a well-preserved diwan or meeting place set in a dramatic setting at the entrance to a very narrow passage between two sets of rock cliffs within Mada'in Saleh. The diwan is built into the rock and contains stone benches on three sides. The Nabataeans used this diwan for religious meetings, as well as for banqueting and entertainment. You will have a chance to sit on the same stone benches as the Nabataeans and contemplate the activities that took place on this location. A cartouche in the ancient Nabataean script can be seen directly opposite the opening of the diwan along with other cuneiform inscriptions on the rock face. Visitors with sturdy footwear can walk a few metres through the *siq*, the narrow gap between the rock face past the diwan to the opening beyond, but no further.

**Al Faqr Tomb** This dome-shaped rock contains several tombs that are now clearly being taken back to nature by the weather. It is possible to make out some of the tomb façades, but others have little but the entrance hole to the tomb remaining.

It is set back from the road a bit, so look carefully from the bus. The bus will also drive by a nearby Nabataean well and one of several rectangular stone watchtowers containing a row of windows towards the top.

**Jebel al Ahmar** Following a visit to the Handicraft Pavillion, the final stop on this tour is Jebel al Ahmar, where there are more than 80 tombs scattered on a plain in several clusters. The tour provides an opportunity for guests to walk around approximately 18 of these tombs and to observe the differences in how the façades were designed and the varying conditions they are in today. It is also where the bones of Hinat (or Haina) – the name given by archaeologists to the skeletal remains of a 2,000-year-old Nabataean woman – were found by archaeologists in 2014, along with bits of fine-quality cloth and a necklace, revealing a bit more information about the wealth of Nabataean culture.

***Dadan Tombs*** [212 B4] (SAR60 pp inc tour of Jebel Ikmah, 10mins away on the same bus – book through Experience al Ula, page 223) These tombs may only be visited on an organised tour. Independent travellers who make their way to the site will be turned back to Winter Park. The tour begins at Winter Park and requires a ticket.

Believed to have been carved out of rock faces more than 2,500 years ago, hundreds of these tombs, about 50m high with squarish-shaped openings, are a strong reminder of the ancient civilisation of the Liyhanite and Dadan kingdoms who lived in Dadan, now the site of modern day al Ula. These pre-Islamic people worshipped multiple gods. The Lion Tombs, named for the carvings above some of the tombs, are indicative of the high status of the occupants, perhaps including royalty. Along with the Minaeans from further south on the Arabian Peninsula, they were also key in providing a trading post for the trade routes running throughout the Middle East and beyond.

Visitors will be welcomed with Arabic coffee, water and dates at stop one, which is **Dadan South**. There is a small museum which provides a very good timeline of the area from the Palaeolithic and Bronze Age to modern times. The guides are knowledgeable and comfortable answering guests' questions. There is also an interesting explanation of the various local alphabets used throughout time, giving visitors a platform to reflect on the different rock inscriptions found in the area. Although there is a stone path and steps that lead to the base of the tombs about 500m away, visitors are not permitted to go further as archaeologists are still active in the area. Binoculars are provided for those who want to get a better look of the tombs from the viewing platform at the back of the museum.

Dadan South also takes in a second bus stop at the ruins of an early Islamic fort which once had a tower in each of its four corners and rooms surrounding an open courtyard. The fort is to the front of a rock-strewn area that is ripe for further excavation.

**Dadan North**, the tour's third bus stop, focuses on the city of Dadan, where the ruins of a stone carved temple worshipping Dhu Ghaybah, the most important god of the Liyhanites, can be explored. Shards of pottery and decoration are still on display out in the open. It is also possible to see the ancient well towards the palm grove beyond the temple if you are prepared to take a short walk along a rocky path. The Dadan Tombs phase of the tour ends at a small gift shop with a modest selection of merchandise.

***Jebel Ikmah*** ✷ [212 B4] Jebel Ikmah, known as the Outdoor Library, is an astounding site, which can be visited as the second part of the tour that begins with Dadan Tombs (see opposite). Visitors will be awed by the proliferation of inscriptions in Aramaic, Dadantic, Thamudic, Minaic and Nabataean languages, leaving a lasting testimony to the importance of these diverse historical kingdoms that go back at least to the 1st millennium BCE. The site also gives a template for understanding the development of the Arabic language. Many of these inscriptions were paid for, upon which stone crafters then created the requested message, often containing little more than what would be considered graffiti. You will also be able to spot a rich display of rock art depicting people and animals in scenes of everyday life. Journeys and pilgrimages are also shown in petroglyphs.

The setting itself is unforgettable, much of this work being on clusters of rock formations on both sides of a narrow opening. Visitors walk in from the fenced entrance after the bus parks, and golf buggies are available for the short ride to the beginning of the path into the mountains. There is a well-maintained rock path that leads into the rock art about 300m from where the path starts. Although it is reasonably smooth at the beginning, it becomes less so nearer to the rock art, so wear appropriate footwear.

***Maraya*** [212 A3] (Ashar Valley) Maraya means mirror or reflection in Arabic and aptly names this concert hall. The structure is made of nearly 10,000 mirrored panels, reflecting the sand and mountain landscape in the near distance, creating a fascinating mirage. Opened in 2019, Maraya serves as a conference venue, concert hall, performance centre and more, with a seating capacity of 500 people, and has been recognised by the *Guinness Book of World Records* as the world's largest mirrored building. Maraya cannot be visited solely as a tourist attraction. Visitors must hold tickets for an event or a confirmed reservation to gain access via the security gate at the entrance just off Route 375.

***Al Ula Town redevelopment area and al Ula*** (Rte 375 about 5km south of Winter Park) Many of these points of interest can be visited independently and for free. However, those who are looking for more in-depth information might consider taking a guided tour, where the tour leader will provide more context.

## WINTER AT TANTORA

Closely affiliated with al Ula Season, Winter at Tantora presents a calendar of world-class music, art, sport and other cultural events. The first festival was held in the winter of 2018/19 and made global headlines, both for its ground-breaking social reforms in the Kingdom, where live music and gender mixing would not have been possible previously, and for the globally renowned performers who agreed to showcase their talents in this unique venue. Winter at Tantora has also promoted desert polo, horseracing, cycling events, hot-air ballooning and even a fashion show. Artists including Alicia Keys, Andrea Bocelli, Craig David, Enrique Iglesias, the Gipsy Kings, Jose Carreras, Lang Lang, Lionel Richie, Nancy Ajram and many more have performed in the Maraya Concert Hall, the mirrored stage in front of the dramatic backdrop of the region's rock formations.

*The Winter at Tantora season runs from December to March with details published through Experience al Ula (w experiencealula.com).*

**Al Jadidah Arts District** [215 B1] This is the first area reached on Route 375 from Winter Park and is rapidly becoming pedestrianised, so parking is limited. Look for the designated car parks to the north and south if you can't find on-street parking. Street conditions currently range from unpaved with shifting sand underfoot to beautifully patterned walkways. There are about 900 houses, 40 shops and five district squares: Art Square, Cinema Square, Gathering Square, Muayada Square and Oasis Square. All are destined for restoration, which is likely to result in a range of purposes from artist studios to quirky accommodation.

**Al Ula Old Town tour** (Rte 375, south of al Jadidah; SAR70 pp booked through Experience al Ula, page 223) Al Ula's Old Town [215 B2] was inhabited from the 12th century until the 1980s. The lower level is where the original settlement of al Ula remains mostly in ruin. Points of interest include **Masjid al Izm** [215 B2] (or the Mosque of Bones), named when the Prophet Mohammed indicated the direction of Mecca with bones during his visit; and **Mousa bin Nusair Fort** [215 B2] (or al Ula Historic Castle), which was built as defence for the settlement in during the 6th century BCE. It also affords a good view if you are prepared to climb its 190 steps to the top, which is 45m above the town. There is an antiques shop in the bazaar and a growing number of atmospheric restaurants and cafés as restoration continues. The upper level is where **Old Town Walk** [215 B2] can be found. This regenerated pedestrianised street has quite a few coffee shops and restaurants and a few souvenir shops worth popping into for a quick look.

There are many other discoveries to be had in al Ula not far from the official Old Town area. You can spot ruins along the road when exploring the wadi or just by taking a random turn off the beaten trail. Rumour has it that much of this is scheduled for restoration/redevelopment. Note that the modern town is to the south near the Hejaz Railway station and hospital.

**Ottoman (Hejaz) railway station and railway cars** [215 D4] (Just south of the roundabout at the eastern end of King Abdullah Rd, at the south of al Ula) This railway station is unrestored, with 100-year-old wear and tear. The station is fenced in and closed but you can get a good feel for the exterior. There are no rails left on site but two original carriages can be found over the road, turned on their sides. It is still possible to have a close-up look at the carriages.

### *Elsewhere nearby*

**Al Fursan Village** [212 D4] (Hwy 70, about 9km east of Winter Park; ⌚ seasonal) Al Fursan Vilage is a purpose-built centre that hosts a variety of upscale outdoor events mostly in the winter season, including horseracing, polo, guided hiking and other outdoor pursuits. Check for any specific events you may be interested in by stopping by the village.

Past cultural events have included **Desert X**, an international art exhibition organised in collaboration with the Royal Commission of al Ula to support cultural dialogue through art. There is a large car park next to the grand entrance. A café and gift shop are on site for when you want a bit of retail therapy or simply to relax.

**Harrat Viewpoint** ✷ [215 A1] (⌚ 10.00–22.00 daily; admission free) If you like vistas and have a head for heights but don't want to ride in a helicopter, then this will work for you. Follow the road leading away from Winter Park roundabout. You will almost immediately encounter dramatic rock formations that are well worth taking time to photograph from many angles depending on the sunlight. Continue along the road, passing the turn to the al Ula Adventure Hub after about 4km. After approximately another 2km, you will start to climb, reaching an elevation of 1,919m. There is a series of steep switchbacks on roads where edges shouldn't be trusted, so make sure you stay within the cats' eyes. You may think you have arrived after climbing to the top but keep going for another 8km to the end of the road just past the mobile phone masts. There are good viewing areas just beyond, but they are unshaded so take care when the weather is hot and bundle up when the weather is cold. Ahead is a spectacular panoramic view of al Ula Old Town in the near distance and al Ula's natural beauty in all directions. To the left is the stunning view of the valley you just drove through, which can be seen from a smaller viewing platform, again open to the elements. Total distance is about 17km from Winter Park and 12km past the adventure hub. Well worth it just to take in the beauty.

**Elephant Rock (Jebel al Fil)** ✷ [212 C4] (Off Rte 375; turn left about 200m past al Fursan Village; ⌚ access 24hrs daily) In a region filled with rock formations that fuel the imagination, Elephant Rock is particularly popular. Nature's highlight is the 52m-high rock itself, which looks remarkably like an elephant from all directions. Looking from either side, visitors can see the shades of colour change as the sun moves throughout the day. Once existing in relative isolation, Elephant Rock has now become a trendy destination for relaxation. Local Saudis and tourists alike hang out in the open-air seating that gives a brilliant view of the sunset. Key Café and a branch of SALT are here, very near the rock, complete with visitor parking to the east side just a few steps away. The cafés open sometime after 16.00 and stay open until late.

**Mahlib al Naaqa Temple** [212 B4] (1km north of the Dadan Visitor Centre on the same road; ⌚ 09.00–17.00 daily) When we visited, we found the temple ruins fenced off and closed. However, it's still worth a drive by and short stop as it's possible to see quite a lot from the road. It is believed that the temple was built by the Lihyanites in the 6th–7th centuries BCE. It contains three steps along the northern side of its interior wall. The wall is still standing with the help of some restoration. At the entrance is the temple's purification basin, which measures about 3.75m in diameter and is about 2.15m tall. Most of the site looks primed to undergo further restoration.

**Zahra Stable for Arabian Horses** [212 B4] (On the unnamed road running parallel to the east of Rte 375, 1km south of Hwy 70; ☎ 054 733 3716; ⌚ 09.30–18.30 daily; contact via WhatsApp for prices) Here is an opportunity for adults and children alike to ride these majestic animals. The grounds are well maintained and set in a stunning location surrounded by palm groves and mountains.

**KHAYBAR خيبر** The drive from al Ula dramatically changes from rock formations sculpted by nature to basalt lava fields that feel like nature became angry, burning the earth and leaving it deserted. Although many people choose to travel between al Ula and Madinah along the Hejaz Railway route, others prefer to take in the history of the region by travelling via Khaybar. This journey takes a bit more than 2 hours and covers a distance of about 220km, leaving al Ula on Route 375 east before turning on to Highway 15 south. It is a further 150km along the highway to Madinah.

Khaybar is an oasis settlement that has been inhabited for thousands of years. Some of the lowest points of the oasis store water that can be accessed year-round. In pre-Islamic times, the population included Arab tribes, as well as a significant number of Jewish Arabs – until Khaybar purged much of its Jewish population, at the hands of the pre-Islamic Ghassanid Christian King al Harith bin Jabalah and the Prophet Mohammed and his followers during the Battle of Khaybar in 628CE.

There were a total of seven castles built on the hills surrounding Khaybar: Naem, al Saab, al Zubayr, al Nizar, Abi, the fortress of al Kamous aka al Qamus, and al Watih al Salalem. Some accounts list a total of up to 13. Although the Jewish castles of Khaybar were well fortified, they were also a long way apart from each other, allowing the conquerors victory as they could not defend one another. Upon defeat, the Jewish population was initially allowed to stay in Khaybar due to their agricultural productivity, but only by paying a steep tariff. After the death of the Prophet Mohammed, Jews were expelled by the Caliph Umar in 642CE. Most were sent to various locations in the Levant. Khaybar remained an important stop on the caravan route used by Islamic pilgrims for the next several centuries until modern times. Referenced by its earlier name of Hibra, Khaybar is mentioned on the Stela of Herran found in what is now Turkey by the last King of Babylon.

**Where to stay and eat** Most people visit Khaybar as a day trip from al Ula or when passing through on Highway 15 to or from Madinah. Accommodation is so limited that we cannot recommend any venues. There are a few mostly Saudi fast-food restaurants along Highway 15, including a Kudu that will be more visitor and female friendly than some locally owned venues.

**What to see and do** Note that, at the time of research, many of the key sites in Khaybar were blocked off by police barricades preventing visitors from exploring them. We expect that the Saudi Tourism authorities have these sites earmarked for restoration as part of the wider development of tourist sites in Medina Province. If this is the case during your visit, you can still get a feel for the town and the importance of the oasis during a quick stopover.

***Khaybar Fort*** Also known as al Qamus, this was the strongest of the Jewish forts found in the region and is more than 1,400 years old. It is the location of the Battle of Khaybar. Perched on top of a prominent hill, this fort also provides a brilliant view of the historical city about 1km below. The road to the fort is physically blocked and also displays a police warning not found at most other tourist sites, suggesting this is not the place to attempt an impromptu self-guided tour. We hope that any restoration work keeps the character of this important fort intact.

***Old Khaybar Historical City*** This site contains a large number of buildings in ruins, revealing homes, shops and mosques that were in use from many centuries ago until as recently as the 1970s. The buildings are constructed on stone bases, revealing their earliest history perhaps as far back as the Bronze Age; the upper parts, built of mud-brick as found in many other settlements in the region, reflect more recent building methods.

***Funerary avenues*** Khaybar continues slowly to reveal its ancient secrets. Archaeologists recently discovered funerary road tombs near the town. These round and pendant-shaped structures are estimated to date back to the 3rd millennium

BCE, and represent some of more than 17,000 tombs believed to be in the Khaybar and al Ula governorates in Medina Province. The majority of these tombs are positioned along ancient roads leading from the key oases of the region, especially around Khaybar. Although it is not possible to visit these tombs at present, the Royal Commission for al Ula has developed a plan called The Journey Through Time, which will provide an opportunity for the public to learn more about these structures and the associated cultures by 2030.

## MADINAH المدينة

*Note: Here we provide detailed information on accommodation, restaurants, shopping and places of interest that are accessible to all visitors, including non-Muslims. Information on these topics within the al Haram area is intentionally more general and is aimed at independent Muslim visitors only.* Chapter 10 *contains further information.*

Also known today as Medina and al Madinah al Munawwarah (المدينة المنورة), which means 'The Enlightened City', and as Yathrib (يثرب) in pre-Islamic times, Madinah is believed to be at least 3,000 years old – meaning that it existed for more than 1,500 years before the founding of Islam. The city is situated in an area of now inactive volcanos, the last eruption having occurred in the 13th century, and is surrounded by the lava fields Harrat Khaybar to the north and Harrat Rahat to the south, which explains the roughness of its terrain even within the desert environment of the Kingdom. Madinah has a population of about 1.4 million, making it the Kingdom's fourth largest city. It is also a modern city, making important contributions to the economy that go beyond religious tourism, including agriculture and manufacturing. With its hot desert climate, temperatures regularly reach the mid to upper 40s (°C) in the summer. Winters are pleasant with warm days and cooler nights.

Together, Mecca and Madinah form the cradle of Islamic culture and civilisation, with Madinah the location of many battles and other key events that led to the lasting establishment of this relatively new faith. The city's main site is Masjid al Nabawi, also known as the Prophet's Mosque, which contains the Prophet's Tomb. Other key mosques are: the Masjid Quba (or Masjid Quba'a), Madinah's oldest mosque and where it is believed that the Prophet Mohammed laid the first stone upon arrival in Madinah from Mecca; and the Masjid al Qiblatain (also known as Masjid al Qibletayn and the Mosque of the Two Qiblas), where Muslims believe that the Prophet Mohammed received instructions to change the direction of Islamic prayer towards Mecca instead of Jerusalem.

### DRESS CODE FOR MADINAH

Madinah is unsurprisingly a very conservative city and expects all visitors, including non-Muslims, to adhere to the most modest aspects of the dress code. This applies to men as well as women, and to boys and girls who have reached puberty. Men should wear full-length trousers and long-sleeved shirts. However, non-Muslim men should not adapt Islamic dress such as thobes as this can be interpreted as mockery and thus offensive. Women should wear a plain black abaya (subtle dark trim is just about acceptable), and also a headscarf that covers all of their hair at all times, including at tourist sites, restaurants and in public areas of their accommodation. Women never need to cover their face with a niqab.

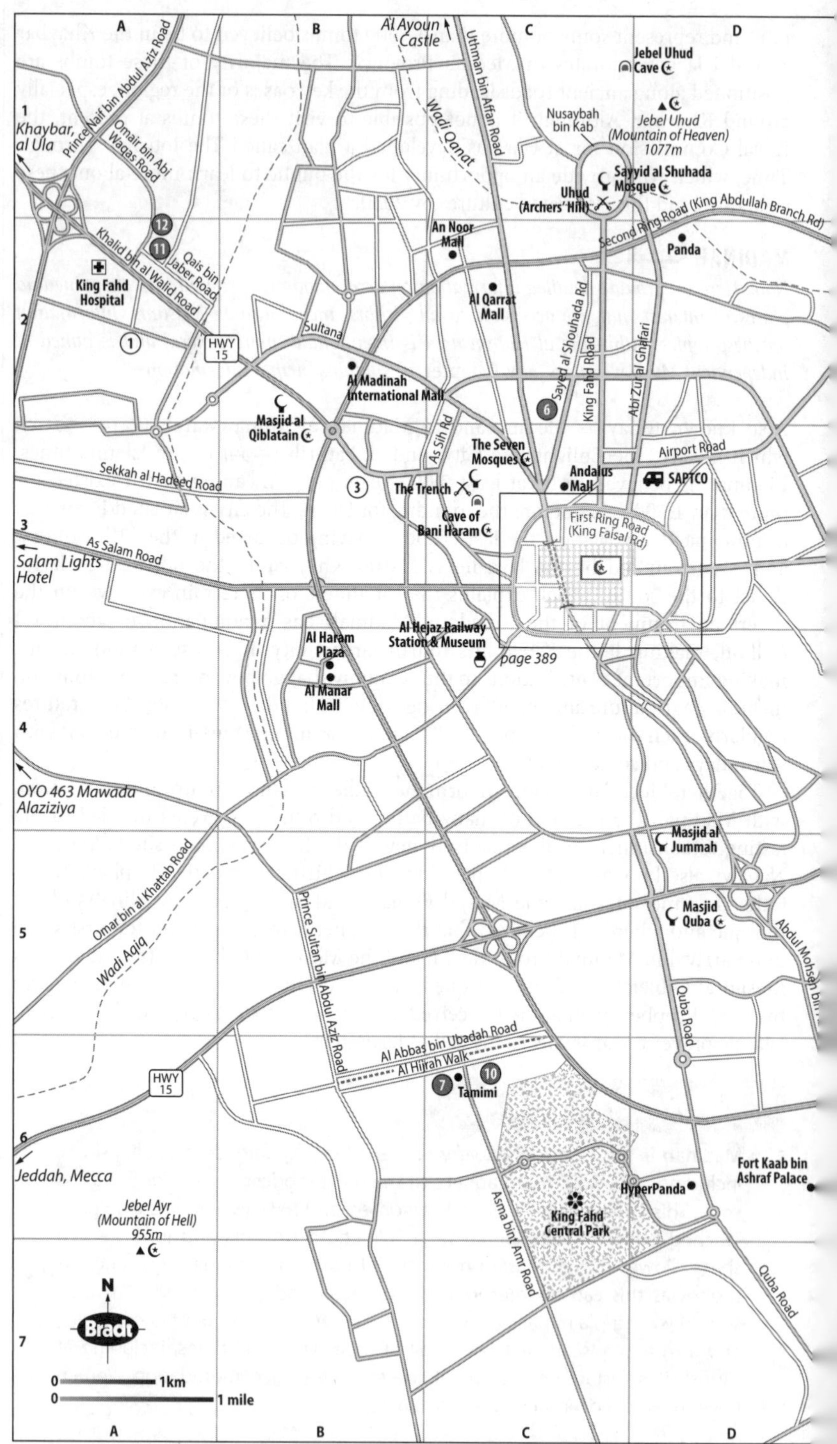
Al Ayoun Castle
Khaybar, al Ula
Prince Naif bin Abdul Aziz Road
Omair bin Abi Waqas Road
Qais bin Jaber Road
Khalid bin al Walid Road
King Fahd Hospital
HWY 15
Sultana
Uthman bin Affan Road
Wadi Qanat
Jebel Uhud Cave
Jebel Uhud (Mountain of Heaven) 1077m
Nusaybah bin Kab
Sayyid al Shuhada Mosque
Uhud (Archers' Hill)
Second Ring Road (King Abdullah Branch Rd)
Panda
An Noor Mall
Al Qarrat Mall
Al Madinah International Mall
Masjid al Qiblatain
Sayed al Shouhada Rd
King Fahd Road
Abi Zur al Ghafari
As Sih Rd
The Seven Mosques
Airport Road
Andalus Mall
SAPTCO
Sekkah al Hadeed Road
The Trench
Cave of Bani Haram
First Ring Road (King Faisal Rd)
As Salam Road
Salam Lights Hotel
Al Haram Plaza
Al Manar Mall
Al Hejaz Railway Station & Museum
page 389
OYO 463 Mawada Alaziziya
Omar bin al Khattab Road
Wadi Aqiq
Masjid al Jummah
Masjid Quba
Abdul Mohsen bin
Prince Sultan bin Abdul Aziz Road
Quba Road
Al Abbas bin Ubadah Road
Al Hijrah Walk
Tamimi
Jeddah, Mecca
Fort Kaab bin Ashraf Palace
HyperPanda
King Fahd Central Park
Asma bint Amr Road
Jebel Ayr (Mountain of Hell) 955m
N
Bradt
0 1km
0 1 mile

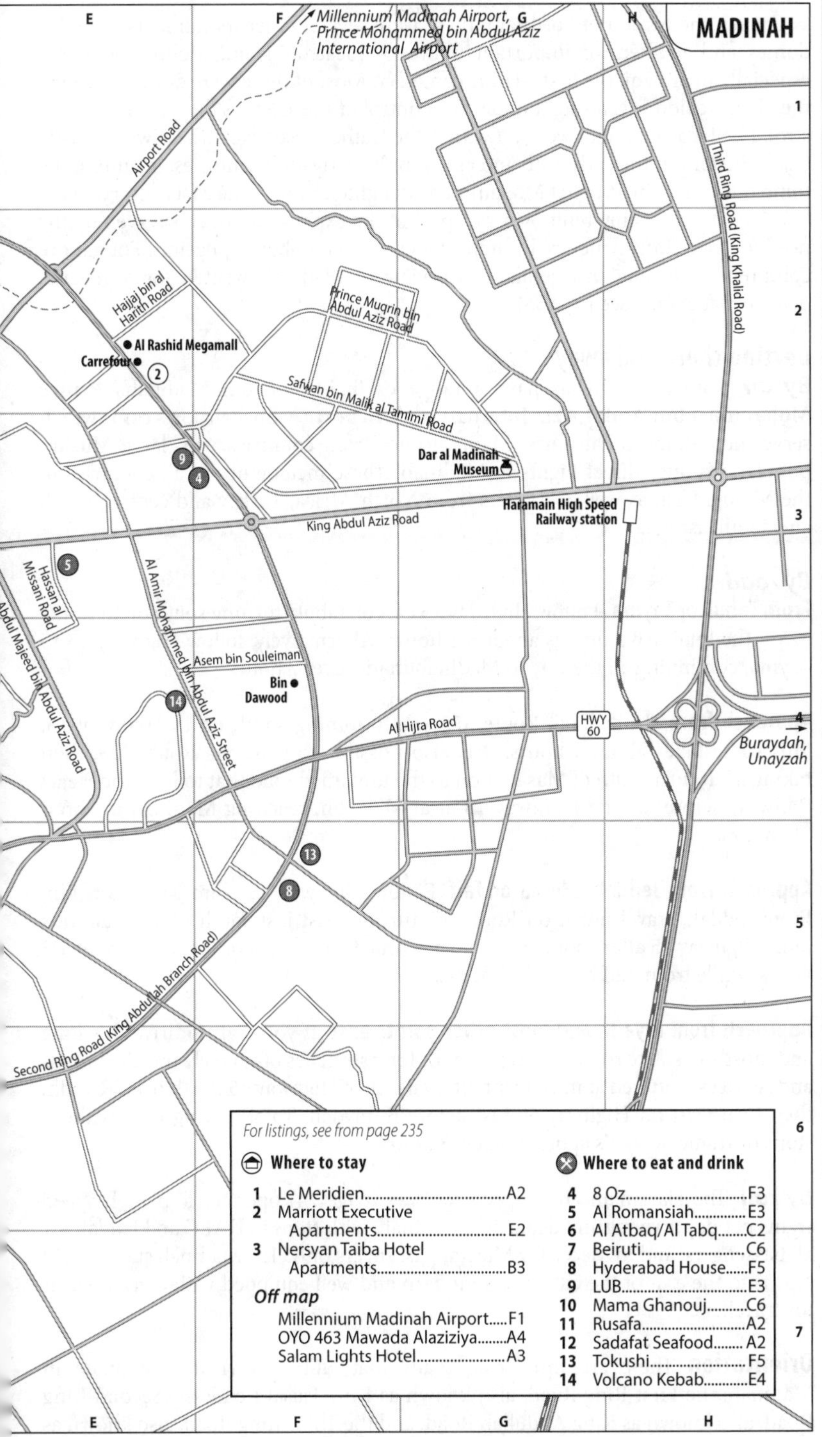
MADINAH
E
F
G
H
1
2
3
4
5
6
7
Millennium Madinah Airport, Prince Mohammed bin Abdul Aziz International Airport
Airport Road
Third Ring Road (King Khalid Road)
Hajjaj bin al Harith Road
Prince Muqrin bin Abdul Aziz Road
Al Rashid Megamall
Carrefour
Safwan bin Malik al Tamimi Road
Dar al Madinah Museum
Haramain High Speed Railway station
King Abdul Aziz Road
Hassan al Missani Road
Abdul Majeed bin Abdul Aziz Road
Al Amir Mohammed bin Abdul Aziz Street
Asem bin Souleiman
Bin Dawood
Al Hijra Road
HWY 60
Buraydah, Unayzah
Second Ring Road (King Abdullah Branch Road)
For listings, see from page 235
Where to stay
1 Le Meridien....A2
2 Marriott Executive Apartments....E2
3 Nersyan Taiba Hotel Apartments....B3
Off map
Millennium Madinah Airport....F1
OYO 463 Mawada Alaziziya....A4
Salam Lights Hotel....A3
Where to eat and drink
4 8 Oz....F3
5 Al Romansiah....E3
6 Al Atbaq/Al Tabq....C2
7 Beiruti....C6
8 Hyderabad House....F5
9 LUB....E3
10 Mama Ghanouj....C6
11 Rusafa....A2
12 Sadafat Seafood....A2
13 Tokushi....F5
14 Volcano Kebab....E4

During the earliest era of Islam, there were several other monuments – tombs, domes and markers of important figures – located in and around Madinah, especially in al Baqi, the first Islamic cemetery. Most of these were destroyed when the Hejaz region was brought under the control of the al Sauds on account of their strong belief against idol worship within the frame of Salafism. These were mostly lost to history in the early 19th and again in the early 20th centuries, including the tomb of Fatima, the Prophet Mohammed's daughter. Even in the 21st century, many historic sites are being built over as a part of the expansion projects driven by the need for more infrastructure to support a growing number of pilgrims. For a more comprehensive religion-orientated overview of Madinah written for a general, diverse readership, see page 387.

## Getting there and away

***By air*** Saudia and flynas have a range of flights to/from Madinah's **Prince Mohammed bin Abdul Aziz International Airport** (w tibahairports.com) which serve most domestic airports. Many airlines from countries with large Muslim populations offer direct flights to Madinah. These include nearly all countries in the Middle East, as well as carriers from North Africa, Turkey and central, south and southeast Asia.

### *By road*

**From Tabuk or Tayma** Follow Highway 15 east of Tabuk, turning south on to Route 375 – the total drive time is about 6½ hours. Alternatively, follow Highway 15 to Tayma, continuing all the way to Madinah in just over 7 hours.

**Approach from al Ula** Take Route 375 south, joining south on to Highway 15. This route takes about 4 hours. It is also possible to drive via Route 328, then taking a left turn south of Masader on to the unnamed road that follows the Hejaz Railway, before joining Highway 15 at al Malaylih, reaching Madinah in about 3½ hours.

**Approach from Jeddah, Mecca or Taif** Follow Highway 15 from Mecca or Taif. From Jeddah, travel north on Route 55, turning east just south of Thuwal. This joins Highway 15 after about 5km. Journey time from Mecca or Jeddah is about 4½ hours, while from Taif it's about 5 hours.

**Approach from Riyadh and most other points east** If you plan to drive this long and mostly desolate route, be prepared for long stretches of sparsely travelled roads and services scattered at infrequent intervals. Take Highway 65 north from Riyadh, then turn west on Highway 60 just before Buraydah. Total driving time without stops or traffic delays is approximately 8 hours.

***By rail*** The Haramain High Speed Railway (page 74) operates four high-speed trains per day arriving and departing Madinah, with stops in KAEC and Jeddah for all passengers, and to Mecca for Muslim passengers only. The Madinah station [233 H3] is to the east of the city and is modern and well equipped with conveniences for travellers.

**Orientation** There are three ring roads that will help visitors orientate in Madinah: the First Ring Road, also known as King Faisal Road; the Second Ring Road, also known as King Abdullah Road; and the Third Ring Road, also known as

## ☪ RELIGIOUS AND MUSLIM-ONLY SITES

The ☪ symbol is used in this chapter to indicate all religious sites in the city of Madinah, both those within and beyond the al Haram area.

We advise non-Muslims to show utmost respect when passing these sites and for the religious pilgrims visiting them. The same symbol is used alongside other information within the al Haram area accessible by Muslims only. We recommend that non-Muslims do not attempt to visit religious sites, either in the al Haram area or sites outside elsewhere in the city, although there are many reports of some non-Muslim visitors doing so.

King Khalid Road. The First Ring Road is less than 500m from Masjid al Nabawi, with the Second and Third ring roads increasingly further away.

Important Islamic sites can be found both within and beyond the **al Haram area**, which, historically, was defined by clearly placed entry/exit arches positioned, broadly speaking, in the proximity of the Second Ring Road, and which were, until relatively recently, actively enforced by the religious police. Only Muslims are permitted to visit within the al Haram area, although it is now possible for non-Muslims to visit some places between the First and Second ring roads, including the Hejaz Railway Station and Museum. However, you should be aware this is still a grey area as there do not appear to be any official publications indicating these boundary changes.

Non-Muslims are able to visit the remaining areas of the city, and those who choose to do so respectfully will have a unique opportunity to see how the historic, religious and modern aspects of this important city work together and provide a distinctive vibe.

**Where to stay** Accommodation options in Madinah include high-end luxury global brands and mid-range chain hotels both within and outside the al Haram boundary. The listings below indicate hotel locations relative to the al Haram boundary.

### *Outside the al Haram zone*

**Le Méridien** [232 A2] Khalid bin al Waleed Rd; 014 846 0777; w marriott.com. Located between 2nd & 3rd Ring rds near King Fahd Hospital & the King Salman Convention Centre, this old but refurbished hotel was the place to stay for non-Muslims when options were much more limited than they are now. The service is a bit tired but is eventually delivered. The restaurant does a decent job trying to cater to all tastes. There are beautiful gardens, ample covered parking & security at the entrance. The rooms are spacious but could do with more electrical outlets. **$$$**

**Marriott Executive Apartments** [233 E2] 2nd Ring Rd to the northeast, attached to al Rashid Megamall; 014 835 9333; w marriott.com. This is a good choice for longer stays or for families & groups. The rooms are of the standard expected of an upmarket Marriott although the halls are labyrinthine & can feel like an echo chamber at times. There are compact gardens interwoven between apartment wings that are lovely to access if the weather is good. There is a good b/fast but limited room service menu that relies mostly on deliveries from the food court in the shopping mall. The property has its own dedicated, free covered car park that allows direct access to the hotel. Note that reception, male health club & some other services are on floors you might not expect them to be, so read the directory at the lifts carefully. **$$$**

**Millennium Madinah Airport** [233 F1] King Salman Rd at Prince Mohammed bin Abdul Aziz International Airport; 014 813 5000; w millenniumhotels.com. This hotel has all of the usual amenities & services expected of an upscale hotel near the airport. The focus is on 1-night stays, especially for visitors about to fly, & staff do their best to respond quickly to any requests. There is a free airport shuttle bus. **$$$**

**Nersyan Taiba Hotel Apartments** [232 B3] Just off Sekkah al Hadeed Rd; 050 806 0816. Located just inside King Abdullah Branch Rd between 1st & 2nd Ring rds, the property's nondescript exterior hides an above-standard budget interior. The rooms & suites are spacious, & all have basic kitchens. There is no restaurant or room service, but there are plenty of options nearby if you don't want to use the kitchen facilities. Decent Wi-Fi & underground parking make this a good place to stay for those on a budget who are happy with no-frills functionality. **$$**

**OYO 463 Mawada Alaziziya** [232 A4] Salma bin Ali off al Imam Muslim Rd, just beyond 3rd Ring Rd; 011 293 2743; w oyorooms.com. This is one of more than a dozen OYO properties between 1st & 2nd Ring rds, most of which lie west, north & east of the al Haram area. **$$**

**Salam Lights Hotel** [232 A3] al Salam Rd between 2nd & 3rd Ring rds, west of Taibah University; 056 677 3386. This is a basic but clean small hotel with free parking at the front. There are small kitchens in some of the rooms adequate for heating up a simple meal. **$**

### *Within the al Haram zone*

*Map, page 389*

*Note: Accommodation within the al Haram area of Madinah is restricted to Muslim visitors only.*

Since many pilgrims will be travelling on a tour package that includes accommodation, the information offered here is intended to aid *independent* Muslim travellers. Many of the following hotels offer a shuttle bus service to pilgrimage sites beyond the al Haram area.

Upmarket properties, some with luxury price points, include the Crowne Plaza (**$$$$$**), Golden Tulip al Shakreen (**$$$$**), Movenpick (**$$$$$**) & Pullman Zamzam (**$$$$$**) on the **southern perimeter** of the Masjid al Nabawi, where many more modest properties can also be found, including the OYO 377 Marina Palace (**$$$**).

On the **northern perimeter**, top-end hotel options include the al Rawda Royal Inn (**$$$$$**), Dar al Taqwa (**$$$$$**), Frontel al Harithia Hotel (**$$$$$**), 6 additional Golden Tulip properties (including al Ansar & al Zahabi; **$$$$–$$$$$**), 2 Intercontinental hotels (Dar al Hijrah & Dar al Iman; both **$$$$$**), the Oberoi (**$$$$$**) & the Ruve al Madinah & Shad al Madinah by Accor (both **$$$$$**).

## Where to eat and drink

### *Outside the al Haram zone*

**Sadafat Seafood Restaurant** [232 A2] Cnr Omair bin Abi Waqas & Qais bin Jaber rds, next door to Rusafa; 056 050 9059; w 6lb.menu/Sadafat; 13.00–01.30 daily. This upscale restaurant's décor has a nautical theme, including blue lights that are switched on at sunset. There is a choice of indoor, outdoor or rooftop seating. The fish & shellfish are fresh, despite Madinah's inland location, & are selected from the restaurant's fish counter. You have a choice of how to have it prepared. **$$$$**

**Tokushi** [233 F5] King Abdullah Branch Rd, just north of al Amir Mohammed bin Abdul Aziz St; 014 869 1766; 13.00–01.00 daily. This upscale restaurant has a good mix of Japanese-inspired décor & accommodates Saudi modesty in the discreet family section. There is a good variety of classic sushi & sashimi complemented by Saudi-Japanese fusion starters & mains. The service is attentive but not overbearing. **$$$$**

**Beiruti** [232 C6] Al Abbas bin Ubadah Rd, about 200m west of Asma bint Amr Rd along the al Hijrah Walk; 014 841 2111; 13.00–01.00 daily. This restaurant to the south of Madinah strikes a careful balance between casual & upscale. The menu is robust & covers Lebanese classics, from snacks & mezze to mixed grills & traditional main courses. The décor includes comfortable open-table seating in the singles section & lovely Levantine touches that enhance the privacy of the family-section booths. There is another branch at Bir Uthman off Sultana Rd, just west of King Abdullah Branch Rd & not far from an Nour Mall to the northwest, which is more casual but the food just as delicious. **$$$**

**LUB** [233 E3] Cnr King Abdullah & Prince Mouqrin bin Abdul Aziz rds; 053 680 5805; w l-u-b.business.site; 06.00–01.00 Sat–Thu, 06.00–11.00 & 13.00–02.00 Fri. If you are looking for a good b/fast, then this is the place to go. The outstanding bakery selection will tempt even the most stoic resisters, with lots of coffee options that are very good but nothing unusual. Although the focus is on b/fast, LUB also has a full post-b/fast menu of salads, pasta, Western dishes & more. The modern décor is complemented by the spacious seating downstairs, upstairs, & on the rooftop weather permitting. $$$

**Rusafa Restaurant** [232 A2] Omair bin Abi Waqas Rd at the junction of Qais bin Jaber Rd; ☎054 003 0977; ⏲ 13.00–01.30 daily. This reasonably priced Turkish restaurant is also a delight on the eye, with a lovely courtyard with tiled floors & a calming water fountain for outdoor dining during pleasant weather. The indoor dining area is well decorated with flowers scattered throughout but is otherwise not over the top. Excellent meats, moutabal & salads are all recommended. Save room for the Turkish desserts on the menu if you have a sweet tooth. $$$

**8 Oz** [233 F3] Cnr King Abdullah & Prince Mouqrin bin Abdul Aziz rds; ☎055 794 6177; ⏲ 24hrs daily. If you want a wider variety of coffees than LUB has to offer plus French toast or full-on desserts, then try this coffee shop next door. $$

**Al Atbaq/al Tabq** [232 C2] Cnr Sayed al Shouhada & al Khilal rds; ☎014 838 8222; ⏲ 11.00–02.00 daily. Found between 1st & 2nd Ring rds to the north, this well-established Pakistani restaurant has been operating since 1983 & still draws the crowds. It is worth the trip, & you won't go wrong with any of the Pakistani curries. There are a few options for vegetarians &, as is common in Saudi Arabia, Chinese noodles & a few other items are also on the menu. $$

**Al Romansiah** [233 E3] Cnr King Abdul Aziz & Hassan al Missani rds; ☎9200 00144; w alromansiah.com; ⏲ 10.30–00.30 Sat–Thu, 12.15–01.00 Fri. Located between 1st & 2nd Ring rds, this large branch of the popular national chain delivers classic Saudi cuisine. Order at the front counter of the singles or family sections. There are conventional tables & private traditional floor seating behind curtains. $$

**Hyderabad House** [233 F5] Cnr King Abdullah & Hammad bin al Jiad rds; w hyd-sa.com; ⏲ 13.30–midnight daily. Not to be confused with the restaurant of the same name at Nour Mall. Stretching the cuisine beyond its name, the menu offers a blend of classic biryani & tandoori dishes with additional nods to a few Saudi, Western & Chinese-inspired options. Usual singles & family sections with a small outdoor terrace seating area. $$

**Mama Ghanouj** [232 C6] Cnr al Abbas bin Ubadah & Asma bint Amr rds; ☎055 501 6704; ⏲ 05.00–14.00 & 17.00–02.00 daily. Less than 300m east of Beiruti Restaurant along the al Hijrah Walk, this casual Lebanese restaurant is another b/fast favourite. Order at the counter. Not as you might expect, the walls are decorated with cartoons & superheroes, & characterful seating can be found both downstairs & upstairs in the family section. $$

**Volcano Kebab** [233 E4] al Amir Mohammed bin Abdul Aziz St, just south of Shehab al Senaani Rd; ☎059 913 2200; ⏲ 13.00–02.00 daily. Enjoy the Syrian-inspired chicken or beef kebabs at this popular casual restaurant & take-away. There is a variety of skewers, plates & sandwiches. The *toum* (garlic sauce) & tahini are gorgeous, as is the flatbread with sesame & nigella seeds. It's an Arabic-only menu but someone will help. Although there is seating & a family section to the side, this is more of a take-away place. $$

### *Within the al Haram zone*

For pilgrims who wish to dine away from their hotel, popular restaurants within the al Haram zone include **Arabesque** ($$$), **al Modeef** ($$$), **Sea Spice Restaurant** ($$$$) & **Zaitoon** ($$). In addition to branches of recognisable fast-food outlets & some global coffee chains, there are local coffee shops on nearly every corner.



## Shopping

You will find branches of the usual **supermarkets** outside the al Haram zone: Carrefour [233 E2], Panda [232 D2], HyperPanda [232 D6], Tamimi [232 C6] and bin Dawood [233 F4], which is at the budget end with lots of cheap home goods. There is also a branch of bin Dawood within the al Haram zone.

Most modern shopping malls outside the al Haram district may open for a couple of hours in the late morning then close until about 17.00, except for the food courts and supermarkets. Most remain closed on Friday until late afternoon.

**Al Madinah International Mall** [232 B2] Sultana Rd between 1st & 2nd Ring rds. This is one of Madinah's first malls. While the trendy shoppers may have moved on, this is an excellent place for those looking for a variety of gold & silver shops.

**Al Manar Mall** [232 B4] Cnr King Abdullah Branch & Abdallah bin Abi Jahm rds. This large modern mall located directly adjacent to the shop al Haram Plaza has everything you'd expect including restaurants & a branch of Panda. Its focus is on women's & children's clothing.

**Al Rashid Megamall** [233 E2] Cnr 2nd Ring & Hajjaj bin al Harith rds. This is a relatively new mall with the usual shops, a Carrefour & a large food court offering a variety of cuisines ranging from decent to dreadful. It is conveniently attached to the Marriott Executive Apartments (page 235).

**Al Qarrat Mall** [232 C2] Cnr 2nd Ring & Uthman bin Affan rds. On the other side of the ring road from an Noor Mall, this is another large modern mall with the usual shops, a food court & Fun World, a large children's play area.

**Andalus Mall** [232 C3] North of the 1st Ring Rd at Sultana, a few metres outside the al Haram area. This is an opportunity to visit a very traditional shopping centre offering a variety of items that were once commonly sold in souqs, including religious souvenirs, traditional men's & women's clothing, perfumes & other scents, & gold.

**An Noor Mall** [232 C2] Unmissable along the north side of the 2nd Ring Rd, this is an upscale Arabian Centre mall with many Western shops, a few American chain restaurants and a HyperPanda.

### ☪ *Shops in the al Haram zone* *Map, page 389*

Unlike the modern shopping malls outside al Haram, it is possible to shop throughout the day within the boundaries of al Haram as many of these shops cater to pilgrims, who may want to pop in any time from early morning until late evening.

There is a cluster of shops immediately north of the Masjid al Nabawi perimeter near the hotels. Have a wander around the area, especially if you are looking for religious souvenirs, clothes and jewellery. The **Anwar al Madinah Mall** is an early modern mall with a mix of everyday items, religious souvenirs and a branch of bin Dawood hypermarket. **Sahab al Andalus Gold Shop** is good for all styles of gold jewellery. Check out the **Taybah Shopping Centre** for its stained-glass dome, striking Islamic columns, large chandelier and other architectural features. The wide range of shops offer something for everyone. **Al Munawwarah Gift Shop** is a lovely gift shop for all things Islamic south of Masjid al Nabawi gates, just off the roundabout along abu Ayyub al Ansari Road. There are other shops to the south of Masjid al Nabawi that are easily found simply by wandering along the roads near the hotels.

## Other practicalities

### *Outside the al Haram zone*

**Al Rajhi Bank** 1st Ring Rd, 100m south of as Salam Rd; ☎ 9200 03344; w alrajhibank.com.sa; ⏱ 09.30–17.30 Sun–Thu

**ANB Bank** Cnr Sulltana & Khalid bin al Waleed rds; ☎ 800 124 4040; w anb.com.sa; ⏱ 09.30–17.30 Sat–Thu

**King Faisal Specialist Hospital & Research Centre** Cnr 3rd Ring Rd & Hwy 60 w kfshrc.edu.sa/en/home/hospitals/Madinah; ☎ 9200 12312

**Nahdi Pharmacy** 2nd Ring Rd, 300m north of al Rashid Megamall; ☎ 9200 24673; w nahdionline.com; ⏱ 07.00–03.00 daily

**Saudi Post** Prince Abdul Majeed St, 200m west of Abdul Mohsen bin Abdul Aziz Rd; w splonline.com.sa; ⏱ 08.00-20.45 Sun-Thu

### *Inside the al Haram zone*

Nearly all mid-range & higher hotels, as well as shopping areas, have ATMs.

**Al Haram Emergency Hospital/Bab Jebreel Health Centre** Opposite Mecca Gate, Masjid al Nabawi; ⏱ 24hrs daily

**Nahdi Pharmacy** abu Ayyab al Ansari and Hussein al Ali St; ☎ 9200 24673; w nahdionline.com; ⏱ 05.00–03.00 daily

**Saudi Post** Omar bin al Khattab Rd, just inside 1st Ring Rd; **w** splonline.com.sa; ⌚ 08.00–23.00 daily

**What to see and do** The following information is written for a general audience. Readers who want more in-depth information about the religious significance of the relevant sites can read more in *Chapter 10*. The following sites are organised using the First Ring Road like a clock, starting at 3 o'clock and going anticlockwise.

***Al Hijrah Walk*** [232 C6] (al Abbas bin Ubadah Rd between King Abdullah Branch & Prince Sultan bin Abdul Aziz rds ) When it's time to take a break from pilgrimage activities and general sightseeing, this clean, public pedestrian space is great for walking or cycling and a good spot for a picnic. At about 2km long, the distance is perfect for fitness fanatics' warm-ups and for an easy self-contained stroll. It's a welcome green space in a city with limited greenery elsewhere.

***Dar al Madinah Museum*** [233 G3] (Safwan bin Malik al Tamimi Rd; 014 865 3049; ⌚ 11.00–19.00 Sat–Thu; SAR25) Located about 200m north of King Abdul Aziz and Hajjaj bin al Harith roads, this is an interesting museum focusing on the history of Islam in Madinah during the life of the Prophet Mohammed, complete with dioramas of key locations. After entering the car park, proceed to the front of the building to the ticket booth. Once inside, in the waiting area you will find a counter selling mostly Islamic books and you will be greeted with Arabic coffee or water. The museum is beyond the waiting room and is packed with artefacts, but the signs and labels are in Arabic only. Guided tours are provided only for groups of two or more people, but you will still be able to wander around the exhibits if you visit alone.

***Fort Kaab bin Ashraf Palace*** [232 D6] (Abdul Mohsen bin Abdul Aziz Rd, about 200m south of the 2nd Ring Rd – take the dirt road access directly off the paved road) Kaab bin al Ashraf was a Jewish leader and poet from the early 7th century who was said to anger the Prophet Mohammed over the Battle of Quraysh during the earliest days of Islam. Many believe that he was conspiring with other Jewish leaders to kill the Prophet. Other reasons were as simple as being a non-believer of Islam. Kaab bin al Ashraf was murdered here, in his own palace. Visitors will find the palace, which was built of black stone but now mostly in ruins, fenced off; but it is clear to see including some restoration works.

☪ ***Masjid Quba*** [232 D5] (Cnr al Hijra & Qiba rds; 014 831 2441; ⌚ 24hrs daily) Also known as Masjid Kuba/Quba'a, the Quba Mosque is believed to be the first mosque built during the time of the Prophet Mohammed, who is said to have positioned the first stones upon arrival from Mecca. The old mosque has been torn down and replaced by the current mosque which was rebuilt and grandly expanded several times as recently as last century. It is one of the most important places for religious pilgrims to visit in Madinah.

***Al Hejaz Railway Station and Museum*** ✷ [232 C4] Omar bin al Khattab Rd; ⌚ 09.00–16.00 & 17.00–22.00 Sat–Thu, 17.00–22.00 Fri; admission free) Situated between First and Second Ring roads and housed in the old al Hejaz Railway Station, this museum is a worthwhile visit for both railway enthusiasts and those interested in the history of the Kingdom. It also has good information about the earliest days of Islam, easily understood by Muslims and non-Muslims alike. The station building has been sensitively restored. Enter from the east side of the station and turn right, where you will see a security desk. A guide will direct you towards the recommended path to follow within the museum, starting with the ground floor with artefacts from pre-Islamic times to the end of the Ottoman era on display which give you a taste of what you will see upstairs. The beautiful wooden stairs leading up to the first floor show the wear and tear from the many people who have climbed them over the decades. The first floor contains several rooms displaying more artefacts, these focusing on Islamic and Saudi culture, from early Qur'ans to antique clothing; some short videos cover more recent history. The path is chronological, with attendants present to guide you to the next room if you are unsure of where to go next. Saudi royal history is also part of the exhibit. The exhibition rooms are well organised, with displays labelled in both Arabic and English. Visitors should be aware that the station is not air conditioned, so the first floor in particular can be very hot in the summer. However, you will be rewarded by the view from the upstairs windows, which overlook the railway yards that contain other outbuildings and a few train carriages. Unfortunately, it is not currently possible to access the yard directly.

☪ ***Cave of Bani Haram (Cave of Prostration)*** [232 C3] (Between 1st & 2nd Ring rds, off as Sih Rd; 🕘 24hrs daily) It is in this cave, on Jebel Sala, where Muslims believe the Prophet prostrated upon receiving a message from Allah via the angel Gabriel. It is also where he rested during the Battle of the Trench, and in the same district as the Masjid Bani Haram, where the Muslim military camped out during the battle. You'll need to be reasonably fit to walk up to the cave, which could be more accurately described as a hole sheltered by a large rock. This rocky walk is a good example of the difficult terrain found in the region and although the small cave itself is physically unremarkable, it has great historical and religious significance. Follow Google Maps to a car park to the east of an ordinary looking neighbourhood, where there is a car park strewn with litter. You will see a 'No Military Zone' sign and a hole in the fence to the back of the car park. Climb through and follow the well-trodden path on the west side of Jebel Sala. The cave is towards the top of the hill to the right of the path

☪ ***The Seven Mosques*** [232 C3] (Khalid bin al Waleed Rd on al Sih Rd; 🕘 24hrs daily) There are seven historic mosques on this large complex not far north of the Cave of Bani Haram. The location is significant as it is adjacent to Jebel Sala where the Battle of the Trench (Ghazwat al Khandaq) took place. From north to south the mosques are: al Fath, Salman al Farsi, Abu Bakr al Siddiq, Umar bin Khattab, Sa'ad bin Mu'adh, Ali bin Abi Talib and the Fatimah az Zahra Mosque. You will notice the large white mosque façade which dominates on the approach to the complex with a large car park in the front for buses and private vehicles. Many pilgrims also climb the hills to access the older mosques, although access is restricted to the exterior of these structures.

☪ ***Masjid al Qiblatain*** [232 B2] (Khalid bin al Waleed Rd, about 500m west of 2nd Ring Rd; 🕘 24hrs daily) Originally built in 623CE, this mosque, Muslims believe, is where the Prophet was commanded to change the qibla or direction of prayer from Jerusalem to Mecca and to reposition the mihrab or directional niche accordingly. It was one of the rare few mosques that contained two mihrabs, one facing Jerusalem and the other, Mecca. When the mosque was rebuilt in the late 1980s, only the mihrab facing Mecca was retained. The mosque is accessed away from Khalid bin al Waleed Road. Go around the back of the mosque where there is a car park and the entrances, the men's to the left and women's to the right.

***Al Ayoun Castle*** [232 C1] (Uthman bin Affan Rd, north of the 2nd Ring Rd) This circular castle from the Ottoman period, now fenced off, used to store ammunition and is a good reminder of the many influences in Madinah over the course of its long history. Although it is very small and perhaps less interesting to some, it is worth a quick stop if you are passing through the area on Uthman bin Affan Road. It is located on the side of the road in between auto-repair shops towards Jebel Uhud.

☪ ***Sayyid al Shuhada Mosque*** [232 C1] (Between King Fahd & Nusaybah bin Kab rds; 🕘 24hrs daily) Contained on an oval 'island' between King Fahd and Nusaybah bin Kab roads, this is another important stop on the pilgrim trail. The mosque is home to the Shuhada Uhud Cemetery, which is the location of the Grave of Hamza bin al Muttaib, the Prophet Mohammed's uncle, who died during the Battle of Uhud. Archers' Hill, where the Battle of Uhud was fought, is also nearby – it is considered sacred ground to Muslims and can be climbed by any pilgrim wishing to do so.

☪ ***Jebel Uhud*** [232 D1] (Beyond Sayyid al Shuhada neighbourhood; 🕘 24hrs daily; see also page 389) At over 1,000m tall, Jebel Uhud dominates the skyline to the north of Madinah. The second biggest battle after the Prophet's migration occurred here which resulted in a defeat of the Muslims by the Meccans. Access to the base of the mountain is via narrow, unnamed streets in the Sayyid al Shyuhada district. The road surface ends at the guard gate but the gate arm is often left up (/// lighter.moon.scale will get you on to the road near the guard gate). If you plan to continue past this point, you'll need to have a 4x4 to climb the mountain further. Most people like to visit during sunrise or sunset as these are the best times to see the reddish hue of the mountain.

☪ ***Jebel Uhud Cave*** [232 C1] (Beyond Sayyid al Shuhada neighbourhood; 🕘 24hrs daily) If you are travelling to Jebel Uhud, you will pass Jebel Uhud Cave just past the last of the houses. It is where the Prophet Mohammed spent time recovering from his wounds during the Battle of Uhud. The Ministry of Tourism has fenced off the immediate area and erected signs shielding the petroglyphs in the cave. The cave can be reached by standard car, but driving up the mountain should only be attempted with a 4x4.

## Inside the al Haram zone *Map, page 389*

☪ ***Masjid al Nabawi*** (🕘 24hrs daily) Also known as the Prophet's Mosque, this is the second holiest site in Islam after Mecca. Originally built in 622CE, it is the second mosque built during the life of the Prophet Mohammed, after the Quba Mosque. It is also the world's second largest mosque after the al Haram Mosque in Mecca. Many Muslims choose to make the pilgrimage known as ziyarat (page 388), which includes visits to this site and other significant sites in and around Madinah. Unlike the hajj pilgrimage to Mecca, ziyarat is not obligatory.

Originally covering an area of about 30m by 35m, the mosque was built with three gates: to the south, the Gate of Mercy (Bab ar Rahmah); to the west, the Gate of Gabriel (Bab Jibril); and to the east, the Gate of Women (Bab an Nisa). In its history, the mosque has been expanded many times, starting with the Rashiduns as early as the end of the Battle of Khaybar in 629CE. Having before contained a qibla pointing to Jerusalem, the qibla now pointed prayers in the direction of Mecca. Subsequent expansions occurred under the direction of the Umayyads, Byzantines, Abbasids, Ottmans and finally the Sauds. The last, completed in 1992CE, increased its coverage to over 160,000m², able to accommodate 500,000 people. A new expansion project is now underway.

Most visitors access the perimeter of the mosque at the southern end of the grounds. There are now a total of 42 gates to the interior of the mosque. Women enter through up to four gates to the north or northwest, often Gate 13. Men can access the interior of the mosque through many of the remaining gates. Some gates are reserved for specific use, such as for imams or administration.

The exterior is mostly a sand colour that suits the environment well. There are a total of 27 domes and ten minarets, including the four minarets from Ottoman times and six additional minarets added during the expansion in the late 20th century. Decoration features black and white stones, marble and elaborate Islamic geometric designs. There are additional prayer areas outside the mosque. *Wudu* stations for ritual washing in preparation for prayer are found in several locations in the courtyard, where large umbrella-shaped awnings suspended over much of the area provide shade. There are also many drinking water stations.

Pilgrims can visit independently, although many arrive in tour groups, proudly wearing their national Islamic dress, adding their country's flag or name to their ensemble. Men are not in *ihram* (page 385) but instead most wear their national Islamic dress, making for an ancillary cultural experience. Security is present everywhere including at the entrances to the mosque perimeter and to the mosque building, but the atmosphere is calm and peaceful, while at the same time both solemn and almost festive, with visitors snapping plenty of photos.

Inside the women's mosque, the green carpets, red dome, white marble floors, gold arched walls and dome lights that display 'Allah' in Arabic are truly awe-inspiring. Some people pray; others read the Qur'an, sleep or simply relax with their female family and friends.

The Prophet's Mosque contains the **Green Dome** at the southeast corner of the mosque. Originally the Prophet Mohammed's youngest wife Aisha's house, the dome was built in 1279CE and has been restored or replaced several times since. It was replaced in its current form in 1818CE by the Ottomans and was first painted green in 1937CE. It covers the **tomb of the Prophet Mohammed** and the first two caliphs, Abu Bakr and Umar. Entry to this area is monitored closely by security and is open only to Muslim men.

Most parking near the Masjid al Nabawi is now closed for security reasons. Public parking is available immediately outside the First Ring Road in car parks opposite the Crowne Plaza Hotel. Fees are modest and are calculated by the hour. The walk from the car park to the entrance to the mosque grounds takes about 5 minutes.

☪ ***Al Baqi Cemetery*** Located to the southeast of the Masjid al Nabawi, this is where many of the relatives and companions of the Prophet Mohammed were buried. Tombs and other buildings were destroyed in this cemetery by Salafists for the first time in 1806CE and again in the 1920s with the permission of King Abdul Aziz ibn Saud in alliance with a Wahhabist militia despite protest from many factions of the Islamic world. The annual Day of Sorrow is still acknowledged by both Sunni and Shi'a Muslims.

***Hop-on Hop-off Bus Tours of Madinah*** (City Sightseeing; **w** city-sightseeing.com/en/125/medina/478/hop-on-hop-off-al-madinah; Hop On Hop Off Bus Tours **w** hop-on-hop-off-bus-tours.com/city/medina-bus-tours; approx US$20 pp) Similar to hop-on hop-off bus tours in other cities, one-day tickets are available to see key religious sites both within and beyond the al Haram area from either of these operators. Tours start at Masjid al Nabawi. There are also stops for the an Nour shopping mall and the Hejaz Railway Museum. There are a total of 12 stops: Stops 1–4 are on the green route, which is in the al Haram area; and Stops 5–12 on the red route, traveling beyond the First Ring Road. Buses are scheduled to run every 30 minutes, but passengers should note that they do not always adhere to the scheduled timings. Bus stops are clearly marked with the official Route Sign posted at each stop, containing all 12 stops. Headphones are provided for this self-guided tour in several languages.

**YANBU المدينة** With a population of a little over 250,000, Yanbu is the second largest city in Medina Province. Although not considered to be of significant tourist interest, the city attracts a number of visitors on account of the sizeable expatriate community working there. It is also a convenient stop for those taking road journeys along the Red Sea, with a range of hotels and restaurants currently not found further up the coast. Most amenities are found in Yanbu city and the Royal Commission to the south of the city centre. Other neighbourhoods include Industrial City adjacent to the Royal Commission. None of these districts should be confused with Yanbu al Nakhel, which is a separate settlement about 50km inland from Yanbu city port, or Yanbu al Bahar, also inland nearby.

## Where to stay

**Holiday Inn** Prince Muqrin bin Abdul Aziz; 014 328 6800; **w** ihg.com. This property delivers what you would expect from a mid-range Holiday Inn, including covered parking, pleasant grounds, outdoor pool & a restaurant. Set a bit away from the city centre, this property offers a quieter environment. **$$$$**

**Novotel Yanbu** Prince Abdul Majeed bin Abdul Aziz, King Abdul Majeed Corniche Rd; 014 398 0000; **w** all.accor.com. In a calming location along the Corniche to the west of the city centre, this Novotel provides a touch of luxury at a reasonable price. It has ample parking, comfortable rooms & a good restaurant where you can choose to eat indoors or outdoors on the terrace overlooking the swimming pool. There is also a children's playground. The front looks out on to a nice view of grass, palm trees & the sea – technically in walking distance if you are brave enough to cross the heavily trafficked road to get to the beach. **$$$**

**Radisson Blu** Abdullah bin Abdul Aziz Rd; 014 322 3888; **w** radissonhotels.com. This hotel is south of Yanbu city on the east side of the port. A good-sized outdoor pool, tennis courts & extensive grounds make it the best hotel in the city for luxury & service. Buffet meals & outdoor table service. **$$$**

**Canary Beach Hotel** King Abdul Aziz Rd; 014 322 2228; **w** canarybeachhotel.com. Value for money for those who are looking for a touch of comfort at a more modest price than many comparable Western chain hotels. This place is in a good location near the city centre & business & historic districts. **$$–$$$**

**Amwaj Yanbu Hotel Apartments** Omar bin Alkhattab Rd, about 2km from the Yanbu Historic District; 014 322 9494. This venue is suitable for longer stays or for those who want a bit of extra space, a kitchen & parking directly in front of the hotel. There is a small coffee shop on the ground floor & a large reception area with plenty of seating, & restaurants & modest grocers are in walking distance. **$$**

**Ibis Yanbu** King Abdul Aziz Rd (Rte 55); 014 354 0666; **w** all.accor.com. Centrally located near the Commercial Port, but not too noisy, with above-average amenities for a typical Ibis. There is an outdoor pool, fitness centre & a restaurant that does a good b/fast buffet & poolside dining later in the day. Parking is in front of the side entrance. $$

**Purple Hotel Suites** Othman bin Affan Rd; 014 391 1777. Near the port but set a few streets inland, with good parking for the area. Suite rates are reasonable for small groups travelling together who want their own rooms. There is a kitchen with a hob, microwave, fridge & washing machine, which may have particular appeal for people who are travelling for an extended period of time. Hotel sign in Arabic only. $$

**Genac Hotel** Omar bin Alkhattab Rd, about 200m from the Yanbu Historic District; 014 322 2220. This hotel's appeal is its low cost & convenient location near the Historic District, restaurants, shops & the port. Basic but clean. Hotel sign in Arabic only; street parking may be tricky at busy times. $

**OYO** w oyorooms.com. There are 6 OYO properties in Yanbu, all in or near the city centre. $

**Where to eat and drink** In addition to the restaurants listed below, there are several casual **seafood eateries** in the Historic District that are worth checking out. There you'll find everything from take-aways and café-style places where you order at the counter, to full restaurants offering table service and alfresco dining.

If you should fancy an **American chain restaurant**, then Yanbu offers a surprisingly wide range of options. Most of these are found in the Royal Commission neighbourhood. There is also a **food court** in the Dana Mall. There is the usual range of Saudi fast-food restaurants throughout Yanbu city.

**Damascene Grill** Cnr Omar bin Alkhattab & Omar bin Abdul Aziz rds; 014 390 6696; 10.30–01.00 Sat–Thu, 13.00–01.00 Fri; w damascenegrill.business.site. If you are missing Levantine specialities like *nakanik*, *kibbe nayah*, *hummus belahm* & *ozzy*, look no further than this family restaurant. The grills won't disappoint. $$$$

**Shangri La Chinese Restaurant Taste Zone** ar Rabban Rd, off King Khalid Rd via al Diyafah Rd; 014 396 0834; 11.00–23.30 Sat–Thu, 14.00–midnight Fri. A large open dining area filled with traditional Chinese décor, right down to the crockery & rosewood furniture. Private rooms are also available. In addition to the usual pan-Chinese menu are a number of Saudi-influenced sushi options. $$$$

**Guzel Saray** King Abdullah Rd between King Abdul Aziz & King Faisal rds; 9200 03652; noon–midnight Sat–Wed, noon–02.00 Thu–Fri. This is an upscale restaurant with a full menu of traditional Turkish dishes & a lovely atmosphere. Those with a sweet tooth will find it very difficult to resist the kunafa & other temptations on display. $$$

**Ostorah Restaurant** King Fahd Rd, just north of al Sahal; 014 393 3331; 11.00–01.00 daily. This restaurant is a good find for those seeking a mix of classic pan-Arabic & Western food, as the extensive menu covers both cuisines well. The focus is on meat & seafood but there are some vegetarian starters & some innovative fresh juice blends too. $$$

**Aryaas Indian Restaurant** Public St Gardens, 1 block east of Rte 55; 054 346 9513; 06.30–midnight daily. This South Indian restaurant makes good use of the local seafood available from the Yanbu fish market. This is also a somewhat friendly place for vegetarians & vegans. $$

**Taste of Damascus** Cnr Omar bin Alkhattab & Omar bin Abdul Aziz rds; 014 390 4593; 11.30–03.00 Sat–Thu, 13.00–03.00 Fri. If you fancy Syrian food but want to keep it cheap & casual, then this shawarma restaurant next door to Damascene Grill will hit the spot. There are a few tables for dining in & counter service with a brisk take-away business. $$

**Shopping** Supermarket chains Farm, Panda and Star are in Yanbu City, Royal Commission or both. The major shopping malls, both in the Royal Commission district of Yanbu, are al Jawhara (off King Fahd & King Khalid rds; 04.00–23.30 Sat–Thu, 14.00–23.30 Fri) and Dana Mall (King Fahd Rd at the junction of Hwy 55; 014 393 5643; w kinan.com.sa; 09.30–midnight Sat–Thu, 14.00–midnight Fri).

The latter has a cinema and a branch of HyperPanda. There is a series of markets centred south of Omar bin Abdul Aziz Road and west of Route 55 selling necessities at rock-bottom prices.

**Sports and activities** If you are a scuba diver or snorkeller, you'll be glad to find this area of the Red Sea is still unspoilt. There are several dive shops in Yanbu where certified divers can organise shore, reef and wreck dives. Snorkellers may also be accommodated if there is space. The following are all PADI dive shops:

**Adventure Diver** aka Diver Adventures; Hwy 55; ☎ 055 530 6292; ⏲ 17.00–22.00 daily

**Diving Bubbles** Off the north end of Omar bin al Khattab Rd; /// backgammon.jeopardy.strangely; ☎ 056 081 0339; **w** bubblesgroup.com; ⏲ 17.00–22.00 Wed–Mon

**Saudi Diving Centre** al Hizam Rd, off King Khalid Rd; ☎ 050 207 0799; ⏲ 10.00–noon & 16.30–23.00 Sun–Thu, 16.30–23.00 Fri–Sat

**Other practicalities** There is a branch of **Riyad Bank** near the Canary Beach Hotel on Route 55 in Yanbu City and a branch of **al Ahli Bank** on King Fahd Road in Yanbu Royal Commission about 1.5km south of al Jawhara Mall. Several branches of **Nahdi pharmacy** (**w** nahdionline.com; ☎ 9200 24673) can be found throughout Yanbu. The branch on King Fahd Road is open 24 hours daily.

**Royal Commission Medical Center** Cnr King Fahd & King Faisal rds; ☎ 014 393 7700; **w** rcymc.med.sa

**Saudi Post** Omar bin Abdul Aziz Rd; ☎ 9200 05700; **w** splonline.com.sa; ⏲ 08.00–21.00 Sun–Thu

**What to see and do** The **Yanbu Historic Area** has been wonderfully restored, with traditional buildings to rival Jeddah's al Balad district. The Night Market is the historic souq, which is now orientated to tourists, with handicrafts heavily featured. Its traditional arches and wooden doors are a lovely change from the architecture of modern shopping malls. There are plenty of choices for dining alfresco where you can catch the evening breeze from the port or simply take a stroll along the promenade.

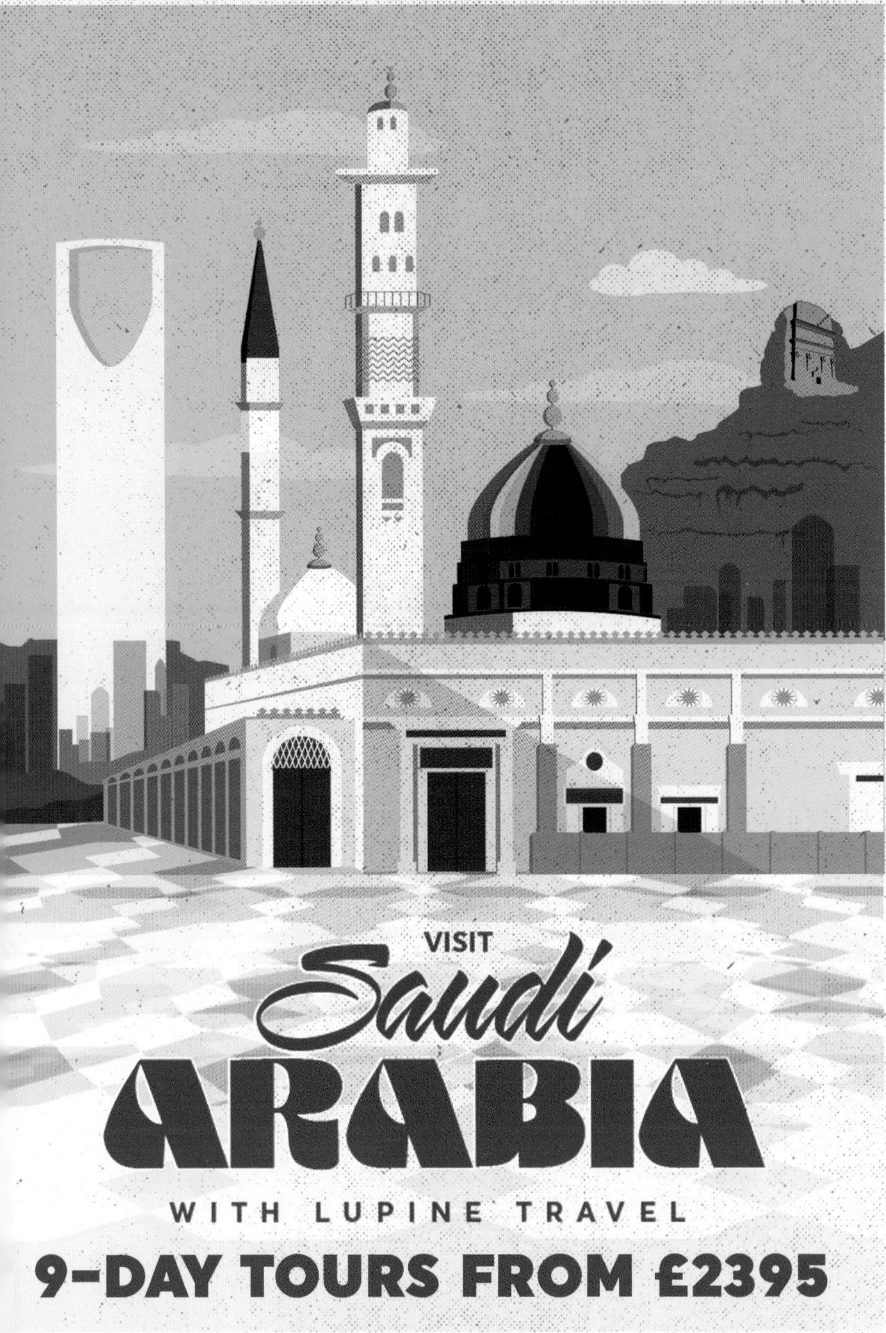

above left (FT/S) With more than 100 tombs on site, Mada'in Saleh – Nabatean sister-city to Jordan's Petra – is a must on any Saudi itinerary PAGE 223

above right (SS) The House of Riffai is a splendid example of an early 20th-century Turkish merchant's house on the remote Farasan Islands PAGE 345

below (R/S) Amara Palace is built in traditional Najrani style, one of the country's many fascinating regional architectures PAGE 331

The drive from Baha to the marble-built Zee al Ayn Heritage Village starts with several kilometres of dramatic switchbacks PAGE 302

above (M/S)

Learn more about the northern reaches of the Kingdom in Sakaka, where Za'abal Castle has defended the population for centuries PAGE 180

right (G/S)

Step back in time at Ushaiqer Heritage Village where traditional homes give visitors a snapshot of early 20th-century life PAGE 153

below (VD/S)

left (AKM/S) For an unforgettable experience, watch the sun set over vast plains from the Edge of the World near Riyadh PAGE 143

below (SW/S) One of many spectacular natural rock formations in al Ula, Elephant Rock is a popular meeting place for coffee as the sun goes down PAGE 229

bottom (H/S) Explorable caves are hidden beneath Jebel Qarah's majestic rock columns PAGE 357

top (H/S)
Remote Wadi Disah in Tabuk Province is the perfect location to get away from it all, whether you prefer to hike, climb or simply picnic PAGE 205

above left (K/S)
Once hunted to near extinction, the Arabian oryx has been successfully reintroduced in protected areas of the Kingdom PAGE 8

above right (H/S)
Hamadryas baboons, Jebel Souda PAGE 318

right (KS/S)
Arabian gazelle PAGE 9

above (AKM/S) Traditional skills can be seen at festivals across the country often promoted through Saudi Seasons. Pictured, a desert safari festival in Buqaiq PAGE 29

below left (AAA/S) Souq Okaz, one of the Kingdom's largest souqs, showcases the full range of Saudi handicrafts PAGE 291

below right (HN/S) The oud is a stringed instrument popular across the Middle East PAGE 38

bottom (GE) Practised by women, the distinctive decorative style of al Qatt al Asiri is found in homes across Asir Province PAGE 310

The *ardah* is a traditional celebratory dance performed by men PAGE 38 above (MHM/S)

Taif's highly valued, world-renowned roses can be brought home as a souvenir in the form of perfumes and oils PAGE 289 below (AJ/S)

above (S/S) The 600m-tall Mecca Clock Royal Tower is a recent addition to the backdrop of Masjid al Haram – Islam's holiest site, which is visited by 3 million hajj pilgrims and several million more umrah pilgrims every year PAGES 284 & 381

below (ALT/S) The green dome of Madinah's Masjid al Nabawi – Islam's second holiest site – is the Prophet Mohammed's tomb, an important place of pilgrimage for many Muslims performing ziyarat PAGES 241 & 388

# 7

# Makkah Province

# منطقة مكّة

*Note: In this guide we use Makkah to refer to the province and Mecca to the city. Road and other names use a variety of spellings, even for the same reference in the same context.*

Also known as Minṭaqat Makkah and Mecca Province, Makkah Province is the most populous in the Kingdom with about 8.6 million people living here. Its three main cities are: Jeddah (population 4.7 million), Saudi Arabia's main port; Mecca (population 1.7 million), Islam's holiest city; and Taif (population 700,000), located in the Sarawat Mountains. Nearly half the population are nationals of other countries, often living and working in the Kingdom for decades.

The original inhabitants in much of the province are people from the Quraysh, Banu Kinanah and Thaqif tribes. When the Ottomans arrived in the 16th century, they took control of most of the Hejaz, including what is now Makkah Province, but were faced with a series of revolts from various Arab groups which dominated much of the 19th and early 20th centuries. Most of the region was later conquered by ibn Saud and became part of the Third Saudi State, now the Kingdom of Saudi Arabia, in 1925.

While modern industry can be found around Jeddah and Taif, historically, the economy of this region has been driven by fishing along Makkah's 700km-long coastline, rich in marine life. Agriculture, especially around Taif, has also been important for centuries. But for more than 1,400 years, famously, Mecca has been an important destination for religious pilgrimage, annually hosting up to 3 million pilgrims during hajj and many more throughout the year. The province is also now a focus of modern secular tourism, with Jeddah a key port of entry into the Kingdom for many visitors. The service industry is therefore well established in Mecca, orientated to religious pilgrims, but also Jeddah more generally.

The geography of Makkah Province is varied, containing the Tihamah coastal plain, the Sarawat Mountains – part of the Hejaz mountain range, which reach up to 2,000m – and the Nafud Desert with its many wadis and oases, located in the east of the province. The climate ranges from hot and humid over the coastal plain to the hot desert climate in the interior, with temperatures reaching the low 40s on the coast and 50°C on the inland plain. Taif and other mountain towns and villages have distinctly cooler temperatures and are generally pleasant year-round, rarely reaching more than the low 30s in the summer months.



## GETTING THERE AND AWAY

**BY AIR** Commercial carriers from all over the Middle East and elsewhere in the world fly into the Kingdom via Jeddah's King Abdul Aziz International Airport (KAIA) – see page 249 for more details. Taif International Airport serves regional

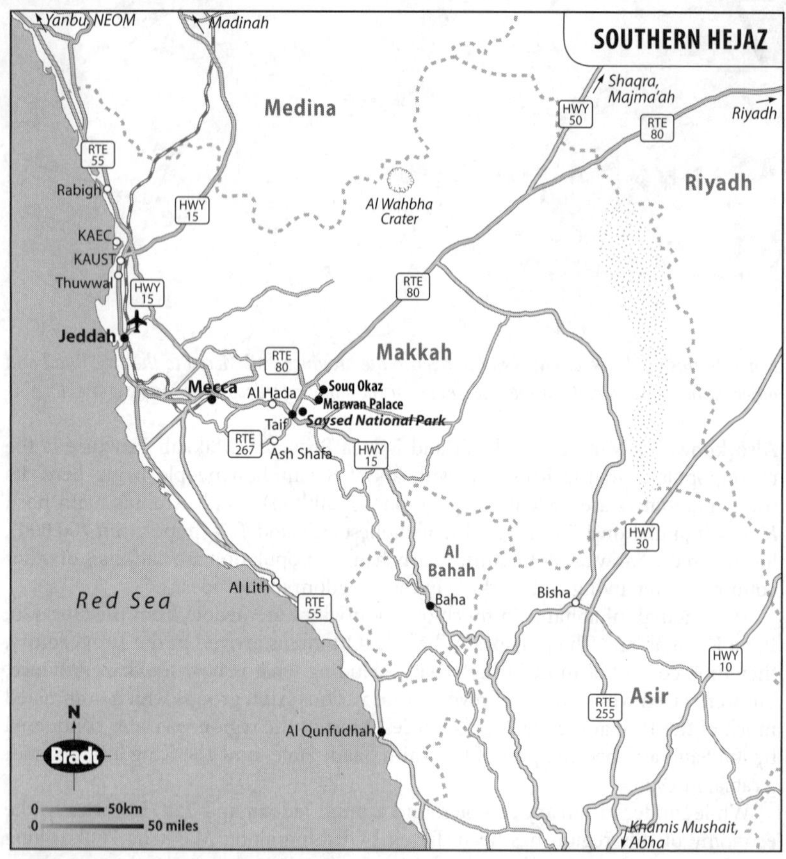


carriers from elsewhere in the Middle East and Turkey. Both airports also have a range of scheduled domestic flights, with KAIA a major hub for Saudia, flynas and flyadeal. Most people travelling to Mecca fly to Jeddah and continue their journey by road or rail.

**BY ROAD** Route 55, which runs along the Red Sea coast for the whole length of the country, is the north–south route into Jeddah. Highway 15 is the major route from the north into Mecca. It continues to the east through Taif and to the south all the way to the Yemeni border. Route 80 is the main route from the east, passing through Taif and Mecca before terminating in Jeddah; however, non-Muslims must be prepared to take a by-pass (page 283) around Mecca. Distances between the main cities are short by Saudi standards, and service stations are found at irregular intervals.

SAPTCO **buses** serve Thuwwal and Rabigh, including King Abdullah University of Science and Technology (KAUST; page 280) and King Abdullah Economic City (KAEC; page 280), as well as Jeddah, Mecca, Taif and some smaller provincial towns.

**BY RAIL** The Haramain High Speed Railway (page 74) serves Makkah from Madinah. Stops in the province include KAEC, two stops in Jeddah, and Mecca.

# JEDDAH جدة

Jeddah (also spelled Jedda, Jiddah, Jidda and Djidda) has a well-deserved reputation as the Kingdom's most progressive city and is often where any social changes in the country first take place. If this is your first visit to Saudi Arabia, Jeddah is a great place to start. It is the Kingdom's second most populous city after Riyadh with about 4.7 million people, and also its most diverse, as Jeddawis' backgrounds extend from indigenous Hejazis to descendants of Muslim pilgrims from all over the world. '*Jeddah Ghair*' (Jeddah is different) is a phrase often heard and it is a fitting motto for this dynamic city.

A trading city for millennia, Jeddah boasts the Jeddah Islamic Seaport, the second largest port in the Middle East after Jebel Ali in Dubai. Fittingly, Jeddah is also referred to as the Bride of the Red Sea. Although there are many theories as to how this important port city got its name, one belief is that it derives from the word *jaddah* (جدة), meaning grandmother. Some believe it is also a reference to the location of the Tomb of Eve.

Jeddah has a tropical arid climate, with warm winters and hot, humid summers. The little rainfall that Jeddah does receive usually occurs in the winter. Owing to the high temperatures and humidity here in the summer, it is best to visit Jeddah between November and April. Summer temperatures typically range from the high 20s to about 40°C.

**HISTORY** Jeddah was originally a fishing port dating back to the 6th century BCE. It is also the gateway to Mecca where most pilgrims arrive in the Kingdom and have done so since the beginning of Islam in the 7th century. During the early days of Islam, Jeddah was controlled by the Rashiduns, followed by the Umayyads and Abbasids, with other groups from the Maghreb attempting to control Jeddah during the first few centuries. The Fattamids, Ayyubids and Mamluks then followed. Jeddah's original walls were built to protect the city from the Portuguese during the time of Vasco da Gama in the late 15th century and who dominated many sea routes of the time. This wall was fortified decades later by the Ottomans, who had gained control of Jeddah in 1521, who then had direct or de facto control for nearly all of the next four centuries until World War I.

The Kingdom of Hejaz was declared by the Sharif Hussein bin Ali al Hashimi in 1916 with the vision of a Hashemite Empire stretching from Aleppo in modern-day Syria and south along the Red Sea Coast to Aden in what is now Yemen. This self-proclaimed Kingdom was defeated by the al Sauds at the end of 1925. The Hejaz region, including Jeddah, was incorporated into the Third Saudi State in 1932, one of the last areas to become part of what is now the Kingdom of Saudi Arabia.

## GETTING THERE AND AWAY

**By air** Jeddah's King Abdul Aziz International Airport (KAIA) is the second major gateway into Saudi Arabia after Riyadh and is the home of Saudia, the national carrier. Scheduled airlines operate out of Terminal 1, which now hosts most international airlines, as well as international and domestic services on Saudia, flynas and flyadeal airlines. This is a welcome new terminal which opened in 2018, finally replacing the old South Terminal. The Haramain High Speed Railway airport station serving the airport and the north of Jeddah is also in this terminal. The North Terminal predominately serves budget regional airlines; the third terminal hosts special hajj and umrah flights.

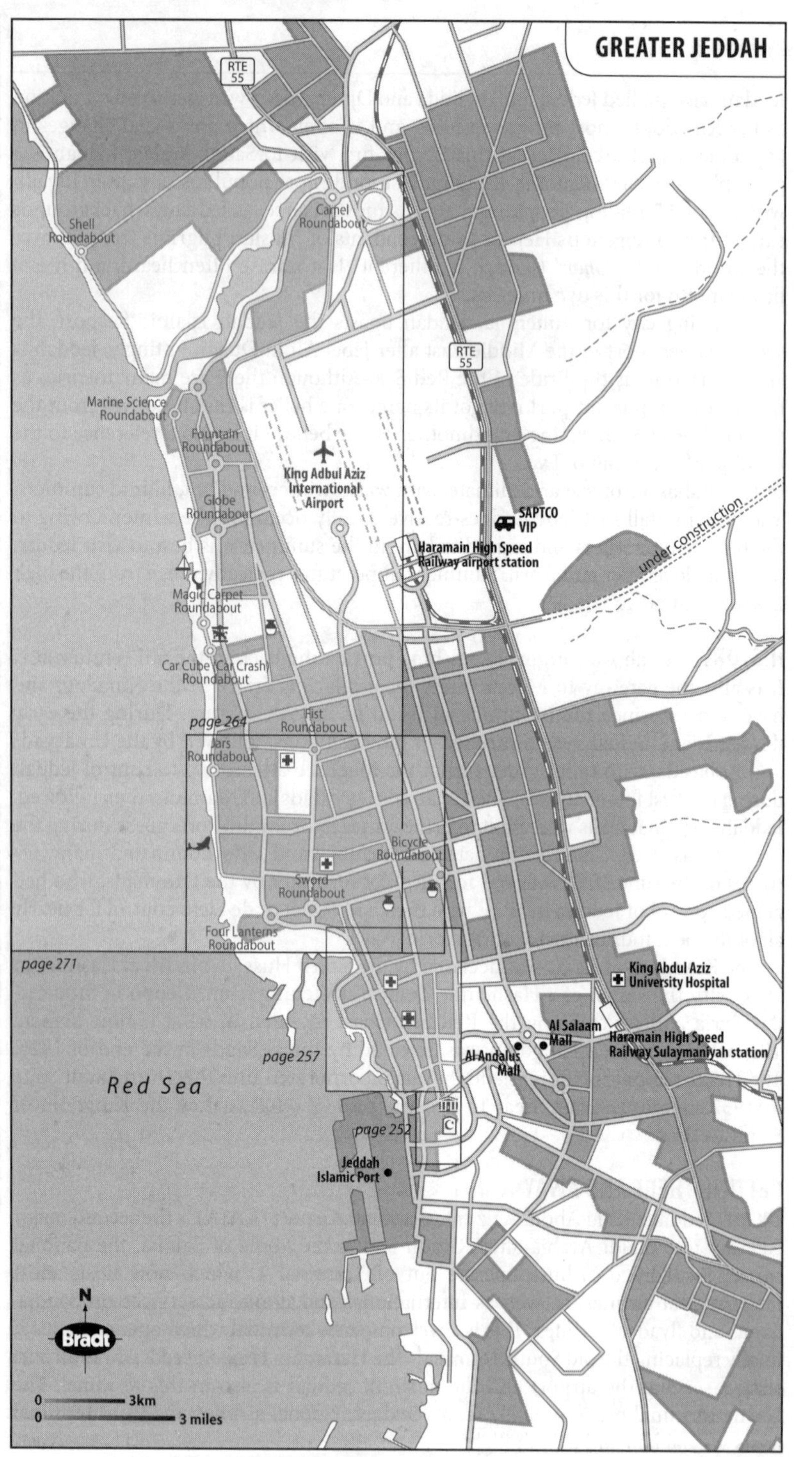
GREATER JEDDAH
RTE 55
Shell Roundabout
Camel Roundabout
Marine Science Roundabout
Fountain Roundabout
King Adbul Aziz International Airport
Globe Roundabout
SAPTCO VIP
Haramain High Speed Railway airport station
under construction
Magic Carpet Roundabout
Car Cube (Car Crash) Roundabout
page 264
Fist Roundabout
Jars Roundabout
Bicycle Roundabout
Sword Roundabout
Four Lanterns Roundabout
page 271
King Abdul Aziz University Hospital
Al Salaam Mall
Al Andalus Mall
Haramain High Speed Railway Sulaymaniyah station
page 257
Red Sea
page 252
Jeddah Islamic Port
N
Bradt
3km
3 miles

**By road** Route 55 is the main route into and out of Jeddah from the north or south, and Highway 80 from the east, although non-Muslims must be prepared to take a bypass around Mecca if arriving in the city from this direction. Highway 15 is the main route from the northeast, via Madinah.

SAPTCO **buses** connect Jeddah to nearly everywhere in the Kingdom. Some services are relatively quick; others seem to stop at nearly every town and village along the way. Jeddah's main SAPTCO station [252 A4], called the Corniche, is located off Baishin (aka Ha'il) Street in al Balad. SAPTCO's VIP station is off the Route 55 Ring Road at Rahmaniya Road near the Donatello Hotel. If you are travelling to Jeddah from Madinah or Yanbu, then you may find SAPTCO's VIP Express more suitable. The non-stop services offer comfortable seating, light food and beverages, free Wi-Fi, personal entertainment screens and toilets. Travel times are similar to the same journey made by private vehicle. For more details, see page 75.

**By rail** The Haramain High Speed Railway operates between Mecca and Madinah via Jeddah (airport and Sulaymaniyah stations) and KAEC. The Mecca station is for the use of Muslims only. Non-Muslims may use the Madinah station as it is located outside of the al Haram zone. The trains can reach a speed of 300km/h, making this an appealing travel option. There is a two-class service and a buffet car offering light snacks. The seats are spacious and have power outlets but do not recline. The stations are new and offer services similar to an airport; security is also airline style. See page 74 for more information.

**By sea** A few cruise ships arrive in Saudi Arabia at the Jeddah Islamic Port in al Balad.

**ORIENTATION** Jeddah has 135 official districts. The key areas that are useful for visitors are outlined below.

The historic district of al Balad is the original walled city in Jeddah's south, adjacent to the northern end of the Jeddah Islamic Port, and designated a UNESCO World Heritage Site owing to its unique culture and architecture. The old town is now mostly populated by expatriates from parts of Asia and Africa. Al Hamra is to the north of al Balad, along or near the Red Sea Coast. Centred around Palestine road (also known as Falasteen), it is the original modern business district, effectively created when Jeddawis first moved out of al Balad. Many of the oldest businesses remain; others have migrated north. This is a bustling and crowded area with people from all walks of life.

Moving north of al Hamra and inland is the district we are calling Tahlia Street and Madinah Road. This area's boundaries are King Abdul Aziz Road to the west and Madinah Road to the east. Both run north to south. Tahlia Street – a main east–west artery – is also known as Prince Mohammed bin Abdul Aziz Road, but Tahlia Street remains in common use. The area around Tahlia Street is known for its luxury hotels and upscale restaurants and shopping and is a great place to see how Jeddah's elite live. Key neighbourhoods here are al Andalus and al Salamah. Madinah Road is a dual carriageway, also known as Route 271, and is home to many of Jeddah's most modern office buildings, business-orientated hotels and a good range of restaurants. Other major north–south arteries are al Safaa, Prince Sultan and Setten roads, where many of Jeddah's newer businesses are located.

Our final area is the Corniche which runs from north of al Hamra to Obhur Bay in the far north of the city, with its eastern boundary around King Abdul Aziz

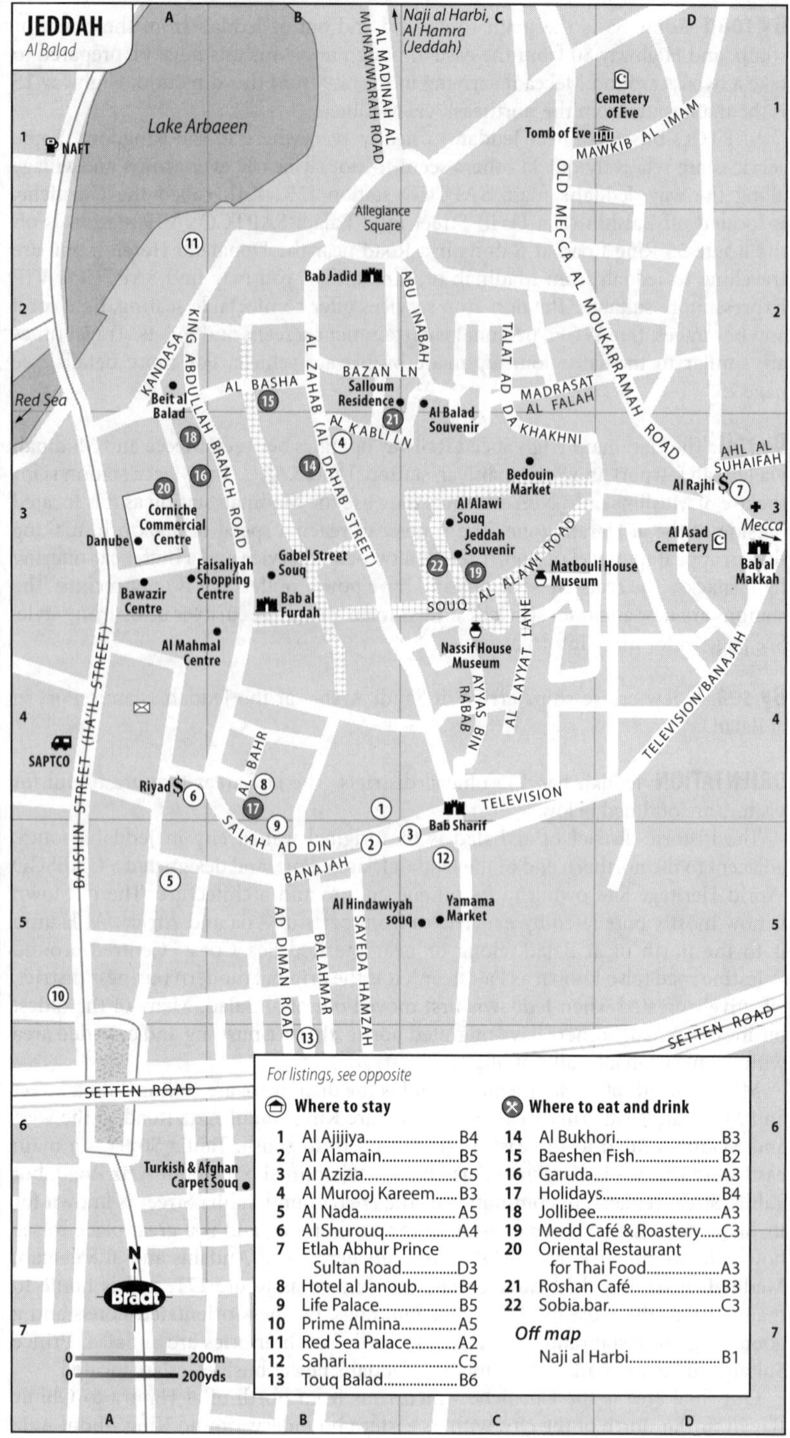
JEDDAH
Al Balad
Lake Arbaeen
NAFT
Red Sea
AL MADINAH AL MUNAWWARAH ROAD
Naji al Harbi, Al Hamra (Jeddah)
Cemetery of Eve
Tomb of Eve
MAWKIB AL IMAM
OLD MECCA AL MOUKARRAMAH ROAD
Allegiance Square
Bab Jadid
ABU INABAH
KANDASA
KING ABDULLAH BRANCH ROAD
AL ZAHAB (AL DAHAB STREET)
AL BASHA
BAZAN LN
Salloum Residence
Al Balad Souvenir
AL KABLI LN
TALAT AD DA KHAKHNI
MADRASAT AL FALAH
Beit al Balad
Bedouin Market
AHL AL SUHAIFAH
Al Rajhi
Corniche Commercial Centre
Danube
Al Alawi Souq
Jeddah Souvenir
SOUQ AL ALAWI ROAD
Matbouli House Museum
Al Asad Cemetery
Mecca
Bab al Makkah
Gabel Street Souq
Faisaliyah Shopping Centre
Bawazir Centre
Bab al Furdah
Nassif House Museum
Al Mahmal Centre
AYYAS BIN RABAB
AL LAYYAT LANE
TELEVISION/BANAJAH
BAISHIN STREET (HA'IL STREET)
SAPTCO
AL BAHR
Riyad
TELEVISION
Bab Sharif
SALAH AD DIN
BANAJAH
AD DIMAN ROAD
BALAHMAR
SAYEDA HAMZAH
Al Hindawiyah souq
Yamama Market
SETTEN ROAD
Turkish & Afghan Carpet Souq
Bradt
0 200m
0 200yds
For listings, see opposite
Where to stay
1 Al Ajijiya B4
2 Al Alamain B5
3 Al Azizia C5
4 Al Murooj Kareem B3
5 Al Nada A5
6 Al Shurouq A4
7 Etlah Abhur Prince Sultan Road D3
8 Hotel al Janoub B4
9 Life Palace B5
10 Prime Almina A5
11 Red Sea Palace A2
12 Sahari C5
13 Touq Balad B6
Where to eat and drink
14 Al Bukhori B3
15 Baeshen Fish B2
16 Garuda A3
17 Holidays B4
18 Jollibee A3
19 Medd Café & Roastery C3
20 Oriental Restaurant for Thai Food A3
21 Roshan Café B3
22 Sobia.bar C3
Off map
Naji al Harbi B1

Road. Key neighbourhoods include Ash Shati to the south, moving north to al Mohammadiyyah, al Murjan and al Basateen before reaching South Obhur at the mouth of Obhur Bay. Less busy than other parts of the city, the Corniche is a good place to come for space and fresh air, and a stroll along the Red Sea shoreline.

**GETTING AROUND** There is no metro or other local train service in Jeddah.

**By bus** The local bus service in Jeddah is run by SAPTCO, though it is used mostly by low-income male expatriate workers and rarely by Saudis; the few women who use these buses must travel at the front of the bus, segregated from male passengers.

There are six routes: 7, 8, 9, B9, 10 and 11, most travelling through al Balad. Most services run approximately every 10 minutes between 05.30 and 23.30, with less frequent service on Fridays. Passengers should purchase a smart card, which costs SAR10 and includes travel credit of SAR5. Single bus journeys cost SAR3. Smart cards can be reloaded at a ticket kiosk, on the SAPTCO app, or with the bus driver.

For detailed route information for Jeddah, visit w saptco.com.sa/buses/transport-services-within-cities/roads-of-jeddah-city.aspx.

**By taxi** Taxis in Jeddah are easier to hail on the street than nearly anywhere else in the Kingdom. All taxis are metered, with rates – as elsewhere – starting at SAR5, plus SAR2 per kilometre travelled; waiting time is charged at SAR30 per hour. These rates can be higher outside the city, in the early hours of the morning, or if you are carrying a lot of luggage.

Realistically, you may wish to consider Uber as an alternative, especially if you're used to using this app in your home country; or Careem, another reliable ride-hailing app (page 76).

**By private car with driver** Many visitors choose to get around Jeddah by hiring a private car and driver through their hotel. The main advantages are flexibility and to minimise hassle with driving violations, accidents, lack of parking facilities and a whole host of general driving challenges. Check rates as they are often set by the hour including waiting time. See page 76 for more information about what to expect.

**On foot** As is the case elsewhere in Saudi Arabia, most people do not walk for any distance longer than from their parked vehicle to their destination. But it is practical to walk around al Balad and parts of al Hamra as these neighbourhoods are compact. When walking around the city, be aware of broken pavements and other hazards, and never trust drivers to stop for you when crossing the street, even if you are already in the road.

**WHERE TO STAY** When considering where to stay in Jeddah, do not underestimate the impact of this city's heavy traffic, lack of parking and general congestion. In addition to morning rush-hour traffic, most of Jeddah's roads are at their busiest from sunset until late in the evening, so you might want to choose a location close to sites and amenities you want to visit to minimise time spent on the roads battling with traffic jams, poor driving and the inevitable delays. Drivers will find it is much easier to park in the Tahlia Street area than in many other neighbourhoods further south. Here you'll find a wide range of Western chain hotels from familiar brands to choose from.

Al Balad, the oldest neighbourhood in Jeddah and now a UNESCO World Heritage Site, was established in the 7th century and is filled with buildings

## DRESS CODE IN JEDDAH

*Jeddah Ghair* translates as 'Jeddah is different' – and Jeddah *is* different Many visitors will notice that, while some **women** wear a plain black abaya, headscarf and niqab, others wear fashionable abayas in the latest on-trend colours with or without a headscarf. A few even push the boundaries by wearing very loose trousers, a knee-length blouse and flowing full-length open robe. The key is to recognise that they cover their bodies with loose clothing from shoulders to toes, all while not revealing their shape. Regardless of what a woman wears, personal grooming and a well-put-together look is very important and shows self-respect.

Female visitors to Jeddah should keep this in mind when deciding what to wear. For some visiting on an organised tour, there is a fair bit of leeway in the dress code as long as you are covered. Some women will feel more comfortable in modest attire from their own culture; others may feel awkward and out of place as soon as they arrive in Jeddah if they are not wearing an abaya.

Independent travellers are advised that it is generally better to err on the side of modesty. It is true that women tend to receive more respect when wearing an abaya, including foreign women. Jeddah is also a great place to shop for abayas once you work out what styles you want to wear. If you do go for the latest trend, keep in mind that it will not be suitable in most of the rest of the Kingdom with the exception of parts of Riyadh, al Khobar and al Ula. Wearing a headscarf is not necessary in Jeddah other than in a mosque if you are able to visit one.

**Men** should remember that they have a dress code too. This includes the same perceptions about modesty, personal grooming and self-respect. Although you may see a few men at leisure wearing shorts in Jeddah, including some that expose the knees, this is still not appreciated by many others. There is some leeway given if actively engaged in exercise. Shorts that cover the knee are fine if it isn't Ramadan. Men should always wear a T-shirt or similar garment that covers their upper body, including upper arms, even at the beach.

*For more comprehensive information about the dress code throughout the Kingdom, see page 100.*

constructed of coral and *roshan* or latticed wooden windows. Most accommodation in this neighbourhood is modest, with many of Jeddah's shoestring options found along Salah ad Din.

The al Hamra and Palestine (Falasteen) area is a good compromise if you do not wish to stay in al Balad but still want to be in the city centre. Accommodation options range from budget to global luxury brands, but parking is generally difficult. If you are on a tight budget but are looking for a more modern option that may not always be available in al Balad, al Hamra is your next best bet.

The Corniche area north of al Hamra is a very popular area to stay. In addition to great Red Sea views, there is a good mix of new and well-established hotels. The area is less crowded by Jeddah standards and much of the Corniche has walking paths, a rarity in the Kingdom. It is also important to note that much of the Corniche north of the Red Sea Mall area is undergoing major building works – it is the location of City Walk, Jeddah Walk Promenade, Formula 1 Street Circuit and other substantial development projects. Although it is near the airport, it is rare to hear flights overhead.

## Al Balad

### *Mid-range*

**Prime Almina Hotel** [252 A5] Baishin St, just north of Setten Rd; ☎ 012 614 1010; w prime-almina-jeddah.hotelmix.co.uk. This hotel is located at the south end of al Balad, conveniently close to both al Andalus & Setten Rds for those looking for quick access to other areas of Jeddah. Overlooking green space, it also has a sense of relative calm. The room options are plentiful, with several suites available for families or groups of travellers. B/fast is included but the restaurant does not offer other meals. There's also a rooftop pool, & tables, from where guests can enjoy views over the city. Convenient on-site parking is a welcome bonus for drivers. **$$$**

**Red Sea Palace Hotel** [252 A2] King Abdullah Branch Rd at Lake Arbaeen; ☎ 012 642 8555; w red-sea-palace.hotels-saudi-arabia.com/en. Located along the Corniche on Lake Arbaeen, this hotel is a good choice if you like to be almost but not quite in the thick of things. It's part of the Saudi-owned Mena hotel group & one of the more comfortable properties in al Balad, complete with a restaurant, fitness centre & pool. It also has rare on-site parking. The property is old but has been refurbished & the service is hit or miss, but it is an oasis of calm in a very busy area. Guests are only a few steps away from the narrow streets of the historic areas & can easily approach from side roads or through Bab al Jadid. **$$$**

### *Budget and shoestring*

Alternatively to those listed below, try al Shurouq [252 A4] (**$**), Life Palace [252 B5] (**$$**), al Alamain [252 B5] (**$**), al Ajijiya [252 B4] (**$**) & al Azizia [252 C5] (**$$**). Be prepared for varying degrees of cleanliness, some male-only accommodation, & noise. Rates for a simple room in the most basic properties start around SAR150 without b/fast.

**Al Murooj Kareem Hotel** [252 B3] Halawah Ln, just east of al Zahab; ☎ 012 644 5052. Part of the OYO group, this hotel has a better reputation for customer service compared with many other OYO properties dotted around the Kingdom & is located in an excellent position just steps away from many of the highlights of al Balad. Most rooms have a balcony. The restaurant is basic but does the job. A lovely seating area next to the hotel entrance provides a front-row seat for people-watching. **$$**

**Al Nada Hotel** [252 A5] al Karantina St south of Salah ad Din; ☎ 012 647 1158; w al-nadah-hotel.business.site. Although this hotel will not win awards for architectural innovation, the property is clean & well located for those who wish to stay in the centre of the bustling markets & near a wide range of restaurants. It is also conveniently near to Jeddah's main SAPTCO bus station. Al Nada offers value for money for the budget conscious without some of the inconveniences often found in this price range. **$$**

**Etlah Obhur Prince Sultan Rd** [252 D3] Old Mecca Rd; ☎ 057 000 1742. The hotel sign is in Arabic only (طريق إتله أبحر الأمير سلطان). Look for red lettering on a white background over the entrance. Located within the triangle of Ahl al Suhaifah & the Old Mecca Rd about 50m from Bab al Makkah, this is a clean apart-hotel in the middle of the hustle & bustle. Some rooms have a good kitchen for self-caterers. There is a small counter in reception where guests can buy soft drinks & snacks. Limited parking; stepped access. **$$**

**Hotel al Janoub** [252 B4] al Bahr, north of Salah ad Din; ☎ 053 889 6861. This accommodation suits those who want to be in the middle of the souq. Steps away from the vegetable market, inexpensive restaurants & many shops selling electronics, this property is basic but does offer a laundry service that comes in handy if you have been travelling for a while. It's over the road from the South Indian Holiday Restaurant & is not too far from the main bus station. **$$**

**Touq Balad** [252 B5] Setten Rd, just east of ad Diman Rd; ☎ 050 811 6822; w touqbalad.business.site. Easily found by its bright yellow & white signs & flags, this hotel is quiet for its location near the souqs & the busy Setten Rd. The rooms can be a bit on the small side if you are used to the often generous-sized rooms in other Saudi hotels, but they are well designed & work for a short stay. A good Arabic b/fast is available at an additional charge & may come in handy as it's a bit of a walk to the restaurants. Parking in front of the hotel. **$$**

**Sahari Hotel** [252 C5] al Zahab; ☎ 012 649 3944. This hotel is about 20m south of Bab al Sharif, with a supermarket on the same street. The rooms are basic but economical. Don't expect many other amenities. This hotel is all about its central location in an area that stays busy until late night. **$**

## Al Hamra and Palestine

### *Luxury and upmarket*

**Crowne Plaza Jeddah** [257 F3] al Mansourah Rd about 100m east of Corniche Rd; 012 260 4900; **w** ihg.com. Set back 1 block from the Corniche, this familiar brand provides the views without being beside the busy road. It's also home to what is considered by many to be the best Japanese restaurant in Jeddah. **$$$$$**

**Narcissus Boutique Hotel al Hamra** [257 B4] Between Corniche & al Woofood rds; 012 261 7700; **w** narcissushotels.com. This Saudi-owned hotel delivers grandeur on a grand scale. It has all of the amenities expected of a 5-star property, delivered with unmistakable Saudi-style hospitality & a selection of restaurants catering to Saudi & Western tastes. The property is located to the south of al Hamra, with easy access to al Balad, & offers views of the Red Sea to the west & city views of the massive Jeddah Flagpole [257 B3] to the east. **$$$$$**

**Park Hyatt Jeddah Marina, Club & Spa** [257 E4] Corniche & al Iskandariyyah near the Bird Roundabout; 012 263 9666; **w** hyatt.com. Here is an oasis of calm in a busy area of Jeddah, with its welcome lawn & paved walk along the Red Sea appreciated by anyone wishing to unwind after a busy day. The lounge & terrace have outdoor seating perfect for watching the sun set over the water, framing the silhouette of the fountain. The service is good, providing everything guests expect at this level, & caters to men & women, with single-sex spas & swimming pools. **$$$$$**

**Ritz Carlton Jeddah** [257 E2] al Corniche Br Rd; 012 231 4444; **w** ritzcarlton.com. Located at the northern end of al Hamra's shoreline, this was once a palace & has long been a fashionable place to stay, dine & simply socialise. It is also a major landmark for businesses who wish to impress with its opulence. Very little is understated in this property. The service is excellent throughout. **$$$$$**

**Intercontinental Jeddah** [257 F3] Hussein Basalamah, Corniche Rd; 012 229 5555; **w** ihg.com. Situated in a prime location overlooking the Red Sea & King Fahd Fountain, this hotel delivers everything you would expect from this luxury brand, including excellent high-end service which can be lacking in some hotels in this category. **$$$$**

**JEDDAH** *Al Hamra & Palestine*
*For listings, see from page 253*

**Where to stay**

1 Al Farhan ........ G4
2 Al Lotus ........ G4
3 Arjan Suites ........ G4
4 Blue Diamond ........ G4
5 Boudl Palestine ........ F1
6 Centro Shaheen ........ C2
7 Crowne Plaza Jeddah ........ F3
8 Emerald ........ C1
9 Hoor Park ........ F4
10 Intercontinental Jeddah ........ F3
11 Mora ........ F4
12 Narcissus Boutique Hotel al Hamra ........ B4
13 OYO 143 Happy Beach Hotel Platini ........ F4
14 Park Hyatt Jeddah Marina, Club & Spa ........ E4
15 Prime Hotel al Hamra ........ F4
16 Ritz Carlton Jeddah ........ E2
17 Rotana Suites ........ F3
18 West Liberty Jeddah ........ F4

**Where to eat and drink**

19 Achaar ........ G3
20 Brasa de Brazil ........ G3
Intercontinental Fish Market ....(see 10)
21 Kandy Restaurants Jeddah ........ D2
22 Marhaba Restaurant Jeddah ........ G3
23 Ramesses ........ E3
24 Saedi Fish ........ E3
25 Sakura ........ F3
26 Saraya Latif ........ F3
27 Shawaya House ........ C3
28 Tikka Express ........ G3
29 Zaatar w Zeit ........ C3

### *Mid-range*

For those looking for mid-range brand name hotels, the Holiday Inn, Mercure, Radisson Blu & Ramada all have properties in this neighbourhood & can be booked directly on their global websites.

**Blue Diamond Hotel** [257 G4] Barh al Arab, just west of al Mashriq al Arabi; 9200 02060; **w** bluediamondhotel.com. This hotel is a good choice for guests looking for top-end luxuries at a more affordable price. Just a few minutes' walk from the Corniche, this newish hotel has well-appointed rooms & a restaurant on the top floor that does a good b/fast buffet as well as à la carte meals later in the day. The underground parking is welcome in this busy neighbourhood. **$$$**

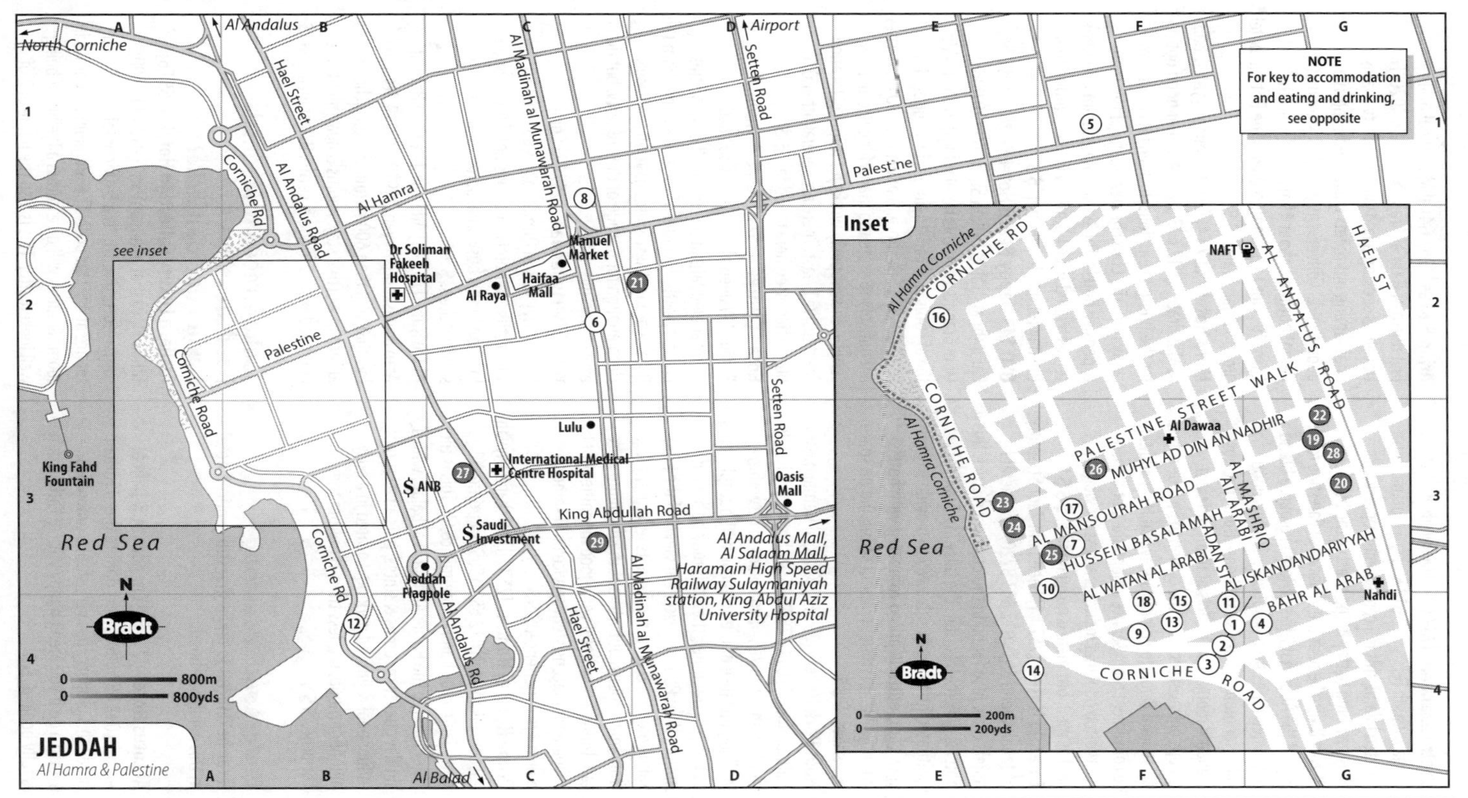
JEDDAH
Al Hamra & Palestine
NOTE
For key to accommodation and eating and drinking, see opposite
North Corniche
Al Andalus
Airport
Hael Street
Al Madinah al Munawarah Road
Setten Road
Palestine
Al Hamra
Corniche Rd
Al Andalus Road
see inset
Dr Soliman Fakeeh Hospital
Al Raya
Haifaa Mall
Manuel Market
Lulu
International Medical Centre Hospital
ANB
Saudi Investment
King Abdullah Road
Oasis Mall
Al Andalus Mall, Al Salaam Mall, Haramain High Speed Railway Sulaymaniyah station, King Abdul Aziz University Hospital
Corniche Road
King Fahd Fountain
Red Sea
Jeddah Flagpole
Al Andalus Rd
Al Balad
800m
800yds
Inset
Al Hamra Corniche
CORNICHE RD
CORNICHE ROAD
NAFT
AL ANDALUS ROAD
HAEL ST
PALESTINE STREET WALK
Al Dawaa
MUHYL AD DIN AN NADHIR
AL MANSOURAH ROAD
HUSSEIN BASALAMAH
AL MASHRIQ AL ARABI
ADAN ST
AL WATAN AL ARABI
AL ISKANDANDARIYYAH
BAHR AL ARAB
Nahdi
200m
200yds

**Centro Shaheen** [257 C2] al Madinah al Munawwarah Rd; ☎ 012 618 8888; w rotana.com. Located inland, this is a convenient property for those wishing to stay in the heart of the business district & also be near the vibrancy of Palestine road. Part of the Abu Dhabi-based Rotana group, a brand renowned for its Arab hospitality, it offers good value for money. Guests can choose from spacious standard rooms & suites to suit many different groups of travellers, with the option to include b/fast. Restaurant & rooftop dining are available, in addition to convenient room service around the clock. There is a rooftop pool that indicates access for women as well as men, but there is no guarantee. **$$$**

**Emerald Hotel** [257 C1] Saeed bin Zaqr St, south of Jabal Aboud St; ☎ 012 663 8220; w emerald-hotels.com. Also found in the business district, this hotel is only metres from the busy Madinah Rd yet is situated just far enough away to provide a quiet stay. Competitively priced compared with hotels with similar amenities without scrimping on space or service. **$$$**

**Hoor Park Hotel** [257 F4] Khalij al Qamar, near Bahr al Arab; ☎ 012 275 5505; w hoor-park.hotels-saudi-arabia.com/en. If you want to be within walking distance of the Corniche without splashing out on a 5-star hotel, then this may be a good option. Hoor Park has excellent views of the King Fahd Fountain & Corniche from its restaurant & from many rooms but without the premium price tag. This is a new hotel with good amenities but be prepared for inconsistent service until some staff gain more experience. **$$$**

**Prime Hotel al Hamra** [257 F4] al Iskandariyyah east of Felkah St; ☎ 012 651 1505; w prime-hotel-jeddah-al-hamra.hotelmix.co.uk. This is the sister hotel to the Prime Almina in al Balad, with a similar quality of rooms & suites, plus a restaurant, indoor pool & limited parking. Located in a busy neighbourhood, it is less than 1km from the Corniche. **$$$**

### *Budget and shoestring*

It can be difficult to find a shoestring-priced hotel in this neighbourhood.

**Al Lotus Hotel** [257 F4] Cnr Adan St & Bahr al Arab; ☎ 012 652 0009. Next door to the al Farhan hotel, this property has very similar amenities. Worth a go if you aren't happy with al Farhan or it is fully booked. **$$**

**Arjan Suites** [257 G4] al Mashriq al Arabi just north of Bahr al Arab; ☎ 054 688 4020. For travellers seeking a laid-back property that is unassuming but meets basic needs, this is a good choice. Conveniently located in a quiet neighbourhood about 1km inland from the Corniche. Not to be confused with the Rotana hotel group's Arjan brand. **$$**

**Mora Hotel** [257 F4] Cnr al Iskandariyyah & Bab al Mandrab; ☎ 012 677 3333. Another good option for the budget conscious, located less than 1km away from the Corniche near many of the more expensive hotels. The Garden Restaurant & Lounge serves a good b/fast buffet & is open throughout the day for lunch & dinner. **$$**

**OYO 143 Happy Beach Hotel Platini** [257 F4] Cnr Bahr al Arab & Felkah St; ☎ 800 820 0063; w oyorooms.com. This hotel is located alongside the al Lotus & al Farhan hotels, just under 1km from the Red Sea shore. While most OYO properties are unlikely to score top marks for customer service, this property works for its price, location & extensive b/fast. There are several other OYO properties elsewhere in Jeddah. **$$**

**Rotana Suites** [252 F3] Cnr al Mansourah & abu al Waleed al Beji; ☎ 012 663 6363; w rotanajeddahhotel.com. Don't confuse this property with the hotel of the same name from the Rotana group. These suites have all the basics & are clean enough for the age of the property, but don't expect any frills. **$$**

**West Liberty Jeddah** [257 F3] Cnr al Iskandariyyah & al Qunaitirah; ☎ 053 769 5055; w westlibertyhotels.com. This hotel is in a good location in this busy area. Some rooms have a small kitchen. **$$**

**Al Farhan** [257 F4] Adan St, between Bahr al Arab & al Iskandariyyah; ☎ 9200 19939. Its good location, less than 600m from the Corniche, makes al Farhan worth a stay. Rooms & apartments are equipped with a fridge & kettle. B/fast included. **$**

## Tahlia Street and Madinah Road areas

### *Luxury and upmarket*

**Assila, a Luxury Collection Hotel** [265 F6] Tahlia St, east of al Aanani St; ☎ 012 231 9800; w marriott.com. This is a 5-star hotel with 5-star service at a 5-star price. The premium amenities in rooms & suites will give guests a feeling of being well looked after. This is also the home of 2 of

Jeddah's best restaurants, Pampas & Aubergine, so you don't need to leave the hotel or even your room to indulge. The rooftop swimming pool has a lovely seating area from where you can enjoy views overlooking the city. **$$$$$**

**Adagio Jeddah City Centre** [265 G6] Cnr Madinah Rd & al Yanooaawi; ☎ 012 233 7911; w all.accor.com. Conveniently located in the heart of central Jeddah, this hotel delivers high-level service at standards usually expected from hotels with grander reputations. The entrance gives directly on to the street & has several steps, so ask for assistance with your luggage & any parking requirements as this is a crowded neighbourhood & parking at the hotel might be full. The venue is focused on functionality over fashion, from the room designs to the shading over the outdoor swimming pool, but it's a great balance for guests who want comfort but don't want to splash out for the bling. **$$$$**

**Casablanca Grand** [265 F1] Madinah Rd, opposite the Mall of Arabia; ☎ 012 222 2203; w casablanca-ksa.com. This hotel boasts spacious rooms & the usual upmarket amenities. Its Lemon Grass Restaurant offers a fusion of pan-Asian cuisine, where you can choose a Japanese-style dish that comes with a performance common in teppanyaki restaurants. The hotel's higher price point reflects its convenience for the airport. **$$$$**

**Hotel Galleria by Elaf** [265 F6] Tahlia St, east of al Foutaihi St; ☎ 012 422 2555; w thehotelgalleria.com. If you want opulence Jeddah style, then this may be just the place. It is situated in the Galleria Mall, next door to Assila. The gym, salon, spa & health club facilities for men & women are particularly welcome – they are single-sex but of equal quality. There are 6 restaurants & cafés to choose from, including Vaquero, an Argentinian favourite. **$$$$**

**The House Hotel** [265 E4] Jeddah City Yard, between Abdul Maqsud Khojah Rd & al Farisi St; ☎ 012 601 5300; w househotels.com. This relaxed boutique accommodation is the first Saudi member of The Design Group of independent hotels, promoting social hubs, sustainability, wellness & creativity, all while maintaining touches of local culture. This is a stay with a difference. The choice of restaurants & coffee shops in the complex is terrific. **$$$$**

**Jeddah Marriott** [265 F1] Madinah Rd, north of Bader Hanin Rd; ☎ 012 236 6668; w marriott.com. This new Marriott replaces the dowager Palestine road property. From the modern design to the friendly service, this is a welcome addition to the Jeddah hotel scene. For those looking for a predictably good experience from an upmarket, brand-name property, this hotel delivers. Don't miss the chance to dine or relax around the rooftop pool. **$$$$**

**Movenpick Jeddah City Star** [265 F1] Madinah Rd, north of Bader Hanin Rd; ☎ 012 618 0000; w movenpick.com. Not to be confused with the older property along Tahlia St, this is a slightly more modest & affordable hotel with all the usual amenities expected of this hotel chain. It's immediately south of the Marriott. **$$$$**

**Movenpick Tahlia** [265 F6] Cnr Abdul Rahman al Tubalshi & Hael St; ☎ 012 213 2000; w movenpick.com. Although this older hotel may have less kerb appeal than some, inside it has been refurbished to a high standard throughout. It is a particularly attractive option for those who want a central but quiet location near Tahlia St. It is home to the Rasoi by Vineet Indian fine-dining restaurant (page 267), & several other upmarket restaurants are in walking distance. **$$$$**

### *Mid-range*

**Ascott Tahlia** [265 G6] Cnr Tahlia & Aalam al Islam sts; ☎ 012 283 2322; w discoverasr.com. This is a chic serviced apartment property that provides the amenities expected from an upmarket hotel, including a restaurant, gym & swimming pool. Guests can choose from studios to 3-bedroom apartments. Each comes with a small kitchen, washer & dryer, making this a good choice if you like your comforts but prefer to self-cater or have simply been travelling for a while & want to take care of your laundry. It's in a great location with a range of restaurants within walking distance. **$$$**

**Boudl al Tahlia** [265 H5] Tahlia St, east of al Hareth bin Jablah Rd; ☎ 012 261 4131; w boudl.com. This Saudi-owned chain offers a selection of rooms & suites that appeal to its many Saudi guests & their families. It's located directly on the busy dual carriageway, so make sure you ask for a quiet room. Underground parking available. Other Boudl properties that usually deliver the same service standards but in properties of differing age include **Boudl Hera** [271 C5] (Hira St, west of al Manahij St; ☎ 012 694 7755; **$$$**), **Boudl Palestine** [257 F1] (Palestine, east of al Afeyah St;

012 670 7000; **$$$**) & **Boudl Qouraish** [265 E1] Qouraish Rd, west of Yahya bin Abdul Muti St; 9200 00666; **$$$**). **$$$**

**Casablanca Hotel** [265 F2] Saqer Qouraish Rd, between bin Nasser & Souhaib bin Sinan sts; 012 682 7771; **w** casablanca-ksa.com. Owned by a Saudi organisation in the hospitality business for decades, this well-located hotel provides a high standard of service. There is a wedding hall on site which may pique the curiosity of some guests who may have yet to see a Saudi wedding. **$$$**

**Centro Salama Hotel** [265 F2] Madinah Rd, south of Saqer Qouraish Rd; 012 230 3333; **w** rotana.com. This is the sister property of the Centro Shaheen hotel in al Hamra & is in a good location for easy access to most areas of north Jeddah. If you are looking for the high standards usually provided by the Rotana group, this property delivers. **$$$**

**Le Méridien** [265 G5] Cnr al Madinah & al Nahdaa rds; 012 283 2322; **w** marriott.com. One of the older properties in this terrific location, Le Méridien has been refurbished but somehow still feels old. It's usually less expensive than other well-known brands in this category & location. **$$$**

**Velvet Inn** [265 E2] Cnr al Sheikh al Sadid & Saqer Qouraish rds; 012 639 4517; **w** thevelvethotel.com. This is the best of both worlds, providing excellent value in a highly desirable neighbourhood that usually demands a premium price. The rooms & suites are equipped with an above-average kitchen that includes a generous fridge, hob, microwave, decent selection of crockery & cutlery, & a washing machine. **$$$**

### *Budget and shoestring*

Tahlia St & Madinah Rd are not the easiest areas to find rock-bottom accommodation. Try your luck on Abdallah al Zawawi & Saqer Qouraish between al Yamamah & Madinah rds, but be prepared to pay more than you may have budgeted for as prices fluctuate frequently by demand, sometimes daily.

**Ahlah an Ayam Hotel** [265 F3] Abbas Hafez & Abdul Rahman bin Ahmad as Sidayri; 012 612 6688. This is a budget hotel from the Capital O range of OYO hotels. It's in a good location, though parking is limited to the few spaces in front of the property. Rooms have a basic kitchenette with a sink & microwave handy for reheating a take-away. The service is above average for this brand. **$$**

**Ibis Jeddah City Centre** [264 B1] Cnr Madinah Rd & al Yanbuaawi; 012 233 7911; **w** ibis.accor.com. One of 2 Ibis properties that will satisfy guests who are looking for brand familiarity at a modest price & a good location. The After Eleven Lounge here has live music. Both properties have a restaurant, gym & swimming pool on site. **$$**

**Ibis Jeddah Malik Road** [265 G6] King Abdullah Branch Rd, south of Urwah bin al Jaid Rd; 012 692 1444; **w** ibis.accor.com. See also Ibis Jeddah City Centre. There is limited underground parking next door. **$$**

**Mirada Purple** [264 C2] Cnr Ahmad al Attas & Abdul Aziz al Khouraiji rds; 012 694 7038; **w** mirada.sa/eng. Located in the al Zahra neighbourhood, with clean & spacious rooms, each with a desk & seating area. There is no kitchen but there are plenty of fast-food & casual dining options in walking distance. **$$**

**Orans Suites 2** [265 F1] Qouraish Rd, west of al Saab bin Jathamah; 012 662 6317. This is a good choice for those looking for a lot of space & a good-sized kitchen. The furniture is old but the location is convenient. **$$**

**Green Leaf Hotel** [265 F1] Qouraish Rd, west of al Khateeb al Tabrizi Rd; 012 619 9994; **w** greenleafhotel.sa. This is about as inexpensive as it gets in this part of Jeddah, located slightly east of Madinah Rd. There is a good Indian restaurant & another good Levantine sandwich shop in the same building, making it a bonus for those uninterested in going far for a meal. **$**

## Corniche

### *Luxury and upmarket*

**Jeddah Hilton** [271 C5] Corniche Rd; 9200 03800; **w** hilton.com. This popular hotel is a favourite for tourists & business professionals alike. Ideally situated at the southern end of the park along the Corniche, as well as the promenade, with the Corniche Beach across the street. Top-notch amenities include the brilliant gourmet Ginger Leaf Indian restaurant & Amwaj, the Saudi-French restaurant. **$$$$$**

**Rosewood Jeddah Hotel** [271 C6] Corniche Rd, south of Said bin Amir Rd; 012 260 7111; **w** rosewoodhotels.com. The entrance is around the corner off Abi Bakr an Nahwi St. The rooms & suites are appointed with every amenity imaginable & come complete with 24hr butler service. The Sky Lounge is a great way to enjoy a perfect sunset view. The small circular rooftop pool is more suited for dipping than for swimming. **$$$$$**

**Shangri La** [271 C5] Cnr Corniche Branch & Jubayr bin al Harith rds; ☎ 012 696 8888; w shangri-la.com. Near the Magic Carpet Roundabout in the centre of the North Jeddah Corniche, this hotel is convenient for every key destination in this prestigious neighbourhood. The rooms & suites have floor-to-ceiling windows with most providing sea views. In addition to the Waterfront Kitchen & a refined coffee shop, the Shang Palace restaurant offers a selection of authentic Cantonese, Szechuan & Yunnan dishes. **$$$$$**

**Waldorf Astoria** [271 C6] Corniche Rd, Qasr al Sharq; ☎ 9200 09565; w hilton.com. Situated next door to the Jeddah Hilton, this might be the most prestigious hotel in Jeddah at present, an oasis of tranquillity in a very busy city. Guests can enhance their well-being in the property's terrific spa. Pure elegance from the rooms to the restaurants to the grounds. As you would expect, the service is reassuringly at the highest of global standards. **$$$$$**

**Four Points Sheraton** [271 B2] Cnr Corniche Branch & Ahmed as Sawi rds; ☎ 012 211 8899; w marriott.com. Note the entrance is to the back & is accessed by turning left off Ahmed as Sawi Rd. Newly built, this friendly hotel is in a prime position on the south shore of Obhur Bay. Rooms are well designed, with practical use of space. The junior suites have a fridge & separate living area that flows rather than isolates. Room service is very good without breaking the bank. The restaurant offers standard international cuisine expected from a global brand. Expect upmarket service & upmarket prices as more travellers discover this surprising gem. **$$$$**

**Radisson Blu** [271 C5] Corniche Branch Rd, south of the Jeddah Corniche Circuit; ☎ 012 511 0000; w radissonhotels.com. This is a reasonably new property situated conveniently along the Corniche not far from the Globe Roundabout, with a great view in both directions. The rooms & suites are comfortable without the distractions meant to impress. Some of the larger suites have separate living & sleeping rooms. Choose from indoor & outdoor dining options. This hotel offers value for money in this class in an upscale area that continues to be developed for the luxury market. **$$$$**

### *Mid-range*

**Al Bilad Hotel** [271 C5] Prince Faisal bin Fahd Rd; ☎ 012 694 4777; w albiladhotel.com. Not to be confused with the al Balad Inn Hotel about 2km south near the Elite Jeddah Hotel. Located just south of the Sheraton Jeddah, this hotel is a great compromise for the budget conscious who still want comfort & a favourable location. The large swimming pool, garden greenery & ample parking are all done well compared with similar mid-range properties. It has a years-long reputation for offering a good Fri brunch. **$$$**

**Elite Jeddah Hotel** [271 C6] Prince Faisal bin Fahd Rd; ☎ 055 993 6438; w luxury-hotel-551.business.site. This hotel is found along the grassy stretch of this road known as the Open Air Museum. It is about 400m north of al Nawras Park, ideal for runners & outdoor exercise buffs. The rooms are spacious & have the basics. Modestly priced for its location, it is only a short walk to several coffee kiosks along the Corniche. **$$$**

**Sheraton Jeddah** [271 C5] Prince Faisal bin Fahd Rd, just south of Car Cube Roundabout; ☎ 012 699 2212; w marriott.com. This venerable hotel remains popular with Saudi guests & business visitors. It's in the fashionable Ash Shati neighbourhood not far from the much more expensive Hilton, Waldorf Astoria & Shangri La properties. The gardens are pleasant with welcome colour from flowering bushes. It has been unevenly renovated, with rooms in the main building brought up to date. Only lower-floor rooms have desks. The rooms in the annexe near the overflow car park feel like a forced exile, requiring an outdoor walk to access hotel facilities, including the restaurants. There is good news, especially for women who wish to swim & anyone who wants a break from the dress code, as the hotel allows guests to access the Red Sea Resort in North Obhur (page 279). **$$$**

**Velvet Inn Hotel Suites** [271 C5] al Najdi, east of Abi al Fadl al Koufi Rd; ☎ 012 288 1600; w velvet-hotel-suites-jeddah.booked.net. This is the sister property of the Velvet Hotel, catering for extended stays or for guests who prefer to use the well-equipped kitchen & in-room laundry facilities. It is further north & closer to the Corniche than its sister hotel & is in a quiet neighbourhood near several restaurants & a branch of Danube supermarket. **$$$**

### *Budget*

The Corniche is not a budget destination. The least expensive properties in this area are generally above US$100 per room per night. These budget properties may be the best choices nearby.

**OYO 148 Diamond Beach Hotel** [271 C5] Hira St, just east of King Abdul Aziz Rd; ☎ 011 510 0453; w oyorooms.com. The rooms have a decently equipped kitchen but don't expect many accoutrements. Service standards are pretty low, to the point that some prospective guests inspect the room before deciding whether or not to check in, especially for cleanliness & fully operational lamps, shower heads, taps & other kitchen appliances. If you need to be in this area of Jeddah & are on a tight budget, this is probably the most economical option. There is decent parking for the area. **$$**

**Quiet Dreams Hotel Qurish Branch** [271 D1] Cnr Quraish Ln & al Madrassah al Saoudiah; ☎ 012 288 0575. Not far from the North Terminal entrance to the airport, this is a basic apartment hotel with modest kitchens. It is a good choice for visitors passing through Jeddah heading north or those who want a low-key stay. Limited parking near the entrance is at an oddly steep angle. There are many restaurants on the other side of the bay that might appeal, saving a longer drive towards Jeddah. There is a branch of the Farm Supermarket nearby. **$$**

**WHERE TO EAT AND DRINK** As you might expect, restaurants in al Balad usually offer good value at a relatively low cost. It is also a good place to sample authentic cuisines from other (non-Saudi) cultures represented in the neighbourhood. Whether you are looking for a gourmet experience, good food in your hotel or a casual spot popular with local residents, the al Hamra and Palestine (Falasteen) area has it all. If you feel spontaneous, then walk along the Corniche or the al Andalus end of Palestine. Walk to see what catches your eye. The Corniche offers a wide choice – various Middle Eastern cuisines, healthy options and good cafés – and views of the Red Sea. If you are looking for the latest trendy restaurant, both for food and the experience, head inland to the areas around Tahlia Street and Madinah Road.

Across the city, Jeddah's sweet tooth is easily satisfied with a wide range of **bakeries**, where you will find everything from traditional French patisserie to Lebanese treats. If you're looking for cakes and other desserts, try local bakery chain Munch; and branches of Al Hatab, the upmarket bakery and deli, are just as good in Jeddah as in other cities.

Coffee aficionados will be happy in Jeddah: **coffee kiosks** are strategically located in places such as petrol station forecourts and there are dozens along the Corniche, so you are never far from satisfying your next caffeine craving. Barns, Emma and Kyan are all popular but there are many more.

Don't hesitate to pop into a **shawarma** place if you are peckish and happen to be passing by – anywhere busy is likely to be a good bet. Finally, a large number of **fast-food** chain restaurants, originating from the Philippines to South Africa to the US, add to Saudi's own favourites throughout Jeddah.

## Al Balad

**Al Bukhori** [252 B3] al Zahab, about 20m south of the al Murooj Kareem Hotel; ☎ 050 231 9026; ⏱ 11.00–midnight daily. You will find traditional Saudi grills & meat-&-rice dishes here, with take-away as well as table & floor seating. **$$**

**Baeshen Fish Restaurant** [252 B2] East of King Abdul Aziz Branch Rd & south of al Basha; ☎ 050 367 4710; ⏱ 13.00–23.00 daily. The restaurant has a thriving take-away business but has limited seating upstairs & outdoors. The simple menu is unpretentious, & guests pay by the weight of their chosen fish. **$$**

**Garuda** [252 A3] al Mawared Alleyway opposite Corniche Commercial Centre; ☎ 053 295 8642; ⏱ 11.00–23.00 daily. Try some authentic

Indonesian cuisine for a change. It's an order-at-the-counter place, with cafeteria-style seating. The menu is in Arabic & Bahasa Indonesian but includes photos. $$

**Holidays** [252 B4] al Bahr, north of Salah ad Din; 012 649 4947; w holidaysgroups.com; 09.30–00.30 Sat–Thu, 13.30–00.30 Fri. This is another restaurant with a popular Indian & Chinese menu. Most of the Indian dishes are south Indian, with many vegetarian choices, some of which are served on a banana leaf. They also serve simple pan-Chinese stir-fry dishes. Dine in or take away. $$

**Jollibee** [252 A3] King Abdul Aziz Branch Rd, south of al Basha; 012 290 7995; 08.00–21.30 Sat–Thu, 17.00–22.00 Fri. Order the Yumburger or Chickenjoy to taste the most popular meals in this famous Filipino fast-food restaurant. $$

**Medd Café & Roastery** [252 C3] Souq al Alawi, about 100m north of Naseem Hse; 08.00–23.00 Sat–Wed, 08.00–midnight Thu–Fri. The sign is above the small window to the right of the entrance in stylised, abbreviated Arabic-only initials, but it is well known so ask if you can't find it. You can't beat the atmosphere here – the lovely interior is in the style of al Balad homes with wood trim, a mosaic floor & outdoor tables both in front of the coffee shop & on the rooftop. The coffee, sandwiches, pastries & other goodies will appeal to Saudis & visitors alike. $$

**Oriental Restaurant for Thai Food** [252 A3] Corniche Commercial Centre, al Mawared Alleyway; 012 644 6263; 10.45–22.30 daily. Despite the name, this restaurant serves a mix of Thai, Indonesian, Malaysian & generic Chinese dishes, many with fish. $$

**Roshan Café** [252 B3] Cnr al Kabli & Qabil Ins; 059 020 3583; probably evenings. This coffee shop, with no published opening hours, is in a traditional Jeddawi house that is now also a museum. Pop in if the doors are open & enjoy a coffee & cake here when you need to take a break. $$

**Naji al Harbi** [252 B1] Cnr al Matthaf Ln & al Madinah al Munawwarah Rd, east of Bab Jadid; 056 590 4533; 07.00–02.00 daily. This well-known restaurant serves legendary beef kebabs with tahini, loved by Saudis for decades. It is a no-frills restaurant but worth a visit for the food & the experience. $

**Sobia.bar** [252 C3] Barhat Amru bin Hilal, around the corner from the Jeddah Souvenir Shop; 050 564 9740; 17.00–23.00 daily. Less than 50m from Naseem Hse, Sobia.bar's rooftop location gives an excellent panorama of much of al Balad. It's a great place to relax once you have finished exploring the area. The *sobia* – a Hejazi cold smoothie made of bread, barley or oats & blended with cardamom, cinnamon & sugar – is excellent, & there's gelato & baked goods too. $

## Al Hamra and Palestine

**Intercontinental Fish Market Restaurant** [257 F3] Inside Intercontinental hotel, Hussein Basalamah, Corniche Rd; 012 229 5555; w ihg.com; 13.00–16.00 & 19.00–01.00 daily. Fish markets have been a tradition in many

**JEDDAH** *Tahlia Street & Madinah Road*
*For listings, see from page 253*

**Where to stay**

1 Adagio Jeddah City Centre....G6
2 Ahlah an Ayam....F3
3 Ascott Tahlia....G6
4 Assila....F6
5 Boudl al Tahlia....H5
6 Boudl Qouraish....E1
7 Casablanca....F2
8 Centro Salama....F2
9 Green Leaf....F1
10 Hotel Galleria by Elaf....F6
11 The House....E4
12 Ibis Jeddah City Centre....G6
13 Ibis Jeddah Malik Road....B1
14 Le Méridien....G5
15 Mirada Purple....C2
16 Movenpick Tahlia....F6
17 Orans Suites 2....F1
18 Velvet Inn....E2

*Off map*

Casablanca Grand....F1
Jeddah Marriott....F1
Movenpick Jeddah City Star....F1

**Where to eat and drink**

19 Adani Bar....E4
20 Al Wazzan....H5
21 Boga Tariq al Hussaini Superfoods....C3
22 Bread Ahead Bakery & School....C3
23 Fogo de Chao....D3
24 Leila min Lebnen....E5
25 Lusin....D6
26 Moon Shell....E4
Rasoi by Vineet....(see 16)
27 The Social Kitchen....E4
28 Toki....C4
29 Vaquero....F6
30 Yemeni Village....F6

*Off map*

Hashi Basha....H3

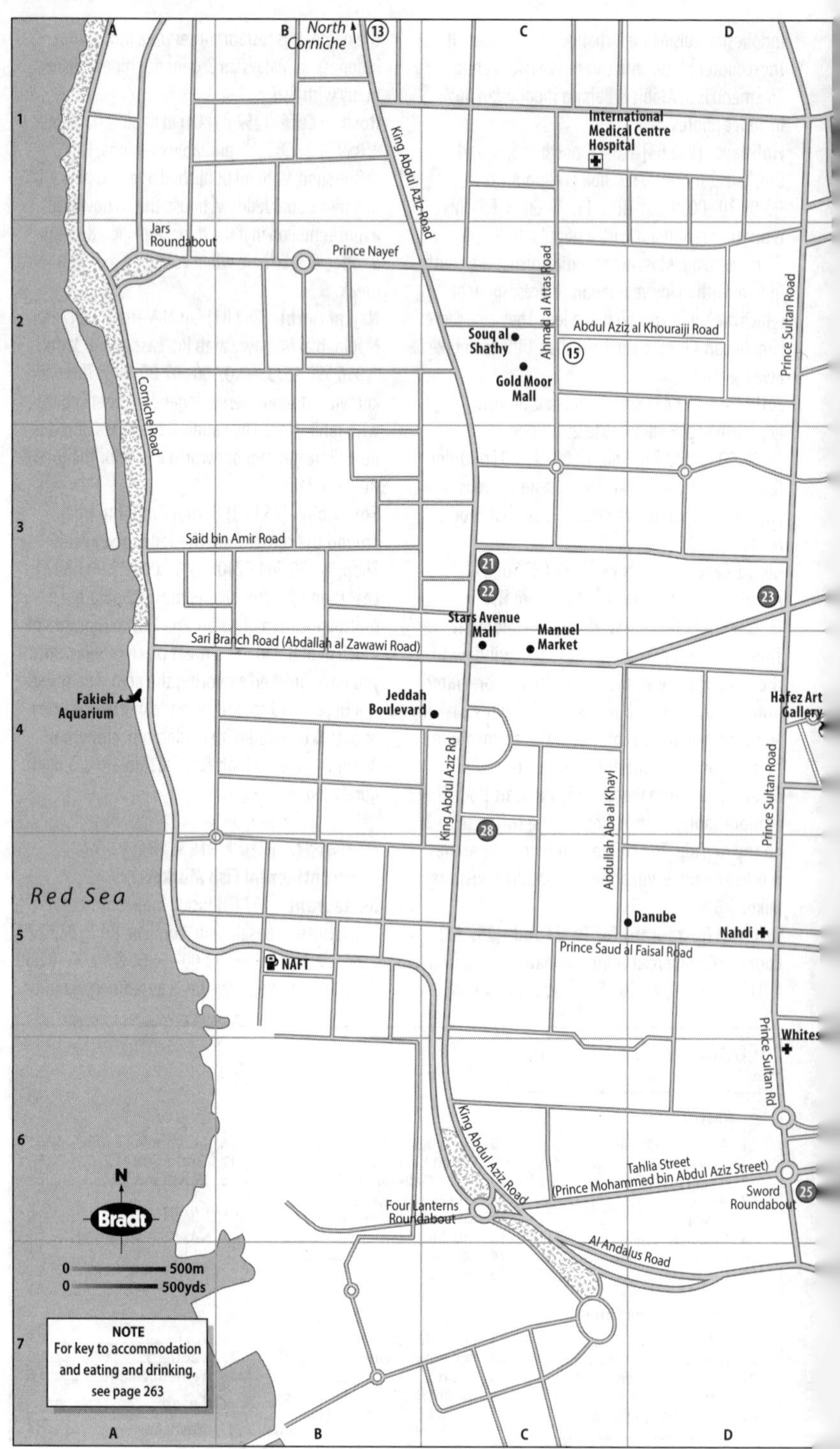

North Corniche
13
International Medical Centre Hospital
King Abdul Aziz Road
Jars Roundabout
Prince Nayef
Ahmad al Attas Road
Prince Sultan Road
Abdul Aziz al Khouraiji Road
Souq al Shathy
15
Gold Moor Mall
Corniche Road
Said bin Amir Road
21
22
23
Stars Avenue Mall
Manuel Market
Sari Branch Road (Abdallah al Zawawi Road)
Fakieh Aquarium
Jeddah Boulevard
Hafez Art Gallery
King Abdul Aziz Rd
Abdullah Aba al Khayl
28
Red Sea
Danube
Nahdi
Prince Saud al Faisal Road
NAFT
Whites
Prince Sultan Rd
King Abdul Aziz Road
Tahlia Street (Prince Mohammed bin Abdul Aziz Street)
Sword Roundabout
25
Four Lanterns Roundabout
Al Andalus Road
Bradt
N
0 500m
0 500yds
NOTE
For key to accommodation and eating and drinking, see page 263
A
B
C
D
1
2
3
4
5
6
7

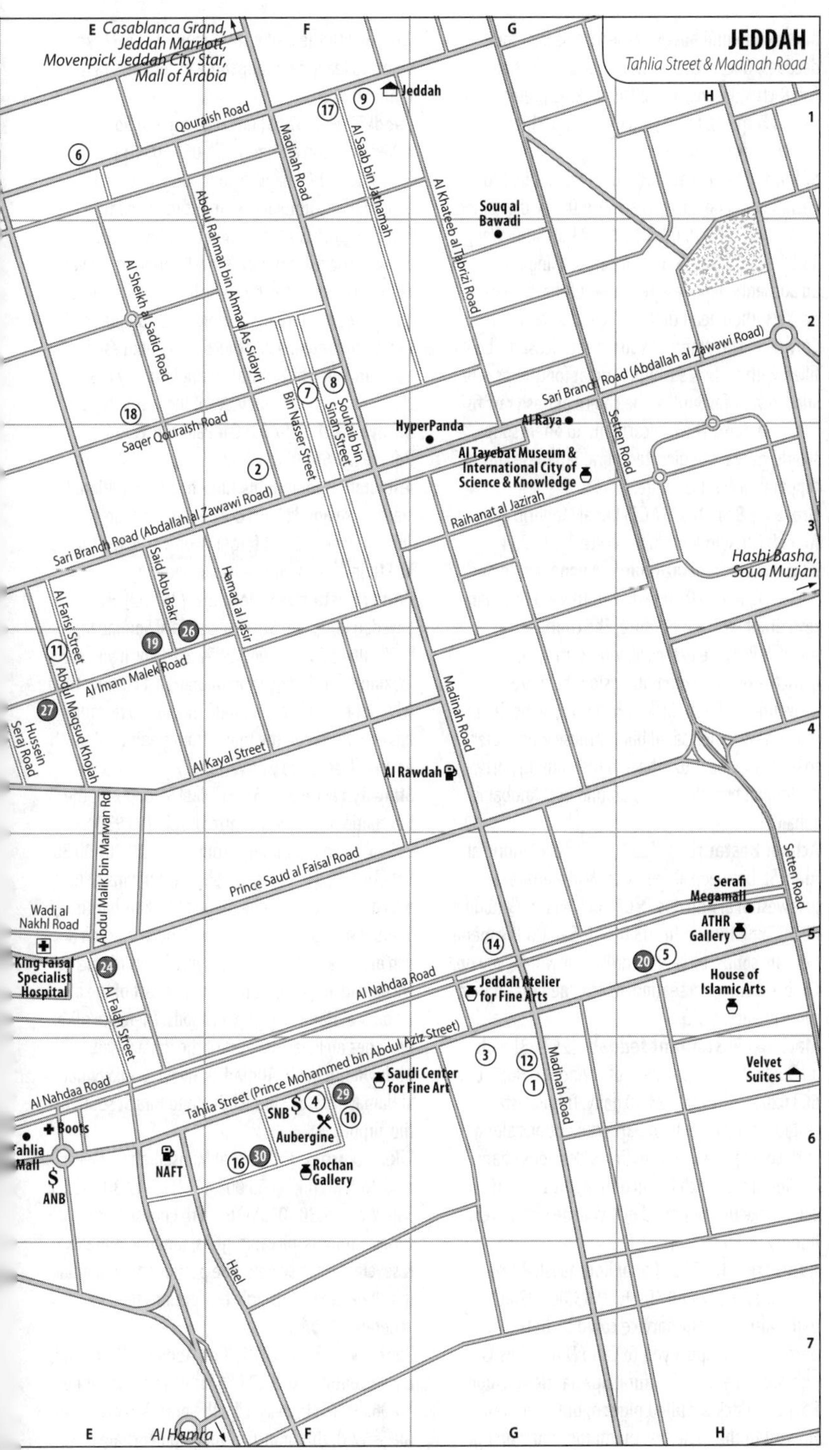
JEDDAH
Tahlia Street & Madinah Road
Casablanca Grand, Jeddah Marriott, Movenpick Jeddah City Star, Mall of Arabia
Jeddah
Qouraish Road
Madinah Road
Al Saab bin Jathamah
Al Khateeb al Tabrizi Road
Souq al Bawadi
Abdul Rahman bin Ahmad As Sidayri
Al Sheikh al Sadid Road
Sari Branch Road (Abdallah al Zawawi Road)
Bin Nasser Street
Souhaib bin Sinan Street
HyperPanda
Al Raya
Al Tayebat Museum & International City of Science & Knowledge
Setten Road
Saqer Qouraish Road
Raihanat al Jazirah
Hashi Basha, Souq Murjan
Said Abu Bakr
Hamad al Jasir
Al Farisi Street
Al Imam Malek Road
Abdul Maqsud Khojah
Hussein Seraj Road
Al Kayal Street
Al Rawdah
Abdul Malik bin Marwan Rd
Prince Saud al Faisal Road
Wadi al Nakhl Road
King Faisal Specialist Hospital
Al Falah Street
Al Nahdaa Road
Serafi Megamall
ATHR Gallery
House of Islamic Arts
Jeddah Atelier for Fine Arts
Tahlia Street (Prince Mohammed bin Abdul Aziz Street)
Saudi Center for Fine Art
Velvet Suites
SNB
Aubergine
Boots
Tahlia Mall
ANB
NAFT
Rochan Gallery
Hael
Al Hamra

Makkah Province JEDDAH

7

Intercontinental hotels in the Middle East for decades. Guests choose from a wide selection of fish & crustaceans, as well as cooking preferences, sauces & spices, to be prepared by the chef. Great for Fri brunch. $$$$$

**Sakura** [257 F3] al Mansourah Rd, about 100m east of Corniche Rd; ☎ 012 260 4900; w digital.ihg.com; ⌚ 13.00–16.00 & 19.00–23.30 Sun–Wed, 13.00–23.30 Thu–Sat. If you are looking for an authentic Japanese restaurant & have deep pockets, then head to this elegant place in the Crowne Plaza. Whether you want to feast on 'boats' filled with sushi & sashimi – great for groups – or stick to your favourites, the choice of fresh raw fish seems endless. The à la carte menu offers soups, salads, gyoza, noodles, tempura, Japanese curries, teppanyaki & much more. $$$$$

**Brasa de Brazil** [257 G3] Cnr al Maghrib al Arabi & Hussein Albasalamah sts; ☎ 012 284 2345; w brasadebrazil.com; ⌚ noon–midnight Sat–Wed, noon–01.00 Fri–Sat. This is a Brazilian restaurant with a difference. The churrascaria meat choices are extensive with camel, deer, ostrich & quail on offer alongside the more conventional beef, chicken & lamb options. There is a large & varied salad bar for those who prefer to leave the meat to others in their dining party. Additional branches can be found in al Khobar & Jubail. $$$$

**Achaar Restaurant** [257 G3] Cnr al Maghrib al Arabi St, between al Qairawan & al Mansourah, just west of al Andalus; ☎ 053 008 4111; ⌚ noon–02.00 Sun–Thu, noon–03.00 Fri–Sat. On the menu here are soups, biryanis & grills that will fill you up. Choose from open seating, or screened seating for more privacy. $$$

**Marhaba Restaurant Jeddah** [257 G3] Muhyi ad Din an Nadhir, just west of al Andalus Rd; ☎ 012 663 6201; ⌚ 13.00–23.30 daily. This Pakistani restaurant has plenty of barbecue options along with vegetable sides or mains & delicious naans, & offers a set-lunch menu option, great if you can't make up your mind of if you are simply very hungry. $$$

**Ramesses** [257 E3] Cnr al Kournaysh Rd & Palestine; ☎ 012 660 4049; ⌚ 13.00–02.00 daily. Although the service could be better, the décor will transport you to Cairo & the view is one of the best in al Hamra. Specialities include Egyptian duck & grilled pigeon, but check out the rest of the generous menu too. You won't go wrong with the garlic chicken *meshawi*. Make sure you leave room for some of Jeddah's tastiest umm ali. $$$

**Saedi Fish** [257 E3] Cnr al Kournaysh Rd & Muhyi ad Din an Nadhar; ☎ 055 503 6346; ⌚ 13.00–02.00 daily. If your budget doesn't extend to the hotel fish markets but you fancy fish along the Corniche, then this may be the answer. The fish counter is lovely, offering a wide range of catch of the day which usually includes *hammour*, crustaceans & more. The fruit juices are freshly squeezed. Ask if there is anything especially recommended as the staff are helpful. Try to sit by the window for a great view of the water. $$$

**Saraya Latif** [257 F3] Cnr Palestine & Ariha Rd; ☎ 012 664 1090; ⌚ 13.00–02.00 daily. This restaurant is thoroughly Turkish, with traditional starters, salads, kebabs & a generous range of Turkish sweets. Don't forget to order the tea served in a tulip glass with or without sugar. $$$

**Kandy Restaurants Jeddah** [257 D2] al Sayedah Rouqaiah St, off al Sayed al Souhadaa; ☎ 053 064 5263; ⌚ 06.30–22.30 daily. If you are looking for a change from Middle East cuisine, then why not try Sri Lankan food? This casual restaurant has everything on the menu from traditional south Asian b/fast to spicy biryanis. $$

**Shawaya House** [257 C3] Hael St, opposite the International Medical Centre Hospital; ☎ 9200 33336; w shawayahouse.com.sa; ⌚ 10.30–00.30 Sat–Thu, 12.30–00.30 Fri. Shawaya means grill, which is the focus of the menu at this authentic Saudi restaurant & take-away. Popular chicken & fish dishes are made with varying levels of spicing. Located in al Ruwais, this branch is east of the al Balad & al Hamra neighbourhoods. There are other branches on Palestine east of the Haifaa Mall, Abdul Rahman bin Ahmad as Sidayr & Sulayyman al Hamawi sts, & 2 branches along Hira St south of the airport. $$

**Tikka Express** [257 G3] al Mansourah just west of al Andalus Rd; ☎ 053 008 4111; ⌚ 12.30–02.00 Sat–Wed, 12.30–03.00 Thu–Fri. Choose from classic samosas, biryanis, grills, tandoor, masalas & several Indian sweets. The portions are generous but there are surprisingly few options for vegetarians. $$

**Zaatar w Zeit** [257 C3] King Abdullah Branch Rd, Liwan Centre; ☎ 055 375 5671; w zaatarwzeit.net; ⌚ 06.00–01.45 daily. Like the branches in Riyadh (page 125), this branch of the popular chain of

Lebanese cafés serves great b/fasts & lunches. There is another branch in Jeddah on Prince Sultan Rd at the al Khayyat Centre. $$

## Tahlia Street and Madinah Road areas

**Fogo de Chao** [271 C6] Prince Sultan Rd, just north of Abdallah Zawawi Rd; ☎ 9200 06815; **w** fogome.com; ⌚ 13.00–01.00 daily. This churrasco experience starts with choosing your beef cut, which is then prepared & carved at your table. Save room for the salad bar. Fine-dining décor & superb service with prices that mean this place is often saved for a special occasion or for a business meal. $$$$$

**Lusin** [264 D6] Cnr Tahlia St & Prince Sultan Rd; ☎ 9200 02690; **w** lusinrestaurant.com; ⌚ noon–01.00 daily. Located in the Teatro Mall, this gorgeous Armenian restaurant is part of the Lusin group in Riyadh (page 123) & offers the same delectable menu & the same impeccable service. $$$$$

**Toki** [264 C4] Douroub al Maarefah Rd, east of King Abdullah Branch Rd; ☎ 012 606 0606; **w** tokiksa.com; ⌚ 13.00–midnight daily. If you are looking for an elegant Chinese restaurant, this ticks all the boxes. The décor evokes the finest of restaurants. The menu is pan-Chinese, ranging from Cantonese dim sum, fiery Szechuan noodles & several Saudi–Chinese fusion options. The front-of-house staff are Filipino, providing attentive but unintrusive service. This is a very expensive place, but the food is very good so worth it for a special treat. $$$$$

**Vaquero** [265 F6] Tahlia St, east of al Foutaihi St; ☎ 012 422 2555; **w** the hotelgalleria.com; ⌚ 18.30–23.30 Thu–Sat. It's probably fair to say this is more of an international restaurant than authentic Argentinian, satisfying beef lovers from all parts of the globe. Located in the Hotel Galleria, the open kitchen fills the dining room with an irresistible aroma. Guests can choose from a range of sauces, as well as salads & other sides. Save room for temptingly gooey desserts. $$$$$

**Leila min Lebnen** [265 E5] Cnr Prince Saud al Faisal Rd & al Falah St; ☎ 9200 07826; ⌚ 09.00–midnight Sat–Wed, 09.00–01.00 Fri–Sat. This spacious restaurant with indoor & outdoor seating offers a classic Lebanese menu with warm & friendly but not overbearing service. The focus is on mezze & grills, with some Leila twists. The Leila Osmailia is irresistible if you like rose & pistachio ice cream. This is a sister restaurant to the property in Riyadh's Diplomatic Quarter. We like this branch better. $$$$

✱ **Rasoi by Vineet** [265 F6] Cnr Abdul Rahman al Tubalshi & Ha'il sts; ☎ 012 213 2000; **w** rasoibyvineetjeddah.com; ⌚ 13.00–16.30 & 19.00–midnight Mon–Sat. Although this award-winning restaurant is in the less-than-inspiring Movenpick Tahlia hotel (page 259), it is in an upscale neighbourhood. What sets this apart from other good Indian restaurants in Jeddah is the imagination of the chef & the pitch-perfect customer service. We loved the chicken Habibi – melt-in-the-mouth chicken pieces covered with malai black olives, marinated in mulukhiyah dust & *makhni labneh*. The nawabi lamb chops, grilled with ginger, pistachio & rose petals served with saffron & pomegranate seed mash is a starter but could easily be a main course, especially with delicious coriander naan with red onion. You might also want to try the date & almond naan that's a nod to the Saudi palate. Don't miss the mocktails, served in an interesting glass with a spout. From the same people at Maharaja East in Riyadh & Maharaja by Vineet in al Khobar. $$$$

**The Social Kitchen** [265 E4] Abdulmaqsud Khojah Road, south of al Imam Malek Rd; ☎ 055 516 3200; **w** wearesocial-sa.com; ⌚ 13.00–midnight daily. This extensive menu is inspired by the Mediterranean, with Lebanese, Greek & Italian dishes all featured. Their bakery products are wide ranging, from pumpernickel bread loaves to lemon meringue 'cruffins'. $$$$

✱ **Yemeni Village** [265 F6] Abdul Rahman al Tubalshi St, just west of al Ghouneim St; ☎ 055 988 1515; ⌚ 06.00–02.00 Sat–Thu, 06.00–10.00 & 13.00–02.00 Fri. If you have never had Yemeni food, this is a great introduction to authentic cuisine at a time when travel to Yemen is off the menu for most travellers. Enter this upscale restaurant through huge wooden double doors, where you will be greeted with great décor & waiters in traditional Yemeni dress. Single men dine on the ground floor, families, women & mixed-gender groups on the 1st floor. Male shisha smokers also have access to the shisha lounge on the 2nd floor. There is also outdoor seating at the front of the restaurant which is very pleasant when the weather is good & it can be enjoyed by all diners. We recommend you try a *mandhi* dish originating in the Hadramaut region. The meat is spiced with black pepper, cardamom, cumin, turmeric & other spices before being cooked in an underground pit & is accompanied by rice. Try to save room for the traditional *areesa* dessert. $$$$

**Adani Bar** [265 E4] Said Abu Bakr, just north of al Imam Malek Rd; 054 282 6054; 07.00–midnight Sat–Thu, 08.00–midnight Fri. This Yemeni-inspired Saudi sandwich shop is a great place to meet friends & catch up. Be sure to try the tuna sandwich. The Adani tea & various coffee blends are elevated with flavours rarely used elsewhere in Jeddah. Choose from indoor & outdoor seating. $$$

**Al Wazzan** [265 H5] Tahlia St, just east of Boudl Tahlia Hotel; 012 660 8909; 24hrs daily. Whether you visit for b/fast, lunch, dinner or a late-night snack, this well-established Lebanese restaurant remains popular for its extensive menu & efficient service. There is a large dining area in addition to a brisk take-away business. There is even a freezer containing some popular dishes that can be prepared at your hotel if you have a kitchen. $$$

**Hashi Basha** [265 H3] Ali al Murtada, just south of Omaiah bin Abdallah Rd; 053 040 7666; w hashibasha.com; 11.00–midnight daily. This rapidly growing chain of Saudi restaurants specialises in *hashi* – camel meat. Try the *nafar kabsa hashi* if you are not sure what to order. Those who prefer to skip the camel can opt for the chicken version of this dish. It is in a neighbourhood east of al Hamra past the al Andalus & al Salam malls. The restaurant sign is in Arabic (حاشي باشا) only but the logo includes an image of a camel so it is easy to spot. There is another branch near Mohammed Saleh Nassif Rd east of Prince Majid Rd in the al Safa neighbourhood in the far east of Jeddah. $$$

✷ **Moon Shell** [265 E4] al Imam Malek Rd, east of Abdullah Nawfal St; 059 000 6969; 07.00–midnight daily. This mostly plant-based café is a welcome relief for those who may have struggled to find vegan options elsewhere in the Kingdom. There is a healthy choice of imaginative fruit bowls along with some vegetarian. Be warned that there are also a few chocolate temptations. The décor captures a feeling of understated Saudi elegance. The restaurant is easily spotted by its stone façade & traditional furniture. There are other branches in Riyadh & al Ula. $$$

**Boga Tariq al Hussaini Superfoods** [264 C3] Abdul Fadl al Koufi, between Abdul Ghanidada & Mohammed Ibrahim al Ghazzawi St; 012 288 9029; 06.30–03.00 daily. Don't expect a menu full of superfoods – instead this place offers more of a mixed menu that ranges from the expected healthy ingredients to items that can be found in more conventional sandwich shops & cafés. There is a combination of veggie & vegan dishes with meat options also available. Look for other branches throughout Jeddah. $$

**Bread Ahead Bakery & School** [264 C3] King Abdul Aziz Branch Rd, northbound, south of Abdul Ghanidada St; 053 843 4670; w breadahead.com; 07.00–midnight Sat–Thu, 13.00–01.00 Fri. This London bakery & school has arrived in Saudi Arabia & is pure indulgence for bread & pastry connoisseurs. Check out the lessons if you want to learn to make these delectables yourself. $$

## Corniche

**Al Riwaq al Omawi** [271 C1] al Kournaysh Branch Rd, opposite Besam Café & Mart; 059 984 8800; w alriwaqalomawi.okm.gg; 13.00–01.00 Sun–Thu, 07.00–02.00 Fri–Sat. This Syrian restaurant is located on the Corniche on the south side of Obhur Bay. The Levantine menu offers something a bit different from the more familiar Lebanese fare. The décor is classic Syrian with nothing held back in terms of bling & there is live music most nights. $$$$

**Urth Caffé** [271 C4] Cnr King Abdul Aziz & al Malik rds; 9200 07498; w urthcaffe.sa; 07.00–00.30 daily. This café's lovely motto is 'People Planet Pleasure' & sustainability is a high priority. The ingredients are chosen for being natural, avoiding additives or genetically modified produce & are organically grown wherever possible. Although this is not a vegetarian restaurant, most items on the menu are vegetarian or vegan. The aim is for healthy eating with room for a little decadence when required! There is another branch located in Le Prestige Mall on King Abdul Aziz Rd & Mitaf bin Awf, with more branches in Riyadh. $$$$

**Zillion Restaurant & Lounge** [271 C6] al Kournaysh Br Rd, just south of Said bin Mohammed; 050 667 0602; w zillion.

yallaqrcodes.com; ⌚ noon–02.00 Sat–Wed, noon–03.00 Thu–Fri. This lounge has a relaxing ambience with ample indoor & outdoor seating & views of the beach & the Red Sea. There is a varied menu of pasta, steak, Turkish kebabs, the ever-popular dynamite shrimp & healthy salads. Parking is about 100m to the south of the restaurant on the slip road. $$$$

**Al Sadda** [271 C5] Cnr Hira St & Qabat bin Ashim; 📞 012 622 8296; w alsaddahrest.com; ⌚ 11.00–00.30 daily. This is the place to go for authentic Saudi folk food. Whether you choose the chicken, goat or camel, expect a hearty dish that can be ordered individually or for sharing. This is also an opportunity for groups to try foods cooked by various traditional cooking methods – *madhabi*, madfoon, mandhi & *mathlothah*. Finish with a warm kunafa & your experience will be complete. You can dine on the floor Saudi style or opt for table seating. There are other branches on Tahlia St & Palestine in Jeddah, as well as in Riyadh. $$$

**Belajio Resort** [271 C5] Cnr al Kournaysh Branch Rd & Ahmad an Nesaai St; 📞 9200 03409; w belajio-ksa.com; ⌚ 09.00–02.00 daily. Located near the Red Sea Mall, this property seems to be giving Las Vegas a run for its money, at least as regards the glitz & bling. There are several seaside restaurants in this complex, offering a wide choice of cuisines, from Thai Tom Yum soup, Belgian waffles & fettucine to grilled hammour. Check out Dar al Qasar or Wave if you want an unobstructed view. There is also a shisha bar with an extensive menu of fruity flavours. $$$

**Blue Ocean** [271 C6] Cnr al Kournaysh Rd & Abdallah Zawawi Rd, next to the Fakieh Aquarium; 📞 012 639 7462; w fakieheats.com/blueocean; ⌚ 07.00–01.00 Sun–Wed, 07.00–02.00 Thu–Sat. If you are looking to enjoy seafood on the Corniche, this is a popular choice. The restaurant claims to be a 'Miami Beach Restaurant', at least through Saudi eyes. There is indoor & outdoor seating, both with large spaces & good ocean views. Outside seating is air conditioned during the day but is a good choice in the evening. In addition to seafood, the menu includes beef & chicken dishes with a nod to Tex-Mex & other Americanised tastes. The Blue Ocean mocktail is its speciality & will work for pineapple lovers. The service is attentive & there is underground parking serving both the restaurant & the aquarium next door. $$$

**House of Salad** [264 D1] al Safaa Rd, north of Manbar al Taqwa; 📞 055 001 9111. Terrific & creative Western & Middle Eastern salads are freshly made in this café, with sandwiches & a few more substantial meals also on the menu. There's a pleasant atmosphere with a nod to plants & other greenery. There are good options for vegetarians & vegans. $$$

✷ **Nakheel** [271 C7] Cnr Corniche Branch & Abdullah Abdul Jabar rds; 📞 9200 06815; ⌚ 17.00–01.00 Sun–Thu, 17.00–01.30 Fri–Sat. Set off the Corniche, entry to this legendary Lebanese restaurant is through a garden which is also home to a family of cats that may say hello if they are in the mood. With its friendly atmosphere, Nakheel is a good introduction to the relaxed side of Jeddah & recommended for first-time visitors & others who are new to the Kingdom. Choose from indoor or outdoor seating. Indoors your meal will be delivered to lovely tiled tables with deep-cushioned bench seating. English-speaking staff mostly from the Levant are helpful & will advise on the extensive menu choices if you want some guidance. Consider sharing a few hot & cold mezze starters. Popular Arabic music videos projected on to screens around the restaurant are loud enough to make some people uncomfortable & others sway to the tunes. This restaurant is good value for money, with ample parking. $$$

**Shrimp Nation** [271 B2] Cnr Corniche Branch Rd & Marine Science Roundabout; 📞 056 209 8999; w shrimpnation.com; ⌚ noon–01.00 Sun–Wed, noon–02.00 Thu–Sat. This place has a cool vibe reminiscent of a Chesapeake Bay crab feast & does a very good job of it, albeit without the beer, complete with brown paper covering the tables so you can be as messy as you like with your shellfish, which makes it fun if you go with a group. Choose your crustacean, your sauce & your level of spiciness. There is another branch between Prince Sultan Rd & al Kuwkabash east of the Fist Roundabout. If you really like shrimp, you might also want to try Shrimp Anatomy (Sari Br Rd & al Solh; 📞 055 090 0379; ⌚ 13.00–01.00 daily), Shrimp Vibes (Prince Sultan Rd & Mohammed bin Abi Bakr St; 📞 055 944 0484; ⌚ noon–02.00 daily) or Shrimp Zone (Sari Br Rd & al Ghaznawi; 📞 054 450 0445; ⌚ noon–02.00 Sat–Thu, 13.00–03.00 Fri) for comparison. All $$$

**SHOPPING** A full range of Saudi supermarkets are found in Jeddah, including al Raya, Carrefour, Danube, Farm Superstores, Lulu, Panda and HyperPanda, and Tamimi. Manuel Market is a small chain found only in Jeddah which offers a similar quality to the larger upscale national brands. Yellow trolley grocers and minimarkets are also plentiful.

It is possible to wander around the souqs of al Balad all evening long and not finish browsing, shopping and people-watching, even without taking a break in the delectable cafés found among the shops. You may stumble upon a favourite place or indeed a place you want to keep secret from the crowds. Try to visit in the evening if you can as this is when Jeddah comes alive. Mornings are quiet with some shops remaining shut. Nearly all shops are closed in the afternoon. Remember to use your best haggling skills and to keep it friendly. There are a few souqs elsewhere in Jeddah, also listed on below, which follow similar trading times and practices as those found in al Balad.

It might surprise some visitors how difficult it is in Jeddah to find **souvenirs**, common as they are in most of the world. Although religious items have been available for centuries, popular souvenir shops are thin on the ground, no doubt due to the fact that general tourism was only launched in 2019. If souvenirs are important to you, then head to al Balad.

## Shopping centres and malls

### *Al Balad*

**Faisaliyah Shopping Centre** [252 A3] King Abdul Aziz Branch Rd; 055 368 7108; 08.00–midnight Sat–Thu,16.00–midnight Fri. Nothing to do with the bling-y mall of the same name in the Faisaliah Tower in Riyadh, this is an old-style shopping centre in al Balad that was a precursor to the modern malls to the north. It's a great place for people-watching, as well as shopping for goods in traditional-style shops. It is adjacent to the **al Balad Corniche Shopping Centre**, which offers a similar shopping experience. Despite the published opening hours, in reality many shops open only in the evening.

### *Al Hamra and Palestine*

**Al Andalus Mall** [257 D3] Southwest cnr King Abdullah & Prince Majid rds; **w** alandalus-mall.com; 09.00–23.00 Sun–Thu, 09.00–18.00 Fri–Sat. Relatively convenient for those staying in al Hamra & al Balad, this well-established, popular mall has something for everyone, including a cinema, shop brands from all over the Gulf, a cinema, children's play area, large food court & a HyperPanda supermarket.

**Al Salaam Mall** [257 D3] Southeast cnr King Abdullah & Prince Majid rds; 9200 00262; 10.00–02.00 Sat–Thu, 13.00–02.00 Fri. Located across the dual carriageway from al Andalus Mall, this is slightly larger but of the same vintage & popularity. It has a similar mix of mid-range & upscale but practical shops, including a branch of Marks & Spencer. It also has a cinema, kids' zone & a large Danube supermarket.

**Haifaa Mall** [257 C2] Cnr Palestine & abu Feras al Salami Rd; 10.00–02.00 Sat–Thu, 14.00–02.00 Fri. Situated on the edge of al Hamra, this is a smaller, more manageable mall than most of the newer malls, but with many of the same types of shops. It also has a good branch of Manuel Supermarket.

**Oasis Mall** [257 D3] Northeast side of King Abdullah & Setten rds; 012 650 1603; 08.00–23.30 daily. Situated in the al Worood neighbourhood about 1km west of the al Andalus Mall, this is a consolidation of gold shops, many of which relocated from various premises in old neighbourhoods. Oasis has now become a convenient destination for one-stop shopping for all of your gold purchases.

### *Tahlia Street and Madinah Road areas*

**Mall of Arabia** [265 F1] al Nouzhah, east of Madinah Rd; 9200 00262; 09.30–02.00 Sat–Thu, 14.00–02.00 Fri. This recently refurbished & extended mall is now Jeddah's largest. Located at the south end of the airport, it is convenient for anyone staying in the north of Jeddah. The shops are mostly recognisable European brands, with plenty of coffee shops, cafés, a food court

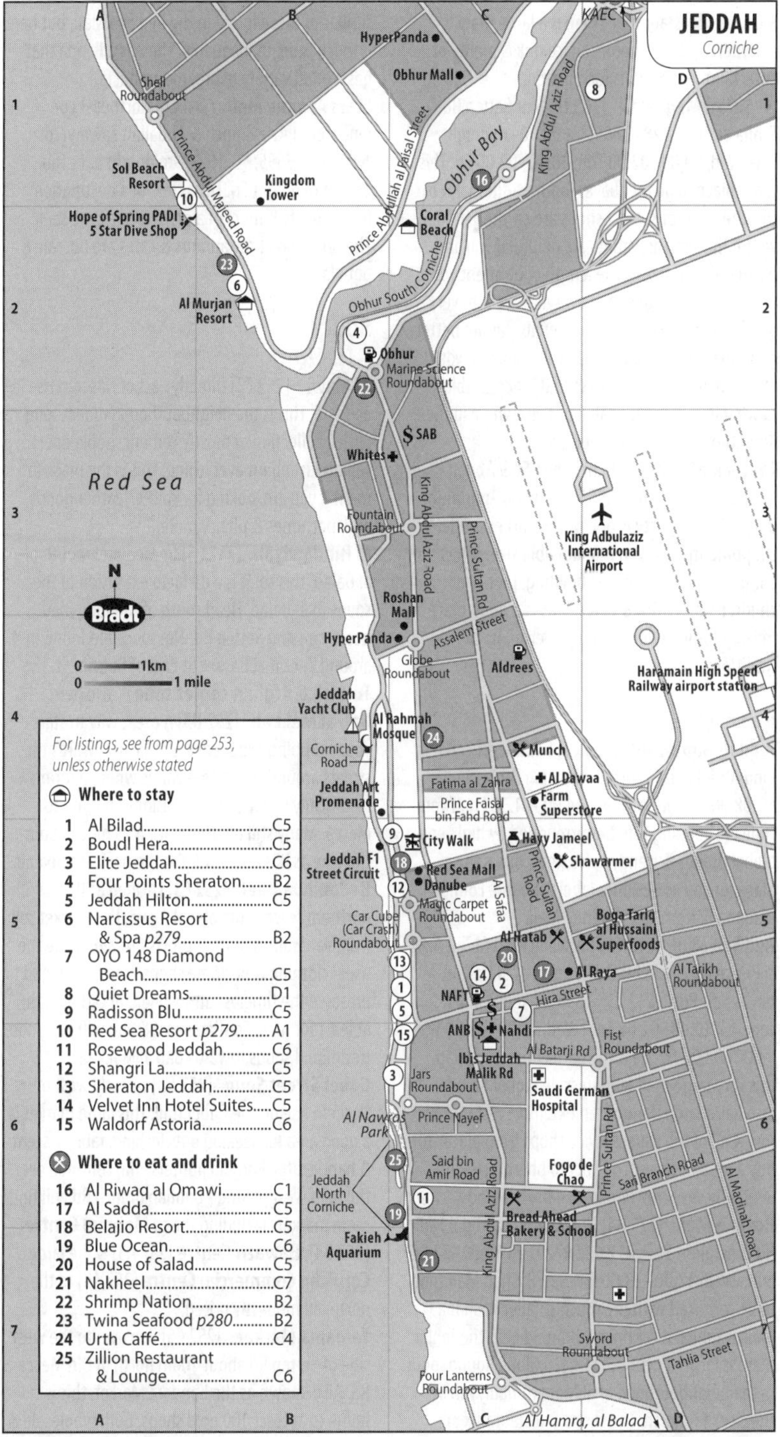
JEDDAH
Corniche
KAEC
HyperPanda
Obhur Mall
Shell Roundabout
Prince Abdul Majeed Road
Sol Beach Resort
Kingdom Tower
Hope of Spring PADI 5 Star Dive Shop
Prince Abdullah al Faisal Street
Obhur Bay
King Abdul Aziz Road
Coral Beach
Obhur South Corniche
Al Murjan Resort
Obhur
Marine Science Roundabout
SAB
Whites
Red Sea
Fountain Roundabout
King Abdul Aziz Road
Prince Sultan Rd
King Abdulaziz International Airport
N
Bradt
0 1km
0 1 mile
Roshan Mall
HyperPanda
Assalem Street
Globe Roundabout
Aldrees
Haramain High Speed Railway airport station
Jeddah Yacht Club
Al Rahmah Mosque
Corniche Road
Munch
Fatima al Zahra
Al Dawaa
Jeddah Art Promenade
Prince Faisal bin Fahd Road
Farm Superstore
City Walk
Hayy Jameel
Prince Sultan Road
Shawarmer
Jeddah F1 Street Circuit
Red Sea Mall
Danube
Magic Carpet Roundabout
Al Safaa
Car Cube (Car Crash) Roundabout
Al Hatab
Boga Tariq al Hussaini Superfoods
Al Raya
Al Tarikh Roundabout
NAFT
Hira Street
ANB
Nahdi
Ibis Jeddah Malik Rd
Al Batarji Rd
Fist Roundabout
Saudi German Hospital
Jars Roundabout
Al Nawras Park
Prince Nayef
Said bin Amir Road
Fogo de Chao
Prince Sultan Rd
Sari Branch Road
Al Madinah Road
Jeddah North Corniche
Bread Ahead Bakery & School
Fakieh Aquarium
King Abdul Aziz Road
Sword Roundabout
Tahlia Street
Four Lanterns Roundabout
Al Hamra, al Balad
For listings, see from page 253, unless otherwise stated
Where to stay
1 Al Bilad C5
2 Boudl Hera C5
3 Elite Jeddah C6
4 Four Points Sheraton B2
5 Jeddah Hilton C5
6 Narcissus Resort & Spa p279 B2
7 OYO 148 Diamond Beach C5
8 Quiet Dreams D1
9 Radisson Blu C5
10 Red Sea Resort p279 A1
11 Rosewood Jeddah C6
12 Shangri La C5
13 Sheraton Jeddah C5
14 Velvet Inn Hotel Suites C5
15 Waldorf Astoria C6
Where to eat and drink
16 Al Riwaq al Omawi C1
17 Al Sadda C5
18 Belajio Resort C5
19 Blue Ocean C6
20 House of Salad C5
21 Nakheel C7
22 Shrimp Nation B2
23 Twina Seafood p280 B2
24 Urth Caffé C4
25 Zillion Restaurant & Lounge C6

& choice of restaurants. There is a large branch of HyperPanda, a cinema, an ice rink & plenty of entertainment options for children.

✷ **Serafi Megamall** [265 H5] Cnr Setten Rd & Tahlia St; 012 284 4885; 09.00–midnight Sat–Wed, 09.00–02.00 Thu, 16.30–02.00 Fri. This is the place to go for abayas, both traditional & in the latest designs. Most shops are on the 1st floor, where the shop assistants are helpful if you are unsure of your size or the length of garment you need. Quality ranges from everyday wear to very good; those looking for designer abayas are better off in the top-end shops. As well as abayas, you'll also find other modest dress that is acceptable to wear in most of Jeddah if not elsewhere in the Kingdom. Prices are competitive.

**Tahlia Mall** [265 E6] Cnr Tahlia St & Abdallah al Matari Rd; 012 675 5555; 09.00–midnight daily. This property is one of the earlier modern shopping malls & is a manageable size. It has a mix of shops, as well as bowling, plenty of children's activities & cafés. This is a good place to shop for jewellery if you prefer malls to traditional souqs.

### *Corniche*

**Jeddah Boulevard** [264 C4] Southwest cnr King Abdul Aziz Branch & Abdallah Zawawi rds; 08.00–01.00 Sat–Thu, 14.00–01.30 Fri. If your style of shopping is to be surrounded by high-end global brands & trendy cafés, then this is the place for you as designer labels abound. Found diagonally from Stars Avenue Mall.

**Red Sea Mall** [271 C5] Between King Abdul Aziz & Prince Faisal bin Fahd rds, north of al Hakam bin as Salt Rd; 012 215 1551; **w** redseamall.com; 10.00–01.00 Sat–Wed, 10.00–02.00 Thu, 13.00–02.00 Fri. Near the Corniche in Ash Shati, this very large mall with upscale global brands also has a large Danube, an extensive restaurant row & all of the usual service shops from places to buy a mobile phone contract to pharmacies. It is generally very crowded from early evening.

**Roshan Mall** [271 B4] Northwest cnr Abdul Fadl Rd & Assalem St; 012 622 6720; 10.00–23.00 Sun–Wed, 17.00–23.00 Fri–Sat. Roshan Mall (not to be confused with the much smaller Roshana Mall at Tahlia St & Prince Sultan Rd near the Tahlia Mall) is located near the famous Globe Roundabout in the neighbourhood of al Mohammadiyyah in the city's far north. The shops & restaurants are similar to those found in the Red Sea Mall, but here is much more manageable. There is a Panda that has a good variety of organic products.

**Stars Avenue Mall** [264 C4] Northeast cnr King Abdul Aziz Branch & Abdallah Zawawi rds; 012 675 5555; 10.00–midnight Sat–Thu, 13.00–midnight Fri. This is less of a destination for shoppers & more of a place to see & be seen. The selection of restaurants & cafés are upscale & popular.

## Souqs

### *Al Balad*

**Al Alawi** [252 C3] Directly east of Naseem Hse in al Balad. This is the neighbourhood's oldest souq with a collection of mostly Yemeni shopkeepers selling just about everything. This is the place to roam if you are looking for spices, leather goods, oud, perfumes & plenty more.

**Al Hindawiyah** [252 C5] Immediately south of al Balad, this souq is a de facto extension of the souqs of al Balad. Head south of the Touq Blad hotel, crossing Setten Rd. The souqs are found in & around Zahrat al Basant St east of Baishin St. The **Turkish & Afghan carpet souq** is also here.

**Bab al Makkah** [252 D3] A great way to start your shopping experience is to head towards the streets around this gate – this is where pilgrims historically shopped for provisions en route to Mecca. Many still do. This place is as much about the vibe as it is about finding the perfect souvenir.

**Bedouin Market** [252 C3] Located at the northern reaches of Souq al Alawi, this market sells fruit, vegetables & other provisions alongside the usual clothing & perfume shops. It has managed to preserve the timeless atmosphere of Old Jeddah, at least for now. Continue east & you will find more traditional souqs towards Bab al Makkah.

**Gabel Street Souq** [252 B3] Directly west of Naseem Hse on the Qabel Trail. This large market is a good area for seeking out clothing, fabrics, scent & handicrafts. Bargain hunters who continue over the road west of King Abdullah Branch Rd will find more markets including the **al Mahmal Centre** [252 B4], **Bawazir Centre** [252 A3] & the large **Corniche Commercial Centre** [252 A3] to the north, all modestly priced.

**Yamama Market** [252 C5] Pop over to the west side of Setten Rd about 100m north of Old Mecca Rd. Also known as the Kandara Market, this is home to at least 100 gold shops, both wholesale &

retail. Note that gold prices are quoted by weight for many items, so make sure you know the official rate per gram before you set out.

### *Other Jeddah souqs*

**Gold Moor Mall** [264 C2] Head to Ahmad al Attas in the al Zahra neighbourhood to find this gold haven. It's neither really a souq nor a modern shopping mall but something in between, where you will also find cosmetics & homeware shops, a play area for children & a Mira Mart supermarket which is open throughout the day & into the early morning hours. There is a car park that serves this mall & Souq al Shathy.

**Souq al Bawadi** [265 G2] This series of shops can be found along Setten Rd in the neighbourhood of the same name. Everyday items for the home are sold alongside handicrafts, gold & jewellery. The abaya market at the north end of the souq, with Its mind-boggling selection, is legendary.

**Souq al Shathy** [264 C2] Adjacent to the Gold Moor Mall. Also known as al Shatea & al Sha'ta, this souq is dedicated to women's clothing & inexpensive abayas.

**Souq Murjan** [265 H3] Also known as the Syrian souq, this souq is located in the al Safa neighbourhood & is the place to go for clothing, perfume & oud. It feels like a souq in a mall.

### Souvenir shops

**Al Balad Souvenir** [252 C2] Qabil Ln, off abu Inabah just over 200m south of Bab Jadid; 053 165 7556; w baladsouvenir.com; 09.00–noon Sat–Thu & 16.30–22.00 daily. Note that opening hours are unreliable, so try to visit during the evening when activity picks up throughout al Balad as it may not open in the morning despite its listed opening hours. Items proudly displayed & for sale include models of iconic Jeddawi buildings & doors alongside the more usual magnets, hats, souvenir clocks & wall decorations.

**Jeddah Souvenir** [252 C3] Abdullah Omar al Matbouli St, about 50m north of Naseem Hse; 050 181 8979; 10.00–14.00 & 17.00–23.00 Sat–Thu, 17.00–23.00 Fri. The shop may not always open during the published morning hours. There is an interesting array of figurines in local dress in addition to the expected souvenir T-shirts, coffee mugs, key rings & other items that are easy to bring home.

**OTHER PRACTICALITIES** If you need to withdraw cash, **ATMs** can be found in nearly every petrol station forecourt found throughout Jeddah. There are ATMs in most supermarkets other than the smallest family-owned businesses, as well as at banks. Some banks also have free-standing ATM kiosks.

The **central post office** [252 A4] (w splonline.com.sa; 08.00–21.00 Sun–Thu, 16.00–21.00 Fri–Sat) in Jeddah is located on Hael just south of al Mahmal Centre in al Balad.

### Banks

#### *Al Balad*

**Al Rajhi Bank** [252 D3] Cnr Ahl al Suhaifah & Old Mecca Rd; w alrajhibank.com.sa; 09.30–16.30 Sun–Thu

**Riyad Bank** [252 A4] Cnr bin Rafia & Banajah; 012 647 4777; w riyadbank.com; 09.30–16.30 Sun–Thu

#### *Al Hamra and Palestine*

**ANB Bank** [257 B3] Cnr al Andalus Rd & Fayd al Nour; w anb.com.sa; 800 124 4040; 09.30–17.30 Sat–Thu

**Saudi Investment Bank** [257 C3] Ghosn al Salam, off King Abdullah Br Rd west of Reyah al Amal; w saib.com.sa; 800 124 8000; 09.30–16.30 Sun–Thu

#### *Tahlia Street and Madinah Road areas*

**ANB Bank** [265 E6] Cnr Tahlia & Mohammed al Bakri sts; w anb.com.sa; 800 124 4040; 09.30–17.30 Sat–Thu

**SNB Bank** [264 C5] Tahlia St next to Assila hotel; w alahli.com; 800 760 0000; 09.30–16.30 Sun–Thu

#### *Corniche*

**ANB Bank** [271 C6] Cnr King Abdul Aziz Rd & Urwah bin al Jaid; w anb.com.sa; 800 124 4040; 09.30–17.30 Sat–Thu

**Riyad Bank** [271 C5] Hira St, next to McDonald's; w riyadbank.com; 9200 02470; 09.30–16.30 Sun–Thu

**SAB Bank** [271 C3] King Abdul Aziz Br Rd & Abdul Malik bin Juraih; w sab.com; 012 603 5959; 09.30–16.30 Sun–Thu

## Hospitals

Along with Riyadh, Jeddah is a medical hub for Saudi Arabia & the wider GCC. The following hospitals are top-quality facilities.

**Dr Soliman Fakeeh Hospital** [257 B2] Cnr Palestine & Abdul Wahhab Naib al Haram Rd; 9200 12777; w en.dsfhjeddah.fakeeh.care

**International Medical Centre Hospital** [257 C3] Cnr Hael St & al Sefat al Hamedah Rd; 9200 12777; w imc.med.sa/en

**King Abdul Aziz University Hospital** [257 D3] Cnr abu Leila al Ashaari & Mohammed Sourour al Sabban rds; 012 640 8222; w hospital.kau.edu.sa

**King Faisal Specialist Hospital & Research Centre** [265 E5] Cnr Abdul Malik bin Marwan & Wadi al Nakhl rds; 012 667 7777; w kfshrc.edu.sa/en/home

**Saudi German Hospital** [271 C6] Cnr al Batarji & Souweid bin Houbairah rds; 9200 07997; w jeddah.saudigermanhealth.com

## WHAT TO SEE AND DO

**Al Balad** Jeddah's original neighbourhood may be quiet during the day, but it comes alive in the evenings when the souqs start to trade and the coffee shops and cafés start to fill. Although most residents may be expatriates from parts of Asia and Africa, Jeddawis still find their way back to al Balad to get a good deal on traditional goods and simply to socialise and sometimes reminisce.

Historic Jeddah, referring to al Balad, earned recognition as a UNESCO World Heritage Site in 2014 for its cultural significance dating back to the 7th century CE. Already a trading port, it grew in importance from the dawn of Islam as the port for Mecca, less than 85km inland, which also contributed to Jeddah becoming a multicultural city. Distinct architecture such as the coral buildings, usually decorated with roshan or latticed wooden windows are recognised, as are historic mosques and souqs. Roshan are also known as *mashrabiyya*, referring to the boxed window designed to enhance airflow in a pre-air-conditioning world. Some say UNESCO rescued historic Jeddah in the nick of time as many of these unique buildings appeared to be destined for the wrecking ball. Happily, the uniqueness of the neighbourhood is now appreciated by Saudis and visitors alike, with renovations and development driven by Saudi Vision 2030 and the Ministry of Culture.

The perimeter of al Balad can be defined broadly by its four gates: Bab Jadid (to the north), Bab al Makkah (east), Bab Sharif (south) and Bab al Furdah (west). Each has its own character, determined by its surroundings. Many visitors approach from Bab Jadid [252 B2] as it is most easily accessed from the modern city. Bab al Makkah [252 D3] is surrounded by particularly interesting shops as it has served as the gateway for pilgrims about to embark on the last leg of their journey to the Holy City. Bab Sharif [252 B3] illustrates how the old city started to expand a long time ago, with shops well beyond the original boundary represented by the gate. Bab al Furdah [252 B3] leads to some of the early purpose-built modern shops of the mid 20th century.

The key attraction in al Balad are the souqs, which are described in more detail on page 272. Visitors also come to al Balad to appreciate the architecture, discovering that some of the roshan have been painted bright green or blue. There's something to marvel at around every corner. The streets are relatively quiet during the day but visitors can easily wander the area without the worry of getting lost as there's always someone around to give directions. A few signs in Arabic and English will also lead you to some key landmarks. Cafés are plentiful and never far away when you need a break. At the time of research, there were no published walking tours, although it is possible to arrange a guided tour through some hotels. This is almost certain to change as visitor numbers grow and the building works are closer to completion.

***House museums*** Some houses in al Balad have become museums, with beautifully decorated interiors and artefacts on display from the houses' golden era. It is possible to visit these house museums, but it's important to note that they do not adhere to their published opening hours – be prepared to find the doors closed when you visit. A total of more than 50 houses are scheduled to be restored as tourism grows.

**Beit al Balad** [252 A2] (King Abdul Aziz Branch Rd, near al Basha) is more than 200 years old and has been beautifully restored. The building's interior and museum are currently closed, but it is possible to walk around and admire the exterior of this traditional house. Built in the unique coral structural tradition of Old Jeddah, **Matbouli House Museum** [252 C3] (Souq al Awali, just east of al Layyat Ln; 🕘 17.00–22.00 daily; SAR10) has been standing since the 17th century. This three-storey house is dedicated to the authentic Jeddawi way of life, albeit a very materially wealthy one. Men's and women's diwans indicate the common tradition of gender separation extending to the home when guests are present. The rooftop, affording great views of the neighbourhood, is currently closed.

Easily found by the beautiful tree slightly to the left of the main entrance, **Nassif House Museum** [252 C4] (cnr Ayyas bin Rabab & Souq al Alawi; 🕘 08.00–23.55 Mon–Sat, 08.00–noon & 18.00–23.55 Sun; admission free at time of writing) is one of al Balad's late 19th-century mansions, built by Omar Nassif Efendi. Now a museum and cultural centre, the building has been carefully restored to its former glory. Its most astounding features are the ramps built wide enough to allow camels to walk up to the roof. **Salloum Residence** [252 B2] (al Kabli Ln, between Salamah & Qabil lns; SAR10) was built by Abdullah bin Obaid Salloum in the late 19th century, and is another example of life that has been mostly lost to the past, if only relatively recently. The signs are only in Arabic, but there is a lantern suspended from the arched entrance and what looks like a garden fence along the roof that let the visitor know they have found the right place.

***Tomb of Eve*** [252 D1] (Mawkib al Imam, just east of Old Mecca al Moukarramah Rd) Yes, *that* Eve. Also known as Mother Hawwa's Tomb, it was destroyed and the surface covered in 1926 as the religious authorities believed visiting tombs was akin to idol worship and thus forbidden. The site was later sealed in 1975. Access to the cemetery, deemed by many to be a significant site of pilgrimage, is controlled by a security guard who appears at random times and determines who can enter.

**Al Hamra and Palestine (Falasteen)** This area is in the heart of the business district with many important government offices as well as being a good place to socialise, especially along the Corniche. Do as the Jeddawis do: visit as the sun goes down and make an evening of it.

***King Fahd Fountain*** [257 A3] Built offshore in the Red Sea, this has been described as the world's tallest fountain, reaching over 200m high. Water from the Red Sea is propelled into the air from what looks like a very large gold incense burner. The fountain can be seen from many vantage points in al Hamra, al Andalus and beyond. The al Hamra Corniche is a lovely spot, with plenty of cafés where you can settle and watch the world go by with the fountain in the background. The sunset views can be terrific.

***Palestine Street Walk*** [257 F3] This promenade lined with shops, cafés and restaurants runs from the al Hamra Corniche to al Andalus Road and has helped to regenerate the neighbourhood, which was once a fashionable area of Jeddah. It's a popular walk in the evening. See the beautiful sunsets over the Red Sea at the western end of the route; this is also a good spot to view the King Fahd Fountain when it lights up in the evening.

**Tahlia Street and Madinah Road areas** Although better known for its collection of hotels, restaurants and shops, don't miss one of Jeddah's more interesting places to explore if you are a foodie or a trendy shopper.

***Al Tayebat Museum and International City of Science and Knowledge*** ✷ [265 G3] (Raihanat al Jazirah, near the southwest junction of Setten & Abdallah al Zawawi rds; ☎ 056 386 6984; w museum-942.business.site; ⌚ 08.00–noon & 17.00–21.00 Sat–Thu; admission free to the complex, museum SAR80) This complex was built in 1987 under the direction of the philanthropist Sheikh Abdul Raouf Hassan Khalil Rahmatallah. It is spread over 10,000m$^2$ and contains over 300 rooms in 12 buildings, including a green-domed mosque and the four-storey Museum for International Civilisation. The museum is a treasure trove of pre-Islamic and Islamic artefacts that reflect life around every region of the Kingdom. The architecture is in the traditional Hejazi style, with its highly decorated doors, distinct arches, minarets, elaborately latticed wooden roshan that beautifully contrast with the white walls, and inner courtyards. There is a row of shops in a small souq along Raihanat al Jazirah Road on the southern permimeter of the complex. Al Tayebat is a gem that has to be seen to be believed.

**Corniche** The Corniche extends from al Hamra to Obhur Bay in the far north of the city and can be accessed via the road of the same name, often spelled al Kurnaysh. National and city parks are dotted along the seashore for almost 30km and can be visited by the public. The parks give access to a combination of sandy and rocky beaches, as well as food kiosks, picnic areas, grassy spaces and much more. Prospective sunbathers and swimmers must take note that this is a modest dress place, so Western swimwear for both women and men are out of the question. Parts of the Corniche road near the Hilton and slightly further north have a pedestrianised area in the centre of the dual carriageway where you can see visitors and locals (men and women) exercising, walking, jogging and generally enjoying themselves.

***Fakieh Aquarium*** [271 C7] (Cnr al Kurnaiysh Bridge & Abdallah Zawawi rds; ☎ 012 606 6144; w fakiehaquarium.com; ⌚ 10.00–23.00 Sat–Thu, 13.30–23.00 Fri; SAR55, plus SAR80 for the dolphin show) This is the only aquarium in the Kingdom. Popular with families, it has more than 200 species of marine life on view from all over the world, plus several shops that will delight children. Swimming with dolphins and a seal show are the aquarium's latest attractions. Purchase your admission tickets at the booths on site to the right in front of the entrance gates. It is also possible to purchase tickets in advance via the website.

***City Walk*** [271 C5] (Abi al Fahdial Koufi Rd; w jeddahwalk.com; SAR50) In spite of the name, this venue should be regarded as an amusement park complete with loud music and the inevitable fast-food establishments. This is the place where many Saudis splash out on their families. Be aware, though, that once inside additional tickets must be purchased for many of the activities, ranging from special arcades to seasonal shows.

***Jeddah Art Promenade*** [271 B4] (North Corniche along Beach St from approx Prince Faisal bin Fahd Rd to Suleiman al Salami Rd; 🕘 16.00–01.00 Sun–Wed, 16.00–02.00 Thu–Sat; ticket prices vary depending on which specialist exhibits are on display, some free) Opened for Jeddah Seasons in late 2021, this is a multi-purpose destination. Whether you are interested in public sculpture, somewhere for children to play, or to take advantage of the 4km walkway, the Promenade provides a lovely opportunity to see where the Kingdom's focus lies for attracting tourists with modern developments. There is also a Saturday Market.

The **Jeddah Formula One Street Circuit** [271 B5] runs parallel to the Jeddah Art Promenade. The race was first held in December 2021 as a part of the Saudi Seasons calendar and appears to be turning into a more permanent fixture...at least until it moves to its future home in Qiddiya, the entertainment district being developed southwest of Riyadh.

***Al Rahmah (Floating) Mosque*** [271 B4] (Corniche Branch Rd, around the peninsula from the Jeddah Yacht Club; 🕘 24hrs daily) Also known as the Fatima al Zahra Mosque, this beautiful structure was built in 1985, on a platform over the Red Sea – which explains its other name, the Floating Mosque. In addition to the main dome, its striking design includes 53 additional domes, as well as 23 umbrella-shaped structures providing welcome shaded areas. Inside, there is a prayer hall for women, as well as one for men. Non-Muslims as well as Muslims are allowed to visit this mosque – a rare opportunity. Be respectful of prayer times, the dress code, gender segregation and other conventions and etiquette. Make sure you visit before sunset, when the last rays of light from the Red Sea create a wonderful silhouette of the mosque. Unfortunately, access is difficult as the nearby road is blocked due to the Jeddah Formula One circuit nearby and the ongoing development of several new hotels along this stretch of the Corniche. Try to park at the nearby Jeddah Yacht Club and walk in.

***Obhur Corniche*** [271 B2] Running along Obhur Bay from the Faculty of Marine Studies, past the Four Points Sheraton, this stretch of the Corniche provides a snapshot of contemporary local life. This area is especially popular with young, modern Saudis in particular and remains busy until sunrise – here visitors can indulge in everything from fishing to boating, jet-skiing, promenading or simply sitting and enjoying a coffee or a picnic. Turn on to Corniche Branch Road from

## ROUNDABOUT ART

Jeddah has been a creative city for a long time. In the 1970s, Saudi and international artists were asked by the then Mayor of Jeddah, Dr Mohammed Said Farsi, to create sculptures, bronzes and other works of art that could be displayed in the centre of Jeddah's many roundabouts. The result was more than 20 individual exhibits, which were then installed on many of these roundabouts throughout the Jeddah, mostly near the Corniche. Works include the *Bicycle, Boat, Camel, Car Cube* aka *Car Crash, Cosmos, Fist, Four Lanterns, Globe, Magic Carpet, Marine Sciences, Qiblah, Seagull, Sword, Verse,* plus many more, and give the roundabouts their name. How many can you find?

the Marine Services Roundabout and follow the coastline along the bay; there are plenty of parking spaces along the coast road.

**Jeddah's art galleries** Saudi, Arab and sometimes other artists have long taken inspiration from Jeddah's relatively progressive, open and tolerant environment. Since the announcement of Saudi Vision 2030, many new galleries have opened in the city, some of which are confident enough to give artists a chance to exhibit content that would have been unthinkable until relatively recently. While some of the work on display may seem quite tame compared with exhibits on show in other galleries worldwide, remember that Saudis are embracing the modern art scene in a way that would have been impossible only a few years ago. Many artists in the Kingdom are encouraged by visitors' support of their creativity.

***ATHR Gallery*** [265 H5] Cnr Setten Rd & Tahlia St; 012 284 5009; w athrart.com; call for opening hours) Located on the fifth floor of the office building next to Danube supermarket in the Serafi Megamall, the entrance is not obvious so ask someone if you cannot find it. This gallery was founded in 2009 and focuses on contemporary art from Saudi nationals and others from elsewhere in the Middle East and beyond. Opening times are not published and are somewhat dependent on exhibits. The gallery also holds lectures.

***Hafez Art Gallery*** [264 D4] Ahmed bin Abbas Rd, just west of Hussein Seraj Rd; 055 551 7000; w hafezgallery.com; 14.00–20.00 Sun–Thu during exhibitions) Founded in 2014, this gallery in the upscale neighbourhood of Rawdah is dedicated to sharing Saudi culture and displays works from Saudi and other artists from elsewhere in the GCC and wider Middle East region. The ground-floor building has a generous exhibition hall. Ring the bell at the gates for entry if they are not open.

***Hayy Jameel*** [271 C5] (Arwa bint Abdul Mutalib St, al Muhammadiyah; w hayyjameel.org; 10.00–20.00 Sun–Mon & Wed–Thu, 14.00–20.00 Fri, noon–20.00 Sat; admission free) You will be asked to register upon arrival at the reception desk. Hayy Jameel is a cultural centre set up to encourage the creative arts. It opened in 2021 and is currently home to Hayy Arts Museum, Hayy Cinema, Hayy Learning and Studios which provide courses, and the performance centre of Fenaa Hayy. Exhibits change frequently, but all focus on various Islamic arts. In among these buildings is the Saha central courtyard where visitors can relax and reflect on their full experience of this lovely venue. Hayy Jameel is part of the Art Jameel, a collaborative body founded by the philanthropist Jameel family. Global partners of Art Jameel include the Delfina Foundation (London), the Metropolitan Museum of Art (New York), the Prince's Foundation School of Traditional Arts (London) and the Victoria and Albert Museum (London).

***House of Islamic Arts*** [265 H5] (Southwest cnr Tahlia St & Setten Rd; w iarts.sa; 10.00–22.00 Sat–Thu, 17.00–23.00 Fri; SAR30 with concessions for children, students & pensioners) Located next to IKEA in Jeddah Park on the fourth floor, this is a hidden gem. Ask if you can't locate it as there are no obvious signs. There are six rooms filled with pieces from various eras. English-speaking tour guides will help people navigate the intricacies of the exhibits, including non-Muslims. There are also Arabic and English-language audio programmes for those who prefer to do a self-guided tour.

***Other galleries*** Well-established gallery **Jeddah Atelier for Fine Arts** [265 G5] (Cnr al Nahdah al Hadeethah & al Moustaqbal al Moudee sts, just north of Tahlia St; 012 664 0710; admission free) proudly exhibits paintings and sculptures showcasing the Saudi modernist style. **Rochan Gallery** [265 F6] (al Juhdal Mukhlis & al Taifi St; 012 665 5630; w rochanfinearts.com; 08.00–18.00 Sat–Thu, 17.00–22.00 Fri; admission free), located in an upmarket residential area convenient for those staying in al Hamra or around al Andalus, is a deceptively large gallery showcasing paintings of contemporary life. With its collection of paintings, sculpture, porcelains and ceramics, **Saudi Center for Fine Art** [265 F6] (Rahman al Islam, south of Tahlia St; 053 144 7888; w saudiarts.com; 10.00–13.00 & 17.00–20.00 Sat–Thu; admission free) explores regional cultures within the Kingdom and beyond. It also offers art courses for men, women and children.

## AROUND JEDDAH

**NORTH OBHUR أبحر الشمالية** Long a popular place to escape the city for the weekend, North Obhur is rapidly developing into a well-to-do neighbourhood in its own right. There are a growing number of restaurants, a branch of HyperPanda, and the new Obhur Mall [271 C1]. Most visitors will find the beach resorts to be the main draw. The Narcissus Resort and Spa (see below), al Murjan [271 B2], Coral Beach [271 C2], Red Sea (see below) and Sol Beach [271 A1] resorts are all popular, each with its own vibe. Some resorts maintain the Saudi dress code.

The incomplete **Kingdom Tower** [271 B1], which dominates views from the beaches, the bay and most residential neighbourhoods in North Obhur, is promising to be the world's tallest tower, standing at 1,000m when finished. Building work was suspended in 2017 and remains so at the time of research, leaving an unintentional silhouette of abandoned cranes on the skyline which looks like a work of art to complement – or compete with – Jeddah's roundabout art.

Scuba divers will be delighted to find the **Hope of Spring PADI 5 Star Dive Shop** [271 A2] (056 222 0007; w hopespringdive.com) on site at the Red Sea Resort. Dives can be organised on most days, with night dives on offer as well. There are many more dive shops in North Obhur, found mostly along Prince Abdul Majeed Road. Double check PADI certifications, opening hours and other information by contacting the shop directly or better yet drop in for a visit.

### Where to stay

**Narcissus Resort & Spa** [271 B2] Prince Abdullah al Faisal St, at the southern end of the North Obhur Corniche; 9200 00777; w narcissushotels.com/abhor. This resort is part of the Narcissus group with properties in al Hamra & in the Olaya district of Riyadh. It is very popular with wealthy Saudi families & offers activities day & night. The outdoor swimming pools are strictly for men & children, while women have access to an indoor pool. Opt for a villa with a private pool if you want to sunbathe. **$$$$$**

✷ **Red Sea Resort** [271 A1] Obhur Branch Rd, parallel to Prince Abdullah al Faisal St; 012 656 2199; w redseamarina.com/red-sea-resort. Note that access is through an unmarked double set of security gates in a break in a parade of nondescript shops – look for the cars parked in front. Red Sea is a private resort that has agreed to allow access for guests of the Sheraton Jeddah hotel. You will be asked for your room number at the reception office immediately after the security gates. Use the car park immediately to the right past the security gates if you prefer to park on site. Once inside the resort, Western dress is allowed, including beachwear. Bungalows can be rented for the day or overnight with b/fast. Note that families, mixed-gender groups & women will be welcome, but it is possible that single men & groups of men may be denied access. As you walk down the path towards the Red Sea, you will pass a tennis court, the saltwater swimming & wading pools & the gym before reaching the outdoor beach restaurant & separate ice cream shop. The restaurant has casual food as you would expect, with especially good grills & salads. The beach is an elevated area filled with comfortable loungers & umbrellas so sunbathers can enjoy the view & the breeze in the sun or shade. Access to the shallow water is via the boat ramp area of the resort. Be careful of the coral & slippery rocks that will almost immediately greet waders. There is also ladder access to waist deep & deeper water for swimmers, divers & snorkellers. **$$$**

### Where to eat and drink

**Twina Seafood** [271 B2] North Obhur Beach Rd, next to Narcissus; 9200 28284; **w** twina.net; 09.00–23.00 Sat–Thu, 13.00–23.00 Fri. This popular establishment is both a fish market & a restaurant. Order at the fish market. Select your fish or shellfish from the fish market at the front, noting that prices are by the kilo. You have a choice of preparation method & don't forget to order side dishes. The baba ganouj & *syadieh* rice are particularly good. After ordering, follow the path to the restaurant which is a few minutes' walk or short buggy ride towards the beach. The restaurant has both indoor & outdoor dining, & there is a minimum spend per table of SAR300. There are other branches in al Hamra near the Aya Mall & Abdallah Zawawi Rd aka Sari Branch Rd at Prince Sultan Rd. **$$$$**

**KING ABDULLAH ECONOMIC CITY (KAEC)** مدينة الملك عبد الله الاقتصادية (*madina malak Abdullah al aqtasadia*) Located about 100km north of Jeddah, this megacity, announced in 2005, was designed to attract a diverse collection of businesses to reduce the Kingdom's over-reliance on oil revenues. Along with KAUST (see below), KAEC was also an early experiment in liberalising some of the social norms that remained in place elsewhere in the Kingdom such as removing gender segregation in the work environment and supporting a modest relaxation of the dress code. It was projected to see a population of 1 million by 2020, but the population is currently estimated to be about 7,000. KAEC is the home of a Haramain High Speed Railway station, the Bay Le Sun Hotel, the newer View Hotel and Residences, a lovely beachfront and a few restaurants, mostly along the Corniche. It is also home to Royal Greens Golf and Country Club. Although businesses do operate in KAEC, in an area that was meant to exceed the size of Washington, DC, little growth has been seen in the years that followed the death of King Abdullah, the king who spearheaded the project and lent it his name. This is a good example of how megaprojects associated with a specific king do not always thrive or even survive once there is a new ruler. KAEC is not specifically tourist orientated, but those travelling along the Red Sea coastline may wish to make a convenient overnight stop in KAEC as accommodation becomes more scarce further north and east.

**KING ABDULLAH UNIVERSITY OF SCIENCE AND TECHNOLOGY (KAUST)** جامعة الملك عبد الله للعلوم و التقنية (*jamiat al malik Abdullah lilulum was teqniyya*) KAUST was built as the first mixed-gender university in Saudi Arabia as another key project under King Abdullah. Located in the village of Thuwwal 20km south of KAEC, it opened in 2009. Most visitors, whether for business or who have requested an organised tour, stay in KAEC. There are a few restaurants along or near Route 303.

## MECCA مكة

Also known as Makkah and Makkah al-Mukarramah (مكة المكرمة), Mecca is the Kingdom's third most populous city after Riyadh and Jeddah, home to an estimated

1.7 million people. As the holiest site in Islam – it is the birthplace of the Prophet Mohammed and of Islam itself – the city hosts religious pilgrims throughout the year, swelling its numbers to more than twice their usual size during the hajj, which occurs during specific dates in the 12th month of the Islamic calendar.

Mecca has a hot desert climate and is warm or hot throughout the year. Owing to the high humidity and temperatures ranging from the mid 20s to over 40°C in the summer, it is best to visit for umrah between November and April. Evenings are pleasantly mild in the winter months but remain warm and humid in the summer.

**HISTORY** Mecca is believed to have been founded, in pre-Islamic times, due to its oasis location along an important ancient caravan route from what is now Yemen to the south, running to the Levant and beyond in the north. Some scholars believe it might have been known to several ancient civilisations, including the Greeks, Romans and possibly the Nabataeans, as Thamudic inscriptions have been found referencing what is believed to be Mecca. During the 5th century CE, while other trade routes, especially along the Red Sea coast, were being threatened by various empires, including the Byzantines and Sassanids, Arab tribes, including the Quraish, gained control of Mecca. Many of these tribes were idol worshippers, with the pagan god Hubei featuring prominently. It is believed that, by the 6th century CE, many Arab tribes would converge upon Mecca annually for pagan religious purposes, an event where trade and other disputes were often settled.

In the early 7th century CE, the Prophet Mohammed started to receive revelations about Islam and its Abrahamic, monotheistic beliefs that were at odds with paganism and idol worship. In 628CE, Mohammed was barred from entering Mecca during that year's pilgrimage. Although an agreement was reached allowing Mohammed and his growing number of followers into Mecca for future pilgrimages, this failed after two years. In 630CE, Mohammed led the Conquest of Mecca. As a result of his success, idol worship was crushed, and replaced by worshipping Allah and no other god. However, the annual pilgrimage to Mecca continued, and was established as one of the five pillars of Islam. See page 18 for further information about the early history of Islam in Mecca.

Although Mecca's religious importance was firmly established, as the centuries progressed attention turned to other cities. Successive Muslim leaders established power bases in Damascus, Baghdad, Cairo and al Andalus (present-day southern

## LOST ARCHITECTURAL HISTORY

Many historic sites were razed to the ground to make way for the construction of the Mecca Clock Royal Tower (page 284), which began in 2002; it opened in 2012. Some of these historic places would have been known to the Prophet, including his birthplace and the houses of his wife, Khadija, and Abu Bakr, his companion and father-in-law. Similar demolition has been taking place in Mecca at an accelerated rate since the mid 1980s, and an estimated 95% of these historic buildings from the earliest days of Islam are believed to have been destroyed. Mecca is expanding at a rapid rate, and the areas surrounding the al Haram area are undergoing massive development as part of the Government's Royal Commission for Makkah City and Holy Sites. Most of this building work is aimed at supporting the increasing number of pilgrims who visit Mecca, with more hotels, transport and other infrastructure projects.

Spain), while Mecca itself endured further attacks, by the Umayyads and the Qarmatians.

The Ottoman Turks were in power from 1517 to 1802, when the Second Saudi State took control of Mecca. As the Ottoman Empire was collapsing, the final Battles of Mecca took place, with the Sharif of Mecca ultimately defeated. The region was conquered by ibn Saud and became part of the Third Saudi State, now the Kingdom of Saudi Arabia, in 1925.

## GETTING THERE AND AWAY

**☪ By air** There is no airport in Mecca. The nearest airport, and where most people arrive, is Jeddah's King Abdul Aziz International Airport (KAIA; page 249). If you are arriving from elsewhere in the Kingdom, Taif International Airport is the next closest option, but it is located to the northeast of Taif centre and thus away from Mecca to its west.

**☪ By road** Highway 15 is the main north–south route into Mecca. Those travelling from Jeddah or from the east will likely travel on Route 80, which runs across the Kingdom through the centre of Riyadh and to the Arabian Gulf, terminating near al Khobar. **Taxi**, Uber or Careem services are plentiful from Jeddah and Taif, and their airports. Upscale hotels can also organise a private car and driver if you prefer, ensuring the driver is Muslim and thus permitted to make this journey.

It is possible to travel to Mecca by **bus** from nearly everywhere in the Kingdom. SAPTCO services are frequent and comfortable, with a high standard of amenities such as on-board Wi-Fi. SAPTCO VIP services run to the dedicated VIP station just north of the First Ring Road nor far from the SAPTCO station that receives standard service buses. There are additional stations to the east inside the First Ring Road of the al Haram area. Note that one of the main stations is located on the Old Madinah Road just south of the Fourth Ring Road, so further arrangements must be made to travel to the al Haram area – be prepared if you have chosen this route.

**☪ By rail** The Haramain High Speed Railway operates between Mecca and Madinah via Jeddah and King Abdullah Economic City, and is the fastest way to travel between these cities. The Mecca station is located to the west of the city centre along al Rasaifah Road, south of Route 80. This station is for the use of Muslims only – this is usually checked at the time of ticketing and can be checked upon arrival at the station. The stations in Madinah, KAEC and Jeddah are accessible to all travellers. See page 74 for more information about this service.

**GETTING AROUND** The biggest challenges for drivers in Mecca are the sheer numbers of pedestrians – unlike in other cities in the Kingdom – and the lack of parking spaces. Drive if you must, but most people sensibly leave their car at their hotel or somewhere else away from the city centre, then take other transport, or walk. Alternatively, you may consider utilising the services of a driver. Mecca is always busy, even in the small hours of the morning.

**☪ By metro** The al Mashaaer al Mugaddassah Metro line (قطار المشاعر المقدسة الخط الجنوبي; *qtar al mashaaer al muqaddassah al khat diljanubi*), the first of Mecca's two metro systems, opened in 2010, designed specifically to move Muslim pilgrims around Mecca during hajj. It operates seven days a week in that period and the route, with a total of nine stations, covers Jamarat, Mina, Muzdalifah and Arafat.

## NOT ALL ROADS LEAD TO MECCA

Only Muslims may enter Mecca, and there are checkpoints on all roads as you approach the city where officials will stop at random anyone they wish and ask to see passports and visas. From Jeddah, travelling on Highway 80, the main gate is Mecca Gate, where you will encounter the first of several checkpoints. Travellers will pass under an arch that resembles a *rehal* or Qur'an stand, from which point only Muslims are allowed to proceed. Officials will redirect any non-Muslims to suitable routes that avoid continuing further into the city. Other routes also have a series of checkpoints.

Travelling between Jeddah and Taif, routes that bypass the Holy City are clearly signposted, and are designated for use by all travellers but should always be followed by non-Muslims. These roads have been dubbed collectively the 'Christian Bypass' by expatriates for decades. Travelling via the bypass routes will take longer, but they have a special vibe. There are several bypass routes around Mecca. The route to the south of the city along Route 298 to Highway 15 has been improved in recent years and affords beautiful views of the plains below with Mecca in sight on a clear day once the road starts to climb towards Taif.

The Mecca Metro, also known as Makkah Rail Mass Transit (قطارات مكة للنقل العام) remains in the development phase despite being announced in 2010. Since both systems are incomplete at the time of writing, it is important to check which stations are open if you plan to use the metro.

**By bus** Local buses in Mecca are run by SAPTCO, with services scheduled from 05.30 to 23.30. Unlike in Jeddah and Riyadh, these buses are well used and by people from all backgrounds. Bus tours are also available to book, departing Mecca or Jeddah and covering Mecca's holy and historic sites, including Ziyarat tours. These tours may be a better way to get around, especially if you are considering visiting these points of interest, and are for Muslims only.

**By taxi** Taxis are plentiful and inexpensive around the clock in Mecca and can easily be hailed on the street, though be prepared to wait at very busy times. Taxis can also be arranged through most hotels other than the most modest properties. Check to make sure the driver switches on the meter before setting off.

Uber and Careem both operate in Mecca and can be an excellent alternative to taxis, especially in busy periods.

**On foot** Mecca's al Haram area is compact and mostly pedestrian friendly, though walking can present the same challenges as in other Saudi cities – don't expect cars to stop for you if you venture on to the road to cross. Police are often present to help the flow of both motorised and foot traffic, so wait for their signal to walk to minimise your risks. Walking is usually the most sensible option, as long as you are fit, as distances between sites can be long and some routes involve hills; remember to stay well hydrated during the hotter months.

**WHERE TO STAY AND EAT** When you consider where to stay, do not underestimate the impact of Mecca's traffic, both vehicular and pedestrian. Mecca has grown organically, with little consideration for organised parking and general congestion.

Try to choose your accommodation to minimise spending more time than necessary on the roads.

Many people travel to Mecca on hajj and umrah package tours, which usually include accommodation and meals. Those who are travelling independently can choose from a wide selection of hotels. As accommodation is accessible only for Muslim visitors, we only provide basic information to give you a flavour of what is on offer.

There is no shortage of five-star hotels in Mecca. They tend to be in great locations within walking distance from the south and west of Masjid al Haram. Familiar chains include Hilton, Hyatt Regency, Intercontinental, Jumeirah, Le Méridien, Marriott, Millennium, Raffles, Movenpick, Pullman, Sheraton and Swisshotel. You may also wish to check out the al Marwa Rayaan, Anjum or Makkah Clock Royal Tower, a Fairmont hotel, for somewhere a bit different in this category and price range. Mid-range and budget hotels can also be booked by independent travellers but are often block-booked by pilgrimage tour operators and are usually a bit further away.

Restaurants featuring cuisines from all over the world can be found throughout Mecca. Whether you fancy a gourmet meal, prefer to grab a quick bite at a Saudi fast-food restaurant or take away a shawarma, the choice appears endless. Most top-end restaurants are, unsurprisingly, located near the top-end hotels.

**☪ SHOPPING** If you want to bring home a souvenir from your pilgrimage, you can choose from shops, souqs and shopping malls. Head to the souqs to the south of Masjid al Haram as this is the most obvious and convenient area to look for religious items and souvenirs, from prayer rugs to wall art to models of the Ka'aba. Check out 'Souq Mecca Gate – Jabal Omar', 'Souq al Khalil – Jabal Omar' and the Abraj al Bait Shopping Centre, all conveniently located near the major upmarket hotels. They are not really traditional souqs anymore but busy shopping centres, and most are open 24 hours.

If you are looking for a modern shopping mall, then head to the north and west, where you will find Al Difaya Mall, Al Hijaz Mall, Makkah City Centre and Saraya Mall. The popular Makkah Mall is located to the southeast of al Haram on King Abdullah Road. Most of these malls are open from around 09.00 to midnight daily.

Al Raya, Carrefour, Danube, Panda and HyperPanda supermarkets all have branches in Mecca. Smaller shops are abundant throughout the city.

**☪ OTHER PRACTICALITIES** **Pharmacies** are plentiful throughout Mecca and offer the full services found in pharmacies in other large cities throughout the Kingdom. As they are used to customers from all over the world, they are often an excellent source of information and advice. Pharmacies are located in shopping malls, hospitals and free-standing buildings. Many are open throughout the day and into the late evening, with some keeping their doors open 24 hours a day. Some of the most popular and well-regarded pharmacies are Al Dawaa, Boots and Nahdi, as well as independent chemists that might be recommended by your hotel. The **Emergency Centre Campus** and **Haram Emergency Hospital** are located within the al Haram complex.

**☪ WHAT TO SEE AND DO** Also known as Abraj al Beit (أبراج الساعة), the **Mecca Clock Royal Tower** is currently the world's fourth tallest building, standing at a height of just over 600m. It is located on the southern boundary of the Masjid al Haram, but can be seen from some distance away as you approach the city.

As Mecca is not a destination for general tourism, we refer readers to page 380 for a better overview of the main places of interest in the city visited by Muslim pilgrims.

## TAIF اَلطَّائِفُ AND AROUND

Taif is the second most populous city in Makkah Province and the sixth largest in the Kingdom, with about 700,000 people. It is known as the City of Roses (*madinat al wurud*), reflecting its rich agricultural heritage. It was once known as Wajj, from the nearby valley of the same name. The name Taif is believed to be derived from *tawaf*, meaning circumambulation.

The Banu Thaqif people have been the dominant tribe in the area since pre-Islamic times and it was they who built the ancient wall that originally encircled the settlement. They are still important residents of Taif. The Ottomans indirectly ruled Taif and much of the Hejaz until the short-lived Hashemite Kingdom was established in the early 20th century. Reverting back to the Kingdom of Hejaz, Taif became part of the Third Saudi State, now the Kingdom of Saudi Arabia, upon independence in 1932.

Taif is situated at an elevation of nearly 1,900m, making for a pleasant climate in the summer. It is a popular destination for Saudis from elsewhere in the Kingdom who take to the mountain resorts in the summer months, escaping the worst of the heat in their cities. Although Taif is very pleasant during the day throughout the year, temperatures can drop to single digits once the sun goes down in the short winter. Taif is well situated as the gateway to al Bahah and Asir provinces and other destinations to the south for those travelling through along Sarawat Mountain range.

### GETTING THERE AND AROUND

**By air** The Taif Regional Airport is located about 30km northeast of the city. Flights operate to most larger cities in the Kingdom, with Saudia the main carrier and additional services on flynas and flyadeal. There are international flights to other Middle Eastern countries and to Turkey and Pakistan.

**By road** Highway 15 is the main road into Taif from Mecca to the west and from points south. For those arriving by road from the east, most travel on Route 80 before turning on to Route 267 for the city centre.

SAPTCO **buses** serve Taif, offering routine services to and from most points throughout the Kingdom. The bus station is located on Airport Road near Khaled bin Ouday Street. Care must be taken when planning travel to Jeddah as any services passing through Mecca are for Muslims only.

Although a public transport plan was announced in 2022 to provide local bus services in Taif, this will take a long time to establish. Realistically, the only public transport in Taif are taxis, Uber and Careem, which all operate throughout the city and to the airport. Otherwise, expect to self-drive. It is possible to explore some of Taif on foot.

### WHERE TO STAY *Map, page 286*

Taif has a growing number of properties to choose from, although top-end accommodation is still mostly absent. If you are prepared for more modest rooms and service that may not reach the standards of Jeddah but are nevertheless welcoming, you will find your home from home in Taif.

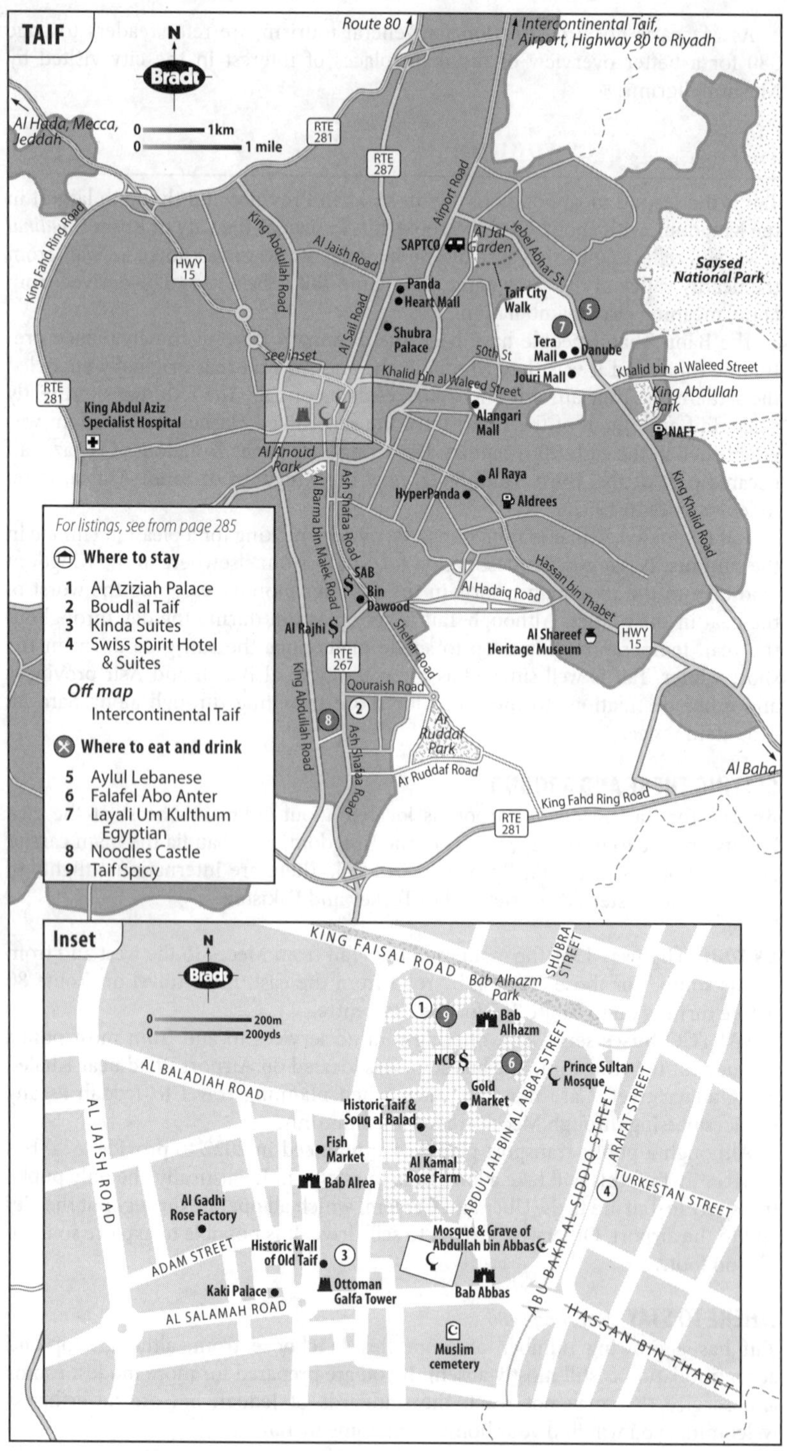
TAIF
Route 80
Intercontinental Taif, Airport, Highway 80 to Riyadh
Al Hada, Mecca, Jeddah
0 1km
0 1 mile
RTE 281
RTE 287
Airport Road
King Fahd Ring Road
King Abdullah Road
Al Jaish Road
SAPTCO
Al Jal Garden
Jebel Abhar St
Saysed National Park
HWY 15
Panda
Heart Mall
Al Sail Road
Taif City Walk
Shubra Palace
Tera Mall
Danube
50th St
see inset
Khalid bin al Waleed Street
Jouri Mall
King Abdullah Park
King Abdul Aziz Specialist Hospital
Alangari Mall
NAFT
Al Anoud Park
Al Raya
HyperPanda
Aldrees
King Khalid Road
Al Barma bin Malek Road
Ash Shafaa Road
Hassan bin Thabet
SAB
Bin Dawood
Al Hadaiq Road
Al Rajhi
Shehar Road
Al Shareef Heritage Museum
RTE 267
Qouraish Road
Ar Ruddaf Park
Ar Ruddaf Road
Al Baha
King Fahd Ring Road
For listings, see from page 285
Where to stay
1 Al Aziziah Palace
2 Boudl al Taif
3 Kinda Suites
4 Swiss Spirit Hotel & Suites
Off map
Intercontinental Taif
Where to eat and drink
5 Aylul Lebanese
6 Falafel Abo Anter
7 Layali Um Kulthum Egyptian
8 Noodles Castle
9 Taif Spicy
Inset
KING FAISAL ROAD
SHUBRA STREET
Bab Alhazm Park
0 200m
0 200yds
Bab Alhazm
NCB
Prince Sultan Mosque
AL BALADIAH ROAD
Gold Market
ABDULLAH BIN AL ABBAS STREET
ARAFAT STREET
Historic Taif & Souq al Balad
Fish Market
Al Kamal Rose Farm
AL JAISH ROAD
Bab Alrea
TURKESTAN STREET
ABU BAKR AL SIDDIQ STREET
Al Gadhi Rose Factory
Mosque & Grave of Abdullah bin Abbas
ADAM STREET
Historic Wall of Old Taif
Ottoman Galfa Tower
Kaki Palace
Bab Abbas
AL SALAMAH ROAD
HASSAN BIN THABET
Muslim cemetery

**Intercontinental Taif** Airport Rd, Rte 267; 012 750 5050; w ihg.com. Once the only true upmarket option, this hotel has undergone renovation to ensure it's still the most comfortable place to stay in the area. Its position near the airport may not suit some, but it's a good choice for those looking for a bit of pampering who also have their own transport. The b/fast & dinner buffets make it easy to relax. **$$$$**

**Boudl al Taif** Cnr Ash Shafaa & Qouraish rds; 012 743 3030; w boudl.com. Boudl's selection of rooms & suites plus on-site restaurant makes this reputable brand a good choice, especially for visitors headed to ar Ruddaf Park. **$$$**

**Al Aziziah Palace Hotel** King Faisal Rd, near Bab Alhazm; 012 733 0800. This hotel is in a great location on King Faisal Rd at the north end of Historic Taif. The rooms have a fridge & some also have a small kitchen. It is in walking distance to several restaurants & the Taif fruit & vegetable market. **$$**

**Kinda Suites Hotel** Off al Salamah Rd, next to Abdullah bin Abbas Mosque; 012 732 5859. Located near to Bab al Abbas at the south end of Historic Taif, this hotel is in a great spot & has all the basics & more. The rooms are spacious, with a living room & well-equipped kitchen, giving guests plenty of flexibility. Parking will be paid by the hotel if you ask. **$$**

**Swiss Spirit Hotel & Suites** Abu Bakr al Siddiq Rd & Turkestan St; 012 737 7774; w swissinternationalhotels.com. This centrally located property is just to the east of Historic Taif, giving good access to the city centre, as well as to the souq. It is better than most in this price range but be aware that it is located on a busy stretch of Hwy 15, so choose your room aspect carefully. **$$**

## WHERE TO EAT AND DRINK *Map, opposite*

Most restaurants here are unpretentious. Anywhere that is busy is a good sign, suggesting that the food will be delicious regardless of cuisine, so drop in to wherever appeals. All the usual major Saudi and Western fast-food restaurants can also be found in Taif.

**Aylul Lebanese** King Khalid Rd; 012 742 1000; w easymenu.site/restaurants/Aylullubnan; 07.00–01.00 daily. Located just north of the Tera Mall, offering a wide range of classic Lebanese dishes from morning to late at night. The ambience is elegant without going overboard, with rooftop dining in a garden-like setting in season. **$$$**

**Layali Um Kulthum Egyptian** King Khalid Rd; 050 967 9944; 07.00–01.00 Sat–Thu, 13.00–01.00 Fri. Named in honour of Um Kulthum, one of Egypt's most revered 20th-century singers, this restaurant is an atmospheric treasure. The décor is unmistakably Egyptian, complete with murals of many famous entertainers on the walls. The menu is authentic Egyptian, including national favourites such as koshari & umm ali, as well as tea. **$$$**

**Taif Spicy** North end of Historic Taif; 056 611 9980; 11.00–01.00 daily. This south Indian restaurant is next to Bab Alhazm, near the al Aziziah Palace Hotel. Its menu has a variety of delicious curries, with a surprising number of non-veg dishes. **$$**

**Falafel Abo Antar** Souq al Balad, east side, opposite Prince Sultan Mosque; 012 737 1070; w falafelaboantar.com; 06.00–midnight Sat–Thu, 06.00–11.00 & 13.30–midnight Fri. One of the oldest restaurants in Taif, this falafel place remains one of the most popular for a quick bite. You can build you own wrap to dine in or take away. Other branches can be found on al Jaish Rd about 1km northwest of the souq, Hwy 15 just north of the Centennial Roundabout, & Hwy 15, known as Hassan bin Thabet Rd, near Rte 25. **$**

**Noodles Castle** Ash Shafaa Rd, north of Sakhar al Jubir Rd; 050 765 3763; 13.00–03.00 daily. If you are hungry after a long day & are looking for a change from Middle Eastern menus, this Chinese take-away offers dishes with a focus on lo mein & other noodles, as the name suggests. It's handy for guests staying at Boudl, which is about 500m north. **$**

**SHOPPING** Taif's **supermarkets** include branches of al Raya, bin Dawood, Danube, Panda and HyperPanda; there are also many smaller grocers throughout the city. The two major shopping malls near the city centre are the **Alangari Mall**

with its many women's and children's shops, and the **Heart Mall** in the Shubra neighbourhood. Along King Khalid Road towards the newer neighbourhoods to the east are the **Tera Mall** and the large **Jouri Mall**, which is part of the prestigious Arabian Centre collection of malls found throughout the Middle East.

**OTHER PRACTICALITIES** As is the case throughout the Kingdom, ATMs can be found in most petrol forecourts, banks and shopping centres.

**Al Rajhi Bank** Ash Shafaa Rd & Arwahbin Masaud al Thagafi Rd; w alrajhibank.com.sa; ☎920 003344; ⏲ 09.30–16.30 Sun–Thu

**NCB Bank** Souq al Balad, next to Bab al Hazm; w alahli.com; ☎012 733 3033; ⏲ 09.30–16.30 Sun–Thu

**SAB Bank** Shehar St, 20m north of bin Dawood supermarket; w sab.com; ☎012 740 0182; ⏲ 09.30–16.30 Sun–Thu

**King Abdul Aziz Specialist Hospital** King Fahd Ring Rd & Al Salamah; w moh.gov.sa; ☎012 731 0800; ⏲ 24hrs daily

**Saudi Post** Airport Rd, 200m south of Prince Mansour Military Hospital; w splonline.com; ☎9200 05700; ⏲ 08.00–21.00 Sun–Thu, 16.00–21.00 Fri–Sat

**WHAT TO SEE AND DO** Although Taif may not be a top destination for many visitors, it is a pleasant stopover on the way to the mountains of the south or to break up a long journey as it is the last major city before reaching Madinah to the north and Riyadh, a very long distance to the east. If you are planning a short stay in Taif, here are some attractions that you might consider visiting.

**Historic Taif and Souq al Balad** (Bordered by King Faisal & Abu Bakr al Siddiq rds to the northeast & al Salama & al Baladiah Rd to the southwest) Historic Taif is now dominated by Souq al Balad as much of the older historic city has been razed. Not to be confused with the neighbourhood of the same name in Old Jeddah, this is one of the Kingdom's more interesting souqs, each sector with its own appeal.

**Bab Alrea** is the west gate located on the east side of al Baladiah near the fish market. Follow the unnamed lane to the right immediately past the OYO hotel that parallels al Baladiah. In just under 200m, you will find the ruins of the **Historic Wall of Old Taif**, which was built by the Banu Thaqif, and the **Ottoman Galfa Tower**. **Bab Abbas** is found to the southeast. Just west of this gate is the **Mosque and Grave of Abdullah bin Abbas ☪**, cousin of the Prophet Mohammed. Access to this mosque is for Muslims only, though it is possible for everyone to appreciate the exterior of the mosque from Uqbah bin Naaf Street.

**Bab Alhazm** is the entrance you want if you are interested in heading directly to the **Gold Market**, which is only a couple of minutes' walk south. Ask if you get lost on the zigzag route through unnamed lanes. **Kaki Palace** (al Salamah Rd, on the west side of the roundabout) was originally the home of a wealthy merchant. The exterior of this ornate property can be admired if you wander a few metres beyond the Historic Wall and Ottoman castle ruins.

**Shubra Palace** (Abu Bakr al Siddiq Rd, 200m south of the Heart Mall; ⏲ no fixed opening hours; admission free) Shubra Palace was built in 1904 under the instruction of the Emir and Grand Sharif Ali Abdullah bin Aoun Pasha during his short reign in the waning years of the Ottoman Empire. As the Ottomans were defeated and the Third Saudi State was established in the Hejaz, this palace became the summer residence for ibn Saud and King Faisal, serving as the seat of government during these months. Later, King Fahd converted it to the Taif Regional Museum. The museum, like many others in the Kingdom, was closed during our visit, but watch for developments as activity under the umbrella of Saudi Vision 2030 progresses.

**Taif City Walk** (Between Wadi Waj Rd & Jebel Abhar St, near al Jal Garden; w taifcitywalk.com) This outdoor destination is lined with clothing shops, cafés and a cinema, and is a popular destination for Saudi youth to hang out.

**Al Shareef Heritage Museum** (Off Hwy 15 to the southeast of the city centre, southeast of al Hadaiq Rd; 055 570 0008; 16.00–22.00 daily; SAR20) Similar to many other heritage museums throughout the Kingdom, this home contains a display of everyday artefacts, mostly from the mid 20th century. There is also an interesting collection of vintage motor vehicles.

**Parks and gardens** Take advantage of Taif's pleasant climate and green spaces. There are several small parks (most 24hrs daily), which you may stumble upon in most neighbourhoods in Taif. **Ar Ruddaf Park** is surrounded on three sides by ar Ruddaf Road. This large triangular park is located to the south of the city and filled with lots of children's activities. It is the home of many cultural festivals, as well as water shows, throughout the year and is especially popular in the evening and at weekends, with many families choosing the park as a good place for a picnic and

## TAIF'S ROSES

The Taif area produces more than 300 million Taif rose flowers a year. Growing centres are concentrated in nearby al Hada and Shafa. Because of Taif's high altitude and other climatic factors, this 30-petal variety produces an intense scent that is desirable to parfumiers from all over the world. The Taif rose is closely related to the Bulgarian Kazanlik rose and arrived in Taif along with the Ottomans as far back as the 16th century; it is believed to have originated in Persia.

Its rose oil, known as attar, is considered by many to be among the best and most valued in the world. It takes about 40,000 Taif roses to produce just 10g of attar, which has a stronger scent than the more familiar Damask rose, and attracts a high price. Pure rose oil is sold by the *tola*, *tolah* or *tullah*, an ancient Indian measurement of about 11.66g. One tolah of pure Taif attar sells for hundreds of US dollars. Taif roses also produce highly desired rosewater, used in cooking.

The harvesting season is in the spring, so if you are travelling to Taif in March or April, you may have a chance to visit the Taif Rose Festival. The main event takes place in ar Ruddaf Park but activities take place all around the city. Follow your nose to the Souq al Balad in the historic district to see how Taif rose oil has been sold for centuries – but remember that most shops are closed for much of the day, opening from early to late evening.

**Al Gadhi Rose Factory** (Also spelt al Qadhi & al Kady) Located on Adam St which runs from al Baladiah Rd west of Souq al Balad to al Jaish Rd.

**Al Kamal Rose Farm** Souq al Balad. This is in the middle of several unnamed lanes in the centre of Souq al Balad. This shop is well known, so ask someone in the souq if you are unable to find it.

to relax. It is also the location of Taif's Flower and Rose festivals which are held in the spring. **Al Anoud Park** is nearer to the city centre along Wadi Waj Road and al Barma bin Malek Rd to the southeast. This park will appeal to children as it has many playground areas.

**AL HADA** الهدا If you prefer to stay away from the city, then consider the resort village of al Hada. The service isn't always up to scratch but the views will make up for that. If you have children or are young at heart, then you many want to explore the nearby theme parks. **Green Mountain Resort** (Hwy 15, known as Mecca–Taif Rd along this stretch; 058 397 6946; 14.00–04.00 daily; admission free plus extra for rides) is a favourite of Saudi children and includes a Ferris wheel, dodgem cars, a toboggan run and many food stalls and cafés. **Rawabi Land Park** (056 515 1334; 14.00–midnight Sat–Wed, 14.00–02.00 Thu–Fri; admission free) is located less than 5km east of the Green Mountain Resort along the same road and offers many of the same experiences at similar prices.

**Where to stay and eat** If you are looking to stay in familiar accommodation, then it's worth knowing that the properties listed here are significantly less expensive than their counterparts elsewhere in Makkah Province. Most people are likely to eat at their resort if staying in al Hada. However, you'll find casual restaurants along the al Hada Ring Road which serve up everything from Yemeni food to pizza. Local grocers are found along the same road.

**Le Méridien al Hada** al Hada Ring Rd, off Hwy 15; 012 754 1400; w marriott.com. Part of the Marriott group, this 5-star hotel has beautiful grounds, a children's playground &, from its hilltop location, panoramic views of the area, including the fog from the valley when it rolls in. The hotel interior offers plush décor & all of the amenities expected of this standard (other than women's access to the pool), although some of the rooms feel dated. **$$$**

**Ramada by Wyndham** al Hada Ring Rd, next to the al Hada Cable Car station; 012 754 5558; w ramada-alhada.com. This property is perched on the edge of the cliffside with brilliant views of the mountain road from the direction of Mecca to the west. **$$$**

**MARWAN PALACE** (40km to the northeast of Taif & a winding 22km from Taif International Airport; 24hrs daily; admission free) Turn right at the cloverleaf on Route 80 east, passing the Okuz Market Theatre, arriving after another 7km at the palace. Home of the Bani Adwan tribe, Marwan Palace was a stronghold to counter the Ottomans. It was built by the military leader Sheikh Mohammed bin Jamhour al Adwani and was used as a headquarters during the times of the First Saudi State. Now in ruins, the palace has stone walls, wooden doors and a palm-frond roof. Some of the rooms are underground and show evidence of restoration. The views are lovely, so it might be worth a look around if you have time on the way to al Wahbha Crater or onward to Riyadh, especially if you have already travelled as far as Souq Okaz.

**AL WAHBHA CRATER** (Off Rte 8454 to al Wahbha Crater Rd; admission free) Whether you are travelling from Taif, Madinah or anywhere else, it's several hours' drive to this remote crater. But if you like craters, the journey is worth the effort. The roads are decent and the traffic is sparse, but services are few and far between so top up your petrol before it drops below half a tank. You will get a very good feel about how vast and how rugged much of the Kingdom still is. Don't forget to bring plenty of water.

From Madinah take Route 8010 to 8454. Turn left at the Al Fafeah sign a few kilometres before reaching Hafr Kashab. You will be travelling through massive lava fields most of the way with a lot of camels and some wandering goats to break up the monotony. Take note of the wadi flood signs along parts of the road if it has rained recently. From Taif take Route 80 to 4420 to 4252 to 8454. The crater is clearly signposted from Route 8454. Turn right when directed and travel about 4km to the crater. There is a big car park, toilets, a welcome building that probably opens for tour groups, and a security guard who warns not to climb down to the bottom of the crater. The view from the top is awe inspiring and takes in the crater base, which contains a large salt flat covering most of the surface. Walking around the top perimeter is allowed; protective stone walls have been built around the edge. There are five viewing platforms that provide spectacular views of the crater from slightly different angles.

**SAYSED NATIONAL PARK** (30mins east of Taif centre) Saysed is not the best national park in the country and is underdeveloped, but it does give a feel of the land and is near enough to Taif to attract quite a few visitors. It has a stream that flows after rain, surrounded by trees that display their greenery when the water does its work. There is an Umayyad-era dam within the park, as well as cuneiform inscriptions. To get there, take the on airport road before turning on to Sulaiman al Rajhi Road.

**SOUQ OKAZ** (40km northeast of Taif off Rte 80) One of the largest and best-known markets in the Islamic world, Souq Okaz was originally established in the earliest days of Islam; it first operated in the lead-up to the hajj season to cater to the needs of pilgrims. It was destroyed in the 8th century CE and rebuilt on what is believed to be the same site in modern times. The souq still operates on a seasonal schedule, now focused more on tourism and exhibitions of poetic endeavours in addition to the numerous shops. Performances usually take place in the Okaz Market Theatre in August as part of Taif Season events.

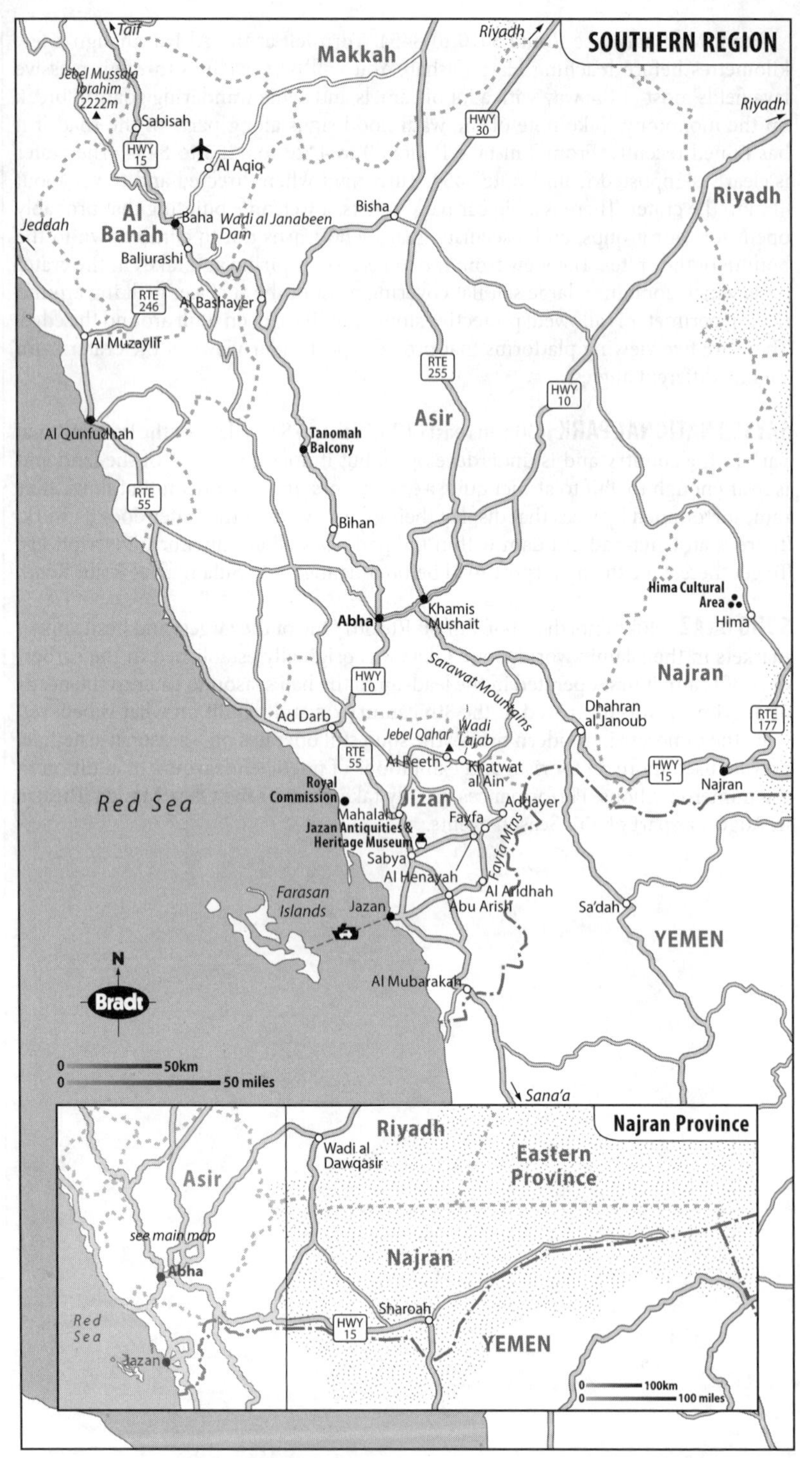
SOUTHERN REGION
Taif
Riyadh
Makkah
Riyadh
Jebel Mussala Ibrahim 2222m
Sabisah
HWY 15
Al Aqiq
HWY 30
Riyadh
Jeddah
Al Bahah
Baha
Wadi al Janabeen Dam
Bisha
Baljurashi
RTE 246
Al Bashayer
Al Muzaylif
RTE 255
HWY 10
Al Qunfudhah
Asir
Tanomah Balcony
RTE 55
Bihan
Hima Cultural Area
Hima
Khamis Mushait
Abha
Najran
Sarawat Mountains
HWY 10
Dhahran al Janoub
RTE 177
Ad Darb
Jebel Qahar
Wadi Lajab
RTE 55
Al Reeth
Khatwat al Ain
HWY 15
Najran
Royal Commission
Red Sea
Jizan
Addayer
Mahalah
Fayfa
Jazan Antiquities & Heritage Museum
Fayfa Mtns
Sabya
Al Henayah
Al Aridhah
Farasan Islands
Abu Arish
Sa'dah
Jazan
YEMEN
N
Al Mubarakah
Bradt
0 50km
0 50 miles
Sana'a
Najran Province
Riyadh
Wadi al Dawqasir
Eastern Province
Asir
see main map
Najran
Abha
Red Sea
Sharoah
HWY 15
YEMEN
Jazan
0 100km
0 100 miles

8

# The Southern Provinces

Saudi Arabia's southern region, comprised of al Bahah (اَلْبَاحَة), Asir (عَسِيرٌ), Najran (نجران) and Jizan (جيزان) provinces, is distinct from the rest of the Kingdom. It's a long way from Riyadh, and in many ways, the region feels more Yemeni than Saudi, reflected in the architecture, clothing, cuisine, religious beliefs within Islam, and more. Affinity with tribal rulers, customs and traditions reinforce this attitude.

Defying expectations held by many people, much of the south is mountainous and green, with temperatures in al Bahah and Asir comfortable in the summer yet cold enough to need a warm layer of clothing in the winter. Travelling to the deserts of Najran is another matter, though, with blazing hot conditions that fit Saudi's weather reputation to a tee. Jizan catches the southwest monsoon, making the summer months rainy at times, moderating the temperature when it does rain.

The four provinces are located actually in the southwest corner of the Kingdom, from the southern Hejaz Mountains of al Bahah to the Sarawat Mountains that run through Asir Province to the Yemeni border. Najran Province extends along the Yemeni border to the remotest part of the Eastern Province (page 348). Much of its land beyond Najran city is in the Empty Quarter and is mostly uninhabited due to the extreme conditions. Jizan is tucked away in the southwestern-most reaches of the Kingdom between Asir and Yemen and is much more geographically diverse than its landlocked neighbours. In addition to mountains rarely explored by outsiders, wadis that feed vital water supplies to agricultural land and a 300km shoreline along the Red Sea, the province has something for everyone.

## HISTORY

The southern region is situated in the northern reaches of what were the kingdoms of Sheba and Himar, in present-day Yemen, which was known by the Romans as Arabia Felix (Happy Arabia) for its pleasant environment. Settlements have existed here for millennia, with rock art and cuneiform inscriptions found in many areas, providing substantial evidence as to the ancient ways of life. As the incense trail and other important trade routes between what is now Yemen and north beyond the Arabian Peninsula pass through this region, control has been challenged over the centuries. During the centuries immediately preceding the birth of the Prophet Mohammed, military campaigns took place between the local populations of Arabia Felix and the Romans, Egyptians and Arabian Kingdoms from the north. These local communities included the first Christian community in the southern Arabian Peninsula, as well as ancient Jewish communities. For most of these groups, the ultimate goal was of controlling the route from the south to Mecca, an important trade city at that time. The Prophet Mohammed also formed a pact with the Christian community, which held for as long as 200 years.

From 1517, the region was part of the Ottoman-controlled Vilayet of Yemen, which covered a wide expanse from northern Yemen to the outskirts of Taif (in Makkah Province of modern Saudi Arabia). While the local population resisted Ottoman rule throughout much of that empire's conquest of the Arabian Peninsula, the Ottomans reigned in various parts of the southern Arabian Peninsula for almost 500 years.

Through the 19th century, conflicts between the influential Shi'a Zaidi Caliphate and the Ottomans continued, culminating with the Zaidi revolt led by Yahya bin Mohammed in the first decade of the 20th century. The Idrissi Emirate, located in what is now Asir, Jizan and northwestern Yemen, and which were closely associated with the Zaidis, also revolted. The region was ultimately defeated by the Ottomans and Hejazi powers, leading to the Treaty of Daan in 1911. However, in the lead-up to World War I, things changed again when the Anglo-Turkish Treaty of 1914 saw the modern borders between what would become Saudi Arabia and Yemen drawn.

After the collapse of the Ottoman Empire at the end of World War I, the Kingdom of Yemen still had control of parts of Asir and Jizan. In 1920, ibn Saud sent Bedouin Ikhwan warriors to Asir, where they defeated the Idrissi leader. With protection given to ibn Saud's warriors from the ruler of Yemen, the area fell under the control of the Third Saudi State. This was the last geographic region to do so, formalised in the Treaty of Taif in 1934. The map of modern-day Saudi Arabia was now complete.

## AL BAHAH PROVINCE منطقة الباحة

*Note: We will refer to the province as al Bahah and the city as Baha. The 'al' is often dropped when referring to either.*

Al Bahah Province (also spelled al Baha) is the Kingdom's smallest province by area at just under 10,000km$^2$. And it is the second least populated, with about 476,000 people, most of whom, about 365,000, live in the city of Baha (or al Bahah) with another 65,000 residing in Baljurashi. Most of the remaining population lives in small, often remote mountain villages. Many of al Bahah's inhabitants are descended from the Azad Shenou'a tribe, the province's original settlers, represented today through the Ghamed and Zahran branches who dominate the region, especially in the southwest of the province. The Ottomans ruled much of the Hejaz including what is now al Bahah for almost 500 years. The region was conquered by ibn Saud and became part of the Third Saudi State, now the Kingdom of Saudi Arabia, in 1925.

Al Bahah's economy remains mostly agricultural, with grains and fruit the dominant crops. It is also known for its honey, regarded as very high quality and celebrated with its annual International Honey Festival (page 301). Tourism now makes a significant contribution to the region's finances.

A mostly mountainous province, with peaks reaching more than 2,500m, al Bahah is growing as a centre for outdoors adventure. It is also known as the Garden of Hejaz for its many parks and forests, and its natural beauty, which along with its moderate summer climate attracts Saudis and other visitors to the region. Temperatures typically range from 12°C to 32°C, with winter temperatures dropping to single digits at night in the winter. Unlike elsewhere in the Kingdom, rainfall occurs throughout the year, with cloud cover sometimes engulfing towns and villages and filling the valleys below. Al Bahah's sparsely populated southwest is part of the Tihamah Plain, though it does not reach the Red Sea. The climate is much hotter and drier there than in the rest of the province.

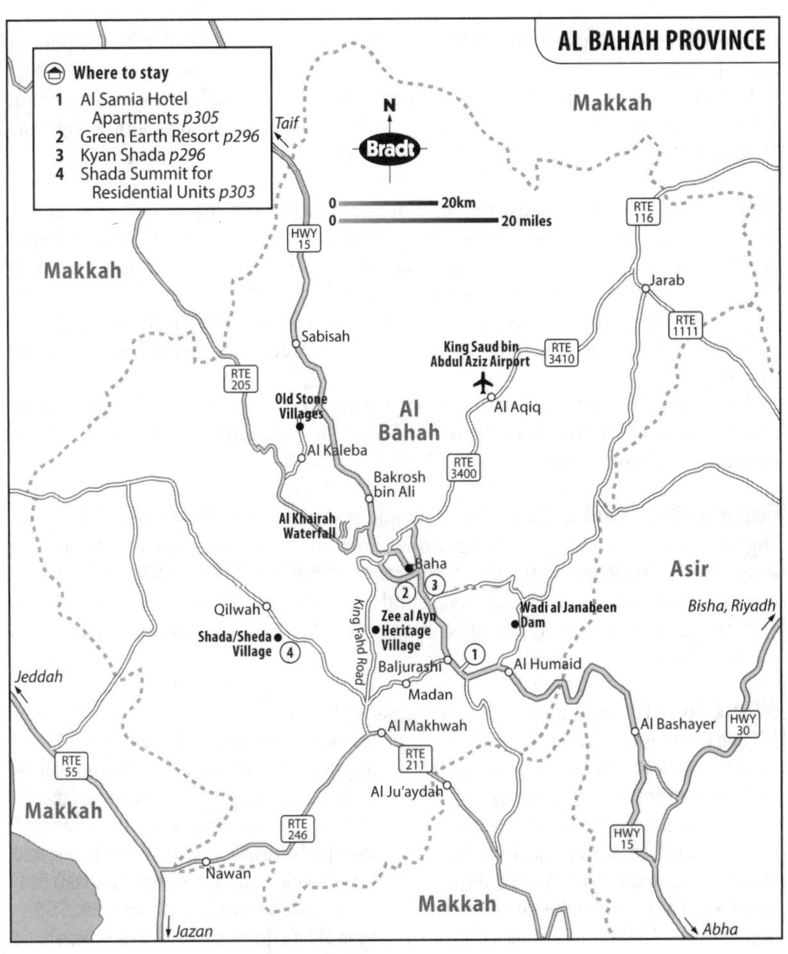


Regardless of when you decide to visit al Bahah, it is a good idea to be prepared for all eventualities – bring something warm and something waterproof to throw on as the weather dictates. The best time to visit is in the summer as many places close during the winter months.

## GETTING THERE AND AWAY

**By air** King Saud bin Abdul Aziz Regional Airport is located in al Aqiq about 45km northeast of al Bahah and has limited services on Saudia, which serves Dammam, Jeddah and Riyadh, and flynas, serving Abha, Dammam and Riyadh.

**By road** Highway 15 is the north–south road taken by most people travelling into Baha city. It is possible to travel to and from Baha along Route 246, which joins Route 55 near al Muzaylif just before entering al Bahah Province from its southwest border. Since al Muzaylif is several hundred kilometres from both Jeddah and Jizan Province, this remote route is rarely used. From Riyadh, the journey of almost 1,000km is mostly along Highway 30, an even more desolate drive. As much of al Bahah Province is very mountainous, make sure your vehicle is able to manage steep inclines. It is also important to check your tyres and windscreen wipers in case of rain.

SAPTCO **buses** serve Baha and Baljurashi and many smaller towns throughout al Bahah Province. Look at the SAPTCO website to locate the stops along Highway 15 near al Baik and about 9.5km north of Saf Hotel.

**BAHA اَلْبَاحَة** Also known as the Pearl of Resorts, Baha is the capital of al Bahah Province and is one of the Kingdom's most pleasant cities. It sits at an elevation of 2,155m, with temperatures ranging from 7°C to 32°C and low humidity. The rainy season is mostly April–August, but it can rain during other months, so make sure you bring waterproofs. Even when it isn't raining, you may find yourself in a cloudforest that drops the temperature enough to warrant wearing a jumper, even in summer.

Although there are supermarkets, shopping malls and other amenities, Baha retains the feel of a provincial capital and a bridge between the modern world and its recent traditional past.

**Getting there and around** Most people travel to Baha along the north–south Highway 15, which briefly changes direction, running east–west and becoming King Abdul Aziz Road, in the city. Its junction with Route 3400, or King Fahd Road, marks the city centre. Although taxis and Uber do operate in Baha, having your own transport is essential if you wish to access the gardens, ancient villages and other attractions.

## Where to stay *Map, page 298, unless otherwise stated*

**Al Faleh Hotel** Hwy 15, about 5km north of the city centre; 017 724 1980. A mid-range hotel away from the city centre, offering hotel rather than resort services, this provides basic 3-star amenities. The rooms are spacious with a good workspace & some have a kitchen. There is a restaurant on site & an indoor pool & fitness centre for men. Al Faleh is situated along the highway, so choose a room facing the rear if you are disturbed by traffic noise. Parking is in front of the hotel. **$$$**

**Green Earth Resort** [map, page 295] On an unnamed road off Hwy 15, about 10km before Baha; 050 896 8834. Clearly signposted from the highway, this resort is a good option for those looking for a reasonably quiet place to stay. The property is landscaped & well maintained with a tranquil seating area where you can hear the fountains. The apartments & chalets are spacious & are a good choice for self-caterers, but be prepared to make a trip to the supermarket if you don't find enough cutlery or crockery for your needs. **$$$**

**Kyan Shada** [map, page 295] Bani Kabeer; 053 069 4448; **w** kyan-shada-albaha.business.site. From Hwy 15, an exhilarating drive on winding roads takes you to this property situated on a mountain near the village of Bani Kabeer between Baha & Baljurashi. You will travel through several neighbourhoods, each revealing a new vista of the mountains. Take care as the roads are narrow

### GREEN BAHA

Rain, fog, cloudforests – there is a reason Baha is green. Although cloudforests may be more closely associated with Monteverde in Costa Rica or Chiang Mai in Thailand, here is a chance to experience the same phenomenon in a country known usually for its vast desert landscape. Frequent low-level clouds and fog here keep the land moist, allowing grass, flowers and trees to thrive; and with more than 40 parks and gardens in the vicinity, nature lovers will find plenty to do. Enjoy the unexpected.

with several switchbacks & many sections wide enough for only 1 vehicle. Kyan Shada is popular with Saudis & welcoming to visitors. The English-speaking receptionist will give you a chance to inspect your room before checking in. You will also get a tour of the common areas, including the separate women's & men's lounges on each floor, & the communal laundry & kitchen areas. The rooms are equipped with sink, kettle, microwave & plenty of kitchen storage, but little else, so you'll need to provide your own cooking utensils, crockery & cutlery if you are planning to cook. The bathroom is small & few towels are supplied. It's all worth it for the clean rooms & the views from the balcony to the valley below. Have the Arabic b/fast in the lounge overlooking the mountains & watch the sun do its magic if you are an early riser. There is ample free parking in front. B/fast inc. **$$$**

**Raghadan Tourist Complex** Hwy 15 about 500m north of al Faleh Hotel; 017 724 1008. Not to be confused with Raghadan Village (see below), this apartment complex strikes a good balance for those looking for clean, comfortable accommodation with 1–4 bedrooms at a fair price. Each unit has a living area, a sufficiently equipped kitchen with dining table, & 1 bathroom. Many staff speak English & provide a high level of customer service. The al Bustan restaurant (**$$$**) is located in the complex & offers room service, as well as dining in & take-away options. There are several modest supermarkets nearby for stocking up. **$$$**

**Raghadan Village Resort** King Abdullah Rd, opposite gate 1; 017 727 4444. The main advantage of this resort is its location at the entrance to Raghadan Forest Park. Accommodation is in detached chalets with 1–3 bedrooms, but they have seen better days & are in various states of repair & cleanliness. All chalets have a living area, kitchen & indoor & outdoor dining areas. Be aware that the heating & AC units may not do their job well in the larger chalets. **$$$**

**Swiss Spirit Hotel & Suites** King Abdul Aziz Rd, Hwy 15, just west of al Shaikh Ibrahim al Ibrahim St; 017 723 0330; w swissinternationalhotels.com. Probably the best hotel in the centre of Baha, with a high standard of cleanliness & customer service, & polished rooms & suites. The larger than average property is centrally located in walking distance of the souq & several restaurants. The 2 on-site restaurants cater to a global palate, with the Grill Room enjoying an excellent reputation. There is also a business centre & a shisha bar. Parking is good for this city-centre location. **$$$**

**Sky Blue Hotel** King Abdullah Rd, al Zarda; 055 612 5588. Set back from Hwy 15 on King Abdullah Rd, this hotel is less than 3km from the entrance to Raghadan Forest Park & convenient for nearby restaurants too. Room furnishings are of varying age & cleanliness so ask to see the room first before agreeing to check in. There is a small, practical kitchen for light cooking. Parking is limited, with few alternative options nearby. **$$**

**Traveler's Hotel** Hwy 15, just east of King Khalid Rd; 054 421 3490. Another hotel that is well located for the souq, supermarket & restaurants. Some of the rooms are carpeted – unusual at this end of the market in the Kingdom. This property is better than many others in this price range, but on-street parking may be a problem. **$$**

**Al Eairy Furnished Apartments 1** King Abdul Aziz Rd, Hwy 15, just east of Shaikh Ibrahim al Ibrahim St; 017 727 0399. This hotel is old & tired with little service, but that is made up for by its brilliant location in easy walking distance of several restaurants & the souq & rock-bottom prices. There's also parking at the front. **Al Eairy Furnished Apartments 3** & **4** are along the same road within 1km of al Eairy 1; **Al Eairy 2** is 100m north of al Faleh Hotel near Raghadan Park. **$**

## Where to eat and drink *Map, page 298*

**Soul** King Fahd Rd, just south of King Khalid Rd; 050 880 0004; w sggroup-ksa.com/soulalbaha; 07.00–01.00 Sat–Thu, 13.00–02.00 Fri. Conveniently located near the town centre neighbourhood, this upscale restaurant is tastefully decorated & has indoor & outdoor seating. The menu is wide ranging, with an offering of mostly Western soups, salads, pizza & pasta, alongside a selection of popular Indian masalas. The service is attentive without being overbearing. **$$$$**

**Fifth Season** King Saud Rd, about 50m west of King Fahd Rd; 017 724 0444; w sggroup-ksa.com; 13.00–midnight daily. This restaurant is probably as close as it gets to a trendy venue in Baha. Women & mixed groups will be invited upstairs to the family section, where seating on the 1st-floor balcony is lovely. The menu is a mix of Lebanese & Adana

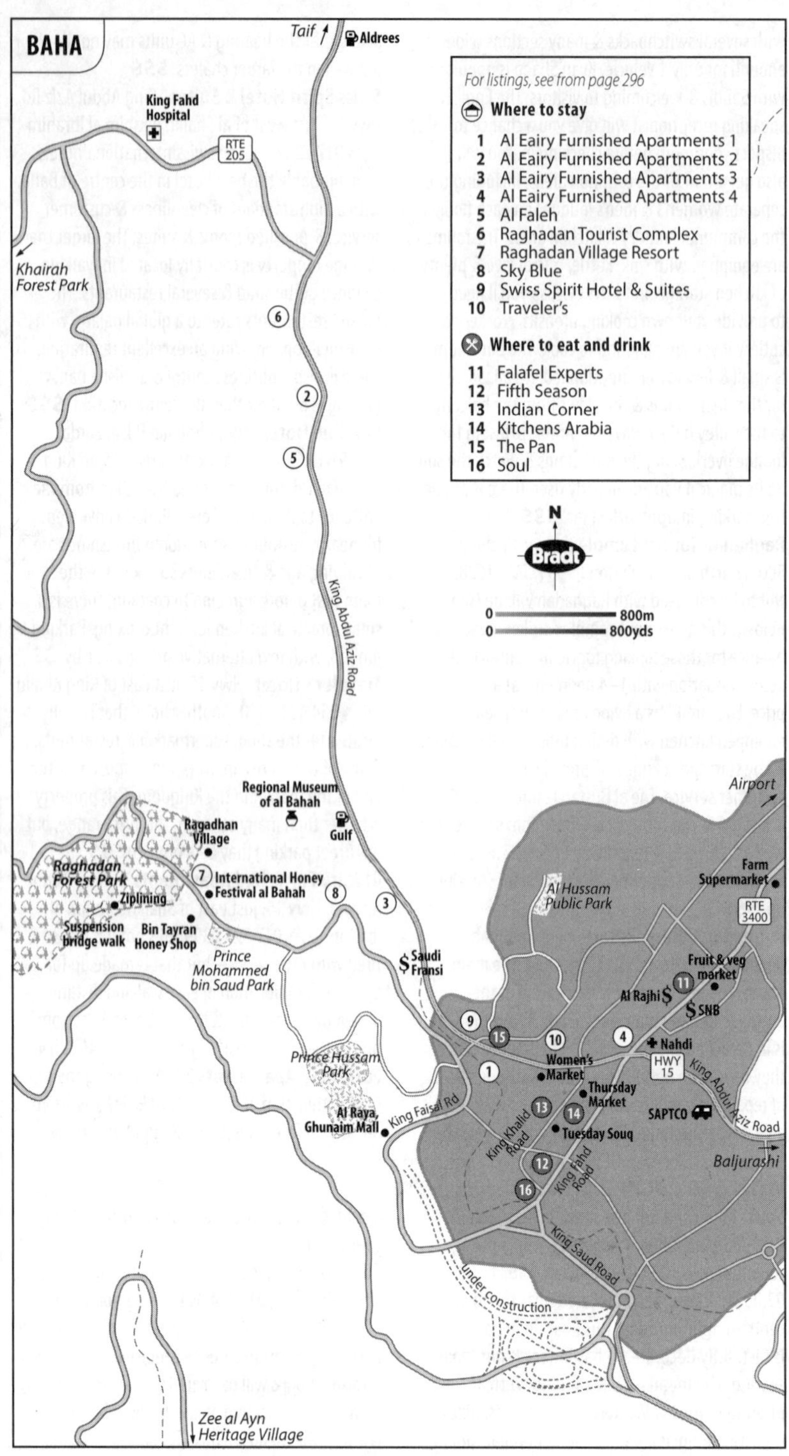
BAHA
For listings, see from page 296
Where to stay
1 Al Eairy Furnished Apartments 1
2 Al Eairy Furnished Apartments 2
3 Al Eairy Furnished Apartments 3
4 Al Eairy Furnished Apartments 4
5 Al Faleh
6 Raghadan Tourist Complex
7 Raghadan Village Resort
8 Sky Blue
9 Swiss Spirit Hotel & Suites
10 Traveler's
Where to eat and drink
11 Falafel Experts
12 Fifth Season
13 Indian Corner
14 Kitchens Arabia
15 The Pan
16 Soul
N
Bradt
0 800m
0 800yds
Taif
Aldrees
King Fahd Hospital
RTE 205
Khairah Forest Park
King Abdul Aziz Road
Regional Museum of al Bahah
Gulf
Ragadhan Village
Raghadan Forest Park
International Honey Festival al Bahah
Ziplining
Suspension bridge walk
Bin Tayran Honey Shop
Prince Mohammed bin Saud Park
Saudi Fransi
Prince Hussam Park
Al Raya, Ghunaim Mall
King Faisal Rd
Airport
Al Hussam Public Park
Farm Supermarket
RTE 3400
Fruit & veg market
Al Rajhi
SNB
Nahdi
HWY 15
Women's Market
Thursday Market
Tuesday Souq
SAPTCO
King Abdul Aziz Road
Baljurashi
King Khalid Road
King Fahd Road
King Saud Road
under construction
Zee al Ayn Heritage Village

Turkish cuisine, which is good but not outstanding. The baba ganouj is imaginative, as are the Adana lamb ribs. The service is good, with some English spoken, but make sure you review your order so there are no misunderstandings. $$$

**The Pan** King Abdul Aziz Rd, Hwy 15, just east of al Shaik Ibrahim St; 053 161 2825; 13.00–02.00 daily. If you are craving a beefburger, chicken sandwich or other Western-style fast food, try this restaurant near the Swiss Spirit Hotel. The menu has a Saudi spin down to the satisfying jalapeño-topped cheesy chips. Enjoy the music & modern vibe in a region where it is sometimes in short supply. $$$

**Indian Corner** King Khalid Rd, just west of King Fahd Rd; 055 892 6307; noon–midnight daily. Located in the town centre souq area, this unpretentious south Indian restaurant & take-away has a good selection of authentic Keralan dishes. Ground-floor seating is for singles, with family seating upstairs. English-speaking staff & all-around great value. $$

**Kitchens Arabia** Cnr King Fahd & Prince Musaad bin Abdul Rahman rds; 017 725 4451; 08.00–23.00 daily. This traditional Saudi restaurant serves the usual barbecue, *mandhi laham* & other favourites. There is a choice of traditional floor or table seating, & although there is no family section, women will not be turned away. $$

**Falafel Experts** Cnr King Fahd & King Salman rds; 050 722 2450; 06.30–midnight Sat–Thu, 16.00–midnight Fri. This take-away spot has a good choice of all things falafel, from sandwiches to plates. Check out the creative Egyptian sandwiches & Turkish pie. $

**Shopping** Farm, Panda and al Raya **supermarkets** offer the most variety here – don't expect to find a hypermarket as in the large cities. There are also more modest grocers that will sell the basics, and several branches of Nahdi (and others) should you need a pharmacy. The **Ghunaim Mall** (King Faisal Rd; 08.30–23.00 Sat–Thu, 16.30–23.00 Fri) offers the closest thing to modern shopping. Al Baha's **Thursday Market** and **Women's Market** are located around Highway 15 and King Fahd Road, and there is a **fruit and vegetable market** further north off King Fahd Road that is open in the mornings until dhuhr prayer. Parades of shops in Baha generally open after about 17.00, though some may open from about 10.00 until dhuhr prayer as well. Don't be surprised if these hours are not strictly adhered to. Nearly all shops accept MADA; some accept Visa; all accept cash.

***Tuesday souq*** Tucked into the southwest corner of the junction of Highway 15 and Route 3400 is the Baha souq. This is worth a visit especially on Tuesdays, when the otherwise typical souq becomes one of the most active in the region, with traders travelling here from as far away as the coastal plains to sell their wares. Local produce, from honey to *kadi*, a leaf that is valued for its antioxidant qualities and in cooking, are particularly prized. This is an opportunity to observe how tribal culture works, with bonds that go back for generations that are evident when people meet in this market.

### TRADITIONAL AL BAHAH ARCHITECTURE

Many buildings in al Bahah Province are traditionally made of stone, often granite. Roofs and doors are made of juniper, *sidr* or olive wood. Quartz, used for decoration as well as for its strength, is built into the structure to reinforce windows and doors, which are often carved with elaborate geometric designs. Homes are usually built over two storeys, with the lower level used for livestock and living quarters above. Although al Bahah has not been spared from the construction of nondescript modern housing, traditional architecture can still be seen throughout the province.

## Other practicalities

**Al Rajhi Bank** King Fahd Rd, 200m north of the junction of Hwy 15; **w** alrajhibank.com.sa; 920 003344; 09.30–16.30 Sun–Fri

**Banque Saudi** Fransi Hwy 15 southbound from Taif direction, adjacent to al Eairy Furnished Apartments 3; **w** alfransi.com.sa; 017 725 0660; 09.30–17.00 Sun–Thu

**SNB Bank** al Ahli Rte 3400 & Prince Sultan bin Abdul Aziz Rd; **w** alahli.com; 017 725 4545; 09.30–16.30 Sun–Thu

**King Fahd Hospital** Rte 205 about 1km west of the junction of Hwy 15; 017 725 4000; **w** moh.gov.sa; 24hrs daily

**Saudi Post** Prince Naif bin Abdul Aziz Rd, 100m southeast of Rte 3400; **w** splonline.com; 017 725 2104; 08.00–21.00 Sun–Thu

## What to see and do

***Raghadan Forest Park*** (King Abdullah bin Abdul Aziz Rd; 08.00–midnight daily; admission & suspension bridge walk free, zipline experience SAR120) Raghadan Forest Park is a large park within an urban setting with cafés and kiosks, picnic areas and plenty of activities for children keen to burn energy. Gate 1 is the busier of the two main gates to the park. Activities in this area include a **suspension bridge walk** and **ziplining**. The zipline ticket office (and the end of the zipline itself) is found towards the exit of this section along the one-way road system; zipliners will be driven to the starting point at Besat al Reeh above Gate 2. Men and women have separate spaces to change into their kit for the experience. Gate 2 is a lovely, peaceful area with beautiful views overlooking a cloudforest and substantial space for a picnic beside green grass. There are baboons nearby so keep an eye out as they can be very quick to steal your picnic if you aren't careful.

To get there, head west from Baha, joining King Abdullah Road off Highway 15 from any number of junctions. At the roundabout, turn right where you join King Abdullah bin Abdul Aziz Road. You will know you are on the right road to the park when you see boys and men wearing Yemeni clothing selling strings of flowers laced with marigolds and other seasonal posies to wear on your head.

***Other parks*** There are several smaller parks within Baha city, all free to enter. Some are less crowded and more peaceful than others, so try your luck. Parks are often relatively quiet until the afternoon. **Prince Hussam Park** (on an unnamed road off King Faisal Rd; 08.00–midnight daily) is more imaginatively designed than most as it is built in a basin shape with grassy sides and water features at the bottom with small footbridges. It's a great place for strolling, picnicking and people-watching. Turn right at the 65 Burger in Happy Market Shopping Centre and you will find the car park after about 1km on the right. **Al Hussam Public Park** (unnamed road off Ghabah Shuhbaha Rd, west of Rte 3400; 07.00–midnight daily) is a family-friendly park near the city centre with football pitches, as well as water features, a children's playground and food stands.

With lots of manicured lawns, **Prince Mohammed bin Saud Park** (King Abdullah bin Abdul Aziz Rd; 055 580 3798; 09.00–22.00 daily) is ideal for picnicking and an especially popular park to take young children to as there are several play areas.

***Ragadhan Village*** This traditional, still-inhabited village is along the way to Raghadan Forest Park, and is clearly signposted off King Abdul Aziz Road. It's a very quick detour of only a few minutes that provides a glimpse of sleepier everyday life beyond Baha city and the parks, with mid-twentieth-century unmodernised buildings. Although there does not appear to be much activity at the time of

## HONEY HONEY HONEY

Al Bahah is known for producing some of the Kingdom's, and arguably the world's, best varieties of honey. The annual International Honey Festival, first held in 2007, attracts beekeepers and fans of this sweet treat from around the region. If you happen to be in Baha city in July, then have a wander through the pavilion (King Abdullah Rd) opposite the entrance to Prince Mohammed bin Saud Park, and see what all the fuss is about. If you miss the festival, then stop by the family-run **bin Tayaran Honey Shop** (King Abdullah Rd, 500m south of festival site, on the roundabout; 055 883 2068; w bintayaranhoney.com). This boutique shop will lay on a honey-tasting session where you can experience first-hand many different varieties and flavours of locally produced honey. Prices vary, but expect to pay a premium for 'top-shelf' products. The shop will wrap the jars suitably for export if you plan to bring some home. Note that the opening hours are erratic, but try to stop by after asr prayer until late evening when the shop is most likely to be open.

research, the large stone-built **Regional Museum of al Bahah** is being built, holding promise for visitors keen to learn more about the heritage of the province.

### AROUND BAHA

**Khairah Forest Park** (Off Rte 205 to Kheera Forest St, on the outskirts of Baha towards Taif; 08.00–02.30 daily; you'll find the name of this park spelled several different ways) If you are looking for an unspoilt natural outdoor experience, then this may be the place for you. Although there are a few concessions for children, most of the grounds have been left in their original state. There is also an arched structure that looks like a viaduct but is positioned more like a gateway. Camping is possible but bring everything you need as there are no shops on site. This is a good choice for hikers who prefer their experience in nature without the 'enhancements' found so often in Saudi parks. The terrain is hilly, sometimes terraced but more often sloping, with loose rocks and other underfoot hazards. Several kilometres of trails, where they exist, are unmarked, so this is better suited to experienced hikers. The views are lovely throughout, with water flowing for much of the year.

To reach the park, head towards Taif on Highway 15, turning west on to Route 205 after about 1.5km. The road continues for a total of about 3km, winding and very steep, and takes about 15–20 minutes to drive. If you make this journey after it has rained, and continue on for a few minutes, you will find the splendid **al Khairah Waterfall** at the bottom. Within the forest park about 15km from Baha, the waterfall is seasonal and may dry up if it has not rained recently, but if you time it right, it's a good outing away from the city, and ideal for those short on time. Visitors should note that the waterfall is located beyond the end of the road and can only be reached on foot. Although there is a path of sorts, it is not signposted. Ask around if you are not sure as most Saudis in the park will be able to steer you in the right direction.

**Old stone villages** To the west of Highway 15 approximately 50km northwest of Baha, and less than 10km from al Mahawiyah, is the first of many old stone villages to be seen near Sabisah and al Kalebah. Leave the highway southbound, making a

## WATCHING OVER AL BAHAH

The mountainous landscape of al Bahah is dotted with stone towers called ***qasaba***. Nearly square at their base, these usually four- to five-storey towers taper gently up to the top, where each corner features a triangulated point. While some historians believe that qasaba may have been used originally for storing grain, others believe they were built as watchtowers. Archaeological evidence suggests that similar structures may date back to the 3rd century BCE.

It is said that there are 1,000 of these towers, which indeed seem to be perched on every hill or high ground in the province both on public and private property. They are in various states of repair, from near total ruins to those that appear to be in excellent condition. Although most qasaba stand alone, they can also be found in the walls of some fortresses.

right turn at Sabeha al Olaya opposite the Gulf petrol station on the opposite side of the highway. You can see Sabisah from the viewpoint just north of the turn-off.

Follow the road for approximately 2km, where you'll encounter several qasaba (see above) on the approach to the village. These towers built of dark stone have contrasting smaller white stones laid in strips with triangles mixed into the pattern.

Park anywhere it is safe to do so along the road but beware of the baboons. The village can be reached on foot up a small but steep hill from the road – any paths have nearly disappeared. In the village you'll notice the walls made of layered flat stones, used both for the construction of buildings and for marking boundaries. Terraced stone walls are commonly seen along the hillsides between villages. Some of the buildings, their palm-frond roofs in various states of disrepair, have wooden window frames. You will have already seen many qasaba on the approach to the old village.

There are many more old stone villages around Baha, including al Mousa Heritage Village, Bani Zabian Villages and al Atawila al Shamlani Heritage Museum. Although the villages are not formal tourist attractions, they make for a pleasant place on a long drive to stop and stretch your legs. The **al Atawila al Shamaini Heritage Museum** (🕘 24hrs daily; admission free), also a collection of ruins, is a bit more organised. You will see many more if continuing south past Baha and throughout the province before they end near the border with Asir.

**Bakrosh bin Ali Heritage Castle** (Admission free) About 10km further south back on Highway 15 towards Baha, you can explore Bakrosh bin Ali Heritage Castle – on the outside (🕘 24hrs daily), and inside if it is open. Bakrosh, or Bakhroosh, was a military commander of the early 19th century, who fought alongside the First Saudi State against the Ottomans. This was his castle, built in 1803–04. It has a traditional qasaba complete with windows and a white-trimmed decorated entrance protected by a round turret.

**Zee al Ayn Heritage Village** ✷ (King Fahd Rd, about 35km south of Baha; 📞 055 678 8776; 🕘 09.00–17.00 Sat–Thu, 15.00–18.00 Fri; admission free) Also known as Thee al Ayn and Dhee al Ayn, this striking village is on the UNESCO World Heritage Site tentative list and for good reason. Built of local white marble and stone on a prominent hill, it contrasts beautifully with its backdrop of the Sarawat Mountains and is named after the permanently flowing natural spring at the base of the hill it has been built on. Estimated to be about 400 years old, the village was also a site of conflict between local tribes and the Ottomans from when it was built until the last years of the Ottoman Empire.

The drive from Baha begins almost immediately with a series of tunnels built through the mountains, followed by kilometres of dramatic switchbacks. The views are other-worldly, with rugged, fog-shrouded mountain peaks that seem almost to pierce the sky. With each hairpin bend another stunning vista is revealed. Fortunately, there are many places where you can stop, park up safely off the road and enjoy the view – but do be aware that health-and-safety features at cliffs are non-existent, so be particularly careful with small children and anyone distracted when taking photos.

As you approach the area, you will see Zee al Ayn slightly to the left of the road. There's a contemporary white mosque on the right and a sign indicating the left turn off the road to the historic village. To the front is a rich oasis of palm trees and gardens nourished by the spring. Keep driving around the oasis to the car park at the end of the road. The site is accessed directly from the car park via a stone path.

The Saudi authorities are in the process of restoring this site, but it remains open to visitors. A visitor centre is also being built along with a row of shops, toilets and a children's playground.

Take care along the paths as some of the steps leading up the hill to the village may be loose. To the left are 49 marble-and-stone homes and other structures with mud-built walls reinforced by wood, stone columns and cedar roofs. The buildings range in size from one to four storeys tall, many with wooden doors and window frames still in place. Although it was possible to explore the buildings at the time of research, the Saudi Tourism Authority is developing this site, so be prepared for some rule changes. Most homes no longer have any accoutrements but still offer a good idea of how they were built.

There is a small stone-built mosque complete with minaret on the right side of the path – visitors can take the steps on to the top of the mosque which gives a nice view of the oasis back towards the road. Continue down past the mosque to reach the spring at the bottom which runs down from a knotty tree, as well as the elevated garden now used as a place to rest and take refreshment. There's also a short hiking trail for visitors further along the edge of the village.

**Shada (Sheda) Village and Jebel Mussala Ibrahim** (Approx 50km southwest of Zee al Ayn) Continue on King Fahd Road to the northern outskirts of Makhwah to Shada Road. Turn west on to Shada Road near al Makhwah University and continue to Jebel Mussala Ibrahim in the Shada Mountain Reserve. Best reached by 4x4, this adventurous drive to the remote village involves a narrow road in poor condition in places, especially after it has rained, steep inclines, and a series of switchbacks as you approach the reserve. The mountain rises to more than 2,200m, with dramatic granite peaks soaring 1,700m from the wadi below. The village is at an elevation of about 1,600m partway up the mountain. The abandoned village is a curiosity, containing abandoned stone dwellings, with many in the village which were built in caves with stone supports at the entrance. It's a great side attraction to the main event at the top of the mountain.

For adventure enthusiasts, Jebel Mussala Ibrahim is also a **mountain-biking** destination that will challenge even experienced cyclists. It is possible to wild camp on the mountain – plan carefully, bring your own provisions and take all necessary precautions as in this remote location help will be far away should you need it. It might be possible to stay at the **Shada Summit for Residential Units** [map, page 295] (050 476 1341 – use WhatsApp; **$**).

**BALJURASHI بَلْجُرَشِي** Located along Highway 15 about 30km southeast of Baha, Baljurashi is the former capital of the Ghamid and Zahra tribes, established after the arrival of the al Sauds in 1925. (The capital reverted to Baha later in the 20th century.) Sitting at an elevation of about 2,000m, Baljurashi has similar weather to Baha, with cool winters and temperatures that do not generally rise above 30°C in summer. The terrain is similar to that of Baha and offers similar activities in the mountains and outdoors.

## Where to stay *Map, below, unless otherwise stated*

**National Park Hotel** King Abdul Aziz Rd, Hwy 15 opposite Panda; 017 722 2273; **w** nationalparkgroup.com. This 4-star hotel has been updated recently but is still showing its age in places. The rooms are comfortable & the AC & Wi-Fi work well, but it would benefit from more electrical outlets. There is an indoor pool, fitness centre & a small café on the ground floor. The Park Restaurant is the main restaurant in the hotel, offering a full b/fast buffet & all-day dining. However, it is much less popular than the outdoor restaurant to the side & back of the hotel (see opposite). **$$$$**

**Gardens City Resort** Unnamed road off Hwy 15, northbound direction, opposite Baljurashi National Park; 055 418 1234; **w** gardens-city-resort.business.site. Although this property is only about 3km from the city centre, it feels a world away. The detached & semi-detached chalets offer 1 or more bedrooms, a living space & kitchen. Some rooms have a small private indoor swimming pool. **$$$**

**Saf Hotel** Hwy 15, 4km north of the city centre; 017 722 2000. Although this is a 3-star hotel on paper, it offers similar services to the 4-star

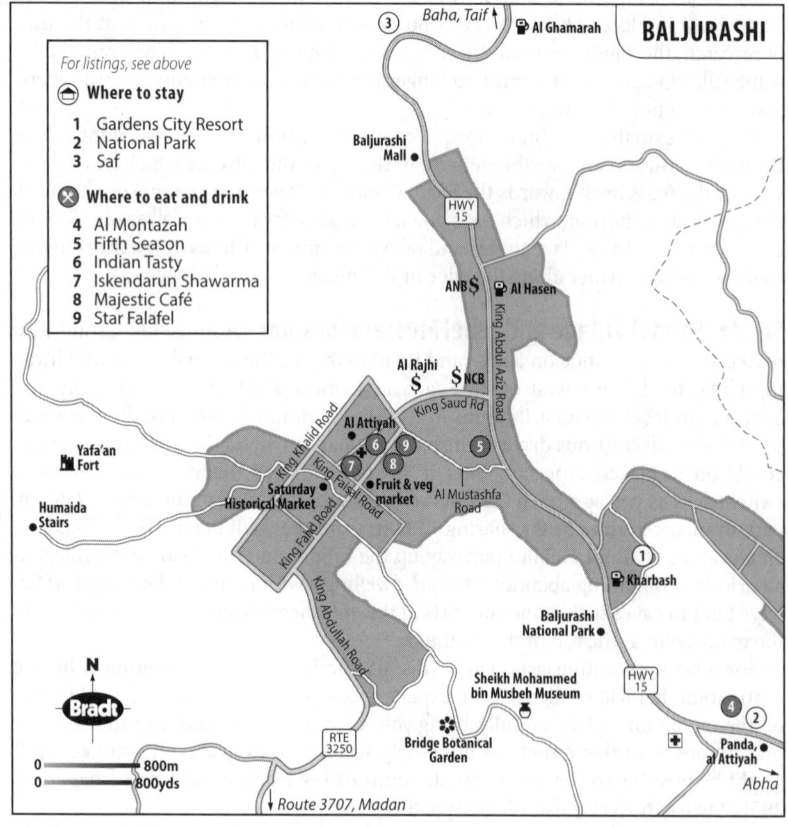

National Park Hotel at a slightly more favourable price. Amenities include a restaurant, fitness centre, traditional diwan seating area & rooftop seating area with great views, weather permitting. With its meeting room facilities, it's also a popular business hotel. **$$$**

**Al Samia Hotel Apartments** [map, page 295] Farsha Rd, off Hwy 15 in the al Bekeer district; /// amplifier.timer.homily; 017 722 7007. These hilltop apartments are spacious & include a small kitchenette, with a handy market on the premises. There is parking to the front of the entrance. Good if you want to stay a bit away from Hwy 15 but still be near the attractions. **$$**

## Where to eat and drink *Map, opposite*

✱ **Al Montazah Restaurant** To the west & down a path to the back of the National Park Hotel; 017 722 2277; 08.00–01.00 daily. The menu here has everything from steaks to tagine with Italian & Lebanese dishes, salads & sandwiches in between. This restaurant's outdoor courtyard setting has open tables, as well as curtained privacy tables for mixed-gender groups, which seem to be used by all combinations of diners. Good service, including a summons button at the bottom of the QR code display. Shisha is also available. **$$$$**

**Fifth Season** Hwy15 southbound, cnr King Abdul Aziz & al Mustashfa rds; 017 753 0444; w sggroup-ksa.com/fifthseason; 13.00–01.30 daily. This is a branch of the same restaurant in Baha (page 297) & provides a similar service. **$$$**

**Indian Tasty** King Saud Rd, a few doors up from Iskendarun; 055 048 4466; 07.00–midnight daily. This restaurant has a few tables for those who prefer to dine in, but the business is orientated to take-away. Most substantial items on the menu are only available from around 18.00. There is a mix of classic Indian tandoor & masala dishes alongside Chinese-inspired noodle options. It does the job when you crave a straightforward curry. **$$**

**Majestic Café** King Fahd Rd near al Mustashfa; 050 665 5109; 09.00–midnight Sat–Thu, 13.00–midnight Fri. This pleasant coffee shop with croissants, sandwiches, desserts & a variety of coffees & teas is a good place to relax. **$$**

**Iskendarun Shawarma** King Saud Rd, off Hwy 15 in the city centre; 053 674 1306; 16.00–midnight daily. This simple take-away is the place to go for freshly made toasted chicken shawarmas with your choice of the usual toppings & tahini or spicy sauces. **$**

**Star Falafel** al Mustashfa Rd just south of King Fahd Rd; 053 512 7435; 06.30–12.15 & 16.30–23.30 daily. Clean & cheap with a menu that also has burgers, broasts & wraps in addition to good falafel. Broasting is a cooking style very popular in Saudi Arabia that combines broiling (grilling) & roasting, usually for chicken. **$**

## Shopping

Shops in Baljurashi generally open after about 17.00, though some may also open from about 10.00 until dhuhr prayer in addition to the evening. There is a fruit-and-vegetable market just north of King Fahd and King Faisal roads which is open in the mornings until dhuhr prayer, and also the Baljurashi Mall (Hwy 15, 2km north of the city centre; 09.00–23.00 Sat–Thu, 16.00–23.00 Fri).

## Other practicalities

**Al Rajhi Bank** King Saud Rd, 500m west of the junction of Hwy 15; 9200 03344; w alrajhibank.com.sa; 09.30–16.30 Sun–Fri

**Arab National Bank** Hwy 15 opposite McDonald's; 017 722 2920; w anb.com.sa; 09.00–16.00 Sun–Thu

**NCB Bank** King Saud Rd immedately east of al Rajhi Bank; 017 722 2440; w alahli.com; 09.30–16.30 Sun–Thu

**Prince Meshari bin Saud General Hospital** Cnr Hwy 15 & Rte 3200; w moh.gov.sa; 017 722 0100; 24hrs daily

## What to see and do

***Saturday Historical Market*** (Saturday Market St, off King Fahd Rd just south of the junction of King Faisal Rd near the gold shops; 24hrs daily) This multi-level historical market is constructed of stone in the traditional provincial style. It was built several hundred years ago and is in the slow process of being renovated. It's a great visit as you can explore each level and get the feel of what it was like in times gone by. Walk into the small open courtyard to the right up to a small level and you can still see the hooks on the ceiling of what would have been the butcher's market, sitting alongside other contained areas selling other wares. There is a small stone mosque complete with stone minaret further up the hill that you can enter. Once inside, you will see the decorated wooden door, palm-frond roof, and prayer rugs that remain on the floor. The open window gives a view of the town below. There are modern chairs and tables at the base of the historic market, where local people relax in the evening when things become more active, as well as some traditional seating just a bit further up to the right. The market still sells mostly local produce on Saturdays. Try to go in the morning.

***Bridge Botanical Garden*** (5km off Hwy 15 on sealed but narrow unnamed roads; /// subtitles.resolved.commentator; 055 651 7744; 06.00–22.00 daily; SAR20 pp plus SAR20 pp for suspended bridge) Set in a neighbourhood with lovely farms and a peaceful ambience, these gardens provide a burst of colour with a range of marigolds, daisies and more. You will also see cactuses and many fruit trees such as pomegranate, quince and fig. A 100m-long bridge is suspended above the gardens – for an additional fee visitors may walk over the bridge or cycle using a specially modified bicycle. Those who wish to walk will need to don a safety harness before starting their wobbly adventure. Anyone risking the chance of a photo must take extreme care as other walkers can cause a sudden jolt. There is a shaded grove and traditional chairs and tables in the open where visitors can sit and enjoy the atmosphere, and a small kiosk sells drinks. At the end of the garden is a surprising Peppa Pig-themed children's playground. Tickets are purchased at the entrance to the property. Parking is on the roadside, but choose your spot carefully as the entrance is on a bend along a narrow road.

***Sheikh Mohammed bin Musbeh Museum*** (Near the Bridge Botanical Garden; 055 651 7744; 08.30–noon & 16.00–19.00 Sat–Thu, 16.00–19.00 Fri; SAR10) The museum was closed during our visit but it does look like it opens more at the convenience of the owner than at any published times. The sign at the museum's entrance promises displays of historical photographs, domestic items and traditional doors, among other treasures; it is probably worth a quick visit if you are also visiting the botanical gardens down the road.

***Yafd'an Fort*** (On unnamed roads in the general direction of Humaida Stairs; /// sunbeam.instigator.dinosaurs; alternatively follow Google Maps, which references the fort in Arabic only حصن جفعان) The fort is situated in a strategic position on a hilltop overlooking Baljurashi and the farming valley; you will see a qasaba and a prominent rock near the summit. Take the road to the north of the hill and you will be rewarded with a panoramic view of the crumbling fortress, with trees and flat land to the front.

***Humaida stairs*** (About 3km from Baljurashi centre on sealed but narrow unnamed roads; /// carriage.pulleys.interpreting; 24hrs daily; admission free) This trail is for serious hikers and is not suitable for young children or anyone without a good level of fitness. About 8km in length, descending to the village of Madan, it has been in existence for at least 200 years and used by traders wishing to travel between Madan and Baha. Most people report the hike takes between 2 and 3 hours down and as much as 6 hours back up.

As you approach the site, you will see a large concrete pavilion directly ahead with a small place to park to the right. Don't be surprised if you are greeted by a troop of baboons frolicking among the rocks. This is where the trail starts, descending an initial set of stone stairs to the right of the pavilion at the end of the car park. These stairs end after about 100m, then the rocky adventure really begins. The trail is obvious if you follow the flat rocks. Enjoy the stunning views of the valley and Jebel Shada in the distance.

Unfortunately, there is a shameful build-up of litter at the top of the trail and little evidence of it being cleaned up anytime soon. Ideally walk in pairs or with a group and tell someone where you are going and when you expect to return. Bring everything you may need – you might encounter rain in the rainier months and clouds may appear at any time.

***Wadi al Janabeen Dam*** (Off Hwy 15, 20mins' drive south of Baljurashi towards Abha; free parking just off the road) For those continuing towards Asir, try to make the time for this diversion. Travel to the village of al Humaid, turning on to Route 3699 to the northeast, where you will see old stone towers at the beginning of the road and sometimes grazing donkeys on the verge. Follow this road for almost 8km (approx 10mins), where you will reach the wadi, revealing rich greenery on both sides of the road from the al Ahab spring. If you are driving an off-road vehicle, it is possible to do a bit of wadi bashing from either side of the road. Continue less than 1km up the hill from the wadi on the paved road and you will be able to enjoy a good view of the dam from two different parks less than 500m apart. Anyone who appreciates dramatic scenery and nature will find this detour well worth it.

## ASIR PROVINCE منطقة عسير

Nestled in the southwest corner of the Kingdom, Asir (or Aseer) Province gives the visitor a very different experience to the rest of Saudi Arabia. Asir Province is Saudi Arabia's fourth smallest by land mass, with an area of almost 77,000km$^2$. It borders Jizan Province to the southwest, Najran Province to the southeast, Riyadh Province to the east and al Bahah and Makkah provinces to the north. Most of the population of over 2.5 million people live in Abha, the capital, and Khamis Mushait, the province's most populous city.

The religious mix of modern Asir includes Sunni populations and sects from Ismaili and Zaidi or Fiver branches of Shi'a Islam, similar to that found over the border in northern Yemen, and are often branches of the same families. The Qatanis, also spelled Khatani, are the dominant tribe in the region and have significant power and influence. They are also associated with the traditions of the Flowermen, who continue to live semi-autonomously according to their tribal laws. The Shahranis, another dominant group, are historically associated with agricultural pursuits.

The Asir Mountains, part of the Sarawat mountain range, run through the province and contain the Kingdom's highest peaks, including Jebel Souda (approx 3,000m). Mountain temperatures rarely exceed 30°C, often being much lower. Summer in this region is particularly appealing to many Saudis wishing to escape the extreme heat elsewhere as this is the rainy season, moderating temperatures sometimes to the low 20s. Summer is also the season when fog often descends on the province, shrouding the capital and other high elevations like a cool blanket. Humidity remains relatively low in the mountains. Winters are typically cold, with

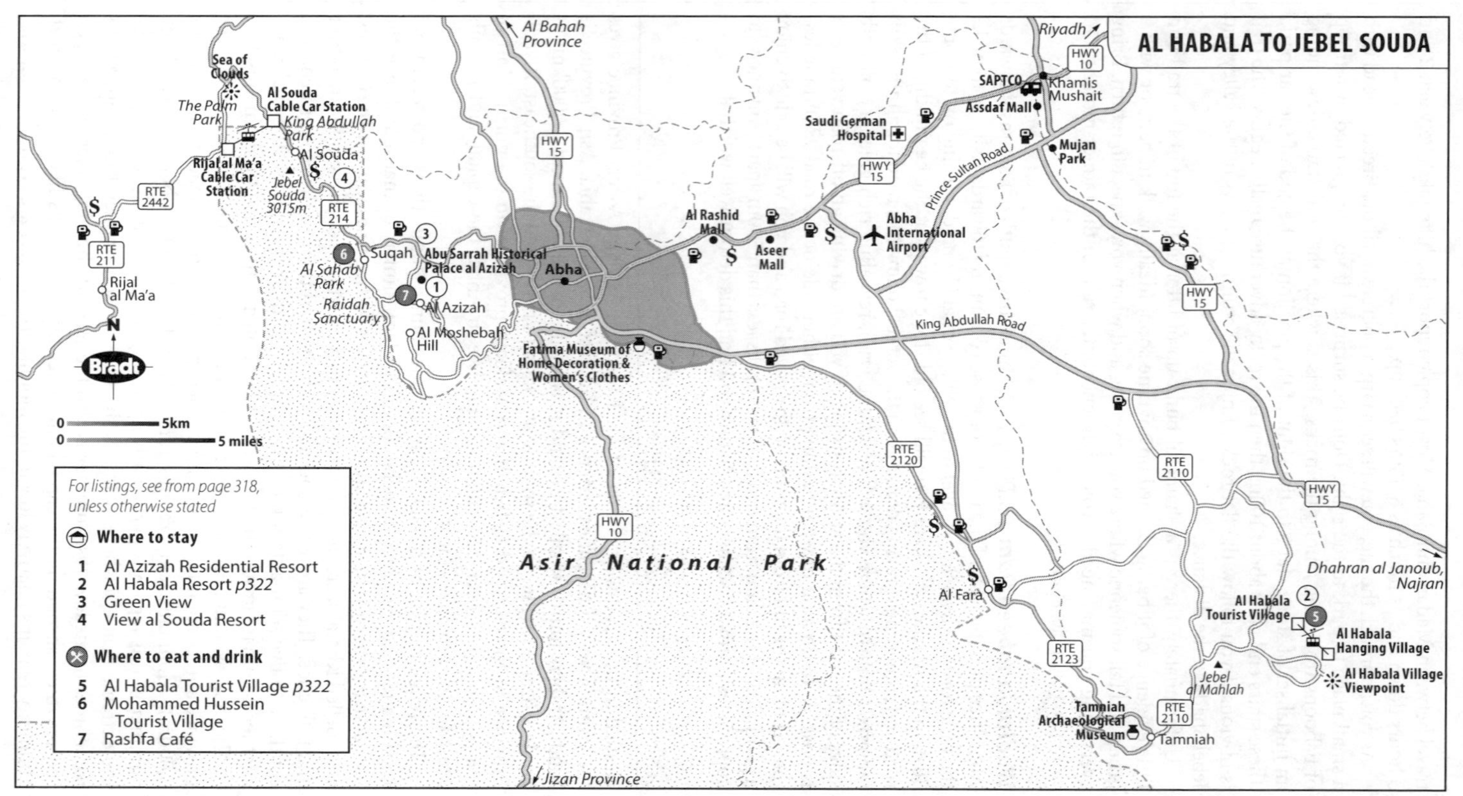

AL HABALA TO JEBEL SOUDA
Al Bahah Province
Riyadh
HWY 10
SAPTCO
Khamis Mushait
Assdaf Mall
Mujan Park
Saudi German Hospital
Prince Sultan Road
HWY 15
Abha International Airport
Al Rashid Mall
Aseer Mall
Abha
Abu Sarrah Historical Palace al Azizah
Al Azizah
Al Moshebah Hill
Suqah
Al Sahab Park
Raidah Sanctuary
Fatima Museum of Home Decoration & Women's Clothes
King Abdullah Road
Sea of Clouds
The Palm Park
Al Souda Cable Car Station
King Abdullah Park
Al Souda
Rijal al Ma'a Cable Car Station
Jebel Souda 3015m
RTE 214
RTE 2442
RTE 211
Rijal al Ma'a
N
Bradt
0 5km
0 5 miles
Asir National Park
Jizan Province
RTE 2120
RTE 2110
RTE 2123
Al Fara
Tamniah Archaeological Museum
Tamniah
Jebel al Mahlah
Al Habala Tourist Village
Al Habala Hanging Village
Al Habala Village Viewpoint
Dhahran al Janoub, Najran
For listings, see from page 318, unless otherwise stated
Where to stay
1 Al Azizah Residential Resort
2 Al Habala Resort p322
3 Green View
4 View al Souda Resort
Where to eat and drink
5 Al Habala Tourist Village p322
6 Mohammed Hussein Tourist Village
7 Rashfa Café

single digits overnight not uncommon. If you plan to visit Asir, go between June and early October. The height of Asir's season is July and August, when children are out of school, so keep in mind that accommodation may be full and tourist sites may be very busy, especially in the evenings. Many places close outside of the summer season. Further east, the province turns to desert as it approaches the Empty Quarter, with extreme temperatures and low humidity. Asir also extends down to the Tihamah Plain, with a short border along the Red Sea, where both the temperature and humidity are high.

Asir Province benefits from Saudi Vision 2030's focus on diversification of the economy and growth in tourism. Many attractions are a short distance from the provincial capital of Abha. Asir National Park, established in 1981, was the Kingdom's first real organised attempt at environmental preservation. Hiking, camping, nature, wildlife and adventure activities all appeal to visitors to this corner of Saudi Arabia.

**HISTORY** Asir Province has been ruled by outsiders for much of its history, starting with the Romans, who tried to control these key north–south routes on the Arabian Peninsula during the earliest days of its empire. Rock art inscriptions give evidence of military activities from Yemen that reached Asir, again for the purpose of controlling trade. These are believed to be during the reign of Himyar kings in the 5th and 6th centuries CE. One of these campaigns was led by Abraha al Ashram, whose army included elephants, thus giving the invaders' route the name Road of the Elephant and the invaders the People of the Elephant. In early Islamic times, the Abbasid Caliphs of Iraq, followed by the Zaidi Dynasties, closely associated with neighbouring Yemen, arrived in the region, eventually replaced to an extent by the Ottomans, who arrived in the region in 1517. After a short period of self-rule during much of the 19th century, the Ottoman Empire gained control, placing Asir under the administration of the Ottoman Vilayet of Yemen. Asir was designated a *sanjak* (an administrative division within a vilayet) of Yemen in 1872. Yemeni influence is strongly felt in much of Asir to this day, including in the dress, food, distinctive mud-brick architecture (page 333) and some religious affinity that is not found elsewhere in Saudi Arabia.

During World War I, local leader Mohammed bin al Idrisi rose to power, establishing the short-lived Idrisid Emirate of Asir in 1917. Regional threats to the emirate from Hejaz and Yemen led to an alliance with the House of Saud in 1926. Ibn Saud became the first King of Saudi Arabia as the country gained independence in 1932. Asir Province was the last region to join the Kingdom in 1934 with the signing of the Treaty of Taif by Saudi Arabia and Yemen.

Asir still shares a short, remote border with Yemen. The Saudi–Yemen conflict that started in 2014 has had an impact on Asir, most notably the bombing of the arrivals hall of Abha airport in 2019. It was repaired quickly and is fully operational once more. Check your travel insurance to make sure you are covered if you travel to this part of the Kingdom.

## GETTING THERE AND AWAY

**By air** Abha International Airport is about 20km equidistant between Abha and Khamis Mushait and has scheduled flights to most domestic destinations on Saudia and flynas, and to Dammam, Jeddah and Riyadh on flyadeal. There are additional flights on flydubai and Air Arabia to Dubai and Sharjah respectively, as well as flights to Cairo and Kuwait on other regional carriers.

**By road** Most people travelling to Asir Province will arrive on Highway 15 from al Bahah to the north or from Najran to the south. Visitors from Jizan Province travel

## ASIRI ARCHITECTURE

Like in other regions in the south of Saudi Arabia, traditional Asiri architecture is distinctive. Houses are built on a wide rectangular stone base with mud walls rising layer by layer, reinforced with flat stones at intervals. The buildings are usually built in contrasting shades ranging from dark brown to a golden tan. Squarish windows, some outlined in white, let just enough light in without exposing the structure too much. This design is intentional as it makes the building more difficult to breach and resistant to attack, an important consideration in this historically troubled region, where neighbours are not always friends. The roofs are flat, with triangulated corners also often accented in white.

Although some buildings rise to as many as eight storeys high, most are more modest at three or four storeys. The stone layers protrude from the walls, giving them the look of a layer cake. The ground floor was usually used for livestock with living quarters on the upper floors, including at least one diwan for receiving guests. The highlight of most Asiri buildings are the elaborately decorated interior walls, an artistry known as 'al Qatt al Asiri', which involves stripes, repetitive geometric designs and general symmetry along the walls and often extends towards the ceiling, framing the room's windows. These designs are often completed at the top with triangles, all in the brightest, most celebratory colours possible, with paints made using flowers that grow locally. The artists are mostly women, who are recognised for their artistic skills and contributions to the local culture more generally.

on Highway 10 from the southwest. Whether you travel along Highway 15 or 10, the mountain views are a highlight of a road journey to Asir.

Abha's main SAPTCO bus station [312 B1] is situated at the junction of Highway 15 and the Route 213 Ring Road to the north of the city. There is also a station in Khamis Mushait. These are the main stations in Asir. Bus services are limited to long-distance travel within and through the province.

Both Uber and Careem **ride share** services operate within Abha and Khamis. Visitors might be able to organise trips outside of these cities during the summer season, but don't rely on this.

**APPROACHING ABHA FROM THE NORTH** For those driving from al Bahah towards Abha on Highway 15, as you cross into Asir Province you will begin to notice that the stone qasaba have a different appearance, with smaller windows and smaller pointed corners. Houses become flatter and squarer, with horizontal double lines providing contrast in the walls and decorated windows also framed in contrasting colours becoming more prominent as you travel further south into the province. Mosques feature two prominent minarets and are more decorative than elsewhere. It remains very green in the mountains with cloud cover and fog that can come and go unexpectedly. If you are driving in the fog, make sure you enable your hazard lights and follow the white and yellow lines that are thankfully all along the highway, as are cats' eyes. The view from the escarpment between the small villages of Bani Amr and al Adwa reveals stunning terraces and a mix of old stone village buildings and modern structures in use today. Several heritage villages and museums signposted as open for visitors are a good way to take a short break from your journey.

**Tanomah Balcony** (Off Hwy 15, Tanomah; 🕘 24hrs daily) This beauty spot with dramatic cliffs is about 180km from Baljurashi and 115km from Abha. Driving in from the north, you will know when you are near as, less than 1km from the site, you will see a wall marked with a huge outline of the boundaries of Saudi Arabia which also contains the national symbol of the crossed swords and palm tree. Tanomah Balcony includes a park, waterfall, children's play area and the escarpment beyond the park. You will be able to see the waterfall from the highway; it is a good place to stretch your legs if you are driving a fair distance. A children's playground is to the left of the stairs that lead up to the park and waterfall and a tree-lined area can be found on the first level just a few steps away. Climb one more set of steps and you will be at the base of the waterfall. There are benches, handy if you want to relax, but beware of the baboons. The waterfall is artificial but is still a nice break. For those with a moderate level of fitness, you can take a 5km hiking trail that skirts the cliffs as you go beyond the waterfall.

**ABHA أَبْهَا** Abha is situated at an altitude of 2,270m, making it the highest provincial capital of Saudi Arabia. It has a population of 1.1 million people, swelling to many more during the summer. Abha is a lovely place, with historical sites and a growing cultural scene. It is also a sensible base for visitors planning to explore the region as it is centrally located and has the widest choice of accommodation outside of the seasonal mountain resorts. Do be aware that some hotels and resorts in Abha close in the off-season, usually from November to May.

**Where to stay** Most visitors to Asir are likely to stay in Abha, from where it is convenient to explore the province in all directions. If you prefer to stay in a resort, you can choose from options in and around Jebel Souda (page 318).

### *Luxury and upmarket*

**Abha Palace Hotel** [312 A3] Unnamed road off al Beheira St; ☎ 017 229 4444; w abhapalace.com.sa. Favourably located in the Abha al Jadidah neighbourhood to the west of Abha Dam, this 5-star hotel offers deluxe rooms & suites to satisfy those who prefer elegance over opulence. The 5th-floor Nahran restaurant provides panoramic views of the lake & the city & offers a range of Arabic & Western options. There is also a wellness centre, with a spa, pool, tennis court & even a bowling alley. **$$$$$**

**Al Nozha Tourist Complex** [312 A3] Unnamed road off Nahraan Rd; ☎ 017 224 5400. This recently refurbished apart-hotel to the south of Abha Dam is another choice for those who prefer understated décor in a relatively quiet but convenient location. 1- to 3-bedroom apartments include a kitchen plus balcony or patio with views of the lake. No restaurant. **$$$$**

**Assalam Palace** [312 B2] Off King Khalid Rd & al Imam Mohammed bin Saud; ☎ 017 228 1000; w assalamabha.com. Well situated at the eastern end of the Art Street less than 1km from the al Basta District, this hotel offers rooms & suites that have views of the city, mountains or garden. There is a revolving restaurant on the top floor that offers buffet & à la carte Arabic options. For those who need a business centre, this is also provided as is welcome private parking in this crowded area. **$$$$**

### *Mid-range*

**Azd Hotel** [312 B2] King Faisal Rd; ☎ 017 238 8777; w azd.hotels-saudi-arabia.com. This medium-sized hotel is in the heart of the city centre less than 400m north of al Maka Mall towards Shamsan Castle. There is a restaurant & a basic kitchen for those who prefer to self-cater. **$$$**

**Blue Inn** [312 B2] King Saud St; ☎ 017 230 5000; w blueinnabha.com. If you are looking for a mid-range hotel in the heart of Abha, this may be a good choice. The rooms & suites are comfortable with access to a fitness centre & indoor swimming pool. The Roof restaurant is convenient as is the Jawahrat al Majd supermarket located in the same complex if you don't fancy the mostly Pakistani restaurants that cater to male labourers nearby. **$$$**

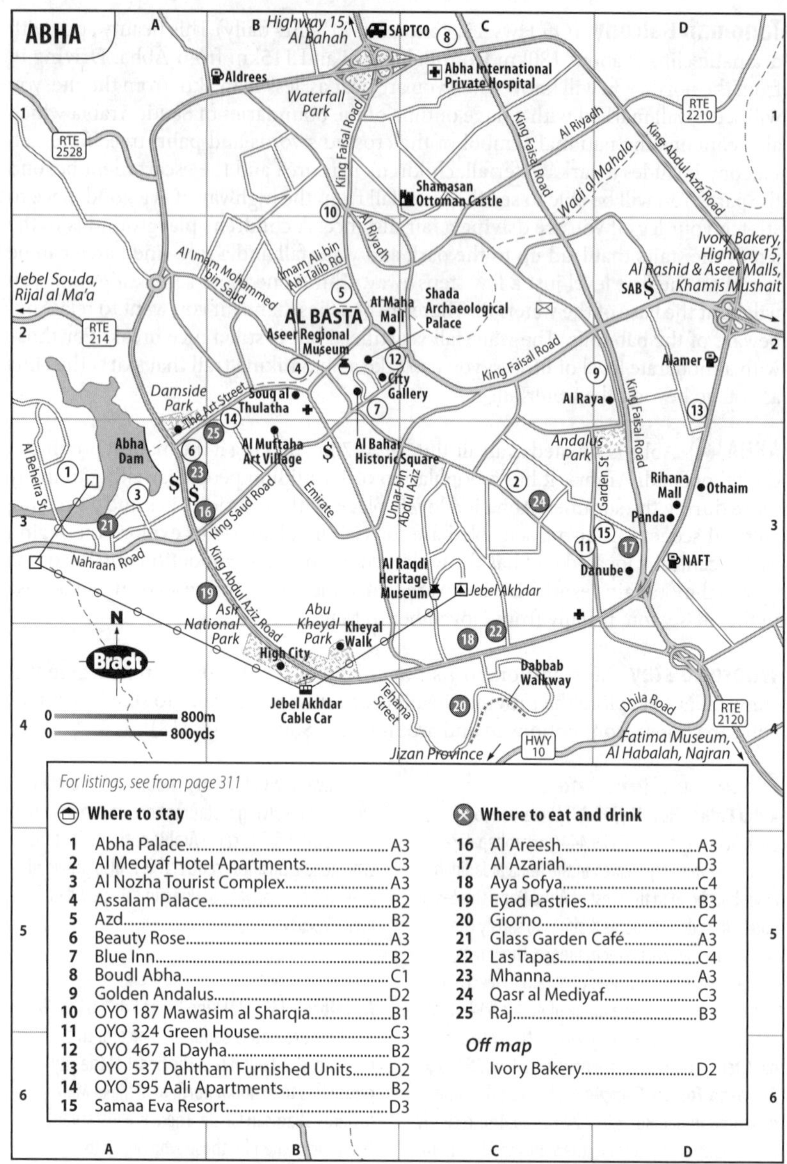


**Boudl Abha** [312 C1] King Abdul Aziz Rd, about 500m east of Waterfall Park; 017 232 2222; w boudl.com. This apart-hotel is part of the upmarket Saudi chain, with a small coffee shop offering room service for b/fast. The rooms & suites are reliably clean, with good service from reception. **$$$**

**Samaa Eva Resort** [312 D3] Garden St, about 200m south of Andalus Park; 050 837 5559. What this place lacks in kerb appeal is made up for by its central location, good-size executive suites & helpful staff, especially housekeeping & bell hop services. The kitchen is functional for preparing light meals, though check to make sure you have enough cutlery & crockery. If not, you can try the Danube supermarket nearby, or the Panda in the Rihana Mall. **$$$**

### *Budget and shoestring*

**Al Medyaf Hotel Apartments** [312 C3] King Abdul Aziz Rd; w qasr-al-midiaf.hotels-saudi-arabia.com. We recommend you use a reputable booking site from your home country if you wish to stay here. This is a rare property that will suit all but the tightest shoestring travellers at the budget end of the spectrum. The studios & 1-bedroom apartments are all en suite & equipped with a fridge, & some with a basic kitchen. There is a coffee stand on site. **$$**

**Beauty Rose Hotel** [312 A3] King Abdul Aziz Rd, just south of King Khalid Rd; ☎ 055 855 5956. This property is conveniently located between High City & the Art Street & offers good value for money in this popular area. All rooms have a living area, & some come with a kitchen. Try to get a room away from the busy road if you are a light sleeper. **$$**

**Golden Andalus** [312 D2] King Faisal Rd; ☎ 017 226 6699; w golden-andalus-hotel abha.business.site. This budget option will suit those who want to be near major highways, with a selection of clean & well-maintained studios, & 1- & 2-bedroom apartments, all at a very affordable price. **$**

**OYO 595 Aali Apartments** [312 B2] King Khalid Rd; ☎ 050 991 4161; w oyorooms.com. Located opposite the Art Street, this is one of the best-situated OYO properties in Abha. As is usual for this chain, do not expect much other than a basic room with a bed & an en suite, with very little service. In a city where inexpensive accommodation can be difficult to find, those on a tight budget may be happy to note that there are several other OYO properties in Abha, all at affordable prices. Some of the properties situated near points of interest or otherwise conveniently located include **OYO 187 Mawasim al Sharqia** [312 B1] (King Faisal Rd), **OYO 324 Green House** [312 C3] (cnr King Abdul Aziz & Garden sts), **OYO 467 al Dayha Hotel** [312 B2] (off King Khalid Rd, 200m south of al Maha Mall & Gold Market) & **OYO 537 Dahtham Furnished Units** [312 D2] (Rte 213, King Abdul Aziz Rd). There are others. **$**

**Where to eat and drink** On the east side of the city, **Ivory Bakery** [312 D2] (Wahhab bin Massara St, about 250m south of Eyad Pastries; ☎ 053 500 2213; w eyadco.com; ⏲ 08.00–midnight Sat–Thu, 13.30–midnight Fri; $) is the place in town to go for croissants.

### *Above average*

**Aya Sofya** [312 C4] King Abdul Aziz Rd at roundabout; ☎ 053 226 0330; ⏲ 05.30–10.30 & 13.00–01.00 Sat–Thu, 13.00–01.00 Fri. The loosely inspired Turkish restaurant offers a mix of Turkish items & Saudi favourites. This is a place for meat lovers, with great-quality lamb. The restaurant has several items on the menu that comes with a 'Fireshow', where an employee dressed as an American cowboy complete with Stetson & handlebar moustache flame-cooks your meat at your table. The salad menu presents vegetarians & the health conscious with several good options. Creative baklava dishes bring you back to Turkey. Mixed-gender seating can be found indoors on the ground floor, with outdoor seating overlooking very busy roundabout traffic. **$$$$**

**Glass Garden Café** [312 A3] al Beheira St; ☎ 053 362 2644; ⏲ 13.00–21.00 daily. More of a café than a restaurant, the focus is on coffees, juices, salads & light snacks, although the menu does offer a few main courses. The cuisine is trendy Saudi with a Western flair. Pizza & pasta lovers will also be happy. The service is slow but the views are lovely so if you come to relax, this won't be a problem. **$$$$**

### *Mid-range*

**Al Azariah** [312 D3] King Abdullah Rd, close to King Abdul Aziz Rd near Danube; ☎ 9200 29226; ⏲ 11.00–01.00 Sat–Thu, 12.30–01.30 Fri. This is another classic restaurant with soup, kabsa, *mandhi* & other Saudi favourites on the menu & is a great place for sharing platters if you are with a group. The venue is large, clean & has table & floor seating. The service is attentive even when it's busy. **$$$**

**Giorno** [312 C4] Tehama St; ☎ 055 258 0280; ⏲ 05.30–01.30 daily. The key attraction of this restaurant is its location overlooking Dabbab Walkway & people-watching. The 1st floor is actually 2 storeys upstairs from the ground floor & has mixed-gender seating. Try to sit by the windows which open from the top. If it is foggy, the room also becomes foggy. The menu has typical Italian-style dishes – pizza, pasta, salads & a few meat dishes. Juices & mocktails including the unusual Splasheer (a combination of grape juice & 7Up) might appeal to your inner child. The service is attentive with several English-speaking waiters. $$$

**Las Tapas** [312 C4] King Abdul Aziz Rd, 100m east of the roundabout; 017 226 8459; 13.00–midnight Sat–Wed, 13.00–01.00 Thu–Fri. We're not sure why this is called Las Tapas. The décor is a reproduction of Tex-Mex kitsch; the menu is a mix of American & Italian with salads & sandwiches in the mix. If you fancy a break from Middle Eastern food, then this might be the place for you. $$$

✱ **Raj** [312 B3] King Khalid Rd about 200m east of King Abdul Aziz Rd Rte 213; 017 222 3555; 13.00–02.00 daily. If you crave a good masala, then this is the place for you. The restaurant was designed in the traditional way with downstairs & upstairs dining but is now mixed seating. Try to find a table on the balcony on either level as this provides a lovely breeze & overlooks the Art Street. The menu is extensive, with fresh juices & mocktails, lovely soups, starters, masalas, tandoori grills & especially delicious naans. As is usual in Indian restaurants in the Kingdom, there are also Chinese-inspired options on the menu including noodle dishes. This is a good place for vegetarians & has an upmarket vibe at reasonable prices that all diners can enjoy. $$$

### *Cheap and cheerful*

**Al Areesh** [312 A3] King Abdul Aziz Rd Rte 213, just north of Nahraan Rd; 055 579 8006; 05.00–14.00 & 17.00–02.00 daily. This stylish venue is kitted out with traditional design features blended with metal sculptures of bicycles & carriages bearing plants & flowers. Somehow it works. There are loads of household artefacts, tiled & wooden tables with classic cushions on the seats & benches. There is a choice of open mixed-gender seating indoors which extends to covered & open outdoor dining with a traditional well out front. The menu is unsurprisingly Saudi with b/fast particularly popular. The service is average. $$

**Eyad Pastries** [312 B3] King Abdul Aziz Rd, between High City & the Art Street ; 055 507 6824; w eyadco.com; 09.00–midnight Sat–Thu, 14.00–midnight Fri. This is a popular dessert shop with traditional Saudi & other Arabic sweets along with cakes & other goodies, with tables & take-away service. There are other branches on Rte 213 about 600m north of the Rihanna Mall & Wahhab bin Massara St to the east of the city. $$

**Mhanna Restaurant** [312 A3] King Abdul Aziz Rd, just south of King Khalid Rd; 017 226 7000; 06.00–midnight daily. Whether you drop in for an early b/fast, a late-night shawarma or falafel anytime, this casual restaurant serves street food that hits the spot. Order at the counter, with an option to dine in or take away. $$

**Qasr al Mediyaf** [312 C3] King Abdul Aziz Rd (not Rte 213 with the same name); 056 130 2629; 12.30–midnight daily. This very popular traditional restaurant closes during prayer times & has strict singles & family sections. Make sure the family section is open if you need this seating as it is not always open during quieter times. The menu is robust with the usual Lebanese starters. The grills will satisfy carnivores for their variety & flavour. This is a very crowded neighbourhood with parking difficult. $$

**Shopping** Also known as the Tuesday Souq, **Souq al Thulatha** [312 B2] (off King Khalid Rd, just east of the Art Street; 055 849 6668; 06.00–18.00 daily), is open daily, but do try to go on a Tuesday as the tradition remains. It sells an array of local handicrafts, as well as practical items for the very budget conscious, some of which, though, is of very low quality. It's easy to walk around if you want to see what Abha's traditional merchants have on offer.

The popular **supermarkets** al Raya [312 C2], Danube [312 D3], Othaim [312 D3] and Panda [312 D3] all have branches here. Abha also has its modern shopping centres – al Maha, City Gallery and Rihana malls are all in or near Abha city centre.

**Al Maha Mall** [312 B2] King Faisal Rd near the junction of King Khalid bin Abdul Aziz St; 053 923 2329; claims 24hrs daily. Best to go in the evening.

**Al Rashid Mall** [312 D2] King Abdul Aziz Rd; 10.00–midnight daily. An upmarket mall about 10km east of Abha along Hwy 15.

**Aseer Mall** [312 D2] 3km east of al Rashid Mall; ☎ 9200 09467; w aseer-mall.com; ⏰ 09.00–01.00 Sat–Thu, noon–01.00 Fri

**City Gallery** [312 B2] Off King Faisal Rd, 300m southeast of al Maha Mall; ☎ 017 226 5555; ⏰ 09.00–23.00 Sat–Thu, 16.30–23.30 Fri

**Rihana Mall** [312 D3] King Abdul Aziz Rd; ☎ 017 229 4444; ⏰ 08.30–midnight Sat–Thu, 16.30–midnight Fri

**Other practicalities** There's a **Nahdi Pharmacy** (☎ 9200 24673; w nahdionline.com; ⏰ 24hrs daily) on King Khalid Road.

**Al Rajhi Bank** [312 A3] King Abdul Aziz Rd, 200m north of Nahraan Rd; w alrajhibank.com.sa; ☎ 9200 03344; ⏰ 09.30–16.30 Sun–Thu

**Riyad Bank** [312 B3] King Khalid Rd & Imam Abdul Rahman bin Faisal bin Turki Rd; w riyadbank.com; ☎ 9200 02470; ⏰ 09.30–16.30 Sun–Thu

**SAB Bank** [312 D2] King Faisal Road & Amber St; w sab.com; ☎ 017 274 3278; ⏰ 09.30–16.30 Sun–Thu

**SNB Bank** [312 A3] al Ahli King Abdul Aziz Rd, 100m north of al Rajhi Bank; w alahli.com; ☎ 800 124 2000; 09.30–16.30 Sun–Thu

**Abha International Private Hospital** [312 C1] Off Hwy 15, east towards Ibrahim al Hadithi St from Waterfall Park; w aph.med.sa; ☎ 017 238 7800; ⏰ 24hrs daily

**Saudi Post** [312 C2] King Khalid Rd; ☎ 9200 05700; w splonline.com.sa; ⏰ 08.00–21.00 Sun–Thu, 16.00–21.00 Sat

## What to see and do

***Al Bahar Historic Square*** [312 B2] (al Imam Mohammed bin Saud St) The old city centre is nowadays more of a modern government and business area, but provides a very good example of how to blend traditional architecture with the functional needs of modern buildings. Notice the layered design of the modern mosque's minaret and the white-accented tops of the contemporary low-rise buildings. If you go around the back towards **Shada Archaeological Palace** [312 C2] (Alaa bin Saad St, 100m behind the square), you will discover some traditional buildings with blue and green contrasts which give them the appearance of an iced layer cake. The palace itself was built in 1927 in the traditional Asir style, with small, unadorned windows along the tower wall and topped with triangulated corners. It was the seat of the provincial emir. These crumbling ruins are undergoing a much-needed restoration and will eventually house artefacts from the recent past.

Also adjacent to al Bahar Historic Square is the **Asir Regional Museum** [312 B2] (al Imam Mohammed bin Saud St; ☎ 017 230 7307). However, as is the case with most regional museums throughout the Kingdom, this one is temporarily closed. The building itself is a nice blend of modern and traditional Asir style – it's worth walking around its exterior if you are already in the area.

***Al Muftaha Art Village*** [312 B3] (al Farzadaq St, off King Khalid Rd next to the Talal Maddah Theatre) This creative enclave was an artists' village until its temporary closure, with a thriving parade of handicraft shops. The modern buildings are constructed in the Asiri style, with distinctive decorative layering on the exterior walls of contrasting cream and brown shades. These modern buildings reflect the values of being a Centre for Conservation and Preservation of Islamic Architectural Heritage, and can still be seen from the perimeter until it reopens.

***The Art Street*** [312 A3] (Off King Abdul Aziz Rd, alongside King Khalid Rd; ⏰ 24hrs daily) Stretching for about 200m, the Art Street – the name a nod to a few decorated concrete walls along the edge of this outdoor green space – is a promenade very popular with young Saudis as a place to gather once the sun goes down. There are several coffee kiosks along the Street and restaurants nearby where a take-away order can turn into a picnic. There are grassy areas and benches that provide a good spot to relax and watch the world go by. There is easy access from the street a few steps down although parking can be a nightmare at busy times.

***Abha Dam*** [312 A3] (Off Nahraan Rd, west of Rte 213; ⌚ 24hrs daily) The lake by Abha Dam provides a welcome watery sight in the middle of the city. Check out the views near the al Nozha Tourist Complex and the Damside Walk in Damside Park, to the east of the dam.

***Al Basta District*** [312 B2] (al Imam Ali bin Abi Talib Rd; ⌚ 24hrs daily) The last of the remains of the old traditional homes in this district north of al Bahar Historic Square have been saved from demolition in the nick of time. Dating back to the Ottoman era, the houses are mostly abandoned, but the vibe of this era remains. They are earmarked for restoration by the Saudi Tourism Authority. Simply park along the road and walk into the neighbourhood if you want to take a closer look, but be careful as some of the buildings are in a very poor state of repair.

***Shamsan Ottoman Castle*** [312 C1] (Shamsan neighbourhood off King Faisal St; ⌚ 24hrs daily; admission free) The drive to the castle is up a very steep hill through Shamsan, an older area of Abha. Once at the top, there is good street parking immediately in front. This castle dates from the early Ottoman period, believed to have been first built in the 16th century with some archaeologists suggesting older structures could have pre-dated it as evidenced by artefacts found on the site. The rectangular stone structure measuring 90m by 50m has undergone recent renovation. You can walk around all sides of the castle, allowing you to explore each of the three towers closely, and there are good views of the city below from the terrace in front. The castle entrance is on the west wall behind the terrace. There is also a floor plan, in Arabic only, that provides a good idea of the interior layout – though you may be unable to visit inside owing to further ongoing renovation.

***Jebel Akhdar (Green Mountain)*** [312 C3] (Green Mountain St, off an unnamed street near al Raqdi Museum) Translated as Green Mountain, Jebel Akhdar is a key landmark in Abha. There are many temporary closures for renovations throughout the Kingdom, but it still might come as a surprise that the authorities have closed the mountain. If it has reopened by the time you visit Abha, it does give an excellent view over the city with the giant KSA flag wafting in the breeze below. Fog cover is frequent in the summer and winter, so consider visiting either mid morning or after sunset for the best chance of clear skies. There was a lovely café at the top that will hopefully be reopened at some point as well. The **Jebel Akhdar Cable Car** [312 D4] (Prince Faisal bin Khalid Rd; SAR70), currently closed, transports passengers to the mountain from the station next to the Abha Palace Hotel. It is also possible to drive or walk to the top.

If you want a quick peak at more family artefacts on the way to the mountain, **al Raqdi Heritage Museum** [312 D3] (unnamed road, off King Abdul Aziz Rd, west of the roundabout; 📞050 575 3329; ⌚ 16.30–23.00 daily; admission free) makes for a convenient pop-in before or after visiting the mountain top.

***High City*** [312 B4] (King Abdul Aziz Rd, Asir National Park; admission free) Situated in Asir National Park, High City is a hybrid destination that combines open parkland with a robust development of restaurants and coffee shops, which are the true destination for most visitors. It feels much more like an outdoor mall with some good views than an experience with nature. Asir National Park extends from the Tihamah Plain that borders the Red Sea in the west to the outskirts of Abha. If you are looking for tranquillity in this popular green space within High City, you will be disappointed, but if you are looking for yet another newly developed trendy place to see and be seen, then it may be for you. There are loads of coffee shops where you can enjoy your favourite brew while relaxing in the park. Although there is plenty of green space, the walkways feel like the artificial urban development that they truly are. When it isn't foggy, there are great views of the city with Jebel Akhdar (see opposite) in the foreground and Asir National Park (page 318) to the back; High City appears to be overtaking the previous role of Green Mountain in attracting visitors looking for the best views above Abha City. This is a very popular venue so be patient with the traffic, especially at night. The parking is poorly planned so drivers park along the roads wherever they fancy.

***Abu Kheyal Park*** [312 B4] (King Abdul Aziz Rd) Situated to the east and over the road from High City at the far end of Asir National Park, abu Kheyal Park is a family-orientated park and a much calmer place than its neighbour, with lovely trees and general greenery. It's a great location for a picnic and has a similarly great view of Jebel Akhdar and the city.

***Dabbab Walkway*** ✷ [312 C4] (Tehama St; 🕒 24hrs daily) This is a lovely promenade where friends and family picnic with a beautiful view of the wadi below if it's not foggy. The walkway is long enough for a good stroll and, although it gets crowded during the evening, you can find a bit more space away from the road. There are plenty of coffee shops and a few restaurants nearby, which are useful if you don't bring your own picnic. To get here, exit King Abdul Aziz Road at the roundabout, heading south on Wadi Marra Street, then turn right on to Tehama Street. Park wherever you can.

***Fatima Museum of Home Decoration and Women's Clothes*** ✷ [312 D4] (Off King Abdullah Rd; 📞 050 574 9843; 🕒 11.00–20.00 daily; SAR20 for full access) Everyone is welcome at Fatima's museum. The first house, in front, is the women's museum, where you will be greeted and invited to look at the arts and crafts of Asir that are beautifully displayed in this artist's home. In addition to paintings, you will also be able to appreciate the jewellery and wonderful clothing exhibits.

You will then be invited to a second house, to the left. This contains a large diwan where an 8-minute informative film is shown in Arabic and English describing the culture of the region and how it is woven into the artwork found upstairs on the first floor, where Fatima's workshop is located. If you are lucky, she will be in the process of creating her next work. Her focus is on the importance of recognising women's contributions to local culture and she is deserving of all the support you can give her.

The specific art style produced in Fatima's studio is the local al Qatt al Asiri, which was traditionally created by women of the region and was inscribed on UNESCO's list of Intangible Cultural Heritage in 2017. Fatima is teaching young women how to preserve this beautiful decorative art form used on clothing and home goods, as well as canvasses. Her work has been recognised as culturally significant and has been displayed at the United Nations. Fatima is warm and welcoming but does not speak much English. An English-speaking man named Ali gives an excellent talk about the museum and culture and is happy to answer questions. Much of Fatima's work in the workshop is for sale. There is also a gift shop on site. Try not to miss this wonderful experience. We recommend you go in the late afternoon or early evening.

To get there, from Abha take King Abdullah Road eastbound and turn off about 1.5km after a cluster of coffee kiosks. From here go straight up the unnamed road to the first ridge, then turn right. If you go past the SASCO station, you have gone too far. Immediately after turning, you will see Fatima's traditional house beyond an open gated entrance.

**WEST OF ABHA** Covering a total of nearly 6,500km², Asir National Park extends from Saudi Arabia's western coast on the Red Sea, and including part of the coastal Tihamah Plain, to the east as far as the outskirts of Abha. Established in 1981, this is the Kingdom's first national park. It is home to many birds, nature trails and hiking paths among a number of juniper forests. The Sarawat Mountains, part of the larger Hejaz mountain range that runs along the Red Sea coast, are at their most dramatic here, providing the perfect area to commune with nature. The jewel in this range's crown is Jebel Souda, claimed to be the Kingdom's highest peak and offering breathtaking scenery and opportunities for more outdoor activities.

**Jebel Souda** Jebel Souda (also spelled Jebel Soudah, Soodah, Sawda and Sawdah) is the highest mountain peak in Saudi Arabia at approximately 3,000m. The exact height of the mountain is disputed, some claiming 2,998m, and others as high as 3,021m. The mountain is a popular beauty spot, tourist resort and adventure hub, where Saudis and other Gulf nationals from the region have been spending holidays away from the desert heat for decades – though people from around the world are now beginning to discover the appeal of this region. Jebel Souda is very popular in the summer as the temperature stays comfortably in the mid 20s, often lower when fog enshrouds the peak. Winter months are cold, with temperatures averaging single-digit figures between November and February, and when most resorts and restaurants close their doors.

From Abha, follow Route 214 west. This road is being expanded to become a dual carriageway part way from Abha. Be prepared for many drivers to suddenly pull over without warning to take a photo, stop at one of the many vendor stalls along the way, or suddenly set up a picnic at the side of the road. Baboons are everywhere and especially favour lay-bys, so take care if you also stop to sightsee, especially if you have food.

### *Where to stay* *Map, page 308*

In this area, accommodation most often caters to Saudi, rather than international, tastes and conventions. It is also possible to camp in the national park, with designated campsites dotted around Jebel Souda. More information about campsites can be found at **w** splendidarabia.com/asir-national-park.

**Al Azizah Residential Resort** Unnamed road off Rte 214, east of al Azizah; ☎056 766 4549. If you prefer furnished apartments, then consider staying at this resort tucked away near al Azizah with a view of al Moshebah Hill. The upmarket apartments are well appointed & make guests feel at home. Nice touches extend to the garden. **$$$$**

**View al Souda Resort** Unnamed road off Rte 214, southeast of al Souda; ☎050 050 3683. These 2- & 3-bedroom villas are in a terrific location situated high on the mountain, leaving the traffic far below. Well-appointed living areas & kitchens make this a good choice for those who want comfort & are happy to self-cater after an active day out. **$$$$**

**Green View Hotel** Rte 214 near al Azizah; ☎055 180 0880. This hotel is in a good location just a bit further down the mountain from most other properties with fewer traffic problems in peak season. It has all the basic 3-star amenities with some rooms including a desirable balcony for those who want to enjoy the view from their room. **$$$**

### *Where to eat and drink* *Map, page 308*

There are plenty of fruit and vegetable stands along Route 214 in addition to numerous small grocers for those who prefer to picnic alfresco.

**Mohammed Hussein Tourist Village** Rte 214, Suqah; ☎050 674 8380; ⌚ noon–midnight daily. This restaurant has a family-style menu serving Saudi classics, with indoor cushioned floor seating, as well as tented seating outdoors. Come here for the view. **$$**

**Rashfa Café** al Azizah; ☎050 494 1900; ⌚ noon–23.00 daily. A branch of this popular café provides an excellent view of the mountains from the cushioned sofas & chairs on the outdoor terrace. There is some indoor seating with traditionally decorated walls. This is another coffee & dessert shop that is a step above so many others found throughout the Kingdom. **$$**

***Sports and activities*** Many visitors come to Jebel Souda for **hiking, mountain biking** and **camping**. All of these can be done independently or on a guided tour. As ever, do keep in mind that tourism is in its infancy in Saudi Arabia and may not always be reliable or meet expectations of some visitors, so be flexible. Asir Province has been off the map even for many expatriate residents, so most tours are organised through hotel staff's personal contacts and can range in quality from very good to abysmal. Visitors planning for outdoor pursuits should ensure they have sufficient travel insurance in case of accidents.

**Paragliding** is on offer around Jebel Souda, with launches at The Palm Park (page 320), the Abha Paraglider Zone and other spots. We cannot recommend a specific organisation, but there are several. Keep in mind that this is a seasonal activity. Expect prices to start around SAR500 per person.

### *What to see and do*

**Abu Sarrah Historical Palace al Azizah** (Unnamed road) Follow the brown sign as you head towards Jebel Souda on al Souda Rd westbound and turn left at the sign. You will descend a steep road for a few hundred metres before climbing again. The old palace towers are more than 200 years old. They will be visible from the decline, with many traditional homes and buildings dotted along the village roads. Although there are no published opening hours for the historical palace, you might be invited to visit if the owner is around, but this cannot be counted on. This area is a popular spot for Saudis to relax and is worth a short detour if you are heading further up the mountain and want to explore and get a glimpse of traditional village life, with fewer crowds than are found towards the summit.

**Al Souda Cable Car** (Rte 214, just west of King Abdullah Park; ☎017 229 1500; ⌚ May–early Oct 09.30–17.00 daily; SAR100) This cable car runs from near the top of Jebel Souda to the misleadingly named Rijal al Ma'a station and should be regarded more as a ride than transport to Rijal al Ma'a as it is several kilometres away, north of the village of al Ous. If you just want an experience soaring above the greenery, the views from the cable car are lovely. Note, however, that operating hours are seasonal and not reliable.

**Parks** Located south of the village of Suqah, the beautiful **al Sahab Park** (🕘 24hrs daily) has a Cloud Corniche from where you can enjoy dramatic 360° vistas when it is clear at the top. Turn south from Route 214 towards the village and follow the signs. It is adjacent to the **Raidah Sanctuary**. Managed by the National Center for Wildlife (w ncw.gov.sa), the sanctuary is home to many protected birds and animal species and requires a permit to enter. Contact them for further details.

**King Abdullah Park** (Rte 214 along the village of al Souda) is conveniently located and a popular spot for families who want to picnic, let kids run around and generally relax surrounded by beauty in every direction; but note that it gets very crowded in the afternoon and evening. If you want to break up your journey to Rijal al Ma'a and take a break from the switchbacks, stop at **The Palm Park** (on Rte 2442, about 3.5km below the junction of Rte 214) below the al Souda viewpoint. This small park has a children's play area, some welcome benches and a grassy area with paved walkways in the shape of palm fronds, which make this park suitable for wheelchair-users. The views are breathtaking when it isn't foggy.

**Sea of Clouds** This vista can be overlooked from several viewpoints towards the top of al Souda Road in the summer season. The spectacular view of clouds blankets the Raidah Sanctuary reserve and captures the imagination. Simply pull over to the side of the road safely at any point along the way, ideally near an ad hoc area for a picnic or at least where you can enjoy a coffee while contemplating the wonder of nature.

**Rijal al Ma'a** Most people visit Rijal al Ma'a from Abha via Jebel Souda. Once past Jebel Souda, turn left from Route 214 on to Route 2442. There is a descent of about 30km on extremely steep and narrow roads with unimaginably tight switchbacks to add to the sense of adventure. As well as other, less-than-cautious, drivers, watch out for the ubiquitous hamadryas baboons. Some of the journey is likely to be in the fog as it is adjacent to the Sea of Clouds. The reward is the village, with its architecture and cultural vibe that is both very Yemeni and Asiri.

***Where to eat and drink*** Small grocers and rustic cafés can be found at al Shabain village to the north of Rijal al Ma'a near the Clock Roundabout along Route 211 near Wadi Hali. Note that this is not the way back to al Souda. Instead, return to the Clock Roundabout and turn on to Route 2442 when you are ready to return to Abha.

**Hot & Cold** Off Rte 211 directly opposite Rijal al Ma'a Heritage Village; 📞059 800 0250; 🕘 07.00–23.50 Sat–Thu, 13.00–23.50 Fri. Complement your artisanal coffee with a cheeky snack if you are felling peckish at this small modern café situated in a perfect spot near the heritage village. $$

**Rijal al Ma'a Heritage Village Tea House** Rijal al Ma'a Heritage Village; 🕘 08.00–midnight daily. Located to the right on the 2nd-floor terrace, this is a great place to catch your breath & enjoy a tea, coffee or soft drink. It overlooks many more buildings in the same style further down the valley. $

### *What to see and do*

**Rijal al Ma'a Heritage Village** ✷ (Rte 2442; 🕘 08.00–midnight daily, hours vary by season; SAR20) The well-preserved village of Rijal al Ma'a (also Rijal, Rejal and Ragal al Maa/alma) is on the tentative list of Saudi UNESCO World Heritage Sites and is a true highlight of any visit to the Kingdom. If you only have limited time to visit Asir, this is the place to prioritise. Located in a valley on the major trade route from Yemen to the north towards Mecca and Madinah, its remote position was isolated enough to protect against invaders for much of its history. The Ottomans tried to conquer most of the Hejaz and southern region of what is now Saudi Arabia and mounted

## THE FLOWERMEN FESTIVAL

Held in late August or early September, the Flowermen Festival takes place in Rijal al Ma'a and other locations around al Souda, celebrating the distinct culture of the Asir Mountains and the resilience of its people. Rijal al Ma'a has particular significance as it is where the Qatanis defeated the Ottomans in 1825. Men from the Qatani tribe perform traditional ardah dances, wearing their distinctive headdresses made of reddish-orange and yellow flowers interspersed with herbs, recognising their rural heritage, fierce independence and preservation of their way of life in harmony with nature. Women weave these beautiful garlands and are also celebrated for their craftwork. Music, handicrafts and head garlands are all available to buy at very reasonable prices. The Saudi Ministry of Culture supports this festival and is promoting the local culture as a part of its bid to add Rijal al Ma'a to its growing collection of UNESCO World Heritage Sites.

a military campaign to do so in Asir during the early 19th century. Although Abha and Khamis Mushait fell, the Ottomans were defeated in Rijal al Ma'a, leading to the recognition of parts of Asir as independent from the Ottoman Empire.

The village is a cluster of 60 mostly high-rise buildings situated on the side of a hill, some of which are eight storeys tall, with stunning architecture that dates back 900 years. The walls are made of stone, mud clay and wood and are accented in imaginative patterns using white quartz around the rooftops and above the windows, some of which frame orange, yellow, green and blue window insets. There are even a few once-elaborate wooden frames known as *roshans*, although they are in poor condition now. Visitors can walk the village's stone-built paths, with steps mostly left in their original condition – they are uneven and have no safety features at the edge.

Many buildings are open, so don't miss exploring the interior of these fascinating structures. Most have stunning decorations in the traditional al Qatt style. If you want to get an authentic feel of what a house was like back in the day, then visit the **Rijal Museum**, which is included in the ticket price and is a couple of levels up and to the left within the village. The highlights are the beautifully decorated wooden doors, vibrantly painted walls, intricately woven textiles, traditional costumes and more.

Tickets are purchased towards the back left of the large ground-floor courtyard. There is also a gift shop next to the ticket office.

**Turshi Museum** (Side street less than 100m opposite Rijal al Ma'a Heritage Village; 056 552 2140; 10.15–20.15 daily; SAR20. Opening hours vary and are unreliable) This is another example of enterprising Saudis converting their homes into a living museum of the recent past. Although the interior repeats the theme of coins, textiles and vintage traditional clothing displays, the brightly painted outbuildings are interesting to explore as they also contain locally designed furniture and tools.

**SOUTHEAST OF ABHA** Most visitors will take day trips from Abha or sometimes Khamis Mushait to visit this part of Asir Province. The distances are short and the roads are good, but the al Habala Resort provides options for an overnight stay should you need it.

**Al Habala and around منطقة الحبالة** Asir means 'difficult' in Arabic. It is an apt description for much of the topography in the province, as well as the living conditions of the people. Escaping the reaches of the Ottoman Empire in the late 17th century, many settled in remote niches within the escarpments of the Asir Mountains. The most famous of these is the now abandoned but preserved 'hanging village' of al Habala. Al Habala is located about 65km southeast of Abha and 50km south of Khamis Mushait.

### *Where to stay and eat* *Map, page 308*

**Al Habala Resort** Next to the Tourist Park (see below). The resort entrance is to the left of the Tourist Village entrance. Ring at the security gate. This property offers chalets of different sizes, all with living & dining areas & a basic kitchen. There's an on-site restaurant serving a selection of Arabic cuisine. The chalets are best for an overnight stay, with the views from nearly every aspect of the resort by far the best thing about this location. Self-caterers should note that the nearest grocery store is a few kilometres away in the village of al Hedilah on Rte 2110 & may want to consider doing their shop in Abha before setting off. **$$$**

**Al Habala Tourist Village** Eastern end of Rte 2112, near Anqarah. The tourist village is a park with a collection of shops & food kiosks, and a lovely terrace with covered tables giving visitors a jaw-dropping view over the edge of the escarpment. It is also where the cable cars descend to the hanging village. **$**

### *What to see and do*

**Hanging Village of al Habala** ✸ The so-called hanging village of al Habala was built by the Qatani tribe about 400 years ago as a way of escaping the Ottomans. It perches on a ledge about 400m from the top of the escarpment at an elevation of 2,270m. The name of the village is derived from the Arabic word for rope, as the early residents accessed the village using rope ladders.

The now abandoned village is terraced and dotted with stone buildings with their wooden doors and windows in the Asiri style, including traditionally designed homes, shops and a mosque. Have a wander along the steps and paths to take in the stupendous views around every turn. Don't miss the diwan with faded al Qatt designs on the three walls, open to the canyon below.

Nowadays there's no need for rope ladders as a cable car makes the journey down to this fascinating village, the only way the village can now be accessed. Park at the **al Habala Tourist Park and Cable Car** (eastern end of Rte 2112, near Anqarah; ⌚ May–Oct 10.00–20.00 daily, limited access out of season; entrance to the tourist park & parking SAR20, plus cable car SAR70). The cable cars are allocated so that each party does not share a pod with strangers. You will arrive at the lowest point of the historic village which gives an excellent view of the valley far below. As you wander along the path from the cable car station, you will see cacti, flowering bushes and other bursts of colour provided by nature.

**Al Habala Village Viewpoint** ✸ After you've visited the hanging village (or even if the cable car isn't running), from the tourist park return to the road and take the first left at the roundabout to the viewpoint about 500m further down, where there is ample parking. From here the panoramic view of the hanging village is spectacular and a great place to contemplate the massive achievement of its original builders. Not to be missed!

**Jebel al Mahlah جبل المهلهل** (Located by road about 1km southwest of a signpost for 'al Habala Cable Car Service' – not to be confused with al Habala Tourist Park & Cable Car) In a land of vistas, the mountain top of Jebel al Mahlah is special. It is still possible to approach the sheer drop overlooking what can only be described as Saudi Arabia's Grand Canyon. There are rust-coloured fences in places, but other areas are a health-and-safety nightmare with no protection for visitors from the cliff rocks to the canyon below. The view is always magical, but especially so when the clouds roll in beneath you. People may be wild camping nearby; and local children, already learning to become good traders, convincingly engage visitors when trying to sell their traditional flower wreaths.

**Tamniah Archaeological Museum** ✷ (Off Rte 2110, Tamniah village; 050 575 0784; ⌚ 08.00–20.00 daily, but may be closed for prayers & during the afternoon; SAR10) Tamniah is about 15km southwest of al Habala. If you are looking for a heritage museum visit that is a bit special, then check out this gem. Nestled below Jebel Ferwa, the Kingdom's second highest peak, only 10m lower than Jebel Souda, the museum is well signposted from the road to the village. You will pass open farmland and ruins from the original neighbourhood on the right, abandoned only a few decades ago. You will know you have arrived when you spot the antique cars out front.

This home turned museum was built about 250 years ago by a prominent family from the al Shahrani tribe in the traditional Asir style, with contrasting beige and brown layers, rectangular windows and a white rooftop balcony. The walls are thick enough to provide natural climate control throughout the year. If you are fortunate, a young English-speaking man from the family will be summoned, if he is not already on site, and will give guests a brilliant tour of his ancestral home, which was the family's main home only a generation ago. Upon entering, you'll pass by a collection of 20th-century consumer goods, from Coca-Cola bottles to children's toys, all accompanied by original and unusual Saudi portrait art. In the ground-floor reception room, displays of jewellery, civilian and military costumes, weapons, tribal rugs and folk furniture can be viewed with plenty of photos from the era on the walls. The ground floor was originally used for animal pens, following local tradition.

Things get even more interesting up the multicoloured painted stairs. You will notice the wooden doors in contrasting colours, adding to the vibrancy. Doors and passageways between the rooms are very low, designed both for ventilation and also to deter anyone from making a quick escape in this historically volatile region. The colour continues with the walls, beautifully decorated in the al Qatt style in the main diwan and throughout the interior of the upper floors, which are the living quarters of this multi-generational home. One of the highlights once you reach the first floor is the antique bridal canopy that is designed to be affixed on top of a camel, concealing the bride as she is transported to the wedding ceremony. You will also be able to see several bedrooms, as well as the original kitchen complete with its utensils and storage holes in the floor that were used as natural refrigeration. It may come as a surprise to find that one of the food storage rooms is located in the animal pen. Make sure you climb on to the roof terrace as it gives a lovely view of the village, farmlands and the mountain, and coffee may be served by the family from the late afternoon in the high season.

**KHAMIS MUSHAIT خميس مشيط** Also known as Khamis Mushayt or simply Khamis, this is the Kingdom's fifth largest city with a population of 1.3 million people. Its name is derived from its Thursday market – *khamis* meaning Thursday. With an economy that has been based traditionally on agriculture, the city is home to the large Shahran tribe, known both for their agricultural pursuits and for their historic rivalry with the Qatanis. At an elevation of 2,000m, it enjoys a similarly pleasant climate to that of Abha. Although not a tourist destination, Khamis has an expatriate population mostly associated with its prominent military base. If you are visiting friends and family, or simply want to stay in Khamis before a long journey further south, a few options are available to suit all budgets.

## Where to stay

**Bayat by Cristal Hotel** King Faisal Rd; 017 226 6666; w bayat.com-hotel.website. Conveniently located for the city centre & Abha's airport, Khamis's most comfortable hotel will appeal to those seeking a pampered stay. A variety of well-equipped rooms & suites have tasteful furnishings & the latest technology. Facilities include a fitness centre & an indoor swimming pool (check access times for men & women), & valet parking. Airport transfers & local sightseeing tours can be arranged in advance. Spacious Le Café, on the ground floor, serves light meals, snacks & hot & cold drinks, while the panoramic views of the city are seen from the hotel's top-floor restaurant, which offers a flexible menu & buffet options. B/fast not inc in room rate. **$$$$**

**Golden Square** Riyadh Rd, north of Prince Sultan Rd & west of Sad bin abu Waqas; 017 221 5450. Book through a reputable hotel booking website. This is a centrally located apartment hotel offering clean, well-maintained 1-bedroom units with separate living area & small kitchenette. Although there is no restaurant on site, there are several basic options nearby. The service is very good, but parking is severely limited. **$$$**

**Qasr Asir Hotel Suites** King Abdullah St, north of King Fahd Rd. Book through a reputable hotel booking website. This budget property is conveniently located, with a nice touch of al Qatt décor on the wall in reception. The rooms & suites are basic & are available with or without kitchenettes. Do not expect much in terms of customer service, but if location & price are your priority, this is a good alternative to the similar OYO chain. **$**

## Where to eat and drink

**Craving Club** King Fahd Rd, about 1km east of HyperPanda; 054 210 7964; w cravingclub-ksa.com; 11.00–01.30 daily. This American restaurant will take care of your cravings if they include wings, onion rings, burgers, steaks, lots of dishes with cheese, & gooey desserts. The décor is stylish & there is a large outdoor seating area with good views. Seating is mixed gender & the vibe is relaxed. Service is attentive, US-style. **$$$$**

**Hot Chow** Less than 500m east of the Craving Club; 050 465 8000; noon–00.30 daily. Continue east on Hwy 15 & take the 1st exit at the roundabout. Hot Chow is next to the Aramex building. This is a build-it-your-way Chinese-inspired noodle bar. Select your style of noodles, from Thai, Japanese & more, then choose your protein & veggies, then have it all mixed with your preferred sauce. There is a limited selection of salads, sushi, dumplings & the ubiquitous dynamite shrimp for those who prefer something other than noodles. Take away or eat in at indoor or outdoor tables. **$$$**

**Maharani Restaurant** Imam Mohammed bin Saud Rd, about 1.5km west of Salahuddin Rd; 017 237 2111; 12.30–00.30 daily. This is an Indian restaurant that offers popular north Indian cuisine but also an extensive menu including Chinese, Middle Eastern & pan-Western favourites. There are separate singles & family sections. **$$$**

✷ **Butter Bakery** King Khalid Branch Rd, Hwy 15; 053 192 0222; w butterbakery.co; 07.30–01.00 Sat–Thu, 15.00–01.00 Fri. This upmarket bakery has it all. Whether you are looking for a buttery croissant, sweet pastry, manakish or a dessert treat, this is the place to go. The spacious indoor & outdoor seating is welcoming whether you are in a rush to start your day or plan to spend a while socialising. **$$**

**Shopping** In Khamis, Assdaf Mall and Mujan Park are the go-to modern malls, along with the popular **supermarkets** al Raya, Danube, Othaim and Panda. **Souq al Khamis**, also known as the Thursday Souq, on and around King Fahd Road, is the place to visit if you want to sample the traditional, generations-old ways of shopping in this part of Asir, whether you are looking for homewares, bargain clothing, spices or local produce. Part of the market also sells chickens, cows, goats and sheep.

**Other practicalities** Many banks are conveniently located along Highway 15, between Prince Sultan and King Fahd roads. **Nahdi Pharmacy** (King Fahd Rd; ☎ 9200 24673; w nahdionline.com; ⏲ 24hrs daily), 1km east of the Saudi German Hospital, is your best bet for quick, professional service at any time.

**ANB Bank** ☎ 800 124 4040; w anb.com.sa; ⏲ 09.30–17.30 Sat–Thu
**Bank al Jazira** ☎ 800 244 0404; w bankaljazira.com; ⏲ 09.30–16.30 Sun–Thu
**Riyad Bank** ☎ 9200 02470; w riyadbank.com; ⏲ 09.30–16.30 Sun–Thu
**SAB Bank** ☎ 017 221 4080; w sab.com; ⏲ 09.30–16.30 Sun–Thu
**Saudi German Hospital** King Fahd Rd, 300m west of HyperPanda Trolley 15; ☎ 017 235 5000; w aseer.saudigermanhealth.com; ⏲ 24hrs daily
**Saudi Post** al Madinah al Munawwarah Rd about 1km south of al Mahaiah Rd; ☎ 9200 05700; w splonline.com.sa; ⏲ 08.00–21.00 Sun–Thu, 16.00–21.00 Sat

## NAJRAN PROVINCE منطقة نجران

Najran Province is a remote area, covering about 150,000km². It borders Jizan Province to the west, Asir Province to the north, Riyadh Province to the northeast and the Eastern Province well into the Empty Quarter to the east, and extends along the Yemeni border for all but about 200km of the 1,300km border between the two countries. Most of the population of 582,000 lives in Najran, the provincial capital. Fewer than 100,000 people live in the remote villages of the province.

Najran has been on key trade routes throughout the Arabian Peninsula for millennia. The Romans were in the region as early as 25BCE, recognising Najran as part of Arabia Felix, a collection of ancient Yemeni kingdoms. The religious mix of modern Najran includes a Sunni population and sects from Ismaili and Zaidi or fiver branches of Shi'a Islam. Zaidi Islam is also dominant in northern Yemen and is usually practised by extensions of the same families. Najran's dominant tribes are the Yam people, who are part of the Banu Hamdan branch of the Qatanis who are prominent throughout the south. The al Makrami people forged an alliance with the Yam several hundred years ago and are known for their religious leadership within the Ismaili communities.

Much of Najran's economy today is focused on mining, with rock quarries prized for their high-quality granite and marble. Much of the remaining economy is concentrated in the agricultural and trade sectors.

Najran's terrain includes the southern reaches of the Sarawat Mountains, as well as desert. It has many wadis, some of which retain water for much of the year. Wadi Najran dominates the topography of the capital. Najran city sits at an elevation of 1,300m, but due to its latitude, it is warmer than most other desert settlements elsewhere in the Kingdom. Temperatures typically range from 12°C to over 40°C, with winter temperatures pleasant during the day and chilly at

### CHECK YOUR TRAVEL INSURANCE

Najran Province borders Yemen. Highway 15 comes within 10km of the border as you cross into Najran from Asir Province, as does Najran city. The Najran Valley Dam to the southeast of the city centre is situated less than 1km from Yemen. It is crucial for visitors to check their travel insurance to confirm that it is valid for travel to this region as many policies are not valid if they go against your country's official government travel advice.

night. Summer temperatures can be very high although they remain relatively low in humidity. The small amount of rain the province does receive is most likely to fall in the late winter. It is a year-round destination, but best visited outside of the summer months.

## GETTING THERE AND AWAY

**By air** Najran Domestic Airport is located about 25km east of Najran city centre and has scheduled flights to Dammam, Jeddah and Riyadh on Saudia, flynas and flyadeal. There are additional flights on flydubai and Air Arabia to Dubai and Sharjah respectively. SAPTCO buses connect the airport to Najran city.

**By road** Najran is remote. If you are setting out from Asir, you will see stunning scenery as you leave Khamis Mushait and continue southeast past the road toward al Habala. Once you are at a lower elevation, try to spot traditional houses, as they are dotted around the remote villages you pass along the way, or watch for camels, goats, sheep, baboons, cats, birds of prey and other animals.

Most people driving to Najran Province will use Highway 15 from Asir, although a few hearty long-distance travellers may take the long, desolate route bordering the Empty Quarter from Riyadh along Highway 10, turning on to Route 177 for the final 400-plus kilometres. If you are arriving from Jizan Province, this journey involves crossing the mountains before joining Highway 15 at Dhahran al Janub near the Asir–Najran border.

Do not expect to rely on getting around **by bus** in the province as services are limited to longer distances. There are limited long-distance services on SAPTCO from Khamis Mushait, with journey times between 4½ and 5 hours.

**DHAHRAN AL JANOUB ظهران الجنوب (ZAHRAN AL JANOUB)*** If you looking for a good place to break your journey to Najran, then this is the place to do it. Although Dhahran al Janoub is still a few kilometres from Najran in Asir Province, people are most likely to visit on the way to Najran, so we are including it here.

The old village is a hidden gem, preserving the feel of its heyday as a stop on the caravan trade route from Yemen to Mecca and points north. It is located at the junction of Highway 15, Route 2002 leading to Jizan Province and an unnamed road signposting the direction to the Yemeni border. Turn right at the NCB building and you'll find the old village about 200m along on the left behind an unremarkable parade of shops and where it is possible to find basic refreshments if you arrive when the shops are open in the morning. The road ends almost immediately afterwards, so park where you can and simply walk in. Be aware that the dirt paths in the village can be muddy if it has rained recently.

This historic site is well worth the visit. Enter on foot through the pathway with the signs and what looks to be a faded map. The architecture here uniquely combines the styles of Asir and Najran, with its Najrani towering multistorey buildings, decorated wooden doors and windows framed in white and red, growing in size on the higher levels. The roofs, made of wood, straw and mud, are finished with the Asiri-style triangular points at the corners. Wander around the twists and turns of the lanes and you will marvel at the next set of buildings around each corner. Try to find the amphitheatre, old souq area and squares large enough to accommodate caravan convoys.

Although many of the buildings are in poor condition, there are signs that restoration is starting to take place by the local community, which no doubt includes descendants of the villagers that once lived here. Many of the distinct horizontal

### SECURITY

It is important to note that the presence of security in Najran Province is stronger than nearly anywhere else in the Kingdom, with checkpoints that are more attentive and where obvious military traffic is commonly seen along the highway. Although the conflict in Yemen that started in 2014 could be described as a civil war at the outset, it escalated with the decision by Saudi Arabia to enter the conflict in 2015, leading a coalition of other countries becoming involved, including some from the region and from the West. It quickly became a proxy war between Sunni- and Shi'a-backed forces, most notably Saudi Arabia and Iran and their respective alliances. Several skirmishes have spilled over the border into southern Saudi Arabia, including Najran.

Away from military conflict, Yemen has long been identified as a smuggler's paradise, with everything from illegal migrants, cheap car parts, alcohol and drugs including qat, the stimulant that remains legal in Yemen but illegal in Saudi Arabia, trafficked across this porous border. This ongoing problem is not fully under control due to a combination of the border's remoteness, tough mountainous terrain tapering off to inhospitable desert, and interconnected families on both sides of the border, sometimes with mixed loyalties. If you do decide to visit Najran, you will be rewarded with a cultural gem, but go with open eyes and make sure you keep informed of current conditions before setting out.

lines eroded on the exterior walls have been preserved during renovation efforts; other exteriors have been painted in traditional Asiri patterns of bright red, green and yellow with striking vibrancy.

The highlight of this exploration is a visit to the mosque tucked away behind padlocked double wooden doors. If you are fortunate enough to find someone who is in the village with a key, take the opportunity to accept an invitation to enter the mosque. Men must be dressed respectfully, with knees and upper arms covered, women should be wearing an abaya and headscarf, and everyone must remove their shoes before entry. You will see thick whitewashed columns, the red carpeted floor, Qur'an stands and a clock indicating the correct prayer times, all evidence that this mosque is still in use.

**NAJRAN نجران** The origin of the term Najran has multiple roots – it can mean both a door frame and thirsty. Some believe the city and province were named after Najran bin Zaydan bin Saba bin Yahjub bin Yarub bin Qahtan who is believed to have been the first settler in the region. The vibe in Najran is not a whole lot different than in border towns in many parts of the world, with an initial caution when interacting with outsiders followed by warmth and hospitality as trust is gained. Yemeni culture dominates Najran, from food to dress, complete with the jambiya or curved dagger that traces its origins back to the Hadramout region of Yemen.

Most tourists do not find their way as far as Najran, but will be rewarded if they do. The city is modern yet filled with historical attractions that you will probably have to yourself when you visit. This is the chance to experience a unique part of the Kingdom and to have authentic exchanges with people who may be as curious about you as you are about Najran.

**Getting there and away** See page 326. Najran's main SAPTCO bus station is situated along King Abdul Aziz Road to the southwest of the city centre.

## Where to stay *Map, opposite*

**Hotel Le Park Concord** Off King Abdul Aziz Rd, nearly opposite King Khalid Hospital; ☎ 017 544 4488; w leparkconcord.com. This growing Saudi hotel chain was founded in 2015 & is already firmly situated at the upper end of the market within the Kingdom. The rooms & public areas are opulently appointed, with an Arabic buffet in the top-floor restaurant that also provides panoramic views of the city. Conveniently located near the centre of modern Najran but with quick access to the historical points of interest. **$$$$**

**Gloria Inn** Off King Abdul Aziz Rd, almost opposite HyperPanda; ☎ 017 522 5222; w gloria-hotels.com. Easily spotted from Hwy 15; exit on to the unnamed roads. This is probably Najran's most luxurious hotel, with 4 restaurants to choose from, an outdoor swimming pool for men & a shisha bar. Rooms range from basic twins to suites with separate living areas & a well-equipped kitchen. This is a good choice for those who are looking for service & comfort. **$$$**

**Park Inn by Radisson** al Hussein bin Ali bin Abi Talib St next to King Saud Park; ☎ 017 544 7800; w radissonhotels.com. If you are looking for a mid-range property with a familiar brand name, then this centrally located hotel, part of the Radisson group, provides all the amenities expected from this chain. The restaurant's b/fast buffet is substantial & specialises in Western & Arabic grills throughout the day, with a room-service option. The hotel has good indoor & outdoor parking & is convenient for King Saud Park & several restaurants. **$$$**

**Florida Inn** Off King Abdul Aziz Rd, east of al Khazan St. If you are looking for a great location in between Wadi Najran & the city centre, this hotel is in the right place. Most staff speak English & provide a high standard of customer service. The rooms are comfortable & have heavy blackout curtains that light sleepers will appreciate. It is near some of Najran's most popular restaurants & has a coffee shop that serves salads & hot snacks if you prefer to stay in. The property also has a gift shop on site that sells locally made handicrafts & other souvenirs. **$$**

**Najran Hotel** Altufail bin Abi Rd, next to the Multipurpose Cooperative Society supermarket; ☎ 017 522 2004. This 3-star hotel feels more like a 4-star property for its polished appearance & is good value for money. The hotel entrance is wheelchair friendly with a sensible ramp to the side of the stairs, with the interior of the property more accessible for those with mobility issues than most. The rooms are clean & spacious & come with a fridge. Pleasant indoor & outdoor patios are what really set this property apart from others in the same price range. Although there is no restaurant on site, the property is in easy walking distance of several restaurants & a supermarket. **$$**

**OYO 380 Crown Hotel** King Abdul Aziz Rd, about 50m south of Ata bin Yasar Mosque; ☎ 800 820 0063; w oyorooms.com. Another property from this budget chain. The best thing about this hotel is its location. The rooms are basic with b/fast included & some parking, but don't expect much in the way of service. **$**

## Where to eat and drink *Map, opposite*

Anyone who is in a hurry or simply fancies fast food will be glad to find the usual Saudi chains as well as a branch of Shrimp Nation, with American fast food from Dunkin Donuts, McDonald's and Subway added to the mix. Najran also has no shortage of coffee kiosks, including the popular Barns and Kyan brands.

**Makan Indian Fine Dining** Abu Bakr al Siddiq St, south of King Faisal Rd; ☎ 050 572 7776; w qr.finedinemenu.com/makan-indian-fine-dining/menu; ⌚ 12.30–midnight daily. This upscale restaurant is among the best in Najran. The décor has been given a lot of thought with a clear nod to India but avoiding most of the clichés. The menu leans to north Indian dishes but there are additional choices from all over the subcontinent. Choose from open seating, private dining suitable for modesty & outdoor tables when the weather is good. **$$$$**

**Two Rivers Restaurant Iraqi Food** Abu Bakr al Siddiq St, south of King Faisal Rd about 100m

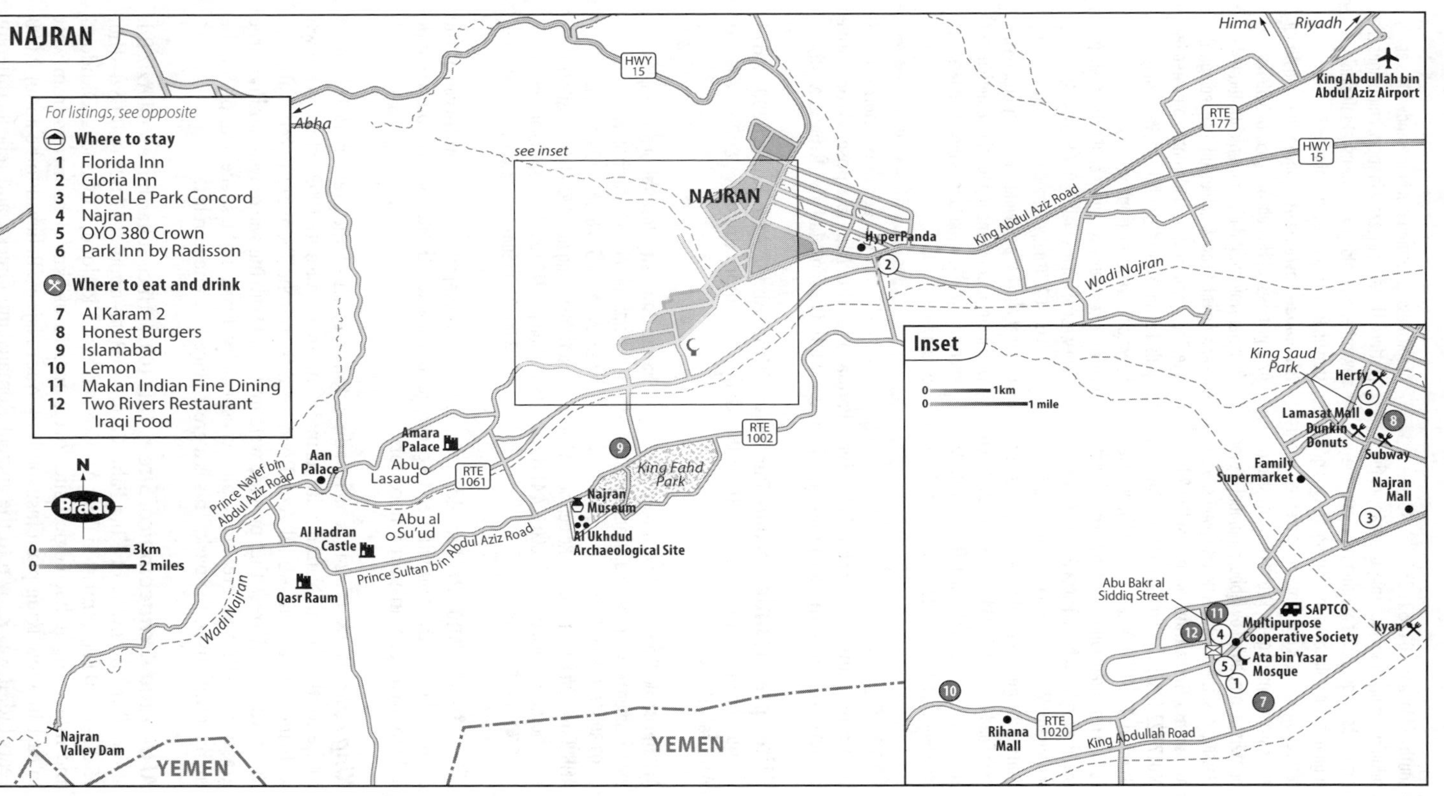
NAJRAN
For listings, see opposite
Where to stay
1 Florida Inn
2 Gloria Inn
3 Hotel Le Park Concord
4 Najran
5 OYO 380 Crown
6 Park Inn by Radisson
Where to eat and drink
7 Al Karam 2
8 Honest Burgers
9 Islamabad
10 Lemon
11 Makan Indian Fine Dining
12 Two Rivers Restaurant Iraqi Food
N
Bradt
0 3km
0 2 miles
Abha
HWY 15
see inset
NAJRAN
HyperPanda
King Abdul Aziz Road
Wadi Najran
Hima
Riyadh
King Abdullah bin Abdul Aziz Airport
RTE 177
HWY 15
Amara Palace
Aan Palace
Abu Lasaud
RTE 1061
Prince Nayef bin Abdul Aziz Road
Abu al Su'ud
Al Hadran Castle
Qasr Raum
Prince Sultan bin Abdul Aziz Road
Wadi Najran
Najran Valley Dam
YEMEN
YEMEN
RTE 1002
King Fahd Park
Najran Museum
Al Ukhdud Archaeological Site
Inset
0 1km
0 1 mile
King Saud Park
Herfy
Lamasat Mall
Dunkin Donuts
Subway
Family Supermarket
Najran Mall
Abu Bakr al Siddiq Street
SAPTCO
Multipurpose Cooperative Society
Kyan
Ata bin Yasar Mosque
Rihana Mall
RTE 1020
King Abdullah Road

south of Makan; ☎ 017 523 3388; ⏰ 13.00–midnight daily. Iraqi food may use many of the same base ingredients as other cuisines in the region, but it's all about the spicing. This is a good restaurant to check out some of differences with its extensive menu of grills, kebabs & many sharing platters accompanied by kibbe, moutabal & other classic sides. The family section is upstairs. $$$

**Al Karam 2 Restaurant** King Abdullah Rd; ☎ 017 522 1085; ⏰ 07.00–03.00 Sun–Thu, noon–04.00 Fri, 11.00–03.00 Sat. This is a Saudi-style Turkish restaurant with an extensive menu that covers everything from dolma to mixed grills. The restaurant does not have a family section. $$

**Honest Burgers** King Abdul Aziz Rd, just south of King Saud Park; ☎ 055 244 8234; ⏰ 11.00–02.00 Sun–Thu, 13.00–03.00 Fri–Sat. This is a Saudi fast-food burger joint where you can decide the level of spiciness. Customers can order sandwiches or platters. There are mozzarella sticks, onion rings & a few other sides along with the usual soft drinks. A step up from similar Saudi chains. $$

**Islamabad Restaurant** Prince Sultan bin Abdul Aziz, just west of Hussein St; ☎ 059 615 5567; ⏰ noon–midnight daily. Conveniently located near King Fahd Park & al Ukhdud Archaeological Site. The menu includes traditionally prepared fish, grills, kebabs & salads, with an above-average selection of vegetarian options. $$

**Lemon Restaurant** King Abdul Aziz Rd, about 1km west of Rihana Mall; ☎ 017 543 4433; ⏰ 16.00–02.30 daily. A modern take on a casual café that also has a thriving take-away business, with a menu varied enough to offer something for everyone, whether you fancy a broast, shawarma or fatayer. $$

**Shopping** There are a few supermarkets with a good variety of goods on their shelves, including Family Supermarket, HyperPanda and the Multipurpose Cooperative Society. The most modern malls are Lamasat Mall, Najran Mall and Rihana Mall.

**Other practicalities** **Nahdi Pharmacy** (King Abdul Aziz Rd; ☎ 9200 24673; w nahdionline.com; ⏰ 07.00–03.00 daily) is approximately 800m east of Amarah Palace.

**Al Rajhi Bank** King Abdul Aziz Rd, opposite the unnamed cemetery; w alrajhibank.com.sa; ⏰ 09.30–16.30 Sun–Thu

**ANB Bank** Off King Abdul Aziz Rd behind Ata bin Yasar Mosque; w anb.com.sa; ☎ 800 124 4141; ⏰ 09.30–16.30 Sun–Wed

**Najran University Hospital** Junction of Hwy 15 & Hamza bin Abdul Muttalib St; w hospital.nu.edu.sa; ☎ 017 544 6336; ⏰ 24hrs daily

**Saudi Post** King Abdul Aziz Rd, opposite OYO 380 hotel; ☎ 9200 05700; w splonline.com.sa; ⏰ 08.00–21.00 Sun–Thu, 16.00–21.00 Sat

**What to see and do** The old city is near Wadi Najran to the southwest of the current city centre. You will need a car to get to the sites, though some hotels will be able to organise transport if necessary.

***King Fahd Park*** (⏰ 24hrs daily; admission free) This large green park is located to the south of Wadi Najran, with its main entrance on Route 1002, which is known as Prince Sultan bin Abdul Aziz Road on this stretch. There are paved walkways lined with many trees that provide welcome shade during warm weather and large grassy areas that are great for a picnic, especially if you find a space near one of the many fountains in the park. This is a great place to come to relax.

***Al Ukhdud Archaeological Site*** ✷ (Rte 1002/Prince Sultan bin Abdul Aziz Rd, about 4km southwest of King Fahd Park; ⏰ 08.00–noon & 17.00–19.00 Sat–Thu, 15.30–18.00 Fri; admission free) Also known as al Ukhdood, Alokdod, al Okhdood and more, this archaeological site covers an area of 5km², which runs from west to east in a low-lying plain just south of Wadi Najran. Believed to be about 2,000 years old, it was known to the ancient Romans and Greeks, and reflects different eras incorporating the Byzantine, Umayyad and Abbasid periods, illustrating the importance of trade in Najran throughout its history. Here you can witness the impact of the three monotheistic, Abrahamic faiths that resided in Najran for much of its history (page 332).

Access to the site is from a side road to the west of the site. Turn right at Najran Museum and park along the same side of the road in the small lay-by a few metres to the south. The entrance is through a gate after going through a gap in the fence, where you will see a sign on the left that gives the visitor a flavour of what to expect. '*Some historical accounts mention the last king of Himyar known as Dhu Nawwas had rules and embraced Judaism. He revenges on the residents of Najran who believed in Isa (Jesus), son of Maryam (Mary), and he killed more than 20,000. This story is mentioned in Surat Al Burug of the Holy Quran.*' As ukhdud is the Arabic word for a ditch or trench, it is not surprising that this population were known as 'People of the Ditch'.

Head to the security container to your left, which serves as a guard gate and where your visa or *iqama* details will be logged. After crossing an open area of land, you will arrive at the entrance to the stone fort, which measures about 235m by 200m. The walls rise to a height of 4m, and are in various stages of ruin, although there is clear evidence that some of the site is being restored, perhaps too enthusiastically. Keep an eye out for petroglyphs on these walls, which include a horse, camel, snakes and a human hand and foot. Other petroglyphs show hunting scenes that depict weapons such as arrows, spears and sticks. There are also clusters of hieroglyphics, and Sabaean and early Kufic writing. Ruins of an early mosque believed to have been built during the first century of the Islamic era can be found in the northeast of the site. Started in 1997, archaeological work continues and is likely to uncover more artefacts. Walls in an advanced state of ruin hint at the homes and businesses that were once a part of this community.

Situated in front of al Ukhdud Archaeological Site, the **Najran Museum** is temporarily closed, as are most other regional museums. It holds great promise when it does open as it is expected to house many artefacts from the adjacent site.

***Al Hadran Castle*** Located in the abu al Su'ud traditional village, this modest castle was built in 1359AH (1940CE) to keep the southern border in check although at first glance it looks older. The castle is fenced off but it is easy enough to walk up and peek through. The traditional village has a cluster of relatively historic buildings that have mostly disappeared elsewhere in Najran city and is worth a quick look before moving on.

***Amara Palace*** (Off King Abdul Aziz Rd, in the abu Lasaud neighbourhood; ⌚ 09.00–17.00 Sat–Thu, 15.30–18.00 Fri; admission free) Also known as Amarah or Emara Palace, the castle was built in 1942, only a few years after Najran became part of Saudi Arabia. It is a purpose-built, self-contained complex designed in the traditional Najrani style by the governor of the time, Turki bin Mohammed al Madi, with round towers at each of its corners and containing a courthouse, communication centre and governor's residence. The castle has more than 60 rooms in total, with an armoury, livestock area, library, guest quarters, formal diwan and mosque. Visitors are free to wander around once visa or *iqama* details have been provided. Entry to the interior is through a hall that displays many interesting photographs of important visitors from the early days of the castle and a small museum that provides more information about the palace's history. There is a well in the courtyard to the right that is purported to be 2,000 years old. If you are

## PEOPLE OF THE BOOK: EARLY CHRISTIANS AND JEWS OF SOUTHERN ARABIA

It is believed that Christians settled in Najran in the 5th century CE. The Christian community lived alongside a substantial Jewish population in pre-Islamic times and not always in harmony – churches and synagogues were burnt, often as an act of political retribution. Significant persecution of Christians occurred during the reign of Dhu Nuwas, a Jewish convert who retaliated against the destruction of a synagogue during the 6th century, executing the Christian leader Arethas. Further massacres took place when Christians resisted conversion to Judaism, leading to an estimated 20,000 deaths.

This was undoubtedly connected to political alignments of the era. When Islam arrived in Najran, followers of the Prophet Mohammed also attempted to convert the Christian population to Islam. Although Christians and Muslims discussed incompatibilities in their religious beliefs, the Prophet Mohammed accepted that a relationship could be agreed despite these differences. This time, the outcome was more peaceful. The Christian community of Najran entered into an agreement with the Prophet Mohammed recognising an obligation of protection and to be treated fairly. It is believed that Christians remained in Najran until the 9th century CE, when most of Najran's Christian population migrated to either southern Syria near the village of the same name or near al Kufa east of Najaf in Iraq.

Jews continued to reside in the Najran area for centuries, enjoying a comfortable life gained by their high-quality crafting skills. When the al Sauds established their presence in 1934, this community was given a choice to leave or to accept that only Muslims would become citizens of the Kingdom. As the Jewish community was loosely part of the wider community of Yemeni Jews, most opted to abandon Najran and crossed into Yemen. By the late 1940s, the community was settled either in Sa'dah near the border or in Sana'a. Eventually, most subsequently emigrated to Israel.

visiting towards the end of the day, you will also have a chance to see the traditional shopping arcades opposite the palace spring to life.

***Aan Palace*** (Off Prince Nayef bin Abdul Aziz Rd; ⌚ 16.00–20.00 Thu–Sat; admission free) Situated about 1km east of Wadi Najran bridge on the north bank, this four-storey palace is a superb example of traditional Najrani architecture with its white-framed windows, some of which resemble the outline of padlocks, and white lace-like trimmed rooftops. Originally known as Qasr al Saadan, it was built in 1688 by Sheikh Mohammed bin Ismaili al Makrami. The palace has 60 rooms, a mosque and many offices originally used by the emir to hold council. The site also has a separate residential area, stables and a pre-Islamic well in its courtyard that visitors can explore when it is open.

***Qasr Raum*** (📞 055 572 6072; ⌚ 24hrs daily) The ruins of the castle sit atop a hill off Prince Sultan bin Abdul Aziz Road on the south side of wadi Najran, but access is over a bridge from the north side. You will go through a lovely neighbourhood from the north of the wadi off Prince Nayef bin Abdul Aziz Road. Follow online map driving instructions. From the road at the base of the hill, the view of the castle is obscured – but if you are fit, hike to the top, where you will be able to explore the fortress, which has five rooms, a staircase and a palm-frond roof. The stone walls feature balconies that give a brilliant view of Jebel abu Hamdan to the southwest of the valley. Take care as there are no safety precautions and the terrain is rocky.

***Wadi Najran*** It is worth stopping along the way to Qasr Raum or Aan Palace and marvelling at the wide wadi's flowing stream even in the height of summer. The view from the bridge is particularly interesting.

***Najran Valley Dam*** (At the end of Rte 1002) Cross over the bridge to the north of Wadi Najran, then turn left at the junction with Route 1020. It is less than 1km from the Yemeni border, so make sure you check the security situation at the time you plan to visit. You will pass through a tunnel just before reaching the dam. There is a wadi at the bottom of this tranquil spot that hikers may wish to explore.

**HIMA CULTURAL AREA** (100km northeast of Najran city, near the small settlement of Hima) Saudi Arabia gained its latest UNESCO World Heritage Site with the addition of the Hima Cultural Area in 2021. It ranges over an area of nearly 900km$^2$ that encompasses more than 30 sites, with still more being discovered.

The site reveals a number of ancient insights from as long as 7,000 years ago. Hima was a major stop on the incense trade route and is the point where many caravans split the direction of their journey either to continue north through the Hejaz and into the Levant, or to travel east along the edges of the inhospitable Empty Quarter through the Arabian Peninsula to the Arabian Gulf or to Mesopotamia, now in modern-day Iraq.

There are several sites near Hima that contain some of the most striking rock art anywhere in the Kingdom. Note that most of these are off-road and require a 4x4 to get up close. Some sites are fenced for protection, but others are not. The rock art includes petroglyphs of soldiers, hunting scenes and depictions of everyday life – evidence of a very different climate to today's as they contain lions, giraffes and cattle that could not live in the current climate of the area. There are also pre-Islamic religious scenes. Traders left several thousand inscriptions over millennia in their languages, from Greek to Nabataean to Thamudic and more that could be described as ancient graffiti.

Merchants also established wells known as Bir Hima that date back millennia, with some still providing water to this day. It is possible to visit many of these wells, which are located less than 5km north of Route 1230.

To get to Hima, take Highway 15 east to Route 177 north. Turn west on Route 1230 for about 20km, turning north on to an unnamed road towards Hima. Visitors should be aware that this is a remote location with very little passing traffic and

### NAJRAN ARCHITECTURE

Traditional Najran architecture, known as *beit teen*, is distinctive, with its light tan mud-brick walls often rising to six or seven storeys, decorated in a way that make the exterior walls look like a layer cake. The ground floor was usually used for livestock, with living quarters starting on the first floor. White-framed rectangular windows are often larger in size towards the top floors, where white hollowed-out triangles are found at the top edges of the roof. Decoration along the roof is usually more elaborate than in other regional architecture. Clusters of buildings would often be built around a communal courtyard.

should take sensible precautions before setting out on the road. There is a petrol station at the junction towards Hima, but check opening hours as they are likely to close during the afternoon.

## JIZAN PROVINCE جازان منطقة

*Note: We refer to the province as Jizan and the provincial capital as Jazan.*

Jizan Province (also spelled Jazan, Gizan and Gazan) is the Kingdom's second smallest province by area, covering just over 11,600km$^2$, and is the most densely populated with about 1.6 million people. Although the city of Jazan is the largest city here, there are substantial populations in smaller towns and villages in the wadis and mountains, including Sabya, Aldhabyah and abu Arish.

Owing to Jizan's coastal location, its economy remains heavily reliant on fishing, and also agricultural pursuits. It was also a key player in traditional pearl harvesting as recently as the 20th century. Abundant crop yields of coffee, grains, mangoes and many other fruits have been produced for centuries and continue to be the cornerstone of the regional economy. Heavy industries, mostly related to the oil business, are concentrated in Jizan Economic City (JEC) about 70km north of Jazan city. JEC is also a growing port city.

Jizan is bordered by Asir Province to the east and enjoys a coastline of about 200km along the Red Sea, stretching from Makkah Province in the north to Yemen in the south. The geography of Jizan is mountainous to the east with some peaks in the southern edge of the Sarawat Mountains reaching more than 2,500m. To the west, Jizan lies on the Tihamah Plain. Temperatures typically range from 31°C to well over 40°C, with winter temperatures in the mountains often in the 20s during the day and dropping to about 15°C at night in the winter. The southwest monsoon more closely associated with south Asia also affects Jizan, bringing rain in the summer months and temporary relief from the heat and humidity. When you decide to visit will depend on whether you plan to spend most of your time in the mountains or along the coast, and the monsoon.

**HISTORY** Historians note that the first known traders of the region were King Solomon and the Phoenician King Hiram, operating from the Gulf of Aqaba to Bab al Mandeb which merges with the Gulf of Aden. The southern end of the Arabian Peninsula is believed to be the Kingdom of Sheba, which extended north as far as Jizan. Over millennia, trade flourished between the indigenous Qatani tribes and empires as far flung as the Nubians, Egyptians, Romans, Sassanids of Persia, and various Indian peoples.

The Prophet Mohammed's cousin Ali visited Sana'a in Yemen in 630CE. As a result, the entire region of northern Yemen, which includes what is now Jizan, embraced Islam during the earliest days. The Ottomans arrived in the 16th century and had substantial control until the dying days of their empire in the early 20th century. The area was also part of the short-lived Idrissi Empire which covered parts of northern Yemen and extended into the southern areas of what is now Saudi Arabia. Jizan Province was formally annexed and became part of Saudi Arabia in 1934, as recognised in the Treaty of Taif. But Yemen and many residents who identified more as Yemeni than Saudi continued to claim the province as belonging to Yemen. This was only resolved through a border agreement that was finally reached in 2000. The Qatanis are still the dominant tribe in the region with several branches on both sides of the Saudi Arabia–Yemen border.

### CHECK YOUR TRAVEL INSURANCE

Similar to other provinces that border Yemen, travelling to parts of Jizan could compromise your travel insurance, including to the beautiful mountains in the Fayfa area. Jazan city is about 50km from the Saudi Arabia–Yemen border. Check with your insurance provider as well as your country's official government travel advice.

## GETTING THERE AND AWAY

**By air** King Abdullah bin Abdul Aziz Airport is the only commercial airport in Jizan Province, with flights to Jeddah, Riyadh and Dammam, as well as flights from Cairo, Dubai and Sharjah. Commonly referred to simply as Jizan Airport, it is located in the eastern outskirts of Jazan city. Taxis, Careem and Uber are available from the airport to the city centre.

**By road** Many visitors to Jizan are likely to travel on Highway 10 from Abha through the Asir Mountains descending to the Tihamah Plain. The journey starts through dramatic jagged mountain passes with a few villages here and there. Once the mountains have been left behind, the topography changes to very green wadis supporting a range of agricultural activity.

If you decide to take the long coastal journey from Jeddah to Jazan, be aware that this 8-hour drive along Route 55 is mostly desert road from as soon as you leave the southern reaches of Jeddah. Al Lith, which is a good place to stop for a picnic along the Corniche, is about 220km from Jeddah. After driving through another 160km of mostly nondescript scenery but passing many camels and goat herds, the next town you reach of any substantial size is al Qunfudhah, still in Makkah Province. This is another good rest stop before continuing to Jazan. You will get a chance to catch glimpses of mangroves and hidden patches of sandy beaches, where coral reaches the shoreline almost begging snorkellers to enter the water. However, these areas are completely devoid of recreational swimmers and everyone else. Once in Jizan Province, the land becomes noticeably greener with agriculture the main business until reaching the Royal Commission and its heavy industry.

SAPTCO have a few long-distance bus services from Abha or Jeddah, but these are rarely more economical than flying.

**JAZAN جازان** Jazan is the largest city along the southern Tihamah coastal plain. Its population of about 320,000 is mostly of Arab descent, from tribes closely associated with those over the border in northern Yemen; the culture here is distinctly Yemeni, from food to traditional dress.

The oldest part of Jazan city centre is al Shamiyyah, around King Faisal and King Fahd roads, and includes the port area and Souq Dakhli. Jazan is the gateway to the Farasan Islands, with the MACNA ferry services running the only commercial access, from Jazan Port, to the islands. The modern city centre is ar Rawdah, encompassing the Prince Sultan Road, al Mutalla Street and Airport Road areas along with the al Rashid Mall. Many of the newer hotels and restaurants can be found in the trendier North Corniche area near the park of the same name.

Jazan has a hot desert climate, with temperatures ranging from the pleasant high 20s in the winter to hot and humid temperatures exceeding 40°C in the summer. The monsoon rains moderate these hot temperatures, at least for a short while.

**Getting there and around** See page 335 for details of routes and travel options to Jazan city. Whether you arrive by long-distance bus or by air, you will be reliant on a vehicle in Jazan. In addition to taxis, Uber and Careem both operate in the city.

**Where to stay** In addition to the accommodation options listed below, there are two OYO properties, **OYO 295** [337 B3] and **OYO 414** [337 B3] (800 814 6590 for both properties; w oyorooms.com; both **$**) on King Fahd Road, about 2km from the Ferry Terminal and thus handier for the port than most other properties.

**Radisson Blu Resort Hotel** [337 B1] Makkah Corniche Roundabout; 017 323 9200; w radissonhotels.com. This familiar hotel group has a prime location at the end of the North Corniche. Situated on sprawling manicured grounds, it also has a large swimming pool popular with children. Don't expect much from the beach as it suffers from the ubiquitous litter problem found in so much of the Kingdom. The rooms, restaurant & usual amenities that accompany this upper-end property are what you would expect. Splashing out for this brand-name resort will get a good level of service in an oasis just far enough from the city to be relaxing. **$$$$**

**Courtyard Marriott** [337 C3] 7B St, in the al Rashid Mall; 017 312 9999; w marriott.com. The Courtyard is a quiet hotel in a good location between the city centre & North Corniche, & not too far from the port. It also has direct access to a modern mall with a food court & a good branch of Panda. **$$$**

**Novotel Jazan** [337 B4] King Fahd Rd; 017 315 0000; w all.accor.com. Situated just north of the Corniche Park about 2.5km south of the Ferry Terminal & port in the older city centre, the Novotel Jazan is a comfortable hotel. Take advantage of the outdoor dining & pool or walk along the Corniche on the other side of the road. **$$$**

**Residence Inn** [337 C3] In the al Rashid Mall; 017 312 9999; w marriott.com. This Marriott hotel offers a bit more luxury than the Courtyard (see above), & is located at the opposite end of the same shopping mall. As an extended-stay property, it offers suites, some of which have kitchens in addition to well-appointed standard rooms. There is an indoor pool & an on-site restaurant, & room service if you prefer this to the mall food court options. **$$$**

**Almaali Hotel** [337 C2] Khalid bin al Waleed Rd, east of the Corniche; 017 322 0100; w almaalihotel.com. This Saudi hotel is in the desirable North Corniche neighbourhood near the park. It has everything most visitors need, including comfortable rooms, a restaurant & coffee shop, room service, covered parking, & customer service that surpasses most hotels. This is an excellent choice for those looking for a good standard usually associated with the chains but with a local style & favourable price. **$$**

**Diamond Elite Hotel** [337 C3] 29 St, off Prince Sultan Rd. This is a good budget option if you want to be near the al Rashid Mall & city centre. Guests can choose various room types including 2-bedroom apartments, which are equipped with comfortable furnishings. This hotel stands above many others in the same range as it also offers a high level of helpful customer service. Although there is limited parking, it is conveniently located in walking distance to many casual restaurants. **$$**

**Jizan Park Hotel** [337 C1] Corniche Rd; 017 340 5111. Make your reservation via a reputable booking site. Located about 200m north of the Makkah Corniche Roundabout, this property benefits from its location in the fashionable North Corniche area. Rooms & suites come with a seating area, fridge & the possibility of booking access to the executive lounge. The rooftop restaurant has a good b/fast buffet, à la carte options for other meals & views of the Red Sea in the distance. **$$**

**Where to eat and drink**

✷ **Happy Hospitality Seafood Restaurant** [337 B5] King Fahd Rd, about 400m south of the Novotel; 055 776 7712; 12.30–midnight Sat–Wed, 12.30–01.00 Thu–Fri. Also known as Happy Times Fish Restaurant, this is a lovely place to choose your own fish from the on-site fish counter. Although shrimp is popular & prepared many ways, it's also a good place to choose fresh hammour. Meals come with additional sides, salads & fresh juices & just the right level of attentiveness, making the customer service top notch. The seating is mixed-gender with a few open tables overlooking the Red Sea, as well as private curtained booths. The décor is interesting with nice local design touches. $$$$

**Ocean Basket** [337 B3] Corniche Rd, about 400m south of North Corniche Park; 017 323 2685;

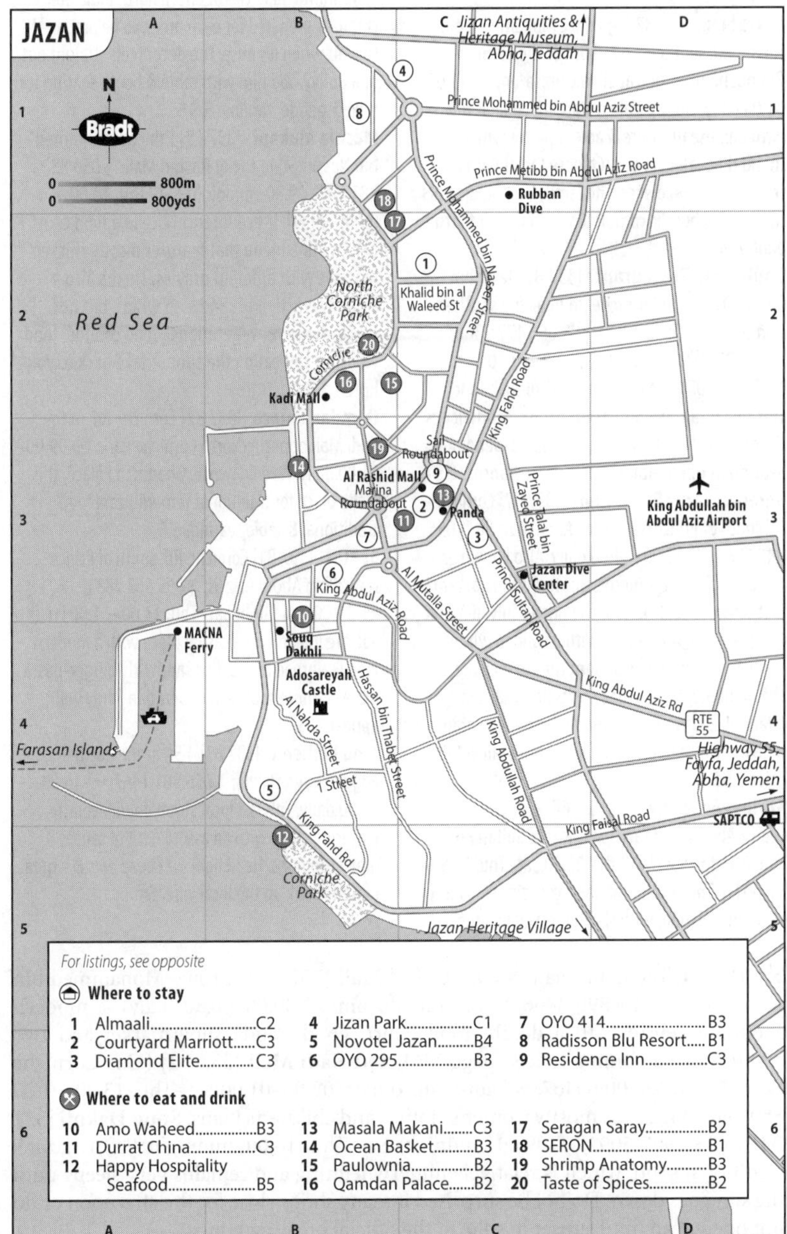

w oceanbasketksa.com; 11.00–01.00 Sat–Thu, 13.00–02.00 Fri. Rising above the string of American fast-food restaurants along this busy part of the Corniche, this Jazan favourite goes beyond shrimp to calamari, mussels, fish & chips & a welcome sushi menu. The ambience is casual & friendly. $$$$

**Durrat China** [337 C3] Prince Mohammed bin Nasser Rd, southeast quadrant of the Marina Roundabout; w durratchina.com.sa/en; 13.00–01.00 daily. This upscale restaurant chain is filled with Chinese furniture & accent pieces with a menu that caters to pan-Chinese tastes with a focus on shrimp dishes. The family section upstairs has privacy booths complete with a buzzer for the waiter. $$$

**Paulownia Restaurant** [337 B2] Tariq bin Zayed St, east of Corniche Rd near the southern end of North Corniche Park; 056 177 7360; 07.00–01.00 Sat–Thu, 07.00–10.30 & 16.00–02.00 Fri. Serving casual Turkish food, this restaurant is popular for b/fast, sandwiches & light meals with a choice of mixed-gender seating at open tables or in private booths. $$$

**Seragan Saray Restaurant** [337 B2] Corniche Rd south of Prince Nawaf bin Abdul Aziz St; 055 445 5184; 13.00–01.00 daily. Also known as Ciragan Sarayi Restaurant, this Turkish restaurant is just south of SERON. Note the sign is only in Arabic (مطعم سيراغان سراي). With its gilded white walls & ceiling, the restaurant tries to recreate the opulence of the palace of its namesake in Istanbul. You won't go wrong whether you order a hearty clay pot, pide, kebabs or grills, all at fair prices. $$$

**Shrimp Anatomy** [337 B3] 6B St, between Prince Abdullah al Faisal St & Prince Sultan Rd; 050 158 5855; 13.00–02.00 Sat–Thu, 14.00–02.00 Fri. This restaurant has a very similar concept to Shrimp Nation, with shrimp served in almost any style imaginable, a minimalist décor, paper on the table, & gloves & bib that give you permission to be messy. $$$

**Taste of Spices** [337 B2] Cnr Corniche Rd & Tariq bin Zayed St; 050 282 7430; 11.30–01.00 Sun–Thu, 12.30–01.30 Fri–Sat. This is a popular restaurant where classics from north India are carefully prepared for each order, so be prepared to wait when it's busy. The décor feels straight out of a Bollywood film with table & booth seating for mixed-gender groups. $$$

**Masala Makani** [337 C3] Prince Mohammed bin Nasser St, in the al Rashid Mall; 050 832 3818; 09.30–midnight Sat–Thu, 13.00–midnight Fri. It's counter service in a food court here, with a menu that features mostly chicken masalas with different gravies. There's also a good selection of sandwich wraps, but not much choice for vegetarians. Good comfort food whether you eat on the spot or take back to your hotel. $$

**Qamdan Palace** [337 B2] Corniche Rd, in the Kadi Mall opposite North Corniche Park; 09.00–01.00 daily. Also known as Ghamdan Palace, this is the place for traditional Yemeni Jizani food. Traditional & table seating. $$

**SERON** [337 B1] Corniche Rd, south of Prince Nawaf bin Abdul Aziz St; 055 563 7883; 11.00–midnight Sat–Thu, 13.00–01.00 Fri. If you are looking for a casual place with a modern vibe & a broad menu, this sandwich-burger-pasta-pizza-&-more spot next to Seragan Saray will appeal. $$

**Amo Waheed** [337 B3] 4 St, at the northern edge of Souq Dakhil; 056 981 1463; 16.00–01.00 daily. This is a local street-food favourite, featuring chips with an assortment of sauces & gravy toppings. Head here for cheap eats & a great place to soak up the local vibe. $

**Shopping** The main malls are **al Rashid Mall** [337 C3] (Prince Mohammed bin Nasser Rd; 013 899 4466; w rashidmall.com; 09.00–00.30 daily), a modern shopping centre with a decent food court, good Panda supermarket and two comfortable adjoining hotels (page 336); and **Kadi Mall** [337 B2] (Cnr Corniche Rd & 2B St; 9200 09467; w kadi-mall.com; 09.00–01.00 Sat–Thu, 13.00–01.00 Fri), which features mostly women's clothes and children's items. **Souq Dakhli** [337 B4] (055 907 5092; 09.00–midnight Sat–Thu, 16.00–midnight Fri) is Jazan's traditional souq, which is relatively underwhelming and remains very sleepy until the sun goes down. Do not be surprised if many shops close for the afternoon or do not open at all until sunset in spite of the official opening hours.

**Activities** With Saudis still getting used to general tourism, it is important to remember that many dives in Jizan are live-aboards organised from overseas. We strongly recommend that prospective divers who are planning to do a day dive visit the **Jazan Dive Center** [337 C3] (cnr Prince Talal bin Abdul Aziz St & Prince Sultan Rd; 050 066 0852; 16.30–22.30 Sun–Thu, 18.00–23.30 Fri) in person, in advance of any dives, as they usually need time to co-ordinate with the dive master and any other interested divers. This PADI five-star dive shop is also a good place to ask about hiring dive gear for the Farasan Islands. Experienced divers may find the lack of an appealing storefront, regular hours and polished level of customer service disappointing. Ask plenty of questions to decide whether this is for you, but they do get good reviews. **Rubban Dive** [337 C1] (Prince Metibb bin Abdul Aziz Rd, just west of 36C St; 055 770 0685; w rubbandive.com; 09.00–noon & 16.00–22.00 Sat–Thu, 16.00–22.00 Fri) is Jazan's other PADI five-star centre and might suit some divers better.

## Other practicalities

**ANB Bank** Prince Mohammed bin Nasser Rd opposite al Rashid Mall; 017 322 0520; w anb.com.sa; 09.30–16.30 Sun–Thu

**Banque Saudi Fransi** Cnr Corniche Rd & Prince Abdullah al Faisal St; 9200 00576; w alfransi.com.sa; 09.30–16.30 Sun–Thu

**Alemeis Hospital** 34B Street & King Abdul Aziz Rd; w alomeis.com; 017 326 6633

**Lemon Pharmacy** Airport Rd, 100m west of 9B St; 9200 13770; w lemon.sa; 08.00–04.00 Sat–Thu, 13.00–03.00 Fri

**Nahdi Pharmacy** Corniche Rd opposite McDonald's & Kadi Mall; 9200 24673; w nahdionline.com; 07.00–03.00 daily

**Saudi Post** King Fahd Rd & 121 St; 9200 05700; w splonline.com.net; 07.30–21.00 Sat–Thu

**What to see and do** For visitors who wish to enjoy the seafront and generally good outdoor weather, the Northern Corniche is a pleasant area to stroll or picnic in. If you are staying to the south of the city near the Novotel, then the Corniche Park is more convenient. Both are open 24 hours daily.

***Adosareyah Castle*** [337 B4] (Off al Nahda St, between 1 & King Abdul Aziz sts; 24hrs daily) Built by the Ottomans in 1810, this hilltop structure is defined by its sandstone colour, four corner turrets and military ramp. Although access to the castle was closed during our visit, it is still possible to appreciate the exterior and the views overlooking the Red Sea from the fenced-off area.

***Jazan Heritage Village*** [337 C5] (Off King Abdullah Rd at the 2nd roundabout on the southern edge of the industrial area; 17.00–23.00 Sun–Wed, 17.00–midnight Thu–Sat; admission free) This is a recreation of a traditional village, complete with a castle, round houses and a tower. Most structures can be entered, where the visitor will see artefacts from the recent past, with some historic information displayed. Not quite a museum or an amusement park, the village is surrounded by attractions, including a parade of souvenir shops, but don't expect many quality items. There are donkey rides, which may appeal to children, from the large car park adjacent to the village and a relatively quiet stretch of the Corniche over the road.

***Jazan Antiquities and Heritage Museum*** (Rte 55, King Abdul Aziz Rd at the junction of Rte 1670, Amjad) Located about 35km northeast of Jazan, this museum is temporarily closed, similar to other provincial museums at present. We are optimistic this museum and others will eventually be a good visit once the authorities complete their Kingdom-wide renovation and upgrade project.

***Further afield*** In spite of the long drive from either Jazan (2hrs) or from Asir (nearly 3hrs), nature lovers will be rewarded by a visit to **Wadi Lajab**, a beautiful green wadi with flowing water and pools deep enough for a swim. Bring a modest swimming costume and cover-up if this destination appeals to you. It also offers hiking opportunities for those with time and stamina. Be prepared to walk in from the road unless you have a 4x4 as access to the wadi is unsuitable for conventional vehicles. The wadi is located off Route 158 about 1km west of the village of Khatwat al Ain.

Serious hikers with a sense of adventure and with the ability to manage a rocky climb may wish to continue on from Wadi Lajab to **Jebel Qahar**, a paradise for hikers, nature lovers and anyone reasonably fit who simply wants to enjoy spectacular scenery.

**FAYFA MOUNTAINS**✷ Part of the Sarawat Mountains, the Fayfa Mountains (also known as Faifa or Fifa Massif), make for a spectacular road trip that can easily be done in a day, albeit a long one, from Jazan. Fayfa is about 100km to the northeast of Jazan and can be reached along routes 55 and 160 or routes 140 and 156. Don't forget to bring your camera, and be prepared to be awestruck.

We recommend continuing along Route 160 as far as the village of Addayer (also ad Dayir and several other spellings). This is a Flowermen village, where most men wear Yemeni dress, complete with *futa* or *ma'waaz* (wrapped skirts) typical in the mountains in the region, distinctive long hair, and either a turban – these can be in a variety of colours and patterns that often contain dark red – or sometimes the traditional wreath of flowers on their head instead. You will know when you reach Addayer when you see the huge Saudi flag painted on the rockface at road level. This is a good place to start your mountain adventure as we believe this is the better direction for appreciating the views that almost defy description. You will be travelling along Route 1671, turning south at the petrol station and small grocers, a journey that will bring you within 5km of the Yemeni border. Travel this route for about 40 spectacular kilometres.

This drive can be done with a standard 2WD vehicle but the tight switchbacks and steep inclines require some experience of driving in mountains, so make sure you and your vehicle can manage these conditions. Although the roads are generally in good condition, safety barriers at the edge of the road can be missing, even on sheer cliffs, so beware, especially when encountering vehicles travelling in the opposite direction. Where barriers do exist, some are either decorated with white-accented stones or are colourfully painted similar to the style found in the local architecture and inside some homes. It is also important to be aware of falling rocks.

Along the way, you will marvel at ancient village ruins in among modern multi-storey homes perched on mountain tops that look like they are signalling the end of the earth with only sky behind them. Inhabited villages are tucked around corners every few kilometres, often far from the road where terraced land, complete with views of valleys and wadis in the far distance, provide stunning scenes representing time immemorial.

Jizani architecture includes what looks like steps at the corners of rooftops. You will pass by mosques on this journey that are built in this design. Other mosques have a variety of decorations that are generally more elaborate, contrasting dramatically with the dominance of plain Salafist mosques found in most other parts of the Kingdom. You will also be able to spot dozens of old stone watchtowers, and plenty of goats, sheep, baboons and camels in some of the flat areas. Unfortunately, you will not be able to avoid the flies.

The highlight of this circular drive is **Jebel Fayfa**, the highest mountain in Jizan Province at about 2,600m. Go to the Faifa Hotel (/// designing.overmuch.posing; 053 917 6134) and head to the rooftop café (**$$**), which has public and private tables and reveals breathtaking views from the cliffside towards the mountains that are in both Saudi Arabia and Yemen, often with cloudforest below. If you decide to carry on past the hotel, you will find a few shops and take-aways about 400m in both directions.

Continue along Route 1670 for another 15km, where you will reach the town of al Henayah and routes 1679 and 1680, both of which will return you to Jazan.

**FARASAN ISLANDS جزر فرسان** This archipelago of more than 80 coral islands is the largest island group in the Red Sea. Believed to have been first settled by the Sabeans in pre-Christian times, the Farasan Islands have also felt the presence of Romans, Aksumites, Arabs, Ottomans, various European explorers in the following centuries including Germans as recently as World War II. After the Ottomans, in the early years of the 20th century, the islands were part of the Idrissi Emirate until they were annexed by ibn Saud into Saudi Arabia in 1934 along with the rest of Jizan Province.

Three of the islands are inhabited. Farasan al Kubra (big) is the largest and is where most of the 20,000-strong Farasani population lives, including the town of Farasan. Sajid is to the north of Farasan al Kubra and connected to it by the Maadi Bridge. Qummah is situated to the south of the main island and is reached by boat. The smaller two islands together are known as Farasan al Soghra (little). The economy is mostly dependent on fishing and a very young tourist industry.

Many mangroves fringe the islands' coastline, including the Mangrove Forest which can be seen immediately after leaving Farasan Port and where the coral reefs are plain to see along the road after leaving the port. Other areas of the island are flat, sandy desert. The Farasan Islands Marine Sanctuary is a protected area home to dolphins, dugongs, manta rays, whale sharks, and the Critically Endangered green and hawksbill turtles. Good work is being done to preserve the natural resources here, though the Farasan gazelle, hunted nearly to extinction, remains in a fragile state. The islands are a birdwatcher's paradise, with flamingos, white-eyed gull, osprey, pelicans and falcons all resident.

**Getting there and away** As there is no airport, the only way to reach Farasan is by **ferry**, which takes vehicles and foot passengers. The ferry is free for all cars, drivers and passengers, but you will need to book your tickets in advance in Jazan at the Farasan Island Ticket Centre (MACNA; King Fahd Rd; opposite the ferry port) as space for vehicles is limited. The office will log your passport details and those of any passengers with you, as well as your vehicle details – you'll need to present your official car card supplied by your hire car company. Ferries are currently running at 07.00 and 13.00 in each direction, but check for changes as the information is only reliable at MACNA. Travellers must arrive no later than 90 minutes before departure or they will be turned away. Travellers with vehicles are strongly recommend to queue well in advance if they have not secured a pre-booked reservation for their vehicle as space is limited. Be aware that both ports practise strict airport-style security for all passengers, and sniffer dogs are used around cars. Drivers will stay with their vehicle and clear security separately from their passengers, who will undergo formalities in the waiting room. As your travel group will board the ferry separately, it's a good idea to decide which part of the ferry you plan to sit in, keeping in mind the ferry is segregated into singles, women's and family sections. The journey itself takes just over 1 hour and is picturesque, passing by several uninhabited islands before reaching the port on the eastern tip of Farasan al Kubra at the end of Route 1901.

**Getting around** You'll need your own vehicle to explore the two largest inhabited islands, Farasan al Kubra and Sajid. Taxis are effectively non-existent. For visiting the island of Qummah, note there are no formal roads, so you will be totally reliant on the boat to get there and back, and must be prepared to explore the island by foot. For all of the Farasan Islands, shade is very limited so make sure you wear appropriate clothing, use sunscreen and drink plenty of water. Regardless of where you go, the roads are nearly empty and the vibe is very laid-back, so take your time to get into the slower pace of life.

Other than routes 1901 and 1910, which form the east–west artery of Farasan al Kubra, the roads on the islands are unnamed. Try to find your destination on Google Maps, which does a reasonable job with most points of interest. This may also be the time to try out What3Words.

## Where to stay *Map, opposite*

The mid-range and basic hotels here will suit most if you are prepared to prioritise the experience of being somewhere very special over hit-or-miss service. Do not expect luxury. You may encounter a delay when checking in or out of your accommodation, often due to the inexperience of receptionists who may not encounter foreign visitors very often, so bear this in mind if you have a ferry to catch.

Farasan hotels are not on booking websites. It is best to book via WhatsApp if possible or have someone from the mainland help you call, especially if you do not speak Arabic. Have some patience if it takes some time to reach someone. If this fails, it is usually possible to find somewhere to stay upon arrival, but be careful around both Eids and the school holidays as demand tends to increase during these times.

**Farasan Park Hotel & Resort** 500m south of Rte 1910, near Farasan Town; /// rare.roamed.powering; 017 316 0000. This property was previously known as the Farasan Coral Resort. Situated directly on the beach, it has a feel similar to other resorts elsewhere in the Kingdom. Many rooms have balconies; others have walled access to the beach that preserves privacy, but are otherwise adequate rather than luxurious. There are garden grounds & a restaurant featuring local fish & other Saudi favourites on the menu. It's the accommodation of choice for those looking for the most comfortable place to stay in the archipelago. **$$$**

**Farasan Hotel** North of Rte 1910, along the southern perimeter of the Farasan General Hospital, Farasan Town; /// clarify.abashed.cucumber; 017 316 1166. Not to be confused with the Farasan Park Hotel, this property is just far enough away from the town centre for those who prefer a quiet stay, but still within walking distance. The villas & rooms are old but well-enough maintained with parking in front of each unit. The customer service is good from this English-speaking family, who can also help organise boat trips & other excursions. The restaurant serves good-quality Indian cuisine. **$$**

**Hotel Saso Suites** Along the north side of the dual carriageway, Farasan Town; /// torches.cheaply.refines; 054 800 3425. Located opposite the Maritime Company for Navigation (MACNA), this is a good, basic, mostly clean hotel that works for a short stay. The rooms are not spacious but they have what you need at this price point. The upper floors are reached by stairs only & visitors should note that an extension is being built towards the dual carriageway which might disturb late risers staying near this end of the property. There is a lovely small garden in the courtyard & plenty of parking near the hotel entrance. Note that this property only accepts MADA or cash. **$$**

**Rahaf Residential Units** Opposite the fish auction, Farasan Town; 017 316 2000. This

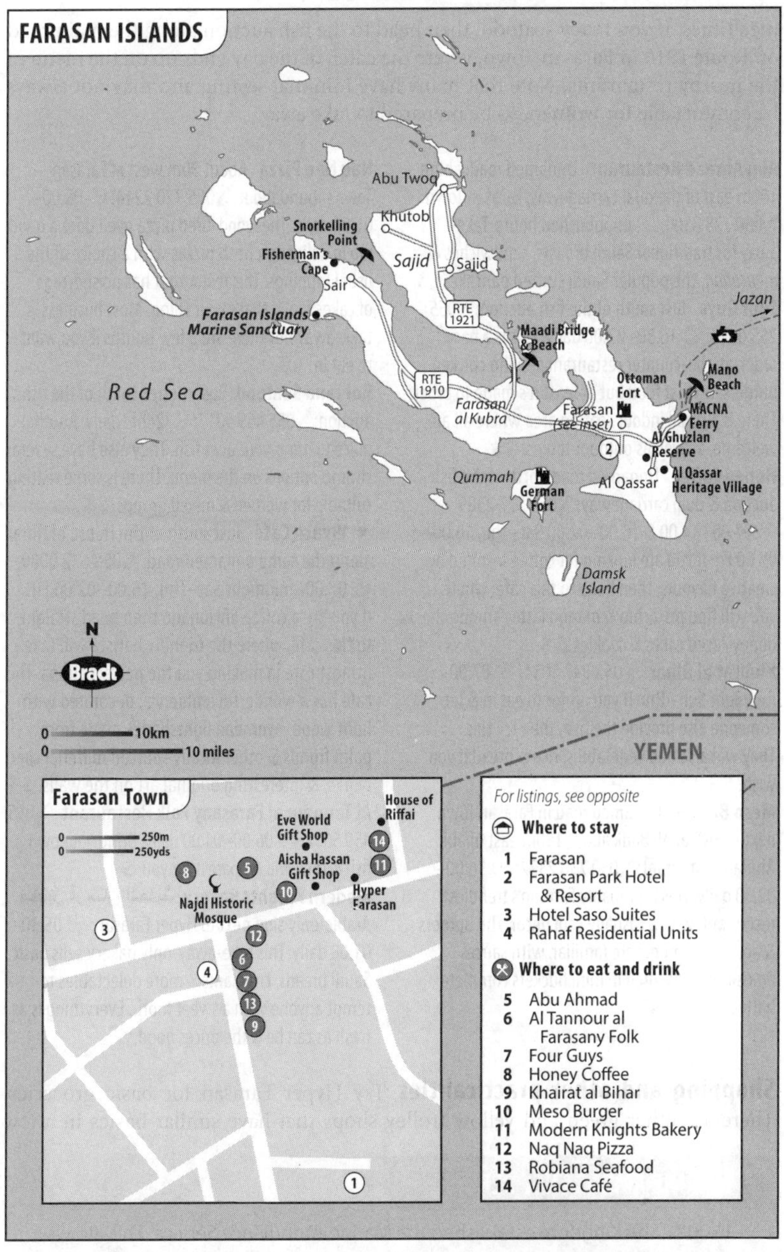


relatively new hotel has clean rooms, parking to the front & is centrally located in walking distance of several restaurants. It's probably the best value for money in Farasan Town. **$**

## Where to eat and drink *Map, above*

Nearly all restaurants, which are located on Farasan al Kubra, close for prayer times. Most do not adhere to published opening hours, so try to visit during peak mealtimes. If you fancy seafood, then head to the fish auction along the main road off Route 1910 in Farasan Town, where the catch of the day ends up on the menu of the nearby restaurants. Note that many have minimal seating and may not always be comfortable for women, so be prepared to take away.

**Abu Ahmad Restaurant** Unnamed road, about 100m east of the dual carriageway, Farasan Town; 050 228 8500; unpublished hours. Take-away for traditional Saudi broasts, sandwiches & *moutabaq*, the popular Saudi stuffed pancake. $$

**Four Guys** Just south of the fish auction; 055 255 6615; 16.30–02.00 daily. This is a basic order-at-the-counter restaurant serving chicken burgers. It's fast food but at least it's made to order. There is a small indoor seating area where all are welcome, as well as outdoor tables. $$

**Honey Coffee** Unnamed road north of the fish auction & dual carriageway; 055 577 2389; 07.00–14.00 & 16.00–02.00 Sat–Thu, 16.00–02.00 Fri. If you are looking for coffee inspired by creative flavours, then head to this café, where you will find pistachio & mango lattes among the honey-laced cakes & cookies. $$

**Khairat al Bihar** 053 547 5034; 07.00–midnight Sun–Thu. If you prefer to eat in & let someone else provide the fish, then try this. They will also add vegetables, rice & bread if you wish. $$

**Meso Burger** Unnamed road in Farasan Town, next to SNB al Ali Bank about 150m east of abu Ahmad Restaurant; 050 738 2322; 16.00–02.30 daily. This is probably Farasan's trendiest restaurant, with a casually cool décor. The burgers & accompaniments are familiar, with sauces amusingly presented in mini buckets complete with a spade. $$

**Naq Naq Pizza** About 30m west of Farasan Town's roundabout; 055 720 2214; 08.00–05.00 daily. The wood-fired pizza oven does a good job in delivering fresh pizzas with a choice of the usual toppings. This restaurant has no shortage of cakes too, if that's your thing. Most business is take-away but there are a few booths if you want to eat in. $$

**Robiana Seafood** Just metres south of the fish auction; 055 459 5017; 24hrs daily. Another place to bring your own fish. They also have several shrimp options on the menu. There is some seating suitable for women & mixed groups. $$

✷ **Vivace Café** Just south of the House of Riffai along the same unnamed road; 058 672 0089; 07.00–midnight Sat–Thu, 16.00–02.00 Fri. If you are a coffee aficionado then head straight to this café, where the friendly barista will take utmost care in making you the perfect cuppa. The café has a wonderful ambience, decorated with light wood, overhead lightshades made from palm fronds & other locally sourced material that works, & interesting original art on the walls. $$

**Al Tannour al Farasany Folk Restaurant** 055 459 5017; 06.00–01.00 daily. Bring your own fish & they will prepare it for you. $

**Modern Knights Bakery** مخابز فرسان الحديثه Arabic-only sign next to Hyper Farasan; 05.30–01.00 daily. This take-away-only bakery sells basic Saudi breads, croissants & more delectables to tempt anyone with a sweet tooth. Everything is as fresh as can be & the prices good. $

**Shopping and other practicalities** Try Hyper Farasan for basic groceries. There are other green and yellow trolley shops that have similar basics in a few

### MARINE AMBULANCE SERVICE

In 2021, the Kingdom established the Marine Ambulance Service. This allows medical professionals to transfer a patient to Jazan Port in about 45 minutes. One of its three beds is equipped as a floating ICU. It is a vast improvement on the basic Farasan General Hospital. If you are travelling to the Farasan Islands and especially if you are planning to dive, snorkel or hike remotely, it is critical to ensure your travel insurance is robust enough in case you require evacuation.

built-up areas. Gift shops appear to be non-existent although Eve World Gift Shop and Aisha Hassan Gift Shop claim to sell souvenirs. All are located in Farasan Town centre.

Do be aware that the Farasan Islands is still a cash society, with few bank cards accepted. ATMs can be found on Farasan al Kubra. There is a pharmacy in Farasan Town which stocks the basics, as well as a post office. Farasan General Hospital is also found in Farasan Town if you are in need of emergency care until you are able to reach the mainland.

## Farasan al Kubra فرسان الكبرى

***Al Ghuzlan Reserve*** (Rte 1910, just west of the junction with Rte 1901; ⌚ 07.00–10.00 & 16.00–sunset daily; admission free) This is your best chance to see the Critically Endangered Farasan gazelle in their natural environment. Visitors must first stop at the ticket office to gain access to the reserve, which is usually organised in advance for one of the next few days. You must provide a passport as well as your vehicle details. A 4x4 is necessary. The tour lasts about 15 minutes. You will follow a guide in another vehicle.

***Al Qassar (Qessar) Heritage Village*** (Southwest of the junction of rtes 1901 & 1910; ⌚ 08.00–18.00 daily; admission free) Follow the unnamed road to the village for about 500m, where you will find a car park. Once parked, enter via the gate ahead or, if it is closed, use the smaller door within the gate. This ancient stone village dates back to Roman times and was originally used by residents of Farasan al Kubra during the summer season, following the *hareed*, or parrotfish, fishing festival (page 346). There are more than 400 homes, shops and a mosque, most of which are numbered with small signs, although we could not find any printed information available beyond this. The village has been partially restored in a mostly sympathetic way, with some houses furnished with traditional pieces from the mid 20th century. The small, shaded café in the centre of the village is most welcome after wandering around in the hot sun.

***Fisherman's Cape*** This is a lovely authentic fishing harbour another 500m further along the road from Snorkelling Point and where the road ends. It's a surprisingly busy place where you can simply sit and reflect on this timeless way of life here, or take in the sunset.

***House of Riffai*** ✷ (Unnamed road, Farasan Town; /// motor.modest.obligations; ⌚ 24hrs daily) Take the road northbound off Route 1910 at al Taj petrol station and continue straight for about 1.8km, then turn left on to unnamed roads in a residential neighbourhood. The House of Riffai is at the end of the road in front of a T-junction. Ask someone on the street if you are lost. Also known as Beit al Refai (among other spellings), as well as the Turkish House, this splendid home was built in 1922 by the wealthy local pearl merchant Ahmed Munawar al Refai. The exterior walls are made of ornately carved coral and stone that show artisans' work at their best. Exterior archways, also elaborately decorated, lead into the building and to the side of the main house. The style is an inspired blend of Indian, Yemeni and Islamic influences and incorporates accents of coloured glass on many interior doors, windows and interior walls, as well as a vibrant blue painted ceiling.

There are two areas to explore in this otherwise unassuming neighbourhood. Across the road from the main house, a few metres away, there is another arched gate at the entrance to the house of **Uthman al Rifai**, where visitors can enter and

## PARROTFISH FESTIVAL

Parrotfish, known locally as *hareed*, are brightly coloured coral fish that usually reside among coral reefs. The fish respond to their coral habitat's natural breeding cycle, gathering en masse at the shoreline when the coral releases its eggs. This release is determined by the moon and water temperature and is a once-a-year event, usually occurring in late April or early May. In Farasan Town, when the fish gather in this way, they are netted by the local fishermen who are then celebrated according to the size of their catch. Celebrations, which last from three to seven days depending on the fish, are public, with traditional dancing, general merriment and plenty of hareed on the menu.

explore a warren of rooms. Although the complex is in various states of disrepair with no obvious sign of restoration or protection, it is worth the visit simply to appreciate its architectural beauty

***Najdi Historic Mosque*** (Unnamed roads in Farasan town centre; /// silkworm.blabbed.adoration) This mosque was constructed in 1928 under the instruction of Ibrahim al Tamimi Najdi, a pearl merchant originally from central Najd. Although its age and size are modest, it is an excellent example of the influences of Ottoman and south Asian design as the architecture incorporates a blend of these styles within the local southern Arabian context. The materials were imported from India, and constructed by architects from India and Yemen. You will see the ornately carved white exterior walls constructed of gypsum, stained-glass windows and once inside, carved stonework, painted wooden touches and the spectacular dome. Note that the mosque is still in use today. If you plan to visit, try to go outside of prayer time if you are not Muslim. Enter from the car park to the left, where you will see the men's prayer hall to the right of the shoe rack and the women's prayer hall up a couple of steps to the left of the shoe rack. Visitors are reminded to remove their footwear and for women to wear their headscarf before opening the wooden doors to the interior.

***Ottoman Fort (al Othmaniah Castle)*** The fort is just outside town on the same road off Route 1910 towards the House of Riffai. Continue along this unnamed road and instead of turning, go past the neighbourhood for another 500m. The castle is located on a hill to the west of the road. It is fenced off but it's possible to climb up the small hill and walk around a bit. The fort was built in about 1832 and was used as a military facility near a well that can still be seen.

***Snorkelling Point*** Coral reefs can be seen above and below the waterline at this beach area along the northwest coast of Farasan al Kubra, and access to the water is relatively easy. Snorkellers will be able to observe a variety of fish among the reefs in very clear water. Although men and women cannot swim in Western-style swimming costumes, you can just about get away with wearing cropped trousers and a very thick baggy dark T shirt, especially if there is no-one else around. Travel west on Route 1910 until it ends at the village of Sair. Turn north at the roundabout where some interesting ruins will be in front of you, then follow the road past the village for about 2km where you will see the point to your right. Park anywhere off-road before walking about 50m to the shoreline.

**Sajid Island جزيرة ساجد** Maadi Bridge connects Farasan al Kubra to the smaller island of Sajid. Leave Route 1910 and travel north for about 4km, where you will pass a beautiful beach to the right of the bridge before the crossing.

***Abu Twoq*** If you are looking for even more peace and tranquillity than on the main island, drive to the end of Sajid, where you will reach abu Twoq. The road is mostly straight with a gentle bend towards the village. To the right of the bend are stone ruins with homes scattered among the crumbling structures. People on the island live very traditional lives and you may see women carrying bundles of firewood destined for the kitchen. When you reach the end of the road, there is a park and garden which provide a great spot for a picnic. There is also a lovely beach a short distance away. As you return to Farasan Town, head towards any of the other small settlements along the way if you want to take a peek at the rhythm of these small villages. Always be respectful if you wish to take photographs.

**Qummah Island جزيرة** Access to Qummah Island is by boat from Farasan Town, which will need to be organised locally through your hotel. There are no scheduled services.

On the north shore of the archipelago's least-populated island is a 20th-century **German Fort**, which can be seen in the distance from the southern shore of Farasan al Kubra, with binoculars. It is probably a more impressive site from the boat than at ground level. Although there are no formal visiting hours, you can walk around this abandoned structure and reflect on the historically strategic location of the Farasan Islands stretching from ancient to modern times. Qummah also has a good reputation for **scuba diving**, but this activity must be organised in advance (page 339) as there are no dive shops on the Farasan Islands.

**Other islands** It is possible to organise a short boat ride to **Square Island** and **Mano Beach** which are both relaxing day trips and both near Farasan port. Visitors may also be interested in having a quick look around **Damsk Island** (also known as Jazirat al Dumsuq) south of Qummah, visited by the French adventurer Henry de Monfreid and other explorers. All of these destinations are for the self-sufficient as there are no facilities on the islands. They are, however, perfect destinations for peace and tranquillity. You may have an entire island to yourself if you are fortunate.

# 9

# Eastern Province

# المنطقة الشرقية

Also known as Sharqiyah, the Eastern Province is Saudi Arabia's largest province, covering an area of over 672,000km$^2$. It extends from Iraq and Kuwait in the north to the Rub' al Khali (the Empty Quarter) that borders Oman to the south. To the east the province shares borders with Qatar and the United Arab Emirates, and is also connected to Bahrain via the King Fahd Causeway. To the west, it neighbours Najran, Riyadh and Northern Borders provinces. The majority of the province's population (approx 5 million) lives in the Tri-Cities of Dammam, al Khobar and Dhahran, with significant numbers also living in Qatif, Jubail and Hofuf. Although Sunni Islam dominates Saudi Arabia as a whole, a significant percentage of the Eastern Province's native population are the Baharma people, who are followers of the Shi'a Twelver branch of Islam.

While various industries are represented here, the oil industry dominates the scene and currently represents approximately 60% of the Kingdom's GDP. Indeed, nearly all of Saudi Arabia's oil fields are located in the Eastern Province – including Ghawar, the world's largest oilfield, and Safaniya, the world's largest offshore field.

The province is also filled with natural wonders, with a long coastline along the Arabian Gulf. The highlight of any visit to this region has to be Hofuf. The entire al Ahsa area was declared a UNESCO World Heritage Site in 2018 for its unique natural features. In addition to being the largest oasis in the world, it features mountains, canals and lakes, hidden caves, and a number of buildings of archaeological and historical importance from Neolithic times to the beginnings of the unification of Saudi Arabia. Hofuf is also on the edge of the Empty Quarter, an area that runs along most of the Kingdom's southern borders, with intriguing sand dunes and Bedouin traditions.

It is best to visit the Eastern Province from November to March as it gets unbearably hot in the summer. Temperatures often reach 50°C, and most people find it impossible to stay outside for more than a few minutes during the hottest months of the summer. High humidity levels along the entire coast add to the misery. Hofuf is marginally less humid but can be even hotter during the day.

Watersports such as boating and fishing are popular activities here, as are horseriding, golf and racquet sports. Although there is some scuba diving in the Eastern Province, it is better to save this for the Red Sea if you can. Desert activities such as dune bashing, wadi bashing and camping are all options in the cooler months.

The Eastern Province has a reputation for being more relaxed than other provinces in the Kingdom. Many Saudis here are outward looking and are used to expats living and working alongside them. Visitors should find a welcoming reception, as long as social rules are respected.

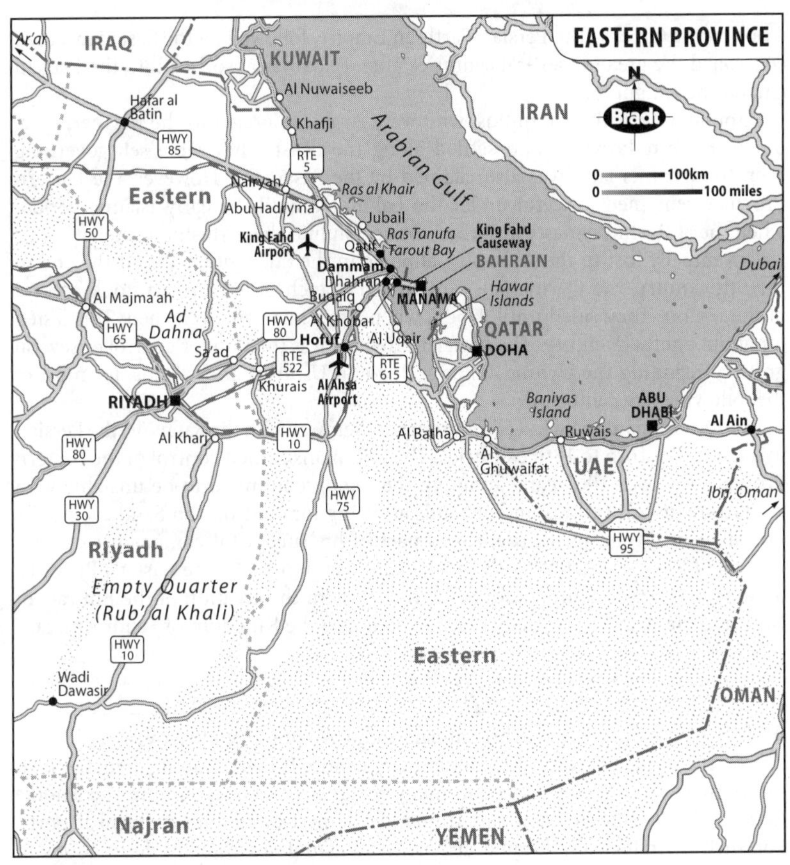


## HISTORY

It is believed that the Eastern Province has been populated since the Bronze Age, substantiated by the existence of *tumuli* or mounds of earth covering as many as 3,000 graves near the settlement of Yabrin in the north of the Empty Quarter. The same tumuli are found on the island of Bahrain, more than 300km away.

Centred in what is now Bahrain, the Dilman Empire (dating from about 4000 to 800BCE) stretched from al Ahsa to Tarout Island in modern-day Saudi Arabia and possibly as far north to what is now Kuwait. It was first referenced in Sumerian cuneiform writing found in Uruk, Mesopotamia, now in southern Iraq, and was described as a paradise. The Dilmans dominated trade routes from Mesopotamia, Oman, Persia and India, trading in agricultural products for most of this time until climate change impacted the fertility of the land and piracy disrupted trade. During these times, the Eastern Province was also part of the caravan route from Yemen, which traded goods with these same empires, arriving by inland routes from along the borders of the Empty Quarter. By 567BCE, Dilman was under the rule of the Babylonians, and collapsed a few decades later.

After the Dilman Empire, from about the 6th to 3rd centuries BCE, most of the Eastern Province was controlled by the Achaemenids, the Persian Empire eventually absorbed by Alexander the Great from Greece in the 3rd century CE. It was named

Tylos by the Greeks. The Persian Parthian Empire, followed by the Sasanians, then controlled the area for several centuries after Tylos was absorbed into the Persian Characene Kingdom.

Around 300CE, the Lakhmids, who were Arabs, migrated to the northern part of the Eastern Province and settled along the coast. They were self-governing even though this land was also claimed by the Sasanians. However, the Eastern Province remained peaceful under the Lakhmids until the early Islamic period, when the al Rashid dynasty absorbed the region into their Muslim Caliphate. This was eventually lost to the Abbasid Caliphate in the 8th century CE. At the end of the 9th century, the Qarmatians, an Ismai'li branch of Shi'a Islam, took control of the region. They ruled until 976CE, when Abyssinian rule returned. This lasted for about another century. The Eastern Province was then under control of several groups, including the Uyunid Empire, Bedouin Usfurids and Jabrids, for most of the following five centuries.

The Ottomans arrived in 1551 as a part of their war with the Safavids, the Persian dynasty of the 16th to 18th centuries. The Ottomans gained control of the Eastern Province for over 100 years, although the region continued to be unstable with the Ottomans, al Rashids and al Sauds all vying for control. Ibn Saud eventually prevailed in the Eastern Province as part of his successful campaign to regain control of Riyadh and by extension Najd and Hasa in 1902. The Eastern Province became part of the Third Saudi State in 1913 with the creation of the Emirate of Nejd and Hasa, and eventually consolidated into the Kingdom of Saudi Arabia.

## GETTING THERE AND AWAY

**BY AIR** Dammam's **King Fahd International Airport** (w kfia.gov.sa) is located approximately 45km west of Dammam city centre. It is the hub for flynas, which serves most domestic airports and many regional cities elsewhere in the Middle East. Saudia also flies to Dammam from most domestic and some regional airports. For such a strategically located airport, it does not serve many destinations in Europe other than Amsterdam on KLM and Frankfurt on Lufthansa. Flights to and from south Asia are more common. Hofuf's **al Ahsa** airport has limited services on flynas.

**Bahrain International Airport** (w bahrainairport.bh) can be more convenient for people travelling to parts of the Eastern Province, including al Khobar and Dhahran. Many people prefer to fly into Bahrain and then make the crossing over the King Fahd Causeway to their destination in Saudi Arabia. Border formalities take place midway across the causeway. Before travel, check the entry requirements for your nationality. Visitors from most Western countries are able to purchase a visa upon arrival; most others will need to organise their visa in advance.

### BY ROAD

#### By car

***From Riyadh to Hofuf*** It is straightforward to self-drive the 340km (3½hrs) from Riyadh to Hofuf, but take note that services, should you need them, on this route are mostly found on Route 80. Leave Riyadh via Route 80 and drive eastbound for about 120km. Turn right near Sa'ad on to Route 522 and head east towards al Thuhaimyah for about 180km. Traffic is much sparser after you leave Route 80 until you reach the outskirts of Hofuf. Continue east on HIghway 75 until you reach Route 615, then straight on Route 615 until you reach Hofuf after about 40km.

***From Riyadh to Dammam*** It is even easier to self-drive from Riyadh to Dammam, al Khobar or Dhahran. Leave Riyadh via Route 80 eastbound for about 120km as above. At Sa'ad, this stretch of the route changes to Highway 40. Follow Highway 40 all the way to Dammam, turning left on to Route 605 to reach the city centre. Total journey time from Riyadh is about 4 hours and the distance about 410km; there are several service stations along the way.

**By bus** SAPTCO serves all major cities and towns in the Eastern Province. The journey will take about 4½ hours from Riyadh to Hofuf, with fares from about SAR135. It will take about 6½ hours from Riyadh to Dammam at a similar cost. See page 75 for further information.

**By taxi or private car** It is also possible to travel from Riyadh to Hofuf by taxi. Rates will vary depending on when you want to travel and other factors, and it is probably best to negotiate a flat fee. Try to achieve around SAR600 if you are a good negotiator, but it could be much more. Uber costs start at about SAR750.

If you prefer to travel to Hofuf by **private car** with a driver, costs will probably be closer to SAR800–1,000 depending on where you organised transport and the quality of the vehicle. If you are being dropped off in Hofuf or anywhere else in the Eastern Province, then you will probably also pay for the cost of the driver returning to Riyadh or other starting point.

**BY RAIL** There are usually five daily trains between Riyadh and the Eastern Province stations of Dammam, Buqaiq/Abqaiq and Hofuf in each direction. Single fares from Riyadh to Hofuf cost about US$6. Single fares from Riyadh to Dammam are about US$8. See page 73 for further information.

## AL AHSA آلْأَحْسَاء AND HOFUF آلْهُفُوف

*Note: We use Hofuf when referring to the city and al Ahsa when referring to the region. The exception is when referring to the Emirate of Nejd and Hasa.*

Owing to its plentiful water, the region of al Ahsa has been inhabited since prehistoric times. Hofuf (also known as al Ahsa and al Hasa), the metropolitan area of the al Asha region, is the jewel in the crown of the Eastern Province and must be the most underrated and under-visited area of the Kingdom. It is located about 330km east of Riyadh and 130km southwest of Dhahran, and has a population of about 900,000.

Whether you are interested in history, nature or archaeology, al Ahsa is a must-see to discover a beautiful part of desert life that is rare elsewhere, culturally distinct and filled with natural wonders. Although it is relatively far from the more well-known tourist areas in the west of the Kingdom, al Ahsa is worth a diversion.

### WHERE TO STAY *Map, page 352*

In addition to the listings that follow, there are several properties suitable for those on a tight budget. These include **al Nakhlah Furnished Units** (King Fahd Rd; ✆013 584 4344), **Grand Lily Hotel Suites** (junction of Dhahran & Mecca rds; ✆013 531 0135; w grandlily.business.site), **Lily Hotel Suites Hofuf** (al Khalij Rd; ✆013 580 8484; w staylily.com), **Lily Hotel Suites Mubarraz** (Ammar bin Yasir Rd; ✆013 582 1621) and **Lily Palms Hotel** (Prince Talal St; ✆013 582 0089;

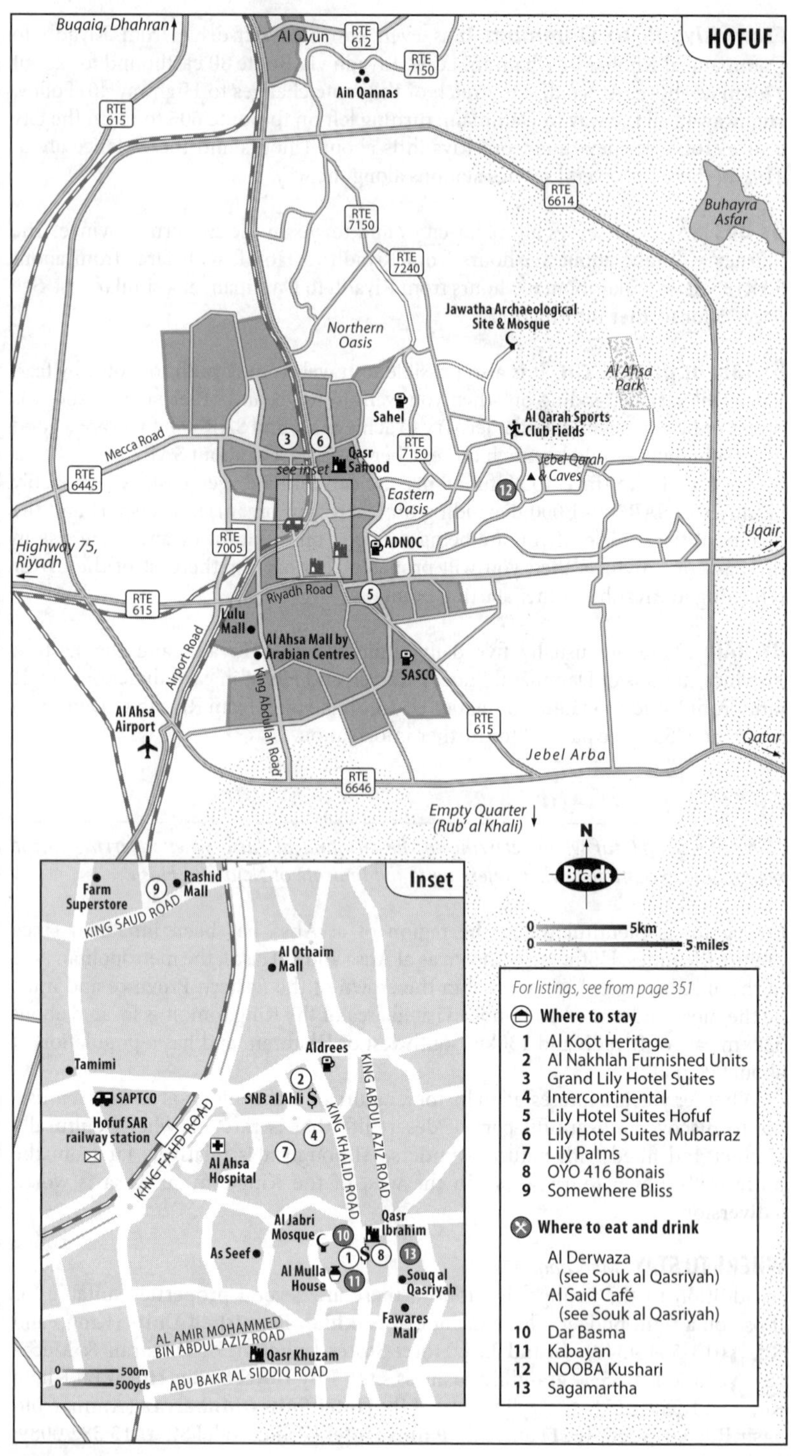
HOFUF
Buqaiq, Dhahran
Al Oyun
RTE 612
RTE 7150
Ain Qannas
RTE 615
RTE 6614
Buhayra Asfar
RTE 7150
RTE 7240
Jawatha Archaeological Site & Mosque
Northern Oasis
Al Ahsa Park
Sahel
Al Qarah Sports Club Fields
Mecca Road
RTE 7150
Qasr Sahood
see inset
Jebel Qarah & Caves
RTE 6445
Eastern Oasis
ADNOC
Uqair
Highway 75, Riyadh
RTE 7005
Riyadh Road
RTE 615
Lulu Mall
Al Ahsa Mall by Arabian Centres
SASCO
Airport Road
King Abdullah Road
Al Ahsa Airport
RTE 615
Qatar
Jebel Arba
RTE 6646
Empty Quarter (Rub' al Khali)
N
Bradt
0 5km
0 5 miles
Inset
Farm Superstore
Rashid Mall
KING SAUD ROAD
Al Othaim Mall
Aldrees
Tamimi
SAPTCO
SNB al Ahli
Hofuf SAR railway station
KING FAHD ROAD
Al Ahsa Hospital
KING KHALID ROAD
KING ABDUL AZIZ ROAD
Al Jabri Mosque
Qasr Ibrahim
As Seef
Al Mulla House
Souq al Qasriyah
Fawares Mall
AL AMIR MOHAMMED BIN ABDUL AZIZ ROAD
Qasr Khuzam
ABU BAKR AL SIDDIQ ROAD
0 500m
0 500yds
For listings, see from page 351
Where to stay
1 Al Koot Heritage
2 Al Nakhlah Furnished Units
3 Grand Lily Hotel Suites
4 Intercontinental
5 Lily Hotel Suites Hofuf
6 Lily Hotel Suites Mubarraz
7 Lily Palms
8 OYO 416 Bonais
9 Somewhere Bliss
Where to eat and drink
Al Derwaza (see Souk al Qasriyah)
Al Said Café (see Souk al Qasriyah)
10 Dar Basma
11 Kabayan
12 NOOBA Kushari
13 Sagamartha

w lily-palms-hotel.business.site); most are furnished apartments with varying states of cleanliness and service. There are also a few OYO hotels: **OYO 416 Bonais** (King Abdul Aziz Rd, 50m south of King Faisal Rd; 011 510 0453; w oyorooms.com) is very basic but is conveniently located near many tourist sites in the centre of Hofuf.

**Intercontinental** King Khalid Rd, about 2km north of Hofuf city centre; 013 533 5555; w ihg.com. This is the only real top-end hotel in Hofuf. It does not quite reach the standards of other properties in the Kingdom from this well-respected brand, but it does offer a good level of luxury that is missing elsewhere in the city, as well as a good range of business services that may be difficult to find elsewhere. Although the service is excellent, this large property is old & some of the guest rooms are in need of renovation. The upscale al Bustan Lebanese restaurant is in a lovely setting in the outdoor gardens, with al Maha lounge & Med restaurant offering more casual dining options. There is an indoor pool; check for times for separate men's & women's hours. You will have a long walk or short ride to most of places of interest. Free parking. **$$$$**

✷ **Al Koot Heritage Hotel** King Khalid Rd, almost opposite Qasr Ibrahim; 013 582 2279. Step back in time & enjoy the traditions that are maintained in this stunningly beautiful property. More of a home than a hotel, it will dazzle you with the sheer quantity of original artefacts that are scattered throughout: carpets & woven fabrics in a range of tribal designs, traditional wooden & palm reed furniture & accessories, & original art pieces hung in recesses on the walls. The comfortable guest rooms are appointed with more traditional touches, as well as all the modern amenities, although some areas have patchy internet service. Road-facing rooms may be noisy, while many interior rooms do not have windows & some at the back are adjacent to the al Fateh mosque (which is also worth a visit for Muslims). The interior courtyard has been converted into a decent restaurant serving meals at b/fast, lunch & dinner – ask about timings, as they seem to change from day to day. Service is slow but helpful; most of the staff do not speak much English. Al Qasiriyah Souq & most other Hofuf landmarks are walkable from the hotel. There is free parking in the SAB car park over the road. This property is not wheelchair accessible. **$$$**

**Somewhere Bliss Hotel** King Saud Rd, adjacent to al Rashid Mall; 013 535 5555; w ksa.somewhere-hotels.com. If you don't mind staying a little way out from the city centre, then this relatively new Saudi-owned hotel may be for you. The upper mid-range rooms & suites are large & offer good value for money, & there is a choice of cafés & restaurants: al Andalusia offers a Saudi-Spanish fusion that is unusual in the Kingdom. Other facilities include an outdoor pool & spa, business centre & executive lounge. The Rashid Mall next door has many good shops & a Carrefour supermarket. **$$$**

## WHERE TO EAT AND DRINK *Map, opposite*

There are quite a few Saudi and south Asian restaurants serving local communities near the south end of the al Qasariyah Souq and Fawares Mall. Some of these choices may not welcome women.

✷ **Dar Basma** Off King Khalid St & the gently curved unnamed road just south of King Faisal Rd & immediately north of al Koot heritage hotel, near the children's park & garden; 056 360 6888; w dar-basma.com; 13.00–23.30 daily. Translated as 'Basma's house', this lovely restaurant is run by a local family. Behind the traditionally decorated heavy wooden doors, you'll find a sympathetically restored interior with a sophisticated & trendy atmosphere. There are stairs up to the restaurant entrance & more stairs inside for those dining towards the back of the restaurant. There is also a wheelchair-friendly large outdoor dining area to the front of the restaurant, where you have a perfect view of the children's park & for general people-watching. Seating is mixed gender throughout, & the English-speaking staff offer attentive service without being intrusive. The menu (in Arabic & English) is a contemporary interpretation of traditional Saudi cuisine & portions are generous. Start with the pomegranate molasses fatteh, a local speciality – wonderful combination of aubergine, mince & bread topped with tahini, tomato sauce & pomegranate molasses, which could be a meal on its own. Try the *ghuzi* if you like lamb, which falls off the bone & is blended with rice, saffron & cashews served with *maboug*, a seeded hot chilli paste. If you can, save room for the imaginative Arabic sweets & cakes. There are vegetarian choices, & staff can also provide suitable options for vegans. Local musicians add to the atmosphere (check for timings, as they vary). $$$$

**Al Derwaza** On the north side of Aisle 1 in al Qasariyah Souq, about 150m from Gate 1; 058 361 7888; 07.30–11.30 & 15.30–23.30 Sat–Thu, 15.30–23.30 Fri. This traditionally yet imaginatively decorated café is friendly to mixed groups & has outdoor seating. Order the *kerak chai* for a wonderful blend of black tea leaves, cardamon, saffron, sugar & evaporated milk. Anyone with a sweet tooth will find it difficult to narrow down the choices of cakes & pastries, so bring friends & share. $$

**Al Said Café** Aisle 8 in the north end of al Qasariyah Souq; 07.30–11.30 & 16.00–22.00 Sat–Thu, 16.00–22.00 Fri. This small, popular tea shop is worth a visit to experience centuries-old traditions. The décor is in keeping with the souq's style & holds Saudi artwork & artefacts. Although traditionally a male-only environment, its location in a growing tourist attraction means that women are starting to visit this café as well. Go for a traditional b/fast of *balaleet* (a cardamon, saffron & rosewater omelette over vermicelli noodles), or *balila* (stewed spiced chickpeas). You may prefer to stop in for afternoon tea, when you can try the regional dish of dried fish & prawns dipped in a spicy sauce. $$

**NOOBA Kushari** In front of Jebel Qarah & Caves; 013 599 0095; noon–midnight daily. For lunch near the Jebel Qarah & Caves, don't miss this Egyptian restaurant – the *kushari* & falafel are both excellent choices. The highly decorative entrance provides a taster of the restaurant's eclectic interior décor. $$

**Kabayan** al Fateh St west of King Khalid Rd, al Koot al Naathil; 013 575 5964; 09.00–22.30 daily. If you want a break from Middle Eastern food, but don't fancy the usual alternatives of south Asian or international cuisine, why not give Filipino food a go? This canteen-style restaurant has a good selection of meat, fish & vegetarian dishes & also has an all-you-can-eat offer for anyone interested in sampling a bit of everything. The singles section downstairs is not nearly as fun as the family section upstairs, which has table tennis & videoke, the Philippines' answer to karaoke. $

**Sagamartha** al Fateh Rd, east of King Abdul Aziz Rd; 058 034 2495; 09.00–23.00 daily. Located in the north end of al Qasariyah Souq, along the north side of al Fath Rd among the perfume shops, this casual Nepalese restaurant is a great find for vegetarians & vegans. Join the local Nepalese community & enjoy *dal bhat*, *momo* (dumplings) & *thakali khana* among other dishes. The menu is only in Nepali & is modestly priced. $

**SHOPPING** For grocery needs, Farm Stores and Farm Superstores, found throughout the region, are prominent in Hofuf. There are also branches of Tamimi and a Lulu hypermarket. For a traditional shopping experience, visit Souq al Qasriyah (page 356).

**Al Ahsa Mall by Arabian Centres** King Abdullah Rd; 9200 00262; w mall.cenomucenters.com; 09.30–23.00 Sat–Thu, 14.00–23.30 Fri

**Al Othaim Mall** Cnr King Fahd & Dhahran rds; 9200 08331; w othaimmalls.com; 09.00–23.00 Sat–Thu, 13.00–midnight Fri

**Al Rashid Town Square Yard** (Rashid Mall) Cnr King Saud & Dhahran rds; 055 840 5223; w alrashidtownsquare.com; 08.00–23.00 daily

**Fawares Mall** Cnr King Abdullah & Abu Bakr al Siddiq rds; 013 585 5959; 09.00–noon & 15.30–23.00 daily

**Lulu Mall** Cnr King Abdullah & Prince Naif rds; 013 582 7334; w luluhypermarket.com; 08.00–01.00 daily

## OTHER PRACTICALITIES

**SAB Bank** King Khalid Rd, just south of King Faisal Rd; ☎ 013 586 6000; w sab.com; ⏰ 09.20–16.30 Sun–Thu

**SNB Bank** al Ahli Prince Talal bin Abdul Aziz St, just west of King Faisal Rd; ☎ 920 001000; w alahli.com; ⏰ 09.30–16.30 Sun–Thu

**Al Ahsa Hospital** Prince Talal bin Abdul Aziz St; ☎ 013 538 4666; w alahsahospital.com.sa

**Nahdi Pharmacy** Cnr Abu Bakr al Siddiq & King Abdul Aziz rds; ☎ 9200 24673; w nahdionline.com; ⏰ 07.00–02.00 Sun–Thu, 13.00–01.00 Fri–Sat

**Saudi Post** Ain Negm Rd; w splonline.com.sa; ⏰ 08.00–21.00 Sun–Thu, 16.00–21.00 Fri–Sat

**AL AHSA UNESCO WORLD HERITAGE SITE** Officially known as 'al Ahsa, an Evolving Cultural Landscape', this UNESCO-listed gem qualifies for its natural characteristics, as well as sites of historical and cultural importance. Encompassing Hofuf and the surrounding al Ahsa area, this is a treasure trove of oases, palaces and a fantastic souq. Twelve separate locations have been defined as part of the 'cultural landscape': Eastern Oasis, Northern Oasis, as Seef, Souq al Qasriyah, Qasr Khuzam, Qasr Sahood, Qasr Ibrahim, Jawatha Archaeological Site and Mosque, al Oyun village, Ain Qannas archaeological site and Buhayra Asfar. If you have limited time in this beautiful and intriguing part of the Kingdom, at least try to visit as many of the sites highlighted below. You will need transport to visit the sites outside Hofuf.

### Hofuf

Hofuf is a walking city during the good weather. Online street map information is mostly accurate but opening hours may not be.

***Old Koot*** Compact and easily explored on foot, the al Koot al Naathil neighbourhood is among the oldest in the heart of Hofuf, with boundaries broadly defined by the curving King Faisal Road, and Abu Bakr al Siddiq and King Abdul Aziz roads. Whitewashed houses are built with traditional mud-brick and straw, and although many of the buildings are crumbling and others are being knocked down, the place gives the visitor a feeling of past times. Think of this area as an open-air museum before restoration and curation. If you are Muslim, then it's worth a quick visit to the restored al Jafri Mosque.

***Al Mulla House (Beit al Bai'ah)*** ✷ (al Fateh St between S4 W1/42 & S4 Q1/20 sts; ☎ 013 562 3100; ⏰ 08.00–16.00 Sat–Thu; admission free, though you might want to pay the attendant a small tip as he is informative even with limited English) The gem of Old Koot is undoubtedly al Mulla House. Also known as the **House of Allegiance**, it is important for both its architecture and its history. Built by the Governor of al Ahsa Sheikh Abdul Rahman al Mulla in 1787–88, the mud-brick building has been sympathetically restored and mixes Arab and Ottoman architectural styles. Ceilings are beautifully decorated with contrasting colours of the wood supports and straw. The upper floor has gorgeous wooden balconies suspended over the inner courtyard.

The future king of Saudi Arabia, ibn Saud was hosted by Sheikh Abdullatif bin Abdul Rahman al Mulla in this residence in 1913. This was where ibn Saud facilitated the peaceful annexation of the Emirate of al Ahsa to the Emirate of Nejd, a significant step in the unification and current borders of the Kingdom of Saudi Arabia.

Palatial for its time but physically modest by today's standards, this house was able to provide a comfortable environment for its VVIP guest. Entrance is through a set of wooden double doors decorated with rivets in the regional style, with the majlis, or male reception room, to the right. To the left is a room containing a water well, and along the corridor to the right of the majlis an interior courtyard. On the first floor you will find the main hall, the female majlis, a room used for the storage of palm dates, the kitchen and several bedrooms that lead off the hall in all directions. Other smaller rooms and small recesses are scattered throughout the house and are labelled according to their use, including where women stored their clothing and jewellery. Clothing and soft furnishings are displayed in each of the bedrooms along with other artefacts of everyday life.

The anteroom and bedroom to the left of the stores room was where ibn Saud slept. The museum displays the original furniture of this era, complete with the bed used by the king. The most important room is the al Bai'ah room, where regional rulers all pledged allegiance to ibn Saud. Photos of several key people from this era are on display. Spend some time in the Historic Documents room, where documents from the agreement are displayed along with swords and other artefacts. Even if you don't read Arabic, you will sense this room's significance. Step next into the Story Behind al Ahsa Annexation room, where there is an excellent narrative, in Arabic and English, of the events that unfolded between the Ottomans, regional Arab rulers and ibn Saud. These family names remain prominent in the Kingdom and throughout the Arabian Peninsula to this day. Delivering the powerful history of unification towards what Saudi Arabia has become today, al Mulla House is not to be missed.

***Qasr Ibrahim*** (Cnr King Khalid & King Faisal rds; 013 562 3100; 08.00–16.00 Sun–Thu, 16.00–20.00 Fri, 09.00–13.00 Sat; admission free) This castle is unusual as it blends the styles of Islamic and military architecture. It sits on an entire city block and has a total area of 16,500m$^2$. In the centre of the structure stands the al Qubba mosque, built by the Ottomans in 1555, with its distinctive white dome and Turkish-style minaret with spiral stairs. The mosque is surrounded by thick walls, observation windows and towers on each corner. Inside the castle, there are also remnants of barracks, a weapons warehouse, the commander's residence and meeting room. There is also a steam bath. The walls are made of mud-brick, and the ceilings of palm wood and sandalwood. The entrance to the castle is located on the south side and leads to a museum. Ibn Saud announced the annexation of al Ahsa to the Nejd Emirate in the mosque in 1913. If you find the museum closed, as it was on our visit, the informative signs along the walls of the palace make it still worth a visit. There's free parking in the adjacent SAB bank car park.

***Souq al Qasriyah*** ✷ (East side of King Abdul Aziz Rd, north of Abu Bakr al Siddiq St; 08.00–11.30 & 16.00–23.00 Sat–Thu, 16.00–23.00 Fri) This souq is one of the most authentic and beautiful souqs to be found anywhere in Saudi Arabia. Although many historians date the souq to the early 19th century, others believe it has its origins at least 600 years ago. It suffered from a major fire in 2001, but it has been restored in a sympathetic way while adding modern conveniences such as a flat floor that makes for good wheelchair and buggy access. Try to enter through Gate 1 at the southern end of the souq. The gate itself is multistorey and contains a large, pointed arch surrounded by symmetrical rounded arches, topped by a viewing platform and wooden window covers above. Inside, there are more than 400 shops, built into clay structures and adorned with wooden doors. Traditional *dakas* or terraces overhang the shops to protect customers from weather extremes, and high ceilings throughout the souq provide for ventilation, keeping it cooler in the summer.

The souq is remarkably well organised, with well-signposted aisle numbers in Arabic and English making it easy to keep track of your location. Most of the shops at the southern end of the souq sell household goods ranging from Saudi-style coffee pots and *mabkhara* (incense burners) to ordinary, everyday items. There are also many small food stalls and mini-markets that remain very popular with local Saudi customers. The north end shops are a delight for anyone looking for traditional Hofuf clothing, for men and women, which incorporates tribal decorations distinct from elsewhere in the Kingdom. This part of the souq is a particularly good place for *bishts*, the robes usually adorned with gold trim and worn by prominent Saudi men over their thobes. Wool-lined, soft leather winter waistcoats beautifully crafted in the al Ahsa style are a more practical purchase as, unlike bishts, which should only be worn by Saudi men, these waistcoats can be worn by visitors. If you like dates, the local *khalasi* variety, grown in al Ahsa, are a great treat and souvenir – you may find it a struggle to avoid eating your purchases before you get home. It is much better to visit after sunset as many shops do not open until then despite published opening hours.

You may also be interested in visiting a cluster of perfume shops on al Fath Street just west of Abdul Aziz Road opposite the north end of the souq. Just a few more steps to the west, you can find the al Amara Mosque, with its wooden doors and white-framed windows with colourful arches, and the minaret containing a number of rectangular panels that could be mistaken for stained glass.

## Beyond Hofuf

***Eastern and northern oases*** Travel to the north or east of Hofuf and you will find yourself in forests of palm trees, agricultural canals and communities on the edge of the oases that still follow centuries-old traditions. Be inspired by the beauty of this unique environment which is an example of sustainability between nature and its local population.

***Jebel Qarah and caves*** ✵ (15km northeast of Hofuf; ☎ 013 598 2888; 🕘 08.00–23.00 daily; SAR50; free parking) These spectacular mountains and caves are a highlight of any visit to al Ahsa. The site is well developed and reasonably well signposted in both Arabic and English, and wheelchair users will find good access until the caves narrow. The mountain, which rises about 75m from its base, is formed of limestone which has eroded into interestingly shaped columns, several of which could be described (politely) as mushroom-shaped, many giving home to birds, which nest at the top. Throughout the day, the colour of the stone changes, ranging from a light yellowish tan to reddish brown. Many of these columns contain rock art and calligraphy, often but not always with an accompanying description or plaque providing additional information.

Access to Jebel Qarah and caves is through the visitor centre, where entrance tickets are sold. The visitor centre has a few small shops including a reasonably good souvenir shop and professional photo shop. There were no guidebooks available on our visit, but we hope this will change soon due to the growing popularity of the site.

Visitors will follow a Land of Civilisation theme, starting with a short walk along a slight uphill gradient, where there is a resting area to your immediate right with traditional Arabic seating and a red woven Bedouin carpet. Beyond this, the site is mostly flat. As you follow the paved path to the left, you will encounter a natural amphitheatre called the Dilmun Kings Theatre, now used as an outdoor performance space. To the right of the theatre, you continue along the path, lined with pottery, past several information signs and a pair of decorative concrete scrolls.

The signs lead to the cave entrance. Well lit with natural and artificial lighting, the caves are naturally temperature controlled, maintaining a steady 20°C throughout the year. They display a range of natural colours throughout the day where light comes through space between the rocks above, away from the artificial lighting installed in the dark recesses and along different cave paths. Everyone can enter the caves, including people with buggies and wheelchairs, but the accessible path ends when you reach the first of several stairs. The footpath narrows, leading to many nooks and crannies that are diversions from the main paths along the way. It is important to note that there are 28 separate paths in the caves, with a total length of nearly 2km. It can be easy to lose your way, especially as the centre does not provide maps, so you might want to hire a guide if you plan to explore the caves more extensively.

Down the hill just past the main car park are a few shops and cafés. Stop by Gooricafe, where the welcoming owner may extend the traditional hospitality of Arabic coffee and dates if you are friendly and are up for a bit of a chat. There's also a small kiosk selling perfume, traditional oud scent and *bukhoor* wood chips that are traditionally burnt in a special wood burner similar to that used for frankincense. The al Ahsa Heritage Site, which contains a museum, was closed during our visit but looks modern.

**Getting there** From Hofuf, follow routes 7150 and 7240 to the large roundabout adjacent to the al Qarah Sports Club fields. Continue towards the right for about 1km to the next roundabout, then towards the left through the small village of al Twaitheer. Turn right after about 1.5km, just before al Ahsa National Park. You will go past the Floating Rock on the right and Jebel abu Hsas Altoithir on the left. Continue over the next roundabout, where you will enter an area with a tricky one-way system. Proceed south for about 3km, where you will then find the car parks on the right. Entrance from the car park to the visitor centre is between gates 2 and 3.

***Jawatha Archaeological Site and Mosque*** (Northeast of Hofuf; free parking & free access to the mosque if you are Muslim; park: SAR10, under-5s free) Jawatha Mosque is believed to be among the oldest near-ruins in Saudi Arabia and the first mosque built in the Eastern Province, in about 630CE. Occupying an area of about 30m by 25m, it has wooden doors, male and female prayer room entrances, and two turrets with a crumbling staircase alongside the southernmost turret. It is possible to walk around the exterior of the mosque but not the interior, although the main room of the mosque has been heavily restored. Visitors will also find a modern, family-friendly park on the north side of the car park.

To get there, follow routes 7150 and 7240 to the large roundabout adjacent to the al Qarah Sports Club fields. Turn left (north), travelling alongside the fields, turning left at the next roundabout after about 600m. After another 300m, turn right near al Adalah Football Club and continue about 5km to Jawatha Park.

***Jebel Arba*** Located about 30km southeast of Hofuf, on the edge of the Empty Quarter, Jebel Arba is a great place to escape the city. These four mountains seem to rise from nowhere. The two westernmost mountains appear to be joined and look like circus tents. The third is somewhat smaller and seems also developing its 'big top' as wind erosion does its work. The fourth, easternmost, mountain is larger and nearest to one of the main dirt roads that you'll drive on to get here. Around the mountain bases enough sand has collected to provide a bit of an adventure climbing the drifts on foot or by 4x4. They are also popular picnic sites at night as evidenced by the litter strewn everywhere.

To get there, take Route 615 south of Hofuf. Continue to the left when this road merges with Route 6446. The mountains are about 2km from here, and are visible from the road on the north side. You will need to travel past the site to the junction of Route 6614, where you can reverse direction back on to Route 615. Leave this road near the dairy, date farm and plant nursery; from here you will travel along a number of well-worn dirt roads to the mountains.

***Buhayra Asfar (Yellow Lake)*** This lake, in a somewhat remote but serene spot, dates back at least to early Islamic times. It is worth a visit to see the water in various shades of yellow that change depending on the time of day and to enjoy the silence here that is broken only by birdsong. Water levels vary throughout the year, dependent on agricultural drainage water that sustains the reed-surrounded lake nowadays and whether it has rained recently, though it remains shallow. You will see salt patches when the water levels are very low, where birdlife abounds.

Access to the lake is off Route 6614 northbound. Keep an eye out for the sign pointing towards the lake, as there are no other landmarks to guide you. Follow the sign on to the dirt road to the east which leads towards the southwest corner of the lake. After about 2km, you will see a 'No Fishing' sign, marking where the lakeshore once was. Turn left and follow the west shore – still 100m away – around the lake, using power pylons as a visual guide. After a long 10km or so, you will reach the north shore of the lake and the area described as 'Yellow Lake Best View'. The view is certainly rewarding – if you have the time and patience to navigate the dirt paths to get there. The lake is just about reachable by 2WD but you should consider a 4x4 as it is easy to get trapped in sand or high ruts in the road. It is also possible to travel the east shore of the lake, where you can take in stunning sunsets over the water. Do not attempt to do this drive on your own after dark – use a guide or drive in a vehicle convoy if you prefer more independent travel if you plan to be at the lake once the sun goes down.

**BEYOND AL AHSA: THE EMPTY QUARTER** Known in Arabic as Rub' al Khali, the Empty Quarter is the place to go if you *really* want to get away from it all. Huge sand dunes, flat plains and lakebeds await. Depending on where you go, you can see birds, as well as scorpions, snakes and spiders. Larger animals such as desert cats, wolves and foxes also live here, but you would be extremely fortunate to see any of these. There are also archaeological items scattered though the area from when this was a more habitable environment, with evidence of shells, water buffalo and even hippopotamus. Never attempt to travel to the Empty Quarter alone. Good guides and tour operators will provide full safety instructions. Check with a reputable hotel as to which guide or tour operator they recommend as this is a new venture for the tourism industry. You will need a satellite phone in case of emergency, and make sure you have adequate insurance that covers you for this excursion. There are also Empty Quarter tours originating from Riyadh and Najran provinces.

If you plan to drive between Saudi Arabia and Oman, it's worth knowing that the road between the two countries through the Empty Quarter is now open, having been completed in 2021. Although hundreds of kilometres from Hofuf, it is located in the remote reaches of al Ahsa Governorate and hugs the border with the UAE for most of the way. You will get a bonus taster of the Empty Quarter simply by making this journey. Join Route 95 from near al Batha and be prepared to cover a total distance of 725km.

## AL UQAIR العقير

If you are driving from Hofuf to the Tri-Cities, try to take the less direct route via al Uqair if you can. It's a good stopover, especially for history buffs. The Uqair Protocol was agreed here in December 1922, defining the borders – still recognised today – between the Mandate of Iraq, the Sheikhdom of Kuwait and the Sultanate of Nejd which covered much of what is now central and eastern Saudi Arabia. As a result, Kuwait lost more than two thirds of its land and had no say in the matter, leading to negative attitudes towards the British-led protocol.

From Hofuf set off on Route 7110, which turns into Route 6448 after approximately 15km. You will reach the coast at al Uqair in about an hour.

**UQAIR ANCIENT PORT** The ancient port of al Uqair is believed to be the first seaport established along the Arabian Gulf and dates back at least to the beginning of Islam. Some archaeologists date the site further back to the Dilmun people in the 3rd century BCE.

The ruins that are being restored today were built 300 years ago during the Ottoman occupation, with warehouses, administration buildings and the Uqair fort which dominates the abandoned port area. Although the buildings are mostly fenced off, it is still possible to get a good impression of how important this area has been over many centuries. If you are fortunate enough to enter the main gate, you will find a large courtyard. Near the north end of the courtyard are a series of columns that are the remains of the souq. There are also living quarters and a mosque.

Although you won't find remains of ancient dhows here, there is a boat prominently displayed by the Saudi border authority at the north end of the village, overrun with families of cats that now seem to run the port!

**UQAIR BEACH** (Admission free) Uqair Beach is a great find for beach lovers seeking tranquillity. There are separate singles and family beaches, with singles directed towards the eastern edge of First Reef Lake and families to the gulf-side beaches. There are at least 14 separate family gates that lead to substantial car parks, children's play areas and semi-private 'cabanas' that look like multicoloured mini-bunkers, complete with barbecue huts. It's a great place to relax, but don't expect Western-style sunbathing.

Gate 1 leads to the main beach with a metal and wood pier, a large children's play area, go-karting and a sand carving area. Many of the other gates are quieter; and it's possible to camp or park a caravan at gate 7. Between gates 9 and 10 there is a modern reproduction of a Roman amphitheatre where events are held. Bring your own food and drink to whichever beach you plan to visit. Saudi Aramco has its own private beach clearly signposted at the north end of the peninsula, but it is not open to the public.

To get here from al Uqair, take the coastal Route 612 northbound for about 20 minutes, then turn right at the top of First Reef Lake to the entrance of Uqair Beach.

**HALF MOON BAY** Leaving Uqair Beach, turn north on to Route 5, which runs along the western shore of Half Moon Bay. You will see many beaches and resorts along the way before reaching Dhahran in about 1 hour.

Some of the more popular beach resort hotels from south to north are the Tamara Beach Resort (Rte 5; ☎053 499 9625; **$$$$$**), Radisson Blu Half Moon Bay (Rte 5; ☎013 851 8700; **w** radissonhotels.com; **$$$$**) and Dana Bay Resort (Rte 5; ☎013 899 9900; **w** dbr.sa; **$$$$$**). You will be reliant on the services of these resorts as there are no supermarkets or restaurants nearby. Children and the young at heart may want to visit the **Loopagoon Water Park** (Rte 5; ☎013 829 3080; w loopagoon.com; 🕘 13.00–20.30 Mon–Sat; SAR230, with concessions for under-13s, seniors, nannies & visitors with disabilities) just north of the Dana resort. If you are looking for a quieter beach experience, then check out Half Moon Beach and Amwaj Beach, which are public and free to use. Both have basic facilities, toilets and a barbecue area, but plan to bring your own food and anything else you want for the beach.

Although there are also resorts on the eastern shore of Half Moon Bay, they are either older, not as well maintained, or privately owned and members only. They are also less expensive. Go if you don't have enough time to make it to the west.

## THE TRI-CITIES: DAMMAM الدمام, DHAHRAN الظهران AND AL KHOBAR الْخُبَر

The Tri-Cities of Dammam, Dhahran and al Khobar have developed into one expansive metropolitan area and are often treated as such. Many people live in one city, work in a second city, and shop in the third city on a routine basis. Dammam and al Khobar have a very similar early history and were settled by the same people. However, each city does have its own distinctions.

**Dammam** is the capital of the Eastern Province, with a total population of 1.2 million people, and is the Tri-City with the most Saudi vibe. Of the three, it is the least visited by outsiders, but try to stop by for a short while if you are in the Eastern Province. Modern Dammam was established in 1923 by the Bedouin Shi'a Dawasir tribe, who migrated from nearby Bahrain with the permission of King Abdul Aziz. Prior to 1923, Dammam was a small fishing village. With the discovery of oil, the city grew rapidly. While Dammam may have the most Saudi vibe, **al Khobar** is the most socially relaxed of the Tri-Cities and is favoured by many resident expats. Like Dammam, al Khobar was established in 1923 by the Bedouin Shi'a Dawasir tribe and saw rapid development after the discovery of oil here. Its current population is just under 500,000. Unlike sleepy Dammam and corporate Dhahran, al Khobar is vibrant, with a restaurant scene and lively Corniche that extends for almost 15km along the waterfront. **Dhahran**, west of al Khobar, was developed in the late 1930s as a company town – Saudi Aramco has its headquarters here – with gated communities, air bases and other private facilities. The population of about 150,000 is mostly expatriate and works in the oil industry.

### Getting there and away

For details of air and bus travel, see pages 350 and 351 respectively.

### By road

***From Riyadh and other points west*** Most people will drive to the Tri-Cities on Route 80, which will bring the traveller directly to Dhahran and on to al Khobar. Route 613 southbound is another route to al Khobar, leaving Route 80 after it turns into Highway 40 on the outskirts of Dammam. For those headed for Dammam, upon arrival in the Tri-Cities area, turn northbound on Route 613 before heading east on Route 605 to the city centre. The main roads between Dammam and al Khobar are coastal Route 617 and the more inland Route 605. Routes 610 and 619 lead more directly to Dhahran.

***From Hofuf*** Coming from Hofuf, you will arrive either on Route 615 through Buqaiq or Route 5 if you are travelling north from Uqair.

***From Bahrain*** Once across the King Fahd Causeway, continue on Route 80 for Dhahran, or you can turn north on to Route 617 (King Abdul Aziz Rd) immediately after the toll booths, which leads directly to the al Khobar Corniche. Route 617 becomes Prince Turki Street, which is the old Corniche road and the main thoroughfare for vehicles. If you continue on this road north past the end of the Corniche, you'll reach Dammam.

**By rail** Trains from Riyadh take about 3½ hours and terminate at the Dammam Railway Station just east of the centre (see page 73). There is a taxi rank outside the station. Uber and Careem are also options for onward travel into the Tri-Cities.

**By sea** A small but growing number of cruise ships arrive in Saudi Arabia at the King Abdul Aziz Seaport east of Dammam city centre.

**WHERE TO STAY** Al Khobar is a pleasant suburb where many people from all over the world live and socialise. The accommodation in this area is generally in the form of either business-orientated hotels or longstay apartments, mostly on or near Prince Turki Street near the Corniche. Dammam's hotels are significantly less expensive than those in Riyadh, Jeddah and even al Khobar. Most hotels in Dhahran are very business orientated and can also be less expensive than in al Khobar.

## Al Khobar

### *Upmarket*

Away from the Corniche, top-end hotels near the business districts include the **Intercontinental** [363 C3] (al Bassam al Andalusi St; 013 845 2888; w ihg.com; **$$$$**), **Kempinski al Othman Hotel** [363 B1] (King Saud Branch Rd; 013 829 4444; w kempinski.com; **$$$$**) & **Park Inn Radisson al Khobar** [363 C1] (King Faisal bin Abdul Aziz Rd; 013 810 0800; w radissonhotels.com; **$$$$**).

✷ **Le Méridien** [363 D3] Cnr Prince Turki Rd & Corniche Bd; 013 896 9000; w marriott.com. This hotel is well situated between the Khobar Corniche & the newer North Corniche. Although it's an older property, it has been refurbished recently. The rooms are a bit smaller than you might expect, but the views are terrific. The garden is a welcome oasis of calm. There are separate male & female fitness centres, but the lovely outdoor pool is for men & children only. The hotel restaurants offer a wide variety of choices, though you may prefer to walk to any number of restaurants along both corniches. **$$$$**

**Movenpick** [363 C2] Prince Turki St, at the al Fozan roundabout; 013 810 9800; w movenpick.com. This is a newer property than most with all of the amenities expected of a 5-star hotel. Better than average service. **$$$$**

**Sofitel** [363 D4] South Corniche Rd; 013 881 7000; w allaccor.com. This hotel is situated on the southernmost reaches of the Corniche & is the nearest top-end hotel to the King Fahd Causeway. It is an older but well-maintained property. As expected from this French chain, the food is great & so is the service. **$$$$**

### *Mid-range*

Away from the Corniche you could try the **Crowne Plaza** [363 B3] (King Abdullah St; 013 814 8900; w ihg.com) or **Hilton Garden** [363 B2] (al Khobar King Saud bin Abdul Aziz Rd; 9200 20064; w hilton.com).

**Golden Tulip** [363 C4] Prince Turki St, north of 30th St; 013 889 3222; w al-khobar.goldentulip.com. Slightly north of the Sofitel, this budget-friendly hotel has a spectacular view of the Salman bin Laden Mosque that appears to be floating in the Arabian Gulf. **$$$**

**Hawthorne Suites by Wyndham** [363 C3] Prince Majed St, between 8th & 9th sts; 013 899 6111; w wyndhamhotels.com. This property is good for larger families or groups. Some rooms are in need of renovation, but the location is in walking distance of Adjan Walk & the Corniche. **$$$**

**Holiday Inn al Khobar** [363 C2] King Khalid Rd, north of 18th St; 013 867 1111; w ihg.com.

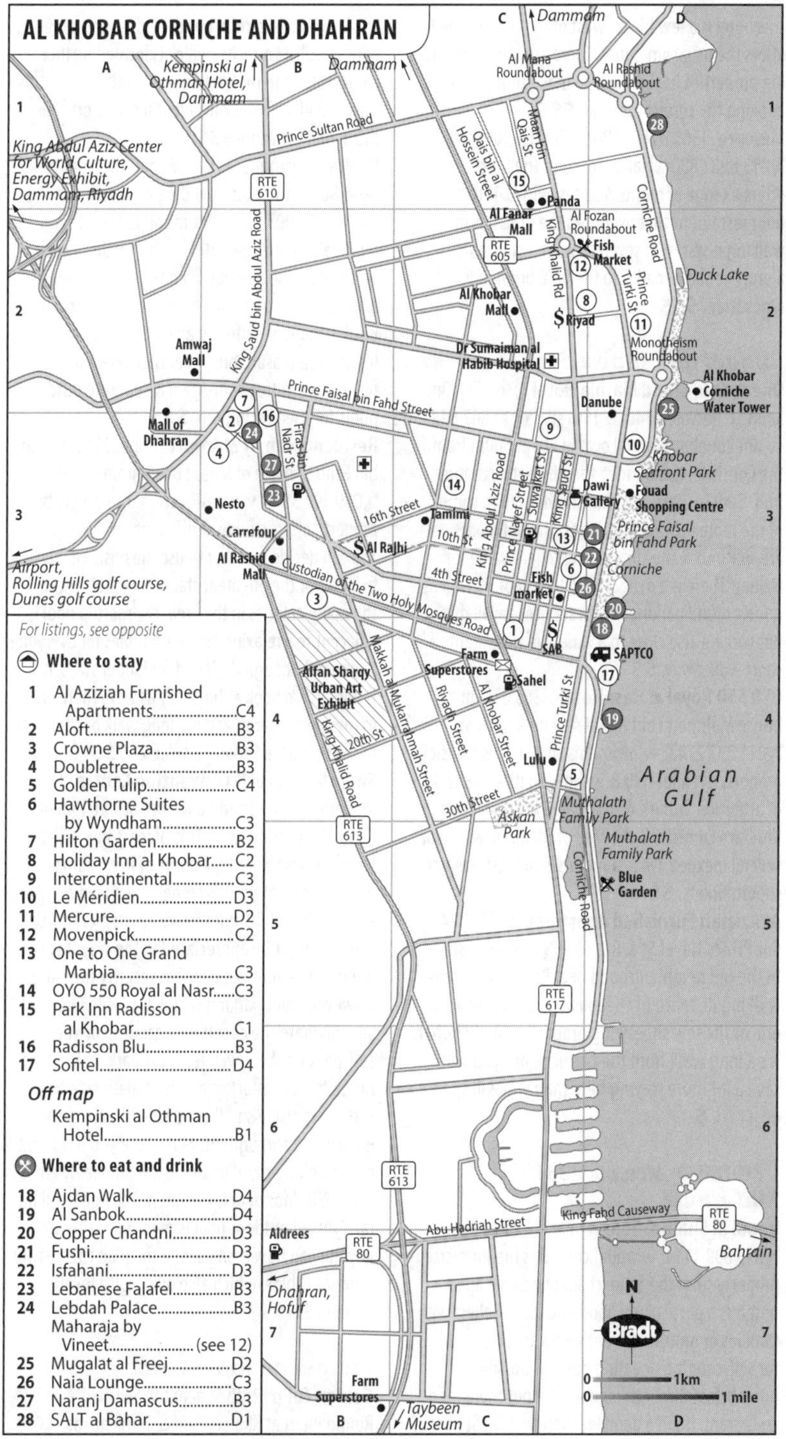
AL KHOBAR CORNICHE AND DHAHRAN
Kempinski al Othman Hotel, Dammam
Dammam
Dammam
Al Mana Roundabout
Al Rashid Roundabout
King Abdul Aziz Center for World Culture, Energy Exhibit, Dammam, Riyadh
Prince Sultan Road
RTE 610
Qais bin al Hossein Street
Maan bin Qais St
Panda
Al Fanar Mall
Al Fozan Roundabout
King Khalid Rd
Fish Market
Corniche Road
RTE 605
Prince Turki St
Duck Lake
Al Khobar Mall
Riyad
King Saud bin Abdul Aziz Road
Amwaj Mall
Dr Sumaiman al Habib Hospital
Monotheism Roundabout
Al Khobar Corniche Water Tower
Prince Faisal bin Fahd Street
Danube
Mall of Dhahran
Firas bin Nadr St
Khobar Seafront Park
Dawi Gallery
Fouad Shopping Centre
Nesto
16th Street
Tamimi
10th St
King Abdul Aziz Road
Prince Nayef Street
Suwalket St
King Saud St
Prince Faisal bin Fahd Park
Carrefour
Al Rajhi
Al Rashid Mall
4th Street
Corniche
Airport, Rolling Hills golf course, Dunes golf course
Custodian of the Two Holy Mosques Road
Fish market
SAB
Farm Superstores
SAPTCO
Makkah al Mukarramah Street
Alfan Sharqy Urban Art Exhibit
Sahel
Riyadh Street
Al Khobar Street
Prince Turki St
King Khalid Road
20th St
Lulu
Arabian Gulf
30th Street
Askan Park
Muthalath Family Park
Muthalath Family Park
RTE 613
Blue Garden
Corniche Road
RTE 617
RTE 613
King Fahd Causeway
RTE 80
Abu Hadriah Street
Aldrees
RTE 80
Bahrain
Dhahran, Hofuf
Bradt
0 1km
0 1 mile
Farm Superstores
Taybeen Museum
For listings, see opposite
Where to stay
1 Al Aziziah Furnished Apartments....C4
2 Aloft....B3
3 Crowne Plaza....B3
4 Doubletree....B3
5 Golden Tulip....C4
6 Hawthorne Suites by Wyndham....C3
7 Hilton Garden....B2
8 Holiday Inn al Khobar....C2
9 Intercontinental....C3
10 Le Méridien....D3
11 Mercure....D2
12 Movenpick....C2
13 One to One Grand Marbia....C3
14 OYO 550 Royal al Nasr....C3
15 Park Inn Radisson al Khobar....C1
16 Radisson Blu....B3
17 Sofitel....D4
Off map
Kempinski al Othman Hotel....B1
Where to eat and drink
18 Ajdan Walk....D4
19 Al Sanbok....D4
20 Copper Chandni....D3
21 Fushi....D3
22 Isfahani....D3
23 Lebanese Falafel....B3
24 Lebdah Palace....B3
Maharaja by Vineet....(see 12)
25 Mugalat al Freej....D2
26 Naia Lounge....C3
27 Naranj Damascus....B3
28 SALT al Bahar....D1

This hotel is a few blocks west of the Hawthorne & offers the usual amenities. There are other Holiday Inn properties in al Khobar so make sure you are booking the correct location. **$$$**

**Mercure** [363 D2] Cnr Prince Turki & 10th sts; ☎013 898 9880; **w** all.accor.com. The hotel offers a range of rooms & suites, with a 10th-floor restaurant that overlooks the Gulf. It is in walking distance of several casual restaurants along the same road & to the Gulf, but needs renovation. **$$$**

### *Budget and shoestring*

**One to One Grand Marbia Hotel** [363 C3] King Saud St, between 14th & 15th sts; ☎013 867 8223; **w** one2onehotel.com. Located about 500m from the Corniche, this budget-friendly hotel is a rare find. Built in 2007, it is more modern than some of the more upscale properties. The dbl rooms are spacious & the suites are excellent value for money. There is a gym & an indoor pool, as well as underground parking. Room service is available, but you are also close to a variety of restaurants a short walk away. **$$**

**OYO 550 Royal al Nasr Hotel** [363 C3] Cnr Prince Mahmoud bin Abdul Aziz Rd & 17th St; ☎011 293 2743; **w** oyorooms.com. This is a basic property even for OYO & is showing its age & lack of attention, but it's well situated in between al Khobar's Corniche & the Mall of Dhahran, & is near several inexpensive restaurants & at least 3 major supermarkets. **$$**

**Al Aziziah Furnished Apartments** [363 C4] Cnr Prince Nayef St & Rte 605; ☎013 831 1384. In the old neighbourhood of al Khobar & within walking distance of cheap eats, this is probably one of the few shoestring properties in al Khobar. It's a long walk from the Corniche but you will save a lot more staying here than you will spend on a taxi. **$**

## Dammam *Map, page 366*

### *Mid-range*

**Boudl al Shatea** 10th St near al Shatea Mall; ☎013 809 1114; **w** boudl.com. This medium-sized property from the Saudi chain of upscale apart-hotels is a particularly good find for travellers with families or groups of friends who are prepared for self-catering or eating out. It is possible to order b/fast through room service but there is no restaurant. It's in a good location on 10th St near al Shatea Mall. Be careful not to confuse this property with Boudl al Corniche, which is located further along 10th St to the east. In spite of the name, this other Boudl is more convenient for the port than the actual Corniche. **$$$**

**Braira Dammam** Prince Mohammed bin Faud Rd north of Fakhr al Dine al Moushasib Rd; ☎9200 00555; **w** brairahotels.com. This relatively new large hotel is a bit further north on the peninsula, away from the more congested centre. It is also part of the Saudi Boudl group. Book a room or suite & stay in Saudi-style luxury at a reasonable price. There is an on-site restaurant, coffee shop, gym & separate outdoor pools for men & children. **$$$**

**Residence Inn by Marriott** Prince Mohammed bin Fahd St north of Muazz bin Aljjmmouh St; ☎059 392 3888; **w** marriott.com. This newly built property offers studios & different-size suites. You can decide whether to use the basic kitchen facilities or the on-site restaurant or step out to the many eateries in the area. The rooftop pool is adjacent to a relaxing area with tables for everyone to enjoy. Although designed for longer stays, it is possible to book a short stay as well. There are many shops nearby, & it is a long walk or short ride to the Corniche. Parking available. **$$$**

**Sheraton Hotel & Convention Centre** Prince Mohammed bin Fahd Rd & 10th St; ☎013 834 5555; **w** marriott.com. This place is in a great location & is the *grande dame* of Dammam's established hotels. It is somewhat dated but not tired, although its impressive 12-step entrance can no longer be appreciated in the way it was meant to be due to extensive security measures. However, valet parking is still available once you navigate the circuitous entrance, or you can self-park on the lower-level car park. The rooms range from comfortable dbls to elaborate suites & there is also a small concierge lounge. Service is excellent throughout. Make sure you request a non-smoking room if you do not smoke. There is a spa & indoor pool for women. The beautiful but rarely used outdoor pool is men only, although anyone can have a snack or a meal on the nearby outdoor tables, which also overlook a lovely garden. **$$$**

### *Budget and shoestring*

**Golden Tulip** 18th St near the Seashell Roundabout at Khaleej/Gulf & Corniche rds; ☎013

852 7777; w goldentulip.com. With relatively modest prices, a highly rated b/fast buffet & a fantastic location almost on the Corniche, this property has wide appeal. There is an indoor pool & gym for men only. Make sure you ask for a recently renovated room. $$

**Ramada by Wyndham** Ahmed bin al Nafis St off Gulf Rd; 013 833 3322; w wyndhamhotels.com. This property is not far from the Golden Tulip & may be a suitable alternative for those keeping a close eye on their budget. It has a range of smoking & non-smoking rooms & suites, a restaurant, coffee shops & 24-hour room service. There is a fitness centre & outdoor pool for men. Free parking on site. It's good value but don't expect anything special. $$

**OYO 427 Nujoom al Sharqia 2** Off al Aqiq Rd, 1 block east of the Esam Bulbul Mosque; 013 809 9812; w oyorooms.com. This chain of Indian-owned hotels has several locations in Dammam; this property is the most convenient for the Corniche, shops & restaurants. The basic rooms have a TV, fridge, kettle & free Wi-Fi. Free parking in front of the hotel. $

## Dhahran

Most of Dhahran's hotels are located east of the Mall of Dhahran near King Saud bin Abdul Aziz Rd. Prominent ones (all $$$) include **Aloft** [363 B3] (21st St; 013 816 4444; w marriott.com), **Doubletree** [363 B3] (21st St; 013 331 1144; w hilton.com) & **Radisson Blu** [363 B3] (Dhahran Zaid bin al Khattab St; 013 801 0080; w radissonhotels.com).

**WHERE TO EAT AND DRINK** There are many restaurants, coffee shops, ice cream shops and pop-up stands along Dammam's Corniche, mostly along the King Abdullah Sea Front on the Ash Shati al Gharbi (east side of the Corniche). Check out any of these restaurants, for atmosphere as well as the menu, as they are great locations to watch the sunset. (Those at the south end also enjoy views of the spiral tower on Murjan Island.) Most have outdoor seating when the weather is cooler and the majority open after 16.00. Al Romansiah ($$) and other Saudi chains are also present in Dammam; other cheap eats can be found near the women's souq area, a collection of shops around King Khalid Street which includes Dammam Souq Sha'bu for Abaya.

There is an abundance of good restaurants in al Khobar, particularly along the Corniche. Whether you want fine dining, a casual meal or take-away for a picnic, you will be spoilt for choice with everything from Japanese to American and almost all options in between. Good-quality cheap eats can be found near Suwaiket Street in the centre of old al Khobar. It's also worth checking out any of the modest restaurants and cafés that cater to the Pakistani expat community – the busier the place is, the better it will be. Note that some may not be used to women customers, but are likely to accommodate you if you are especially polite.

Dhahran, on the other hand, has plenty to offer if you're happy eating at American chain restaurants, shopping mall food courts and other fast-food places, and there are a small number of good independent eateries to be found if you explore.

## Al Khobar

For those planning to dine along the Corniche, here are a few recommendations. This is just the beginning – there are plenty of other restaurants along the way that are also appealing.

**Maharaja by Vineet** [363 C2] Inside the Movenpick hotel (page 362); 013 898 4999; w movenpick.com; noon–15.00 & 18.30–23.00 daily. This Indian restaurant is a favourite in Riyadh (Rasoi by Vineet; page 267) & its sister branch here is just as special. $$$$$

**Al Sanbok** [363 D4] Corniche Rd, south of the Sofitel Hotel; 9200 08000; w alsanbok.com; 11.00–midnight daily. This is a great seafood restaurant in a prime location at the southern end of the Corniche where the view towards the causeway & Bahrain adds to the atmosphere. It's known for its use of the freshest ingredients, with signature dishes such as salmon & hammour

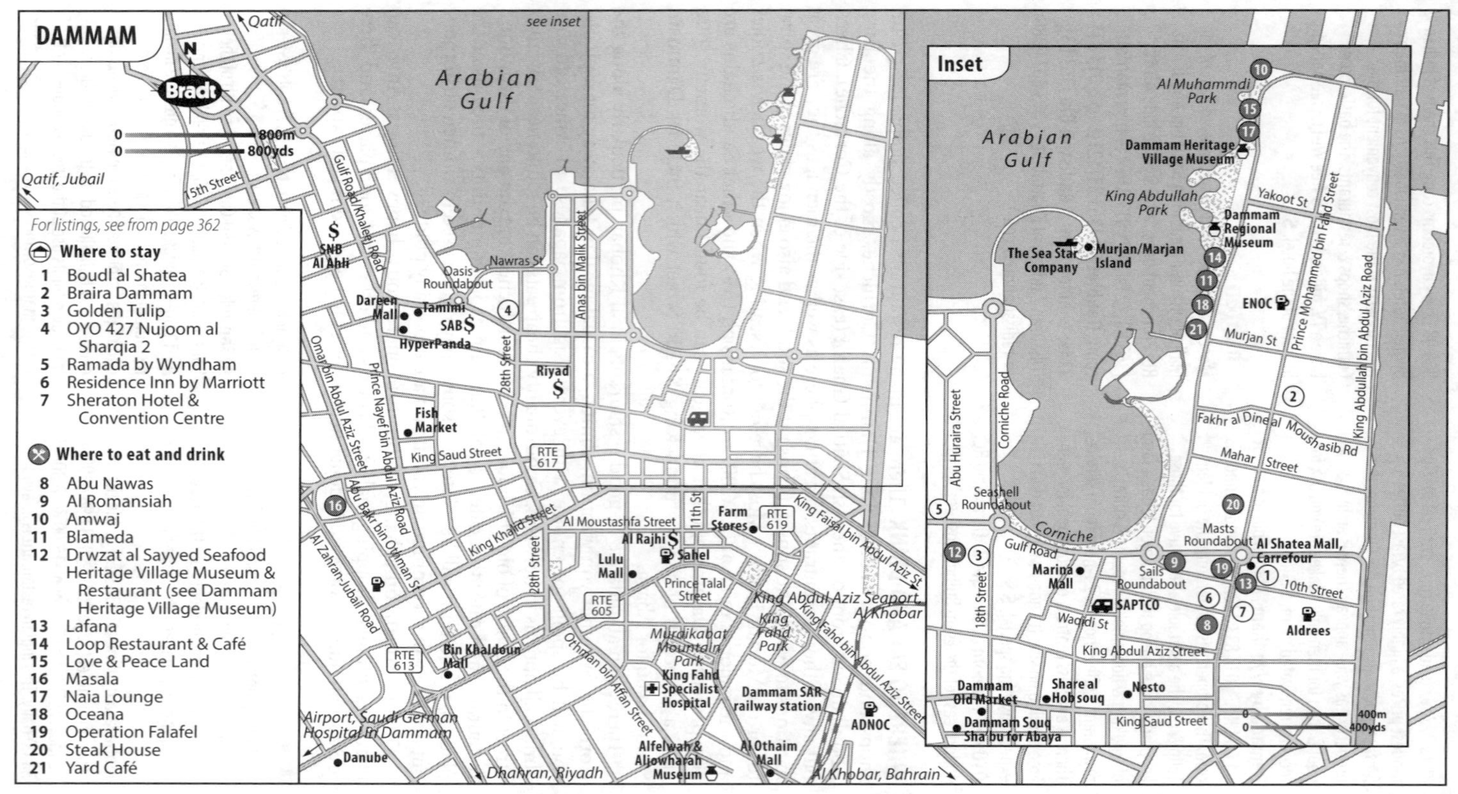
DAMMAM
For listings, see from page 362
Where to stay
1 Boudl al Shatea
2 Braira Dammam
3 Golden Tulip
4 OYO 427 Nujoom al Sharqia 2
5 Ramada by Wyndham
6 Residence Inn by Marriott
7 Sheraton Hotel & Convention Centre
Where to eat and drink
8 Abu Nawas
9 Al Romansiah
10 Amwaj
11 Blameda
12 Drwzat al Sayyed Seafood
Heritage Village Museum & Restaurant (see Dammam Heritage Village Museum)
13 Lafana
14 Loop Restaurant & Café
15 Love & Peace Land
16 Masala
17 Naia Lounge
18 Oceana
19 Operation Falafel
20 Steak House
21 Yard Café
Arabian Gulf
see inset
Qatif
Qatif, Jubail
15th Street
Gulf Road/Khaleej Road
SNB
Al Ahli
Oasis Roundabout
Nawras St
Dareen Mall
Tamimi
SAB
HyperPanda
28th Street
Riyad
Anas bin Malik Street
Omar bin Abdul Aziz Street
Prince Nayef bin Abdul Aziz Road
Fish Market
King Saud Street
RTE 617
Abu Bakr bin Othman St
King Khalid Street
Al Moustashfa Street
11th St
Farm Stores
RTE 619
King Faisal bin Abdul Aziz St
Al Rajhi
Sahel
Lulu Mall
Prince Talal Street
RTE 605
King Abdul Aziz Seaport, Al Khobar
King Fahd Park
King Fahd bin Abdul Aziz Street
Al Zahran-Jubail Road
RTE 613
Bin Khaldoun Mall
Othman bin Affan Street
Muraikabat Mountain Park
King Fahd Specialist Hospital
Dammam SAR railway station
ADNOC
Airport, Saudi German Hospital in Dammam
Danube
Dhahran, Riyadh
Alfelwah & Aljowharah Museum
Al Othaim Mall
Al Khobar, Bahrain
Inset
Al Muhammdi Park
Dammam Heritage Village Museum
King Abdullah Park
Yakoot St
Dammam Regional Museum
The Sea Star Company
Murjan/Marjan Island
ENOC
Murjan St
Prince Mohammed bin Fahd Street
King Abdullah bin Abdul Aziz Road
Abu Huraira Street
Corniche Road
Fakhr al Dine al Moushasib Rd
Mahar Street
Seashell Roundabout
Corniche
Masts Roundabout
Al Shatea Mall, Carrefour
Gulf Road
Marina Mall
Sails Roundabout
10th Street
18th Street
SAPTCO
Waqidi St
Aldrees
King Abdul Aziz Street
Dammam Old Market
Share al Hob souq
Nesto
Dammam Souq
Sha'bu for Abaya
King Saud Street
0 800m
0 800yds
0 400m
0 400yds

with coral sauce & lobster ravioli all good choices. If these don't appeal, then we recommend you make your fish selection from the market, where you then advise the chef how you would like it seasoned & cooked. The options take inspiration from nearly 20 countries, & all are delicious. There is an additional focus on Thai & Indian seafood specialities. Limited options for vegetarians & vegans. Top-end dining at top-end prices makes this a restaurant for special occasions. $$$$

**Copper Chandni** [363 D3] Off Prince Turki St near Ajdan Walk; 013 895 1188; w copperchandni.com; noon–00.30 daily. If you are looking for upscale Indian cuisine, then you are in luck. This is a branch of the same restaurant in Riyadh (page 124), in a much lovelier location on the Corniche. $$$$

**Ajdan Walk** [363 D4] Off the Corniche Rd; 9200 00658; w adjan.com; 07.00–01.00 daily. Adjan Walk is a mixed food court with better-than-average casual dining options. Familiar international names such as PF Chang's & Texas Roadhouse rub shoulders with Middle Eastern joints like Lebanese Babel & Operation Falafel. If you are looking for a quieter venue, there are loads of cafés a bit further along at the end of the Walk, on the waterfront. Here you will find the ever-popular Café Bateel & newer Mantorose Café, as well as the stylish Cay Café. $$$

**Fushi** [363 D3] Prince Turki St, just north of Jarir Bookstore; 013 898 9595; w sofushi.com; 12.30–midnight Sat–Wed, 12.30–00.30 Thu–Fri. The clue is in the name. This is a Saudi take on Japanese fusion. You will find authentic enough miso & mushroom soups, yakitori dishes, gyoza, bento boxes, a range of ramen & soba noodle options, tempura, katsu curry, Japanese-inspired salads & an especially generous sushi menu. Astonishingly, these sit alongside fried cheese balls, mac & cheese, breaded chicken fingers & some popular Thai dishes. Go for the sushi, which has a very good reputation, & enjoy the better-than-usual customer service. $$$

**Naia Lounge** [363 D3] West side of Prince Turki Rd behind Hardee's & KFC; 058 333 6262; noon–01.00 Sat–Thu, 14.30–02.00 Fri. More Asian fusion than pan-Chinese, this is a destination restaurant, with mixed seating, at which to see & be seen. You won't go wrong with the plentiful seafood, noodle & sushi choices. It's also a popular place for young Saudis to celebrate birthdays, even a few years ago when it was frowned upon more than it is now. There is outdoor dining when the weather is more temperate. You will pay a premium for the atmosphere. There is another branch in Dammam. $$$

**Naranj Damascus Restaurant** [363 B3] West side of Firaz bin al Nadr St; 050 844 6622; w naranj.net; 11.00–02.00 daily. This is the place to go to for a top-rate Levantine meal that blends Syrian & Lebanese traditions. Soup, cold & hot starters, salads, BBQ & grills. Go for a hot mixed mezze & the Aleppo-style kebab Halabi. They also do a good *arayes*, pita stuffed with lamb, which sounds like a lighter option but is substantial. Better yet, try the local *tajins* that are difficult to find outside of Syria. There are meat, prawn & vegetarian options, as well as a good selection of fresh juices. Worth the short journey away from the Corniche towards the eastern reaches of Dhahran. $$$

**Isfahani Restaurant** [363 D3] Prince Turki St, just north of Jarir Bookstore; 013 893 0133; w isfahanigroup.com; noon–23.00 Sat–Thu, 13.00–23.00 Fri. Possibly one of the last remaining Persian restaurants in KSA. If you need a fix & can't get over the causeway to Bahrain & its endless choice of Persian cuisine, then this restaurant will suffice. Although the décor is tired, with a few tiles & very worn small rugs of what was once a grand dining room, visitors can feel its former splendour. The big windows remain with a pleasant view of the Corniche & sea for diners in both the singles & family sections. The menu offers a decent range of traditional dishes, although they may not always have everything available when you visit. The food is mid-range both in price & quality. Try the *koobideh* as they are better than the lamb chops. The *faloodeh* & *bastani* are good enough to fulfil a craving but are not memorable. Isfahani is tucked away on the 1st floor of a building shared with Segfredo's; pass into the interior alongside Segfredo's & look for the small sign on the right. There is a lift directly in front – take this to the 1st floor. $$

**Mugalat al Freej** [363 D2] North Corniche, just south of al Khobar Tower; 053 380 6993; 06.00–11.30 & 13.00–midnight Sat–Thu, 06.00–10.30 & 13.00–midnight Fri. This restaurant serves authentic Eastern Province cuisine. & is popular for b/fast, especially at w/ends. However, it remains busy throughout the day & into the late evening. Reservations recommended. Singles, families & outdoor seating. $$

**SALT al Bahar** [363 D1] North Corniche, just before the al Rashid Roundabout; ☎ 9200 24788; **w** indpt.com; ⌚ 13.00–02.00 daily. Created in Dubai to appeal to trendy customers, SALT has come to Saudi Arabia. Located on the far North Corniche on a clean stretch of white sand beach, it's a great place to have fun. There are loads of activities for children, while young adults almost sway to the music in this mixed venue that would have been impossible only a few years ago. SALT is very casual, featuring a simple selection of sliders (mini burgers – or at least mini from a Saudi perspective) & chips. Both are ordered with your choice of calorie-laden sauces; fire sauce is particularly popular. Save room for the lotus soft serve ice cream. $$

## Dammam *Map, page 366*

### *Corniche*

**Amwaj** King Abdullah Park, off Corniche Rd; ☎ 055 132 0888; **w** amwajbeach.business.site; ⌚ claims to be open 24/7. We are including this restaurant simply for its great location at the top end of the Corniche just beyond al Muhammdi Park, at the northern end of King Abdullah Park. Amwaj tries to appeal to every palate. Its menu focuses on chicken & prawns, which are prepared in a variety of ways – generic 'Western', in pastries, sandwiches, kebabs, Chinese-style stir fry & in Italian-inspired pasta dishes. There are also Arabic starters & soups. This is a great place to come if you are part of a group that can't make up their minds. The location is the key draw, with great sunset views. There is also a popular shisha bar that gets lively after dark. $$$

**Blameda** Corniche; ☎ 053 161 5404; ⌚ 06.00–01.00 Sat–Wed, 06.00–02.00 Thu–Fri. Blameda offers a mixed menu with some pasta & other Western cuisine along with Arabic options. $$$

**Loop Restaurant & Café** Corniche; ☎ 056 536 6373; ⌚ 05.30–midnight daily. If you are looking for upscale dining along the Corniche, then check out Loop with its strong Lebanese influence. $$$

**Love & Peace Land** South of Amwaj restaurant; ☎ 055 349 2064. Love & Peace Land is, unsurprisingly, geared towards couples & special occasions. The menu is upmarket with a bit of everything. $$$

**Naia Lounge** Corniche; ☎ 054 303 0528; ⌚ 11.00–02.00 Sat–Thu, 12.30–02.00 Fri. This is a good night-time spot for café comfort food & shisha. See the listing of its sister lounge in al Khobar for more information (page 367). $$$

**Yard Café** Corniche; ☎ 050 199 3996; ⌚ 12.30–02.00 daily. Yard offers a mixed range of cuisines. $$$

**Oceana** Corniche; ☎ 050 388 8929; ⌚ noon–01.30 daily. Most people would expect a restaurant called Oceana to focus on seafood. Not so here – their menu is pan-Indian & pan-Chinese. $$

### *Elsewhere*

**Drwzat al Sayyed Seafood** abu Huraira St, south of Khaleej/Gulf Rd; ☎ 013 832 9991; ⌚ noon–midnight daily. This is the place for seafood lovers. The eclectic décor is striking, capturing a blend of traditional Gulf items with more than a splash of colourful furnishings. Fresh hammour, lobster, prawns & more are complemented by mezze & salads. The menu is in Arabic only. $$$

✷ **Heritage Village Museum & Restaurant** King Abdullah Park along the seafront; ☎ 055 843 2232; ⌚ noon–midnight Sat–Wed, noon–01.00 Thu–Fri; SAR20 pp for the restaurant & museum. Popular with local Saudi nationals, as well as expats & visitors, the main restaurant in this wonderful property is the Lobby Café, immediately behind the entrance on the ground floor. As a reproduction of traditional Saudi dining, it features modern tables as well as heritage seating, where you will sit on the floor surrounded by low cushions & eat from communal plates, as is traditional, laid on a tablecloth in the centre; you can order individual meals if you prefer. Be prepared to eat with your (right) hand. This is the place to try authentic Saudi cuisine. Don't miss the *lahm mandi*, the Yemeni special meat dish cooked in an underground pit. Bring your appetite or a large party so you can also try soups, different mezze starters & local Saudi desserts. $$$

**Steak House** Prince Mohammed bin Fahd St, near Prince Talal St; ☎ 013 833 5468; **w** steakhouse.com.sa; ⌚ 11.00–midnight daily. Sometimes you just fancy a break. If you're in the mood for beef, from steaks to burgers & everything in between, then you have come to the right place. They also have a terrific salad bar. $$$

**Abu Nawas** Prince Mohammed bin Fahd Rd, north of Osamah bin Zeid Rd; 013 895 2225; noon–02.00 daily. This casual Lebanese restaurant remains as popular as ever. Try their signature broasted chicken if you want something a bit different & delicious. The usual mezze & mixed grill are also excellent choices, & their famed *toum* (garlic sauce) deserves its superb reputation. Seating is in single & family sections. Be prepared for a bit of a wait when the restaurant is busy, but it's worth it. Afterwards, pop round to the irresistible Saadeddin Pastry a few doors down, if you have space for more treats. $$

✷ **Lafana** al Ashriah St, next to al Shatea Mall; 013 809 1115; noon–23.00 daily. This is a lovely opportunity to dine in a beautifully converted home run by a friendly Iraqi family. The patriarch speaks better English than the younger men in the family, though they are all gracious & helpful; any attempt at speaking Arabic will be well rewarded. Singles dine in a ground-floor room to the left of the small reception room. The kitchen is also behind reception. A brisk take-away business is in evidence by the number of people waiting to collect their orders. Families & mixed-gender groups will enter to the left side of the building & climb a flight of stairs to a lovely open room with curtained booths along the walls. Although the singles section is elaborately decorated, the family section has more character with a water fountain, Iraqi artwork & tiling. The menu is in Arabic only but a friendly chat with any of the family will see you through. This is one of those rare restaurants where anything you order tastes like home cooking. Try the mutton kebab with shredded carrot, onion & tomato sprinkled with sumac & a whole green chilli served on Iraqi flatbread. Fish lovers must try the *masgouf*, the Iraqi national dish. Juices are excellent. $$

**Masala Restaurant** Cnr Abu Bakr bin Othman & Suleiman bin al Athir sts; 013 832 7614; w masalahouse.business.site; 11.00–00.30 daily. This aptly named restaurant, with singles & family sections, features Mughlai food but also mixes it up with pan-Indian, Chinese, Pakistani & generic Arabic food. It's all good & it won't break the bank. Worth the short journey away from the Corniche & most hotels. $$

**Operation Falafel** Khaleej Rd at the Masts Roundabout; 9200 02970; w operationfalafel.com; 07.00–01.00 Fri–Tue, 07.00–02.00 Wed–Thu. If you are looking for Middle Eastern street food with a difference, come here to try creatively constructed falafel, shawarma, hummus & salads in a modern, relaxed atmosphere. $$

## Dhahran

For a good Levantine meal in this area, also try Naranj Damascus Restaurant (page 367).

**Lebdah Palace Restaurant** [363 B3] 21st St, behind the Aloft hotel; 013 830 1515; 11.30–22.30 Sat–Thu, 12.30–22.30 Fri. Serves delicious kabsa & other Saudi specialities. $$$$

**Lebanese Falafel** [363 B3] Firaz bin al Nadr St, towards al Khobar; 06.00–23.30 Sat–Thu, 06.30–10.00 & 16.00–23.30 Fri. Good Levantine food. $$

**SHOPPING** Most of the large supermarkets and hypermarkets are found in the Tri-Cities, including Carrefour, Danube, Lulu, Nesto, Panda and Tamimi.

## Al Khobar and Dhahran

### *Shopping malls*

Smaller than al Rashid, other malls that may be worth dropping in to are **al Fanar** [363 C1] & **al Khobar** [363 C2].

**Al Rashid Mall** [363 B3] Cnr Firaz bin al Nadr St & Custodian of the Two Holy Mosques Rd; 09.30–23.00 Sat–Thu, 14.00–23.00 Fri. This mall may not be quite as large as the Mall of Dhahran (see right), but it is at least as popular. It has similar amenities plus a large Carrefour Hypermarket. This mall has the advantage of uninterrupted opening hours .

**Amwaj Mall** [363 A2] Prince Faisal bin Fahd Rd, opposite the Mall of Dhahran; 9200 09467; 09.00–23.00 Sat–Thu, 16.00–23.00 Fri. This mall is smaller than its over-the-road neighbour, with more practical shops & a few cafés, including Café Meow, where cat lovers can visit the felines in residence. It is also next to a large IKEA that draws customers from all over the Eastern Province.

**Mall of Dhahran** [363 A2] Cnr King Saud bin Abdul Aziz Branch & Prince Faisal bin Fahd rds;

🕘 09.30–23.00 Sat–Thu, 16.00–23.00 Fri. The Mall of Dhahran is one of the Kingdom's largest malls & has the full range of upscale shops, children's play areas & a cinema. Many of the shops still operate split hours so keep in mind that they are closed from approx noon until 16.00.

### Traditional shops and markets

If you are looking for a traditional shopping experience, then check out the shops in & around **Suwaiket St** [363 C3], near the mosque of the same name. This is al Khobar's oldest shopping area, where bargaining is still the norm. There is also a **fish market** [363 C3], off King Abdul Aziz Rd & the Two Grand Mosques Rd.

## Dammam

### Shopping malls

**Al Othaim Mall** Cnr Rte 619 & al Khansaa St; ☎9200 08331; w othaimsmalls.com; 🕘 10.00–23.00 Sat–Thu, 13.00–midnight. The most popular & upmarket shopping mall.

**Al Shatea** Cnr Prince Mohammed bin Fahd Rd & al Ashriah St; 🕘 10.00–01.30 daily. Useful for its supermarket & other practicalities.

**Bin Khaldoun Mall** King Fahd Rd; 🕘 09.30–midnight Sat–Thu, 09.30–10.30 & 13.00–midnight Fri

**Dareen Mall** Khaleej Rd; ☎9200 09467; w dareen-mall.com; 🕘 10.00–23.00 Sat–Thu, 13.00–23.00 Fri

**Lulu Mall** Cnr Prince Bandar bin Abdul Aziz & 18th sts; ☎9200 22330; 🕘 08.00–23.00 daily

**Marina Mall** On the Corniche, Khaleej Rd & 11th St; ☎013 809 9966; 🕘 10.00–midnight Sat–Thu, 14.00– midnight Fri

### Souqs and other markets

Dammam still has a **traditional souq area**, where narrow streets & packed shops can be found in the area west of 11th St from al Moustashfa St to King Abdul Aziz St. The **Share al Hob souq** specialises in gold & jewellery. **Dammam Old Market** & **Dammam Souq Sha'bu for Abaya**, within the women's souq, are great for finding abayas & other women's clothing at reasonable prices, & are located off King Khalid & 18th sts. Other goods on offer in the souqs range from spices & perfumes to carpets & ceremonial swords. The souq area is also a good place to find cheap eats. Keep in mind that there is minimal trade in the morning, then shops close for the afternoon. The souq comes alive once the sun goes down & stays open late.

Dammam's **fish market** is off Prince Nayef bin Abdul Aziz Rd.

**OTHER PRACTICALITIES** There are branches of the **King Fahd Specialist Hospital** (Ammar bin Thabit St; ☎013 804 3333; w kfsh.med.sa) and **Saudi German Hospital** (King Fahd Rd; ☎9200 07997; w dammamsaudigermanhealth.com) in Dammam, and the **Dr Sumaiman al Habib Hospital** in Al Khobar [363 C2].

For **golfers**, the Dunes (☎055 255 2218) is a public 18-hole sand course located on the Old Abqaiq Road. Rolling Hills Golf Course is a private members' 18-hole grass course located on Saudi Aramco property. If you are lucky enough to have a connection, this offers an active social scene.

## WHAT TO SEE AND DO

## Al Khobar

***Corniche*** Al Khobar's Corniche is a pleasant area, with pedestrian paths, gardens and plenty of restaurants and entertainment. A great place to exercise and catch some fresh air if it isn't too hot, it is also popular with cyclists, joggers and those simply wanting to relax with family and friends. Picnics are popular.

Al Khobar's Corniche starts in the south at the aptly named Corniche Road. Travelling northbound, you will find the landmark Blue Garden [363 D4] and Oriya Restaurant on a spit of land shared with Crystal Hall, an events venue. Further on, you will reach the Sofitel hotel.

Most visitors will find the area north of the Sofitel more interesting as it is the heart of the al Khobar Corniche. You have arrived once you reach Adjan Walk (page 367). If you have the time, and weather permitting, continue walking north towards Le Méridien hotel. Beyond this you will find many American chain restaurants. Stop at the Khobar Seafront Park [363 D3], where you can catch a decent sea breeze while looking over the water to a clear view of Bahrain when the weather co-operates.

Opposite Le Méridien hotel, by the Fouad shopping centre, the Corniche Road bends to the east. This is the start of the New Corniche, beginning with the al Khobar Corniche Water Tower [363 D2] and Duck Lake [363 D2] landmarks and ending near the SALT al Bahar at the al Rashid Roundabout. The New Corniche is quieter and is popular with Saudi families.

***Dawi Gallery*** [363 C3] (Cnr 22nd & King Saud sts; ☎ 013 802 7412; w dawigallery.com; ⌚ 09.00–noon & 16.00–23.00 Sun–Thu, 16.00–23.00 Sat; admission free) Photography and paintings by contemporary Saudi artists are on display in this elegant gallery founded by Riyadh-born artist Madawi Albaz. Albaz also conducts fine arts courses and seminars to advance the arts in the Eastern Province and wider Kingdom.

***Alfan Sharqy Urban Art Exhibit*** [363 B4] Wander through this street art display in the historic Bayoniya and Thuqbah neighbourhoods of al Khobar to see how the artists have brightened up tired buildings with colourful graffiti, murals and calligraphy. This project is supported by the Dawi Gallery and sponsored by Princess Abeer bint Faisal al Saud of the royal family and is a terrific example of the changing times in the Kingdom as this relative freedom of expression would have been unimaginable only a few years ago.

***Taybeen Museum*** [363 C7] (al Sheraa, 1 block west of OYO 409 Enjin hotel; ☎ 050 800 7333; w altaybeen.net; ⌚ 16.00–22.00 Mon–Sat; SAR25, concessions available for under-16s from SAR15) If you have ever wondered what Saudi childhood was like during the 1970s to 1990s, then this place is worth a visit. Located in a district of historic al Khobar that would otherwise be overlooked by most visitors, the small museum, created by Majid al Ghamdi as a project to preserve his childhood memories, is quirky if not downright eccentric. On display are vintage toys, games and popular food product packaging from the era. His collection of Coca-Cola bottles, Sesame Street nostalgia and Barbie dolls are certainly a great surprise.

**Dammam** Although Dammam activities can be underrated, there is a lot to do, especially if you are interested in the history of the Eastern Province.

***Alfelwah and Aljowharah Museum*** (Cnr 9th & Usrah sts, al Nuzha neighbourhood; ☎ 055 188 6880; ⌚ 18.00–21.30 Mon, by appt at other times) Established in 2018, and set in a palatial villa, this is a private museum (open to the public on Monday evenings) established by local philanthropist Abdul Wahhab al Ghunaim from his love of history and collection of artefacts. The museum now houses more than half a million items including a 500-year-old copy of the Holy Qur'an and vintage cars, many of which are from the early to mid 20th century. Some of King Abdul Aziz's personal possessions are on display too.

***Dammam Regional Museum*** (Located in the south of King Abdullah Park along the seafront; ☎ 013 826 6056; ⌚ 08.00–noon & 16.00–19.00 Sat–Wed; SAR50) This newly built museum focuses on the early history of the Eastern Province. Its six halls exhibit various artefacts dating from pre-Islamic times including Palaeolithic tools and other instruments. Its more modern history is exhibited through displays of regional Bedouin costumes, jewellery and craftworks. It was temporarily closed at the time of research, but we hope it will reopen within the lifetime of this guide.

***Dammam Heritage Village Museum*** ✷ (1km north of Yaqoot St in the King Abdullah Park along the seafront; ☎ 055 843 2232; **w** heritage-village.com.sa; ⏲ noon–midnight Sat–Wed, noon–01.00 Thu–Fri; SAR20) Not to be confused with the Dammam Regional Museum nearby, the Dammam Heritage Village Museum is a perfect combination of museum and restaurant (page 368). Pass by the ground-floor restaurant to the back of the building where you will find lifts to the upper floors. There are a total of five floors to explore.

On the first floor are rows of traditional doors elaborately painted in the regional designs of Asir, Baha and Taif. The colours and patterns are fascinating. Moving up to the second floor, shoppers looking for Saudi heritage items and souvenirs will be happy to roam the recreation of a typical village market. Shops are filled with traditional clothing, reproduction crafts and homewares, jewellery and other mementos. You will also find the Village Café and Sea View Café on this floor. The Sea View Café is a great place to take a break and admire the view over the water.

Still on the second floor, the main entrance to the museum is to the right if you are overlooking the restaurant from the open centre of the building. Follow the arrows on the floor. You will see an astonishing range of items on display as you roam through the upper floors. Work your way through the exhibits of coins and antiquities, and other antiques from incense burners to early-/mid-20th-century radios to heavy flat-irons, typewriters and similar technology, weapons, paper and publications, and mummified animals. There is a lovely display of the topography and key architecture for each province and photographic scenes of people in motion. The car museum on the top floor features some vehicles belonging to early kings. As expected in the Eastern Province, there are lots of interesting photos of early Aramco oil discoveries and snapshots of everyday life during these early days.

Back on the ground floor, in addition to the restaurant, you can also explore recreations of diwans from different regions of the Kingdom. Between the entrance and the exit, you will find the king's Masmak diwan near the Najd sign. You will also find the Asir sign leading to traditional architecture, as well as the private dining area where families who require additional modesty can dine.

***Corniche*** The Dammam Corniche extends in an arc surrounding the bay in the Arabian Gulf to the immediate north of the city centre. Stretching for more than 10km, there is something here for everyone. Starting from the northeast end of the arc, you will find the peaceful and calm King Abdullah Park seafront, containing lovely gardens, as well as many welcome restaurants and cafés for when you need a break. As you continue south, you will see a large building site in the distance – this will become the King Abdullah Cultural Centre. Re-join the green space of the Dammam Corniche proper at the cradle of the arc nearest the city, where you will find more cafés, children's play areas and plenty of people-watching opportunities. There is a 4km walking trail for those seeking gentle exercise at their own pace. Continuing around to the west side of the bay, you will pass SEVEN, a large recreation project under construction. Further north, you will find Dolphin Village and Morjan Resort which are located at the southern end of the bridge leading to Murjan Island. Like many other outdoor activities in the Kingdom, the Corniche is often quiet during the day and comes alive once the sun goes down. The best months to fully enjoy the Corniche are from late October to April. Try to avoid the summer as temperatures and humidity are extreme even in the late evening.

***Murjan/Marjan Island*** Once you reach the bridge near the Morjan Resort, the vibe changes. If you are here very early, you will see a brilliant sunrise from this spot that beautifully frames the spiral tower on the island. People are already fishing from various spots along the bridge. Continue over the bridge and you will reach Murjan Island. There is a large car park, green parks with walking paths, and children's play areas. Unfortunately, the island is also strewn with litter. For many visitors, the highlight is the opportunity to take a short (30mins) cruise out to sea, from where you can look back at the dominating Dammam skyline. The Sea Star Company (☎055 850 0460; ⌚ 10.00–22.00 daily; SAR80 pp, with concessions for children) can be found at the entrance to the island. Expect increasingly long queues in the afternoon and evening.

**Dhahran** Dhahran is all about oil. Why not start by visiting exhibitions dedicated to the discovery of this commodity which modernised the Kingdom.

***King Abdul Aziz Center for World Culture*** [363 A1] (Off H E Ali Naimi St & Rte 613; ☎013 816 9799; **w** ithra.com; ⌚ 09.00–22.00 Mon–Thu & Sat, 16.00–23.00 Fri; general admission free, fee for special events) Also known as Ithra, meaning 'enrichment', this centre was built on the site where oil was first drilled in the Kingdom in 1938 and remains closely linked with Saudi Aramco. The building dominates the Dhahran skyline with its 18-storey Knowledge Tower, built in a modern, curved design. In addition to a library, theatre and ideas laboratory, there are galleries exhibiting all things oil. There is also a children's museum. Check the website for what's on during your visit.

***The Energy Exhibit*** [363 A1] (Adjacent to King Abdul Aziz Center for World Culture; ☎800 122 1224; ⌚ 09.00–21.00 Mon–Thu & Sat, 16.00–21.00 Fri) Most easily reached via the free shuttle buses running from the King Abdul Aziz Center, the Energy Exhibit is an interactive experience for children and adults to learn about oil, from discovery to how it is processed for modern use, even incorporating a range of exhibits featuring alternative energy sources. Some are free to enter; others charge a fee – check **w** ithra.com for more details.

## QATIF ألْقَطِيف

Located about 20km to the north of Dammam, Qatif is one of the oldest settlements in the Eastern Province, dating back to Dilmun times as far back as 3500BCE. It has a population a little over 500,000 and is also home to the Kingdom's largest Shi'a population. Qatif has been an important port for most of its history – until the discovery of oil, when the port of Dammam became more prominent. Once part of the Province of Bahrain before the arrival of the Ottomans, and under various periods of Portuguese and Ottoman rule from the 15th to the early 20th century and the rise of the Third Saudi State, Qatif has had a volatile history. The city also has a recent history of uprisings, especially during the upheavals of 1979, the so-called Arab Spring in 2011 and more difficulties between 2017 and 2019. Much of the unrest here is caused by discrimination against the Shi'a which results in anti-Royal sentiment and perceptions of being treated unfairly compared with other Saudis owing to differences in religious beliefs. Despite this background, Qatif is safe to visit – but do be careful to keep up to date with the news and be aware of any protests, which often happen after Friday midday prayers. If you do visit, you will be rewarded with historic castles in various states of restoration and other off-the-beaten-path gems.

**GETTING THERE AND AWAY** If you are travelling to Qatif from Dammam, take the Corniche Road to the Gulf Road, which will lead you to the city centre and also Riyadh Road for Tarout Island in less than 30 minutes, traffic permitting. Alternatively, take Route 613 from Dammam city centre. If coming from Riyadh, take Route 80, then routes 6446 and 605.

**WHERE TO STAY AND EAT** Most people visit Qatif from Dammam, which is less than 20km away. See page 362 for accommodation options there.

**Atlal Shamea** Uhud Rd at King Faisal bin Abdul Aziz St; 013 808 8440; w app.foodbit.io; noon–01.00 daily. Syrian restaurant with delicious soups, salads, mezze, BBQ & shawarma. $$

**Kumari Restaurant** Near the Darin roundabout, 70m east of the Palace of Mohammed bin Abdul Wahhab Faiha; 056 453 6159; 05.00–15.00 & 16.00–23.00 daily. This restaurant is a real find if you are looking for authentic Tamil & Keralan Indian cuisine, complete with Tollywood dramas on the TV for all to watch. English-language menu with a surprisingly high number of meat dishes. Excellent value for money. $$

**Tarout Loaf Bakery** Opposite Tarout Fort; 013 824 8838; 12.15–midnight Sun, Tue & Wed, 06.00–midnight Mon & Thu, 24hrs Fri. This bakery will tempt you with its fantastic bread, sandwiches, sweets & much more. Drop in & indulge after working up an appetite visiting the ruins of the castle. There is another branch on Uhus Rd on the island. $

**SHOPPING** Located on Tarout Island just over the Riyadh Road bridge, **Qatif City Mall** (09.00–23.00 daily) is the premier shopping mall in Qatif with the usual mid-range shops and fast-food court. Despite its published opening hours, don't expect to find all shops open on Friday.

### WHAT TO SEE AND DO

**Abu Loza's Bath** (Just off the southwest corner of al Khabbaqah cemetery, adjacent to the ruins of the al Abbas mosque, off al Nudher bin al Haretj St) An early example of Turkish baths, these ancient ruins date back to the 10th–11th century. This bath was restored during both the Ottoman and Nadj empires and the site is in good enough condition that it can be explored if you are careful in the interior with its uneven floors and low ceilings.

**Qatif Fish Market** (07.30–19.00 daily) Conveniently located off Gulf Road near the bridge to Tarout island, this fish market is one of the largest in the Eastern Province. The buildings are modern but the fish traders sell their catches of the day just as their ancestors did. You can also check out the spice, fruit and vegetable souqs nearby in the same trading complex.

#### Tarout Island

***Tarout Castle*** This crumbling castle is located in a living village at the top of the island's highest hill. The site is believed to date back to the Dilmun period as Mesopotamian inscriptions and artefacts have been found at the base of the castle walls. The castle itself was built in the 16th century, most likely by the Portuguese to defend from the Ottomans. There is another theory that it was built earlier, during the Uyunid Period, on the base of a Phoenician temple and could date to the 12th century. Three of the four towers remain. The castle's oval interior is relatively small. There is a tourist sign but the castle is fenced off for renovation. Try to find a local guide to gain entry. If this is not possible, then after admiring the building's exterior, explore the immediate neighbourhood of winding streets and traditional houses complete with ornate wooden doors which are still inhabited to this day.

Tarout Castle is easy to find. Cross on to the island from Qatif on the Riyadh Road causeway, then continue straight for about 3.5km. Turn left on to Jafer al Tayyar Road, weaving through a small village after 1km. Turn left at the T-junction and continue for about 500m until you reach a major roundabout adorned with a sculpture of a crescent and two fish at its centre. You will see the castle on your right along this road. Turn right on to Hajer bin Udal Street, then take an immediate right where you will see the tourist sign. Park on the street.

***Palace of Mohammed bin Abdul Wahhab Faihani*** (50m from Darin Corniche) This important palace was originally built in the 16th century by the Faihani family, prominent pearl merchants known throughout the Arabian Gulf, and restored in the late 1880s. The two-storey building contained warehouses, lounges and a round tower. Close to the Corniche, it is easy to imagine people trading in these buildings in busier times. Today the palace lies in near-total ruin, and it is hoped it's not too late to restore it – for the moment it is fenced off by the Saudi authorities. Nevertheless, visitors will be able to see the castle tower and several arches along the exterior walls. There is just enough to imagine how lavishly this family lived at the height of its wealth.

The ruins can be reached by turning right from Riyadh Rd on to Jafer al Tayyar Rd. Continue along this road, keeping the Darin cemetery to your left. Turn right at the al Ruzaihan shopping centre, then travel south, staying to the left at the fork in the road. The palace is on the right shortly before you reach the Darin roundabout, with parking along the road.

***Darin port*** In the southeast corner of Tarout Island is Darin, the place where, in 1915, the Treaty of Darin was signed by the British and ibn Saud, who, at the time, was ruler of the important Emirate of Nejd and Hasa. This was the first international recognition of what would become the Kingdom of Saudi Arabia. It also helped define the borders of Kuwait, Qatar and the Trucial States (modern-day UAE). Today Darin has an attractive Corniche and fishing port. Although there is no specific site to visit, the Corniche is a peaceful place to contemplate this important snapshot of history.

***Ramlet al Bayda Beach*** If you have time, take a short road trip along the east coast to Ramlet al Bayda Beach. Like most Saudi beaches, this is not the place to expect to sunbathe, but it is a lovely place for a picnic in pleasant weather. Bring your own provisions.

## JUBAIL الجبيل

Jubail is located about 80km north of Qatif and about 100km south of Ras al Khair and has a population of about 700,000. The three main areas of the metropolitan area from south to north are Jubail City, Jubail Industrial City and the residential area of Fanateer. Jubail is not known as a tourist destination, but since many expats live and work here, some visitors come to spend time with friends and family.

Jubail's old city has a few hotels, restaurants and a souq. Counterintuitively, Jubail Industrial City and the residential neighbourhood of Fanateer are the places to go. Visitors may be surprised to discover that Fanateer has been developed to look like a middle-class Floridian beach community complete with all of the US chain restaurants, as well as Western-style shopping malls.

**GETTING THERE AND AWAY** Whether you are driving along the coast or coming from Riyadh, Route 613 is a pleasant drive. Head north from Qatif past the Aramco development of Ras Tanufa; you will arrive in Jubail city centre after about an hour (80km). If you are headed for Jubail Industrial City and Fanateer, leave Route 613 and join Expressway Route 1.

**WHERE TO STAY** *Map, opposite*

Jubail's top-end hotel is the Intercontinental, but there are also several other hotels in the Fanateer area that are gentler on the wallet.

### Jubail city centre

If you plan to stay in & explore the old city centre, try these mid-range hotels. All are reasonably priced.

**Al Reem Village Hotel** E Expressway 1; 013 342 5555; **w** alreemhotel.com.sa. The lovely outdoor pool & seating area are highlights of this property. **$$$**

**Hilton Garden Inn** King Faisal N; 013 342 9800; **w** hilton.com. This mid-rise modern property has great views of the Corniche & Arabian Gulf. **$$$**

**Al Farhan Hotel Suites** King Abdul Aziz Rd; 013 363 8388. Situated to the south of Jubail city centre. **$$**

**Al Shaiki Hotel** Cnr King Abdul Aziz Rd & al Madrasah St; 800 820 0063; **w** oyorooms.com. This is the most centrally located of several OYO locations, all of which are good for the budget-conscious traveller. **$$**

**Coral Jubail Hotel** King Faisal W; 013 362 8800; **w** hmhhotelgroup.com. Once considered to be a top-choice hotel before the big brands arrived, Coral is doing its best to keep up with the amenities available in other properties in Jubail. **$$**

### Jubail Industrial City and Fanateer

✷ **Intercontinental** Rd 101, south of Rd 6; 013 356 4000; **w** ihg.com. This older but well-loved business-orientated property has been recently renovated to a high standard & has the vibe of a private members' leisure club. Inside, the hotel dining options are all good & the service is impeccable; outside, the private beach is accessible to women & men, with changing facilities & a beach bar offering non-alcoholic drinks & light snacks. Fishing trips, jet skiing, banana boats & row boats & a mini-golf course are all available; horseriding is organised on Fri & Sat. **$$$$**

**Boudl al Jubail Suites** Darin Harbour; 013 345 4111; **w** boudl.com. This modern hotel located at the north end of the Fanateer Corniche provides traditional Saudi hospitality & lovely views of the bay. **$$$**

**Holiday Inn & Suites** al Salam Rd, east of Rd 6; 013 345 1555; **w** ihg.com. Functional business hotel with a small outdoor pool & fitness centre. **$$$**

**Park Inn by Radisson** Cnr Deira Rd & Rd 6; 013 343 7500; **w** radissonhotels.com. With similar amenities to the Holiday Inn & Suites, this property is situated in the quiet end of the Fanateer Peninsula. It also has an outdoor shisha bar. **$$**

**Warwick al Jubail Hotel** al Wajeha Rd; 013 347 2316. This hotel offers all of the basics. The highlight is its location along the Fanateer Corniche, within walking distance of several restaurants & cafés. It's a great option for those on a modest budget looking for convenience & comfort. **$$**

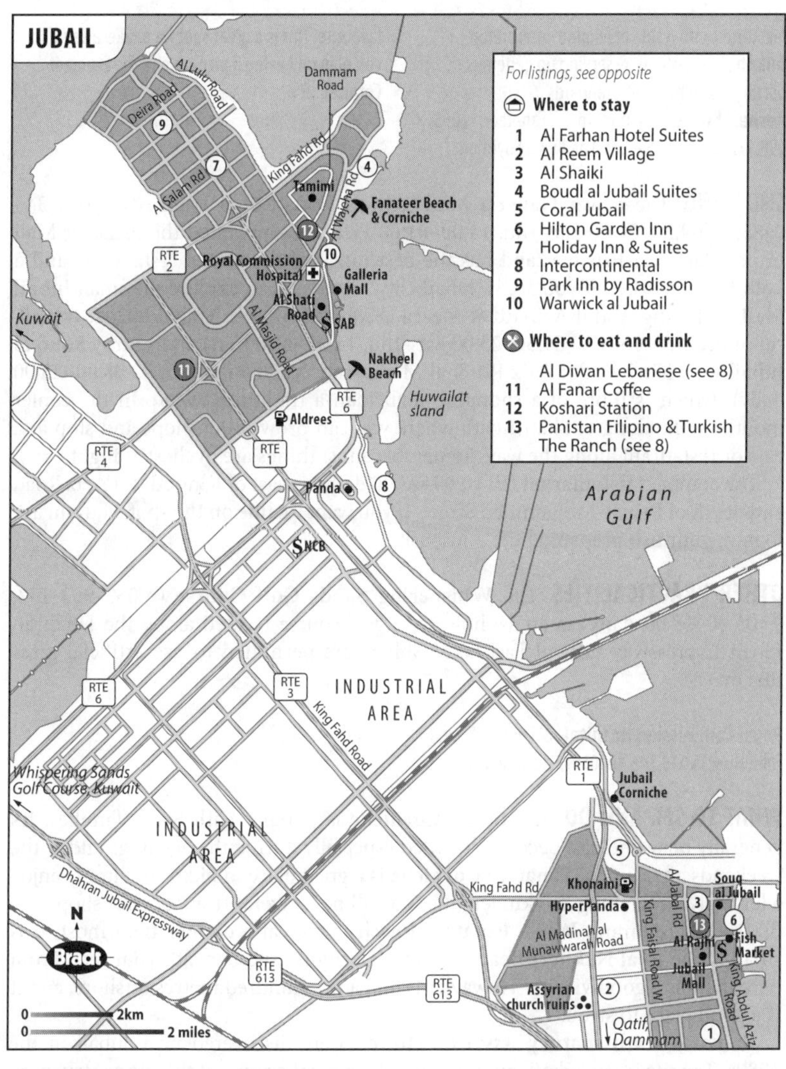


## WHERE TO EAT AND DRINK *Map, above*

There are many bakeries and coffee shops to choose from, including several branches of **al Fanar Coffee**. The Fanateer branch on al Wajeha Road is an excellent alternative to the nearby Starbucks. Otherwise, American chain restaurants and fast food are in abundance here and can be found in most shopping areas if this is what you crave. King Abdul Aziz Road in Jubail Centre is a good place to start.

**Al Diwan/The Ranch** In the Intercontinental; see opposite; both ⌚ noon–15.00 & 19.00–22.30 daily. The Intercontinental's Lebanese restaurant, al Diwan, offers an elegant setting, as well as a delicious menu, while The Ranch is ideal if you fancy Tex-Mex. Both are good if pricey. $$$$

**Pansitan Filipino & Turkish Restaurant** Cnr King Abdul Aziz Rd & Mecca St; 📞 056 630 1565, 050 823 6814; ⌚ 10.00–22.00 Sat–Thu, noon–22.00 Fri. For an interesting change, try this popular casual eatery, which offers what is probably best described as a blend of Filipino favourites with a side of Filipino-interpreted Turkish meat options, & serving up generous portions even by Saudi standards. $$$

**Koshari Station** Dammam Rd, Fanateer; ☎055 988 1728; ⏱ 12.15–23.00 daily. An Egyptian favourite. This is a great spot for a take-away if you plan on having a picnic along the Fanateer Corniche. $$

**SHOPPING** The newer **Galleria Mall** (cnr ad Danah & al Wajh rds; ☎013 345 0385; ⏱ 09.30–01.00 Sat–Thu, 14.00–01.00 Fri) has supplanted the Fanateer Mall in popularity in Fanateer and has the best range of shops and restaurants and a Lulu Hypermarket. If you are in Jubail City, then you can explore the small **Jubail Mall** (cnr King Abdul Aziz Rd & Mecca al Mounawwarah; ☎9200 00262; w mall.cenomicenters.com; ⏱ 09.30–23.00 Sat–Thu, 14.00–23.00 Fri) and nearby **Souq al Jubail** (cnr King Abdul Aziz Rd & al Madrassah; ☎056 055 0977; ⏱ 08.00–23.00 daily), which is more of a shopping mall than a traditional souq. In the cooler months walk along al Shati Road, where you can browse the shops and stop at a café or restaurant along the way. Remember most things are liveliest at night.

The compact **fish market** (⏱ 10.00–23.00 daily) is east of King Abdul Aziz Road and north of Prince Mohammed Street. If you want to dine on the spot, you can ask to have your fish prepared here – just ask.

**OTHER PRACTICALITIES** The **Whispering Sands Golf Course** (☎053 962 132; ⏱ 05.00–18.00 daily) is an 18-hole sand golf course located along the Dhahran Jubail Expressway near al Fasl lake. Golfers are permitted to use artificial grass turf mats.

**Royal Commission Hospital** al Lulu Rd & King Fahd Hwy; ☎013 346 4000; w rchsp.med.sa

**WHAT TO SEE AND DO** The **Jubail Corniche** is popular with Saudi families. It's generally busy and can become crowded especially during the evenings and at the weekends after lunch. **Fanateer Corniche** is a great place to picnic or simply enjoy a leisurely stroll along its 4km length. You will never be far from a coffee shop, café or casual restaurant. While **Fanateer Beach** is nice and cleaner than most, it is small, so go to **al Nakheel Beach** if your priority is sand beneath your feet. From here there is a good view of Huwaylat Island a few hundred metres offshore, and it is a good place to stroll.

Ruins of a **4th-century Assyrian church** were discovered near Jubail in the 1980s. The site is fenced off, but it is possible to see the ruins of this stone structure. There are four recesses that may have contained ancient stone or wooden crosses. Although recognised by the Saudi government, the site remains vulnerable to ongoing vandalism. The site is not signposted. Leave Route 613 southbound just after the junction of King Faisal bin Abdul Aziz Road. Take the first right and go past the Gulf Steel Camp and other industrial camps. When the road bends, take the second right and follow it until you see the fenced-off site. You may need to ask someone local to guide to you but be aware that some people may be reluctant to help.

## NORTH OF JUBAIL

**To Kuwait** Continuing on Route 5 north of Jubail, you will reach the border town of Khafji at the junction of routes 5 and 6643. Border formalities take place about 20km further north near Manfadh al Khafji.

**To the Northern Borders** Continue on Route 5 north of Jubail as far as the junction with Highway 85, about 3km south of abu Hadriya. Turn on to Highway 85 westbound towards **Nairyah**, about 60km away. As distances are very long, take the opportunity to fill up with petrol and buy some snacks at Nairyah. The next town of any significant size is the border town of **Hafar al Batin**, more than 270km further west, towards the western reaches of Kuwait. If you need to break up your journey, then this is the best place to do so as it has some decent hotels including Boudl and al Farsan. There are also quite a few Arabic, south Asian and American fast-food options. Given its remote location, this town sees very few outsiders, so you may attract attention, especially if you are travelling alone or if you are female travelling without men. Continuing on Highway 85, you cross into the Northern Borders nearly 100km further west past the small settlement of abu Nazim.

# 10

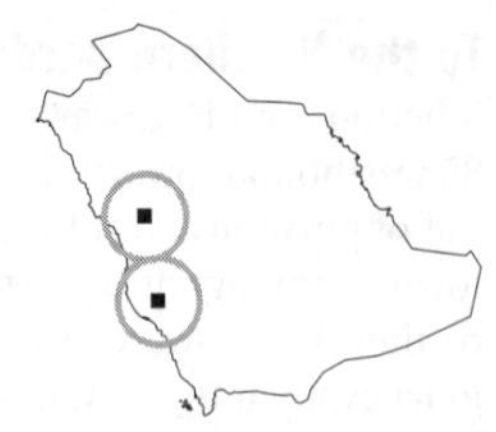

# Mecca مكة and Madinah المدينة

The purpose of this chapter is to give an overview of the significance of Mecca and Madinah in the Islamic world and to provide an overview to understanding pilgrimages for all readers, including non-Muslims. It is not intended to provide specific guidance for pilgrims.

## MECCA مكة

Pilgrimage to Mecca, or hajj, is the fifth pillar of Islam. Mecca's great mosque, the Masjid al Haram, is the main site where pilgrims start to perform their rituals, and where the Ka'aba (see opposite) is found. The Ka'aba is believed by Muslims to have been built by Ibrahim – an Islamic Prophet, also known in Judaism and Christianity as Abraham – and Ishma'il (Ishameal), his son.

Muslims believe that, during his lifetime, Ibrahim received a command from God to leave his wife, Hajar, and son, Ishma'il, behind in Mecca. With Ibrahim gone, Hajar went to find water, running back and forth seven times between the two hills of Safa and Marwah in her search. She was unsuccessful, but upon returning home, she saw water spring from the spot where Ishma'il was making scratching movements on the ground with his foot. These early events have become important foundations of hajj.

Mecca has been an important settlement on key trade routes throughout history. By the 6th century CE, many Arab tribes were converging upon Mecca annually for pagan religious purposes, and it was during this event that trade and other disputes were often settled. At this time, the Ka'aba was surrounded by many pagan idols, which were worshipped by a substantial number of pilgrims. This, and pre-Islamic times more generally, was considered to be *jahiliyyah* or 'The Time of Ignorance'.

In the early 7th century CE, the Prophet Mohammed started to receive revelations about Islam and its Abrahamic, monotheistic beliefs, which were at odds with paganism and idol worship. Jebel al Nour's Hira Cave, located in the northeast outskirts of Mecca, is where Muslims believe that the Qur'an started to be revealed to the Prophet. The Prophet Mohammed preached these 'new' ideas, but met with much resistance and eventually migrated to Madinah in 622CE. For more detail about the Prophet Mohammed's life during the following years, see page 387.

In 628CE, The Prophet Mohammed was barred from entering Mecca during that year's pilgrimage. Although an agreement was reached, allowing The Prophet Mohammed and his growing number of followers into Mecca for future pilgrimages, this failed after two years. The Prophet Mohammed then led the successful conquest of Mecca. As a result idol worship was crushed and replaced by the worship of Allah

## HAJJ AND UMRAH VISAS

All pilgrims must obtain a special visa in order to perform hajj. In order to control numbers, these hajj visas are issued via a lottery-style system by nationality. Hajj pilgrims travel on an organised tour, usually with other pilgrims from their home country and/or nationality. Hajj visas are valid usually for just 30 days and only within the miqat zone (see below); pilgrims must generally depart the Kingdom no later than 10th Muharram.

It is possible to perform umrah (but not hajj) on a tourist visa. Most nationalities eligible for a tourist e-visa simply visit Mecca with this visa outside of hajj season. However, as a tourist visa does not indicate your religion, be prepared to show you are Muslim if stopped by the authorities. Alternatively, an umrah e-visa now exists for 51 countries that mostly align with tourist e-visa countries. Umrah visas are usually limited to two weeks' duration and, like the hajj visas, are valid only within the miqat zone.

*For more information about hajj and umrah visas, visit the official Saudi Ministry of Hajj website (w nusuk.sa).*

and no other god. The Prophet Mohammed performed his last pilgrimage to Mecca in 632CE, the year of his death, instructing his followers in the rituals that have become the hajj rituals performed to this day.

### MIQAT ZONE *Map, page 382*

Pilgrims should arrive at the miqat zone already prepared for their pilgrimage. Reaching far beyond Mecca itself, the zone includes Jeddah, as well as the outskirts of Taif and Madinah. The specific boundary points are Dhatu Irq and Qarn al Manazil to the northeast of Mecca, Yalamlam to the south, the Red Sea and al Jufah to the northwest and Dhul Hulayfah to the north.

### ☪ AL HARAM ZONE *Map, page 384*

The al Haram zone defines the area around Mecca where non-Muslims are forbidden to travel. There are signs indicating exits for non-Muslims on all approach roads towards the city, leading them away from the al Haram zone. Checkpoints are found along these approaches, where you can be stopped and asked to show your passport and visa. Non-Muslims will be turned away.

### IMPORTANT SITES

☪ **Masjid al Haram** ٱلْمَسْجِدُ ٱلْحَرَام The Masjid al Haram is the world's largest mosque, and is the most significant site for pilgrims to Mecca. The mosque complex, covering some 400,800m², has nine minarets towering 90m high and a total of 210 gates, and surrounds several important landmarks. It has been damaged, rebuilt and expanded throughout its history and currently claims a capacity of up to 4 million people. Unlike mosques worldwide, within the boundaries of the Masjid al Haram men and women are not separated. However, they are expected to go to separate designated areas during *salat*. Prayers here are believed to count for 100,000 prayers elsewhere.

☪ ***Ka'aba*** ٱلْكَعْبَة Also known as the Cube or Bayt Allah (House of God), the Ka'aba is the holiest site for all sects of Islam. The area in front of the Ka'aba where pilgrims

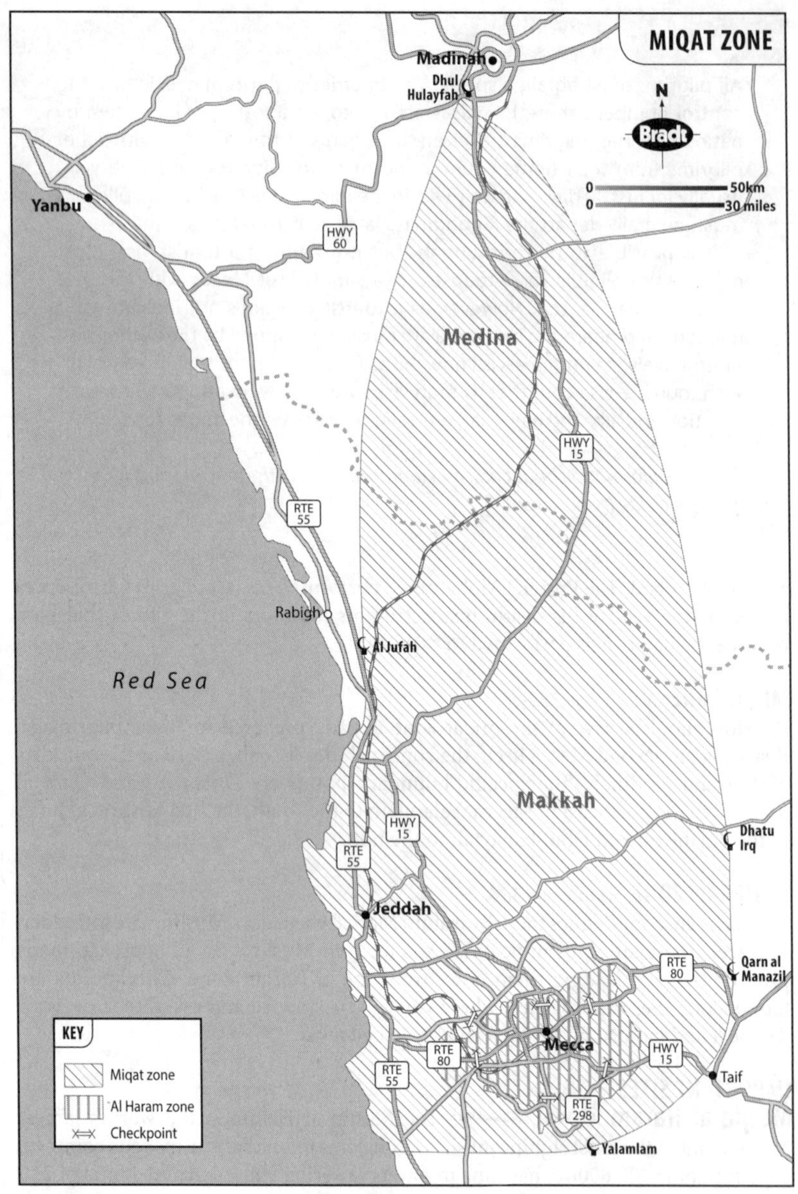


circumambulate (page 385) is known as the *mataaf*. Wherever they are in the world, Muslims pray in the direction of the Ka'aba (during the Prophet's lifetime, prayer was performed in the direction of Jerusalem).

**Kiswah** This is the elaborate black cloth that covers the Ka'aba. The tradition of covering the Ka'aba pre-dates Islamic practices and continued with the Prophet Mohammed after the conquest of Mecca. Woven into the cloth, and positioned about one third of the way from the top of the cube, is a *hizam* or belt of Islamic calligraphy from the Qur'an. Covering the door of the Ka'aba is an additional elaborately decorated curtain known as *sitara*. The Kiswah is replaced annually on 9th Dhu al Hijjah.

☪ **Hajr al Aswad** Also known as the Black Stone, this rock is set in a silver frame and attached to the eastern corner of the Ka'aba. It is believed that the Prophet Mohammed originally placed it – now in several pieces, but reassembled – into the wall of the Ka'aba in the early 7th century, when the stone was intact. Revered in Islam, but not worshipped, the Black Stone is believed by Muslims to have been brought from heaven by the Angel Gabriel and has had religious significance since pre-Islamic times.

☪ **Multazam** This is a 2m area between the Black Stone and the Ka'aba door that is regarded as especially holy, where *du'a* or supplications are accepted from pilgrims.

☪ **Hijr Isma'il** This is an extension of the Ka'aba that was originally built as a shelter. Also known as *hateem*, it is thought by some to be the burial place of Ishma'il and Hajar.

☪ **Maqam Ibrahim (Station of Ibrahim)** Muslims believe that when Ibrahim was building the Ka'aba, a rock appeared, allowing him to reach higher. It is said that this rock – situated next to the Ka'aba, now in a crystal dome – contains Ibrahim's footprint.

☪ ***Zamzam well*** This is the well that opened for Hajar, Ibrahim's wife, when she returned home after searching for water, and where their son Ishma'il was scratching the ground with his foot (page 380). Muslims believe also that the Prophet Mohammed's grandfather rediscovered the well's position after it had closed many centuries before. It is found within the mosque about 20m east of the Ka'aba. Many pilgrims drink from the well, but pilgrims are only allowed to buy Zamzam water at Jeddah airport to take home. At present you are allowed to export only one 5-litre container.

☪ ***Safa and Marwah*** These are two small hills located within the northeast to southeast sectors of the Masjid al Haram and are about 450m apart. It is believed that Hajar ran between these two hills seeking potable water. The space between these hills is known as al Mas'aa.

☪ **Ghar Hira (Hira Cave)** This is where it is believed that the Prophet Mohammed started to receive the Qur'an from the Angel Jabril or Gabriel. It is near the top of Jebel Noor less than 10km northeast of Masjid al Haram. The hike to the cave is about 1.5km and requires a reasonable level of fitness.

☪ **Ghar Thawr (Soor Cave)** This cave is situated in the southeast of Mecca about 10km from Masjid al Haram. It is where the Prophet Mohammed and his companion Abu Bakr sheltered in preparation for *hijra* or migration from Mecca to Yathrib, now Madinah. The climb of about 600m will take fit pilgrims close to 2 hours to complete as the terrain is challenging.

☪ **Jannat al Mu'alla cemetery** Located less than 1km north of Masjid al Haram, this is the cemetery where many of the Prophet Mohammed's relatives are buried, including his first wife, Khadija. Domes covered the tombs until 1925, when the Third Saudi State destroyed them as part of their belief that it was wrong to worship graves.

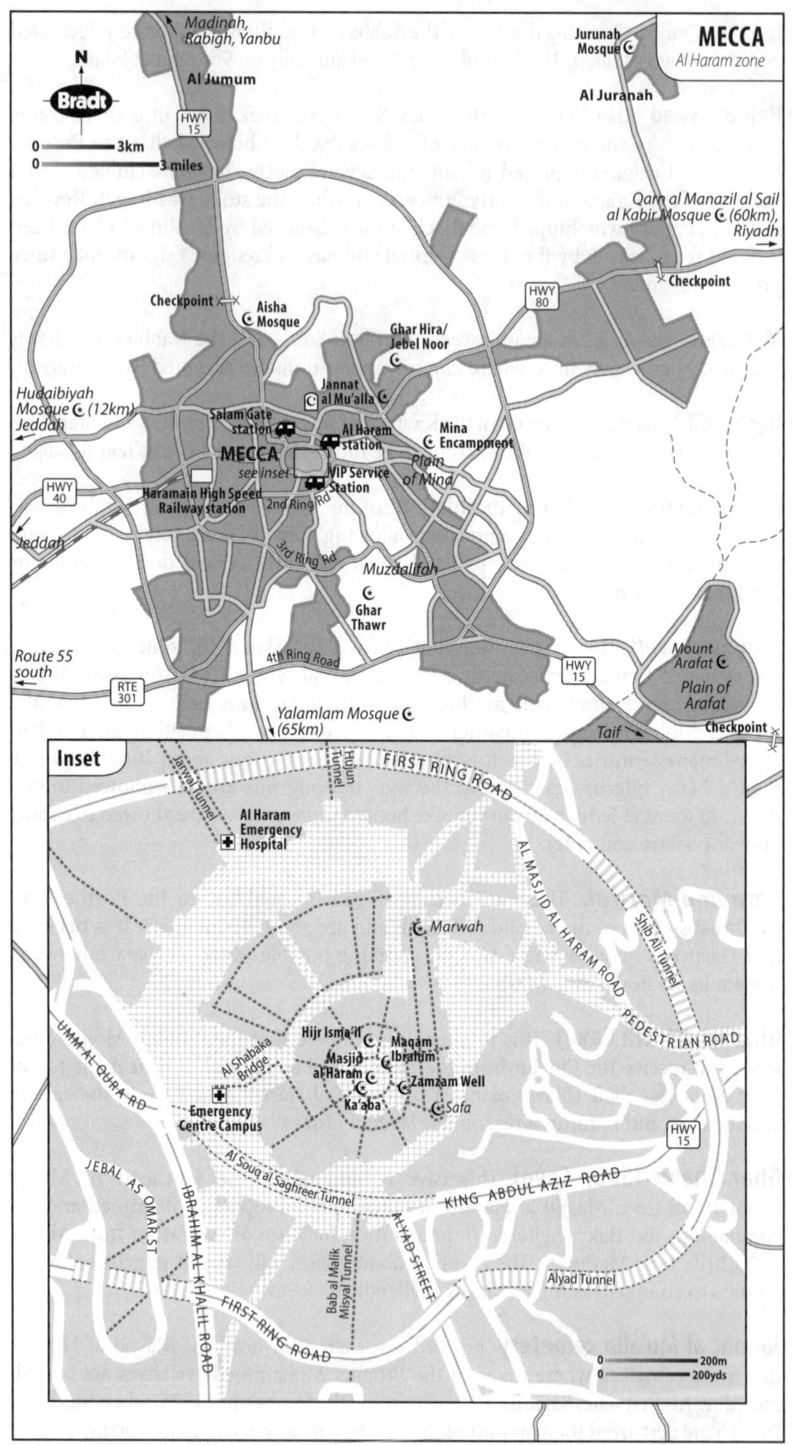
MECCA
Al Haram zone
Madinah, Rabigh, Yanbu
Al Jumum
HWY 15
0 3km
0 3 miles
Jurunah Mosque
Al Juranah
Qam al Manazil al Sail al Kabir Mosque (60km), Riyadh
Checkpoint
HWY 80
Checkpoint
Aisha Mosque
Ghar Hira/ Jebel Noor
Jannat al Mu'alla
Hudaibiyah Mosque (12km)
Jeddah
Salam Gate station
Al Haram station
Mina Encampment
MECCA
see inset
VIP Service Station
Plain of Mina
HWY 40
Haramain High Speed Railway station
2nd Ring Rd
Jeddah
3rd Ring Rd
Muzdalifah
Ghar Thawr
Route 55 south
4th Ring Road
HWY 15
Mount Arafat
Plain of Arafat
RTE 301
Yalamlam Mosque (65km)
Taif
Checkpoint
Inset
Jarwal Tunnel
Hujun Tunnel
FIRST RING ROAD
Al Haram Emergency Hospital
AL MASJID AL HARAM ROAD
Shib Ali Tunnel
Marwah
PEDESTRIAN ROAD
Hijr Isma'il
Maqam Ibrahim
Masjid al Haram
Zamzam Well
Ka'aba
Safa
Al Shabaka Bridge
UMM AL QURA RD
Emergency Centre Campus
HWY 15
Al Souq al Saghreer Tunnel
KING ABDUL AZIZ ROAD
JEBAL AS OMAR ST
IBRAHIM AL KHALIL ROAD
ALYAD STREET
Bab al Malik Misyal Tunnel
Alyad Tunnel
FIRST RING ROAD
0 200m
0 200yds

**HAJJ حَجّ** Hajj (also spelled haj or hadj) is the pilgrimage to Mecca and the fifth pillar of Islam. All Muslims who are physically and financially able are expected to perform hajj once in their lifetime. It takes place on 8th–12th Dhu al Hijjah, the 12th month of the Islamic calendar, with about 3 million pilgrims fulfilling this obligation each year. Unlike holy sites of most other faiths, Mecca is exclusively open to Muslims; non-Muslims are not allowed to visit or perform hajj. As a reminder, all pilgrims require a hajj visa (page 381). Women over 45 years old are now allowed to perform hajj on an organised tour without a mahram.

**Preparation** **Ihram** is a state of purification or ritual cleansing that must be performed by men, women and children prior to both hajj and umrah. In addition to cleansing rituals, ihram garments are worn. It is spiritual as well as physical, cleansing the mind of impure thoughts and worldly vanities. When in ihram, sex, smoking, swearing and many other behaviours considered as unclean are forbidden. Someone who is in a state of ihram is known as *muhram*. Pilgrims must be in a state of ihram when crossing into the miqat zone. There are signs on the ground indicating miqat zone boundaries and will usually be announced on hajj flights and regional flights to Jeddah.

During ihram, special clothing must be worn for the purpose of all being equal in front of Allah. Men generally wear open sandals and two pieces of white cloth wrapped around the upper and lower body. No knots or stiches are allowed; nor is deodorant or scent. The head is uncovered. The dress code for women is less defined. Many women continue to wear the abaya; some a white abaya. All abayas must be unadorned, though they can be stitched. Women are allowed to wear a headscarf but are forbidden from wearing a niqab, gloves, make-up and jewellery. They also cannot perform hajj when they are menstruating, but a pregnant woman may perform hajj.

**Pilgrimage steps** During hajj, pilgrims follow specific rituals. Men, women and children perform these rituals together. Upon completion of all the steps, pilgrims are entitled to use the honorific *hajji* (men) and *hajjah* (women). However, children under the age of discernment will not have met their obligation and must perform hajj again when they are mature enough.

### *Day 1: 8th Dhu al Hijjah*

**Tawaf** Tawaf is the ritual of walking around the Ka'aba seven times in an anticlockwise direction. This is followed by prayers and drinking water from the Zamzam well. It symbolises the monotheism of God.

**Sa'i** Also spelled Sa'ee, this ritual emulates Hajar's search for water. It takes place between the hills of Safa and Marwah and involves running back and forth between these hills seven times.

**Mina** After Sa'i, pilgrims travel to the neighbourhood of Mina in the east of Mecca and stay overnight in tents.

### *Day 2: 9th Dhu al Hijjah*

**Wuquf** Pilgrims leave Mina and travel onwards to the Plain of Arafat below Jebel Rahma (also known as Mount Arafat or Arafah), where they perform *wuquf*: they stand or sit from noon to sunset praying for forgiveness and offering up supplications. This site is significant as it is where the Prophet Mohammed gave his last *khutbah* or sermon.

**Muzdalifah** At sunset, pilgrims travel to this plain between Jebel Rahma and Mina where they stay overnight, collecting a minimum of 49 stones or pebbles in preparation for the ritual of *rami* or Stoning the Devil, which is performed the following morning.

### *Day 3: 10th Dhu al Hijjah*

**Rami** At sunrise, pilgrims return to Mina, where *rami* is performed. This is the ritual that symbolises the stoning of the devil. Pilgrims take aim at three pillars that represent the devil's temptations. These are the large Jamrat al Aqaba, the medium Jamrat al Wusta and the small Jamrat al Sughra.

**Qurbani** Qurbani is the first day of Eid al Adha, the feast of the sacrifice. An animal, usually a sheep or a goat, is slaughtered for each pilgrim. Although some pilgrims dispatch the animal themselves, it is possible to purchase a voucher for someone to do this on their behalf.

**Halq and taqsir** After qurbani has been completed, it is obligatory for pilgrims to cut their hair. Many men choose to undergo halq, the ritual shaving of the head. Women perform taqsir, trimming their hair. Men can choose taqsir if they prefer.

**Tawaf ziyarat** Pilgrims return to the Masjid al Haram and perform tawaf again.

***Days 4–6: 11th and 12th Dhu al Hijjah*** On day 4, pilgrims drink again from Zamzam well, emulating Ishma'il. After this, although the obligatory rituals of hajj are now complete, many pilgrims may wish to repeat them. Other pilgrims might wish to travel to other significant sites in and around Mecca such as Ghar Hira, Ghar Thawr and Jannat al Mu'alla. Others are content to shop or relax.

***Tawaf al Wadaa*** This is the final circumambulation ritual performed before departing Mecca. It is performed on whatever day pilgrims finish their stay in the city.

**UMRAH عُمْرَة** Umrah is a pilgrimage to Mecca at times of the year other than hajj. It is encouraged but does not fulfil the obligation of hajj. Nearly 20 million Muslims perform umrah annually, and as with hajj non-Muslims are not allowed to perform this pilgrimage. Although many people prefer to travel with a tour operator for umrah, it is possible to travel independently. Women over 45 years old are allowed to travel on an organised tour without a mahram, as is the case on hajj.

It is possible to complete umrah in a much shorter time than hajj, often in less than one day, involving fewer rituals. Tawaf is performed, with the first three circuits performed at a faster pace than the remaining four, followed by Sa'i between Safa and Marwah. At the end of umrah, halq can be performed by men. Taqsir is performed by women and is an option for men if they prefer this to halq. (For a definition of these rituals, see from page 385.)

**PRACTICALITIES** Mecca is crowded throughout the year and there is **security** everywhere, especially around Masjid al Haram; guards are uniformed and are generally polite and professional. In addition, the Saudi authorities have established a Health Emergency Centre Campus adjacent to Masjid al Haram. For more pressing medical emergencies, the al Haram Emergency Hospital is located in the northwest corner of the Masjid al Haram area inside the First Ring Road.

**Roads** to Mecca are very busy during hajj season, especially from Jeddah, and in the city, with most people getting around on foot, large pedestrian groups crossing the roads frequently disrupt the traffic. Parking is a nightmare. The expansion projects that have been ongoing since the 1980s and have accelerated in recent years under the reign of King Salman, especially near Masjid al Haram, as well as building sites and surrounding roadworks, present further challenges both for vehicles and pedestrians. Be patient and follow any instructions given for motorised and pedestrian traffic.

As the holy sites and surrounding areas are crowded, be cautious about getting lost or becoming separated from your group. Although crowd control has improved in recent years, it can still pose a risk, especially to children, the elderly and people with mobility challenges. The weather is hot for most of the year, so it's vitally important to stay hydrated – there are vendors near the sites if you need more water. Wear sturdy footwear, especially if you plan to climb anywhere, as much of the terrain is loose underfoot. Finally, you will probably be sharing your experience with cats as they are everywhere.

For basic information about hotels, restaurants and shopping, see from page 283.

## MADINAH المدينة

Muslim pilgrims around the world regard Madinah as the second holiest city in Islam and recognise the importance (but not obligation) to undertake *ziyarat* (page 388) in this destination.

Known as Yathrib يثْرِب in pre-Islamic times, Madinah is now formally known as al Madinah al Munawwarah. It was populated by Jewish and Arab tribes for at least 1,500 years before the arrival of the Prophet Mohammed. These tribes had a history of both cooperation and control over one another.

The Prophet Mohammed undertook the hijra or migration, leaving Mecca on the equivalent of 16 July 622CE. This date marks the start of the Islamic calendar. The *muhajirun* are the Prophet Mohammed's companions and early followers who migrated with him to Yathrib. These new arrivals were initially able to mediate between rival tribes, to convert many residents to Islam and to give a level of respect to Jewish tribes as they were also recognised as People of the Book. However, due to shifting alliances, times remained turbulent. Key battles fought include the Battle of Uhud (625CE) and the Battle of the Trench (627CE). Over the next several years, while based in Yathrib, the Prophet Mohammed and his muhajirun also continued their attempts to reconquer Mecca.

The Treaty of Hudaybiyyah was an agreement struck between the Prophet Mohammed, who represented Madinah, with Mecca's dominant Qurayshi tribe. Agreed for ten years in 628CE, it was enforced for only two. In 630CE, the Prophet Mohammed left Madinah, leading the successful conquest of Mecca.

Upon the Prophet Mohammed's death in 632CE, the first three caliphs Abu Bakr, Umar and Uthman continued to operate their caliphates in Madinah, expanding the Islamic Empire. However, the fourth caliph, Ali, moved the centre of the caliphate to Kufa, in what is now Iraq, leading to a decline in Madinah's power and influence.

The Prophet Mohammed was buried in his wife Aisha's house, in the exact place where he had died. Many of the Prophet's family and friends also came to be buried beside the Prophet or in the nearby al Baqi cemetery. The Green Dome over the Prophet Mohammed's Tomb was originally built in 1297, and over the next centuries other tombs were also enhanced. With the main exception of the

Prophet's Tomb, most of these shrines were destroyed during the First Saudi State – efforts by the 19th-century Ottomans to restore the damage were only met with a second round of destruction by the Third Saudi State after the collapse of the Ottoman Empire in the 1920s.

**AL HARAM ZONE** The al Haram area of Madinah is a Muslim-only zone and is defined as the area within the First Ring Road, also known as King Faisal Road. There are no formal checkpoints in operation at the time of research. Unlike hajj, pilgrims do not enter into a state of ihram for travel to Madinah.

**ZIYARAT SITES** Ziyarat is a pilgrimage to the sites important to Islam, especially those related to the life of the Prophet Mohammed and his family and associates. These sites include mosques, cemeteries, battlefields and natural features such as caves and mountains. Many Muslims perform ziyarat to Madinah, either after they complete hajj or on a separate journey. Although not obligatory like the hajj pilgrimage to Mecca, ziyarat includes visits to the Masjid al Nabawi and other significant sites in and around Madinah. The following information describes the usual ziyarat route pilgrims are likely to take. Ziyarat sites fall both within and outside the al Haram zone.

### Ziyarat sites within the al Haram zone

***Masjid al Nabawi* المسجد النبوي** As the second holiest site in Islam, most pilgrims regard this mosque, known as the Prophet's Mosque, as the most significant place to visit in Madinah and it is often used as the starting point when setting off to tour other important ziyarat sites. Muslims believe that when they pray here, their prayers are equal to 1,000 prayers elsewhere. It's a peaceful place, and many pilgrims spend many hours or days reflecting on their faith within the mosque itself or in other prayer areas within the courtyard. The interior of the mosque and all prayer areas are strictly gender segregated, but the outside areas are not. See page 241 for more detail.

**The Prophet's Tomb ٱلْقُبَّة ٱلْخَضْرَاء** Also known as the Green Dome or al Qubbah al Hadra, the Prophet's Tomb is located in the southeast corner of the mosque and is visited by Muslim men in conjunction with Masjid al Nabawi. Women are strictly forbidden and will be waved away by security if they attempt to approach the entrance.

**Al Baqi Cemetery** Although tomb worship was curtailed by the destruction in the 19th and 20th centuries of headstones, mausoleums and the like, not just here but in many other cemeteries in the Kingdom, pilgrims still visit this cemetery because of its religious and historical significance. It is located to the front and east side of the Prophet's Tomb.

***Masjid Abu Bakr Siddiq*** This stone mosque has one dome and is located just past the southwest corner of Masjid al Nabawi, built on the site of Abu Bakr's house. It is the smaller of the two mosques in the same area and is where the Prophet Mohammed led Eid prayers.

***Masjid al Ghamamah*** This mosque is situated a few metres southeast of Masjid Abu Bakr Siddiq and is another place where the Prophet Mohammed gave Eid prayers. Similarly built of stone, it is larger and has several domes.

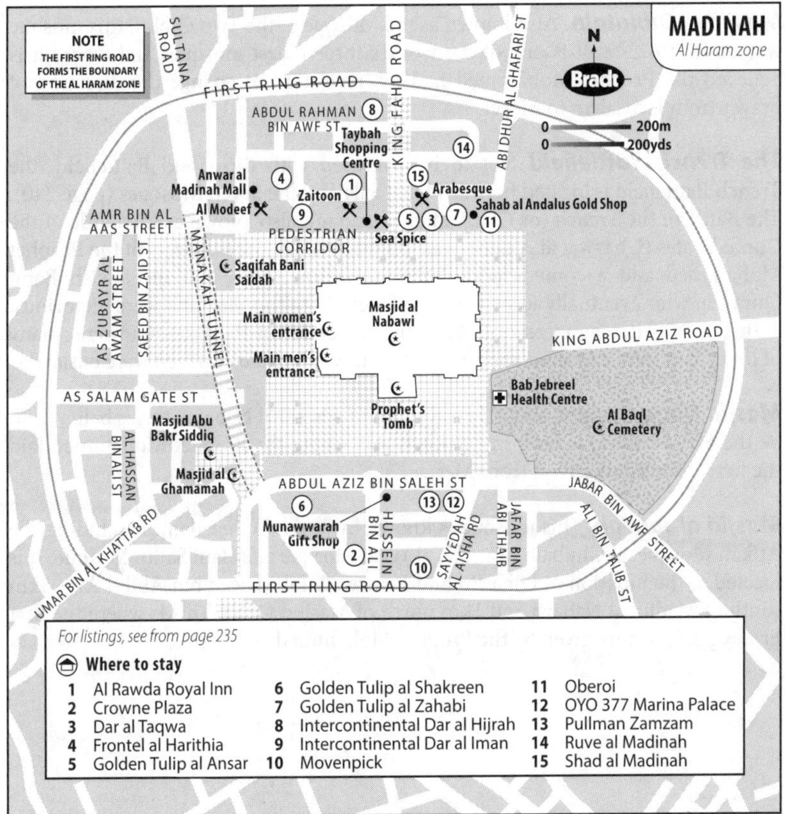


***Saqifah Bani Saidah*** Also known as Soqaifat Bani Saedah, this site, located less than 100m from the northwest corner of Masjid al Nabawi, once contained a roofed structure where it is believed many of the Prophet Mohammed's companions pledged allegiance to Abu Bakr after the Prophet's death.

**Ziyarat sites outside the al Haram zone** Many pilgrimage sites are located around Madinah beyond the al Haram zone. Many of these sites have been described in *Chapter 6*, where more detail can be found (page 239).

***Jebel Uhud and Jebel Ayr*** Also known as the Mountains of Heaven and Hell, these mountains are visited by many pilgrims. Rising to over 1,077m, **Jebel Uhud** (Mountain of Heaven) is the highest peak in Madinah and is located about 7km from the Shuhada Cemetery at the site of the Battle of Uhud (see below). The road to the mountain passes by caves where it is believed the Prophet Mohammed sheltered during the battle (page 241). **Jebel Ayr** (Mountain of Hell), located 10km southwest of the al Haram zone, is the second tallest mountain in Madinah at 955m and can be accessed by 4x4 only.

***Uhud Battlefield*** The Battle of Uhud took place at the base of Jebel Uhud and is a key place for most pilgrims as it is where the Prophet Mohammed and his followers were defeated by Meccans who objected to the Islamic faith and its growing influence.

☪ ***Masjid al Qiblatain*** Also known as the Mosque of the Two Qiblas, this mosque was built in 623CE. It is one of the world's three oldest mosques and where it is believed the Prophet Mohammed had his revelation to change the direction of prayer from Jerusalem to Mecca.

☪ ***The Trench Battlefield*** Not to be confused with the Uhud Battlefield, the Trench Battlefield is located between Jebel Sala and the Seven Mosques (page 240). The Battle of the Trench (or Ghazwat al Khandaq), also known as the Battle of the Confederates (Ghazwat al Ahjab), was fought between the followers of the Prophet Mohammed and a confederation of non-Muslim tribes and the Jewish Banu Qurayza, who eventually joined the confederation. The Muslims were victorious, with the confederacy in retreat. After the surrender of the Banu Qurayza, many of their men were executed and many of their women and children were enslaved.

☪ ***Masjid Quba*** Located about 3.5km south of Masjid al Nabawi, this is believed to be the earliest mosque built in Madinah and where the Prophet Mohammed laid the first stone upon arrival from Mecca.

☪ ***Masjid al Jum'ah*** This mosque is known by several other names including the Atikah Mosque, al Ghubaib Mosque, al Wadi Mosque and Bani Salim Mosque. It is located at the junction of Qiba Rd and Prince Abdul Majeed bin Abdul Aziz 3km south of Madjid al Nabawi and 1km north of Masjjid Quba. This is where the first Friday prayers were given by the Prophet Mohammed.

# Appendix 1

## LANGUAGE

The official language of Saudi Arabia is Arabic, a Semitic language – others in this group are Amharic, Hebrew and Maltese. About 300 million people worldwide speak Arabic as their first language, and it is the official language of 22 countries stretching from Mauritania and across North Africa, and throughout the Arabian Peninsula to the Arabian Gulf. It is estimated that another 100 million people speak, read or understand Arabic to varying degrees of proficiency in addition to their native tongue. These are often Muslims who learn Arabic as part of their religious education as Arabic is also the language of Islam.

In Saudi Arabia, Arabic, and English more and more, are the primary languages of business. English remains less widely spoken than in other Gulf countries, though this is increasing, especially among younger Saudi nationals and Saudis who have been educated abroad.

It is said that Arabic is one of the hardest languages to learn (Rosetta Stone, a prestigious language learning organisation, places it in its highest Category IV ranking for difficulty and time needed), but it is possible to learn basic vocabulary and other 'survival' Arabic without too much effort and this is highly recommended if you are an independent traveller. From a practical perspective, most visitors should concentrate on speaking more than reading.

**ARABIC BASICS** Arabic is a 'root language' based on three-consonant clusters of words with related meanings. For example, k t b are the root consonants for the words *kitab* 'book', *kātib* 'writer', *maktūb* 'letter', *maktab* 'desk' and *maktaba* 'library'.

Arabic is written from right to left and is written in lower-case letters only. For each letter, however, there are four different written formats determined by a letter's position within a word: isolated (written alone such as in a list); initial (beginning of a word); medial (in the middle of a word); and final (at the end of the word). Vowels are mostly not written, and although there are annotation symbols to assist with vowel sounds, these are generally used only for young children's books or in Arabic language lessons.

The language has masculine and feminine genders, where verbs change depending on whether you are speaking to a male or female. Nouns can be masculine or feminine and adjectives, which follow the noun, must 'agree' with the noun, similar to French and many other European languages. There are complex sets of pronouns that account for gender and single/dual/plural references.

**Alphabet** The Arabic alphabet has 28 letters. The table on page 392 gives the different formats of each letter and a pronunciation guide. There are also various additional vowelling diacritics and constrictive throat sounds without any real approximate in English.

| Final | Medial | Initial | Alone | Transliteration | Pronunciation |
|---|---|---|---|---|---|
| ـا | | | ا | aa | as in '**a**fter' |
| ـب | ـبـ | بـ | ب | b | as in '**b**ut' |
| ـت | ـتـ | تـ | ت | t | as in '**t**in' |
| ـث | ـثـ | ثـ | ث | th | as in '**th**ink' |
| ـج | ـجـ | جـ | ج | j | as in '**j**am' |
| ـح | ـحـ | حـ | ح | H | emphatic, breathy '**h**' |
| ـخ | ـخـ | خـ | خ | kh | as in the Scottish 'lo**ch**' |
| ـد | | | د | d | as in '**d**en' |
| ـذ | | | ذ | dh | as in '**th**at' |
| ـر | | | ر | r | as in '**r**ed' |
| ـز | | | ز | z | as in '**z**ero' |
| ـس | ـسـ | سـ | س | s | as in '**s**it', hard 's' |
| ـش | ـشـ | شـ | ش | sh | as in '**sh**ut' |
| ـص | ـصـ | صـ | ص | S | emphatic, strong '**s**' |
| ـض | ـضـ | ضـ | ض | D | emphatic, strong '**d**' |
| ـط | ـطـ | طـ | ط | T | emphatic, strong '**t**' |
| ـظ | ـظـ | ظـ | ظ | Dh | as in Dhofar |
| ـع | ـعـ | عـ | ع | ' | guttural stop, hardest sound for non-Arabs to make, called 'ayn. |
| ـغ | ـغـ | غـ | غ | gh | like a gargling sound |
| ـف | ـفـ | فـ | ف | f | as in '**f**ire' |
| ـق | ـقـ | قـ | ق | q | like a guttural 'k' |
| ـك | ـكـ | كـ | ك | k | as in '**k**ing' |
| ـل | ـلـ | لـ | ل | l | as in '**l**ady' |
| ـم | ـمـ | مـ | م | m | as in '**m**at' |
| ـن | ـنـ | نـ | ن | n | as in '**n**ot' |
| ـه | ـهـ | هـ | ه | h | as in '**h**at' |
| ـو | | | و | w | as in '**w**ill', or 'oo' as in 'f**oo**d' |
| ـي | ـيـ | يـ | ي | y | as in '**y**et', or 'ee' as in 'cl**ea**n' |

| | |
|---|---|
| alif hamza | أ |
| waw hamza | ؤ |
| ya hamza | ئ |
| alif madda | آ |
| ta marbuṭa | ة |
| alif maqsura | ى |

**Pronunciation** Some letter sounds used in English do not exist in spoken Arabic, most notably 'p' and 'v', and in some dialects also the hard 'g'. Conversely, there is no equivalent in English to the Arabic "ayn", which can sound like guttural swallowing; the Arabic 'q', pronounced somewhere between an English 'q' and 'gh', that almost resembles a gulp but with distinct aspiration; and 'kh', which sounds like clearing your throat. A few other sounds are familiar but expressed in a way that may seem exaggerated.

**Numbers** Just to keep things interesting, numbers are written from left to right in Arabic, just as they are in English. Indo-Arabic, or Eastern Arabic, numerals are used more often in Saudi Arabia than they are in other Gulf countries, but Western Arabic numerals, familiar in much of the rest of the world, are also commonly used. Using your phone to display any numbers you need, such as when out shopping, is an easy way to avoid any misunderstandings.

| Western Arabic | Eastern (Indo-) Arabic | Pronunciation |
|---|---|---|
| 0 | ٠ | *sifr* |
| 1 | ١ | *wahid* |
| 2 | ٢ | *ithnan* |
| 3 | ٣ | *talatah* |
| 4 | ٤ | *arba'a* |
| 5 | ٥ | *hamzah* |
| 6 | ٦ | *sitta* |
| 7 | ٧ | *sab'a* |
| 8 | ٨ | *tamaniyyah* |
| 9 | ٩ | *tis'ah* |
| 10 | ١٠ | *ashar* |
| 11 | ١٠ | *hidashar* |
| 12 | ١٠ | *ithnashar* |
| 13 | ١٠ | *talatashar* |
| 14 | ١٠ | *arba'a ashar* |
| 15 | ١٠ | *hamsa ashar* |
| 16 | ١٠ | *sitta ashar* |
| 17 | ١٠ | *saba'a ashar* |
| 18 | ١٠ | *tamaniya ashar* |
| 19 | ١٠ | *tis'a ashar* |
| 20 | ٢٠ | *ishrun* |
| 21 | ٢١ | *wahid wa ishrun* |
| 30 | ٣٠ | *talatun* |
| 40 | ٤٠ | *arba'un* |
| 50 | ٥٠ | *hamzaun* |
| 60 | ٦٠ | *sittun* |
| 70 | ٧٠ | *sab'un* |
| 80 | ٨٠ | *tamanun* |
| 90 | ٩٠ | *tis'un* |
| 100 | ١٠٠ | *mi'a* |

## USEFUL WORDS AND PHRASES

### Basics

| | Transliteration | Arabic |
|---|---|---|
| Yes | *na'am / aywa* | نعم / ايوة |
| No | *la* | لا |
| OK (ie: I agree; general acknowledgement) | *tammam / tayyib* | تمام / طيب |
| Shame on you | *haraz ealayk* | ح |
| Sorry | *assif* | آسف |
| Please | *min fadlik / min fadlak* | من فضلك |
| Thank you | *shukhran* | شكراً |
| [response] | *afwan* | عفواً |
| Open | *maftouh* | مفتوح |
| Closed | *maghlaq* | مغلق |
| Help (assistance) | *messaede* | مساعده |
| Help (information) | *talimat* | تعليمات |
| It doesn't matter | *ma'alesh* | معلش |
| No problem | *la mushqila* | لا مشكلة |

## Greetings

| | Transliteration | Arabic |
|---|---|---|
| Hello (formal) | *as salaam aleikum* (lit: peace be upon you) | السلام عليكم |
| [response] | *wa aleikum salaam* (lit: and unto you peace) | وعليكم السلام |
| Hello (informal) | *marhaba* | مرحبا |
| Welcome | *ahlan wa salan* | أهلاً وسهلاً |
| How are you? | *kaif halek / kaif halak* | ؟ كيف حالك |
| [response] | *al hamdulillah* (lit: praise be to Allah) | الحمدلله |
| Goodbye | *ma'a salaama* (lit: with peace) | مع السلامة |
| What is your name? | *ma ismak* | ؟لاً وسهلا |
| My name is… | *isme…* | اسمي |
| God willing | *insh'allah* | إن شاء الله |

## Travel

| | | |
|---|---|---|
| accident | *haditha* | حادثة |
| airport | *matter* | مطار |
| bus | *hafila* | الحفيلة |
| bus station | *mahattat hafilat* | محطة الحافلات |
| car | *sayyara* | سيارة |
| car park | *mawqif sarayat* | موقف سيارات |
| driving licence | *rakhsa kayada* | رخصة قيادة |
| embassy | *sifara* | سفارة |
| flight, trip | *rahla* | رحلة |
| full (petrol) | *malla binzeen* | بنزين ملء |
| go | *dahab* | ذهب |
| how far | *kim yibad* | كم يبعد |
| left | *yasar* | يسار |
| Let's go | *yallah* | يلا |
| lost | *mafqood* | مفقود |
| museum | *mothef* | متحف |
| passport | *juaz safer* | جواز سفر |
| petrol station | *mahta binzeen* | محطة بنزين |
| railway station | *mahattat qitar* | محطة القطار |
| reverse | *yarija* | يَرْجِع |
| right | *yamin* | يمين |
| roundabout | *darawan* | دوران |
| shopping mall | *markaz souq* | مَرْكَز تَسَوّق |
| slow | *yabteh* | يبطئ |
| stop | *waqef* | وقف |
| straight ahead | *mobashera* | لمباشرة |
| street | *sharie* | شارع |
| suitcase | *haqiba* | حقيبة |
| taxi | *taksi* | تاكسي |
| ticket | *tedkira* | تذكرة |
| traffic police | *sharta al marour* | شرطة المرور |
| train | *qitar* | قطار |
| turn | *enataf* | انعطف |
| visa | *visa* | فيزا |

| | Transliteration | Arabic |
|---|---|---|
| **Accommodation** | | |
| check in | *nazal fi (al funduq)* | نزل في الفندق |
| check out | *aldafe* | الدفع |
| entrance | *madkhal* | مدخل |
| exit | *khuruj* | خروج |
| hotel | *funduq* | فندق |
| housekeeping | *al tadbir al manzali* | التدبير المنزلي |
| I need… | *ana bahaja…* | أنا بحاجة |
| loo, toilet, restroom | *hamam* | حَمَّام |
| key card | *bataga al moftah* | بطاقة المفتاح |
| reservation | *hajz* | حجز |
| room | *gharfa* | غرفة |
| double room | *gharfa muzdawijat* | غرفة مزدويجات |
| single room | *gharfa mofreda* | غرفة مفردة |
| twin room | *gharfa tom* | غرفة توأم |
| toilet roll | *lefa al hamam* | لفة الحما |
| towels | *manashef* | فـشانملا |
| Wi-Fi code | *rams wifi* | رمز واي فاي |
| …doesn't work | *…la yeamel* | ل ا يعمل |

## Food and eating out

### *Food and drink*

| | | |
|---|---|---|
| apple | *tefah* | تفاح |
| beef | *lahm al baqr* | البقر لحوم |
| bread | *khubz* | خبز |
| butter | *zabda* | زبدة |
| cheese | *geben* | جبن |
| chicken | *djaj* | دجاجة |
| coffee | *qahwa* | قهوة |
| dairy | *al alban* | الالبان |
| date (fruit) | *tamr* | تمر |
| eggs | *bayed* | بيض |
| fish | *samak* | سمك |
| fruit | *fakha* | فاكهة |
| honey | *assel* | عسل |
| juice | *usair* | عصير |
| lamb | *kharuf* | خروف |
| mango | *anbaj* | أنبج |
| meat | *lahm* | لحم |
| milk | *halib* | حليب |
| orange | *bertkali* | برتقالي |
| pomegranate | *raman* | رمان |
| sugar | *sukkar* | سكر |
| tea | *shay* | شاي |
| vegetables | *khudarrat* | خضروات |
| water | *al maa* | الماء |
| watermelon | *battikh* | بطيخ |
| yoghurt | *laban* | لبن |

| | Transliteration | Arabic |
|---|---|---|
| ***Eating out*** | | |
| bakery | *mokhabez* | مخبز |
| bill | *fatoura* | فاتورة |
| Bon appétit | *shahia geida* | شهية جيدة |
| breakfast | *fattour* | فطور |
| dinner | *ashaa* | عشاء |
| less | *akal* | أقل |
| more | *akther* | أكثر |
| menu | *gaema* | قائمة |
| restaurant | *matam* | مطعم |
| vegetarian | *nabati* | نباتي |
| **Shopping** | | |
| cash | *naqad* | نقد |
| cheap | *rakhis* | رخيص |
| credit/bank card | *bitaqat aitiman* | بطاقة إئتمان |
| discount | *khassam* | خصم |
| expensive | *ghaly* | غالي |
| How much? | *bikam* | بيكام ؟ |
| mall | *mol* | مول |
| market | *souq* | سوق |
| size | *hajam* | حجم |
| supermarket | *sobermarkt* | سوبرماركت |
| **Colours** | | |
| black | *aswad* | اسود |
| blue | *azraq* | أزرق |
| brown | *bonny* | بنّي |
| gold | *dhahabi* | ذهبي |
| green | *akhdar* | أخضر |
| grey | *rumadi* | رمادي |
| orange | *bertkali* | برتقالي |
| pink | *wardi* | وردي |
| purple | *benfesji* | بنفسجي |
| red | *ahmar* | أحمر |
| silver | *fadhi* | فضي |
| white | *abyad* | أبيض |
| yellow | *asfar* | أصفر |
| **Medical basics** | | |
| ambulance | *sayyara asraf* | سيارة إسعاف |
| arm | *dharra* | ذراع |
| back | *daher* | ضهر |
| chemist | *sedle* | صيدلي |
| chest | *sadar* | صدر |
| dentist | *tabib al asnaan* | طبيب الأسنان |
| doctor | *tabib* | طبيب |
| ear | *azan* | أذن |
| eye | *ayn* | عين |
| foot | *qaddem* | قدم |

| | Transliteration | Arabic |
|---|---|---|
| hand | *yed* | يد |
| head | *ras* | رأس |
| hospital | *mustashvi* | مستشفى |
| ill/unwell/sick | *mareed* | مريض |
| leg | *sak* | ساق |
| medicine | *taba* | طب |
| mouth | *fem* | فم |
| neck | *raqba* | رقبة |
| nose | *and* | أنف |
| stomach | *maada* | معدة |
| tooth | *sen* | سن |

## Time

***Days*** Notice that the days of the week, starting with Sunday, are variations of the numbers one to seven.

| | | |
|---|---|---|
| Sunday | *al ahad* | الأحد |
| Monday | *al athnayn* | الاثنين |
| Tuesday | *al thalatha* | الثلاثاء |
| Wednesday | *al araba* | الأربعاء |
| Thursday | *al khamis* | الخميس |
| Friday | *al juma'a* | الجمعة |
| Saturday | *al sabt* | السبت |

***Months*** Note these are the Islamic months from the first to the twelfth month. Conventional months are generally referred to in English, albeit with various pronunciations.

| | | | |
|---|---|---|---|
| *muharram* | محرم | *rajab* | رجب |
| *safar* | صفر | *shaban* | شعبان |
| *rabi al awwal* | ربيع الأول | *ramadan* | رمضان |
| *rabi ath thani* | ربيع الثاني | *shawwal* | شوال |
| *jumada al ula* | جمادى الأولى | *dhu al Wa'dah* | ذو الوضعة |
| *jumada alakhirah* | جمادى الآخرة | *dhu al Hijjah* | ذو الحجة |

### *Other time words and phrases*

| | | |
|---|---|---|
| day | *yawm* | يوم |
| early | *mubakir* | مبكر |
| evening | *al masaa* | المساء |
| hour | *sa'aa* | ساعة |
| last (year) | *(sanna) al maady* | (...) المعضي |
| late | *matakher* | متأخر |
| minute | *degiqa* | دقيقة |
| month | *shahr* | شهر |
| morning | *al sabah* | الصباح |
| next (week) | *(asboua) al qadim* | (...) القديم |
| second | *thahn* | ثان |
| today | *elioum* | اليوم |
| tomorrow | *ghada / bukra* | غدا / بكره |
| week | *asboua* | أسبوع |

| | Transliteration | Arabic |
|---|---|---|
| year | *sanna* | سنة |
| yesterday | *amas* | س‌مأ |

## Question words

| | | |
|---|---|---|
| How? | *Keef* | ؟ كيف |
| At what time… ? | *Ma al waqqat* | ؟ما الوقت |
| What? | *Maza* | ؟ ماذا |
| When? | *Mette* | ؟ متى |
| Where? | *'Ayn* | ؟ أين |
| Who? | *Minn* | ؟ من |

## Other handy words

| | | |
|---|---|---|
| after | *baad* | بعد |
| Be careful! | *Intebah* | !انتبه |
| before | *qabel* | قبل |
| boy | *sibi* | صبي |
| cold | *barad* | برد |
| done, finished, over | *hallas* | هالاس |
| first | *'awal* | أول |
| girl | *sibiya* | صبية |
| here | *hanna* | هنا |
| hot | *har* | حار |
| last | *acher* | آخر |
| later | *fima baed* | فيما بعد |
| man | *rajul* | رجل |
| next | *muqbal* | مقبل |
| now | *alaan* | الآن |
| only | *fakat* | فقط |
| there | *hanak* | هناك |
| too | *al da* | ايضا |
| with | *mae* | مع |
| without | *bidoon* | بدون |
| woman | *amra* | امرأة |

# Appendix 2

## GLOSSARY

| | |
|---|---|
| *abaya* | a long black robe worn by women and older girls as part of Saudi national dress |
| *abi* | my father |
| *abu* | father of |
| *adhan* | also *azhan*; call to prayer |
| *agal* | a black rope-like band worn on top of the ghutra as part of male Saudi national dress |
| *al qatt* | distinct Asiri interior design |
| *allah* | god |
| *ardah* | a traditional sword dance |
| *areesa* | also *arika*; a Yemeni dish made of dates, bread, honey and condensed milk |
| *asida* | Maghrebi wheat-based dough made with butter and often eaten at breakfast |
| *asr* | the third prayer time held in the afternoon |
| *attar* | rose oil |
| *bab* | gate |
| *bahira* | lakes |
| *balaleet* | a cardamon, saffron and rosewater omelette over vermicelli noodles |
| *balila* | stewed, spiced chickpeas |
| *Basic Law* | Saudi law similar to a constitution and based on the Qur'an |
| *beit teen* | Najran architecture |
| *bin* | son of |
| *bint* | daughter of |
| *bisht* | a robe worn by men over a thobe, often by VIPs |
| *boshya* | a woman's headscarf |
| *broast* | a popular method of pressure cooking marinated, spiced meat |
| *bukhoor* | wood chips soaked in perfume |
| *burj* | tower |
| *dakas* | terraces that overhang shops, offering protection from the weather |
| *dallah* | the traditional Arabic coffee pot |
| *dhuhr* | also *zhuhr*; the second prayer time, held when the sun is at its peak in the sky |
| *duf* | also *raq*; a handheld drum-like instrument that can be square or round, used in traditional music |
| *fajr* | the first prayer time, held at dawn |
| *fatayer* | Arabic pie made of meat, or sometimes spinach, originally from the Levant |

| | |
|---|---|
| *fatteh* | aubergine, mince and bread topped with tahini, tomato sauce and pomegranate molasses |
| *fatwa* | opinion on legal and social matters |
| *fawhat* | craters |
| *futa* | Yemeni wrap-skirt worn by men; also *ma'waaz* specific to the Fayfa mountains |
| *fuul* | fava beans stewed with olive oil and spices, often eaten at breakfast |
| *gapama* | stuffed pumpkin dish – an Armenian speciality that has become popular in Saudi Arabia |
| *ghazal* | love poems |
| *ghutra* | a plain white or red-checked headcloth worn as part of male Saudi national dress |
| *ghuzi* | also *quzi*; Iraqi slowed-cooked spiced lamb and rice dish |
| *ha'ia* | formal term for the religious police; see also *mutawa* |
| *hadith* | sayings and anecdotes during the time of the Prophet Mohammed |
| *hajj* | the fifth pillar of Islam, obliging Muslims who are able to undergo the pilgrimage to Mecca during a specific time in the Islamic calendar |
| *hamasah* | poetry focused on military prowess |
| *hammour* | a fish, similar to cod |
| *hareed* | Farasan parrotfish |
| *harrat* | basalt fields |
| *hashi* | camel meat |
| *hijra* | migration of the Muslim community from Mecca to Madinah during the life of the Prophet Mohammed |
| *hijri* | Islamic lunar calendar |
| *hisba* | Islamic morals |
| *hizam* | the belt of Islamic calligraphy woven into fabric found on the Ka'aba; the word hizam can also refer to a decorated waist belt often embellished with coins, coloured beads and glass worn by both men and women |
| *hneini* | also *hanini*; dessert similar to areesa |
| *ibadi* | a third branch of Islam found mostly in Oman |
| *iftar* | the meal eaten to break the fast at sunset during Ramadan; or breakfast more generally |
| *ihram* | a state of readiness for pilgrimage to Mecca which includes ritual cleansing and special clothing |
| *imam* | Muslim religious leader |
| *iqama* | formal residency document similar to an internal passport |
| *isha* | the fifth prayer time, held at dusk |
| *jad* | grandfather |
| *jaddah* | grandmother |
| *jamal* | camel |
| *jambiya* | a curved dagger originating in Yemen |
| *jebel* | mountain |
| *jummah* | Friday midday prayer |
| *ka'aba* | the stone-and-marble cube found in the centre of Islam's holiest mosque in Mecca. Muslims pray in the direction of the Ka'aba |
| *kabsa* | the Saudi national dish, made with basmati rice, fruit, nuts, vegetables and meat |
| *kafala system* | the set of rules about work and residency rights for expatriates |
| *kahf* | cave |
| *kalava* | red thread worn on the wrist by many Hindus |

| | |
|---|---|
| *kerak chai* | a black tea flavoured with cardamon, saffron, sugar and evaporated milk |
| *khareef* | southwest monsoon |
| *khasm* | escarpment |
| *khokha* | a small door within a larger door |
| *khutbah* | an Islamic speech similar to a sermon |
| *koobideh* | traditional spiced Persian kebabs usually made of lamb or chicken |
| *koshari* | the Egyptian national dish of pasta, rice, lentils and onion in a tomato sauce |
| *kunafa* | syrup-drenched pastry topped with cheese, pistachios or cream, served warm |
| *kuttab* | religious primary school |
| *laban* | fermented milk |
| *labneh* | strained yoghurt used in many cuisines from the region, similar to soft cheese or Greek yoghurt, depending on its thickness |
| *ma'waaz* | see *futa* |
| *mabkhara* | incense burner |
| *maboug* | seeded hot chilli paste |
| *madfoon* | a Yemeni meat-and-rice dish cooked in a pit |
| *madhabi* | one of several traditional meat-and-rice dishes popular in Saudi Arabia, this one originating from Yemen |
| *madih* | eulogy poems |
| *madrassa* | religious school |
| *maghrib* | also *maghreb*; the fourth prayer time, held at sunset, also meaning west and a common reference to North Africa |
| *mahram* | a male guardian for women and girls (such as her father, husband, brother or even her son) who traditionally oversees a female family member's life, especially in public |
| *majlis* | meeting room |
| *malik* | also *malek* or *melek*; king |
| *manakish* | a pizza-like flatbread topped with olive oil, cheese, and za'atar, or cheese and za'atar half and half |
| *mandhi* | a meat-and-rice dish similar to madfoon, originating in Yemen and very similar to Saudi kabsa |
| *manjur* | a tambourine-like percussion instrument with goat hooves around its circumference; the musician wears the instrument tied around the waist and when he moves the hooves make a rattling noise which is used to set a rhythm |
| *mashrabiyya* | boxed window |
| *mathlothah* | a meat-and-rice dish similar to madfoon, but Saudi in origin |
| *melwi* | a twisted silver bracelet for women |
| *meshawi* | a garlic chicken dish from Egypt or the Levant |
| *mihrab* | notch in a mosque indicating the direction of Mecca |
| *mimbar* | similar to a pulpit from where an imam addresses the audience in the mosque |
| *miqat* | zone within which pilgrims must be prepared for their pilgrimage |
| *mirwas* | a two-sided cylindrical drum used to set rhythms, often to accompany poetry |
| *mizan* | a type of scales, or weighing balance, with two baskets that contain the items being weighed, for example rose petals before oil extraction. *Mizan* is also used figuratively meaning 'balance', used when assessing a Muslim's good deeds and sins |

| | |
|---|---|
| *mizmar* | a flute-like wind instrument with five holes; also a dance |
| *moutabaq* | Saudi stuffed pancakes |
| *muezzin* | a man who issues the call to prayer |
| *muhram* | a person who is in a state of ihram |
| *mukhtasar* | the private room near a majlis, used for private conversation |
| *mutawa* | informal term for the religious police; see also *ha'ia* |
| *nabati* | Bedouin poetry or the people's poetry |
| *nargelah* | a water pipe used to smoke flavoured tobacco; also known as shisha or hubbly-bubbly |
| *niqab* | face veil for women that usually covers everything but the eyes |
| *nisba* | family name used adjectivally as part of the name of a place or country, eg: al Saud in Saudi Arabia, as well as a tribal or other ancestral affiliation |
| *nitaqat* | the Saudi work scheme to promote the employment of Saudi nationals |
| *osmailia* | a Levantine dessert with crunchy noodles filled with cream, syrup and nuts |
| *oud* | a scent, a type of wood, or a pear-shaped stringed instrument |
| *pbuh* | Peace Be Upon Him; used when referencing the Prophet Mohammed in writing *saws* in Arabic |
| *qasaba* | stone towers in al Bahah |
| *qibla* | indicator of the direction towards Mecca |
| *raq* | see *duf* |
| *ras* | headland |
| *rawi* | a knowledgeable tour guide |
| *reem* | gazelle |
| *rehab* | a wooden instrument typically played with a bow made of horsehair, used to accompany the recitation of poems |
| *rehal* | also *rehat*; Qur'an stand |
| *risha* | an elongated pick for playing stringed instruments, specifically the oud |
| *roshan* | latticed wooden window frame |
| *sadu* | weaving |
| *sahra* | desert |
| *salat* | the second pillar of Islam, ritual prayers performed five times a day |
| *samri* | a dance where men sitting in two rows clap and sway and poetry is sung to the beat of the *duf* |
| *sawm* | the fourth pillar of Islam, fasting during the month of Ramadan |
| *shahada* | the first pillar of Islam, the profession of faith |
| *shakshouka* | a dish of spiced eggs and tomatoes from the Maghreb, often eaten at breakfast |
| *shamal* | wind from the north |
| *Shari'a Law* | Islamic Law derived from the Qur'an |
| *shawaya* | grill used for cooking meat. This term is also used similarly to the English use of the word grill in 'mixed grill' |
| *shayla* | see *boshya* |
| *Shi'a* | the second most populous group of Muslims, who believe in hereditary leadership |
| *sidari* | a heavy waistcoat often made of wool and leather worn by men |
| *simsimiyya* | a lyre with steel wire strings |
| *sobia* | a smoothie made of bread, barley or oats and blended with cardamom, cinnamon and sugar; famous in the Hejaz region |
| *souq* | a traditional market |

| | |
|---|---|
| *suhoor* | the meal eaten during Ramadan prior to dawn to sustain the faster for the day |
| *sunnah* | traditions and practices of the Prophet Mohammed |
| *Sunni* | the most populous group of Muslims, who believe in consensus leadership |
| *ṭabl* | drum |
| *taqiyah* | a white, rounded skullcap worn by men |
| *tar* | a tambourine made from goatskin stretched on to a wooden frame |
| *tardiyyah* | a style of poetry that recounts successful hunting |
| *tarha* | see *boshya* |
| *thobe* | the long white robe worn by men and older boys as part of Saudi national dress and which may be worn in other dull colours during the winter |
| *tola* | also *tolah* or *tullah*; an ancient Indian measurement equivalent to about 11.66g |
| *toum* | garlic sauce |
| *tumuli* | mounds of earth covering graves |
| *ukhdud* | a ditch or trench |
| *umm* | mother of |
| *ummah* | global community of Muslims |
| *ummi* | my mother |
| *urg* | sand desert |
| *uruq* | sand dunes |
| *wadi* | a dry riverbed |
| *waha* | an oasis |
| *wudu* | ritual washing performed in preparation for prayers |
| *wusum* | specific tribal signs that signify ownership of camels |
| *zakat* | the third pillar of Islam, charity |
| *ziyarat* | pilgrimage to sites associated with the Prophet Mohammed, usually in Madinah |

# Appendix 3

## FURTHER INFORMATION

**BOOKS** There are a lot of negative publications about Saudi Arabia out there, many of which give an unfair portrayal of both the country and its culture. But there are also those that provide a more balanced view of the Kingdom, and which are worth seeking out.

Most of the titles listed below were published as social reforms were just beginning and are referenced here so that visitors can appreciate how much the country has already changed in only a few short years. We have avoided the recommendation of other books that are perceived to have a political position considered as controversial within Saudi Arabia.

al Sanea, Rajaa *Girls of Riyadh* Penguin, 2008. By one of the first Saudi women to write about contemporary life in the Kingdom, these are the stories of four modern young women and how they balance contemporary life with the conservative expectations of their society.

al Sharif, Manal *Daring to Drive: A Saudi Woman's Awakening* Simon & Schuster, 2018. Now living in Australia, al Sharif is associated with high-profile campaigns to allow women to drive. Read about how her actions led to both reform and suppression, and the impact on her own life, as she left the Kingdom.

Cuddihy, Kathy *Anywhere but Saudi Arabia! Experiences of a Once Reluctant Expat* Barzipan Publishing, 2012. Authored by a Canadian woman who turned her presumptions upside down.

Ferraris, Zoë *Finding Nouf* Houghton Mifflin Harcourt, 2008. Also published as *The Night of Mi'raj*. *City of Veils* and *Kingdom of Strangers* round out this thriller fiction series by this controversial American author, who lived in Saudi Arabia for a short time with her Palestinian husband and his Saudi-based family. It's a good example of how outsiders interpret and misinterpret the Kingdom's conventions.

Gardner, Frank *Blood and Sand* Bantam, 2014. British author and security reporter for the BBC, Gardner recounts his time reporting for the BBC in Saudi Arabia.

Ghattas, Kim *Black Wave* Wildfire, 2021. A deep exploration of the relationship between Saudi Arabia and Iran and how the Iranian revolution impacted Saudi society.

Hubbard, Ben *MBS: The Rise to Power of Mohammed bin Salman* William Collins Publishing, 2020. The author, a *New York Times* reporter, gives a good account of the politics of Saudi Arabia's true power behind the King.

Jones, John Paul *If Olaya Street Could Talk* The Taza Press, 2007. Jones, an American expat and author, captures the transition of the Kingdom in the late 20th century to a modern country.

Lacey, Robert *Inside the Kingdom* Arrow, 2009. An update of the author's original 1981 work, a generation later.

Lacey, Robert *The Kingdom* Harper Collins, 1981. Early history of the modern Saudi royals, written by a respected British author and royal historian.

Thesiger, Wilfred *Arabian Sands* Penguin, 2007. This classic, originally published in 1959, tells of Thesiger's travels during the late 1940s in Arabia's 'Empty Quarter'.

Trofimov, Yaroslav *The Siege of Mecca* Penguin, 2008. Understanding how the events of 1979 were pivotal to the conservative resurgence of Saudi culture.

**MAGAZINES** Until recently, most Saudi magazines were business orientated. There are now a few titles that may be of interest to visitors. Localised editions of fashion magazines such as *Vogue* are also popular. All of the magazines below are published online, in Arabic and English.

*Destination Magazine* **w** destinationksa.com. Lifestyle magazine that offers a window on contemporary culture. It has a regional focus covering Jeddah, Riyadh and Eastern Province.

*Directions KSA* **w** directionsksa.com/en. Publication covering contemporary culture.

*Time Out* **w** timeoutriyadh.com; timeoutjeddah.com. Magazine concentrating on current social events. Specific information for Riyadh and Jeddah.

*What's On Saudi Arabia* **w** whatsonsaudiarabia.com. Covers a wide range of activities throughout the Kingdom.

## WEBSITES

**Tourist information** There are quite a few tourist-orientated Saudi websites, of varying quality, in these early days of tourism in the Kingdom. Do bear in mind also that websites commonly stagnate or disappear, especially in Saudi Arabia. At the time of writing, the following websites are recommended.

**w** **experiencealula.com** This is the go-to site for everything visitors need to access activities in the al Ula area. Excellent-quality information.

**w** **saudiarabiatourismguide.com** Especially recommended for return visitors who want to go beyond the tourist highlights.

**w** **vacaay.com/middle-east/saudi-arabia** An itinerary-planning website with a variety of activities in Saudi Arabia (and other destinations) catering to a wide audience.

**w** **vision2030.gov.sa/v2030/v2030-projects** Curious readers can learn much more about the projects that are underpinning a significant part of the massive economic changes within Saudi Arabia, including current and future plans in the tourism industry.

**w** **visitsaudi.com** The official Saudi tourist information website – a good place to start. This is also the official website for e-visas.

**Blogs** Many blogs are incomplete, out of date, out of touch or unfairly negative. Good blogs can disappear when expat authors leave the Kingdom. Readers should conduct their own searches and determine what sites are most suitable for them. We suggest the following as a good place to start.

**w** **blueabaya.com** An award-winning blog written by a Finnish woman who started expatriate life in Riyadh. She met her Saudi husband there and settled, with their two children arriving in the following years. Covering most of the Kingdom, this comprehensive, well-respected and useful website and blog is of interest to many resident expats, business visitors and tourists.

**w** **susiesbigadventure.blogspot.com** 'Susie of Arabia' is an American woman, married to a Saudi man, who moved to Jeddah, together with their teenage son, after decades of living together in the US. Although this blog has been less active in recent times, her information and observations are a good read.

**W thepinktarha.com/ksa** This long-running blog is a winner of the Saudi Excellence in Tourism Award. The Pink Tarha is Riyadh based and is written from the perspectives of Filipina women.

**Other useful websites** The following two websites provide practical information about prayer times, Islamic dates, and much more: **W** islamicfinder.org; **W** muslimpro.com.

### *Banks*

**Al Rajhi** **W** alrajhibank.com.sa/en
**Arab National Bank** (ANB) **W** anb.com.sa
**Banque Saudi Fransi** **W** alfransi.com.sa/en
**Riyad Bank** **W** riyadbank.com
**SAB Bank** (HSBC) **W** sab.com/en
**Saudi National Bank** (SNB) **W** alahli.com

### *Currency exchange*

**Tahweel al Rajhi** **W** tahweelalrajhi.com.sa/en

### *Newspapers*

Both English-language Saudi newspapers.

**Arab News** **W** arabnews.com
**Saudi Gazette** **W** saudigazette.com.sa

### *Restaurant delivery apps*

**Hungerstation** **W** hungerstation.com/sa-en
**Talabat** **W** talabat.com/ksa
**Uber Eats** **W** uber.com/en-sa

### *Telephone companies*

All of these companies have shops & kiosks throughout the Kingdom & in the major airports where visitors can purchase a local SIM.

**Mobily** **W** mobily.com.sa
**Saudi Telephone Company** (STC) **W** stc.com.sa
**Zain** **W** sa.zain.com/en

### *Transport*

#### Airlines

**flyadeal** **W** flyadeal.com
**flynas** **W** flynas.com
**Saudia** **W** saudia.com

#### Ride-hailing apps

**Careem** **W** careem.com
**Uber** **W** uber.com/sa/en

#### Train, bus and ferry

**Haramain High Speed Railway** **W** sar.hhr.sa
**Marine Transportation Company** **W** macna.com.sa. Runs the Jazan-to-Farasan Islands ferry service.
**SAPTCO** **W** saptco.com.sa. Saudi national bus company.
**Saudi Arabia Railways** (SAR) **W** sar.com.sa

# Index

Page numbers in **bold** indicate main entries; those in *italics* indicate maps

## INDEX OF ADVERTISERS